SIR HALLEY STEWART TRUST PUBLICATIONS

ELIZABETHAN NONCOMFORMIST TEXTS

Volume VI

THE WRITINGS OF JOHN GREENWOOD AND HENRY BARROW

1591–1593

SIR HALLEY STEWART TRUST PUBLICATIONS

CARTWRIGHTIANA
Elizabethan Nonconformist Texts—I

THE WRITINGS OF ROBERT HARRISON AND ROBERT BROWNE
Elizabethan Nonconformist Texts—II

THE WRITINGS OF HENRY BARROW, 1587-1590
Elizabethan Nonconformist Texts—III

THE WRITINGS OF JOHN GREENWOOD, 1587-1590
Elizabethan Nonconformist Texts—IV

THE WRITINGS OF HENRY BARROW, 1590-1591
Elizabethan Nonconformist Texts—V

THE WRITINGS OF JOHN GREENWOOD AND HENRY BARROW, 1591-1593
Elizabethan Nonconformist Texts—VI

CIVITAS DEI
by Lionel Curtis

DISABLED CITIZENS
by Joan Clarke

THE SOCIAL TEACHING OF THE CHRISTIAN CHURCHES
by Ernst Troeltsch

THE SPIRITUAL CRISIS OF THE SCIENTIFIC AGE
by G. D. Yarnold

THE UNMARRIED MOTHER AND HER CHILD
by Virginia Wimperis

THE SIR HALLEY STEWART TRUST LECTURES

EQUALITY
by R. H. Tawney

HEALTH AND SOCIAL EVOLUTION
by Sir George Newman

THE WORLD'S ECONOMIC CRISIS
by Sir Arthur Salter, Sir Josiah Stamp, J. M. Keynes
Sir Basil Blackett, Henry Clay, Lord Beveridge

THE WORLD'S ECONOMIC FUTURE
by A. Loveday, J. B. Condliffe, B. Ohlin, E. F. Heckscher
S. de Madariaga

RICH MAN, POOR MAN
by John Hilton

THE ATOMIC AGE
by P. M. S. Blackett, D. W. Brogan, Lionel Curtis, R. F. Harrod
M. L. Oliphant, Bertrand Russell

THE WRITINGS OF
JOHN GREENWOOD AND HENRY BARROW

1591–1593

Edited by
LELAND H. CARLSON
PH.D. LL.D

Published for
THE SIR HALLEY STEWART TRUST

GEORGE ALLEN AND UNWIN LTD
RUSKIN HOUSE
MUSEUM STREET LONDON

FIRST PUBLISHED IN 1970

SBN 04 809002 6

Printed in Great Britain
in 11 on 12 point Baskerville
by Alden & Mowbray Ltd
at the Alden Press, Oxford

THIS BOOK IS DEDICATED TO

THE STAFF OF

THE HENRY E. HUNTINGTON
LIBRARY AND ART GALLERY
SAN MARINO, CALIFORNIA

WITH GRATITUDE FOR
BOOKS AND MANUSCRIPTS, FAVORS AND FRIENDSHIPS

PREFACE

THIS is Volume VI in my series on "Elizabethan Nonconformist Texts." It brings to completion the writings of Barrow and Greenwood, which began with Volumes III and IV for the years 1587–1590, published in 1962, and which were continued with the publication in 1966 of Barrow's works for 1590–1591. The writings of Greenwood and especially of Barrow proved to be more extensive than I anticipated. The work on the manuscript material has been slow, tedious, and exacting, and the need for collating the manuscripts has required considerable time and travel. I envy those who live near the British Museum and the Public Record Office, but I appreciate the privilege of residing near the Huntington Library.

My obligations are many. For the use of books and manuscripts, I feel especially thankful to the many friends at the British Museum, the Public Record Office, Lambeth Palace Library, Dr. Williams's Library, the University of London Library, the Bodleian Library, the Cambridge University Library, and the library of Corpus Christi College, Cambridge. In the United States the Pierpont Morgan Library, the Folger Shakespeare Library, and the Huntington Library have been especially helpful, as well as the Honnold Library at Claremont University Center.

To Mrs. Orin Tramz I am deeply indebted for efficient and accurate typing of perplexing Elizabethan documents. Somehow, the transition from rough notes and rewritten sentences and reworked paragraphs to a neat typed page gives me a joy no less than that of seeing galley and page-proof. To S. T. Bindoff, Patrick Collinson, Joel Hurstfield, J. E. Neale, Anthony G. Petti, A. L. Rowse, Robert Palmer, and A. Scoufas I express my thanks for suggestions, solutions, and seminars, as well as for personal friendship.

I have been saddened by the recent news of the death of my publisher, Sir Stanley Unwin, chairman of the firm of George

Allen and Unwin Ltd. For more than eighteen years I have known him, and I shall treasure the memory of our first discussion in 1950 on the long-range project—Elizabethan Nonconformist Texts—which has become my major field of research. I should like to record my gratitude for visits in his home, discussions in his office, social luncheons, and tennis games which he played up to the age of eighty or so. He will live in the life of the books he published, in the hearts and minds of the authors and readers thereof, and in the books he himself wrote—such as *The Truth about Publishing* and *The Truth about a Publisher*.

To Barbara Clapham and the trustees of the Sir Halley Stewart Trust I express my continuing appreciation, and to the American Philosophical Society I wish to record my special gratitude for aiding my research.

LELAND H. CARLSON

Claremont, California
December 10, 1968

CONTENTS

INTRODUCTION

Part I

The first part of this book pertains to the writings of John Greenwood in the period 1591–1593. The earlier writings of Greenwood for the years 1587–1590, together with those works which he issued jointly with Henry Barrow, were published as Volume IV in the series, "Elizabethan Nonconformist Texts," and approximated 273 pages. Thus, it is clear that Greenwood, compared with Barrow, was not a voluminous writer.

Greenwood's "A Breife Refutation of Mr. George Giffard His Supposed Consimilitude betwene the Donatists and Us," was a rejection of any parallels between the Donatists of the fourth century and the Separatists of the sixteenth century. It was also a refutation of Gifford's book, *A Plaine Declaration*, the first part, pp. 1–69.

Greenwood's second refutation of Gifford is entitled "A Fewe Observations of Mr. Giffard's Last Cavills," and should be carefully distinguished from Barrow's "A Few Observations to the Reader," which was also directed against Gifford. Greenwood deals specifically with the use of stinted read prayers and devised liturgies in the worship services of the Church of England. Both of Greenwood's treatises first appeared in Barrow's *A Plaine Refutation* (1591), and were reprinted, the first in 1605 and the second in 1603.

The third, fourth, and fifth items are transcribed from manuscripts. The material in Chapter III is especially useful, since it provides new information on the Separatists' views on marriage, adultery, and re-marriage.

Part II

There are ten items or chapters which contain Barrow's writings in the period 1591–1593. Of these items four are taken from printed sources (VI, VIII, XIV, XV). When the Separatists printed Barrow's "Letter to an Honorable Lady" in 1604—eleven years after it was written—they may have used a copy of the original in the possession of the Countess of Warwick. For years I have searched various manuscript collections in the hope of finding the original, both in the Netherlands and England. It may have been lost or destroyed after the Countess died in February, 1603/1604, but there is a slim possibility that it may be extant. Since it is such a moving letter which expresses the final sentiments of Barrow only a few hours before he was hanged, it would be a priceless memento which could be reproduced in facsimile. The remaining six items (VII, IX, X, XI, XII, XIII) are all extant in manuscript, and we are fortunate to have them. This is especially true of the longest item—VII—which is an unusual example of marginalia. I suspect that even specialists have been unaware of the existence of VII and IX, for they have never been printed. Thus, in Part II, about two-thirds of the material comes from manuscript sources.

Part III

Part III consists of thirty-five chapters, but actually comprising about eighty-nine items, all from manuscripts, and providing new material for the Separatists. The chapters are categorized under four divisions: criticism, trials, examinations, and petitions. It is my hope that the basic sources of the radical Puritans will become better known. They should make possible a more meaningful monograph on the rise of the Separatists in England, the Netherlands, and the New World. They should also contribute a chapter to the broad history of Puritanism and to the even larger movement of nonconformity. For the significance of this movement, students should read the thoughtful article by Charles F. Mullett, "Religious Nonconformity: A Central Theme in Modern English History," in *The Historical Magazine of the Protestant Episcopal Church* for September, 1968.

PART I

THE WRITINGS OF JOHN GREENWOOD

1591–1593

I

A BREIFE REFUTATION OF MR. GEORGE GIFFARD HIS SUPPOSED CONSIMILITUDE BETWENE THE DONATISTS AND US, WHEREIN IS SHEWED HOW HIS ARGUMENTS HAVE BENE AND MAY BE BY THE PAPISTS MORE JUSTLY RETORTED AGAINST HIMSELF AND PRESENT ESTATE OF THEIR CHURCH

In 1587–1588 Barrow, Greenwood, and Gifford carried on a polemic in manuscript treatises. About May, 1590, Gifford issued his second answer in a printed book, *A Short Treatise against the Donatists of England, Whome We Call Brownists.*

One portion of this work (pp. 7–46) pertained to the accusation of false worship, and much of the argument revolved around the subject of read prayer (pp. 21–46). To this subject of false worship and read prayer, Greenwood addressed himself, and during the summer of 1590 his book appeared, *An Answere to George Gifford's Pretended Defence of Read Praiers and Devised Litourgies.* On February 25, 1590/1591, Gifford's third answer was entered in the *Stationers' Register*, with the title: *A Plaine Declaration That Our Brownists Be Full Donatists, by Comparing Them Together from Point to Point Out of the Writings of Augustine. Also a Replie to Master Greenwood Touching Read Prayer, Wherein His Grosse Ignorance Is Detected, Which Labouring to Purge Himselfe from Former Absurdities, Doth Plunge Himselfe Deeper into the Mire.* It will be seen from the title that Gifford's book dealt with two issues: Donatism and read prayer, which constitute the two main divisions of the book. Greenwood proceeded to answer both charges. About March, 1591, he wrote *A Breife Refutation of Mr. George Giffard His Supposed Consimilitude betwene the Donatists and Us, Wherein Is Shewed How His Arguments Have Bene and May Be by the Papists More Justly*

Retorted against Himself and Present Estate of Their Church. This work, which is a denial of the accusation of Donatism, constitutes a reply to the first part of *A Plaine Declaration* (pp. 1–69), and it was published, about April, as one section of the 1591 edition of Barrow, *A Plaine Refutation of Mr. George Giffarde's Reprochful Booke* (pp. 207–234). It is also included in the 1605 edition of *A Plaine Refutation of Mr. Giffard's Booke, Intituled,* A SHORT TREATISE GAINST THE DONATISTES OF ENGLAND (pp. 209–236).

Some time during the early spring of 1591 Greenwood wrote another reply to Gifford. This time he devoted himself to the second portion of *A Plaine Declaration* (pp. 70[72]–126), which is a defence of read prayers in the Church of England. He entitled his reply, *A Fewe Observations of Mr. Giffard's Last Cavills about Stinted Read Prayers, and Devised Leitourgies.* This was also published, about April, as a part of the 1591 edition of *A Plaine Refutation of Mr. George Giffarde's Reprochful Booke* (pp. 235–256). It was also included in the 1603 edition of *An Aunswer to George Gifford's Pretended Defence of Read Prayers and Devised Leitourgies* (pp. 45–66), and therefore was excluded from the 1605 edition of *A Plaine Refutation,* which now included for the first time a section with a similar title, *A Few Observations to the Reader of M. Giffard His Last REPLIE* (pp. 237–260), written in 1591/1592 by Barrow in answer to Gifford's *A Short Reply unto the Last Printed Books of Henry Barrow and John Greenwood, the Chiefe Ringleaders of Our Donatists in England* (entered in the *Stationers' Register* on December 6, 1591).

[207]

A BREIFE REFUTATION OF MR. GEORGE GIFFARD HIS SUPPOSED CONSIMILITUDE BETWENE THE DONATISTS AND US, WHEREIN IS SHEWED HOW HIS ARGUMENTS HAVE BENE AND MAY BE BY THE PAPISTS MORE JUSTLY RETORTED AGAINST HIMSELF AND PRESENT ESTATE OF THEIR CHURCH[1]

Mr. Giffard a man inexpert in discerning the times and seasons, having long skirmished with vaine titles, and assuming the matter in question, undertaketh now to deface all God's inviolable ordinances with a certayne dialogue betwene Augustine and the Donatistes,[2] and to make Christ's ordinances and our persons odious, as he supposeth, to all men therby, to heale the wounde of the beaste and dawbe up the whole table of the Romish ministerie, lawes, worship, government, which al men of anie judgment know to be received from the pope. He taketh upon him to compare us to the Donatistes, and without considering the causes and persons from which and from whome they separated, as also the times and ages. He sclanderously wresteth some perticular doctrines about separation, and wee therupon must needes be Donatistes. But we have learned that we ought al to take heede to the most sure Word of God, and that he that speaketh ought to speake as the wordes of God, and to this lawe and this testimonie if anie speake not, it is because there is no light in him. We refuse utterly to be drawen into this kinde of fruictlesse strife, and will not intermedle either with the Donatistes' nor Augustine's persons, nor yet with their causes or maner of pleading them; but only shewe in a fewe breif notes how unjustly this godlesse quarrelous man hath dealt herein, even in the thinges he hath set downe, leaving the better veiewe thereof to such as will bestowe their time that waye, and those to due consideration, and unpartiall triall by the Worde and Spirit of God.

At his first entrance into his discourse, he denyeth us to be Christians, saying, all that are gathered by Christ's doctrine only unto Christ alone, as it is written, "one is your Doctor, even Christ," Matthew 23, are only by his title called Christians. But we are

[1] By John Greenwood.

[2] *A Plaine Declaration That Our Brownists Be Full Donatists, by Comparing Them Together from Point to Point out of the Writings of Augustine* [pp. 1–69]. *Also a Replie to Master Greenwood Touching Read Prayer* [pp. 72–126].

wicked schismatickes, therfore we must be called by the first aucthors or chief maintayners thereof.[1] To which we answere, that Mr. Giffard and his collegiates have given out for undoubted doctrines, that such as hold the fundamental doctrines of justification by faith in Christ alone, are to be holden Christians; and to cleare our selves a litle further, we seeke to be gathered and ruled by Christ's doctrine only, and by Christ alone as our King, Priest and Prophet, [208] yea, therfore we suffer, because wee wil not denie this faith. But by his owne argument he hath turned himself and their whole church and priesthood out of the folde, whiles they are not gathered unto Christ alone by his doctrine only, but maintaine Antichriste's lawes and orders; his servantes they are to whome they gyve themselves to obey.

To prove his former reason, hee aledgeth the custome of the olde time in God's church and the Scripture it self, Revelation 2, where the Nicolaitanes are mentioned, Arians of Arius, Montanistes of Montanus, Novatians of Novatus, Pelagians of Pelagius, Donatistes of Donatus.[2] The doctrine we do graunt, that wicked heretikes and scismatikes may justly be named of the aucthors and leaders. But heresie and schisme we denye to be maintayned by us. And you, having never convinced us of heresie, neither can prove your churche to be the true apparant established church of Christ, must gyve accompt for your malitious sclandering of us, and numbring us

[1] *Ibid.*, p. 1.

[2] *Ibid.*, p. 1. The Nicolaitans are mentioned in Revelation 2:6, 15. They are also mentioned by Irenaeus and Hippolytus, as followers of Nicolas, who was a proselyte from Antioch. See Acts 6:5. Arius was a presbyter in the Alexandrian church, a student of Lucian, and the staunch opponent of Athanasius at the Council of Nicaea. Arius advocated the view that "the Son has a beginning but that God is without beginning." The Son, Jesus, is like the Father, but not identical with Him. Arius represented the homoiousian position and Athanasius supported the homoousian doctrine. Montanus came from Phrygia, in Asia Minor. About 175 he advocated the early return of Christ, emphasized prophecy, stressed purity of life, and claimed to be the special mouthpiece of the Paraclete or Holy Spirit. Tertullian was a convert to Montanism and strengthened it in Carthage. Novatian was a presbyter in the church at Rome, opposed lenient treatment for the *lapsi* or weak brethren who had yielded to the Decian persecution, and promoted a schism by his opposition to the bishops of Rome, Fabian (236–250), and Cornelius (251–253). Pelagius was a British monk who taught that free-will and indeterminism are true, that the doctrine of original sin was wrong, that a child is born without sin, that some men are sinless, and that men should lead a life of moral austerity by the strength of their own wills. His views provoked Augustine to write his anti-Pelagian denunciations. Donatus was the opponent of Caecilian and the successor of Marjorinus. Elected bishop of Carthage in 316, Donatus the Great gave his name to the schism that developed first in 311 and continued until the Vandals and Arabs overran northern Africa. Augustine wrote trenchantly against the Donatists.

among such hatefull heretickes as the Arians, etc. If wee be Christians, then must you gyve accompt for this offence, which is not only done to us, but to his truth and to himself. You affirme in an other place that you had rather gyve accompt for to[o] much charitie shewed to the wicked, yea, for justifying an evil man, than for condemning the just,[1] being ignorant that the woe is pronounced against both. But here you have forgotten your self herein, and by sclandering the truth you know what danger you incurre. Luke 17:1, 2. Matthew 18:7.

He draweth the original of Brownisme (as he termeth it) from Donatus, and saith Browne was the cheife renewer therof,[2] yet afterward saith ther was a church of them eighteene yeeres agoe in London, wherin one Bolton was a cheife doer, whose fearful end is not forgotten.[3] For the original of our profession we fetch it from Christ and his apostles and practize of the church in the apostles' time, as all the martyres from time to time have done, according to the light they sawe. For Donatus and Browne, they must answere for themselves. We are buylt upon the foundation of the apostles and prophetts, Jesus Christ being the chief corner stone. Other foundation than this can no man lay; wee offer our workes to be tryed hereby. It is Mr. Giffard himself that so wel may remember the fearfull end of Bolton, for it is true that (as I have heard) he stood against your ministerie for cappes, surplus [surplice], crosse, with many other your Romish trynckets, as I have heard your self have done;[4] after [later] revolting and become a conformable member of your churche, hanging himself, it is a remembrance for apostates.

Donatisme (saith he) "in old time about twelve hundreth yeares past was condemned, as approued [a proud] detestable schisme and

[1] *A Plaine Declaration*, signature A 2 *recto*.

[2] See Albert Peel and Leland H. Carlson, *The Writings of Robert Harrison and Robert Browne*. See also Dwight C. Smith, "Robert Browne, Independent," *Church History*, VI (December, 1937).

[3] John Bolton was a member of the Plumbers' Hall Congregation and of the Privy Church of Richard Fitz in the period 1567–1571. He was elected an elder in the Privy Church, recanted publicly at Paul's Cross, was excommunicated, probably regretted his recantation, and hanged himself. See Burrage, *Early English Dissenters*, I, 80–93; II, 10, 12, 140. Gifford speaks of Bolton and the church "twenty yeares past" (1590/91–1570/71), and his reference to "eighteene yeeres agoe" suggests 1572–1573 as the date for Bolton's death.

[4] During the 1580's Gifford was a Reformist, joined the classis movement in Essex, refused to conform, was suspended as vicar at Maldon, Essex, but was permitted to continue as minister or preacher of God's Word. See John Strype, *Annals*, III, Part I, 354, 691; III, Part II, 479. John Strype, *Aylmer*, pp. 71–73. John Strype, *Whitgift*, I, 301; II, 190.

heresie." The Brownistes and Donatists shal appeare to "agree together as two peices of cloth that are of the same woll, same threed, colour, working, and bredth."[1] If this man had read with judgment the Holy Scripture as concerning the general defection and apostasie, with the encrease and decrease of Antichriste's kingdome, hee would have blushed to have entred this comparison. For the Donatistes wee have not to deale, yet if the right eye were not blinded, hee [209] might have considered better the Donatistes' causes of separation and ours, and it woulde not have seemed so like together; the times, causes, persons from whome and maner of their separation must be better weighed, which because he hath taken in hande to perticulate afterward, I wil only shew one here wherin we make such a difference, as al his other are but trifles. The Donatistes held still the same worship, government, offices, officers, entrance, and the same administration of sacraments, etc., that the other did from whome they did separate, and as it seemeth received whole citties and contries to be the church as before; so that their separation was more like the sectes and schismes amon[g]st your selves; you from the papists, the Martinistes[2] from you, the forward predicants (as they are called) from the bishops,[3] than any such separation as we by the commandement of God make from the false church, false ministerie, false sacraments, antichristian government, etc., unto the true ordinances of Christ. Heretickes and sectaries make schisme; but this true convertion from the evill to the good, from the false to the true, fewe find it, although it be the plaine commandement of God, Revelation 18:4, and the way to salvation, Acts 2:40.

For indeed it is not enough to forsake the false wayes, but to seeke the antient wayes of the Lord, and to walke in them, that wee may finde rest to our soules. Mr. Giffard his setting downe of the causes of the Donatistes' separation, bewrayeth himself to seeke onlie the defamation of the truth, without shew of reason.

First he sayth that in the persecutions by the Romish emperours,

[1] *A Plaine Declaration*, p. 2.

[2] The Martinists were the writers and followers of the Martin Marprelate point of view in 1588–1590. See William Pierce, *An Historical Introduction to the Marprelate Tracts*. See Henry M. Dexter, *The Congregationalism of the Last Three Hundred Years*, Lecture III, 129–202.

[3] Some of the forward predicants, or Reformist preachers, were Thomas Cartwright, Laurence Chaderton, William Charke, Stephen Egerton, John Field, William Fludd, Richard Gardener, George Gifford, John Knewstub, William Perkins, William Proudlove, Walter Travers, John Udall, and Robert Wright.

manie being (as they were then termed) proditors and traditors[1] of the bookes of God, the holy vessells, their bretheren, etc., there was a rumor that such offences had bene committed by some. Nowe (saith he) "there came certaine bishops from Numidia to Carthage, a famous citie in Africa, to ordeyne a bishop, and found Cecilianus[2] alredye ordeined and placed in the seate," etc.[3] Thus farre I trust it will be granted me his peeces of cloth are not both of a woll; for the difference, I refer to the obstinate and heynouse transgressions wherwith we have chardged these parrish assemblies. Further, the Brownistes (as he in the spirit of blasphemy termeth them) approve of no such bishop or bishoprickes, no such seate nor ordination as they came about.

Well, the bishops of Numidia "were wroth that they could not ordeine."[4] In this poinct his threeds are not proportionable. Wee thrust not our selves beyond our lyne in these actions, neither do any thing in the high matters of God through ambition. These things are all founde amongst your selves, the kingdome through envie divided; for al your chiefest strife hath bene, whither a synode of parrish priestes [a Presbyterian classis or presbytery], or a lord bishop should create your priestes;[5] this being your principal

[1] Proditors and traditors are betrayers, traitors. During the persecution of Diocletian (303–305–313) some Christians saved their own lives by delivering up their sacred books and vessels and even betraying their friends. Secundus, Bishop of Tigisis in Africa, refused to deliver up the Scriptures to the officials, and said: "I am a Christian and a bishop, not a traditor."

[2] Cecilianus, or Caecilian, was a deacon in the church at Carthage. In 311 he was chosen bishop to succeed Bishop Mensurius of Carthage. Some of the zealous martyrs and sufferers regarded Caecilian as a traitor or traditor, and refused to recognize him as bishop. Subsequently, a council of seventy bishops declared his ordination by Bishop Felix invalid, and a new bishop, Majorinus, was elected and consecrated. His successor in 316 was Donatus "the Great", from whom the Donatist schism is named. The most recent work on Donatism is W. H. C. Frend, *The Donatist Church. A Movement of Protest in Roman North Africa* (Oxford, 1952).

[3] *A Plaine Declaration*, pp. 2, 3. [4] *Ibid.*, p. 3.

[5] This is a reference to the controversy which had been waged during the past two decades between the Presbyterians and the Anglicans. It began in earnest with the dismissal in December, 1570, of Thomas Cartwright from his Lady Margaret professorship and from his fellowship in September, 1572. The appeals to Parliament, the Admonition Controversy, the appearance of Walter Travers' *A Full and Plaine Declaration of Ecclesiasticall Discipline* (1574–1575), and the rise of the Separatists in Norwich complicated the struggle. Above all, the rise of the classis movement in the 1580's helped to spread Presbyterian ideas.

A new phase began in 1584 with the publication of *A Breife and Plaine Declaration concerning the Desires of All Those Faithfull Ministers*, a work generally attributed to William Fulke and known by its running title as "The Learned Discourse." In 1587 Dr. John Bridges, dean of Salisbury, issued his lengthy (1401 pp.) and discursive work, *A Defence of the Government Established in the Church of England for*

contention, the one side must needs be Donatistes. He procedeth and saith, these bishops of Numidia "joyned together, and layd a crime upon Cecilianus; they say his ordeyner delyvered the holy books and was a traditor [traitor]; whereupon they would have Cecilianus reputed no minister of Christ, but the sonne of a traditor [traitor]."[1] In this Mr. Giffard discerneth not colours. The Brownistes [210] separate not for anie one man's person through envie, they shewe other causes whie they repute your whole ministerie to be a false and antichristian ministerie and not the true ministerie of the gospel; they allowe not ordination by one man, but prove the offices, entrance, and administration of your ministerie to be wholly antichristian; and hereupon we repute them no true ministerie of Christ. For the triall of this matter (sayth hee) "there was no assemblie of learned pastors to judge in this case according to Christ's ordinance," but *furor*, *dolus*, *tumultus* did beare the swaie.[2] Here Mr. Giffard saith, it is Christ's ordinance that an holie assemblie should judge in such cases. Howe will this agree with the office of your arch-bishop? Further (as a man ignorant in the Scriptures) he would have the people excluded in their synods.[3] The Holye Ghost setteth before us another order. Acts 15. And for a christian trial of our cause, wee have everie way sought it by supplication and all maner of wayes, but could never obteine it. But your whole broode have not only refused it, and shewed al exquisite tyrannie upon our bodies so farr as they had powre, by close emprisonment, rending us from our trades and families, and al ordinarie meanes of live[li]hood, but set their priestes everiwhere to crye out in their pulpits, gyving out lyes and sclanders openly and

Ecclesiasticall Matters. It was answered by Dudley Fenner in *A Defence of the Godlie Ministers* (1587), by Walter Travers, *A Defence of the Ecclesiastical Discipline* (1588), partly by John Udall in *A Demonstration of the Trueth of That Discipline Which Christe Hath Prescribed* (1588). In 1588 and 1589 the Martin Marprelate pamphlets were published, and in January 1588/1589 Bishop Thomas Cooper issued his *An Admonition to the People of England*.

[1] *A Plaine Declaration*, p. 3. Felix, bishop of Aptunga, was the one who consecrated Caecilian, but the charge against him of delivering up the holy books to his persecutors is debatable. Even if the charge were true, the "sins" of the bishop should not be imputed to others, and the consecration should not be regarded as invalid.

[2] *Ibid.* The expression "fury, deceit, and tumult," is from St. Augustine, "Psalmus contra Partem Donati," *Sancti Aurelii Augustini Hipponensis Episcopi Opera Omnia*, Tome IX (Paris, 1837), p. 44. Augustine wrote: "Non testes, non documentum, quo possent crimen probare; sed furor, dolor, tumultus, qui regnant in falsitate."

[3] The Elizabethan Presbyterians or Reformists minimized the role of lay elders. The classis movement, being secret, consisted of meetings of clergymen, professional get-togethers, without laymen.

secretly, in articles,[1] in printed bookes,[2] in private complaints and false suggestions, wherin Mr. Giffard hath not bene behinde, yet never vouchsafed us free conference, nor have or can convince us of crime or error maintayned by us. In whom then is this *furor*, *dolus*, *tumultus* now found, but in these godlesse priestes, that cannot abide the light, because their workes are evill?

He procedeth now to shew what tryalls [hearings, conferences] were granted the Donatists before the emperour, and by his apointment.[3] Wherein there wil be founde little consimilitude betwene our estate and theirs: for these antichristian bishops usurpe such powre, as the magistrate may not cal their actions into question, shutting up the benefit of the common lawe against us, suffring no jurie to passe upon those they murther in pryson, nor no bayle for anie they commyt. I mervel you could set forth these trialls alowed the Donatistes without blushing, and make such havock amongst God's children now without anie trial granted them.

Further it is rehersed how these men, the Numidian bishopps and their companie, condemned "all churches through the worlde, as wrapped together in the guyltines of those churches of Africa," al polluted, al uncleane, al "fallen from the covenant of God through [the pollution of] such as had committed sacriledge and were not separated." They said there was no true ministerie, no true church, no true sacramentes.[4] To which wee answere, that wee are not to pleade the Donatistes' cause; but setting their persons and causes aside, I trust it wil be granted me, that the defection and apostasie under Antichrist was generall, in which defection you wil stil remaine in obstinate confusion, not only retayning that ministerie, worship, lawes, offices, etc., but rejecting Christ's prescribed and for ever commanded in his testament; which your ministerie, lawes, worship [211] and government we are able to prove false and antichristian. So that there is no consimilitude in the Donatistes' separation and ours in this poinct; their matter being about sinnes committed in the church, where there was lawful office, worship, government, as they did not denie; and our cause being about the not having of a church gathered unto Christ from the apostasie, from all them that remaine under that apostatical ministerie, govern-

[1] These articles were printed and refuted in *A Collection of Certaine Sclaunderous Articles Gyven Out by the Bisshops*, signature A iv *recto*–B iv *verso*. See Carlson, *The Writings of John Greenwood, 1587–1590, Together with the Joint Writings of Henry Barrow and John Greenwood, 1587–1590*, pp. 103–174.

[2] Greenwood is referring to the books of Robert Some, George Gifford, and Richard Alison.

[3] *A Plaine Declaration*, p. 3. [4] *Ibid.*, p. 4.

ment, and worship, and in that confusion we have warrant to separate, Revelation 18:3, 4.

Now to the poinct: These Numidian bishops taught, that so manie as would save their soules, must separate themselves.[1] Mr. Giffard wil graunt, I doubt not, that if there were no true church, true ministerie, nor no true sacramentes, it was tyme to come out from amongst them, and have no communion with the tables of divells, as the apostle reasoneth, I Corinthians 10. If the Donatistes separated from the true church, we do not so; but we separate according to God's commandement from the false church, false ministerie, worship, and sacramentes. Prove your church therfore a true church, or our separation is just and holy, and the only way to salvation. In the mean tyme let the papist reason thus with you: You separate from our church, therfore you are schismatikes, Donatistes, heretickes. If Mr. Giffard say, no, we hold you the true church, to have the seales of the covenant, to hold many doctrines of faith, to be the temple of God, then we [Separatists] may lawfully hold you still daughters of that damnable harlot, murderesse of the saintes so often accursed, in whose cupp of fornication you are drunken. If he say separation from the false church is a commandement of God, and that they have made a kinde of separation, then all are not Donatistes that make a separation, but the cause must be considered from whome, for which, in what maner, and to what we separate or joyne.

Where he alledgeth that Augustine thought it an unequall thing to condemne as they did at the first all the world for one man's sinne; namely, for the sinne of this Caecilianus, and they thereupon tooke on hand to affirme, "that as the church of Carthage and the churches elswhere in Africa were fallen from God by the pollution of the sacriledge of Caecilianus and others, so all other churches in the world were destroyed by the like sacriledges committed in the dayes of persecution."[2] There is litle consimilitude betwene the Donatistes and us therein; for we separated not at the first for one man's sinne; neither do since condemne the churches we know not; but for the whole ministerie of Christ's testament, worship, lawes and ordinances, which you reject, deface, and pervert, standing subject unto and administring in the apostaticall orders and offices of Antichrist, do wee separate.

But to answere your perticulars as you have filled the printe with rayling, lying, and unfruictfull and impertinent matters, were but to

[1] *Ibid.* [2] *Ibid.*, pp. 4, 5.

trouble the reader and maintaine strife. You bring a storie of their comparison betwene Caecilianus and Judas Iscariot whether [which] should be greater sinner, a repetition of Calvine's *Institutions*, histories out of Augustine, Tertullian, etc.;[1] [212] which your labour, as it tendeth but to a shadowe of defence of your rayling, so I will leave their writinges and you to the judgment seate of God, where everie one must answere for himself, and brieflie proceed to your perticular accusations falsly fathered upon us most of them.

Thus we see (sayth he) "that the Donatistes departed disorderly out of the church, not condemning it for anie poinct of doctrine, for therein they did not disagree."[2] Herein then we cannot be compared, till you have proved your parish assemblies the true church; and we holde that you have poysoned all the fountaines of sincere doctrine, and pervert the whole testament, and turne away the practize thereof by your damnable false expositions, yea, that you teach not one poincte sincerely. Againe, where you say afterward that you will affirme the worship in the churches from which the Donatistes separated as corrupt as yours, and here say they agreed in all poinctes of doctrine, we wonder what [that?] you make your worship to be some things indifferent, as reading, for prayer; men's writings, for Scriptures; homilies, for interpretation; but no doctrine conteined in your worship.

And where you affirme that the Donatistes cryed out, all was polluted, because such as revolted from the faith in time of persecution, returned, and were againe received into the church,[3] you know we hold no such doctrine, but all that God gyveth grace to returne by repentance ought to be received, though no apostate ever to beare office in the church; yet such we take to be wholly purged in the blood of Christ by repentance, which your parish assemblies never did. But this (setting their persons aside) we take to be an undoubted truth of God, that where no separation is made from idolatrous prophane atheistes, heretickes, tyrannicall persecutors, nor no covenant entred by the faithfull unto the obedience and orderly practize of Christe's ordinances, but a generall commixture with the world in sacriledge, in false worship, under a false ministerie; such assemblies are no true churches orderly gathered or established.

[1] *Ibid.*, p. 6. See John Calvin, *Institutes of the Christian Religion*, translated by Henry Beveridge, II (London, 1949), pp. 291, 460, 521. Compare St. Augustine, "Contra Cresconium," Liber IV, *Sancti Aurelii Augustini Hipponensis Episcopi Opera Omnia*, Tome IX, Pars prior (Paris, 1837), pp. 748–752.

[2] *A Plaine Declaration*, p. 6. [3] *Ibid.*, p. 7.

"Now looke," saith he, "upon the Donatistes of England. Antichrist hath bene exalted according to the prophesie of Paule: he hath sat in the temple of God, etc."[1] This man by his whole former discourse and present argument (it semeth) herein chiefly compareth us to the Donatistes, that as they made all their quarrell for Caecilianus his unmeetnes for his office; so we made our quarrell for that Antichrist reigned, or doth reigne (as he after expoundeth it) in the church of God; wherein he affirmeth, that they which submitted or stand still in subjection unto his decrees, jurisdiction, ordinances, ministerie, are yet notwithstanding the true apparant church of God.[2] First we answere, that we take not the word [Antichrist] to be understood of one man's person, but of all the falsly called fathers of the sea [see] of Rome, and more generally of all that exalt themselves above the ordinances of Christ and his church, establishing their owne devises in place thereof, or give life [213] unto the image of the beast; for if the same markes of pride, blasphemie, and tyrannie, erection of a strange ministerie, lifting up themselves above Christ's testament, ordinances, and worship, be found emongst your spirituall lords in England, we see not but Antichrist spoken of by Paul may be also found amongst you. Now if Mr. Giffard had considered Caecilianus his estate (who at the hardest was but uncapable of that lawfull office, and to that lawfull administration, as it was on both sides supposed, and concerning the outward order or maner lawfully ordeyned), there can be no comparison betwene him and Antichrist. And for Antichriste's sitting in the temple of God, Mr. Giffard must know, that manie times the church is called the church, not because it remayneth still under the outward covenant, but because it sometimes did so; yea, and at the first creeping up of that man of sinne, while the iniquitie wrought in a mysterie, it was the church out of which he sprang, and in which he somtimes sat. The Holy Ghost giveth us then hereby to understand, that this Antichrist who should change the holy ordinances, should be an apostata, he should be neither Turke nor pagan, but the bottomlesse pit should be opened by him in more subtile and strange delusions; out of which smoke all your ministerie is proceeded. But when he had changed the ordinances, destroyed every greene thing, caused all high and low, rich and poore, to receive his marke in their hande or foreheade, and suffred none to buye and sell which would not fall downe and

[1] *Ibid.* Paul's prophecy is given in II Thessalonians 2:4.
[2] *A Plaine Declaration*, pp. 2, 8.

worship him, the sunne now covered with sackcloth, the moone turned into blood, the starrs fallen from heaven, the true worshippers murthered if any one stood up, God's curses threatned to all that worshipped the beast or his image, or received his marke in their hand or foreheade;[1] we hope this man will not say it was now the apparant church of God, lest he condemne not only the Scriptures, but al whome God commanded to come out of her, calling her the mother of fornications, the harlot that sitteth upon many waters, hold of all uncleane spirits, cage of all uncleane and hatefull birdes, confused Babell, etc.[2] So that if Mr. Giffard had anie salt of grace, he would better peruse the booke of Revelations, which with all the prophesies of the prophets, of Christ himself, and of his apostles, make manifest this generall apostasie and defection under Antichrist, and not now tell us a tale of Caecilianus. Doth he not see in the whole booke the false church and true lyvely [one] described? The one worshipping the beast, the other following the Lambe; the one persecuted, the other persecuting in most bloody murder of the sainctes.

Well (saith he), but Antichrist "is disclosed by the glorious light of the gospel, his damnable doctrine, cursed idolatrie, and usurped tyrannie are cast forth of this land," "the true doctrine of faith is published, etc."[3] First we must here demaunde, whether these assemblies were then the true church when they were ledd by those damnable doctrines, and lyved in that cursed idolatrie, bowing downe to the beast, and [214] persecuting the sainctes. Secondly, as we are not unthankfull for the abandoning of the pope's person, supremacie, with much of his damnable wares, we demaund of you what you thinke of those persons which set open his shoppes againe, keepe his courtes, and exercise like usurped power and tyrannie that was before. But to answere directly, Antichrist is not discovered in your assemblies, his damnable doctrines, cursed idolatries, usurped tyrannie are not cast forth, the doctrine of faith is not sincerely published.

Againe, what is al this to the proving of a true church, a lawfull ministerie, true worship, and holy government of Christ? Your parish assemblies were received from the pope's hand, without anie conversion by repentance or orderly gathering by doctrine into any communion, the pope's ministerie set over them, the worship, though a litle changed out of Latine into English, some of theirs

[1] Revelation 6:12, 13; 8:7; 9:1, 2; 13:16, 17; 14:9.
[2] Revelation 17:1, 2, 5; 18:2, 3. [3] *A Plaine Declaration*, p. 7.

left out, but al that remaineth either taken from his portesse [portas] or men's devises, these assemblies still governed by those courtes, officers and canons, that [existed, prevailed] before. What place hath now Christe's testament amongst you? How is Antichrist discovered or his damnable wares cast forth? Is it not made subject to these antichristian ordinances, ministerie, worship, governement? Is it not limited, stinted, and apportioned, no further to be opened than to uphold these execrable orders, idolatries, sacrileges? Yea, is not only the bare name therof used as a stale,[1] and doctrine therof perverted to the deceiving of the people in this estate? Moses' law was read everie Sabboth day in their synagogs, when they crucified Christ. But you should have proved you had such assemblies, such a ministeri, such a worship, such a government, as the gospel prescribeth. Being then the same assemblies, contynuing in false worship under the same ministerie, government, al the atheistes, papistes, hereticks, antichristian officers, etc., in one commixture that the pope left, we may wel affirme you to remaine stil the marcked servantes of Antichrist, not speaking here how many Antichristes are here exalted; leaving the damnable doctrines, cursed idolatrie, false preaching of the gospell, to our lardger discourse in due place.[2]

But now Mr. Giffard beholding these things, that they have made no separation, nor drawen the people unto the ordinances of the gospel, is compelled to runne backe againe to justifie the church of Rome, and to maintaine that these assemblies were the true churches of Christ in the deepest defection under Antichrist: "The apostasie having invaded the church, it contynued even then the temple of God in which Antichrist did sit, and that the very idolators were sealed with the seale of baptisme, professed Christ in some poinctes rightly, their children from antient discent within the covenant, the ministeri so far remayning as [that] it was the authentick seale delyvered by them;" the Brownistes not understanding the Scripture, thus "in mad furie lyke blynde hypocrites condemne, etc."[3] Let us reason a litle more coolely, rage will not serve to carie the matter. We will here take it granted that your parishes, ministerie, etc., cannot now be proved the church and ministerie [215] of Christ, except they were so in the time of poperie. We see furder

[1] A decoy-bird, trap, lure, bait, pretext, deception.

[2] This may be a reference to Barrow's *A Plaine Refutation* or to *A Brief Discoverie of the False Church.* More likely, Greenwood is referring to his own work, *An Answere*, published in 1590.

[3] *A Plaine Declaration*, pp. 7, 8.

how wel the gospel is opened or Antichrist discovered with you, when such a famous prophet hath not learned to read the mysterie written in that woman's forehead, which the Holy Ghost recordeth to be this: "great Babilon the mother of whoredomes and abhominations of the earth," Revelation 17:[5]. Again, the Scripture saith, *caput* 14. "If any man worship the beast and his image, and receive a marke in his forehead or on his hand, the same shall drincke of the wine of the wrath of God."[1] Who wil Mr. Giffard make this woman, if not the church of Rome sitting upon the people, tongues, and nations that were seduced or are seduced in this apostasie? And howe hath he read the Scriptures that [who] saith, the seales of the covenant belong to open blasphemous idolators and their seede? God saith, he will punish the transgression unto the third and fourth generation.[2] He [Giffard] saith nay, though they be the children of idolators and contynue in their fathers' steppes, they ought to have the seals of the covenant. Againe, if he say the seale of baptisme in the false church belongeth unto that adulterous seede, howe wil he denie that blasphemous sacrifice and bread God,[3] against which so manie witnesses have gyven their lyves, which is plainely deniing of Christ to be come in the flesh, and imagining him a fantastical body to be in every place? How can Mr. Giffard yeild them one sacrament, and not the other? Further, how ignorantly he speaketh of the covenant, and of a sacrament made by that ministerie, it were too long to discusse.

Wel, in al this he hath forgotten his comparison betwene the Donatistes and us; they had no such controversie with Caecilianus: but now peruse one of Mr. Giffard's reasons. The church of papacie in the deepest defection was the visible temple of God, having the true seales of the covenant.[4] I then reason thus: The church of Geneva, Scotland, Lowe Countries, France, etc., have separated from the church of Rome which is the apparant church of God (for none have the true ministerie and the true authentick seales of the covenant, but the true churche). Therefore they are schismaticks, Donatists, Brownists, hereticks. Againe, Geneva, Scotland, etc., condemne the church of Rome by separating from it; therefore they do also condemne the Church of England, which approveth of and communicateth with the papistes. Moreover, howe wil he answere this: Her Majestie hath expelled the pope, his ministerie, his doctrine, and idolatrous worship; therfore she hath expelled the

[1] Revelation 14:9, 10. [2] Exodus 20:5; Numbers 14:18; Deuteronomy 5:9.
[3] The Eucharist and the doctrine of transubstantiation.
[4] *A Plaine Declaration*, p. 8.

ministerie and worship of the true church? And what followeth by Mr. Giffard his collections, think you? They that reject the ministerie of Christ, reject Christ himself.

But these Brownistes condemne the reformation by magistrates, etc.[1] No, it is a false sclander. We only put difference betwene the reformation by the magistrate's sworde, and the reformation by doctrine;[2] and he is a false prophet that either goeth about to set these at variance, or confoundeth them. The magistrat suppresseth the evil within the church and without the church in their dominions by bodily punishments in equitie, and defendeth the godly. The ministerie of the Word gathereth, guydeth, ordereth, etc., a people unto and under the true or-[216] dinances of Christ, by the Word and Spirit. The prince may and ought suppresse all false worship, false ministerie, idolatrous assemblies; and proclaime and commaund true worship, orderly assemblies, true ministerie, etc.[3] But the workmanship hereof is spiritual, by doctrine, etc., to be accomplished in due order according to the rule of the Word. Stil wee urge you therfore to shewe us this gathering, ordering, and governing of a true church in these parrish assemblies, by the Word of God. In the meane time you bestowe but your oyle, meale, and your whole ministerie and guyftes to dawbe upp idolatrie, confusion, sacriledge. Neither doth the word [*reformation*] agree to your church, for cursed is he that buyldeth the walles of Jericho, not one stone of Babel wil serve for a foundation.[4]

What comparison is there then betwene your reformation, and the reformation by Josias? Shew the perticulars, we wil answere. Ells it shall suffice that he sacrificed the priestes of Baal upon the altar, reduced the people to the true ministerie and ordinances of the

[1] *Ibid.*

[2] The pattern of reformation should be derived from Scripture, not from the State; but the latter should sanction the former. Reformation without tarrying for any, as advocated by Robert Browne, was permissible, but the role of the magistrate was really that of implementing the programme of reform and removing the obstacles. Brownists and Barrowists welcomed the reformation by magistrates—provided that such a reformation was consonant with the Scriptural pattern. What Browne and Barrow and Greenwood found difficult in perceiving was that men could evolve such different patterns from the same Bible. Moreover, they found it more difficult to believe that the pattern, once established, was subject to adjustments and alterations in different times and places, as asserted by Thomas Cooper, Thomas Bilson, Richard Hooker, and Archbishop Whitgift.

[3] Greenwood may not have realized that both Roman Catholics and Anglicans believed this to be a true policy. Intolerance was still the norm.

[4] Joshua 6:26.

temple. If the priestes did not this according to God's Worde, then they were guyltie, and to be punished by his sworde. So that these false prophets, inchanters, counterfeit time-servers (which extol Her Majestie for having granted the freedome of the gospel, true ministerie, true worship, government, etc., and yet themselves do misleade the people in a false way to perdition) shall not only lye open to the magistrate's sword when God shall put in their heart to execute his wil, but answere before the Lord for al this confusion, sacriledge, idolatrie, and filthines maintained by their deceitful tongues. I do not pleade to have them put to death, because they never knew or professed the truth; but to have their false offices abolished, and they compelled to some lawfull calling in the church or common wealth, as they should be thereunto founde meete, and be lawfully called.

Wee are not deceived then in imagining that you woulde make us believe the princes did compell them to be a church which were no church before, without any orderly gathering, guyding, and ordering of them by Christe's lawes, worship, ministerie, and ordinances; for wee deny that your parrish assemblies were in time of popery true churches, or have nowe forsaken all false worship. Prove your assertions, and what discipline belongeth to the false church, judge you.

OF THE POLLUTION BY COMMUNICATING WITH OPEN SINNERS

Where hee maketh the cause of our separation, and (as hee calleth it) our accusing of these parrish assemblies to be utterly fallen from the covenant of God, to be for that they are polluted with communicating with open sinners, he mistaketh, and (I feare) purposly falsifieth our minde and writings; for we have added to this an obstinate and wilful retayning of al sortes of prophane as members of your church, gyving them the sacraments, etc. But as I have donne before, so must [219] you here take my answere, that we deny these parrish assemblies to be true churches, or to have any power or aucthoritie to cast out any according to Christe's ordinance; so that wee cannot reason with you as to make the controversie of open sinners in the church, but as a confused assemblie, not being ever gathered unto Christ, or guyded by his ordinances. We know that in the true church are and shalbe open sinners, yet ther are rules and lawes by due censure to bring them to repentance, or els to cast them out if they remaine obstinate in anie open grosse sinne, of which things we wil not enter into discourse with you, deniing you to have eyther true church, or power to redresse abuses in your parrish assemblies.

And where he demandeth what order of discipline wee have observed in our separation; we have learned that no other censures belong unto the false church, than powring forth the vialls into the ayre, waters, sunne, etc. For this wee have the direction and commandement of God, Revelation 16 and 18:6. Againe, where should we finde your synod of pastors in the whole tayle of the dragon; you have no such order as you prate of unskilfully; your Lord Archbishop or Ordinarie can teach you otherwise than plead for synods of pastors.[1] For anie christian or equal triall either in free conference by the Scriptures, or triall by the common law, we have upon the dispence of our lyves long sued for it, and cannot obtaine anie as wee have said, and finde nothing but *furor*, *dolus*, *tumultus*[2] amongst your broode.

Now after his former discourse, he will from poinct to poinct prove us to agree with the Donatistes. First (saith he) "the Donatistes did accuse and condemne the churche and ministerie of the churches most falslie. And I say" (saith he) "the Brownistes are as false accusers as they, and condemne as injustly in all crimes."[3] Here are bold and sore chardges; but Mr. Giffard's bare word wil not stand.

The Donatistes' cause was not about the orderly gathering of a true church, but for the casting out of the unworthie; not about the office, entrance, or administration of the ministerie, but about the sinnes of such as were in that office. So that if Mr. Giffard would looke againe of the cause, he should finde no cause to keepe this stirr as upon a stage to no end or edifiing. Wee have often told him in our former writinges, that our matter is not about offenders in the church, but about the beeing or not beeing a church. In the meane time he handsomly layeth upon their owne filthines, saying companies and swarmes of drunckardes, gluttons, whoremasters, covetous worldlings, greedie usurers, extortioners, oppressours, bribers, defrauders, lyers, backbyters and sclanderers, envious, hatefull, and contentious persons, swearers and cursers, are suffred and admitted to the Lord's table; this, saith he, in manie or in most of their parrish assemblies, and many of their ministeri such. Where

[1] The Presbyterian faction was effectively blocked by the bishops, and the classis movement was upset in 1590 with the arrest and imprisonment of such leaders as Thomas Cartwright and John Udall.

[2] Fury, deceit, tumult. These words from St. Augustine had been used by Gifford against the Barrowists. [3] *A Plaine Declaration*, p. 10.

[wherein he doth] admit them a church in his owne conceit, let him ad now this more which is as true; that they have no power to redresse these evils by due censure, for that they thus contynue after they have bene long and often reproved for this sacriledge, [218] and we are bold to pronounce the priest as the people, a denne of theives, a cage of uncleane spirits, as the harlot that receiveth all commers, cast together into Jesabel's bed.

Hee further confesseth that the threatnings of the prophets against Israel are due unto them,[1] whereby hee confesseth these assemblies not to be the churches of God. For all the prophets that prophesied against Israel in the defection, pronounce her not to be the churche of God; reade Hosea 1 and 2; Jeremie 3; Ezechiell 23. But, saith he, might not the Donatistes have pleaded that there were manie wicked people and wicked ministers in those churches from which they separated.[2] We answere, that is not the question; for first we denie you to have anie church orderly gathered unto the ordinances, worship, government of Christ, which they did not. And againe we have not to reason what they might have excepted against those assemblies or ministers, but what they made the cause of their separation; wherein you trouble but your self, and with odiouse names deceive the ignorant, to make anie shewe of agreement betwene our cause and theirs.

"It wil be demanded" (saith he) "whither Cyprian and the rest of the godly did worship together with those open sinners" in their dayes, joyning with them in prayer and in the sacramentes, etc.[3] No, the question shal be, Mr. Giffard, whether if they did communicate with the open transgressions of the lawe in their time, they did wel and lawfully therein, or no; for I trust you will graunt that the church hath alwayes power to cast out the obstinate offenders; reade then the fifth [chapter] of the I [Epistle] to the Corinthians a litle more consideratly, and tel us whether they faulted not in keeping in their fellowship the incestuous person, and for not purging out the leaven from amongst them; for what saith the text? "Now I write unto you that you companie not together; if anie that is called a brother be a fornicator, or an idolator, or railer, or a drunckard, or an extortioner, with such an one eate not."[4] Where the words *me synanamignysthai*,[5] be not together commingled; and

[1] *Ibid.*, p. 11. Gifford actually says that "the complaints that the prophets doo make everie where against the church of Israel, may verie well be applied against us" [the Church of England].

[2] *Ibid.*, p. 11. [3] *Ibid.*, p. 14. [4] I Corinthians 5:11.

[5] Mē sunanamignusthai—not to be mixed with, not to be commingled.

after, "with such an one eate not," sheweth a plaine inhibition of communicating with the open prophane or impenitent offendors. For where is this commixture or commixion, if not in that holy banquet and conjunction in the communion and Supper of the Lorde; and if Mr. Giffard could discerne the spiritual things, he might see the outward signes of bread and wyne to be tokens not only of our union with Christ and benefit of his death, but also of our communion with the members of his bodye spiritually, as the Holy Ghost reasoneth, saiing, "The cup of blessing which wee blesse, is it not the communion of the blood of Christ, and the bread which we breake, is it not the communion of the bodie of Christ, for we that are manie are one bread and one bodie, because we are partakers of one bread."[1] For us then to come together in this banquet and spiritual rejoycing with the members of Christ (to our judgment) we have true comfort one with another. But with the open prophane or obstinate open knowen transgressor ther can be no good rejoycing, fellowship or communion; for besides the wicked priest that presumptuouslye blesseth where God curseth, and committeth sacriledge in [219] delyvering the signe of God's covenant with his people in Christ, to the treaders under their feete of his body and blood; so the whole congregation, and every one that participateth with those open wicked, transgresse (in not admonishing and casting out the leaven) against so manie rules as command admonition and excommunication by due order, and partake with the wicked against God by their rejoycing with them as bretheren. But (as I have still pleaded with you), we know better order than blinde separation in pride, for the sinnes committed in the church; denying to reason with you what is to be done in the church, till you have proved your church to be a true church established, guyded by the officers and lawes of Christ; so that all your matter is but the fighting with your owne shadowe and flying the question in hand.

But my purpose is not to follow your gameplay either to justifie the Donatistes, or those learned pastors, neither to reject the truthes, nor maintaine the errors of either of both sides; wee have a better foundation to buyld upon, and a surer Word to trust unto; it is because you have no furniture on your selfe [shelfe?] that you set forth this shew, and fight under other men's names; your savour is lost if ever you had salt. Looke on one of your arguments how well it will prove your matter. The Brownistes use five or six places of Scripture which the Donatistes used; therefore the Brownistes be

[1] I Corinthians 10:16, 17.

Donatistes.[1] Let the Brownistes answere for themselves; but sure I must deny both proposition and consequence. For neither do we agree in the application of these, with them; neither do we aledge all the same places because we alledge some which they alledged for excommunication of the open knowen obstinat wicked in the church, or separation from the false church. Neither doth it follow that because we alledge some places they did, that therfore we are Donatistes. If you allow anie separation from Turke or pope, you must agree with Donatistes in some of these Scriptures, Esaias 52, II Corinthians 6. And in this your exquisit search you have had one place alledged yet now, which if you had well looked upon, you would have bene ashamed to have compared us to the Donatistes. It is written, Revelation 18:2, 3, 4, 5 verses, etc., where your mother church of Rome with all her daughters is proclaymed no longer to be rested in, or communicated with. If your assemblies be such a cage, stand in such confusion, have the same ministerie, lawes, worship, etc., then we must come out of her.

Where in consideration that you would conningly turne away all places that commaund a separation, by other men's expositions, and have not managed your cause in your owne name, I will brieflie demaunde whither you wil maintaine these doctrines or no. For the convincing whereof I shall either refer you to our handling of the four transgressions,[2] or els gyve you answere when you deale particularly in your owne name.

First, beginne to set downe under your owne hande that these Scriptures, "come out from emongst them," depart out of her, "seperate your selves," etc.,[3] are not understood of a separation both of bodye and minde. [220] Secondly, that the minister being a swearer, drunkerd, covetous, worldling, etc., he continuing obstinate in his sinne, in that estate may be suffred to administer, and the godly may communicate with him in sacramentes and prayer.

Thirdly, that it is lawful for the minister to delyver, the parties to receive, the people to communicate with open knowen unrepentant professed whoremasters and multitudes of wicked.

Fourthly, that open sinne may be tollerated in the assemblie.[4]

Fiftly, that when open sinners be common, and such persons manie, it were not safe to use the censures of the church.

[1] *A Plaine Declaration*, pp. 16–18, 37. This is an interesting example of the fallacious principle of guilt by association. [2] In Barrow's *A Plaine Refutation*.

[3] II Corinthians 6:17.

[4] If the reader will preface each of Greenwood's points with the question—"do you really believe"—he will see the force of these inquiries directed to Gifford.

Sixtly, that ther may be a separating in heart, and comming out from them in minde, with whome we communicate in the church.

That ther is no pollution, participation, or communicating with other men's sinnes, but either by doing the same evill, or consenting in heart to the evill; and though they remaine in their open filthines unrepentant, our communicating with them in the sacrament or prayer, or the priestes' delyverie of the sacrament unto them, is no rejoycing with them in their sinne, no communicating with other men's sinnes, no allowance or consenting or approving of them in evill, nor no sinne or transgression in us.

That they which are the temple of the lyving God, and in the middest of a crooked and a perverse nation, apearing as lightes in the world, having the word of life, nothing can infect them which they tollerat for unitie's sake, neither are they put up in any straight [strait, difficulty], because God dwelleth in them and walketh amongst them.

That to separat from such a perverse and crooked generation were dangerous, lest we should seperat in spiritual separation from the good, such separation were seditious.

That David was not separat in body from the open wicked and uncleane in the sacrifice, in his dayes.

That Isaias himself in one congregation with them, did touch the uncleannes which he reproved in the people.

That the Apostle Paule and the church of Corinth did tollerate and communicate with such as committed fornication, though they repented not but continued in their sinne after due admonition.

That in policie for feare of schisme excommunication may not be used against open obstinat sinners, but they may be tollerated and communicated with of the godly.

That when he which for some notorious crime is reprehended hath the multitude [as] his companion, it is not healthful to reprehend or excommunicate, but to tollerat.

That the cause and person of the tares being understood of the open wicked and unrepentant, doth not prejudicate the cause and person of the wheate growing together in the field, and whither [whether] you will interpret this of the church.

That the cause and person of the chaffe doth not prejudicat the cause [221] and person of the corne being together in the same floore, until the last wynowing; the same of the goates and sheepe in the pastures; the fishes good and bad in the net; vessells of honour and dishonour.

The causes and person of the chaffe, bad fishes, goates, vessells of dishonour, being understood of the open knowen wicked, whoremasters, murderers, heretickes, idolators, etc., and the field, floore, pastures, net, howse, etc., of the apparant church, and make the inhibition of plucking up the tares a commandement, then is not only the censures of the church, admonition, excommunication, etc., but the use of the magistrat's sword not only needlesse, but utterly unlawfull to be exercised against anie transgression. Let Mr. Giffard see how he is plunged in Anabaptistrie, ath[e]isme, and blasphemous contradiction of the whole reveiled [revealed] will of God for the cutting downe of sinne. But let Mr. Giffard or his Ordinarie [Bishop Aylmer] in their owne name subscribe these foresaid positions, and he shal heare our answere. We wil not confute them in the persons of dead men.

We then conclude this point thus; that Mr. Giffard hath ignorantly skambled[1] about the sinnes arising in the church, and the order of reprehension, when all our question is of a separation from a false church, consisting of the world, the athiestes, papistes, heretickes, and all sortes of prophane not gathered unto Christ. So that he hath but fought with his owne shadow in comparing us to the Donatistes in this poinct. Againe, al Augustine's reasons are against separation in the church, without discreet and orderly using of the power of Christ by the censure of excommunication; wheras you all confesse you have no discipline to execute, neither belong Christ's ordinances to your antichristian ministerie and Babilonish assemblies, which we denie to hold the head Christ in this their subjection to Antichriste's ministerie, ordinances, worship. It is but then your ignorance to make comparison betwene the Donatistes and us.

TO THE WORSHIP

That the Donatistes did separat themselves from as corrupted a worship as the Brownistes doe, Mr. Giffard will stand to affirme. Saith he, there were prayers and oblations for the dead, then significative ceremonies, superstitious signing of themselves with the signe of the crosse, etc.[2] To which wee answere, that Mr. Giffard affirmed in the sixth page of his booke, "that the Donatistes departed disorderly out of the church, condemning it not for any poincte of doctrine," for therein the other churches and they did agree.[3] Now

[1] Concluded in a haphazard or expedient way, or contrived unscrupulously.
[2] *A Plaine Declaration*, pp. 37–39. [3] *Ibid.*, p. 6.

here he would make a comparison betwene them and us, in disalowing the worship. But it seemeth Mr. Giffard holdeth not anie doctrine to be contayned in the worship, which indeed ought to conteine nothing els, and sure it is a strang worship that is not grounded upon doctrine.

The second thing in this place we will note, is, the time of these corruptions in the worship; namely, as he reckoneth within two hundreth [222] yeares after Christ. If their worship were then as corrupted as ours is now, we merveil how you will defend the platforme of your church government from that tyme that was so corrupt, calling it the primative church. Your fellow priests' argumentes from the primative church (as th[e]y falslie call those times) will be of small weight, if you make their worship as corrupt as this derived from Antichrist. In the forty-fourth page, he graunteth as much of the [discipline or externall] governement, that it was then thus corrupt, when our tyme-servers will only cleave to that paterne, and neither he nor they to the testament of Christ.[1]

Thirdly, he hath forgotten his scope and argument. He should by his promise have prooved that the Donatistes and we were of one judgment in this poinct; and that they made the false worship one principal cause of their separation, as we doe; so that he hath forgotten himself in this place, as a man not knowing where to make shew of something.

Next, where Mr. Giffard grantes that in those assemblies where the worship is idolatrous, it is lawfull to separat a man's self,[2] he (contrary to those expositions of the II Corinthians 6 and other places to that effect) now granteth a separation in body and minde both. I will not rebuke him nor charge him of inconstancie, because I perceive him to contradict his holy pastors of these tymes where he seeth them to erre.

But he by and by returneth to his vomit againe thus: "Ther are many and great corruptions" in the worship "before it come to that": where certeine fundamental poincts of doctrine are holden, the worship cannot be idolatrous;[3] but in the deepest defection in poperie ther were certeine fundamentall poincts holden (as he saith in an other place) wherby they were stil in the church and under the covenant, therfor ther is no idolatrous or blasphemous worship that may in the papiste's church be separated from. Mr. Giffard may be a good subject, but sure his groundes of doctrine

[1] *Ibid.*, p. 44. [2] *Ibid.*, p. 37. [3] *Ibid.*, p. 37.

are popish and pernitious. We here demaund of Mr. Giffard whither [whether] such corruptions and errours as he speaketh of, might be of the godly that knew them such be offered up by themselves or communicated with in the church.

And Mr. Giffard must give us leave to say it cannot be their worship was so corrupt as yours, consisting of so manie patched devises of your learned popes so long hatched, and by so manie heades as have out of that fordge of Sathan's minting howse contrived it, even out of Antichriste's treasurie of deceites. As for errours that have no good foundation, we may shew him twentie for one. Hitherto then Mr. Giffard and his bretheren that have separated from the church of Rome as they would pretend, yet retayning still that worship, are bretheren with the Donatistes, as he pleaseth to deride that holy name of bretheren.

TO THE MINISTERIE

"The Donatistes cried out that the churches" from which they separated "had no true ministers, but that they were all false prophets, Judasses, persecutors of the just, generations of vipers [traitors], because [as] they said [223] they had their ordination from them that were such. The Brownistes lift up their voyces with all their might and call us Baal's priestes, the marked servantes of Antichrist, false prophets, seducers, and such lyke, because (as they say) 'we are ordeyned by antichristian bishops',"[1] therefore we be Donatistes. Mr. Giffard his argument is denyed. Jeremie, our Saviour Christ, and divers of the prophets against Israell, did in this maner pull off the visardes of the false prophets, disclosing their wickednes to the people; were they therfore Donatistes or schismatickes? Calvine and all of you cry out against the pope's ministerie at Rome, are you therfore Donatistes and schismatickes? The matter then must be considered for which they so called them. The Donatistes for no other cause, than for that some of them were ordeyned by Judasses and traytours; the Brownistes, for that these are ordeyned by antichristian bishopps which exercise an other spirituall government than Christ's. Wherein if you had eyes to see, there is no comparison betwene their cause and ours.

First the person that did ordeine satt in a lawful office as the Donatistes supposed; did also ordeine (as they thought) in maner according to the rule of the Word; the partie that was ordeined, meete for the ministerie; the office to which he was called, lawfull;

[1] *Ibid.*, p. 40.

the administration wherein he was to administer, holy and good for anie thing they sawe. The contrarie of all which we finde in your ministerie; and the thing wherein you would have us likened together was never our reason, which is the wickednes of the man's person that doth of his sole authoritie ordeine for manie churches, which we neither approve in the Donatistes or you. Our exceptions in this case I say hath never bene against the person of your Ordinarie [Bishop Aylmer], although we might justly. Take next time your matter together, and looke whose kingdome you administer in, what calling, office, leitourgie, flock, and be ashamed of your comparison, by so much as your ministeri is more wicked.

Again, you here put the cause of our casting of[f] the bishops and their traine into the lake, to be, for that they exercise an other discipline than Christe's,[1] as though this were some small matter, which if you put the word (government of the church) you shall finde it the denial of Christ to reigne in his kingdome, a suppression of al his lawes and ordinances, even the whole testament, and erection and practising of an other. Let him that readeth consider what state all stand in that remaine in this kingdome erected against Christ, and what ministerie the seducers in this foraigne priesthoode exercise of God or of the devill, for Christ hath but one ministerie, one gospell, one government over his church.

Now seeing ther is no comparison betwene the Donatistes' cause and ours, I would (if he would forbeare to conclude me a Donatist for this poinct) demaund this question in their cause if their accusation had bene true, namely, whether one that hath professed the faith, and after so foully apostatat as to accuse his bretheren, denie the faith, persecute the truth he sometimes professed, may without repentance be received into the church againe? Then whether though he repent and be received, he [224] be ever capable of the ministerie or no? Then whether he alone may ordaine an other minister or no; if hee do, whether the other be a lawfull minister or no? But in such cases in the church I could like well to he[a]re some man to perswade to repentance, or to cast out the obstinat by due order; and neither Augustine nor angell from heaven to plead for a tolleration of open transgression; which pleading for sinne maketh us suspect the matter verie deeply, justifiing neither.

Their similitudes, the river from the fountaine, the members, the head, the stock and the plant,[2] in their application wee approve

[1] *Ibid.* [2] *Ibid.*, p. 41.

not, but hold the doctrine erronious that they thought anie thing could be ordeyned from the person of the man in that sort. But your discent from Antichrist and pedegree in that kingedome is an other thing, if you would please to conceive it; namely, that your office, names, livinges, entrance, administration, etc., is of the pope and of Satan, and that when his kingdome shalbe abolished, your office, name, entrance, vicarage, leitourgie and all shalbe cast with the great milstone upon them with all such trafique into the bottome of the sea. Hereupon it is, we say, [that] your discent is from the pope within few degrees, being the children of these antichristian bishops, which are the creatures of the pope, who is the oldest sonne of Sathan, and his vicar generall upon earth, whose image, marke, power and life you beare, and together with him lyve, reigne, stand and fall as the branches with the tree; for when the power, decrees, government, offices, worship, etc., of Antichrist is gone, all your ministerie is vanished for ever.[1] The Lord therfore put in Her Majestie's heart to extirpate the same, and to advance Christ's lawes, ordinances, ministerie, worship, etc., as he is worthie, that every knee may bowe unto him.

But Mr. Giffard affirmeth we shal not be able to prove our accusation of their ministerie, that it is by discent from Antichrist; his reason is, "there is no minister[ie] in England [ordained] by the pope, etc."[2] We shal not here need to seek out a pope in England. If hee will learne to distinguish betwene the pope's person, and his decrees, canons, and orders after the pope's orders of priesthood, he must be driven to confesse their whole ministerie, office, entrance, etc., to be drawen by discent, and wee thinck Mr. Giffard will not hang the life and vertue of holy thinges upon men's persons, but upon the ordinances of God, lest he be a Donatist.

Hee further affirmeth "the ministerie of publishing the gospel [and] delyvering the sacramentes, is not the devise of man, but Christ's ordinance."[3] Do you thinke Mr. Giffard can begg the question to affirme a ministerie whose office, entrance, etc., is of Antichrist, doth publish the gospel? Againe, that they receive it as Christ's ministery, when it is from point to point wholly found to be after the orders of Antichrist?

And when no shift will help him out, he is faine to affirme valiantly, that "the ministery was not utterly destroyed in popery, for there remained the sacrament of baptisme."[4] See here how he

[1] *A Short Treatise*, p. 74. [2] *A Plaine Declaration*, pp. 40–43. [3] *Ibid.*, p. 43.
[4] *Ibid.*

hath plunged himself into the sea of poperie, and overtumbled the doctrines of his learned [225] fathers. T. Co.[1] saith from Malachie, that the ministerie is not tyed to the succession of men's persons, but to the law and ordinances;[2] and what ministerie the pope's is, reade Revelation 9, etc. You chardge Her Majestie verie far, to have cast out the true ministeri out of the land for putting out pope, cardinal, shaven crowned priest, fryer, monke, abbot. And if the baptisme could not be a true sacrament without a lawful minister, then your ministerie being unlawfull, there is no seale with promise, no true church, etc.

Seeing then the Holy Ghost hath described that church to be "the harlot sitting upon many waters," "the mother of fornications," confused Babel, murderesse of the saints, "an holde of uncleane spirits, and a cage of everie uncleane and hateful birde,"[3] neither ministerie, sacramentes, worship, or anie thing remayneth there according to God's ordinance; and at the best you make your self and this whole land schismaticks from the true church, ministeri, sacramentes, if it so stand with the church of Rome and ministeri thereof, and of necessitie you ar al Donatistes by your reasoning, though my purpose is not to defend and prove in this discourse, but to call a fewe notes to your memorie. I wil conclude this poinct, that you are driven to the pope's ministerie for your orders, now desiring you to satisfie us next time concerning the pope's damnable masse or sacrament of the altar; if they be true ministers, whether the church can have one sacrament good and an other evil, one with promise, the other damnable, blasphemous, and accursed; for I take it they cannot be true ministers at the font, and sacriledgious massmongers at the altar. Weigh these things more consideratly, before you publish such doctrines in England again.

TO THE SACRAMENTS

The Donatistes did hold that the sacramentes or efficacie of them, depend upon the worthines and holynes of the man that administreth. But the Brownistes are not of that minde. To this objection hee verie charitablie answereth, that in this great ranke point of

[1] Thomas Cooper, Bishop of Winchester.
[2] Malachi 2:1–9. See Thomas Cooper, *An Admonition to the People of England*, pp. 185–187. This is from the 1589 edition with 245 pages. Two other editions of this same year have 244 and 252 pages.
[3] Revelation 17:1, 5, 6; 18:2, 10. Compare Jeremiah 50:2, which is "Babylon is taken, Bel is confounded," in the King James Version. The Revised Standard Version reads, "Babylon is taken, Bel is put to shame."

Donatisme he can finde no difference at all. "Let the wordes and meaning of both be skanned, and it shall appeare manifestly that they hold the self same thing, neither more nor lesse, but like even bretheren,"[1] or ells Mr. Giffard will be found a common lyer and sclanderer. This man may not be suspected of anie malitious practise to deface the truth, yet is found to make his comparison by his false sclanders, and not of anie direct sentence of ours. What sinne hee is fallen into that so often derideth the word "bretheren," let the godly consider.

The Donatistes held that if the man being a lawful minister were a sinner, the sacrament delyvered by him was no true sacrament. Mr. Giffard confesseth we hold no such thing;[2] where is then the consimilitude?

The Donatistes held that the faith or conscience of the gyver did give faith unto, purge and make cleane the conscience of the receiver; and so of the contrarie the guyltines:[3] which doctrine we holde to be blasphemous; it is only the Holy Ghost that worketh faith, and purgeth from an evil conscience.

[226] The Donatistes held, that if he which did administer were an open sinner, he was no minister, and so no sacrament.[4] We do not hold that every open sinne maketh the minister no minister, seing the high priest manie times sinned under the law, yet his office still retained: but we hold that the minister ought to repent his sinne before he administer, and the church to admonish him of his knowen sinne before they suffer him to administer, and not communicate with him if he be obstinat. If the church neglect their duetie, he and they transgresse, yet do we not say that it is no sacrament that he delivereth, or that his ministerie is disanulled.

But we must put Mr. Giffard in minde how far he is gone from our cause in this comparison. We never disalowed their sacraments as being administred by a lawful minister in a lawful office, yet the man a sinner. But of such counterfeites as have neither lawfull office, entrance, etc., but stand enchanters in Antichriste's kingdom; so that these are not the personal sinnes of a minister in the church; wherein Mr. Giffard's wickednes appeareth to make the question of the man's person or his sinne, when it is the ministery, office, entrance, administration, al which wee hold to be antichristian, and to have nothing to do with the seales of God's covenant in this estate: not here to speake of the altering of the institution in the

[1] *A Plaine Declaration*, pp. 50, 51. [2] *Ibid.*, p. 51. [3] *Ibid.*, p. 52.
[4] *Ibid.*, pp. 52, 53, 54.

maner of administring it, which the Donatistes never either had cause or made question of, as it seemeth.

And whether anie promise is made to the elementes abused in the false, yea, whether to the elementes or to the keeping of the lawes and ordinances in the true church, let Mr. Giffard make answere.

Further, when we affirme the sacramentes of the false church to be no true seales of the covenant, because they are idolatours and idolatrous, the Lorde's ordinances prophaned and lawes wholly violated, wee do not therby conclude it to bee no baptisme concerning the outwarde washing; for wee can put difference betwene a false and none, a false sacrament or counterfeit signe, and none, for the false church is saide to have her peace offringes. And although wee holde them highly to tempt God to their owne condemnation (if they repent not) that wittingly prophane or of wilfull ignorance transgresse those high ordinances, as in the false church to be superstitious of the element where the lawe and covenant is broken, yet do wee not thereupon affirme wee neede anie reiterating of the outward signe, as the Donatistes; but hold this false signe nowe a true signe, sufficient to us concerning the outward washing. Circumcision in the apostasie of Israel, which was without promise to the receivers in that estate, and nothing but sinne in it, yet stood for a sufficient outward cutting when anie of them returned to the church and ate of the passover, whereof it was not lawfull for any uncircumcised to eate; how the signe might have bene reiterated if need had so required, we may see by that of the apostle, I Corinthians 7, for gathering againe their circumcision if it might be gathered againe, then [than?] secondly cut.

Where Mr. Giffard then in stead of performing his comparison saith, [227] that the Donatistes in rebaptising did better of both, because "he that is not baptised ought to be baptised," etc.,[1] he bewrayeth his ignorance, that cannot put difference betweene a false sacrament and none, a false signe and none. The grossnes also he supposeth to have bene in us, is found in himself, that lest he should make the false and counterfeit washing in the false church to be none, runneth to justifie the church, ministerie, sacramentes, etc., at Rome, and so must conclude himself of necessitie a schismaticke or a popish priest, which he will.

And where he demandeth whether he that knoweth he was never baptised can be saved if he seek not to be baptised when he may

[1] *Ibid.* p. 61.

have it.[1] We demande againe how ever true baptisme should be restored, if the false signe of baptisme which was then without promise in the false church, should not now be sufficient concerning the outward signe.

TO THE GOVERNMENT

In the principle of principles, that I say not the verie summe of all causes of our separation from these assemblies, namely, the government which Mr. Giffard termeth discipline, he can not finde any consimilitude between the Donatistes and us; for he confesseth he hath not read that they did take anie exception against it in that tyme.[2] Take your word "discipline" for al the meanes that Christ hath apointed by his lawes, ministerie and censures, to keepe, guyde and governe his church, joyntly and severally to be instructed in their dueties, and see what a dilemma you are come unto, this being granted that herein ther is no agrement, seeing the chief cause of our controversie with you is for the rable of this antichristian and pseudohierarchie courtes, etc., which have no place in the church of God, where Christ's officers, offices, lawes, censures, ought to governe and guyde his church.

But here according to your accustomed maner you goe about to say there were faultes to be found in their government then, yea, as well as in their worship, etc., which you affirmed to be as corrupt as yours is now;[3] wherein (if anie regard were to be had of your words) you would not only make those bishopps [to be] in as evill state as these, that church [to be] as yours now; but have cast into the fire all the platformes that your learned Reformistes have pleaded for, from that falsly so called primative church. Well, I have told you the question is not whether they had the true government or no, whether in that government there were corruptions, defaultes or negligences, but whether the Donatistes separated therfore or no; they had the same offices, officers, lawes, censures, that the other, so that you speake not only false in saying they might have had as just cause in this respect of separation as wee,[4] but also bring the argument to confound your self with your whole church wherin you stand a priest. Thus you are separated from the church of Rome, but retaine still the same hierarchie, worship, government, that they used and have, as the Donatistes of the churches from which they sepa-[228]rated; therfore you in this as in the rest of

[1] *Ibid.* [2] *Ibid.*, p. 44. [3] *Ibid.* [4] *Ibid.*

your argumentes conclude your selves Donatistes, heretickes, and schismatickes from the church of Rome.

But Mr. Giffard will denie that the Donatistes had as great cause to separate from those churches from which they separated, as those English priestes from the graundfather the pope, for it was not so corrupted. The same we answere to you for your government, how then shall we end this matter? I take it, thus; that the priestes of England despise the pope's person, and yet keepe the same orders, lawes, officers, offices that he erected. So the Donatistes kept stil the orders of government that the churches they separated from [possessed]. Now if we can cleare our selves that we retaine not the same government amongst us that the [Anglican] church doth [which] we separat from (which I thinke cannot be denyed), then Mr. Giffard hath in a chief principle put himself and this whole land into the number of Donatistes. The argument is now this. The Church of England separateth from the church of Rome, and yet keepe their government and worship, therfore the Church of England are schismatickes and Donatistes; and an other poinct, that ther can be no true sacraments, no true church under a false government. And Mr. Giffard is yet further out of his way.

TO THE ARGUMENT OF MANIE CHURCHES

He granting that we herein differ from the Donatistes, in that they condemne all churches in the world [and] we do not, will needes notwithstanding have us Donatistes in this poinct also. For (saith he) though they shoote not their arrowes at them, yet their arrowes strike them, their argumentes upon consequence will reach so far, yea, "runne thorough the sides of all churches."[1] This we answere: you must first cleare your selves of those thinges wherwith you are chardged and pressed, and trouble not your self with other men's matters, seing you make this but a cloke for your wickednes to shrowde your self under other men's persons with whome we have not to deale. We utterly refuse to enter into this controversie of the estate of other contries; we knowe the Word of God is neere us (thankes be to God) by which if your cause be good, suffer it to be tryed.

As for the consequence of our argumentes, they are but your owne collections to passe over your owne sinnes, and sett the strife

[1] *Ibid.*

betwene us and other churches, which we wil not be drawen unto. And all men may here behold this sower of wordes and strife maker will counterfeit not only consequence, but argumentes of his owne head, to raise quarrell. In all which he hath forgotten his promise to compare our writinges and theirs together; and flyeth to his owne collection.

In this part of his stage-play he beginneth thus. "The Church of England is esteemed and reverenced emongst the churches as a sister, and so communicated with, yet they all know what her faultes be in her assemblies, in her worship, in her ministerie and government, in asmuch [229] as they are apparant."[1] Unto the first, we suppose your worship, ministerie, church government, are not so apparant unto them as you gyve out. Secondly, we doubt, yea, I may say it is untrue, that they justifie your ministerie, worship, or government. Thirdly, admit they should thus sinne either of ignorance, negligence, or infirmitie, standing otherwise orderly gathered to the practize of Christe's ordinances, they are not for this sinne (till after due convincement and admonition they remaine obstinat) to be presently judged no churches. But what I thinke of their estate, you shall here pardon me, I will not intermedle till I be called.

As for your *Harmonie of Confessions*,[2] if it be not the harmonie of the prophets, Christ and his apostles, it skilleth nothing us what consent you make. Againe, it is not an accord in certeine general articles that can satisfie this matter, when in the perticulars you discent [dissent] to the overthrow of al. Such an harmonie you may very wel make with your mother church of Rome, and a great deale more large. Neither do their Confessions agree with you in the estate of the ministeri, church government, nor worship; Scotland, Geneva, France, etc., have an other ministerie, offices, choise, ordination and ministration, an other government, worship, etc.; but it were too large to discusse. And now hold to your argument, and see what wil follow. The church of Rome have the same confession of faith, which you call your Apostolick Crede, that you have, yea, the Lorde's Prayer (as you cal it), Athanasius' Crede, etc., therfore they and

[1] *Ibid.*, p. 45.

[2] *An Harmony of the Confessions of the Faith of the Christian and Reformed Churches, Which Purelie Professe the Holy Doctrine of the Gospell in All the Chiefe Kingdomes, Nations, and Provinces of Europe* (Cambridge, 1586); *S.T.C.*, 5155. This was first issued in Latin in 1581. See William Pierce, *The Marprelate Tracts*, pp. 26, 27; see also John Strype, *Annals*, III, Part I, pp. 650–651.

you agreeing in this *Harmonie of Confession*, are one body, one church. Againe, these churches, you say, hold you the church of God, and you hold the church of Rome to be the church of God, therfore you are one body al, and then you and al the churches schismatickes from your mother church.

"If the Church of England be antichristian and idolatrous, and worship the beast, etc., then the churches which perfectly know the same and yet acknowledg her a sister, are partakers of her sinne, and so to be condemned with her."[1] The same argument we thus returne you.

If the church of Rome be antichristian and idolatrous and worship the beast, then the Church of England which perfectly knoweth the same and yet acknowledgeth her a sister (as Mr. Giffard doth say) is partaker with her sinnes, and so to be condemned with her.

"Al those churches," saith he, "which know the Church of England" in this estate and do yet "reverence her as a true church of Christ, do condempne those as heretical schismatickes which cal it antichristian and separat themselves from it."[2] We answere, that all those churches he speaketh of do not approve the Church of England in this estate, neither condempne us in the thinges we withstand therein, and receive it againe thus. At the first comming out of papacie, all the churches in the world did approve the church of Rome, and condempne those as heretical schismatickes which caled it antichristian and separated from it. Let Mr. Giffard put to what conclusion he wil. I take it Mr. Giffard must now [230] leave the bare title of church, ministerie, etc., and flee to the proofe of their profession and orderly walking, by the Word of God; which if he do not, yet do we buyld thereupon as upon a most sure foundation.

As to Mr. Calvine, we refer you to his confession of faith printed in the latter end of his owne *Catechisme*,[3] and if he be contrarie to himself in his other writinges, looke you unto it; we do not for the holynes of the man justifie anie of his errours (as no man is without), neither for his errors reject any truth he held; knowing of the one God hath had mercy as we hope, and for the other God's Word approveth it; so that we beleive not any thing because such a man said so, but because by the Word and Spirit we heare Christ himself speak. And you do greatly abuse his writinges, in using them after

[1] *A Plaine Declaration*, p. 45. [2] *Ibid.*

[3] See John Calvin, *The Catechisme, or Maner to Teache Children the Christian Religion* (London, 1580). For "The Confession of Faith," see signature K iii *verso*–K vii *recto*.

your owne sense in his name contrarie to his minde and purpose, and by your leave wrasting them to your owne judgment, deceiving others therby. In his confession he affirmeth ther is no true sacrament with promise (as I do remember) but where the minister hath a lawfull office and outward calling to administer;[1] so that all his argumentes must be understood of such a church as have a lawful ministerie in office, entrance, and administration, and cannot be applyed to yours. Moreover, he reasoned against the Anabaptistes and such as held an integritie and perfection in the church, and separated for everie sinne committed, without due seeking of redresse.[2] And if he erred in these or any other doctrines, we do not therfore hold them presently to be no church in which he was minister, or which did in like ignorance receive the said doctrines; it is obstinacie in error that only deserveth casting off, and that by due order.

As for most of your places expounded by his mouth and now received by you to maintaine open sinne and to communicate with the open knowne transgressours, they are so common and stale, that every infant in the faith can shew you your vanitie, if in your owne name you durst propound them. Your learned bretheren have gyven them over as sclender collections, you will now revive them; put them in your owne name, ells we have nothing to say, the man [Calvin] being dead, whose steppes God give you grace to follow in that which is good. But this is a simple course to justifie your owne wayes by men's names and writinges, when God's Word convinceth you of sinne and wickednes. For that place of the Epistle to the Corinthians 11. "Let a man examine himselfe, and so let him eat of that bread and drink of that cup,"[3] it doth not dischardge us of any dutie to others by admonition and due censure, for the same God hath said, "admonish one another, tell thy brother his fault, if he repent, forgive him"; "goe first reconcile thy self to thy brother, then bring thine offring;" "if anie that is called a brother be a fornicatour, etc., be not commingled together, with such a one eat not."[4] So that our examination must be whether we do follow these rules also; and Mr. Calvine himself saith it is sacriledg for the

[1] Calvin wrote: "neither must we in the administration of these sacramentes, folowe manne's phantasie, but as Christ hymselfe hath ordeined, so must they be ministered, and by such as by ordinarie vocation are thereunto called" (*ibid.*, signature K vi *recto*).

[2] John Calvin, *Institutes of the Christian Religion* (London, 1949), I, 519; II, 292–303, 652.

[3] I Corinthians 11:28.

[4] Luke 17:3; Matthew 5:24 and 18:15; I Corinthians 5:11.

pastor to gyve the sacrament to the open unworthie.[1] What communion is ther then betwene him that openly standes under the wrath of God, the minister that committeth sacriledge, and us in that banquet? We may better reason thus then: we are commanded to exa-[231]mine our selves and so eat, therfore I must examine my self also with whome, what, and howe I do come to receive. But what have wee to do to reason what is to be done in the church to the preventing of God's wrath and reprofe of sinne, when our question is of the utter forsaking of the false church with all her wares and stolen waters? So that wee conclude al Mr. Calvine's argumentes must be enforced against such as separate themselves from the true churche, otherwise himself and you all shall be found schismaticks from the church of Rome.

As for the church of Corinth and churches of Galatia, they were separated from idolatours, orderly gathered, established and governed by Christe's lawes, true ministerie, worship, and stood not obstinatly to maintaine and retaine open grosse sinne, and to murder the messengers sent early and late to reprove them, as you doe. So that ther is no comparison to be made betwene you and them; for thus the papist might pleade with you. Ther were sinnes and corruptions in the churches of Corinth and Galatia, but it was not lawfull to separate from them, therfore it is not lawfull to separate from the church of Rome, wherein stil you see your selves concluded schismaticks and Donatistes. But because wee will not intermedle with Calvine nor other churches, let us returne againe to your comparison betwene the Donatistes and us, from which you are so farr and so long digressed, as a man litle regarding wherein hee busieth himself.

CONCERNING THE MAJESTRACIE

In this matter he first termeth us Donatistes, for that we crye out of persecution, and of the false prophets that incense the magistrates hereunto.[2] Wee answere, wee complaine not of impatiencie nor yet for revenge: only (as duty bindeth us) we seeke to the lawfull magistrates for some redresse of our miseries which wee wrongfully sustaine, and shewe the people the ungodlynes of their woefull guydes, or rather wolves; and if you had anie grace you would rather be moved with pitie, than compare us to either schismatickes

[1] John Calvin, *The Catechisme, or Maner to Teache Children the Christian Religion* (London, 1580), signature G viii *recto*.
[2] *A Plaine Declaration*, p. 68.

or hereticks for our just complaintes. But herein our cause differeth from the Donatistes, that wee are persecuted by the clergie, which is armed (according to the order of their bloodie predecessors) with civill power together with their popish ecclesiasticall jurisdiction both in one person,[1] contrarie to the lawe of God: which unlawfull power they only usurp to keep Christ out of his office, suppressing his lawes, offices, people, worship, with al force in all unmercifull crueltie, so far as their hornes will reach pushing poore Israel. And howsoever Her Majestie and Her Honorable Councill see not their wickednes, or suffer them and winke at their doinges (which God grant it be not layd to their chardge), yet wee finde this antichristian prelacie both the false accusers, and hatefull molestours of God's children; so that the persecution is chieflie by that broode. And whether haling unto, and shutting up in most [232] straite close imprisonment till they have murdered them without trial whom they get into their clawes, never loosing their hold till eyther they dye in prison or revolt from the truth, so that manie are made to blaspheme and denie the holy wayes of God through their mercilesse tyrannie; whether this kind of tyrannising without anie free conference or judicial proceeding, thus pulling the husband from the wife, father from children, servant from master, etc., al from their lawful callings and trades, be not barbarous persecution, let al men consider.[2] If we diserve death, let us dye in due execution, if banishment, banish us; but first by order convince us of some crime or errour worthie therof, if you will cleare your selves.

Mr. Giffard after this Ismalitish derision of our persecution, proceedeth to accuse us of some doctrines derogatorie to the prince's aucthoritie. As first; that princes may not make lawes. 2. That wee should hold the prince ought not to reforme the church by their authoritie. 3. That none of the godlye kinges of Juda did compel anie to the covenant. 4. That the people of Christe's kingdome be *spontanei*, etc.[3]

In al which, besides that ther is no comparison betwene the Donatistes and us in these poinctes, hee doth but followe the steppes

1 Archbishop Whitgift was not only the ecclesiastical head of the Church of England, but also a real power in the Court of High Commission and a potent force as a Privy Councillor. As the little "black husband" of Queen Elizabeth, he possessed strong support from her.

2 These charges are true.

3 *Ibid.*, p. 68. Spontanei, from spontaneus, means voluntary, spontaneous, of one's free will. The meaning here is that the Separatists are too independent of the prince, too much given to their own ideas, too little subject to the proper authority of the magistrate.

of that olde perverter of the truth. We wil then first shew briefly how we hold this doctrine, and how far we are from that hee would insinuate into the magistrates' eares, as though we sought to diminish their lawful jurisdiction, power or rule. For lawes' making we hold, that princes are limited by the law of God (as he himself in another place confesseth)[1] and ought not to proclame any law that hath not warrant from God's law either in expresse words or necessary collection from general rules, stil keeping within the equitie. For reforming we hold, that the prince ought to suppresse all transgression of God's law, and punish al persons without partialitie according to the offence within the church or without the church within their owne dominions as wel for the transgression of the first table as the second, and to defend the observers therof in al equity, and that whiles we walke in the wayes of God we are not afraid of that power, but gyve God glorye and them due obedience, whether they be of the church or no. To the fourth [point or doctrine] we hold, that none can be received into the church, but that willingly maketh publick confession of his faith, for neither may the church receive nor they be holden of the church, without this repentance and confession. Yet we grant that the prince may command and compel her subjects to the hearing of the publick doctrine and prayer of the church, but to enter covenant or be received a member it is to be done by doctrine, faith and repentance. Neither did the kinges of Juda compel the priestes to receive anie uncircumcised or idolatours into the fellowship of the church. Faith is the gift of God, wrought by his spirit and Word. The prince may compel to the meanes thereunto, but not enforce faith.

The Donatistes resisted the magistrates so far as they durst (saith he), and when Julian the Apostata shewed them favour, their circumcellions made revel in companies, walking with clubbes and staves, did spoile and beate [233] such as lighted in their handes, etc. The impatient heate of Brownistes is not unknowen, etc.[2] Let this lawlesse man shewe where ever anie of us have resisted the magistrate, or spoken evil of the ruler of the people, or gone about to revenge our selves by any violence or unlawful meanes. As for his prophecie, what we would be if we had power, it layeth open himself to be a malitious false prophet to incitate the magistrate with

[1] Gifford, *A Short Treatise*, pp. 104–106.

[2] *A Plaine Declaration*, p. 68. This page is wrongly numbered 68; it should be 69. Julian the Apostate, successor of Constantius, was Roman emperor from 361 to 363. The Circumcellions were Donatist fanatics who roamed from house to house, arguing and causing trouble.

lying dreames. Let him better consider and he shal find that this antichristian prelacie hath bene not only the procurers but shedders of much innocent blood, usurping civile power. And how they have behaved themselves towards their soveraigne kings and princes, let the records be searched; in your church are found dayly treasons, bloodshed, etc., and most plentifull in your mother church of Rome. This then is but the false report of Sanballat and Tobia to hinder God's temple.[1]

Nowe admiring Mr. Giffard's clearing of the Donatistes' errour, affirming they differed not from the other churches in doctrine, as also [to] manifest or at least protest our innocencie from these and all other errours in the perticular course handled or els where to be found, I will set downe three or fower grosse errours before him, which we detest in the Donatistes; as:

That he which ordeineth a minister (as it seemeth they allowed ordination by one man) is the head of him ordeined, yea, the fountaine, and the other the river; therfore if the head be holy, the other is therby made holy, and so on the contrarie if the first be wicked.

That the conscience of him that gyveth, may wash the conscience of him that receiveth.

That when hee which baptiseth is manifest a good man, hee gyveth faith, hee is the original, the roote, the head of him that is by God's spirit renewed.

That those which are baptised by a wicked man though in a lawfull office, ought to be baptised againe.

That it is lawfull in some respectes to kill themselves.

That the magistrate cannot compel us to that which is good.

That we have free wil after regeneration.

I will not now justifie Mr. Giffard's explaining of their mindes, whether in these or anie other wee handled, I take al in this matter from his record, which I hope hee will not affirme to be false.

As for his learned fathers,[2] how they have wrasted the Scriptures, New Testament and Old, in more than twenty false expositions and

[1] Nehemiah, chapters 2–6.

[2] This is a reference to Tertullian, Cyprian, and Augustine. The anti-Donatist writings of St. Augustine to which Gifford refers are:

1. *contra Epistolam Parmeniani*;
2. *contra Litteras Petiliani*;
3. *de Unico Baptismo contra Petilianum*;
4. *contra Cresconium Grammaticum Donatistam*;
5. *contra Gaudentium Donatistam Episcopum.*

See *Patrologiae Cursus Completus. Patrologiae Latinae.* Tomus XLIII. Paris, 1865.

flat contradictions of the scope of the whole canon of the Worde, to justifie open iniquitie by slightes, and tollerat it in the publick assemblies with all their doctrines of separating in heart and not in bodye, at comon meates and not at holy communion, that all nations should be the apparant church, etc., wee leave them al, denying to enter controversie with dead men, wishing Mr. Giffard to spread such deceites in other men's names no more, but to come orderly to some christian triall by the booke of God. In the meane tyme he seeth wee neither hold of [234] Donatistes nor of Augustine, but follow faith in a pure conscience to our knowledge, readie to be instructed wherein we erre. And when hee hath made such a lardge discourse to prove us Anabaptistes, Montanistes, Arians, Pelagians, Nicolaitans, etc., we shal in stead of conflicting with a beater of the ayre, and unconscionable sclanderous rayler, demand the end and use of his labours, and now leave him to his accompt for his defacing and blaspheming of the truth, wishing all men to beware of such methodes of imposture.

I. G. [John Greenwood]

FINIS

II

A FEWE OBSERVATIONS OF MR. GIFFARD'S LAST CAVILLS ABOUT STINTED READ PRAYERS, AND DEVISED LEITOURGIES

Greenwood's treatise, *A Fewe Observations of Mr. Giffard's Last Cavills about Stinted Read Prayers, and Devised Leitourgies*, was his final reply to Gifford. He felt that he had "no cause of further strife (his former convinced)[1] to intermedle again with perticular handling of his chaffe and smoke, his reasons in effect the same before answered," but he nevertheless wrote an answer of twenty-one pages in print to refute "some few brief poincts," abused by Gifford.

In the summer of 1590 Greenwood's first book was published, *An Answere to George Gifford's Pretended Defence of Read Prayers and Devised Litourgies*. About eight months later, Gifford's book appeared, *A Plaine Declaration That Our Brownists Be Full Donatists, by Comparing Them Together from Point to Point Out of the Writings of Augustine. Also a Replie to Master Greenwood Touching Read Prayer, Wherein His Grosse Ignorance Is Detected, Which Labouring to Purge Himselfe from Former Absurdities, Doth Plunge Himself Deeper into the Mire*. The second half of Gifford's book contained his defence of read prayers in the Church of England. It was this portion which Greenwood answered in his treatise, *A Fewe Observations*. The writing of this reply occurred in the early months of 1590/91, and in April, 1591, it was published as a part of Barrow's book, *A Plaine Refutation*. Unfortunately, the entire edition, with the exception of a few copies, was seized upon at Flushing and consigned to the flames, through the work of the English ambassador, Sir Robert Sidney, aided by Francis Johnson, preacher to the English merchants in Middelburg. Francis Johnson kept one copy and bestowed the other on a special friend. The identity of this

[1] Greenwood's *An Answere to George Gifford's Pretended Defence* (1590).

special friend is not certain, but it may have been Gifford, who obtained a copy and prepared an answer. His reply was entered in the *Stationers' Register* on December 6, 1591, with the title, *A Short Reply unto the Last Printed Books of Henry Barrow and John Greenwood, the Chiefe Ringleaders of Our Donatists in England.*[1] This terminated the controversy, so far as Gifford and Greenwood are concerned, but Barrow prepared two more replies in 1592.

Inasmuch as *A Plaine Refutation* was intercepted by the authorities and burned, Greenwood's treatise contained therein obtained no circle of readers. Therefore, when Greenwood's *An Aunswer to George Gifford's Pretended Defence of Read Prayers and Devised Leitourgies* was reissued in 1603, the editor, probably Francis Johnson, appended Greenwood's *A Fewe Observations of Mr. Giffard's Last Cavills about Stinted Read Prayer and Devised Leitourgies.* For this reason, it was omitted from the reprinted *A Plaine Refutation,* which appeared in 1605, minus Greenwood's *A Fewe Observations,* but plus Barrow's *A Few Observations,* printed for the first time.

[235]

A FEWE OBSERVATIONS OF MR. GIFFARD'S LAST CAVILLS ABOUT STINTED READ PRAYERS, AND DEVISED LEITOURGIES

Having heretofore written *An Answere to Mr. George Giffard's Pretended Defence of Stinted Read Praiers and Devised Leitourgies,*[2] and since received an emptie replie,[3]

[1] Gifford's *A Short Reply* is an answer to *A Plaine Refutation.* The article on Gifford in the *D.N.B.* is wrong in saying that Barrow replied in *A Plaine Refutation to Gifford's A Short Reply.*

[2] Greenwood's *An Answere to George Gifford's Pretended Defence of Read Praiers and Devised Litourgies* was published about July or August, 1590, as a reply to pp. 17–46 of Gifford's *A Short Treatise.*

[3] Gifford, *A Plaine Declaration,* was published about February, 1591. It was divided into two parts. The first part, pp. 1–69, sought to demonstrate the similarity between the Donatists and the Barrowists. The second part, pp. 72 [70]–126, was a reply to Greenwood's *An Answere.* Greenwood's second reply—the present treatise—pertains to this second part of *A Plaine Declaration.*

wherin he doth nothing lesse than yeild to any sound reason alledged, but ungodlily cavilleth at and perversly wrasteth the sence of so much as he toucheth, I seeing no cause of further strife (his former convinced)[1] to intermedle againe with perticular handling of his chaffe and smoke, his reasons in effect the same before answered, have only thought it my dutie to illustrate unto the readers, some few brief poincts abused by him, that they may the better be able to judge of the former writings, whereunto with these few helpes following I refer the trial.

Wheras I alledged out of the eighth [chapter] to the Romans and out of the fourth [chapter] to the Galathians[2] that in the verie time and action of our praiing to God, the spirit of God was the only instructor and the only help, no other help mentioned or that can be collected in the Scriptures, Mr. Giffard having granted that reading prayer is not praying, doth now answere, that howsoever the Scripture doth extol and magnifie outward helpes and meanes, yet when they are compared with God which worketh all in all by them, or when the Scripture will set forth the efficacie and worke to be his alone, they are either not mentioned, or els if they be mentioned, so cast downe, as if they were nothing.[3] "God buyldeth his church" (saith he) "by the ministerie of men, yet Paul is said to plant, Apollos to water, but God to gyve the encrease," I Corinthians 3, "and therfore to gather from those places," Romans 8, Galatians 4, "that there neede or may be no outward help or meanes in the verie action and instant of praying, is far awrye."[4] In which answere it evidently appeareth he is so bent to turne away all truth and raise new strife, as ther can be no expectation of agreement. There is no sequence, neither doth the Scripture alledged prove his owne reason, so that nothing hangs togeather. No man doubteth but that sometimes and in some places of Scripture the outward meanes of begetting and encreasing faith is only recited, and sometimes the secret work of God's spirit only, sometimes both, when yet they are not

[1] That is, his former book, *A Short Treatise*, has been effectively answered and refuted. [2] Greenwood, *An Answere*, pp. 23–25.
[3] Gifford, *A Plaine Declaration*, p. 73. [4] *Ibid.*, pp. 73, 74.

divided but goe together, and all of God both inward worke and outward meanes, though in way of comparison I never so read, but rather the one repeated for both. For shal I say, that when the Word of God and preaching therof is shewed to be the power of God unto salvation, that the inward worke of the Spirit is therfore not mentioned, because the other is of God? Then both inward and outward meanes being of God and God's owne worke, though the one by instrument, that there is silencing of the one in way of comparison, is not true. But all this is [236] nothing to our matter. He should plainly have affirmed, that from these places, Romans 8, and Galatians 4, it cannot be proved, that in the very instant tyme and action of owre praying to God, the spirit only instructeth, without outward helpes of instruction; and he should have seene I could prove (as then I did) the contrarie unto him, Romans 8:26. "The Spirit doth together supplye or help our infirmities, for we knowe not what to pray as we ought, but the Spirit it self maketh request for us with sighes and grones unutterable." In the action of praying the Spirit is here set downe in this place to be the meanes and help of instruction, teaching us to aske aright, no other meanes or helpes of instruction in that instant time and action of praiing mentioned in this way or any other place of Scripture. Therfore in the time of our praying and laying our hearts open to God, the Spirit only doth instruct and openeth our mouth. In this place let the word *synantilambanetai*[1] be wel considered. Againe Galathians 4:6, it is said, "because yee are sonnes, God sent the Spirit of his Sonne into your hearts, crying, Abba, Father." The argument here is the same that [was used] before: this word *crying* sheweth the worcke of his Spirit or rather office, in our continuall occasions of prayer to direct us to unburden and unfold the heart, so that in the instant action we see no other. And where I shewed him that reading in the action of praying could not be caled an help of instruction at that time when we were powring forth our hearts unto God, the eyes and

The sp[irit] only doth instruct and teach us how to pray

[1] Sunantilambanetai—take, take hold of, take part in, undertake, assist in, participate, help—in Romans 8:26.

hands lyft up to heaven, our meditation fixed upon our knowen occasions, and heart and mouth unfolding them, my reason this, that the minde and bodie could not be intent upon two diverse distinct and several exercises and duties of minde and bodie at one time and instant, he inverteth my words, and stealeth them as a new shift to help himself (as he supposeth), returning them thus in way of question, demanding "whether fasting, lyfting up our eyes and hands to heaven, prostrating the bodie and kneeling be praier it self, or outward meanes and helpes to make the prayer more fervent." "Every simple man wil laugh at him" (saith he) "if he make them prayer it self"; and if they be helpes, then I have brought the former proofes not from an idle, but from an unsound brayne.[1] Leave scorning and reproch, and consider what helpes we did al this time intreate of; was it not instruction of the minde by some other spiritual exercise than prayer in praiing? Wil he call fasting, kneeling, etc., instructions of the minde what to pray? Then he must needs plead for his image and al poperye, if these bodily actions and gestures be instruction of the minde, which are but preparations to make the body serviceable and apt to and in this dutie. Further, how learnedly he disputeth to make reading one of these bodily gestures or bodily actions only, let it be considered of. And as he confoundeth these bodily exercises and spirituall exercises, so he sheweth himself ignorant and unable to discerne spiritual gyftes and exercises one from an other, with the distinct use of them; demanding whither [whether] the voyce of an other, an other that prayeth, be an outward help or prayer it self, an outward meanes to make our prayer more fervent. He thinketh I will be laught at, if I say it be prayer it self. Sure if in anie assemblie, or [237] where two or three are in Christ's name gathered together, *epitoauto* and *homothymadon*,[2] unto the same thing and with one minde, for avoyding confusion they do use but one voice, and that by God's order and commandement, the others'

[1] *A Plaine Declaration*, p. 74.

[2] Epi to auto, added together, in the same place; homothumadon, with one accord. See Acts 2:1. In Alexander Souter, *Novum Testamentum Graece,* the reading is homou, together.

hearts going with the wordes and saying *Amen*,[1] they that heare pray not as wel as he that according to God's ordinance speaketh, our publique prayers are not the prayers of the church, but of him that speaketh only. But now God hath otherwise taught, I Corinthians 14, etc., Acts 4. It must needs be, that Mr. Giffard is in great error to thinke none but he that speaketh prayeth. I take then such hearing of an other's voyce, praiing; and this to be a foule error to publish the contrarie; but that prayer both edifieth him that speaketh and him that heareth, and together in heart prayeth, I make no doubt. Yet hereupon to affirme, that there are other meanes of instruction to be used in the instant action of praying than praying it self, were as grosse as the other, and both a confounding of spiritual exercises, and flat contradiction of the Scripture, especially so diverse weightie actions of minde and bodie, as *proseuche*, and *anagnosis*,[2] powring out our hearts to God in prayer, and reading. At other times I did not only allow, but teach, that we have al the dayes of our lyves need to be instructed to pray aright, and that reading is a blessed meanes thereunto. So that you see whiles you of purpose will oppose, you runne your self upon the rocke; in stead of justifiing your accusation of two heresies to be found in my first reason, you have published this follye, which you must retract, if you wil obey the truth.

Mr. Giffard then granting, that reading is but to help to prayer and not praying, and now being shewed that it can be no help in that instant action of praiing, let us proceede to peruse an other of his mistakings and wilful pervertings. I affirming, that the Holy Ghost never enjoyned us to any certaine number of words by stint and limitation in praiing, as commanding the very words to be said over when we pray, he every where in his wrytings as a supposed foundation to their leitourgie and collects, alledged out of Numbers the 6, Matthew 6, Luke 11, example of Psalmes, and now Deuteronomy 26, that the Lord did by commandement bynde them to those verie words saiing over, when they prayed or

[1] I Corinthians 14:16.
[2] Proseuchē, prayer; anagnōsis, reading. See *An Answere*, p. 4.

blessed in those formes which are there prescribed.[1] For my reasons in disproving this popish carnal conceipt, I refer the reader to my former answere to his published pretended defence of reading for praiing.[2] One reason was drawen from the words of the text, Numbers 6:32 [22], where the Hebrew words *Coh Tebaracu*, "thus shal you blesse," do not import a tying them to the verie words of this forme in blessing, but to the rules and instructions there taught them concerning the matter it self for their direction, which I collected by this word *Coh*, which is an adverb of similitude, signifiing with us as much as "after this maner" and therfore cannot be to say the same words, but according to the same instructions. Where first he reprocheth me for that *Tebaracu* was false printed,[3] thereupon chardging me I cannot reade two words right of Hebrue, which were not great ignominie in their priesthood. But shall we say Mr. Giffard cannot reade two words in Latine rightly, because in the [238] twenty-eighth page of his booke he repeateth out of Augustine, *npoli sui*, for *populi sui*?[4] This I mention, as sory to see the defendor of this false hierarchie so emptie, to leave sounde doctrine, and thus to trifle; if he had bene at the print, it should have bene amended, it seemeth. Now to the doctrine gathered of this word *Coh*, Mr. Giffard would invert the words in his owne sense, thus; that where I said, the Lord did not command to say the same words but the like, that is, according to those directions of doctrine, he gathereth, that I should affirme it unlawfull to use those words at all, yea, that they might not use all or anie of these words at anie time. Whether this be a christian interpretation of my words or no, I leave not only to all men's, but chieflie to his owne conscience to be considered. Yet he still covertly persisting in his error, produceth a place of Scripture, where the word *Coh* (as he thinketh) is used for the saying of the verie words. Exodus 3:[14–15].

[1] *Ibid.*, pp. 6, 7. *A Plaine Declaration*, pp. 77, 78, 79. The correct reference is Deuteronomy 26, not 36. [2] Greenwood, *An Answere*, pp. 24–28.

[3] Mistakenly printed as "Teborcu" instead of "Tebaracu" in *An Answere*, p. 7. This is a small detail about how one should transliterate the Hebrew qameç and about the difference between a silent simple shewa and a vocal compound shewa. The word could have been transliterated as "tevareku."

[4] A misprint in Gifford's *A Plaine Declaration*, p. 28.

"The Lord said to Moses, 'Thus shalt thou say unto the children of Israel, EHEIE[1] hath sent me unto yee;' moreover, God said unto Moses, 'thus shalt thou say unto them, The God of your Fathers, etc.'" "According to Mr. Grenewood's interpretation" (saith he) "Moses is not commanded to say those words, but the like." True, he is not here bound to this certeine number of words, or the same words. If then they should say, "what is his name that hath sent thee," he may not say, "EHEIE hath sent me," because God said *Coh*, etc. Now Mr. Giffard sheweth himself a shifter. I did never hold it unlawfull to use anie wordes of the Scripture as need required, it is your slander; where you have in all your bookes affirmed we hold it unlawfull to say, "thy kingdome come," or use anie phrase of Scripture to right use; your woeful wrasting of the tongue for untruths, wil tourne to your further judgment. I proved only by the word *Coh*, which signifieth "after this maner" that God commanded not the very certaine number of words to be said. And where I sayd the word *Coh* was so used in all the prophets (when they say, "Thus saith the Lord") to this end, that neither the Holy Ghost had registred al their verie wordes they spake, nor that they were tyed to the prescript number of words, he would have it thought I should hold those words which are recorded, not to be the words of God; which wrasting of my words, is but his emptie quarreling to turne away this firme doctrine; namely, that God did in those formes of prayer mentioned by him, prescribe the somme of their blessings and petitions, wherunto they ought according to their severall occasions within the limits of these doctrines, frame their suites and desires, and did not tye them to a certaine number of words. Now he finding himself pressed, in that all his proofes are at once brought to be weapons against him rather than warrant, if being prooved unto him that those formes are repeated in other words in other places, and that the priests used other in blessing the people, as Eli blessed Hanna;[2] also that the apostles used other words in prayer, and never

[1] EHEIE, I AM WHO I AM, or I AM WHAT I AM, or I WILL BE WHAT I WILL BE.
[2] I Samuel 1:13.

that verie forme and number of words, he playnly denyeth that our question was about the bynding and limiting to the verie words by commandement, and saith our question was, whither [whether] it were idolatrie to use those [239] prescript phrases or no. Thus the man is fled, not only contradicting all his writinges, making voide his proofes, but granting as much as I affirmed upon the word *Coh*, hath gyven mee the whole cause against his wil. For if these places wil serve to prove an apportioning by number and stint upon commandement, then Mr. Giffard hath no profe for his collects, no, though these had bene so, yet his patched broken massbooke[1] shoulde have bene far from comming in place of true prayer. But that this is a popish dreame to think in prayer they were bound to some certeine number of words saying over, it was also convinced unto him by the Greeke word *houtos*,[2] where Christ commandith his disciples, saying, "When you pray, pray thus, 'Our Father, etc.'" Which word "thus," Mathew 6:9, singnifieth, "after this manner" or "according to this forme, rules, and instructions;" for if the commandement shoulde goe to bynde us to the very words, then this word "*when* you pray" would bynd us never to use other words, for the text saith, "when you pray, say thus." To this he answereth, "that respecting the rules for matters, *when* is as much as [to say] *whensoever* you pray, because we may not depart from those matters conteyned in those general petitions."[3] But in words it is not so there. We must consider to distinguish, etc. Wel, hath he not lost himself, and still against his will yeilded the matter; namely, that wee are not in these formes of prayer bound to the verie words saying over, and that the Holy Ghost did never, by commandement, stint or limit us to anie words in praying, which in deed is common with inchanters. And I take it he will easily yeild me this point, for if he remember Augustine to teach, that then we pray that prayer which Christ taught his disciples, when our prayers are grounded upon those doctrines and

[1] *The Book of Common Prayer*.

[2] This is the Greek adverb and not the demonstrative pronoun or adjective; houtōs, not houtos. [3] *A Plaine Declaration*, p. 100.

instructions, or to that effect.[1] And Calvine to say: the Sonne of man would not prescribe us what words we must usc in prayer, he should have put us to lesse trouble.[2] So that besides his mass-booke was never prescribed by the Lord himself or warrant of his Word, he seeth it unlawful to apportion, limit and stint as by measure and waight certaine members [numbers?] of wordes, sentences, etc., in prayer. As for his examples of the Psalmes, I refer to my former answere, namely, that praying is one thing, and singing a psalme an other.[3]

Now then we have heard that reading is not praying or any help to pray in the instant action of praying, when we should powre forth our owne hearts to God. Also that it is unlawful to bynde man to numbers of words or sentences in praying. Let us come to the first generall argument, which is this.

> "No Apochripha must be brought into the publick assemblies; for there only God's Word and the lyvely voyce of his owne graces must be heard in the publick assemblies."[4]
>
> But men's wrytings and the reading them over for prayer are Apochripha.
>
> Therefore [they] may not be brought into the publick assemblies, eyther for lawes or worship.

Here hee finds fault with the worde: "Apochripha" (although it hath bene an antient word in this sense, and now published in their Bibles to distinguish other wrytings from the authentick Scriptures), willing mee to goe to the matter it self, drawing by firme con-[240] clusion, that nothing is to be allowed any place in the church, which is not that perfect rule it self in writing or without errour uttered in speach, and he wil yeild. This I did prove unto him by an argument hee was not able

1 See John H. S. Burleigh, *Augustine: Earlier Writings*, "The Library of Christian Classics," VI (Philadelphia, 1953), p. 70.

2 See Calvin's commentary on Matthew 6:9 in *Commentaires de Jehan Calvin sur le Nouveau Testament*, volume I (Paris, 1854), p. 178. Calvin wrote: "It was not the intention of the Son of God, (as we have already said), to prescribe the words which we must use, so as not to leave us at liberty to depart from the form which he has dictated."

3 Greenwood, *An Answere*, p. 4.

4 See "Reasons against Read Prayer," in Carlson, *The Writings of John Greenwood, 1587–1590*, pp. 12–15.

to answere, and did leave out the word *Apochripha,* thus.

> "Only the canonical Scriptures and lyvely voice of God's owne graces are to be brought into the publick assemblies for doctrine and prayer.
>
> But men's writings or collections are neither canonical Scripture, nor the lyvely voice of God's graces in such as he hath appointed to speake in the publick assemblies.
>
> Therefore no man's writing may be brought into, nor imposed upon, the publick assemblies" for doctrine and prayer.[1]

Now, where he cavilleth about the perfectnes of the rule and absolute perfectnes of the graces, it doth not help him. For the Word of God being of necessitie by the lawe and ordinance of God, to be read in our owne language, I trust he will not denye it to be the written Word of God for the unperfectnes of the translation, being (to the best search the church can make) skanned by the original tongue and stil amended; or at least the church no further bound to it, than it shal be found to be the perfect rule; so likewise the lyvely voice of God's graces are not for the imperfectnes to be excluded, being God's appointed ordinance; neither is anie fault in the translation to be allowed, and errour in doctrine or prayer are presently to be admonished and repented of. Mr. Giffard then must denye the Bible translated into our owne language to be the canonicall Scriptures, and denye the lyvely voice of God's lawfull officers, and such as are thereunto called, in doctrine and prayer, to be the manifestations of the spirit and utterance of God's graces for the assemblie, or els grant the proposition firme. And if hee can put dead men's writinges into the place of either of these, I will yeild. In the meane time I hold such translations to be the Worde of God, and by God's ordinance put into our owne language, to all our knowledges retayning the words of God, which Word and the lyvely use of God's owne graces in the mouth of such as he thereunto appointeth, are only to be brought into

[1] Greenwood, *An Answere,* pp. 10–12.

the publicke assemblies for prayer and doctrine; for God hath commanded these unto us as his owne ordinances in his assemblies, and no other means wherby either God speaketh unto us, or his people unto him, in the congregation. To this all the Scriptures beare witnesse; the Word is always firme, confirmed with miracles from heaven, and commended to us by Christ, the prophetts and apostles, to be the foundation, canon,[1] light, lanterne, etc., the graces of the Spirit gyven for the interpretation, prayer, doctrine, etc. Christ is ascended up into heaven, and hath given giftes unto men to serve their tyme and minister in their place in this house. These graces stil renewed, not only in those called of God in this service for their dayly administration, but newe workmen thrust forth into this harvest, as the Lord of the house disposeth: which graces of his Spirit are compared to two olive branches, which emptie out of themselves thorow two golden pipes, Zacharie 4:12. And to seven thunders which utter their voices that cannot be written. [241] Away therfore with your patched mass-booke,[2] it may neither stande for a foundation in God's house, nor for the lyvely voyces of these thunders; you make it a monstrous idoll by putting it in either of these uses, yet you will make it serve for both. Wee have nothing to do with your matters of order, as you understand that order for tyme, place, etc.; wee reason of the spirituall action it self, when wee entreat of the meanes whereby God speaketh to us, and appointeth us to speake unto him. Wee can cast out the errours in translation or doctrine or prayer, and yet retaine God's Worde in our owne language, and the lively voice of his graces in the assemblie. When you can do so with your devises and newe hatched leitourgies, wee will give eare unto you and them; till then wee thinck of your conterfeit playes and pleas for your idolls and detestable sacriledge and high prophanation of God's ordinances with Jannes and Jambres[3] to resist the truth. Paraphrases[4] wee hold to

[1] Rule, touchstone. [2] *The Book of Common Prayer*.

[3] II Timothy 3:8. Possibly, they may be identified with the Egyptian magicians, who opposed Moses, and who are mentioned in Exodus 7:11.

[4] Paraphrases were biblical restatements, commentaries and exegetical guides. The paraphrases of Erasmus are extended restatements of biblical verses, with

be men's writinges and expositions, and not the Word of God, nor the lively voice of God's grace of interpretation or prayer, therefore to be excluded this place of service unto God. Thus you see the further you wrastle, the further you make your wares, the best of them, odious to everie godly conscience. You say I deceive the simple by gyving them one crabbe amongst many apples;[1] but you may behold your best apples such as the Holy Ghost hath foretold us, Revelations 18, to be entisements to evil. It is well you will grant my propositions to be sound; and I would wish (if such be God's wil) they might be better favored.

Nowe because I wil not stand either repeating or contending about syllogismes, I will take this much yeilded of your owne conclusions, which is as much in effect as I have affirmed, where you teach me thus to reason. No man's writings are the undoubted truth of God, but have errours and imperfections; therfore men cannot further ground upon them, than they be consonant to the canonicall Scriptures. Againe, the church is builded upon the foundation of the apostles and prophets; therfore our faith is not to rest upon men's writings. Whereupon doth necessarily follow, that if men's writings may not be builded upon nor rested upon, howe should you dreame it lawfull to impose them for lawes upon the publick assemblies, or to have them there read to beare rule as the wordes of God? And this you confessed in an other of your writings,[2] that God spake unto us out of his undoubted Worde, or by his owne

comments woven into the expanded material. See *Desiderii Erasmi Roterodami Opera Omnia*, Tomus VII (Lugduni Batavorum [Leiden], 1706). This volume contains his paraphrases on each book of the New Testament except Revelation. See also *The First Tome or Volume of the Paraphrase of Erasmus upon the Newe Testament* (London, 1548/1549). This volume contains the four gospels and the Acts of the Apostles. See also *The Seconde Tome or Volume of the Paraphrase of Erasmus upon the Newe Testament* (London, 1549). This volume contains the remaining twenty-two books of the New Testament. In the *Short-Title Catalogue*, these two volumes are 2854. See also 10502 for *The First Tome*.

[1] *A Plaine Declaration*, p. 85.

[2] In 1581 Gifford had said, "For looke whatsoever a man findeth in the auncient writers in expounding, he is no further to beleeve them than they prove their exposition out of the Bible" (*A Briefe Discourse of Certaine Points of the Religion Which Is among the Common Sort of Christians* (London, 1581), p. 57.

word. If then God speake not unto us by men's writinges that be of private interpretation, in the assemblie, nor that they can be made groundwork to buyld our faithe upon, or to rest assured upon, it will be granted, I hope, that they are not to be imposed upon the publick assemblies as lawes and rules, but left to everie man's private use in their libertie, as they wil answere for themselves what use they put them to, and whither [whether] they doe not prefer them before the booke of God, or prejudice themselves by them. This first poinct is then plaine, that only God's undoubted Worde is [242] to be imposed, brought in, and maintayned in the publick assemblies as lawes and rules, no other writings being authentick or canonical. But here Mr. Giffard doth in effect affirme, that the Word of God it self is not authentick or canonical, except in the Hebrew or Greeke copie. Wherein he goeth a little beyond the papists, that wil yet allow the Worde of God in Latine. And if it shoulde be defended, that the Worde of God were not the worde it self that wee have in our owne language, it wil follow that no man could have assurance of faith, except he understoode both Hebrew and Greeke, yea, be able soundly to interpret the Scriptures in both. If the translations be so far men's writings that it ceaseth generally to be the Word of God that is not written in Hebrew or Greek, and men's writinges not to be grounded or rested upon, where shall our assurance stand? And might not Mr. Giffard as well say, the Hebrew and Greek copie are but paper and ynck, many faults and errours by the print in vowells, accents, letters; and so conclud we had not authentick or canonical Scriptures at al, except in men's erronious writings [which] might be of equall authoritie in the assemblie that the Scriptures [possess]? Must he not beare with mee in accompting him an atheist or libertine in thus reasoning? Hence, then, we see whiles you go about to abase the canonicall Scriptures, and extol your patched leitourgie, you fall into manie blaphemies, as I have before told you. Wee hold it the Word of God in what language soever, stil rejecting the errours in the print, in the translations, etc.; as they are knowne unto us, and not [objecting] to the Word it self for the imperfections or errours in the translation and print. Now when you can so [in this manner] reject the errours in men's writings, as you can make that which remayneth the undoubted Worde of God, not agreeable only, but an authentick approved canonicall Scripture, authorised from God to be the verie eternall foundation and rules, limitts, and lawes given by himself unto his people, you may lift up your stumped Dagon into this place; if there be some truth in their writings (as what men's writings have not some, and the holy name of God verie much), yet is that truth in the Scripture it self and here so mingled with chaffe, that it were not only unprofitable and a hinderance of the true use of God's Worde, but an abolishing and defacing of the Word it self; the majesty whereof ought to terrifie you from this presumption. And where you say that you "decide not controversies by anie translation, but by the authentick copies of Hebrew and Greke,"[1] I trust you speak only of such as are able by the interpretation thereof so to decide controversies, and holde it not unlawfull for anie such as have not that help, to convince errour by the powre of the Word and conferring [comparing] one place with an other in anie translation, according to the analogie of faith, though I grant we ought to use the best approved. But if this were not lawfull, surely no man might prophesie in the church, which hath not the gift of interpretation of the tongue, neither might any affirme any Scripture to be true, but they which have knowledg of tongues. How blasphemous is this geare, whiles you are igno-[243]rant of the powre, wisdome and agreement of the Word and Spirit, and diversitie of giftes given unto men; the Word and the Spirit approve each other, and beare witnesse ech of other, in what language soever God giveth it, to our understanding. Prophesie and knowledg of tongues are two several giftes, not alwayes given to one member, but distributed as God in his wisdome hath appointed, I Corinthians 12, and prophesie commanded for the more excellent, *caput* 14. But this is sufficient in

[1] *A Plaine Declaration,* p. 85.

this place, that the Word of God is the Word of God in what language soever, and to accompt it being verbatim translated, or at least so far foorth faithfully translated, man's writing, were blasphemies: but men's writings can never be so holden the authentick Scriptures of God, how agreable to the Word soever they be. My argument is then firme, and thus left upon you. Those writings which be not the Word of God being imperfect, and never without error, may not be imponed [imposed] as lawes and canons upon the publick assemblies, or there be read or interpreted, or offred up in worship; but such are al men's writings that be not the authentick Word of God it self. The publick assemblies are only bound to the reading and interpretation of the Scriptures, which God hath ordeined to be read in a knowne language, and for prayer and prophesie hath ordeined the lively voice of his owne graces in the mouth of such as he hath appointed to be the mouth of the congregation unto him, and his mouth unto them. So that your patched leitourgie, paraphrases, songes in rime, homelies, and al your dead men's writings, are cast forth of the publick assemblies, and manifest to be idols when they are thrust into that place.

Now where I alledged that the binding of the publick assemblie, yea, of all assemblies, to certaine writings of men everie day and yeare, their number and portion of words, daylie, monthly and yearly, in al assemblies the same matter and words reiterated, in stead of powring forth their hearts unto God according to their present needs and occasions, was a setting of themselves in God's seate and taking the office of his Spirit, which only knoweth the wantes of the several assemblies according to their diverse occasions,[1] he runneth away from the matter, as one unwilling to heare of this their *tautologia* [tautology] and counterfet babling, demanding whether everie one should utter their owne perticular wantes in the publick assemblie, or should pray nothing but that everie one feeleth the present want of in himself, or should tell the minister before hand what everie one of their wantes were; then how the minister should

[1] *An Answere*, signature Aii *recto* and *verso*, 4, 11, 15, 20.

remember al. Are these any thing but mere cavils? Can any of these follow upon the former doctrine? And let him looke againe, whether he that is the mouth of the congregation unto God in publick prayer, must not consider the present public occasions of that publick assemblie, and thereafter frame his prayers, all the people joyning in heart to his words of petition or thanksgyving, saying *Amen* to so much as he asketh according to the wil of God and neede of the time, yea, and if they have not feeling in such prayers, they are unfeeling members; yet neither doth he intermedle with private or secret wantes, neither neede they tell him [244] them; he is sent for the publick affaires of the church, to commend the several actions general and publick, unto God. And as they are diverse in everie assemblie, so must he be a man of wisdome to know, see and consider them, lest they al rashly step into the house of God to offer up the sacrifice of fooles, and make a counterfeit babling, Ecclesiastes 4. Yet the sinne of this is nothing comparable to the doung your priests cast forth by pratling over your English portuis [portas], which the Lord wil one day cast in your faces. As then in private prayer we are to lay forth our owne wantes and estate of our own soule, which cannot be done by reading an other man's writings, alwayes singing one song, customably repeating in supersticion certaine words, our hearts never ripped up, examined, nor the diseases therof layd open unto God, seeking due cure. So the man that is the mouth of the whole assemblie prayeth, as the mouth of one bodie, for al their open publick present wantes and occasions. Which occasions, considering the persons and actions, are diverse and cannot be written for one assemblie before hand, muchlesse for all assemblies in a whole kingdome, neither by man nor angel. See then the mockerye of your service booke, and what idolatrie is committed by it, to the abandoning true prayer according to the present wantes and occasion.

The next thing to be considered, is, about making of lawes in the worship of God. Where he would persuade us that their whole leitourgie conteining al their publick worship, government, offices and ordinances of their church, be but matters of order and conveniencie.[1] Then the compelling and teaching the publick assemblie to reade over men's writings both as canons and lawes in the church, and publickly and privately to offer them up in stead of true prayer and holy invocation, is a matter of comelines and conveniencie. In the meane time it must be a turning away of the whole order and ordinances of God. For what is the whole Testament of Christ but an order for everie office, person, action in the church, if he wil have it *taxis*,[2] and then must confesse their leitourgie an other order of publick administration, and so as I have said an other gospel, an other Testament, a setting up an other worship. And hereupon I trust I may cal al this an adding to the Word of God; yea, I wil go a litle further, an abolishing and disabling and dishonoring of the Word it self and graces of his spirit. And whither [whether] all this smoke of the bottomlesse pyt may not be reproved with these Scriptures, not only Proverbs 30, verses 5, 6; Deuteronomy 4, verse [12 and] 32; but also Revelation 22, verses 18, 19; let the godly ponder and search; and let the fearefulnes of the threats deterre all flesh from presuming to alter the ordinances, lawes and worship of the most high God. And that the verie reading of an other man's writing for my owne praier, or the prayer of the church, in stead of powring foorth our owne hearts, is a changing of the whole worship into the making men's writing an idoll, which is by these places condemned as an accursed sinne, let the most hard text (as he in carnall wonder exclaymeth) be looked into, Revelation 22, verses 18, 19. The words are plaine: "If anie man put or add any thing unto these," or "if anie man take away from these words," he shalbe [245] judged as followeth. Now if the adding an other whole worship, and suppressing of that God hath appointed, be not an adding to these things written, gyve sentence as you wil answere. O (saith he) but it is said "God wil add unto such al the plagues written in this booke"; and there is in this booke mentioned the lake of fire.[3] As

[1] *A Plaine Declaration*, pp. 106–108. [2] Hē Taksis, arrangement, order.
[3] *A Plaine Declaration*, p. 114.

though the lake of fire is not due for everie sinne, and yet not every one that committeth sinne to be condemned; what sinne is it that deserveth not the eternall wrath of God? Yet not every one that sinneth [is] given over to that judgment, for either it may be of ignorance, or of negligence, and washed away by repentance in the blood of Christ, or it may be repented of and left when wee see it. Mr. Giffard hath read wel the curses of the law and all the curses due for sinne, that seeth not how many curses the law and the prophets pronounced upon sinne, to call the persons themselves to repentance, shewing together the equitie of God's law, and yet withal the free mercye of God to al that truly repent their evil wayes. Al that receive the beast's marke in their hand or forehead, are thretned to be cast with the beast and false prophet into that lake; yet I doubt not but manie that have bene so seduced into that sinne, shal by repentance be saved. Not that I encourage anie to continue in such fearful estate, to harden their hearts against the threatnings of God, but that I would have Mr. Giffard to put difference betwene the curse layed to the sinne, and the condemnation of the person sinning. And seeing he taketh that lake a perticular severe threat to the apostasie under Antichrist, I would he had the grace to consider how it lyeth upon him, whiles he speaketh out of the mouth of the beast, if he repent not to turne from his evil wayes. Let it further be weighed how ignorantly he chargeth me to condemne al churches,[1] for this smale examplifying of this Egiption darknes, idolatrous worship, and exalting men's writings into this defacing of God's Word and true worship, they neither being guylty of such a sacrilegious leitourgie, as this Egiptian calf hatched at Rome, neither are to be presently judged no church for others' sinne, till they joyne obstinacie to their transgression. But shift the matter as you wil, or rather as you can apeare before God, I wil not make lesse the sinne, or the judgment due to sinne, for men's persons, no, not of whole churches, if they shal be guilty therin. My desire is by discoverie of the sinne, to bring men to repentance, and unto the awe of God in his worship; who

[1] *Ibid.*, preface, signature A 4 *verso* and p. 70 (wrongly paged 72).

are guyltie besides your selves in such sacriledge, as to abrogate the leitourgy of Christ, and set up an other, or to restraine God's true worship, and to give life to the image of the beast, it skilleth me not; let sinne be sinne, and God righteous, and then examine your selves, if they or you be cleare, I rejoyce, neither do I think or can charge them with such idolatrie as is here erected. I take it you wil be found the sclanderer of other churches, to hide your owne filthines. But, saith Mr. Giffard, those Scriptures are against the adding of humane preceptes and lawes to be kept as partes of God's worship to bind the conscience to seek righteousnes and the forgivenes of sinnes, or the merit of eternal life in them, or against such rules of government as God hath set [246] to be perpetual.[1] In which we must take your meaning to be this; that you grant where anie humane precepts and lawes be enforced as a part of God's worship, or as lawes to bind the conscience, or when righteousnes is sought in them, and forgivenes of sinnes by observing of them, or merit by them, or if they be against such rules of government as God hath set to be perpetuall, if the additions or constitutions be such as anie of these, then such lawes and constitutions are against the perfection of the Word of God, against christian libertie, and in the chief things which concerne God's worship, against the ground and foundation of our faith, and so a thing most detestable and accursed, which our Saviour Christ refused justly to observe with the blinde Phariseis, wherein you have granted as much as I ever affirmed. For is not your whole leitourgie being an other than Christ's testament, your whole reading men's writings in place and in stead of laying forth your owne present wantes and occasions in prayer to God, humane constitutions, and made a parte of God's worship? At least such pretended worship as you thinke good enough for him? Weygh the matter uprightly. Againe, whither [whether] your whole antichristian government, offices, courtes, and ministerie, be not constitutions and ordinances against such rules of Christ's government as be perpetual, and an innovating of his testament,

[1] *Ibid.*, p. 113.

examine; which you shall soone perceive, if you looke but what Christ's perpetuall ordinances, offices, officers and lawes for the guyding, ordering, and governing of his church be, prescribing everie one their place, dutie and limits joyntly and severally, and not finde your ministerie registered there, but a strange leitourgie and worship borrowed from the pope, which came out of the bottomlesse pit;[1] confesse your sacriledge in suppressing Christ's whole ministerie and ordinances, and erecting an other for the perpetuitie of his, even to everie naile and pyn. The Holy Ghost sheweth that only to be his ministerie, till we be all a perfect body in him, and his whole ministerie and ordinances a kingdome that cannot be shaken, Hebrews 12, Ephesians 4, a commandement to be kept undefiled till the appearing of Jesus Christ; his scepter an everlasting scepter; the Sonne as faithfull in his house as Moses a servant in the tabernacle, who made all things according to the paterne. So that it is to be wondered Mr. Giffard should think anie part of Christ's government should not be perpetuall, that was given by the apostles—the master buylders and layers of the foundation, wherby all actions should be tried to the world's end. May not Mr. Giffard as wel cal into question the perpetuitie of the Testament, as the lawes and rules for the government of his church? Now if your whole false hierarchie, offices, officers, lawes, worship, be plainly other than Christ's, as in our other writings are proved, and shame will inhibit you to denye, how can you be so drunke with the cup of the whore's fornication, to think you have no constitutions, lawes or traditions, which are a part of worship, and against such rules of Christ's government as the apostles have prescribed for the ordring of his howse, and the same ordeyned for all [247] churches til we become all a perfect bodye in him? But if Mr. Giffard wil shew himself so voide of al conscience and truth, to say al their traditionall worship and antichristian offices and ordinances be neither part of their worship nor constitutions disanulling the ordinances of Christ, yet wil he confesse I doubt not this kinde

[1] This phrase, used more frequently by Barrow than Greenwood, comes from Revelation 9:1, 2, 11; 11:7; 17:8; 20:1, 3.

of worship and government to be imposed as matters to binde the conscience, being all the service of God they have, seeing hee woulde also have all that observe them not, to be censured and excommunicat for this merchandize. It were a sore matter a man should be cut off from Christ and his church, gyven over to Satan, and the judgment ratified in heaven against soule and bodye, for a matter that byndes not the conscience. As though the soule and bodye (howsoever some things perteine to the one, or is done by the one as proper worke thereof) were not both to be counted when the conscience shalbe opened to answere for all done in both, or by eyther of both, even whatsoever wee have done in soule and bodye; and Calvine would but divide the soule and the bodye in civile causes. But Mr. Giffard would goe a note further; namely, that in the service of God in such causes as the transgression deserve excommunication, to be no matter bynding the conscience. But it may be Mr. Giffard doth suppose, that except the constitutions ecclesiasticall be such, as righteousness be commanded to be sought in the doing them, and forgivenes of sinnes and merit by them all is wel. Then, besides the other abuses granted, he must be demanded whither those traditions of the Fathers, which our Saviour Christ and his disciples refused to observe, were imposed as meritorious? Wherunto wee answere, No. For in the superstitious washings of cuppes, of beddes, with al such trincketts, wee see to be no such matter, Marke 7: [8], and Christ's words in saying, they layde the commandements of God aside to set up their owne traditions, doth shew wherin the sinne was; namelie, to do and observe such things of vaine glorie, superstition, or custome, as God has not injoyned them, and to leave undone the lawes and commandements of God; which sinne is your transgression at this day. Reade therefore the 7 of Marke and 15 of Mathew more diligently. Further, those superstitious traditions, Galatians 4, and Colossians 2, the observing wherof were the denyall of Christ, were neither held meritorious, nor justification sought by them, manie of them being Jewish ceremonies, sometimes as rudiments commanded of God, now abolished and no further burden to be layde in such outward thinges; no, we reade not that the law of God it self was eyther commanded, or so observed, as to seeke righteousnes by it. Now then to the matter. Mr. Giffard thinketh Christ and his apostles did well in refusing to obey the traditions of the fathers at the Pharisies' commandement, and so [Mr. Giffard] must confesse it lawful and a dutie of us to refuse to observe your Jewish cerimonies and Romish superstitious traditions, which are so manie as even your whole leitourgie and worship conteine nothing els, God's lawes and ordinances not only left undone, but al that pleade for them and seeke to walke in them, persecuted with deadly hatred. And how [248] Mr. Giffard will prove that there is no adding or diminishing to or from the Word of God, by imposing and creating more lawes than God hath made in his worship and government of his church, but such as bee made part of the worship, or bynde conscience, or bee meritorious, or against such rules of his government as bee perpetuall, though I take all your orders, lawes, worship in this compasse; yet howe you can p[r]ove this, I know not; for looke againe upon the Scriptures, Proverbs 30:5, 6; Deuteronomy 4:2 and 12:32; and Galatians 3:15; Revelation 22:18, 19; and you shal finde, that to add, superordeine, innovate, or diminish or take anie thing from the lawes of God already prescribed for his worship, were to abrogate his lawe, to laye further burdens than hee hath layde, to make his lawe unperfect, and set our selves in his seate; yea, whatsoever wee put to which hee hath not commanded or whatsoever we inhibit that hee hath commanded, is here forbidden. For this [thus] saith the Lorde, "Ye shall put nothing unto the word which I command you, neither shall you take ought therefrom that you may keepe the preceptes of the Lorde your God which I commande you," Deuteronomy 4:2. And that this was as well in the outwarde ordinances of the temple as in the judgments, is plaine in the first verse. Againe in the 12 chapter, [verse] 32: "Whatsoever I command you, take heede you do it; thou shalt put nothing therto nor take anie thing therfrom;" and in the Proverbs. "Everie word of God is pure, put nothing unto his wordes lest hee reprove thee and thow bee found a lyer."[1] Now the Scripture speaking so absolutely and generaly against al addition or detraction to or from his ordinances, Mr. Giffard overshooteth himself of his bare word to contradict and limit so expresse commandementes; for these Scriptures (saith hee) are against adding of humane precepts and lawes to bee kept as partes of God's worship, to bynde the conscience, to seeke righteousnes, forgevenes of sinne, merit in them, or against such rules of government as God hath set to be perpetuall.[2] This is true, but this is not all, for the lawe is generall against all inventions, traditions, constitutions, whatsoever God hath not commanded, as the Second Commandment doth also teach. "Thou shalt not make to thy self," etc;[3] so that God hath left nothing to be layde upon his church by commandement, which he hath not commanded. And therfore that place of the apostle to the Galatians 3:15, must be better perused: "If it be but a man's testament, when it is confirmed no man doth abrogate it or superordeine anie thing to it." Christ's Testament then being much more perfect, his whole minde for the ordering of his house manifested therin, it is wicked presumption to alter the ordinances thereof, or to holde them unmeete or unsufficient for anie age or estate. Well, Mr. Giffard could nowe bee content thus far to limit the power of the church; namelie, to have her subject and obedient to his voice; but that he supposeth there may be lawes ecclesiastical made, of things in themselves indifferent; that where the Scripture hath commanded such things to be used at our libertie for order, for comelynes, edification and glorye of God, as matters of place, time, and such circumstance. But hee here mistaketh his text, for the Lorde commandeth by the apostle in that place, I Corinthians 14:[26, 33, 40], that those [249] publique busines and exercises of the assemblies, shoulde be done in order, in comlynes, to edifiing; and doth not leave somthing to bee com manded, which the maister buylders hath not prescribed. For to binde those thinges by lawe which God hath not

[1] Proverbs 30:5, 6. [2] *A Plaine Declaration,* p. 113.
[3] Exodus 20:4. Deuteronomy 5:8.

bound in his worship, wee are to add newe traditions to bring us into bondage of the creatures, which the same apostle denyeth ever to bee brought into bondage unto, I Corinthians 6:12, in his owne person teaching us so to walke; the Lord see in his wisdome cause to leave them in our libertie, knowing there woulde bee no end of such perticular lawes, especially if he had left it to man's wyt to make and unmake lawes therein.

For the orders you speake of then, meaning circumstances of time, place, kneeling, sitting, standing, etc., there can be no further lawes of them, than the apostle hath set, and (as the minister of Christ prescribed) that al be donne to edifying in comlynes, order, etc. Of theis to set perticular lawes, were to break these general lawes of God, whereby he teacheth us the true use of them, and leaveth them in the churches' libertie as need requireth to use them or not use them. Neither can all assemblies bee bound in these thinges to the same in perticular, that being needfull and decent in one, that is not in an other. And in that you woulde have them no further commanded, than they bee needfull, convenient, decent, etc., you condiscend that there can bee no setled lawe in perticular layde upon the church in them. For to use them so far as they bee convenient, necessarie, and to edifiing, is the lawe and commandement of God; and to use them further at anie man's commandement, were both a breach of God's lawe, and making the creatures stumbling blockes, idolles, bondages, and everie way sinnefull. And when the church commandeth them so far to be used as they are commanded of God, the churche doth but ratifye and see God's lawe executed; so that you have lost your selfe, whiles you shoulde have proved your bold assertion: that the church hath power to ordeyne lawes, for to create or make lawes, which you see the folly of, being nowe driven to another shift; that in the perticular thinges whereof God hath given generall lawes, wee may make setled lawes, and yet but for the tyme they be convenient; whereas in deed God's lawe is the same and nothing ells. But because they bee necessarye in one place, that bee not in another, at one tyme, that bee not at another, of some persons, that bee not to other, ther can bee no lawe sett in the perticular one daye for all assemblies in such thinges. Neither shall anye disagreement bee such amongst the several churches, as need anye contention for them, whiles everie assemblye doe that w[h]ich is to themselves most meet, most convenient and necessary in such things, for the present tyme. The pastor and elders were of small discretion if they might not have these things in their libertie; and even these doctrines and examples are in this point against your selfe, which you have alledged from other churches. But my purpose is not to contend about men's writings, nor to be drawne into controversie with other [250] churches, when I am to deale with your present sinne; for the avoiding wherof you thus rage. If your cause be good, plead it by the Scriptures, and I wilbe so farre from casting our darts against al churches, as I wil not deale with their estate, till I be further occasioned; the rather may I omitt this labour, for that you have alledged one place of Scripture which you suppose wil beare up all your matter. If it helpe you not, I see not how you wil defend your assertion. In the 15 of the Acts where it is said the apostles, elders, and brethren at Jerusalem met about the question of circumcision and other ceremonies of Moses' lawe, which some would have burdened the Gentiles with, we see there (saith he) "that the apostles themselves did decree some thing for the time, which afterward were to be altered when the occasion was taken away," namelie, "that the Gentiles should absteyne from blood, and from [things] strangled," for avoiding offence to the weak Jues.[1] First let us see what the decree was, and then it will appeare how litle it serveth Mr. Giffard his purpose; these be the wordes, Acts 15:28, 29. "It seemed good to the Holy Ghost and to us, to lay no more burden upon you than that which is necessary of these thinges, to absteyne from idolothytes, and from blood, and from [things] strangled, and from fornications; from which keeping your selves, yee doe well." For one of these, which is [fornication], we have here no question, it being by the moral lawe alwayes forbiden; for the other Mr. Giffard would thus

[1] *A Plaine Declaration*, p. 112.

reason. The apostles themselves did decree them for the tyme, therfore the church hath power to make and ordeyne lawes in things of themselves indifferent, about the worship of God and publick exercises. For our answere, wee would have Mr. Giffard first learne, that he, in saying the apostles themselves did this by the direction of the Holy Ghost, hath overthrowen himselfe; for these were the maister builders, appointed of God to be law makers for the whole leitourgie and worship of Christ to all posterities, even all the lawes and ordinances of the Newe Testament, confirmed by miracles from heaven, delivered by their ministery unto us. It will not follow, then, if the apostles had made and ordeyned some law here, that therefore everie synode or anie synode may impose lawes and commandements by themselves ordeyned, till they shew they have that power given them [which] the apostles had, and an other leitourgie to be made, which they shall never be able to doe, without a newe Christ. Wee have sure foundation alreadie layd, whereupon all synods and counsells must build, and suffer their actions to be tryed therby; they have not power to injoyne one title, which is not by the Word of God injoyned us. Further, what did the apostles here that they had now warrant for? Neither would they lay anie yoke or burthen. And as for these thinges, they doe as much binde us nowe if ther be like cause, namelie, not in idolothyts,[1] blood, or that which is strangled to offend our weak brethren, if the Jues should be now againe called, neither to offend anie in meate or drinke for whome Christ hath dyed. Neither was ther here any absolute law made of these thinges, nor necessitye for the present tyme, furder than it should bee necessary for the respect set downe; for [251] otherwise it had bene to build againe the thinges destroied; onlye they thus counselled and ad[m]onished the Gentiles to use their libertye in these thinges, as they might gyve noe offence to theyr weake brethren of the Jues, the more to drawe them on in the wayes of Christ;[2] for they doe not injoyne it as a lawe, but tell them they shall doe well if they observe these thinges, by no necessitye inforced. But wee

[1] Things offered to idols; meat sacrificed to idols. [2] Acts 15:19–31.

doe not nowe observe these thinges, the occasions being removed. True, therfore I trust you wil grant, that no man shall bee furder bounde to anye constitution in such thinges indifferent, than there shall bee cause, neyther need wee publick order to retract; so that you leave the matter to me, that wee can bee no further bounde in such thinges, than by those rules of edifiing, order, comlines, occasion shall require, so that wee neither need nor can have setled lawes herein: howe much more bondage and burden is imposed under this antichristian yoke, the thinges being of themselves most lothsome and detestable popery, abrogating and making voide all the true ordinances, lawes and worship of Christ, and so inforced as whot [hot] persecution procedeth against anye that of conscience absteyne from them, let it bee considered. Neither hath there ever bene detracting this thirtye yeares[1] of anye your abhominations, neither is held lawefull for them that seeth them unlawfull, to forbeare them, without deadlye hate, to bee followed to the death. Blessed bee our God, that hath delivered our soules out of such Egiptian servitude; our lives are not deare unto us, neither shall your reproch move us.

Nowe concerning the last places of the *Treatise*,[2] where hee is utterlye mute in this, that all whiche stand under another hierarchie or spirituall regiment than Christ's, bee by outward profession no true Christians, or under the promise of salvation, also for the freedome wee professe in holye obedience to all statutes and ordinances of God; as hee hath left untouched the matter, for which hee aledged the 7 to the Romanes, namelye, the outward professed bondage to a false spirituall government,[3] so I having before largely expressed my minde in that poinct of doctrine, and in such as then were about these thinges opposed, referre anye that desire the truth herein, to ponder the reasons and proofes there set downe,[4] not minding to repeate againe, or to bee set aworke in

[1] Greenwood is writing in 1591. Therefore, from the Act of Uniformity in 1559 to 1591 would be a period of thirty-two years.

[2] *A Plaine Declaration*, p. 118. [3] *A Short Treatise*, p. 44.

[4] Greenwood, *An Answere*, p. 38.

unfolding his troublesome and confuse cavills in abusing this place, or to make further replye, till I see more capeable conceypt in him of such principles of regeneration and sanctification, of freedome and bondage; yet for others' direction, one cavill or two shalbe breifly set in veiwe. First where hee supposing I had bene in error (and he himself fast fettered in heresie and seeth it not) chargeth mee to runne as farre on the other side, as a wheele turned with contrarye [252] motions of the streame,[1] for saying I helde the deare children of God might fall into any sinne, except the sinne against the Holy Ghost, yet bee restored by repentance, God's grace so far abounding, alwayes considered (as then I noted) that obstinacye in anye sinne, made them to us the servants of sinne whiles they so remayned,[2] not speaking this to give leave or incouragement to presume in the least on first step of sinne, lest God leave them to themselves, but to give them hope if they returne that have so fallen. Hee excepteth generally against all presumptuous sinne, saying, of frailty God's children may fall, but of presumption hee maketh great doubt, for anye so sinning to bee renued by repentance, for it is spoken of the *maranatha*[3] to be pronounced in this life to none, but that bee in that sinne against the Holye Ghost; and here to fill his paper (as his common shift is, when hee can neither affirme nor denye) hee putteth me to newe questions: you must (saith hee) "declare howe filthye incest is not [the] sinne against the Holye Ghost, nor if a man kill his father or mother or children," nor witchcraft, nor familiarity with spirites; "is not your meaning that the regenerate man may of presumption and obstinacy commit these?"[4] If Mr. Giffard shoulde thus understand the worde *may*, hee is in the same fault to say

[1] *A Plaine Declaration*, p. 121 (wrongly numbered 115).
[2] Greenwood, *An Answere*, p. 38.
[3] Greenwood is using this word as a curse, as a synonym for anathema. The use of this word in an imprecatory sense was common for many centuries, but it seems to rest on a false exegesis. *Maran atha* is an Aramaic expression, probably used as a concluding formula, meaning, "Our Lord, come." See I Corinthians 16:22 and Revelation 22:20. See also the Didache. See further the article by C. F. D. Moule, "A Reconsideration of the Context of Maranatha," *New Testament Studies*, July, 1960.
[4] *A Plaine Declaration*, p. 121 (wrongly numbered 115).

the regenerate may sinne of frailty. And I answere furder, he coulde understand the worde *may* otherwise, if (as in all his writinges) hee caryed not this minde to take in evill part, to quarell, hee coulde have understood it thus; that God suffereth of his elect to fall into such sinne, yet hee is able to reduce them by repentance, and hath made promise to receive them if they retourne; and not have cavilled in this maner in such thinges, the horrour in the verye naming of which sinnes shaketh the flesh and bones of the godlye to hear or behold; so that his drift is but to cast in a litle wormewood, to deface the truth delivered. Therefore I will onlye proove the generall doctrine before affirmed, and for these perticulars, let him that taketh pleasure in raking in them, being sinnes not once to bee named amongst God's children, answere himself. And much better might hee have put his question thus. Whither [whether] wilfullye committing of sacriledge, and presumptuous continuing to enchant in a false ministery, with Jannes and Jambres resistinge the truth,[1] persecutinge the light against their knowledge, bee not within the compasse of that sinne against the Holye Ghost. That God's elect after regeneration doe fall into presumptuous sinne, and for a time persist in obstinate sinne, and may bee restored by repentance, I thus proove. Manie of God's children may bee excommunicat, and upon the repentance bee received againe, as the incestious person, I Corinthians 5, therefore do for a time remayne in obstinate sinne. Againe, everie sinne is to bee prayed for, but that one sinne against the Holye Ghost, I John 5:16. Therefore presumptuous sinn is committed of God's elect after regeneration. That [253] all presumptuous sinne is not sinne against the Holy Ghost, wee shall see by the discription of that sinne, Hebrews 6 and 10, where there is dispyting of the spirit, accompting the blood of Jesus an unholy thinge, persecuting the light they have sometimes taste of, and such like notes, which are degrees further than presumption; for there is presumption of ignorance, of rashnes, of hope of mercy, and many times do the prophets charge the people with rebellion against God;

[1] II Timothy 3:8.

so that all presumption cannot have the curse *maranatha* pronounced upon it, or the persons not to bee prayed for. But sure I grant, that presumption is neere to sinne, and there cannot bee that high sinne without presumption. But now if all sinne but sinne of frayltie were unpardonable, your clergie were in a wofull case, that thus maynely resist the truth, and persecute God's servants.

Neither is this doctrine anye way contrarye to that I delyvered, namelye, that the regenerat man cannot bee sayd to stande in bondage to sinne after regeneration, and the servant of God at the same time by outwarde profession; for none are in bondage to sinne after their calling to the faith (to our judgment) but suche as contynue obstinate in their open knowne sinne after due admonition: that such stande not by outwarde profession the servants of Christ but of sinne, and are to be excommunicate, hee willingly granteth; and hereupon merveileth how I shoulde gather, that obstinat grosse sinners should not bee excommunicat, which hee might playnlye perceive if hee had eyes; for if al the regenerat bee in bondage to sinne, and so the servants of sinne and of Satan, howe should they cast out an other for bondage out of their fellowship by the power of Christ? If Mr. Giffard say, because the obstinate is in greater bondage than the other; this proveth not that the bond can cast out the bond by the power of Christ. Againe, if all bee in bondage, then none can bee holden without for being in bondage to sinne; so that none should bee excommunicat, none without, the worlde and the church, light and darknes, Christ and Beliall, should bee mingled together. To all which hee hath made no answere, but demandeth certeine questions, and maketh such a formal conclusion, as if all were in bondage unto sinne. His questions I grant al affirmatively, yet denye his consequence. Let him plainely prove therfore by evidence of Scripture, that all that do sinne are bondslaves of sinne; and when hee hath so done, I shall thereupon conclude him a flat Anabaptist in the chief ground of their profession. Verye gladlye therefore would hee leave out the worde "bondage," and falslye accuseth and sclandereth mee, in saying I holde that men can not outwardly appeare sinners, and stand the servants of Christ both at a time, which is an open untruth.[1] It is hee, that cannot put difference betwene sinning, and bondage unto sinne; so that in one worde all his questions are answered. If anie bee in [254] bondage to sinne, hee standeth a servant thereof. Now for the 7 to the Romanes, the apostle setting forth the strift [strife] betwene the flesh and the spirit, speaketh somtimes in the person of the one (if I may so speake) and somtimes of the other; somtimes of the newe man or regenerat part, or of himself so far as hee is regenerat; sometimes of the olde man, which is not wholly slaine, but full of rebellion, [and] striveth for maisterie. Nowe I must demand of him, whether of these two have the preheminence, dominion and rule in the regenerat, the graces of the spirit, or the rebellions of the flesh? The same apostle saith the spirit, and that part of the man renewed therewith, which wee call the inner man. In the 8 *caput* hee maketh it playne, "The lawe of the spirit of life in Christ hath freed mee from the lawe of sinne and of death."[2] What is the lawe of the spirit but the powre, rule, and dominion of the Spirit of God in us? And what is the lawe of sinne, but the powre of sinne, and bondage, wherewith wee were sometimes led headlong by Satan at his pleasure, but are nowe freed, that it no more doth reigne or beare rule in us unto condemnation? Againe, "whosoever are ledd by the Spirit of God, are the sonnes of God";[3] and in the 7 *caput*, [verse] 4, and 6 *caput*, [verse] 16: "knowe you not that to whome you exhibit your selves servants unto obedience, his servants you are to whome you give your selves obedient?" David feeling the great assaultes of sinne in his flesh, and his inhabilitie to keepe the lawe of God, earnestlye prayeth unto the Lorde, "direct my steppes in thy worde" (saith hee) "and let none iniquitie have dominion over mee."[4] After the stronge man is cast out, Christ beareth the rule over us and in us, by his Spirit. So the Scripture everye where pronounceth us saincts by calling, kinges, and priestes, a people set free; not that

[1] *A Plaine Declaration*, p. 120. [2] Romans 8:2. [3] Romans 8:14.
[4] Psalms 119:133.

wee sinne not in thought, word, and deede howrely and daylye, but that sinne hath not dominion over us. If then wee were in bondage to sinne, wee are the servantes of sinne and of death, which God forbid. Where Mr. Giffard therfore reasoneth thus; the regeneration is imperfect, therefore the freedome is imperfect, therefore there is some bondage, it is blasphemie. For first our freedome is perfect in Christ, ells his death is not sufficient. Then though our sanctification bee not perfect, yet is there no bondage, but a rebellion of sinne; which if it shoulde reigne, wee were not the servantes of Christ. And while it seemeth for a time to reigne, and wee obstinatly to cleave unto it, wee are judged (soe far as men can judge) the servantes of it, and so gyven over from Christ unto Satan, till the grace of the Spirit againe to our judgement againe appeare to beare rule. As for David in the whole yeare after hee had commytted adulterye and murther, hee never pleaded for his sinne when hee was reproved, nor did no longer cleave unto it. Soe likewise though wee fall and sinne, and bee ledd awaye with sinne, yet are wee not in bondage thereunto, until wee obstinatly and wilfully give our selves unto it from Christ, [255] which you finde not in the 7 to the Romans but resisting of sinne, a hatred of sinne, a will to doe good, a repentance and continuall recoverye of himself, and flying unto Christ. Soe that your doctrine is false, to saye, the apostle stoode in some spirituall bondage; and my argument still firme, that these ministers and people which stande in a professed bondage to a false government, their prayers are an abhomination unto the Lorde, till they repent and submit themselves unto Christ and his lawes and ordinances. Whiche the Lorde gyve them grace to doe, even speedely to depart out of the house of bondage, and from all subjection of his antichristian hierarchie.

Christ's *unworthie witnes for the truth and freedome of the gospell.*
JOHN GRENWOOD

FINIS

III

NOTES FOR A SERMON AGAINST ADULTERY

This hitherto unused and unknown document is Manuscript 547 in the library of Corpus Christi College, Cambridge. It is interesting to note that this Separatist document has found its final resting place in the library made famous by the great collection of manuscripts presented to the college by the first Elizabethan archbishop, Matthew Parker. It is also interesting to note that Corpus Christi was the alma mater of such Separatists as Robert Harrison, Robert Browne, and John Robinson, as well as of John Greenwood himself.

The manuscript is entitled "Notes for a Sermon against Adultery." This may be correct, but there is the possibility that the document constitutes an attempt to resolve the doubts and questions of a group of Separatists who had asked for help. Greenwood states in the concluding paragraph that he hopes his comments will be profitable to those who will read his observations.

There is no suggestion of a date, and there is no internal evidence that provides a clue. Therefore the date which I have given—1592—is conjectural. Greenwood was bailed about May, 1592, and he attended the meetings of the Separatists during the summer and autumn of that year. On the evening of December 5–6 he was arrested, and he remained in prison during the following four months until his execution on April 6, 1593. Previously, he had been continuously in prison from October 8, 1587, to the spring or summer of 1592.

The Separatists believed that marriage was a civil ordinance. Therefore, they regarded marriage as a contract between the engaging parties. Marriages were sometimes performed in prison, with fellow-prisoners and visitors as witnesses, without the services of a clergyman in the Church of England. To the Separatists the rite of marriage did not belong to the church or the clergyman. It was not necessary that marriages be performed in the church at prescribed times. All that was necessary was the consent of the parents and involved parties, together with faithful witnesses. Barrow and Greenwood denied that they had executed the office of an officiating clergyman, but they admitted that they had witnessed such ceremonies. Although Greenwood was a clergyman, Barrow was a lawyer and did not consider himself eligible for special clerical functions.

Barrow appealed to the simple marriage of Boaz and Ruth, the great-grandparents of King David, and to the marriage at Cana which Jesus witnessed. These were marriages in a private house, not in prescribed places, and seemed to lend sanction from the Old and New Testament to marriage as a civil rite. The Separatists were naturally incensed by any accusation that they would contract marriages lightly and irresponsibly, as suggested by the charge of Bishop Aylmer that they made marriages under a hedge.

Greenwood's observations on adultery indicate not laxity but its very opposite. He is struggling with the problem of the application of outmoded Mosaic legislation to the circumstances of Elizabethan England. With Thomas Cartwright he bemoans the fact that the severe Old Testament laws are not followed by Tudor magistrates.

The Lord has established commandments, precepts, and blessed laws which are holy, perfect, and clear. Nevertheless, the magistrates will not put into practice the death penalty for persons taken in adultery. The consequences are that much confusion, sin, and wickedness abound in the land. Out of this situation emerges the problem: shall an adulterer or adulteress upon repentance be permitted to live with his wife or her husband?

Greenwood regards an open adulterer as an adulterer, despite repentance. Even if the wife desires the continuation of the marriage, such a practice should not be followed where the guilt is clear and publicly known. Once a couple has openly broken God's law, neither party has the power to join what God has separated.

Greenwood makes a doubtful distinction. Where the transgression is publicly known, the case is clear. The wedlock has been broken. But where the transgression is not publicly known, the case is different. Then the repentant party needs to confess his sin to God, but not to his wife. He is not called upon to accuse himself. Wedlock is broken only when it is publicly known. Greenwood denies that an inward lusting after another person, or an affront given to one's own conscience or to God, is a sufficient cause for separation, inasmuch as the sin is not public.

It would seem that Greenwood puts too much importance upon the fortuitous fact of public knowledge and conviction. It would also seem that he gives insufficient thought to the consequences of an enforced separation, upon the parties involved and the children. Also, in his zeal for the Old Testament standard, he may have minimized the law of the New Testament that forgiveness should be given freely. An eye for an eye and a tooth for a tooth may have been an ancient attempt to limit retaliation, and to that extent good, but the higher law of turning the other cheek, walking the second mile, and loving one's enemies, proceeds from the spirit, not the letter, of the divine law.

NOTES FOR A SERMON AGAINST ADULTERY

Psal. 119:126, 127, 128, verses

"It is tyme for the Lord to worke: they have distroid thie law. Therfore love I thie comandements above gold, yea, above most fine gold. I esteme all thie preceptes most just and hate all false waies."

The Lord make his blessed lawes which are most holy, equall, and perfect, plaine and easie to be understand of us his wretched and unworthie servantes, whose eyes in this corrupted age were even as it were utterly darkened in our degenerate estate and now enlightened but in part to behold the unmeasurable wisdom of our al wise God in the whole frame, governement, and order of this whole world, in all degrees reservinge unto him selfe an holy sede, and for the completinge of his elect, and even also to the orderly guidinge of this great house of vessells of honor and dishonor, hath constituted holy matrimonie, and prescribed many excellent lawes and statutes for the holy preservation therof, besides the law and whole order of nature teachinge us the same, with infinit blessinges promised both present and eternall to the observers herof as also judgementes to the wicked, and present punishment bodily to all that break the bandes therof.[1] And such is the bodily punishment by the magistrate's sword to be excecuted to the faithfull and infidell that if it were executed and put in upright practice, the question presently to be handled would easely be decided, and plainely appear void of controversie, namely, if the man or woman taken in adultery were put to death ther could be no question for their separation. But now by reason that God's just law is not without partialitie put in practise, no, not at all executed, much filthines hath covered the land by the defilement therof, not onely by the generall bouldnes in committinge that sinne, but when the wickednes is brought in to question, the parties either suffered to live with their forsaken abused companion as before or els openly to mary againe after thei have bene put awaie for adultery, the matter also for fleshly and earthlie respectes lefte in their choise, I meane in the clear [clean?] parties' choise whether thei shall be divorced or no, where upon the filthines daily practised doth abound, unutterable sinne, these abuses beinge heades and springes of much wickednes to the breach and confusion of God's ordinance and the whole order of nature. Now then our question is not whether every adulterer ought to be put to death or no but whether the adulterer or adulteresse may be suffered upon repentance to live with their former sometymes their husband or wife or no when the majestrate doth not execute that law of God accordinge to his Word. This matter that it may plainely appear I

[1] For a sampling of Puritan views on marriage, see William Bradshaw, *A Mariage Feast* (1620); Thomas Gataker, *A Good Wife God's Gift, and a Wife Indeed* (1623); William Gouge, *Of Domesticall Duties. Eight Treatises* (1622); William Perkins, *Christian Oeconomie* (1609).

will thus in order sett downe and prove. I then by God's Word affirme:

> That no Christian, havinge broken the bands of wedlock by outward adultery knowne to the church by evident profe convinced, may at any hand live with their former sometymes wife or husband though the other partie would agree, yea, that all that live so after thei be convict openly live in adulterie, and under God's wrath, though thei continew not their former wickedness with other but by repentance confesse their sinne, and promise amendment, for this were a defilement to the whole land.

Leviticus 20:10 Dewtr. 22:22

"If a man be found lyinge with a woman maried to a man, then they shall dye even both twaine, the man that lay with the wife, and the wife, so thou shalt put away evill from Israell." Here we see God's irrevocable justice to comand the majestrate to put the adulterour and adulteresse to death, with out exception of person, repentant or unrepentant, and that where this is not executed the land is defiled, now God appointinge them both to be cut of[f] and so the clear [clean?] partie to be free, and appointinge no other remedie for them, either to continnew with the partie against whom they have sinned, nor capable of mariage with any other. It were not onely a thinge with out warrant and so sinne for God's children to allow them to live with their former sometymes wife, or to mary an other, but all this were a polution of the land. Repentance then may appease the wrath of God concerninge the judgement to come, but not restore this breach of wedlock beinge convict in the eyes of all men. It were an abhomination to suffer it. And though no private man may execut this punishment with out the magistrat, yet all men may diswade them from livinge in that uncleanes and not partake either with the magistrates' sinnes or theirs by givinge consent to the contrary.

Jeremie 3:1 Dewtr. 24:4

"They say, if a man put away his wife, and she go from him, and become an other mane's, shall he returne unto her?" Shall not this land be polluted while for the hardnes of the peoples' hartes for other causes than adultery upon dislike they were suffered to put away the wife with a bill of divorsement, when shee had once bene to an other man, and he either dead or by a bill of divorsement also, shee againe made free might not returne againe to the first husband, though otherwise shee were free to mary wher she list, for then the land were polluted. How much more the woman or man that by breach of wedlock hath comitted adultery and bene to an harlott, if shee or he after open conviction shold returne to the first, shold not the land be polluted?

Proverbes 6:32, 33, 34, 35

"But he that comitteth adultery, he is destitute of understandinge, etcetera, he shall fynd a wound and dishonour, his reproche shall never be put awaie, for jelousie is the rage of a man, therfore he will not spare in the day of vengeance, he cannot bear the sight of any rannsome; neither will he consent though thou augement the giftes." Here the spirit of God showeth the greatnes of the sinne of whoredome how much it is more odious than theft both in regard of the magistrate's sword which is to cut it of[f] by death and in respect of the partie to whom the injury is offered, namely, the man or woman which is clean, who cannot nor may not be reconciled any more to the adulterer or adulteresse concerning wedlocke. Wher we may see that though concerninge the fynall judgement together with the rest of the church he may forgive the offence done to him upon the partie's repentance, yet concerninge wedlocke he cannot forgiv or it be [bottom cropped—forgiven unto him?].

I Corinth. [6]:16

"Do you not know," saith the Apostle, "that he which coupleth himself with an harlott is on[e] bodie?" But every man or woman openly convict of adultery is an harlott, namely, [an?] adultererr or adulteresse. Therefore, who so ever coupleth themselves with them, whether their former sometymes husba[n]d or wife, should now be one with an harlotte, etc.

Math. 19:5, 6 Mala. 2:[15]

Though the Lord had other spirits in his power, yet because he would have on[e] holy sede [seed], he made man and wife one flesh, "they two," saith He, "shall be to [becom?] one flesh." [T]his sheweth that the partie once openly convict of whordom can be no more coupled [coupleth?] to their sometymes wife or husband, for that were to make three livinge persones one flesh, which were an abhomination.

Math. 19:6 Againe, "let no man put asunder that which God hath coupled together," saith our Saviour Christ. Whereupon it may be evidently convinced that as the man nor all the world ca[n] separat man and wife, so wedlock openly broken lyeth not in man's will to joyne againe, God havinge separated them by his law.

[Math]. 19:9 For where he saith that "whosoever putteth away his wife except for adultery and mary a[n] other, comitteth adultery," it sheweth that God's law separateth for open convict adu[ltery]. "Mariage honorrable amon[g]st all and the bedd undefiled. But whoremongers and ad[ulterers] God shall judge." Now surely after the publick conviction of adultery, it can not be an holy matrimony or undefiled bedd to couple our selves with an adulterour or adulteresse. The Lord then give grace to his children to kepe them selves in their spirit, that they trespasse not against the wife of their youth.[1]

Hebrew 13:4

Now while we plead for the equitie of God's holy lawes, not openly to suffer such unholy confusion but to shew others the counsells of God, that they might abstaine from evill and all uncleanes, that we beinge bought with a price might glorify God in our bodies and soules. Ther ariseth many scruples in this doctrine, for if the open breach of wedlock utterly disannull wedlock to the parties offendinge, that neither they may mary with any other or live any longer with their former sometymes husband or wife, then is demanded whether a man or woman havinge comitted adultery and it is not knowne to any but to the parties offendinge, whether either of those parties repentinge their sinnes to God may live with their former husband or wife as before. To which we answer yea, for concerninge the outward punishment of this fact the partie offendinge is not to accuse himself or her self, the offence is then onely knowne to God to whom they must confesse their sinne,

[1] For two differing views on remarriage, see Edmund Bunny, *Of Divorce for Adulterie, and Marrying Again: That There Is No Sufficient Warrant So to Do* (1610), and John Rainolds, *A Defence of the Judgment of the Reformed Churches. That a Man May Lawfullie Not Only Put Awaie His Wife for Adulterie, but Also Marrie Another* (1609).

so that it is the [then?] open conviction and the knowledge of the partie to who[m] the wronge is done or the magistrate that must disanull this outward covenant.

Therfor, saith the law, if the man or woman be taken in adultery or can be manifestly convinced, under two or three witnesses, then is the wedlock openly disanulled, so that the other can have no more fellowship with the adulteresse or adulterer when it is so proved. For no man is to accuse him selfe; if God therfor bringe not forth their falt to be judged of man, they have not but to confesse their sinne to God, and not to depart from or put away their former husband or wife, neither can do, for so no wedlock would be kept, neither might we receive the partie's accusation of the partie of himselfe except ther be witnesses, though they were so unwise to shed their owne bloud where God requireth it not. Yet some further reply that after they have bene to an other by adultery, their wedlock is broken to their owne conscience and in God's sight and that therfore when God giveth repentance they are not to couple them selves with their former husband or wife. To which we answer that God hath laid no such burden upon them to accuse them selves to their husband or wife who knoweth not they have sinned, but only confesse their sinne to God. And to say wedlock is broken before men when none knoweth it but the parties offendinge and none openly offended, it is not true, for adultery of the hart as to lust after an other man's wife is breach of wedlock in the eyes of God and to our owne conscience, yet disannuleth not the outward covenant before men.[1]

Mathew 5:[28]

[1] The secondary literature on wedlock is voluminous. Good monographs are: John S. Burn, *The Fleet Registers* (1833); Carroll Camden, *The Elizabethan Woman* (1952); Alice M. Earle, *Customs and Fashions in Old and New England* (1916), Chapter 2; Elizabeth Godfrey [Jessie Bedford], *Home Life under the Stuarts, 1603–1649* (1925); George E. Howard, *A History of Matrimonial Institutions*, 3 vols. (1904), especially I, chapters 3–10, and II, chapter 11; Joel Hurstfield, *The Queen's Wards. Wardship and Marriage under Elizabeth I* (1958); Marshall M. Knappen, *Tudor Puritanism* (1939), chapter XXV; Herbert M. Luckock, *The History of Marriage, Jewish and Christian, in Relation to Divorce and Certain Forbidden Degrees* (1894); Edmund S. Morgan, *The Puritan Family* (1944); Levin L. Schücking, *Die Familie im Puritanismus. Studien über Familie und Literatur in England im 16., 17. und 18. Jahrhundert* (1929).

The first objection against this separation.

Our Saviour Christ saith if thy brother offend against the[e] and say it repenteth him, forgive him, yea, seven tymes a day and seven tymes turne againe, etc. Matthew 18. Luke 17. This forgivenes is spirituall and doth not hinder the execution of earthly punishments by the magistrate's sword nor the divorsement from the adulterour or adulteresse. Hebrewes 10:28. Againe if it were in the free partie's power, either husband or wife, to forgive this breach of wedlock and to live with them as before, then they ought alwaies so to do, seinge we are comanded to forgive as we would be forgiven. But divorcement for adultery are [is] comanded or by al men's confession lawfull; therfor we cannot, neither is it in the free partie's power to receive the adulterour as before. Matthew 5:32.

Objection 2. If it be the magistrate's dutie to putt to death the adulterer and adulteresse, then we should take the magistrate's sword into our handes if we sever by divorse the adulterour, etc.

Answer is easily made that we graunt none but by the magistrate's power can put them to death but by counsell and perswasion to inhibitt them to live in the defiled bed, or to joyne them selves to an adulterour or adulteresse, which counsell they must obey, seinge it is of God, if they will be members of His church, and prevent God's wrath due to the contrary. With us the popish courtes give out divorsementes and not the magistrate. But sure it is the man or woman against whom the offence is comitted hath this power to put away the adulteresse or adulterour. Without any man's leave, the sinne beinge certainely knowne, for when Christ saith he putteth away his wife, except it be for adultery, sheweth that for adultery it is lawfull and accordinge to the law. Joseph when his espoused wife Mary was found to be with child would have put her away privately, etc.

Objection 3. David comitted adultery with the wife of Urya [Uriah] and when he repented the sinne, yet still continued with her as befor. Salamon also had many wives as many other of the fathers.[1]

First we answer, David was then kinge and could not be put to death by any private man or private men. And though he maried not Berseba untill Uria was dead, yet it is said the Lord was displeased with it, but after wardes was appeased by his repentance. But in that place we may see how Urya observed the law that would not companie with Beerseba after David had defiled her, though it were the kinge had donne it, no, not when the kinge would have had him gone to his howse unto her to have covered his owne sinne. II Samuel 11:8, 9. And for havinge ma[n]y wives, which God semed to passe over, wherby that kingdom was encreased, ye leave [leaso[n]e?] it to be considered of others, onely I say it was not so from the begininge. To conclud, no particular example warrant us to transgresse the law of God.

Yet it is objected that Rahab the harlott as they call her was maried to Salman of whom came Christ, to which the Scripture doth answer that though shee were a Gentile, yet was she called to her faith.[2] Hebrews 11:31. And she ought not to be called harlott, for the word signifyeth vittaler or inkeper. Thus we see the Lord to have whordom in such detestation that though the magistrate execute not the law to put them to death, yet may not God's children couple them selves with them in the duties of wedlock, nor they mary any more.

Question. If God should stirr up the magistrate's hart to execut that law, would you have all such put to death as are openly detected of this sinne, all the land for the most part given unto this vice?

No, first the magistrate must proclaime it death accordinge to God's law and that all shall die the death which after comitt that sinne, for after such generall defections ther must first be a new covenant before the

[1] See II Samuel 11:2–27 and 12:1–25; I Kings 11:1–8.

[2] Salmon, the son of Nahshon, married Rahab, whose son was Boaz. Boaz, in turn, married Ruth of Moab, by whom he begat Obed. Thus, both the mother and the grandmother of Obed were non-Israelites. Obed was the father of Jesse and grandfather of David the king.

lawes can be executed least all were cut of[f], some for one sinne, some for an other. Ther is no faith, ther is no mercy, ther is no acknowledginge of God in the land. By swearinge and lyinge and killinge and stealinge and whoringe they breake out and bloud toucheth bloud.

[*Question:*] *If one have comitted adultery in his first wive's tyme and it not brought to light, and he after that wive's death havinge lefte his sinnefull life and marieth an other and then shee findinge it of his voluntary confession or otherwise, whether wedlock be broken to those two or no?*

To this it is first answered that if it be but come to light by his owne accusation, his accusation is not to be taken, neither hath he offended against his second wife; therfore shee is to perform the duties of wedlock unto him and he unto her accordinge to the rule of the Word and that comandment. I Corinthians 7:3, 4, 5.

Thus have I briefely shewed you my simple judgement in those pointes, besechinge God it may be as profitable to you and the rest that shall read it, as I desire to satisfy you. And the Lord pardon all my ignorances.

Christe's unworthie witnes
John Grenewood

IV

GREENWOOD'S EXAMINATION, MARCH 11, 1592/1593

On Sunday, March 11, 1592/1593, Greenwood was examined by the two leading judges of England, Sir John Popham, Lord Chief Justice of the Queen's Bench, and Sir Edmund Anderson, Lord Chief Justice of the Common Pleas. The purpose of the examination was to establish the authorship of several treatises and one book penned by Greenwood, and to ascertain information about the printers and publishers. Greenwood readily admitted his own authorship and that of Henry Barrow. He also admitted having the books in his possession, but would not mention the names of others who had owned or read the books. The one name he reveals frankly is that of Robert Stokes, who had been a chief agent in seeing the books through the press. He mentions his maidservant, Cycely, but does not implicate her. Some time during the autumn of 1592, Stokes had been excommunicated by the newly organized Separatist church, and Greenwood evidently had no hesitation in revealing his name. Stokes had recanted, made his peace with the Church of England, and disowned the Separatists. Although he had been a primary agent in publishing the books of the Separatists, more culpable than Studley, Boull, or Bellot, he was not brought to trial on March 21–23, 1592/1593, when the others were arraigned. To the Separatists, he was an apostate, a renegade, an informer, a traitor.

The original manuscript is in the Huntington Library, San Marino, California, Ellesmere Manuscript 2092. It is printed by John Payne Collier (ed.), *The Egerton Papers* (London: Camden Society, 1840), pp. 171–172.

THE EXAMINATION OF JOHN GRENWOOD, TAKEN THE XIth DAY OF MARCHE, 1592[1593]

A. He confessyth that he knoweth the thre severall bookes showed hym upon his examination, and that for such part of the severall bookes as concernyth thys examination [examinant?] was collected by thys examinant, with which he made Henry Barrow acqaynted; and that which doth concern Henry Barrow, the same Henry dyd collect and sett down, which he, thys examinant, saw or saw part therof, for that the same Barrow and thys examinant were there chamber fellowes together at that tyme.[1]

B. He sayeth he remembreth not to whom they were delyvered after they were thus collected and sett down, whether yt was thys examinant's wyff or not, he doth not well remember.

C. He sayeth the cause why they so sett the same down was to shew Lord Chief Justices, and that those in authoryte myght se what they held concernyng the crymes [synes?] wherewith they were charged.[2]

D. He sayeth that for hym selff he hadd one of every sort after they were prynted, and doth not well remember whether yt was Cycely, then thys examinant's mayed servant, that brought them to thys examinant.

E. He sayeth he hath sene manie of these bookes, but doth not remember in whose handes, or how many.

F. He sayeth that he hath h[e]ard that one Robert Stookes hadd those bookes, as owner of them, but who otherwyse prynted them he knoweth not.[3]

G. He sayeth he hath h[e]ard there shold be a thowsand off them printed, or therabouts; the pryce, as he h[e]ard, was viij^{d} a pece.[4]

By me, John Grenewood

Examined by us,
John Popham Edmund Anderson

[1] These three books were, in all likelihood, *A Collection of Certaine Sclaunderous Articles Gyven Out by the Bisshops*; *A Collection of Certain Letters and Conferences*; and probably *An Answere to George Gifford's Pretended Defence of Read Praiers and Devised Litourgies*. Greenwood was the author of parts of the first two books and sole author of the third one. Conceivably, the third book may have been *A Plaine Refutation*, which contained two sections or treatises by Greenwood. On March 20 Greenwood was questioned about this latter book.

[2] Sir Christopher Wray was Lord Chief Justice of the Court of Queen's (King's) Bench from 1574 until his death in 1592; Sir John Popham succeeded him, 1592–1607; Sir Edmund Anderson was Lord Chief Justice of the Court of Common Pleas from 1582 until 1605.

[3] Robert Stokes financed the printing of these books. Arthur Billet or Bellot served as proof-reader, Robert Boull received them from the printer, and Nicholas Lee helped to distribute them.

[4] Robert Stokes testified that there were about 500 copies printed of each of the three books—1500 in all.

V

GREENWOOD'S EXAMINATION, MARCH 20, 1592/1593

On Tuesday, March 20, 1592/1593, Greenwood was examined a second time within a period of ten days. Preparations were being made for his trial, as well as for that of Barrow, Bellot, Boull, and Studley. The examination supplemented the one of March 11. Greenwood had already admitted his part in writing *A Collection of Certaine Sclaunderous Articles Gyven Out by the Bishops*, and *A Collection of Certain Letters and Conferences.* Although these books did not carry the names of the authors on the title page, they were easily identified by the conferences recorded therein, and his book, *An Answere to George Gifford's Pretended Defence of Read Praiers and Devised Litourgies*, did have his name on the title page, on the final page, and also in the preface.

On March 20 Greenwood was confronted with two more books, which evidently had not been produced on March 11. He was asked about *A Plaine Refutation*, and readily admitted that he wrote two of the treatises contained therein, "A Briefe Refutation" (pp. 207–234), and also "A Fewe Observations" (pp. 235–256). But he denied any participation in writing *A Brief Discoverie of the False Church*, which was considered the most damaging and dangerous book by the judges and critics. In asserting that Barrow had written this book, Greenwood was not divulging any new information, since the book carried Barrow's name in print (p. 263).

It is interesting to note that five of the greatest legal figures participated in this examination. Besides the two chief justices, who had been present on March 11, there was present Thomas Egerton, who had served as Attorney-General since his appointment on June 2, 1592. William Lewin was Dean of the Peculiars. And Edward Stanhope was vicar-general of the province of Canterbury, chancellor to the Bishop of London, and a member of the Court of High Commission.

The original manuscript is in the Huntington Library, San Marino, California, Ellesmere Manuscript 2098. It is printed by John Payne Collier (ed.), *The Egerton Papers* (London: Camden Society, 1840), pp. 176–177. Mr. Collier has misread three words in this manuscript, which was carelessly and hurriedly written by Judge John Popham. He has "confirmation" for consimilitude, "Dyscription" for Discoverie, and "Edw. Stanley" for Edward Stanhope.

THE EXAMINATION OF JOHN GRENWOOD, TAKEN THE XXth DAY OF MARCHE, 1592 [1592/1593]

A. He confessyth that hym selff dyd sett forthe that part of the booke intituled, *A Playne Refutacyon of M. G. Giffard's Reprochfull Booke, Intituled,* A SHORT TREATYSE AGAYNST THE DONATYSTS OFF INGLAND, contynued in the end therof, intituled, *A Breif Refutacyon of Mr. Georg Giffard's Hys Supposed Consimilitude betwene the Donatysts and Us, etc.*, and that also in the end therof intituled, *A Fewe Observacyons off Mr. Giffard's Last Cavilles about Stynted Redd Prayers and Devysed Lyturgies*; for the rest, beyng the former part off that booke, he sayeth that Mr. Henry Barow dyd sett it forthe, as Mr. Barrow sayed.[1]

B. He confessyth for the other boke showed unto hym, intituled *A Breiff Dyscovery of the False Churche,* he taketh that to be sett forth

[1] In the 1591 edition of *A Plaine Refutation*, there are 256 pages. Of these Barrow wrote pages 1–206, which constitute two replies to Gifford's writings. Pages 207–234 comprise Greenwood's work, entitled, *A Breife Refutation of Mr. George Giffard His Supposed Consimilitude betwene the Donatists and Us.* This is a reply to the first part of Gifford's *A Plaine Declaration.* Pages 235–256 also comprise Greenwood's work, entitled, *A Fewe Observations of Mr. Giffard's Last Cavills about Stinted Read Prayers and Devised Leitourgies.* This is a reply to the second part of Gifford's *A Plaine Declaration.*

To make the matter more complicated, and yet to keep clear the record, we should add that in 1603 Greenwood's *A Fewe Observations* was reprinted with his *An Answere.* Therefore, in the 1605/1606 edition of *A Plaine Refutation,* Greenwood's work, *A Fewe Observations,* was omitted, and in its place was substituted Barrow's *A Few Observations to the Reader of M. Giffard His Last Replie,* previously unprinted. This was a reply to Gifford's *A Short Reply.*

by Mr. Barrowe, for he sayeth that Mr. Barow hath hadd such spech with thys examinant of the same booke.

C. He sayeth that Stookes upon that thys examinant and Henry Barow agre[e]d to wryte the sayd bookes, Stookes offered to be the means to gett them printed, and to be at the charg off yt;[1] but he sayeth he remembereth not by whome he h[e]ard thys, but sayeth he h[e]ard Henry Barrow saye yf the same Stookes wold not gett them prynted, that yet hym selff wold use some other means to gett them prynted.

By me, JOHN GRENEWOOD

Examined by us,

John Popham — Edmund Anderson
Thomas Egerton — Edward Stanhope [Stanley?][2]
William Lewyn

[1] Robert Stokes paid for the printing of *A Brief Discoverie of the False Church* (1590) and of *A Plaine Refutation* (1591). Daniel Studley and James Forester copied out the former work for the printer, and Arthur Bellot was the examiner, or proof-reader. These last three men may have served in similar roles for the latter book, *A Plaine Refutation*, but there is no evidence on this point.

[2] John Payne Collier has read this name as "Edw. Stanley" (*Egerton Papers*, 176–177). The manuscript signature is almost a series of careless up and down lines, but Edward Stanhope is a better reading. There was no judge whose name was Edw. Stanley, but there was a younger son of the third Earl of Derby, an Edward Stanley, who died in 1609. However, Stanley does not belong in this group of names, but Stanhope was a frequent examiner.

PART II

THE WRITINGS OF HENRY BARROW

1591–1593

VI

A FEW OBSERVATIONS TO THE READER OF MR. GIFFARD HIS LAST *REPLIE*

This treatise of Barrow should be distinguished from Greenwood's *A Fewe Observations*, which was published in the 1591 edition of *A Plaine Refutation*. Barrow's *A Few Observations* was written in January or February, 1591/1592, too late for inclusion in the 1591 edition of *A Plaine Refutation*. But when this latter work was reissued in 1605, Greenwood's *A Fewe Observations* was eliminated and in its place the editor put Barrow's *A Few Observations*.

The occasion for the work was the publication of Gifford's *A Short Reply*, in December, 1591. We can date Barrow's answer as January or February, 1591/1592, because he says that he and Greenwood have been in prison for a period of four years and three months. Depending on whether we use Greenwood's date of arrest on October 8, 1587, or Barrow's date of seizure on November 19, 1587, we obtain January–February as the time of his reply.

This treatise consists of a few general observations of how Gifford misrepresents Barrow's position. Then follows a summary of Barrow's four main theses. The last portion of the treatise is a refutation of twenty-eight articles which Gifford had appended as a summary of Barrow's errors, in his *A Short Reply*. It is interesting to note that in Barrow's personal copy of Gifford's *A Short Reply* the only pages on which he has no marginal comment are pages 1, 15, and the last two and a half pages listing the twenty-eight articles. Barrow needed more space to reply, and somehow managed to obtain paper to make an extended reply filling ten printed pages. His more detailed answer to Gifford's *A Short Reply* may be seen in "Barrow's Final Answer to Gifford—Marginalia," in Chapter VII.

[237]
[Ij]

A FEW OBSERVATIONS TO THE READER OF M. GIFFARD HIS LAST *REPLIE*

The prelates of these tymes, not having such power as their predecessors to murther the faithful servants of Christ openly, have together with the learned of their clergie taken a more secret course, to make them away in their prisons and there to burie them as it were alive. So that the poore church this day may justly lament under their handes. "They have cut off my life in the prison, and have cast a stone upon me."[1] And not content with this, having them thus fast shut up in in [*sic*] their trusty keepers' handes, where they have no meanes to make knowen their estate and usage, they let loose their prints and pulpits to their servants the priestes, to defame them with slanders to the people, and as their auncestors used the prophet Jeremiah, to smite them with or for the tongue. Among others, Mr. Greenwood and my self have thus ben entreated by them. Now albeit we are and have ben four yeares and three moneths[2] without tryal or relaxation, kept by the prelats in most miserable and streight imprisonment: so as we have at this time scant any meanes to defend or answere for our selves: Yet, beholding this *Replie*[3] of Mr. Giffard unto certaine intercepted books[4] of ours, to

[1] Lamentations 3:53.

[2] By using Greenwood's arrest on October 8, 1587, or Barrow's imprisonment on November 19, 1587, as the starting point for computation, we obtain January–February, 1591/1592 as the date of writing. The preceding sentence confirms the authorship of Henry Barrow.

[3] *A Short Reply unto the Last Printed Books of Henry Barrow and John Greenwood, the Chiefe Ringleaders of Our Donatists in England* (London, 1591).

[4] With the exception of two copies, the entire edition of *A Plaine Refutation of Mr. G. Giffard's Reprochful Booke* was thought to have been seized and burned about June 1591, by Sir Robert Sidney, with the collaboration of Francis Johnson at Middelburg. At the time the latter was serving as preacher to the Company of the English Merchant Adventurers at Middelburg, he collaborated with Thomas Ferrers, deputy governor of the company, and he served as an informer and agent for the English governor. See especially Sir Robert Sidney's letters to Lord Burghley, April 21, 1591, and May 31, 1591, in State Papers, Holland, XLI, ff. 349 *recto* and *verso*, and XLII, f. 82 (S.P. 84/41 and 84/42). These uncalendared letters have now been published. See Carlson, *The Writings of Henry Barrow, 1590–1591*, pp. 370–372, and also pp. 373–377 for William Bradford's account. See also "Governor Bradford's Dialogue," in Alexander Young, *Chronicles of the Pilgrim Fathers of the Colony of Plymouth, from 1602 to 1625* (Boston, 1841), pp. 424–425. See also Strype, *Annals*, IV (1824), pp. 187–192. Of the two copies reserved, one found its way through Attorney-General Thomas Egerton into the Bridgewater Collection and thus to the Huntington Library. After some trouble and numerous false leads, I was happy to find the second copy at Lambeth Palace Library. Johnson probably did not know that Sir

tend not only to the defaming and disgracing of our selves (as he himself proclameth in an Epistle unto us prefixed to his book)[1] but therein to the reproch of the faith we professe and of our suffrings for the gospel, to the hardening of the wicked enemie in evill, to adde to the afflictions of the godly, and to discourage and drive back such as had any zeale or love of the truth, whilest he therin also laboreth to justifie the lawles persons and proceedings of these antichristian bishops; I thought it good, towching this *Replie* of Mr. Giffard to the said intercepted book [books?],[2] to signifie these "Few Observations unto the Reader." The rather for that the books here pretended to be refuted, ar not common or easie to be come by of the reader,[3] who without the same might be easily deceived and greatly abused by this author. Therfore have I written this, yet not so much for an aunswer to his *Replie* as for a demonstration of his dealing unto the reader. Otherwise (to say as it is) I should make aunswere to him, before he hath made replie to any of the matters in question.

For this I testifie and the reader shall finde it true, that in al this *Replie*, Mr. Giffard hath not touched much les approoved the proceedings of his lordes the bishops in any one poinct whereof wee have complained and convinced [convicted] them, nor yet hath

Robert sent six copies to Lord Burghley. The librarian at Hatfield House has informed me that they are not in the Hatfield Library of the Marquis of Salisbury. Two of them may be the copies at the Norwich Public Library and the Lincoln Cathedral Library. Thomas Bodley also received a copy.

It is likely that most of the copies of *A Brief Discoverie of the False Church* were also seized. I have found copies at the British Museum, Cambridge University, and the Folger Shakespeare Library. The evidence for the seizing of this book depends on the ambiguous testimony of Robert Stokes, who says that all the books were taken at Flushing and Brill. But John Payne Collier probably has misread the manuscript, Ellesmere MS. 2094, which he printed in *The Egerton Papers*, pp. 173–175. The phrase "taken at Flushing and Brill" should be "taken at Flushing and Burned." The latter word is indistinct, but the initial "B" and the final "ed" are fairly clear. Since the edition of *A Plaine Refutation* was seized at Flushing, near Middelburg, I conclude that the shipment of *A Brief Discoverie of the False Church* was also captured at Flushing. Gifford said that "some few [of the intercepted books] have escaped, and are dispersed among theyr fellowes" (*A Short Reply*, A 2 *recto*). Flushing [Vlissingen] is a port town in the island of Walcheren, and is about five miles from Middelburg. Brill [Brielle] is about forty-five miles northeast of Flushing and about twenty-five miles west of Dort [Dordrecht]. Since the books were burned in June, 1591, and since the better manuscript reading is "Burned", we may eliminate Brill from the story.

[1] *A Short Reply*, A 3 *recto*.

[2] This implies one book—*A Plaine Refutation*. Yet, in this same paragraph are two references to "books." I believe "book" is a misprint for "books," and that Barrow also had in mind his *A Brief Discoverie of the False Church*.

[3] This implies two books—*A Plaine Refutation* and also *A Brief Discoverie of the False Church*.

mainteined and proved any one of the accusations and charges wherewith he and his said lords the bishops have reproched us, and whereof wee have fully cleared our selves in this intercepted booke. 2. But in stead of this (which [had he] done, all our controversie had presently ceased), he hath by the said his lords' the [238] bishops' privie instigation and open protection set out his book, to the slander, accusation, and defamation of us and our holy cause. Our persons he still with al bitternes and hostilitie reprocheth and inveigheth against with hard wordes and fearful judgments: all this under the pretence of discovering the woolfe, painting out seducers.[1] But let the reader judge this bitter zeale in that it boasteth against the truth and contendeth for corruption, this carnall wisedom in that it departeth from the rules of Christianitie. Mr. Giffard might have sought and founde the woolfe in some more stately places and pallaces, than in loathsome prisons for the testimonie and sincere practise of the gospell of Christ, for the faith and kingdome of our Lord Jesus Christ, if his zeale had ben such to have sought out and discovered the woolves in their dennes.

Whereas he reprocheth our suffrings to be for heresies and other crimes, let the reader know it is spoken with great untruth to cover the tyrannie and evil dealing of his lordes the bishops, who cast and hold us in prison for not subscribing and submitting to their popish power, Romish courtes, and antichristian proceedings. And at length indicted and condemned us at Nue-gate Session, for refusing to communicate with this false ministrie and worship which they erect in this sacriledg and confusion, and this upon the statute made for the papists, where the prelate of London sate our accuser and judge.[2] Other tryall or conviction than this, either of error or crime, we never hitherto had nor could obteine by any meanes. Therfore also hath Mr. Giffard greatly departed from the rules of Christianitie in giving such rash, peremptorie, and publick sentence of heresie, schisme, etc., against us, in such high and most weightie causes, such as concerne the whole church, before his church had either heard or given sentence of these matters, before we had ben duely convinced or refused to heare, yea, whilest by all meanes we most humblie besought and intreated audience and christian triall, with protestation and faythfull promise to yeild to whatsoever should be shewed

[1] *A Short Reply*, A 3 *recto*.

[2] This session was held about February–May, 1588, at Newgate Sessions, Justice Hall, with Bishop Aylmer in attendance "as accuser and judge." The statute referred to is 23 Elizabeth, chapter I, "An Act to Retain the Queen's Majesty's Subjects in Their Due Obedience."

us to be the will of God: yea, and all this, before Mr. Giffard did ever see or speake with us (as himselfe confesseth), although by his lords the bishops he might have had leave and accesse when he would. If Mr. Giffard espied such heinous faults in us, all the world should not excuse us, of most intollerable pride, most high presumption, savage barbaritie, and what not, for taking upon us the office, power, and judgment of the whole church, for rushing into God's judgment seate, giving judgment without the law, before the time, for rending and tearing up the tender plants, the good wheat, etc.[1]

As to the charge of Donatistes, wherwith it pleaseth Mr. Giffard to intitle us,[2] suer it might have ben spared untill he had repaired his former consimilitudes and reasons, which we have so infringed and retorted the whole force of them against himself, his lords the bishops and the rest of the English clergie, for condemning and departing from their mother of Rome, which they judge a true visible church, for that she hath the true seale of the covenant, the true ministrie of Christ, etc. For that they reteyne and exercise the same ministrie, government, courtes, [239] orders, proceedings, etc., and wel nigh worship and administration, that is used in and they fetched from the church of Rome. It will not cleare themselves, or chardge us, of schisme, to say that they have departed from the church of Rome after due conviction, but we depart from them rashly before such due conviction. For though the papist would aske when and in what generall council this was doone, yet not to insist upon the order, me thinks I might justly aske him what by this reason he thincketh of Mr. Luther and of such as came first out of poperie, before the church of Rome was so generally convinced, condemned and forsaken of so many or almost of any but themselves, now how Mr. Luther and those few in those first tymes shal escape the crime of schisme.[3] For sure I see not how the true church may at any tyme for any crime or occasion that can be imagined be condemned or forsaken by any Christians, what writinges of men soever Mr. Giffard may bring to the contrarie. Whilest therfore he wil needs allowe the church of Rome for a true visible church, let

1 Gifford, *A Short Treatise*, pp. 3, 4, 6, 49, 50, 77. Barrow, "A Brief Summe of the Causes of Our Seperation," in Carlson, *The Writings of Henry Barrow, 1587–1590*, pp. 118–150.

2 Especially in *A Plaine Declaration That Our Brownists Be Full Donatists*, but also in *A Short Treatise against the Donatists of England*, both titles including the word "Donatist."

3 See Richard Bernard, *Look Beyond Luther: or, An Answer to That Question Proposed by Our Adversaries, Where Our Religion Was Before Luther's Time.*

him see how he can cleare himselfe and these bishops of schisme, if Christ have but one body, one spirit, one baptisme. To say he doth separat from the tyranny and apostasie of Antichrist but not from the Church,[1] will not hold. For how he can make the same ministrie and people antichristian, apostates, idolators, and true ministers of the gospell, faithfull Christians, unto our sight and judgment, at the same instant, or the church of Rome and her daughters, that great Babylon, that harlot, that mother of all abhomination, the very corruption of the earth (as the Holie Ghost caleth her),[2] and againe that heavenly Jerusalem, the true constituted church, that bride and spouse of the Lambe, unto us at one and the same instant; is very strange divinity, too high a mystery for my conceit. But if the case stoode so as Mr. Giffard supposeth, that they may separat from the tyranny and the enormities of Antichrist in the church of Rome,[3] and yet not separat from the ordinances of Christ and the church of Rome, why then wil not he allow the like favour to us, when we may alleadge the like, yea, the same reason towards them, *viz.*, that we separate not from the true ordinances and church of Christ, but from the tyrannie and enormities of these antichristian bishops and clergie. But sure for any learned sentences I have yet heard, me thinckes it safer with the pore persecuted Christians to cleave to the worde and commandement of Christ, that willeth us to goe out from the harlot being discovered least we be destroyed in and with her, than to follow Mr. Giffard his advise, that willeth us rather to stay with the marke of the beast upon us, buying and selling the whore's wares, until that witch, that murtheres[s] of the saincts, be convinced by churches and men ynowe [enough] to Mr. Giffard his allowance.

There next calumniation wherby Mr. Giffard indevoreth to bring us into hatred with the whole land, is, that we condemne all the persons both the men and women of England which are not of our minde and plucke them up as tares.[4] Wherein hee doth us open wronge, if not against his owne conscience, yet against our expresse writings every where. Mr. Giffard [240] cannot justly reporte this of our behaviour who have alwaies gladly acknowledged and rendered all reverence and honour to our superiours and where it was due, our conversation gentle though simple, our heartes open and

[1] *A Short Treatise*, pp. 53–55. [2] Revelation 17:5.

[3] This is the language of "The Litany" in *The Book of Common Prayer*, in the versions of 1549 and 1552. It disappears from the 1559 version.

[4] *A Short Treatise*, pp. 49, 50.

compassionate to all, pittying their seduction, indevoring by all meanes to bring them to the sight and acknowledgment of the truth.

Hereunto we have not held our owne lives deare, but against all humane wisdome and consultation with flesh and bloode, not after the maner of some in their doctrines, testimonies and sufferings, we have kept back no truth that God gave us sight of, but have most plainly, according to the measure of grace given, discovered the enormities and corruptions of the tymes with the authors and craftesmen therof, not sparing the greatest nor omitting the least, but describing the grievous wolves, and also the little foxes, both by pen and mouth, as our cruel usage above al others by these bishops in their prisons, the common invectives of all the clergie men abroad both in their pulpits and libels against us, declare. Againe, how often have we in our writings signified our good hope of manie thousands, our intire love unto al? Who have more reproved such rash peremptorie final judgment of persons and future tymes, as belongeth only unto God to condemne and again to save and cal whome and when he will? Furder, have wee not commended the faith of the English martyres, and deemed them saved, notwithstanding the false offices and great corruptions in the worship excercised, not doubting but the mercy of God through their sincere faith in Jesus Christ extended and superabounded above all their sinnes seen and unseene.

And what now should let [hinder] that we should not have the same hope where the same pretious faith in sincerity and simplicitie is found, so that they neither neglect to search out the truth further, nor despise the truth when they see it? Let not therfore any godly heart that loveth our Lord Jesus Christ, be drawen into dislike of the truth or hatred of such as bring the same, by these impostures of deceipt. For they shall finde the wounds of a lover more faithful than the kisses of an enimie,[1] the corrections of Christ more comfortable to the soule in the end than the peace of the false prophets. The faithfull servants of Christ, denying the whole constitution and government of this Church of England, may justly deny the people, whilest they remaine in this confusion and subjection to these antichristian bishops and their procedings, to be members of a true constituted church, yet hereby not condemne them with any such peremptorie sentence as Mr. Giffard suggesteth, to cut them of[f] from God his election or from Christ, to roote them up as tares for

[1] Proverbs 27:6.

the fire, but rather to transplant them into the walled watered orchard and paradize of the Lord his true planted and constituted church, where they might growe as incense trees and bring forth their severall and acceptable fruites to the glorie of their God. This I do assure the reader is the worst that we wish or indevour towards them, howsoever Mr. Giffard doe emulate [woo] you amisse.

Yet not content with this to bring us into hatred with our owne [241] nation, he laboreth also to make us odious unto all others by this calumniation, that we condemne al the churches in the world. This indeed he hath earnestly gone about and faine would have brought us unto in his former bookes, by applying our arguments brought against these bishops and their procedings, against other churches, saying that though our words were not directed unto them, yet our reasons perced them through the sides, etc.[1] Whereunto he was alwaies answered, that we wholie bent and ment our speaches to the publick corruptions of the Church of England, and not to meddle with others unknowen. If our arguments extended so far, we could not stoppe the course of the Word of God. Let them look to it to whom it more nearly appertayneth, as also they that so should direct these arguments: deniing utterly to be drawen into this quarrell, or withdrawen from our present purpose therby; often denying to condemne any church; yea, protesting to thincke better of them, as both in my writings and especially often in Mr. Greenwood's, he having more cause to deal therewith, appeareth, who defended the churches against Mr. Giffard, shewing that howsoever they might agree in the confession of many grounds and principles of the faith (as also the church of Rome, in that common creed, Lord's Prayer, etc.), yet they have another, and quite divers ministrie, church offices, an other choyce and ordination, an other worship and ministration, an other church government, orders and ordinances. These I am sure are no variable or indifferent thinges, such as churches may safely differ in, and yet the one and the other be to be held and esteemed true established churches. Christ hath instituted and left unto his church in all places unto the world's end but one and the same ministerie, ministration, worship, government. Mr. Giffard therefore and such as maintaine this Romish antichristian ministerie, ministration, worship, government of the Church of England, must needs condemne these other churches, that so greatly differ from them herein. For suer Christ standeth not a heade to two so divers bodies, having so divers and strange

[1] *A Short Treatise*, p. 72. *A Short Reply*, pp. 2, 8, 35, 96. *A Plaine Declaration*, p. 44.

members, functions, power. Now therfore let the reader judge whither Mr. Giffard or we (accused by him) condemne other churches, and let not Mr. Giffard be halfe so fierce in the poinct.[1]

And as to the places he so urgeth in my writings, I do advertise the reader that he greatly inforceth and wresteth my words contrarie to my meaning, purpose and scope. For in the [*Brief*] *Discoverie of the False Church* I neither did condemne nor ment to condemne any true church, or to intermeddle with their doings. Only being pressed by the adversaries with the writings and practise of Mr. Calvine at Geneva, I was driven simplie to defend the truth, *viz.*, that no true ministery could be in or come out of popery; that the people ought to have been duly called and gathered by the Word unto the faith; that with knowledg they might give their owne publick and willing consent to the obedience of the covenant at their joyning together; that it is not lawful, but were open sacriledge in the whole church to deliver unto or communicate with the open prophane, impenitent offenders, or open un-[242] worthie in the Supper of our Lord.[2] Yet in these howsoever the church of Geneva might erre in their first coming to the fayth out of poperie, not then knowing a better course, yet was it not to be compared to the popish proceedings of the bishops here in England. They erected no such antichristian clergie and hierarchie, no such idolatrous leitourgie, etc., but called all men to the Testament, true worship, ministrie, government of Christ; which we heare they have now amongst them, and have no doubt made greate reformation and more perfectly instructed the people in the waies of God and in the dueties of communion by their faithfull and painfull teaching them in this lardge time, which here in their Church of England is neither doon nor permitted to be doon. Not without great injurie therfor doth Mr. Giffard even in these things compare the church of Geneva unto this Church of England.

And as to my writings, they are to be understood of their first comming out of poperie, and not of the present estate of these foraine churches; howsoever Mr. Giffard will needs abound in his owne sence. No faultes disanull the beeing of a church, untill contempt of God's Word be added thereunto, after due conviction. The faulte and errors of a church may be severely reproved and convinced according to the qualitie thereof, and yet the church not be condemned, as Mr. Giffard could perswade. Again the true church and

[1] *A Short Treatise*, pp. 42, 72. *A Short Reply*, pp. A 2 *verso*, 9–18, 82, 96.
[2] *A Brief Discoverie of the False Church*, pp. 13–45.

faithfull servants of God will be so farr from hating or reproching such as shew and reprove their faltes, as on the contrarie they will most of all love and esteeme them that so do, whilest it is done in love and order. Neither is it to be thought that the churches of Geneva, Scotland, etc., would reproch or persecute[1] in such hostile maner any Christian that should reprove their publike practise and intreat christian audience therunto, as the prelates and their clergie of England do, that "hate him that rebuketh in the gate and abhor him that speaketh uprightlie,"[2] that seeks to take away the life and good name of all such as stand for the ordinances of Christ, the sincerity and upright practise of the gospel, or that reprove any of their proceedings. A man might as wel goe into a leoparde's den or take a beare by the tooth, as come neare any of this Romish broode or within the compasse of their power upon this earrand. Very vainly therfore hath Mr. Giffard exclamed of us as schismatikes, for departing before we had duly convinced their church, especiallie whilest the chief bishop of his church hath shut us up in most close and miserable imprisonment now more than these fower yeares,[3] and wil by no meanes be drawen to lay his pawes of[f] us or give us liberty or so much as audience in bands to discusse our controversies. And what good eare or answere, they have given unto our bookes, this sober *Replie*[4] of Mr. Giffard sheweth. To conclude this poinct, we have desired to go unto other churches for the deciding these matters when we could here obteyne no equall or christian tryall, but could not be suffred. Which sheweth both how well the bishops and clergie of England doo submit themselves and their cause to the triall and censure of God his Word, and also how we doo not condemne other churches.

[243] As to Mr. Giffard his other chardge of condemning Mr. Calvin and al the learned, it is with as litle truth or liklyhood.[5] That which hath ben said of the martyrs, our good hope and liking of many thowsandes, our general and unfained love to all, may keepe the godly reader from giving credit to such reports. Furder of Mr. Calvine we have published our reverend estimation and judgment, commending and propounding his rare faith, knowledg,

[1] But compare Robert Browne's criticism of Scotland's clergy, in Albert Peel and Leland H. Carlson, *The Writings of Robert Harrison and Robert Browne*, p. 519.
[2] Amos 5:10.
[3] In the opening paragraph Barrow speaks of four years and three months in prison. [4] *A Short Reply*.
[5] *A Brief Discoverie of the False Church*, pp. 13–45; *A Plaine Refutation*, p. 97; Gifford, *A Short Reply*, pp. 97–98.

labour, constancie, meeknes, as an example to all men, especiallie to these his untoward disciples of these tymes that chuse rather to insist in [rely upon] his errors for worldly emolument, than in his vertues to be praised of God. Now then whilest unto Mr. Calvine's person there is no wronge doon, we are not to be blamed, if we suffer our selves to be pressed with or follow his writings no furder than they are found consonant to the Word of God. Wherunto he with his uttermost care and study squared them, and himself exhorted al men therby to trie, receive, or refuse them. So then I hope without the injurie of any it may be as lawfull for us to dissent with such sound reason and proof as we have set downe, as for our adversaries to vouche his writings both contrarie to the truth and many tymes to the meaning and scope of their author. In these dayes (if ever) it behoveth men to see what they heare, and to "trie the spirits whether they be of God. For many false prophets and false teachers are gone out into the world."[1]

Other criminations against us hath Mr. Giffard devised, by the consent and counsell no doubt of his good lords and bishops under whom he publisheth them, and these in way of errors by him decerpt [extracted, excerpted] out of our writings, as in those twenty-eight Articles suffixed at the end of his [*A Short*] *Replie* appeareth.[2] Which with what just construction or truth he hath donne, shal by their brief and severall answers to each in the same place be seen.

In the meane tyme let me addresse my selfe to shew the reader a little of Mr. Giffard his behaviour and sounde replie to the chiefe matters in controversie. Which I must advertise and by God's grace will shew, that he hath not in this *Replie* at al touched, but utterly fled and yeilded us the whole cause, spending his whole discours either in vituperie of our persons, in idle strife of words, or impertinent matter.

The chief matters in controversie were altogether about the present constitution and proceedings of the Church of England under these bishops. We blamed and convinced the constitution and proceedings of their church, in the gathering unto, joyning and communion in the faith; in their whole ministerie, offices, choice, ordination; in their worship and administration; in their government, courtes, orders, ordinances, procedings. These we have

[1] I John 4:1.
[2] *A Short Reply*, pp. 96–98. Barrow replies to these twenty-eight articles in the last half of this treatise ([251]–[260]).

required to be approved unto us by the expresse rules of God his Worde; as Moses made al things according to the patterne exhibited of God in the mountaine.[1] Or els wherin they should be found to have erred or swerved from this heavenly rule, they would suffer losse or correction of their worck according to the prescript of God's Word. Protesting on our owne parts, notwithstanding all the cruel usage, defamation, and hostility against us, yet to yeald to the truth and to confesse wher we shal be found to have falted. [244] This might have stayed either Mr. Giffard his rage or his penne, until either some publick or more peaceable course had ben taken, for the deciding these most weightie controversies; or except himself by writing had ben able more fully and sufficiently to handle and determine them. Seeing no Christians in such weightie matters could offer more; but chieflie seeing himself had ben so often before by us blamed for begging and assuming both in general and particular that he should prove, even the greatest matters in question, and in that strong imagination to break foorth into rash judgment and bitter reproches against us, crying out of us as of schismaticks, hereticks, etc., before he had either proved their parish assemblies true established churches, or approved the prelates' proceedings in any one poinct whereof they were by us blamed, much more before we had refused to heare or despised the Word of God. Nor yet for all these warnings and reproves (wherwith that booke of Mr. Giffard's *Refutation* everie where upon due occasions aboundeth)[2] hath he amended his fault, or by any urging can be stimulate to prove the matters in question by the evidence of God his Word directly (which donne all controversie about the same foorthwith had ceased); as if we look a little into his handeling the pointes severally will appeare.

I. First, the whole publick worship and administration injoyned of their church was blamed unto him and refused, as idolatrous, devised by man, after the prescript of a rotten popish leitourgie, and proved such unto him by expresse Scriptures. As in their Romish fastes, Lents, Embers, saincts' and feastes' eaves. In their popish and Jewish feastes, their Hallow-masse, Candlemasse, Christmasse, the day of Christe's circumcision, the day of Epiphanie, their Easter, Pentecost, their Ladie's daies, Apostles' daies, saincts' daies, Innocents' day, Soules' day, angels' day. In their popish and Jewish ceremonies, their comminations, rogations, purifications, tithes,

[1] See Exodus, chapters 19–31 and Deuteronomy, chapters 4–34.
[2] That is, Barrow's *A Plaine Refutation*, refuting Gifford.

offrings, mortuaries to the priest. In their popish and Jewish places, instruments, attires, their hallowed church and church-yard, after the manner of the Jue's temple and walled court, with their porch, battlements, lights, doores, celles, vestrie, chancel or holiest of all, set east and west, their hallowed font, hallowed bells, organes, musickes. Their Juish and popish ministeriall vestures, surplices with sleeves, surplices without sleeves, rich and ordinarie copes broydered and fashioned as the high priestes' ephod, vestiments. Their episcopall and sacerdotal attires, palles, rochets, amices, truncked gounes, sleeved cloaks, square cappes, tippets. Their scholastical or graduates' attires, scarlat gownes, hoodes, habits. Their popish and unholy manner of administring their sacraments, their baptisme with the signe of the crosse, gossips, numbred prayers, a ridiculous dialogue betwixt the parish priest, the parish clerck, the gossip and the infant, and an ungodly and unpossible vow taken of the gossip for the infant. Their severall kindes of baptisme, publick by the priest, private by the midwife. Their baptisme of supposition, and their lords' the bishops' confirmation. Their altering the words of our saviour Christ's institution, in delivering the bread after their popish manner, unto the people kneeling. Their nourturing the priest where and when to stand, to say, [245] pray with prescript and nombred wordes. Their trifling dialogue betwixt the priest, his clerck, and the people. Their wilfull sacriledg and portsale [auction] of the same to al commers for two pence a head. Their privat Supper, *viz.*, the prieste's howseling the sick therwith. The prieste's visitation and absolution of the sick with their service booke. Their priestes' marriing and burying by the booke, with their nombred prayers and dirge over the dead. Their greatest bishops forbidding mariage through the whole land, at certain pope holy times, wel nigh a third part of the yeare. And again his venal licenses to eat flesh or marrie in the times of prohibition. Their set service and worship to all their holy feastes, holy dayes, holy eves, and through everie day of the yeare, and action of their ministrie, how much, what and when to read, to pray, with their set psalmes and lessons, this to their mattens, that to their evensong, this for the first lesson, that for the second. Wherby they banish and reject a great part of God his Word out of their church never to be read there. Their abuse of that they read; as the Scripture caled *The Lord's Prayer*, five times said over at their mattins; and used at al their assaies, mariing, churching, visiting, buriing, sacraments. Their rending and shreding Scriptures to make their epistles and gospels upon their idol dayes, etc. Their reading Apocrypha in place of canonical scriptures in the church. Their stinted erroneous unsesonable and unreasonable prayers, their conjuring Christ in their letanie, etc. These trumperies have I briefly and barely recited unto the reader, because that booke of *Refutation* is intercepted,[1] that he might understand both what miserable stuffe these prelates and priestes mingle unto them in the publick worship and ministration of their church, and also be rightly informed of the matters in question. All these forgeries are by us in the first part of the *Refutation* layed open and by the Word of God confuted, as popish, idolatrous, blasphemous.[2] Not any of these have bene by Mr. Giffard now this third time[3] in this his *Replie* directly approved or justified by the Word of God, though he have ben often urged therunto, and himselfe stand a minister of these wares after this leitourgie.

His only subterfuge and evasion hath ben, that they are not so popish, idolatrous, blasphemous, as we have in our writings set them out. Here about he spendeth his whole discourse, and with many gentle glosses and more favorable constructions he seketh to defend the suspitious places of his service booke, and to divert those hard sentences and rough conclusions by us drawen against this trumperie, labouring with all his learning and cunning rather to cover and hide this stuffe from the people's eyes, than to approve their publick worship and ministration to everie man's conscience by the evidence of God his Word, as the true minister of Christ ought to doe, least by that light their deceites should be espied, and no man buy there [their] wares any more. Therfore with these sleights, he knowing the impossibilitie to justifie these things, hath sought to withdraw the readers' eyes from the true question, which is not, whether these things reproved in their publick worship and administration be so popish, idolatrous, blasphemous; but whether they be not popish, idolatrous, ab-[246]hominable in this present use of them in the Church of England, having no foundation in the Word of God. And therefore such as no true minister of Christ ought to exercise, no true Christian to joyne unto. And in stead of proving or repenting

[1] The edition of *A Plaine Refutation*, with the exception of two copies (plus at least seven "gift" copies), was seized and burned.

[2] *A Plaine Refutation*, pp. 25–50. "A Brief Summe of the Causes of Our Seperation," in Carlson, *The Writings of Henry Barrow, 1587–1590*, pp. 118–150.

[3] Gifford's first answer was in manuscript; *A Short Treatise* is his first printed answer; *A Plaine Declaration* is his second printed answer; *A Short Reply* is his third printed answer. Inasmuch as *A Plaine Declaration* relates more to Greenwood, Barrow probably is thinking of: (1) Gifford's first manuscript answer; (2) *A Short Treatise*; (3) *A Short Reply*.

these doings hee hath also filled the readers' eares with al manner of vituperie against us for writing and suffring against these abhominations, these Jewish and popish reliques. All which (to my seeming by the scope and ends of his writings compared to the matters in question) he hath sought at once to justifie by the practise and writings of the apostles, al these Juish rites and trinckets by Acts 21, where the apostles and the church of Jerusalem received the Jues, notwithstanding they were zealous and still exercised the ceremonies of Moses' law; all these Romish trumperies and toyes by the practise of the apostles, that sought to joyne the churches together in some knowen errors. Romans 14 and 15 chapters. These if he deny or be ashamed of, then hath he left the whole publick worship and ministration of his church utterly without defence, then hath he forsaken and yeilded the cause in these poincts wholly unto us. No cavils or reproches besides the purpose will excuse.

In this stuffe, he shall finde the forreine churches to have no harmonie with their Church of England. Nor yet in these shall he finde us to have any consimilitude with the Donatistes.[1] And this I must say unto the reader, that if all these Jewish and popish errors and forgeries, which hee standeth publickly to administer and defend, were drawen and set out in a catalogue according to the indignities and inconvenienes therof in Mr. Giffard his name, peradventure he would not be so forward to collect and blason other men's errors, especially so unjustly and untruly as hee hath doon. But now let us consider Mr. Giffard his replie unto the Second Transgression.

II. Their Church of England was herein shewed and blamed by us, not to have ben duly called, gathered and joyned in the fayth. But immediatly from high popery and open idolatrie, all without the exception of one person received upon one day (at the happie change of this our prince for her [half] sister) as members of their church.[2] This ministrie, worship, ministration, government, ordinances set over them. No assurance in particular or open profession of their faith and purpose of walking being made, but altogether without any choice of the good, without any repudiation or separa-

[1] Greenwood's treatise was entitled, *A Briefe Refutation of Mr. George Giffard His Supposed Consimilitude betwene the Donatists and Us*, which was a refutation of the first part of Gifford's book, *A Plaine Declaration*, pp. 1–70.

[2] Elizabeth succeeded to the throne on November 17, 1558, was crowned on January 15, 1558/1559, and the following May 8 approved the Act of Uniformity, which went into effect on the Feast of the Nativity of St. John the Baptist—June 24, 1559.

tion of the prophane, open wicked, impenitent, unworthie received, joyned and kept together in these parish churches as members, by this ministrie, in their worship and sacraments. This by us in the *Refutation*[1] was proved to be contrarie to the practise and order of our saviour Christ and his apostles: who even in the kingdom of Judea baptised and received none to the church but such as were wonne to the fayth and made open profession of their owne faith and purpose of heart at their joyning to the church. That admitted not any prophane, or idolator, not as yet having professed their faith, neither any open wicked, impenitent, unworthie that had made such profession unto the Supper and table of the Lord. But our Lord at the leaving of his howse unto his servants set a porter at the door, a steward and wa[tc]hmen within to every one his worck, to all his servants [247] power and commandement to watch, with certaine prescript rules for all things, whom and when to receive, whom and when to cast out, etc. So then it remained unto Mr. Giffard to justifie the gathering, joyning and present communion of the people in these parishes, as also the ministers' delivering the sacraments, and the peoples' receiving them in this confusion and open sacriledge. Hereunto Mr. Giffard hath but gathered and fighteth with the broken stumpes of his old refuted reasons: That the covenant of God indureth to the thowsand generation, albeit neither the forefathers have nor the children do abide in the faith. That the stabilitie of the covenant dependent [dependeth] not upon the workes of men but upon the grace of God, concluding therupon the outward covenant is not to be discerned and judged of men by the outward profession and obedience of God his Word. That open rebellion of the church doth not disanul the outward covenant to our judgment. That Israel in their long schisme, Judea in their greatest apostasie, Rome in their deapest defection and corruption, were in that estate to be judged of us the true visible churches of God. That the true ordinances of God, baptisme and the true ministrie of Christ make the church of Rome a true established church. That Antichrist sitteth in the temple of God. That the baptisme of the church of Rome is a true seale of the covenant. That the godly may communicate with heapes of open wicked, impenitent, unworthy without offence or hurt to them in the Supper of the Lord. That there shal be wicked alwaies mingled amongst the good in the church unto the world's end. That

[1] *A Plaine Refutation* deals with the Four Principal Transgressions, which Barrow has summarized as false worship, membership, ministry, and government.

the prophets and our saviour Christ communicated with the open wicked both priests and people in the temple. That our saviour both heard these wicked priests and Pharisees teach, and commanded his owne disciples, Matthew 23, to heare them. That the true established church of Christ may be without the power of Christ to excommunicate.[1]

To prove these unsound collections and untrue assertions Mr. Giffard again bringeth many Scriptures: how faithfully applied and used, let the reader search: only this I say that I thinke all his frends that be of any knowledg will blush for shame therat, yet in these pointes hath he sore traveled [travailed] and pained himself, spending therin more than halfe his booke, and of the same not a little parte in most bitter invectives against us.

To these reasons I have answered in that intercepted [*A Plaine*] *Refutation*, and if it were extant and but half so commonly as his bookes to be had or seen, I suppose that the shame of the world would have restreyned Mr. Giffard from publishing this [*A Short*] *Replie*, wherin yet with all his labour and skill he hath not proved the gathering, joyning together and communion of these churches in their parishes by the rules of Christe's Testament. Nor yet justified their prostituting the bodie and blood of Christ by their admitting the open unworthy, prophane, or notorious impenitent offenders to the table of the Lord. Or that the godly ought not to refuse to joyne in such open prophanation of the holy things of God, and wilful sacriledg. Especially where they see the whole institution of Christ so highly violate, where they see neither a true minister of the gospel to deliver, nor a faithful people orderly gathered to receive, nor yet the administration according to Christ's Testament. In al these Mr. Giffard for the satisfiing and convincing us ought to have approved his banquet [248] and communion, and not thus to have changed the question to general propositions which concerne not these matters in controversie nearely enough, nor approve their doings in any of these. Wherfore in al this discourse he hath not towched much les proved the question, but fled the points and with impertinent matters sought to cover and tolerate the open confusion and wilfull sacriledg of their church, and turned in all hostile manner the force of his weapons against them that in Christ's name have reproved the same. But as the curse causelesse returneth,[2] so

[1] This is a summary of Gifford's arguments in *A Short Treatise*, pp. 47–70. See especially pp. 48–49, 52–57, 59, 65.

[2] Proverbs 26:2.

the peace of the false prophet wil neither heale these sores, nor hide these heynous sinnes from the sight and wrath of God.

III. The third matter in question, was and is about all the publick ministrie of England, whether it be that true ministrie which Christ unto the world's end hath instituted to his church, or no. The whole ministrie of England we shewed to be the self same that the pope left and used in this land, even their whole governing collegiate and serving ministrie, as their primate and metropolitane, gracious lord arch-bishops; their palatine and lord bishops; their archdeacons, chancellors, commissaries, civill doctors, advocates, proctors, and their attendants, notaries, registers, purcevants, paretors;[1] their deanes, sub-deanes, prebends, canons, peti-canons, gospellers, singing men, queristers, vergiers, sextines; their full priests, half priests or deacons, parsons, vicares, curates, parish-clerckes, church-wardens, sidemen, questmen. All which wee proved to have come out of the smoke of the bottomlesse pit, when that fallen starre, that apostate Antichrist, opened the same; to have no other mention in the Testament of Christ, no place or true use in the church of Christ; to have neither the true offices, the true entrance, or administration of the said offices of christian pastors, teachers, elders, deacons. We blamed Mr. Giffard for his former vaine and light proves [proofs], of their preaching of the gospell, and of the effects therof to the comfort and salvation of others. Where it was shewed him they preached not in any true office or ministrie, and he [was] blamed for balking and begging that he should prove, even the chief thing in question: *vizt.*, their true and certaine office of ministrie, their right entrance into, and administration of the same office, being often and earnestly urged to prove these. He was shewed also that al the preaching of their church was in subjection to the antichristian throne of these bishops, by their licence, prescription, limitation, joyned to all this false worship and administration, not leading the people forward one steppe to the true order of Christ, and sincere practise of his Testament, or so much as shewing them the same; but labouring rather to beate and keepe them back from it, and stil to hold them in bondage of these antichristian bishops. It was also shewed him how unsoundly they taught God's lawes, and drew not the upright obedience of any one law. How they preached for lucre and hire, not for love and conscience. His old and often inculcate reason of the martyres in this ministrie, was fully [249] answered: that wee might justifie the persons of the martyres, as

[1] A paritor, or apparitor, was a summoning officer of an ecclesiastical court.

God no doubt did, yet not justifie their false offices of ministrie, which God never did. Notwithstanding these things largly and fully proved by us in that *Refutation*,[1] yet hath not Mr. Giffard in his [*A Short*] *Replie* proved this ministrie of their church in their office, entrance, and administration, but againe repeated most unreasonablie his former and often aunswered reasons. Not so much as leaving out his former prophane fable of the asse in Aesope,[2] but appliing and inforcing it beyond all christian modestie and almost civill honestie unto me for writing my conscience plainly of this ministrie, their preaching, and proceedings. For which I know not how often in this [*A Short*] *Replie* he termeth me Rabshaka, Sathan transformed into an angel of light, wickedly to blaspheme the operation and motion of God his spirit in the hearts of the hearers at their preaching,[3] with sondrie other false and fearfull reproches, in stead of proving the ministrie of his church, and that himself exerciseth, by the rules of Christ's Testament, in their office, entrance, and administration. Which untill he directly do, he maketh no replie, and but flyeth and yeeldeth the chief matters in question. No vituperie can justifie their ministrie, nor cease the paines of the men that have the marcke of the beast. No other church can approve of this ministrie and government of England, when both themselves have a quite divers and contrary, and these are found so contrary to the Testament of Christ.

IIII. The fourth chiefe matter in controversie is the present government of the Church of England by these bishops and their substitutes. This was shewed and proved by us to be antichristian, such as belongeth not unto, may not be set over, or received by the true church of Christ; for that the arch and lord bishops, archdeacons, chancelors, commissaries, civil doctors, etc., are not true

[1] *A Plaine Refutation*, pp. 102–160.

[2] Gifford used the illustration from Aesop's Fables about the lion and the ass. He had written: "You have put on the lion's skinne, and so imagine, that all the learned doo tremble at yee, and the truth is, they have espied your long eares." He is accusing Barrow of putting on the lion's skin to frighten people, only to have the learned discover his stupidity (*A Short Treatise*, p. 71; *A Short Reply*, p. 79). See *The Fables of Aesop as First Printed by William Caxton in 1484 with Those of Avian, Alfonso, and Poggio, Now Again Edited and Induced by Joseph Jacobs.* 2 volumes (London, 1889), II, 219–220.

[3] The Rabshakeh was an Assyrian officer, of high rank, but subordinate to the Tartan. Sent to Jerusalem with an army, by the Assyrian King Sennacherib, the Rabshakeh demanded the surrender of the city. See II Kings 18:17–37; 19:1–37; Isaiah, chapters 36 and 37. Gifford uses this title at least five times in denouncing Barrow. See *A Short Reply*, pp. 33, 56, 64, 68. See also pp. A 2 *recto*, 4, 13 and 70, where Gifford asserts that Satan in the likeness of an angel has seduced Barrow. See Article XXIII, *infra*, for the last charge.

ministers of Christ's church, such to whom he hath committed the charge, oversight and government of his howse; for that their maner of government in their Romish courtes, offices, canons, proceedings, is not according but quite contrary to the order prescribed in Christe's Testament. This was demonstrate in many particulars, by the inordinate authoritie and absolute power over all churches, ministers, persons, causes, doctrines, usurped by these tyrants the bishops, yea, by that one primate archbishop, that English pope, to sommon, heare, determine, censure, silence, depose, incarcerate, without controlment or redresse either in the church or common wealth, by God's or man's law. By the inordinate and unchristian handeling of causes in their popish courts, prophane comming toether, litigious maner of pleading by their advocates and proctors and not by the parties all maner of causes, where the most vile and inaudible finde their patrons for money, and where without money the most just or poore is not heard; where the causes ar not determined by the Word of God, but by their popish canons and customs. By their impious maner of imposing oathes. By their punishing by the civil sword, prisons, fines, etc., usurping the civil magistrates' author-[250]-itie and office. By drawing into their courts and jurisdiction the judgment and punishment of sundrie civil causes. By their popish maner of excommunication, excommunicating no obstinate offender how heynous soever, but only such as do not or will not appeare at their courtes, and absolving their excommunicate for money. These and sondrie other detestable enormities and unsufferable disorders were alledged and proved in their ecclesiasticall government; all or any of which have found no defence in Mr. Giffard his [*A Short*] *Reply*. But that he might the more slily evade, he hath handled the third and fourth principall causes intermixedly together, to both of them allowed but eighteen pages of his booke,[1] and of the sayd eighteen spent thirteen in impertinent or lesse necessarie matter, and hath ben verie plenteous in proving that princes and the church may make lawes of thinges indifferent, and that such lawes do not binde the conscience, with charge of errors unto us therupon, which in their place shall have answere.[2]

Only here if he thinck or would perswade hereby, that the publick

[1] Gifford devotes pages 78–96 of *A Short Reply* to the third and fourth transgressions.

[2] *Ibid.*, pp. 84–91. Barrow answers this argument when he comes to Article XX. See *infra*, [257].

ministrie and government of the church are thinges indifferent, and that their wicked constitutions and proceedings by law injoyned binde not the conscience, any more than the green gowne, tawny coate, and blue cap he speakes of,[1] he greatly deceiveth and is deceived. These are most high and weighty matters concerning the glorie of God and our salvation most neare. Given of God as the most excellent (if not the only ordinarie) meanes for our instruction in the faith, for our conservation in the order and obedience of Christ. These therfore require some more christian and serious discussing and looking into in the feare, peace, and love of God, than such barbarous hostile usage in their prisons and defamatorie bookes. Which that it may be obteined, let the godly reader and as many as seek the prosperitie of Sion pray instantly and indevour. As I shal not cease to desire of God the assistance of his Holy Spirit unto the reader, that he may be able to discerne betwixt good and evil, to eschew the one and cleave unto the other, that he may find peace unto his soule and stand before the Sonne of man.

Grace to all them that love the Lord Jesus Christ in incorruption. Amen.

Of Mr. Giffard's *Replie*

[Barrow's Answer to the Twenty-Eight Articles].

[251] That it might be seen to all men how constantly Mr. Giffard houldeth and throughly pursueth his purpose to deface and utterly to disgrace us from the beginning to the end of his booke, he hath here suffixed and to that end published certaine defamatorie Articles, by him self observed and collected out of our writings.[2] With what equitie, truth, and conscience, remaineth to be examined, and shal partly appeare by these brief answeres to each one in particular: but more fully to such as have the intercepted bookes,[3] and will

[1] Gifford contended that he could wear in private "a yellow gown, a green hat, white hose, and a tawny coate, without giving offense, but that to appear in public assembly with the same dress would be to sin grievously" (*A Short Treatise*, pp. 87–88). In a later passage (p. 96) he speaks of "blew caps, or greene cloaks."

[2] These are twenty-eight articles which summarize erroneous and "Donatist" teaching in Barrow's *A Brief Discoverie of the False Church* and in *A Plaine Refutation.*

[3] This seems to imply that a few copies of *A Plaine Refutation* got into circulation, but according to Francis Johnson only two copies were saved. Johnson may not have known of the sample copies which Sir Robert Sidney sent to Lord Burghley. I have examined the two copies at Huntington Library and Lambeth Palace Library. Copies of *A Brief Discoverie of the False Church* circulated more freely, but most of them seemed to have been seized at Flushing [Vlissingen].

diligently confer and compare them to Mr. Giffard his suggestions in the places by him cited.

I. The first Article suffixed here against us by Mr. Giffard is this: *That ye do most presumptuously against the expresse rules of God's Word, intrude your selves into the Lord's office, in taking upon ye to condemne the whole Church of England, as separated from Christ.* [A PLAINE] REFUTATION, *page 23* [23–24].

Answer. This is denied. Wee do not there condemne the parish assemblies of the Church of England as separate from Christ; but rather there prove them by the four principall apparant reasons, not as yet rightly gathered to Christ, nor such constituted churches to which the faithfull servants of Christ may resort and joyne. And this by the expresse rules of Christe's Testament (from which the whole frame and proceedings of the Church of England do varie). And therefore without such presumption and intrusion in God's office and judgment seate, as Mr. Giffard (notwithstanding he hath ben so plainly convinced and reproved of us for the same) still shameth not maliciously and falsely to give out.

II. The second article. *That ye condemn al the churches in Europ which professe the gospel, that their people are but heapes of prophane men.* [A BRIEF] DISCOVERIE, *page 33. That their worship is blasphemous idolatrie, in as much as they have leitourgies, which is (as yee say) to have another gospel, another Testament.* Mr. Greenwood's treatment of read prayer, pages 54, 55.[1] *That there is no ministrie of the gospel in Europ.* [A BRIEF] DISCOVERIE, *page 104. That the government of all churches is false and wicked.* [A PLAINE] REFUTATION, *page 74* [*75*], [A BRIEF] DISCOVERIE, *pages 189, 190.*

Answer. This article is above answered and proved a very false and malicious sclander. The foreign churches shewed in the four principal transgressions, whereof the Church of England is by us blamed and convinced, wholy to diffar, and to have no harmonie with the Church of England in their whole ministrie, ministration, government, etc. Neither can these places alleadged out of our writings prove this calumniation of Mr. Giffard. To the first and third places, concerning their people and ministerie, I have already

[1] These page references should be pp. 244–245 of Greenwood, "A Fewe Observations of Mr. Giffard's Last Cavills about Stinted Read Prayers, and Devised Leitourgies," which was printed in the 1591 edition of *A Plaine Refutation.* Gifford has given the correct citation. Furthermore, in 1590–1592, Greenwood's only published book was one of forty-two pages—*An Answere to George Gifford's Pretended Defence of Read Praiers.* His other treatise—"A Briefe Refutation"—was published in both the 1591 and 1605 edition of *A Plaine Refutation.*

shewed my meaning not to be of their present estate, but only of their comming out of popery, when (if these our English divines say true) they received at the first all the people of their territories into the church, still reteyning the same ministrie they [252] brought out of popery. By whose example, so contrarie to the rules of God his Word, not willing to be pressed, I was driven to refell [disprove, reject] the same. Yet this without prejudice of their present estate, of which I thinck much better. Not doubting now but their people may be much better instructed, and the true ministrie of Christ practized amongst them. To the second, concerning their worship and leitourgie, Mr. Giffard hath ben often answered, that the leitourgies of other churches are not so popish, idolatrous, contrary to the rules of God his Word, nor so imposed and inforced as this patchery of theirs in England. Therfore no such comparison or consequence to be made. To the fourth place, of their government, I there fault not the government of other churches so much as in the one place discover the adulterate and corrupt practise of Christe's government, which these sometimes forward preachers sought to erect here in England.[1] And in the place of the [*A Plaine*] *Refutation* do justly dislike some faultes in the ecclesiasticall government at Geneva, being inforced thereunto by Mr. Giffard, yet do not there or therefore utterly condemne their government as antichristian or like to this in England. Therfore in all this Mr. Giffard but accuseth and is become the depraver and reprocher of other churches himself, whose faultes as they are not comparable unto, so will they not excuse the odious faultes of the church men of England.

III. The third article: *That ye confound errors and heresies, as to make all errors, heresies, being convinced to his conscience that erreth and held, and to make none to be heresies, unles he be convinced that erreth.* [A PLAINE] REFUTATION, *page 24.*

Answer. Mr. Giffard in this article, as in all the discourse about the same, but striveth about words. It is true (as in that place of the [*A Plaine*] *Refutation* alleadged) that no error held by any church or Christian may be by us judged heresie in them, untill obstinacy after due conviction be joyned therunto. It is true also that some more great and foule errors considered in themselves, in respect of their danger and contagion, may by sufferance and use of speach,

[1] This is a reference to the classis movement of the 1580's. Some of the "forward preachers" or "reformists" or "Presbyterians" were Thomas Cartwright, Walter Travers, Stephen Egerton, John Udall, John Field, William Charke, Edward Philips, Richard Gardener, Thomas Sparke, and George Gifford.

be called heresies. Neither did wee ever deny or resist this, as Mr. Giffard cavilleth.

IIII. The fourth article: *That with Novatus*[1] *the wicked heretick, ye take away all hope of salvation from those which offend of knowledge willingly, in as much as ye make every obstinate persisting in the least error, to separate from the faith and communion of Christ.* [A PLAINE] REFUTATION, *page 24.*

Answer. This article also but bewrayeth in Mr. Giffard a spirit greatly perverted, and disposed to deprave whatsoever we have written, be it never so true. May we not affirme, that wilfull obstinacie joyned to error or open transgression duly convinced separateth so far as wee may judge from the outward covenant and communion (when the church for such falt is commanded to cut of[f], cast out, deliver to Sathan) but that we must hould this wicked heresie, to "take away all hope of salvation from such as offend of knowledge willingly?" Will Mr. Giffard by no instruction or reprofe [253] learne to put difference betwixt the temporall censures and judgments of Christ in and by his church (which alwaies tend to salvation and not to destruction) and the final judgments of Christ according to God's election or reprobation, which are without repentance and belong only to God? May we not according to this temporal judgment and censures pronounce excommunication against such convinced impenitent, and being excommunicate hold and avoyd them as separate from the outward covenant and communion, but that we must so utterly and finally condemne them? Suer these are strange collections and assertions.

V. The fifth article: *That ye deny the distinction of errors fundamentall and not fundamentall, calling it popish.* [A PLAINE] REFUTATION, *page 26.*

Answer. Though we hold no error to be of the foundation, yet deny we not in use or speach such distinction, so much as withstand such erroneous abuse of that distinction as Mr. Giffard and other divines of these tymes would infer therof: *viz.*, that some seen falts

[1] Novatian was a presbyter, a man of high character, a competent and orthodox theologian, and author of *De Trinitate.* During the Decian persecution (249–251) Cornelius was elected bishop of Rome (251). He favored a lenient treatment of those who had not stood the test of persecution—the *lapsi*—but who had repented. The stricter party, which opposed such lenient treatment for the apostates, elected Novatian as bishop (251), who was an antipope. By encouraging schism, Novatian involved the church in a problem regarded as more serious than apostasy. Extreme puritans within the Catholic Church, such as the Eustathians in Antioch, Donatists in Carthage, and Novatians in Rome, helped to widen and perpetuate schism, whereas lenient treatment and restoration to the faith of weak brethren, as advocated by Bishop Callistus, helped to heal threatening schisms.

and errors are tolerable and wittingly to be committed, because they are lesse and lighter than these other which they call fundamentall: with the papists making some sinnes mortall, others not deadly. Which abuse and error, I in that place of the [*A Plaine*] *Refutation* cited do convince.

VI. The sixth article: *That ye judge of the whole church to bee convinced in conscience as of one man. Page 24* [A PLAINE REFUTATION].

Answer. There are no wordes in the place cited to beare this article. It is there said, that error, obstinatly holden and taught, after it hath ben duely convinced, maketh heresie in that congregation or in that partie, that then so holdeth and teacheth it. If any error can be picked out of these wordes, it is more than I can as yet see.

VII. The seventh article: *That ye hold it a due convincing, not onely of particular persons, but also of whole churches, and such as doth cast them forth as heathen, so soone as any private man doth reprove the least error, and they forthwith do not reforme the same. Page 24,* [A PLAINE REFUTATION].

Answer. This article is verie falsely collected. That place cited conteineth no such matter, but rather the quite contrary, Mr. Giffard being there reproved for arrogating and chalenging the titles, privileges, censures, duties that belong to the true constituted churches of Christ, to these parish assemblies of the Church of England, to which they neither belong, nor can be performed, when all the bishops and governours of their church with one consent reject and blaspheme the holy government of Christ, deny him to reigne over them or their church by such officers and ordinances as he hath appoincted in his last wil and Testament, bring in and set up others of their auncestors' devising, to which all the whole ministery and people of the land stand in bondage. Evill therfore may Mr. Giffard complaine for want of due admonition, when neither himself nor the chief ecclesiastical rulers of his church will suffer admonition or be bound in those bandes.

[254]. VIII. The eighth article. *That ye condemne al without exception, both learned and unlearned, men and women young and old, which professe the gospell in publick assemblies, upon false accusations, without admonition, and in matters wherin if there be errors, yet excellent godly men have erred in them, finally even by your own confession.* [A PLAINE] REFUTATION, *page 182* [*180*].

Answer. This eighth article is a malicious sclander, and above answered. We condemne no man, but hope well of many thousands, and wish well to all. For the faults of their assemblies, Mr Giffard might with credit call them false accusations, if he had proved them such by either justifiing the actions, or clearing his church therof. In the meane time, the ignorance or evil example of the martyres will neither justifie nor excuse such as wilfully continue to sinne against their owne conscience and the knowen truth.

IX. The ninth article. *That ye say the best part of the Booke of Common Praier is no better than a peece of swine's flesh and abomination to the Lord.* [A PLAINE] REFUTATION, *page 48.*

Answer. In that idolatrous use, I may justly say so, and have proved it such in the place cited.[1]

X. The tenth article. *That ye say the greatest minister hath no more power to binde or loose the least member, than the said member hath to binde or loose him: and so, with the Swinckfeldians, destroy the whole power of the ministry.*[2] *Page 37*, [A PLAINE REFUTATION].

Answer. In that place cited, I confute that popish blasphemous absolution of the sick by these parish priests with their service booke, and there I speake not of any true ministrie or ministration. Though in way of admonition and reproofe of sinnes committed each to other or before ech other, every Christian hath like and the same power, though not like giftes, calling, or abilitie, to reprove sinne committed before or unto them, and may in due place and order as wel reprove, reteine, or remitt such sinne of the pastor by the Word of God, as the pastor his. Yet this without derogating any iote of the dignitie, reverence, or power of his ministrie, as Mr. Giffard very ignorantly and unsoundly collecteth.

XI. The eleventh article: *That ye speak so prophanely of singing of*

[1] This caustic and harsh description is found in the earliest Separatist work, "Four Causes of Separation." It is also found in "A Brief Summe of the Causes of Our Seperation, and of Our Purposes in Practise." It reappears in "Certen Wicked Sects and Opinions," and in "A Collection of Certaine Sclaunderous Articles." All of these works were issued before the publishing of *A Plaine Refutation*, and are in Carlson, *The Writings of Henry Barrow, 1587–1590*, pp. 49–66, 118–150, and in *The Writings of John Greenwood, 1587–1590*, pp. 103–174, 292–299.

[2] The Swinckfeldians, or Schwenkfelders, were followers of Caspar Schwenkfeld (1487–1541), a mystic who stressed the importance of man's inner experience of the grace of God. Consequently, he minimized the importance of dogma, ritual, and formal institutions. Active in Silesia, the Schwenkfelders were persecuted, and some of them fled to Pennsylvania in the eighteenth century. See Christopher Schultz, *A Vindication of Caspar Schwenckfeld von Ossig. An Elucidation of His Doctrine and the Vicissitudes of His Followers*, ed. E. S. Gerhard (Allentown, Penn., 1942).

psalms, and so dishonorably of christian people. [A BRIEF] DISCOVERY, *page 180.*

Answer. This article is with great injury and untruth. I have not there spoken against that most comfortable and heavenly harmony of singing psalmes, but against the riming and paraphrasing the psalmes as in your church.[1] Nor yet in that place so much against that as against the apocrypha erroneous ballades in rime songe commonly in your church in stead of the psalmes and holy songs of the canonical Scriptures. And as to your confuse assemblies, I speake of them but as the Holy Ghost doth, Revelation 18:2, allegorically according to the type, Leviticus 11.

[255] XII. The twelfth article: *That most offensively and prophanely, ye terme the articles of our faith, our forged patcherie.* [A BRIEF] DISCOVERIE, *page 76.*

Answer. I tooke the whole Word of God to be the foundation of the faith of Christe's church and servants, and that the whole fayth of the church ought not to be called upon, limited in, or restrayned unto a few articles only. I there spake of that creede of the Church of England, called the Apostles' Creede, because it is given out in the twelve apostles' names, with ech one his peculiar article or symbole,[2] yet is not in that maner found in any of their writings canonicall, than which we may receive none other word, epistle, or revelation, as from them. In this therfore (though otherwise it conteine most holy matter), yet is it to be esteemed but a forgerie. Neither is it, seeing all the true matter therof is much more excellently to be found els where in the canonical Scriptures, to be set up, expounded, and reverenced with such superstition as in the Church of England. Againe as I called it a forgerie in respect of that unsavory and most unsound article of Christ's descension into hell,[3] foysted in, so contrary to the apostles' doctrine, to the evangelists' writings, to our

[1] There are editions for almost all the years of King Edward VI's and Queen Elizabeth's reign. See *The Whole Booke of Psalms Collected into English Meter by Thomas Sternhold, I. Hopkins and Others* (*S.T.C.*, 2419–2510). Later in Holland, the Separatists had their own edition when Henry Ainsworth published his work in 1612, *The Book of Psalms, with Annotations. Englished, Both in Prose and Metre* (*S.T.C.*, 225, 2407, 2411).

[2] One of Erasmus' books was entitled, *A Playne and Godly Exposytion or Declaration of the Commune Crede* (*Which in the Latin Tongue Is Called* SYMBOLUM APOSTOLORUM) *and of the Ten Commaundementes of Godde's Law* (London, 1533). See also Arthur Cushman McGiffert, *The Apostles' Creed: Its Origin, Its Purpose, and Its Historical Interpretation* (New York, 1902).

[3] The Church of England taught, in the Third Article, "as Christ died for us, and was buried, so also is it to be believed, that he went down into Hell." See Carlson, *The Writings of Henry Barrow, 1590–1591*, p. 99.

saviour his expresse wordes, to the truth and ends of his death and passion, and to our whole faith and hope, as no corrupt translations, or construction of that place in the psalme,[1] no popish glosse or devised exposition can hide, as it is there set in their creede, and hath ben a long tyme expounded and received.

XIII. The thirteenth article: *That yee deny men are to joyne in that worship, where any errors whatsoever do appeare, and are not reformed, and so open a most wide gappe unto all schismes.* [A PLAINE] REFUTATION, *page 27.*

Answer. This article will not hide the apparant heynous errors of the publick worship and administration of the Church of England, wherof in the place mencioned I did speake, proving and convincing it not to be such as any faithful ought to joyne or be compelled unto. From which therfore who so departeth, forsaketh not the true worship of God, or the true constituted churches of Christ; neither openeth so wide a gapp unto schisme as Mr. Giffard himself doth, whilest he holdeth and publisheth it lawfull for some causes to separate from and denounce sentence of condemnation against a true visible church, as they do from and against the Church of Rome.

XIIII. The fourteenth article. *That you are so grosly ignorant how the false apostles urged circumcision, and so from the words of St. Paule to the Galathians* [5:3, 4; 6:6] *affirme that paying tithes, or the observing any times as it is in our church, is an error fundamentall.* [A PLAINE] REFUTATION, *page 36.*

Answer. But how if all this grosserie and ignorance layed by Mr. Giffard upon me must faint to retourne unto himself, whilest with all his learning he is not able to perceive either my scope or maner of use and application of the Scriptures by me alledged against these Juish tithes and times reserved and observed in the Church of England. [256] Against the tithes, I do in the page cited alleadge, Hebrews 7:12, to prove that they cannot be joyned to the ministrie of Christ under the gospell. For if that priesthood be chaunged, there must of necessity also be a remove of the law.

And against their Juish feastes, I alledged, Galatians 4:9, 10, 11 verses, where the observation of these beggerly and weake rudiments by the Gentiles (that were not so taught [by] Christ or the gospel) is pronounced a turning from God, a willing bondage, to make the apostles' worck and preaching and even their own fayth vayn, etc.

[1] In Psalms 16:10 or 63:9.

Now let the reader judge what cause Mr. Giffard had thus to insult; or how he and his lords the bishops can colour and excuse the bringing in and imposing all their Juish trumperies now amongst the Gentiles, and that so many hundreth yeares after their utter abolishing, after so great and severe charges against the same. And if I but for confuting them amisse deserve an article of reproch, what then is due to Mr. Giffard that defend[e]th and observeth them?

XV. The fifteenth article: *That yee judge them to be no true churches which have not excommunication.* [A PLAINE] REFUTATION, *pages 54, 74.*

Answer. This fifteenth article is a false charge, there is not any such thing to be found in the places cited. We have before reproved Mr. Giffard for divulging this error in our names.[1] We hould that everie true constituted church of Christ hath the power of our Lord Jesus Christ to excommunicate. Yet acknowledg wee withall, that right famous and excellent churches have neglected and falted, and may neglect or falte in the use of this power. But what is this to the Church of England, that is utterly destitute of this power of Christ, and wholly overruled by the erroneous power of Antichrist in his limbes, these bishops and their clergie?

XVI. The sixteenth article: *That yee deny baptisme to the children of open sinners, which yet remaine in the church.* [A PLAINE] REFUTATION, *pages 58, 59.*

Answer. In the places cited, there is no such thing houlden. Only this, that the prophane, whither infidels in the world, or idolators in the popish church, may not in this ignorance be received as members of the true church, nor yet their seede in respect of these parents be baptised.

XVII. The seventeenth article: *That yee make the stablenes of God's covenant towardes his church to depend upon the worckes of men.* [A PLAINE] REFUTATION, *page 60.* This article also is with great injury and untruth collected and divulged, there is no such matter to be found in the page cited. This error is fully and largely refuted in the sayd [*A Plaine*] *Refutation, pages 89, 90,* and Mr. Giffard there blamed for devising and publishing it in our name.

XVIII. The eighteenth article: *That yee hould circumcision among the ten tribes or in Juda in time of idolatrie, was no true seale of the covenant, and yet yee say that concerning the outward cutting it was true circumcision: the*

[1] *A Plaine Refutation,* pp. 239–242. See also *A Brief Discoverie of the False Church,* pp. 187–221.

like yee say of baptisme administred in popery. [A PLAINE] REFUTATION, *page 64.*

[257] Answer. This article we hold with truth, rightly discerning the times, and as the Holy Ghost teacheth us. That Israel in their schisme was not of us to be judged the Lord his true visible church, and therfore in that estate could not have their circumcision a true seale of the Lord his outward covenant. Yet was not that circumcision either defaced or repeted, when they returned to the true temple and were received by their repentance. Which evidently sheweth that concerning the outward cutting it was heild [held] sufficient. The like in the like times doth well follow concerning the baptisme in the generall apostasie or poperie. Howsoever Mr. Giffard can put no difference betwixt a false sacrament and a true, betwixt a false sacrament and none at all, betwixt the thing sealed or represented, and the outward signe; nor yet can savour or brooke any truth delivered by us; and that which worst is, will not insist [stand, continue steadfastly] in the manifest evidence, judgment, and practise of the Holy Ghost in the self same case, but chuseth rather to be moved and caried about with the winde of men's doctrines, justifying the one sacrament of the popish church to be holy and authentick, damning the other as blasphemous and execrable: with many other inconveniences and absurdities, which he had rather runne into, than imbrace truth with a fewe.

XIX. The nineteenth article: *That in your* [A BRIEF] DISCOVERIE *from page 16 [17] to page 45 and* [A PLAINE] REFUTATION, *page 98, yee take uppon yee to confute almost all which Mr. Calvine hath written against the Donatists and Anabaptists, holding that the prayers and sacraments, and the consciences of all that communicate together are defiled, where any open sinners are admitted.*

Answer. Wee hold with the apostle, that where any open unworthy ar so received to the table of the Lord, the whole lump is defiled. To this doctrine if Mr. Calvine's writings accord not, wee have just cause to refuse; yet in this difference, have we not defended the Donatists or Anabaptistes against him (as Mr. Giffard would secretlye perswade). Whose manifold errors and Mr. Calvin's writings against the same Mr. Giffard either knoweth not, or els uncharitablie dissembled, making no conscience to speake untruth, so he may bring his adversaries into hatred therby.

XX. The twentieth article: *That yee deny the distinction of the external courte, and the court of conscience: and so take away the power of the civile magistrate, and the power of the church in makeng [sic] lawes in things indifferent, taking uppon yee to confute Mr. Calvine.* [A BRIEF] DISCOVERIE, *pages 94, 95.*

Answer. We deny not the distinction betwixt the outward action and the conscience. But we deny and have refuted the ungodly doctrine, that separateth the conscience from the outward action, seing every action doon in this mortall flesh open or secret, the conscience shall accompt before the Lord. In the least and most indifferent things wee are to use our liberty aright, and that as of conscience unto God as they that shall answer the contrary. This most sound and holy doctrine doth nei-[258] ther derogate any thing from the power of the civile magistrate or from the power of the church, as Mr. Giffard in his perverse ignorance giveth out. Nor yet will all those destable enormities which flowe from the throne of these antichristian bishops be brought within the compasse of things indifferent, or be covered with Mr. Giffard his large catechising on this poynct.

XXI. The twenty-first article: *That yee condemne logick, rethoricke, and other liberall artes.* [A PLAINE] REFUTATION, *page 118.*

Answer. This charge also is untrue and unjust. We have there set down in expresse words the direct contrarie, that wee condemne no lawfull or good arts, but only reprove the vaine and pernicious abuse of these arts in the universities under and for Antichriste's kingdome, as wherby they have alwaies fought against the truth, corrupted and perverted the Scriptures, and turned away the simplicitie of the gospel.

XXII. The twenty-second article: *That yee would have al authors (the Bible only excepted) cast aside in the studie of divinitie.* [A BRIEF] DISCOVERIE, *page 146.*

Answer. Mr. Giffard stil even of set purpose maketh no conscience to falsifie the very words he readeth, that he might frame his crimination. The words in the place to which he referreth, are: *In prophesie and doctrine to lay aside their authors, etc.* Mr. Giffard in stead therof saith: *To the studie of divinitie.* As if there were no difference to be put betwixt private study, and those publick exercises of the Word in the church.

XXIII. The twenty-third article: *That ye wickedly blaspheme the operation and motions of God's spirit in the harts of men at the preaching of the gospel, as if they were but the illusions of the divel.* [A BRIEF] DISCOVERIE, *pages 141, 156.*

[Answer.] This article also is a very false accusation, and a most malicious collection without all shadow of likelihood or truth in the places cited. In the one wherof, from our saviour Christe's owne mouth, his prophets' and apostles' writings, I discover the false pretextes and deceitfull stales [allurements, baits] wherwith the false prophets allure and deceive the simple people, and wherwith they cover all their corrupt and evill doings. In the other place, I shew how these preachers in the Church of England mancipate [subject] the gospell they preach to the antichristian throne of the bishops, preaching by their licence, prescription, limitation, joyning their gospell to all the abhominations that flow from the sayd bishops' throne. I there also discover their false and corrupt maner of teaching both the law and the gospel. These things Mr. Giffard should rather have justified or els cleared himself and his fellowes, than thus unchristianly to have reproched us that reprove their faltes, falsifiing our writings. If we were as evill as Mr. Giffard would make us, what would this mend Mr. Giffard and his fellowes' estate, or approve their doings either before God or men?

[259] XXIIII. The twenty-fourth article: *That ye speake so reprochfully of all the most excellent learned divines which God hath raysed up in all churches, condemning them of pride, ignorance, rashnes, sensualities, etc.* [A BRIEF] DISCOVERIE, *from page 140 unto page 191.*

Answer. It is not so. I have not reproched any, but faithfully shewed and discovered the counterfeit behaviour and hypocrisie of these time-serving preachers, whereby they deceive and delude the simple and wel minded. Otherwise we from our soule reverence and rejoyce in the grace of God in any of them that love our Lorde Jesus Christ, and consent to the truth.

XXV. The twenty-fifth article: *That yee stil stand to maintaine, that private men may assemble and erect a church with all the offices and officers.* [A PLAINE] REFUTATION, *page 193.*

Answer. In such times and estate, as we have there put the case, wee justly may so do; having so strongly proved it both by evident Scriptures, and also by the practise of all these churches at their first coming out of this generall defection in the popery, when they were all but private men. We may therfore by good right hould it at the least untill our reasons and proves [proofs] be answered and refuted. Which is not doon in this [*Short*] *Replie*, or by this article.

XXVI. The twenty-sixth article: *That yee affirme there be no true ministers any where to be found upon earth, nor yet any extraordinarie ministers to be looked for, and therefore meere private men are (as ye say) to erect and establish the church.* [A PLAINE] REFUTATION, *page 198.*

Answer. The place is to be understood of the first comming out of poperie, when there was no true constituted church or true ministrie to be found upon earth. I doubt and deny not but since they may have erected the true ministrie of Christ in sondrie places.

XXVII. The twenty-seventh article: *That yee affirme these private men are not to stay for the prince.* [A PLAINE] REFUTATION, *page 198.*

Answer. This is to be understood, where the prince denieth or refuseth the sincere practise of the gospel. And herein I have proved, that wee neither usurpe, or prejudice in any thing the office and authoritie of princes, the worke being spirituall and commanded of God unto his servants. Otherwise we at no hand allow any private men to runne before publick authoritie, where the prince or state wil erect the same.

XXVIII. The twenty-eighth article: *That yee mainteine that no fault is to be tolerated in the church: but if any private man do espie a fault and reprove it, if they will not amend it he is to forsake that church. This is your whole practise.*

Answer. The first part of this last article, we and all godly men affirme, *that no open sinne is to be committed and tolerated in the church.* The second part, is a slander of Mr. Giffard his owne surmising like the rest, save that it is without booke. When he shal prove any such practise allowed in the church here, then let him be beleeved. In the meane time, let the reader know that private men or any members of the church [260] whosoever are not so taught or suffred to walke. When any such matter ariseth, they are shewed a further duety.

Thus are all these defamatorie articles, wherin Mr. Giffard hath bestowed his time and his whole strength against us, found either sclanderous, calumniations of us, perverse collections of his owne, or open gainsaying and reproch of the holy truth of God. Wherby the reader may easily conjecture, what store of other errors Mr. Giffard hath observed and of his charitie conceled, when these are the greatest matters he could any way forge or wrest. Hereby also may the reader partly discerne, with what charitable spirit Mr. Giffard was led, either at the reading of our bookes, or at the writing of this [*Short*] *Replie.* That in the one, could finde and gather no better matter than this he publisheth in our names. In the other quite omitting the chief matters in question wherof he had undertaken the defence, hath wholly and of set purpose framed his whole stile to accuse, reproch, deface, and disgrace his adversaries, in stead of approving the whole constitution, publick ministric, ministration, worship, government, orders, ordinances of his church, by the rules of God his Word. For reproving of which, I know not how often Mr. Giffard in this [*Short*] *Replie*, and now for a conclusion, pronounceth us transformed, seduced and sent by Sathan to seduce others.[1] But herein let the very matters in controversie betwixt us, reproved by the one, defended and exercised by the other, as also the things desired, called unto and suffred for by us, namely, the holy ministrie, order, government of Christ in his church, with the sincere teaching and practise of God his Word, withstood in all hostile maner and repressed by these antichristian bishops, Mr. Giffard and others of their band, judge and shew betwixt us of what spirit and kingdome each one is.

As to Mr. Giffard his prayer to God to open our eyes and to give us some sparcke of his grace to repent,[2] I doubt it scarce of charity or faith whilest he hath before so maliciously, unjustly, and of set purpose labored to deface and utterly to disgrace us to the people. And whilest he continueth thus hardly to judge of us, as to be quite fallen from and utterly destitute of grace, yea, and pronounceth us (article 23) wickedly to blaspheme the operation and motion of God his spirit.[3] Suer in this estate we ought not to be prayed for.

To conclude, I deeme this prayer scarse acceptable, whilest Mr. Giffard still reteineth and exerciseth his antichristian ministry, ministration, worship, etc. Let him therfore "first cast out the beame out of his own eye, and then shal he more throughly see to take the mote out of his brother's eye."[4]

Henry Barrowe

[1] *A Short Reply*, p. 98. [2] *Ibid.*
[3] *Ibid.* [4] Matthew 7:5 and Luke 6:42.

VII

BARROW'S FINAL ANSWER TO GIFFORD—MARGINALIA [1591/1592]

In December, 1591, Gifford's work, *A Short Reply unto the Last Printed Books of Henry Barrow and John Greenwood, the Chiefe Ringleaders of Our Donatists in England*, was entered in the *Stationers' Register*. Gifford was replying to *A Brief Discoverie of the False Church* (1590) and to *A Plaine Refutation* (1591). To this *A Short Reply* Barrow responded about January or February, 1591/1592, with his *general* answer in "A Few Observations to the Reader of Mr. Giffard His Last Replie." But shortly thereafter, he began work on a *detailed* reply to specific points in Gifford's *A Short Reply*. Somehow, possibly through the help of Andrew Smyth or Daniel Studley, he had obtained a copy of Gifford's book, and though he was denied paper, he managed to write his replies on the margin of Gifford's work. When and how long he worked we do not know for sure, but it is clear that he had completed his "A Few Observations" about January or February, 1591/1592. Very likely he then spent the next month writing his marginal replies. There are ninety-eight pages in this book, and all but four of them are filled with replies, written in such a fine albeit clear hand that it is best to read them with a magnifying glass. Whereas Gifford's printed type line is 3⅓ inches wide, Barrow has only a 1-inch margin at the side. Nevertheless, in a not untypical page, Gifford has 374 printed words and Barrow has squeezed in 370 written words on one margin and on the bottom of the page.

Gifford's book with Barrow's marginalia is at the University Library, Cambridge (Bb-11-29). If this book was smuggled out of prison to one of Barrow's friends, it probably passed from friend to friend until it found its way into the library. But if it was one of the writings confiscated by the prison authorities, in their numerous riflings of Barrow's chamber, it is likely that the book became a part of the archbishop's library, and may have found its way to Cambridge during the tempestuous years of the Long Parliament, Archbishop Laud, and the archbishop-hater William Prynne.

Gifford's statements are printed first, and then Barrow's comments—indented in the text—follow.

[A 1 *recto*]

A short Reply vn-
to the last printed books
of Henry Barrow, *and* Iohn
Greenwood, the chiefe ringleaders of our Donatists
in England:

VVherein is layd open their grosse
ignorance, and foule errors:
upon which their whole building is founded.

By *George Gyfford*, Minister of God's holy
worde, in Maldon. [Essex].

Imprinted at London by
Thomas Orwin, for *Tobie*
Cooke: and are to be solde
at the Tygers head, in
Paul's Churchyard.

1591.

[A 1 *verso*] Blank.
[A 2 *recto et verso*] To the Reader.
[A 3 *recto et verso*] to Master *Barrow*, and Master *Greenwood*. [In italics].
[A 4 *recto* = p. 1–N4 *verso* = p. 98] Text.

Barrow's Final Answer to Gifford

[A 2 *recto*] To the Reader.

There were (good christian reader) foure haynous accusations laid against the Church of England,[1] for which the accusers have condemned her, and all her publique assemblies, as most wicked, antichristian, idolatrous synagogues of Sathan. I[A] shewed how falsely they doo accuse, and howe presumptuously agaynst God they doo condemne. And that indeede they are the very same with the auncient Donatists.[2]

[A] You hitherto have not approved the constitution of these parish assemblies in the people, ministrie, ministration and government ecclesiastical therof by the rules of God's word. Nor yet made an aunswere to our reasons in disprofe of the same. Therfore this vitupery wil neither justify them, clear yourselfe or charge us.

They have replyed and published in print their defence, but their bookes are intercepted; yet some few have escaped, and are dispersed among theyr fellowes.[3] Wherefore I hold it needfull to publish some answere,[B] not dealing with every error and absurditie (for that would aske the travaile of some yeares), but onely with the chiefe grounds[B] of their schisme.

[B] In this treatise you both leave the chiefe matters in controversie for which we blame and forsake your assemblies. And also those grounds and criminations of schisme wherof you accused us. And therfore herein [you] doo but abuse the reader.

In this, I trust every simple man that hath a christian heart, shall see the effectual power[C] of Sathan, when he turneth himselfe into the likenes of an angell[C] of light, to seduce ignorant men, which are lifted up in their mindes, with opinion of their knowledge.

[C] Let the antichristian ministry, ministration, government, which we by our writings and suffrings witnes against, what you exercise and mainteine, shew to the reader which of us seduce,

1 "A Breefe Sum of Our Profession" and also in "A Brief Summe of the Causes of Our Seperation." See Carlson, *The Writings of Henry Barrow, 1587–1590*, pp. 81–85 and 118–150.

2 In a manuscript answer, in *A Short Treatise*, and in *A Plaine Declaration*.

3 The entire edition of *A Plaine Refutation*, published in 1591, was seized by Sir Robert Sidney, the English governor of Flushing in the Netherlands. Francis Johnson kept two copies, read one of them, and was so moved that he visited the Barrowists in London, joined with them, and was chosen as their pastor when the church was organized in September, 1592. The two copies came into the possession of the archbishop and the attorney-general, Thomas Egerton. Today the archbishop's copy is at Lambeth Palace Library and Egerton's copy is in the Bridgewater Collection at the Huntington Library. Most of the copies of *A Brief Discoverie of the False Church* were also seized.

speake in the power of Sathan, are those transformed angels. For being men unlearned (onely some little froth[D] excepted).

[D] Our knowledge is according to a meashure of grace received, not builte upon the froth of men's writings but upon the holy Worde of God, which whilest you resist you but stumble at that rock which shal grinde you to powder.

(I speake thus because they pervert that little which they have read in other men's writings, in sundry poynts), yet as if they were sent from heaven with revelations; or as great apostles,[E] they take upon them to confute, and controll, and condemne all churches, and all the most worthy instruments which God hath raysed up in these last times.

[E] May not but apostles defend the truth or reprove error and transgression? Or doo those which reprove the errors and transgressions of the best churches and men therby condemn the said churches and men? Or may the goodnes of any church or man justifie their sinnes and the sinnes of others? If not [then][1] you wrongfully accuse us and slenderly defend yourselves.

For knowe this (good reader) that the foure[F] accusations which they have brought agaynst the Church of England, to condemne her, are also (though with some differences) brought against all churches in Europe, and that in expresse wordes in these their last bookes.[2]

[F] The Reformed churches in other partes have no harmonie with you in your leitourgie, ministry, government, procedings. Therfore you both wrongfully charge us and them. And herein rather condemne them your selfe in that you differ [last line cropped, foot of page].

[A 2 *verso*]

For the prescript[G] formes of prayers, which all the Reformed churches doo use, they [the Separatists] condemne as most horrible and accursed blasphemie. The people[H] (they say) are prophane multitudes. They say, that in all Europe, and in all these knowen partes of the world there is no minister[I] of Christ. The government[K] by elderships, they condemne as a most proude thing, as being without any warrant of God's word.

[G] Though we dislike of all nombred stinted prayers and devised prescribed leitourgies, yet have we not so written or spoken of

[1] Edge of the paper. Only the letter "t" appears.

[2] That is, in *A Brief Discoverie of the False Church* and in *A Plaine Refutation.*

their leitourgies as you here falsly accuse us. It is your popish patched portes [portas] that commeth so neere unto blasphemy.

H We say that the people of your parishes are such. We hope better of others that have had more sincere teaching and government.

I Though we deny the whole ministry of your Church of England, yet doo we not therby condemn the ministry of other churches, as you falsly accuse.

K Neither do we condemn the government by elders as you without truth or shame give out of us. We seeke and suffer for the holy gospell, ministry and government which Christ hath set over his church, and renounce all foreign ministries and governments.

Doo but reade over these fewe things which I have noted out of their bookes: and judge how fit they be for such a work as they have taken in hand, and whether it be like that God hath sent them, even as it were Moses and Aaron, to conduct his people out of Aegipt . . . for so they take it; as appeareth by their owne wordes . . ., page 5 of the Epistle[1] . . . . "Many[L] they see by God's mightie hand (say they) escaped [and delivered], and marching with the banner of the gospell displayed before all the inchaunters of Aegipt and Pharaoh his troupes."

L With what construction this charge may be gathered out of these wordes let the god[ly][2] judge. As also with what spirit you have read and [reduced?][3] our writings.

[A 3 *recto*]

To Master Barrow, and Master Greenwood.

Ye complaine[A] much of hard dealing offered you, and say ye are blasphemed with odious tearmes.

A But Michael the arch angel when he disputed against the divel controverting abought the body of Moses durst not enter[4] sentence of blasphemy. The true minister and servant of Christ ought not to strive but to be meake towards all men instructing the opposite in lenity. II Timothy 2. Prisons and contumely are hitherto the best usage or conviction that the faithful servants of Christ that stand for the true ministry and government which he hath given unto his church can obteine at your hands.

1 *A Brief Discoverie of the False Church*, A iv *recto*.

2 Edge of paper.

3 The word may be "restated," or "receaved."

4 The reading seems to be "enter," but "answer" and "confer" are not impossible. See Jude 1:9.

They that take it to be uncharitable dealing, to disclose, and to paynt out such seducers in their colours, and to disgrace[B] them utterly, to the end that the simple may not be spoyled by them as a praie [prey], doo want some judgement.

[B] Indeed all your writings hitherto savour more of malice and bitternes, than of love or piety. But slander and vitupery wil neither deface us or defend your selfe.

For as it is Christian charitie in the shepheards to deale meekely with the sheepe, so is it high treachery and unfaythfull dealing to Christ and his church, when the woolfe[C] dooth come in sheepe's clothing, not to pluck it off. . . .

[C] If Mr. Gyffard had been minded to have sought where he mought [might] have founde the wolfe, happely his evil conscience would have sent him rather to the princely pallaces of these lordly prelats than to the prisons and dongeons where thei hould Christe's poore servants that wil not submit to their antichristian power and procedingz. But how stoutly he plucketh of[f] their visards and baiteth those greavous wolves from the fould, let the estate of his church, his present ministration, and writings declare.

[A 3 *verso*]

Ye have drawen many into an outragious[D] presumption against God and his people.

[D] When you shall be able to prove this by us, let credit be given unto your words. In the meane time we retorne them as most unjust and untrue slaunders.

Ye have rent out of the hearts of many, all reverence and love towards the preachers of the gospell, and led them into such a presumptuous opinion of their owne understanding, that if they become not heretikes, yet experience doth teach, that many of them growe into irreligious[E] prophanenes.

[E] Sutch heretikes, irreligious and prophane, as are cast out of our churches, are received and reteined in your churches as most holy members.

Master Barrow and Master Greenwood, I doo not know[F] your persons, and I protest unto ye, that there is no private thing hath moved me to seeke your disgrace, but indeede the care of Christ's sheepe. And let it appeare by the things which follow whether I have done ye any wrong.

[F] How greate then is your sinne and presumption that before you either knew us, or your church had convinced or condemned us, durst of your selfe thus to divulge and denounce us. Let the reader judge how wel you knowe or keape the rules of God his Worde herein.

[There are 98 pages of *A Short Replie vnto the Last Printed Bookes of Henry Barrow and John Greenwood, the Chiefe Ringleaders of Our Donatistes in England*; printed in black letter. There are notes on all but four of these pages, altogether 301 in number. Sometimes they are short, and occasionally they fill the margin and overflow to the head or foot of the page. Generally the sentences or phrases underlined in the text are those to which reference is made in the notes; occasionally there is no reference letter or underlining.]

Page 1. [No notes. In two passages Gifford accuses Barrow and Greenwood of "savage crueltie" in condemning the assemblies of the Church of England as "most wicked antichristian synagogues" and himself as a "marked servant of Antichrist."]

Page 2. And if in the chiefe[A] poynts of Donatisme ye be not full Donatists, and so holde sundry poyntes of Annabaptisme, being fallen into their tents and as outragiously fighting against all churches, and with the same weapons that they did . . . . let me be accounted for no better indeed than a lying prophet.

[A] The bitternes of your waters eaven of every worde that commeth out of your mouth bewrayeth the treasures of your hearte and of what sorte your fontaine is. Matthew 15:18. James 3:11. How justly you have charged us in your former writings of Donatistry and Anabaptistry or how wel in this [*A Short*] *Reply* you have repaired those former charges by us refuted, let the reader that hath read those our writings judge. As also how wel you have defended your church in those fower principal enormities for which we blame and come out of the same.

Page 2. Then how much more intollerable is their wicked presumption and intrusion into God's office, which take upon them utterly to condemne[B] as quite separate from Christ all the assemblies in a kingdome, which professing the gospell, have many particular members in them, that earnestly indevour to please God, and are not spotted with any grosse errors or notorious offences?

[B] Unto this you were aunswered that we doe not condemne any tru church or Christian for such errors or faltes. Wherein you did and doo but slaunder us. Also you were shewed but to begge that you should prove whilest you thus strongly assume these parish assemblies for tru constituted churches, whilest thei are founde to have nothing aright according to the rules of God his Worde. Yet wil you stil persist without al shame to slaunder and assume that [which] you are never able to prove.

Page 3. [To the argument that other godly churches give the Church of England the place of a sister and regard her as a mother in Israel], ye have not, (Master Barrow), answered[C] one worde unto al this, but have with deepe silence slipt past it.

[C] You have been often aunswered that no universality, consent or pretext of antiquity could justify the Church of Rome, much lesse now her daughter of England whilest the Worde of God condemneth them. You have been often urged to approve by the rules of God his Worde the constitution and government of your church, in the people, ministry, ministration, procedings. Likewise your stale argument of the martyres hath been often aunswered,[1] not to approve any thing which the Worde of God condemneth. Therfore your church is very crasy that leaneth to these weake proppes. And either your understanding or conscience very bad that perceived not, or now dissembleth these aunsweres.

Further, I now aunswere you and before in the first, third, and fourth transgression aunswered, that no Reformed church in Europe alloweth or consenteth to your ministry, leitourgie, government, procedings. But rather condemneth you in all these in that them selves have a faith divers and contrary. So that both of them can not be aright or of God.

Page 3. But ye say . . . the Church of England . . . holdeth[D] errors

[1] *A Plaine Refutation*, pp. 155, 156, 180–182. See also "A Brief Summe of the Causes of Our Seperation," p. 5.

and is convinced in them, and yet persisteth to defend and teach the same, and therefore it is quite seperated from Christ.

[D] We doo not for the houlding some errors forsake the Church of England as you slily would insinuate. But for that their whole constitution in their communicants, ministry, ministration, government is from the rule and antichristian, we judge them no tru established churches, or such wherwith we may communicate. So that the question is whether these in this estate be true established churches or no. And not whether we forsake them for some errors, etc., as you to evade would change the question.

Page 3. [A man who sins is not to be cast forth as a heathen if he despise private admonitions, but only when he will not hear the church (Matthew 18)]. This ye have not answered[E]. . . .

[E] We have aunswered that the court without the temple is not to be meashured. That the censures of Christ only belonge to the tru established church of Christ. That you alwaise begge the question whilest you affirme these parish assemblies true constituted churches. Againe it was aunswered that any of these parishes or all of them joyned together have not power to redres any thinge that is amisse be it never so evil. Therfore it were vaine to tel them. As for the chiefe ministers and governors of your church, thei blaspheme the censures and holy discipline of Christ as intollerable. Thei persecute and imprison all that seake or stand for the same. Therfore not safe to tel them. All this, Mr. Gyffard, you have balked in evil conscience. And have untruly here given out that we have aunswered nothing.

Page 4. In these words . . . lieth the whole defence[F] and cleering of your selves from that wicked and presumptuous intrusion into God's office, which I have layd to your charge.

[F] It is a ful clearing of us from your slaunderous calumniations for that in abandoning your confuse assemblies we forsake and condemn no true church. Nextly, we forsake them not for such light causes as you pretend. Thirdly, we hould not those erroneous opinions which you have accused us of.

Page 4. I doo indeed greatly wonder[G] to see how strong the illusions of Satan be. . . .

[G] [We] wonder not so much as sorrow to see such counterfeat ministers as you that stand under your king Abaddon,[1] Antichrist, that angel of the bottomles pit, so bitterly to invey against Christ's faithful servants, so to contemne and abuse the Scriptures.

Page 5. I will begin first with the difference which . . . ye have learned to put betwixt error and heresie. The only[H] difference which ye make is the obstinate persisting in it, and teaching it, after it is convinced unto him that erreth.

[H] There was not cause offred me to put any other or further differences. Whilest we only controverted whether any church or member of Christ be to be censured or left before obstinacy after due conviction appeare.

Page 5. [Men are heretics only if they refuse to be convinced and strive to pervert others]. But will it hereupon followe that[I] no error is of it selfe an heresie, unlesse it light into such a man as obstinatly will holde and teach it?

[I] You forsake the matter to strive abought wordes. We had no controversy whither [whether] some error in it selfe might in way of speach be called an heresy. But whether any church or Christian before obstinacy after due conviction may be censured and avoided as heretical. Wherfore in all this you but cavil and flee the point.

Page 5. Agayne, shew us where ye have learned, that every[K] error, even to the least, being in an hereticke, becommeth an heresie.

[K] Our controversy was of such errors as deserve publike censure and separation. Which being obstinatly held, etc., make heresy. Therfore in this also you but pervert our wordes, cavil and flee the point.

Page 6. [To say that] error must be duely convinced unto the conscience of the man that erreth, before he can be so wilfully obstinate, as doth separate him from the faith

[1] Abaddon is the Hebrew name for the angel of the bottomless pit. In Greek he is Apollyon, the Destroyer.

and from the communion of Christ . . . is so farre from cleering ye from presumptuous[L] intrusion into God's office, that it utterly overthroweth ye;

[L] You weary me with shewing how every where you stil continue to begge the chiefe question which you should prove, *viz.*, that these parish assemblies are true constituted churches of Christ. Which we forsake not as some times true churches now obstinate in error, but as never rightly gathered, constituted, ordered, etc. Therfore in all this we condemn no true church, but seake one. Neither intrude into God his judgment seate, but obey God his commandement. Revelation 18:4.

Page 6. [Barrow admits that] those which suffered death for religion in our church [are] godly martyrs, saying . . . "their sinnes, and these false offices and ministrie which they executed in their ignorance . . . being forgiven them."

Page 7. [The same is true of the ignorant which embraced the gospel.] Upon[M] this it followeth, that the Church of England was or might bee a true church, untill such time as she was duely convinced of her errors and found obstinate.

[M] There is no such sequele; you might doo well to draw your argument. The piety of those martyres can not justify the open transgressions in the constitution of these your churches. Or make them true established churches whilest their whole constitution is found so contrary to the rules of God his Worde.

Page 7. [The Church of England is thus still the true church, having] many thousands[N] in her, which are readie to shed their bloud for the holy gospell of Christ.

[N] God hath many deare elected in the church of Rome, yet make thei not the popish synagogs true established churches of Christ, sutch to which Christ's faithful servants ought to resorte and joyne.

Page 7. This is your bare accusation[O] . . . . [to say the church is] so wilfully obstinate in maintayning her errors . . . . that she hath forfaited the covenant, and is separated from the communion of Christ.

[O] Stil you assume the question, *viz.*: that your parish assemblies are true constituted churches to which the censures of Christ belong.

Page 7. [To prove the church has been duly convinced and found obstinate, we must accept the rule] that one brother[P] offending is not to loose the dignitie and place of a Christian [until he obstinately despise the judgment and authority of the church].

[P] But how observe you this rule that before your church hath thus convinced us, or [before] we [be] found obstinate, [you] dare thus to revile and divulge [expose, publicize] us.

Page 7. [Still more does this apply to a church.] All[Q] the true churches have convinced the church of Rome, and condemned her as obstinate. . . . But what churches are they which have convinced the Church of England of such errors and found her so obstinate. . . ?

[Q] If all true churches have thus convinced, condemned, and caste out the church of Rome, how then in this estate doo you alowe her the seale of the covenant, the true ministry, etc., yea, stil to be a tru church of Christ? How shal this be reconciled? But now at Mr. Luther's first comming out of popery and publike writing against the same, how can you in those times shew this general condemnation of the church of Rome? Or what judgment wil you give of Mr. Luther and other Christians that condemned and seperated them selves and others from the church of Rome in those times? Thincke duly of the matter. . . .[1]

Page 8. But what churches are they which have convinced the Church of England of such errors, and found her so obstinate, that they have condemned her and willed all men to forsake her? O Mr. Barrow,[R] you shall finde that all the godly churches are so farre from this, that contrariwise they acknowledge her for a sister.

[R] No Reformed church doth or can alowe the publike ministry, leitourgie, government of your Church of England, seing them selves have made an other and quight divers. Againe al the learned prechers of this land have sought the removinge and utter abolishing of these by Parlament.[2] Wherin they acknowledge

[1] The margin is cropped. The reading seems to be: "Thincke duly of the matter, then give your [reply, answer]."

[2] See Donald J. McGinn, *The Admonition Controversy* (New Brunswick, 1949);

them not to be of Christ. And so condemn them, as hath been often proved and hitherto not aunswered or touched by you. Therfore, Mr. Gyfford, this your exhortation or rather execration might in wisdome have been spared until you had better proved your matter or convinced your adversary.

Page 8. Ye have[S] no way to shift or to colour your wickednes but this, that men may bee convinced of error by particular persons, and that so hath the Church of England beene duly convinced.

[S] This shift and colour is of your own devising. Therfore you had need speake wel of it. For us we have not learned to stay conflicting or disputing in the false church until we have convinced that impudent murtherous harlot. But we are commanded to save our selves and to flee out of Babylon. Sufficieth us that God condemneth her. Revelation 18:4, 5. Jeremiah 50 and 51 chapters.

Page 8. I will follow ye in this, yeelding this scope, to see when[T] or who they be of particular persons which have duely convinced the Church of England and al her assemblies of such errors.

[T] The false church is to be avoided not confuted.

Page 9. Indeede I am of this minde . . . . that right excellent men come[V] short in some things about the ordering of God's church, and especially at the beginning, because time is a teacher.

[V] Our question is not abought faltes in your ecclesiastical constitution, ministry, ministration, government, procedings (as you would torne [turn, twist] this case), but whither [whether] the constitution, ministry, ministration of your church be true or false. If true, though with error, then is the frame to stand, the faltes to be corrected. But if the whole frame be false, then is it to be quight plucked doune and a right one erected.

Page 9. [Such men read the Scriptures, and] might have been able in those days, after twenty years' separation from

J. E. Neale, *Elizabeth I and Her Parliaments, 1584–1601* (London, 1957), pp. 58–83, 145–165, 216–232; Albert Peel (ed.), *The Seconde Parte of a Register* (London, 1915), II, 70–87, 212–218, 258 f.

popery, to see as much as some in these dayes that have been but foure or five yeares from the bowling[W] alleyes.[1]

[W] Speake wel of bowling alles least you mar one of the best exercises of your chiefe ministers.[2]

Page 9. But there lieth the matter howe you can prove that our church[X] is convinced.

[X] You stil[3] assume that [which] you should prove [*viz.*, that] these your assemblies to be true constituted churches.

Page 9. In some ceremonies, and in the manner of government, our church doth differ from other churches. Those churches (indeede) have shewed their reasons, why they use not such ceremonies[Y] and government.

[Y] You must not make the whole ministry, ministration, worship, government, lawes, leitourgie of your church ceremonies and so evade. These are no matters indifferent wherein churches may varie (as you perswade). Such as have not those aright but forged and antichristian can not be esteamed true established churches.

Page 10. [People are not immediately convinced in their consciences by a truth.] There were[Z] thousands in the church of Jerusalem, Acts 21, which erred groslie about the retayning the ceremoniall law, and the holy Apostles were driven to beare with them, when they could not perswade them from it, and that many yeares.

[Z] This ignorance and zeale of those nue called Jues, Acts 21, can neither justify or excuse the procedings or persons of these antichristian prelates and clergie, who have no such warrant for their popish enormities by pretext of God's lawe as those Jues had; yet obtrude their popish and Juish ceremonies by force upon al churches and Christians being Gentiles, which the Apostles them selves did not. No, not upon Jue[s] that knew they were abrogated. Nor yet were these zealous Jues suffred many yeares in that error

[1] This is a caustic reference to Barrow's dissolute mode of life before his conversion. If "foure or five yeares" is accurate, then we may date Barrow's conversion in 1586–1587. Perhaps 1585 is the right date.

[2] Barrow's retort is a reference to Bishop Aylmer, who enjoyed a game of bowls, even on Sunday. Martin Marprelate twitted Bishop Aylmer for his bowling (*An Epistle*, pp. 19, 20, 49).

[3] The word "strongly" is crossed out.

(as Mr. Gyfford falsly alledgeth). This appeareth by al Paule's epistles written from Rome.

Page 10. [Many of the martyrs knew of the form of government of the Reformed churches in Geneva and elsewhere, and some], as Bishop Hooper,[A] and Archdeacon Philpot,[1] were travailers even to that ende and purpose. [And many divines from the churches of the Continent were in England.]

[A] You rather shew your selfe ignorant of the first erection of that state which was doone by Act of Parlament immediatly out of most grosse popery and that by such as never had lived in any tru constituted church, as I saied. For Mr. Hooper and Philpot, they were not of the first erectors but joyned to it being erected. Wherein if thei erred it is neither a president [precedent] for us[2] to follow nor warrant for you to proceed. Neither can the commoration [sojourning] of those strangers with you justify the state of your church. This is not to approve it by the rules and practise of the Apostles.

Page 10. [Who have laid the true pattern before the church more clearly than it was laid before the martyrs. Even the Separatists will not claim that they alone have done so.] Let us then begin with these other, and then come to you. The Church of England at the first (as you confesse) set up the frame as they were perswaded[B] in conscience to be very right and agreeable to God's Word. Since that there hath risen controversie at home about some ceremonies[C] and observations, and about the government.

[B] But I never saied thei set it up according to God's Worde, which where thei did not their worcke must borne [burn].

[C] You may not so hide or put away the most weighty matters in controversy. As the antichristian ministry, ministration, worship, government, lawes, etc.

Page 11. But now the visible[D] Church of England, the prince and

[1] John Hooper, Bishop of Gloucester and Worcester, was burned at the stake February 9, 1554/1555 (John Foxe, *Acts and Monuments*, VI, pp. 636–676). John Philpot, Archdeacon of Winchester, who was examined some fifteen times, was burned at the stake December 18, 1555 (John Foxe, *Acts and Monuments,* volume VII, edited by George Townsend and Stephen Reed Cattley, London, 1838), pp. 605–714. [2] "You" crossed out.

all those which exercise the cheife power therein, have stood and doe stand resolute.

[D] Stil you begg.

Page 11. [The prince and those that exercise the chief power deem the ceremonies, etc., if not agreeable to God's Word, at least tolerable, and the government] is such as is by God's Word most fit and profitable[E] for our church.

[E] Can any other government than Christ hath given be more fit and profitable to the church of Christ than his sacred government? Yea, or is any other tollerable or to be accepted of the church of Christ?

Page 11. Tell me then Mr. Barrow (seeing ye confesse the martyrs were not convinced[F]) [how you are certain that the thousands who accept the ceremonies are convinced and wilfully obstinate].

[F] Though I thinck reverendly of their persons for the grace of God in them, yet may I not therby be pressed to approve of any error thei held or transgression they committed. What conviction belongeth to your church, and how wel your clergie men wil receive it, I have often shewed.

Page 11. You see by the church[G] in Jerusalem that men may ignorantly remayne still in error.

[G] How you abuse this place is shewed. Page 10. in Z[1]

Page 11. We have beene perswaded that the governement ecclesiasticall ought to be by one of these two . . . either by bishops[H] or by presbyteries, and you condemne both.

[H] Your popish lord bishops have no government or place in Christe's church. Again, your fonde distinction betwixt the government of bishops and of presbytries rather bewrayeth your thicke ignorance than excuseth your church. We alwaise toke the government of bishops and of the eldership to be all one. Neither did we ever deny this government of byshops or elders as you slaunder.

Page 12. Ye had abandoned and condemned all without any order.[2]

[1] Note Z, page 10, *supra*, p. 140.

[2] The marginal comment is crossed out, but is still readable: "Al this futility ariseth upon the question begged that ought first to bee proved. *Viz.* That those Parish Assemblies are true Constituted Churches."

Page 13. Satan[I] in the likenes of an angell of light hath most miserably seduced ye.

[I] This is the third time of the use of this phrase against us in these few leaves.[1]

Page 13. Master Barrow, it is a foule hereticall[K] opinion to hold that a man may not joyne with that church which holdeth and maintaineth some faults and errors.

[K] Mr. Gyfford, you slaunder me if you say I ever held it.

Page 13. Doth not St. Paule labour in divers places to joyne them together in peace, which in some matters held and continued in divers judgement?[L]

[L] Yet taught not divers or false doctrines for that were intollerable.

Page 13. Thus much might suffice to shewe your horrible and inexcusable presumption.[M]

[M] Al this futility ariseth upon the question begged, which ought first to be proved, *viz.*, that your parish assemblies are true constituted churches.[2]

Page 13. [You say that if a man persist obstinately in an error and continue to teach it,] wee may safely judge that man to have no faith, nor communion with Christ. The same is to be sayd of a congregation, and so[N] of the whole Church of England.

[N] "And so of the [whole] Church of England" is of your own adding. I spake generally that obstinasie after due conviction, added unto sutch error or transgression as deserveth censure, separateth from communion, etc. I made no such application to the Church of England because I denied it to be a tru constituted church.

Page 14. But it is farre otherwise in a visible church, because in it, there bee sundry sorts of members, which may[O] not be all foulded up together under one sentence.

[O] We reasoned of the outward estate of a church after such due conviction and not of the estate of every perticuler person therin. We doubt not but God hath many elect in the church of Rome, yet condemn we the outward estate therof. There is no comparison betwixt the church of Israel at the time of our

[1] In the preface, A 2 *recto*, pp. 4 and 13.

[2] This is the same note transferred from p. 12.

Savior's birth and these parish assemblies in this estate.

Page 15. No notes.

Page 16. Then seeing there is no man but sinneth willingly, and continueth with some obstinacie in sundrie things, how can you maintaine this, that every wilfull obstinacie in error doth[P] separate from the faith, and from the communion of Christ, but that you must with Novatus,[1] cut all the regenerate from the hope of repentance, seeing all doo transgresse of knowledge?

[P] There are none so pervers as thei that wilfully cavile at the known truth. Mr. Gyfford, you could not be ignorant of my meaning which my plaine wordes often expressed. To be only of that temporal judgment of the present estate of such convicted obstinate. Whom the Lord commandeth to cut of[f], to cast out, to deliver up to Sathan. Yet this not by final sentens (as you of set purpose cavil) but only to bring him to repentans, which sheweth our charitable desire and purpose in this temporal censure. Which yet if he continue hardened no dout shal binde in heaven. So that al this your railing and vituperie is rather against the rule and commandement of the Holy Ghost than against us.

Page 17. Alas, poore man, may not a childe see your follie? When ye confesse there be errors[Q], that a man may erre and dye in, and yet hold Christ the foundation, and so be saved: is it not as much as to say there be errors that are not fundamentall?

[Q] In al this, Mr. Gyfford, you but strive abought wordes. Your selfe here confesseth that I hould not al errors or sins equal or of like indignity. In my writing I set down how no errors were of the foundation. No transgression of God's law, venial without repentance. As you to extenuate and cover your odious transgressions sought to persuade.

Page 17. Now therefore, Master Barrow, and Master Greenwood,

[1] Novatus, or Novatian, was a priest of the third century. He advocated strict or even harsh treatment of the *lapsi,* those who had not withstood the Decian persecution. He opposed the election of Pope Cornelius in 251, set himself up as anti-pope, and began the Novatian schism.

lay all those things together which I have noted touching your confused ignorance,[R] errors, and absurdities.

[R] "Out of the aboundance of the hearte the mouth speaketh."[1] Al this vitupery but addeth to your accompt.

Page 17. The fearefull and odious, yea, most accursed presumption, by which yee take upon ye to abandon and forsake, as utterly separated from the faith, and from the communion of Christ, all the assemblies of the Church of England, and all the[S] particular members of the same.

[S] In forsaking the antichristian constitution of your churches we do no injury to any man much les condemn them (as you accuse), but only in obeying the commandement of God seake to save our own soules.

Page 17. I saide that the fearefull end of one Boltom,[2] about twentie yeares past, would not be forgotten. You have heard (as you say, page 208) that he revolted and became a conformable member of our church, and so fel into that fearefull estate. Seeke better information, Master Barrow[T], seeing the example may touch ye, for the trueth is, he did for the same causes that you doo, utterly condemne the whole Church of England, and was with sundry other separated from it. And (as it is constantly affirmed) he was an elder in their secret church, and afterward falling into deepe dispaire, he could not be recovered, but did hang himselfe. The matter which pressed him so sore was this, that hee had judged and condemned men better than himselfe.

[T] You fare like him that smiteth him that standz next him who so ever made the offens[e]. He that applied your own storie unto you did it upon better evidence and testimony than it seameth your Ordinary hath

[1] Matthew 12:34.

[2] John Bolton was a member of the Plumbers' Hall congregation in London. Arrested on March 4, 1567/1568, for participating in a conventicle, he was released from Bridewell prison on April 22, 1569. He became an elder in the London "Privy Church" of which Richard Fitz was the pastor. After a second imprisonment, he recanted publicly at St. Paul's Cross, and rejoined the Church of England. Excommunicated by the Privy Church, he hanged himself about 1572. See Gifford, *A Short Reply*, p. 17; John Robinson, *A Justification of Separation from the Church of England* (1639), pp. 49 f.; Henry Ainsworth, *Counter-poyson* (1608), p. 39.

given you. He was a minister of the same order [as] that [to which you belong] your selfe. He stood awhile in great zeale against the priestes' attire, crosse, etc., injoined. Not able to indure the prison, he subscribed. And after hange[d] him selfe. I thincke in al this his fearful example toucheth you more neare than me. Yet wil I not refuse any frute or instruction I may gather by the same. Yet feare I not the corse causles[1] or the false prophet's vaine threat whilest I have the Worde of God for what I doo or refuse to doo.

Page 18. Where yee thinke your selves most devine, there Satan[V] hath most deepely deluded yee.

[V] The fourth time of abusing this phrase to blaspheame the Holy Spirit of God in us.[2]

Page 18. Looke also upon your owne booke now printed,[3] and you shall finde, that both in the accusation you have omitted these words (*wilfully*[W] *obstinate*) and also passed by mine answer unto them.

[W] It was omitted by negligence in the printe as all the copies and your own witnes. As also your own writings witnes. These may cleare me of evil dealing in this behalfe.[4]

Page 18. Looke in the tenth page,[5] and see whether I doo not charge ye with an *Annabaptisticall*[X] *freedome.*

[X] With what truth you have charged us or I avoyded your charge, let the godly reader judge to your or my reproofe.

Page 18. And for *The Booke of Common Praier*, although the question betweene us, was not whether there bee faultes in it, but whether it be (as you tearme it) a great pregnant idoll, full of heresies,[Y] blasphemies, and abominations?

[Y] It is to[o] late for you now to change the question, or to evade by these shifts of heresy, blasphemy, etc.

[1] "As the bird by wandering, as the swallow by flying, so the curse causeless shall not come" (Proverbs 26:2).

[2] Barrow has reference to the figure of Satan transformed into an angel of light (II Corinthians 11:14). In this instance Gifford may not have so intended.

[3] *A Plaine Refutation*, p. 25.

[4] In Barrow's first reply, he had charged the English churches to be "heinouslie faultie, and wilfullie obstinate." When this was printed, the phrase was "heinously guiltie" ("A Brief Summe of the Causes of Our Seperation," p. [1]).

[5] *A Short Treatise*, p. 10.

If it be found devised and prescribed by man without warrant of God's Worde, as in our first charge, no Christian that seeth the same ought to communicate, especially when it wil not be amended; but chiefly in the false church. As we esteame yours to bee.

Page 19. And if you (Master Barrow) wil not become a ranke heretick, . . . to maintaine this opinion, that we may not joyne in that worship, where wee finde any imperfections and errors holden, and not reformed: why doo you with wonderment crie out, that this so large an exception of imperfections,[Z] is the odde and onely exception that ever you heard of.

[Z] Your exception was of errors, bleamishes, wants, spottes, imperfections; which made it a joly large exception. But now if you cut it any thing less I assure you it wil be to[o] narrow to cover the bed of your fornications.

Page 19. Or will you refuse to joyne, as the Apostles did joyne with the church in Jerusalem,[A] that held and continued in a grosse error?

[A] I have shewed, page 10, Z: 1. How the Apostles did neither injoyne the legal ceremonies upon the Jues that beleved. 2. Nor yet mix them or joyne them to the gospel in their christian assemblies. 3. Nor yet soffred those weake Jues longe to continue, etc. 4. I shewed no comparison betwixt these antichristian traditions and these ceremonies, which some time were commanded of God. 5. Betwixt this people and that. Let the reader compare and judge how unsofferably you pervert. . . .[1]

Page 19. Doo you not see how by this your doctrine, you open the doore as wide *unto all schismaticks*[B], as ever did the Donatists or the Annabaptists.

[B] It is no schisme to forsake the false church. We have no cause here to reason of the true.

Page 20. Will you not see how you contrarie [contradict] Saint Paule directly, who . . . dooth labour nothing else but to perswade the Christians that held divers[C] opinions touching some things in God's worship, yet to joyne together? Romans 14 and 15.

[1] Last line unreadable because the page has been cropped.

[C] The Apostle Paule never willed to soffer any that publikly taught false doctrine in the church but to obscrvc and avoidc thcm. Romans 16:17. Galatians 1:8. I Timothy 6:3. II John 9. Our controversy is of errors and transgressions publikly taught, committed, and persisted in, yea, injoyned upon others that see the truth. Therfore you greavously falsefy and abuse these Scriptures that only intreate of private ignorances and discrepance in judgment unto the defence of these publike enormities.

Page 20. You charged our church with Romish fasts. I charged you with false[D] accusing.

[D] Your feastes, eaves, saints' eaves, Ember fasts, Lent fasts, etc., are popish fastes. Of these we speake in them selves and not of the opinions the ppsts [parish priests] held of them. Therfore not being able to approve these by the Word of GOD your church remaineth justly charged and you but cavil against the evident truth.

Page 20. You charge us with idoll feastes, as if wee worshipped saints and angels. I told you it is a starke[E] lie, and so I must affirme, our church utterly condemning all that most blasphemous doctrine of popery, touching the meditation of saints or angels.

[E] Your idolle feasts and saints' dayes have been blamed and convinced unto you. It had been your duty either to have defended these your feasts and holy dayes by the Worde of God or els to have yealded to the truth. And not by these cavils to seake to evade, torne [turn] away the question and hide this manifest and most heinouse idollatry.

Page 21. For here to prove the paying[F] of tithes an error fundamentall, and utterly to separate from Christ being obstinately held; you alleage the words of Saint Paule, Galatians 5.

[F] Mr. Gyfford [seeks] to avoide the defense[?][1] of the many Juish ceremonies reteined and injoyned in their church. As their holy courte or churchyarde. Their holy temple. East and west [with][2] foulded doores. Lightes, battlements, cellz, isles, vestries, the

[1] The page is torn. In the next line the letters are "n s e" or possibly "use."
[2] Page torn, but letter "w" seems a good guess—possibly for "with."

holy and most holy, as the chancel for the priest. Their ministerial vesselz, instruments, vestures. Their fonts, organes, copes embroydred and so fashioned, surplices for the priestz and Levites, *viz.*, their singing men. Parish clearkes.[1] Their Juish feastes, Easter, Pentecost. Their purifications. Offrings, tithes, etc. From the present use of these in his church he hath after his maner torned the question to know whither [whether] tithes be an error fundamental.

Page 21. Let me first aske ye then, were the fathers[G] which were circumcised in the time of the law, abolished from Christ, and fallen from grace? [Galatians 5:3].

[G] The fathers sinned not but observed the commandment of God therin. The Apostle and Timothy sinned not whilest their office extendet and thei did this to the gaining of the Jues. The church, Acts 21, neither sinned nor erred. For there was a time of shaking and removing these things to the weake Jues, Acts 15. Romas 14. Hebrews 8. But you, Mr. Gyfford, greatly sinne and erre thus to abuse and pervert these Scriptures to bring in these Juish ceremonies amongest the Gentiles; yea, you shew your selfe ignorant not only of these Scriptures by your selfe so often cited and abused, but of the whole state of the controversy, Acts 15. And of the whole argument of the Epistle to the Gallathians.

Page 21. Whereupon it followeth of necessity, that Saint Paule here to the Galathians,[H] dooth not speake simply of the ceremonie of circumcision.

[H] I would be loth to beginne nue controversies with you, having never had speach hitherto of the argument of this Epistle, wherof to torne [turn] away the approbation of your Juish ceremonies you make so large and impertinent discourse. Yet, suppose I, it wil be harde for you to prove as you affirme that the false apostles or the church of Galatia ever placed merit of eternal life in circumcision and the legal ceremonies. Although indeed, seing thei were commanded of God, made a parte of his worship

[1] Five or six words crossed out: Purifications offeringz Mon[ie?] Tithes & sutch [?].

called *dikaiōmata.*[1] Thei thought and taught that thei could not obeye or worship God aright except thei observed them. And so indeed put righteousnes, that is obedience and not merit in them.

Page 22. Here is the thing then, that the false apostles did joyne the law and Christ together for justification; and Saint Paule testifieth and denounceth, that he which is circumcised with such a minde, as to be justified in part[I] thereby, hee is debtor to keepe the whole law, which is not possible for any flesh, and therefore he shall stand under the curse.

[I] [A long note, occupying the whole of the margin and at times intruding on the text]:
Paul rather sheweth this by necessary consequence that would insue of their observing the ceremonies than of any such position of theirs that thei ever put merit in the ceremonies. Shewing them to have been unto the Jues never meritorius. When Abraham was justified by faith and not by the worcks of the lawe. Shewing them to have been to the Jues but as a garrison or schole wherin thei were shut up. To have been, but temporary. And that but unto infansy, servitude. To have been but elements, principles, shadowes, leeding to other thingz and not the thingz them selves. To have been impotent, poore, not pourging the conscience. To have served but unto Agar and Mount Sina[i] and not unto the spiritual Hierusalem, etc. And therfore sheweth the Gentiles that thei being called in the Gospel unto the thingz themselves unto liberty, unto grace, unto salvation. And that without these ceremonies in going back unto these receive a nue gospel or rather departe from the tru gospel and fall away from grace, liberty, etc., wherin thei are called in soffring them selves to be led backe to this servitude to be borthened with these traditions, etc. Further to shew the impotensie of these ceremonies unto salvation he sheweth God's covenant made without them before the law given to Abraham and his seed before he was circumcised. Abraham to be justified by faith. All the faithful to be his true children, partakers of the same promises. Hagar and

[1] Ordinances, decrees, judgments.

her son not to be partakers of the promises. To be cast out. Exhorting therfore to stand fast in their christian liberty, not to be intangled again or brought in bondage. To receive no such leaven. No such troblers which subvert and destroy their faith by imposing these ceremonies. And now let the reader judge whither [whether] you or I seduce the people: you that receive, exercise, and defend these Juish ceremonies now under the gospell amongest the Gentiles, or I that withstand the same. You that thus falsify, pervert, and abuse the Scriptures to extenuate and excuse the heape of Juish ceremonies imposed upon your church or I that affirme them not to be imposed upon the church without losse of christian liberty. Not to be joyned to the gospel without drawing backe to and reviving the shadowes, which were the losse and denial of the substans of Christ him selfe come and exhibited in the flesh. You that accuse the church of Jerusalem, Acts 21, with error, the Apostles with willing tollerating error. That affirme those zealous Jues not to have placed the worship of God in those ceremonies. That affirme the churches . . .[1]

Page 22. The Church of England, (say you), observeth dayes and times, as Easter, Whitsonday, etc., and payeth tithes, and observeth other ceremonies; therefore Christ[K] can profit yee nothing.

[K] You have priviledge to falsify, change, adde, leave out, invert, or pervert my writings as you liste. You might doo wel in these broken sentences to set down the booke and page. I disproved your tithes by Numbers 18, shewing them ceremonial by Hebrews 7:12, shewing that law with that priesthood to be changed, by I Corinthians 9, where an other maintenanse is prescribed. All these reasons Mr. Gifford hath not touched but by raising and changing the question sought to evade.

[1] Page cropped. One line is missing, but the last word is "merite." In the middle of the page, written in between the lines, is the comment about the Church of Jerusalem: "Those Jues placed the worship of God at that time in the Ceremonies."

Page 23. The church of Jerusalem is not abolished from Christ, but yet erreth grosely,[L] Saint Paul and Timothie sinne not at all thereby.

[L] Or rather you err grosly in so judging of the church of Jerusalem in those times and circumstances.

Page 24. Our church doth renounce[M] and accurse all such doctrine [such as "ceremonies of their owne invention, by which they seeke remission of sinnes"], neither doe we maintaine any Judaisme.[1]

[M] Your church doth revive and injoyne a great number of Juish ceremonies, even the same that were used in the church of Rome. Therfore no boasting of knowledg or renounsing these popish errors wil excuse you from Judaisme. And those judgments denounced against such troblers of the church.

Page 25. [Dare you deny that men have power to forgive sin? In John 20:23 Christ told his Apostles they had such power.] Dare you contradict the flat testimonie[N] of the Scripture?

[N] In all this you but cavil. You see I give not only the minister but every faithful Christian power as kingz and priestes to reprove and to binde sinn by the Worde of God. So that if you wil contradict you must prove that the minister only may remit or binde sinne. And that other Christians may not or else you but skirmish with your own phantasies. Seing I have proved that this power of binding and losing is not tied either to the person or to the office of any minister but only to the Word of [God] received or dispised [disposed?] of the hearers. That the same Worde preached by others which are no ministers hath the same power and operation. I proved also that any private member may in due order reprove the sinne of the greatest minister, as of any other member. These things Mr. Gifford neither distinguishing nor refuting hath exclaimed of my ignorance with open throate.

Page 26. [Answering Barrow's argument that the member of the church has equal power with the minister to forgive sins, Gyfford replies:] Is it not a straunge thing (Master

[1] There are eight other lines of underlining, but no corresponding marginal comment.

Barrow) that such geare should come from you? Will you take away the whole[O] *efficacie and power of the ministrie* which Christ hath ordayned?

[O] You rather take away the dignity, efficasy, and power of the ministry of the Worde, which attribute that to the person of the minister which only belongeth to the Worde of God than I that give alwaies and only this power and effect to the Worde of God whither [whether] it be preached by a minister or by a privat Christian that hath the gift of interpretation.

Page 27. What do you tell us then of that rule of admonishing[P] and pardoning? Luke 17 [Matthew 18:15–18 and Luke 17:1–4].

[P] This was brought to shew that this power of binding and losing sinne was given to all Christians as wel as to the minister. The other you confesse not to be tied to the excellensy of any man's persons but only to the word.

Page 27. But yet (Master Barrow) you should knowe, that it is God's ordinance and good pleasure, to give[Q] a special operation and power unto it [binding and loosing] by the ministrie. Baptisme doth seale by the forgivenes of our sinnes, and hath he not ordayned, that this seale shalbe set to by the ministry?

[Q] It never was denied but the Worde of God hath there the most effect where it is most sufficiently and sincerely taught. But what is this or the administration of the sacraments to confer this power of binding or losing to the person or office of the minister only? I hope you thincke their sinnes are forgiven before and not by the receiving of the sacraments. The minister for the dispensation of these excellent things may be reverenced though this power which is due to God by his Worde be not given to his person.

Page 27. You say that by the place, John 20, wee cannot proove this power of binding and loosing, to bee given onely[R] to the Apostles, there being many disciples both men and women in the place when Christ gave it.

[R] Many faltes no dout through ignorance, haste, negligence, and wante of due correction have escaped me. Neither wil I defend or excuse my maner of handeling this place of John 20, yet this I say, Mr. Gifford, I never thought that weomen or any of the disciples had like commission and authority given with the Apostles. Only my desire there was to prove that the same power of binding and losing was given to others that preached the Word as wel as to the Apostles which though by that John 20 I missed to prove, yet proved I it immediatly after by sending forth the seventy. Luke 10: [1–20].

Page 28. And tell me, Master Barrow, is there not some part of this power of loosing or remitting sinnes by the sacraments[S]?

[S] The sacraments doo not confer but seale grace. Their sins are remitted before and not by the sacraments. Neither is there any consequense or sound religion in your reason to draw the power from the Worde and sacraments administred to the person of the minister.

Page 29. But learne you, Master Barrow, by the Scripture, and remember that God hath given a power to the ministrie of the gospell to forgive sinnes. The power indeede is but ministeriall, and so *The Booke* [*of Common Prayer*] it selfe declareth, where it sayth: He "hath given power and commandement to his ministers, to declare and pronounce to his people being penitent, the absolution and remission of their sinnes."[1] Other power in the minister to forgive sinnes, than this, *The Booke* alloweth none.[T]

[T] Neither wil you shew or see how your church hath received this trumpery and power of the pope. And giveth power to every one of her reading parish priests (which are not tru ministers of Christ) by their portes [portas] to visite, absolve, howsel, etc., their sicke, be thei never so evil or impenitent that require the same. This with their popish and fond maner of doing with their nombred prayers, pistles, gospels, aydes, respons, etc. Some to be said at the howse doore, some at the bed side, Mr. Gifford would not looke or thincke of. But in pure zeale of the truth hath torned [turned] al his force against me

[1] See "The Order for Morning Prayer," or for "Evening Prayer," *The Book of Common Prayer*.

that reprove the same. If the priest may perdon and absolve all the rest, is wel inough.

Page 30. I doo not take it the meaning of *The Booke* [*of Common Prayer*], that it should be uttered[V] of such as make no profession of the holy faith.

[V] It is saied over all whether blaspheamour, heretike, witch, etc.

Page 30. The other is, that we pray for the soule of our brother departed: where we say, that wee with[W] this our brother, and all other departed in the true faith, "may have our perfect consummation and blisse both in body and soule."[1]

[W] This your dirge for the deade is verbatim taken out of the pope's portesse [portas]. Thei hold it no sinne to pray for the dead. But to that purpose made and said these nombred prayers which you use in the same prescript order. The wordz also used in your prayer importe no lesse. Therfore your glosse wille hardly excuse your *Booke*. Thei that made it a parte of the pastor's office to bury the dead and therfore gave him mortuaries, from whom you received your leitorugie, could also teach you to put difference betwixt Limbo and Purgatory, the patriarches, prophetz, etc., and other common Christians. The one not to reade, the other to reade these prayers. This therfore is but a weake defense.

Page 30. [As to considering better] that glorious anthem which wee say at our communion, that we "with angels and archangels and all the companie of heaven lawd and magnifie," etc.[2]—You will not demaund, (that is, you doo in a fine retoricall sort demaund it) but the finenes of this retoricke will not cover the sottishnes[X] of your ignorance.

[X] *Bona verba*, Mr. Giffard. I hope you are not ignorant that the papists from whom you fetched this glorious antheme (which thei used at their high masse and you at your solemn communion upon your high feasts) thought and taught that at that instant in

[1] See "The Order for the Burial of the Dead," *ibid.*

[2] See "The Order of the Administration of the Lord's Supper, or, Holy Communion," *ibid.*

that parte of their masse the angels and all the company of heaven, the spirits of men disceased, did worship and laude God with them. If you thincke not so and would not have others so to thincke, whie use you this popish anth[em] in the same wordes, order, and (so my wordz be not to[o] far inforced) action that thei do?

Page 31. And if that Michael the archangel which strove with the divell about the body of Moses and durst not give rayling sentence, were Christ: yet St. Paule speaketh of an archangell besides[Y] Christ . . . I Thessalonians 4: verse 16.

[Y] That archangel, I Thessalonians 4:16, no doubt is Christ as by the wordes and circumstances of that verse doth appeare. And by other Scriptures to the same effect. Again, Mr. Gifford, Paule speaketh but of one arch angel, your church of many, with angels and archangels, etc. Therfore herin you goo beyound Paule, neither wil this place help you. Againe, according to your own understanding if you make chiefe angels or a chiefe angel, how can it be avoided that you must make degrees of angels.

Page 31. The saintifying the floud Jordain, and all other waters to the mysticall[Z] washing away of sinne, is none other way to be taken, than to say that bread and wine are sainctified to represent the body and bloud of Christ.

[Z] These wordes and the signe of the crosse, etc., added to the water taken out of your halowed fonte, what doo thei else but put superstition and holines in the water to the washing away of sin. Your glosseme[1] wil not excuse the popery and blaspheamy therof.

Page 31. Touching Michael and all angels, we do not worship[A] angels, nor yet make Christ a creature.

[A] You keape a holy day, feast, and worship to the memory of your St. Michael and of al angels.[2] What defense or excuse make you of this?

Page 31. This is but a vayne collection, when prayer is intended for such as are prayed for[B], that they may be turned from their evill. [*Re* the litany.]

[1] Glossēma, the tongue. A possible reading would be—"Glosse we," but the "o" is clearly an omega, the only letter written in Greek.

[2] September 29, Michaelmas, is the day of St. Michael and all the Holy Angels.

[B] This glosse wil neither excuse the first invention or your present use of this letanie.

Page 32. We see there are[C] even anon some which are stricken with thunder: and when the clap is past, it is too late to pray for them.

[C] Your defense of these unreasonable and unseasonable prayers deserves rather a benefice than an aunswere. Yet methinkes you doo some injury to this your leatanie, seing it hath by others been incommended [intrusted] to us as soveraine good for all these things by your to[o] much restreining some general wordes in it.

Page 33. And now touching this that you did affirme the best part of the booke to be but as a peece of swine's flesh, and [an] abomination to the Lord:[1] you goe about to defend your wicked speech[D] by the abuse, which I told you before could be none answer.

[D] You stille but accuse or cavil. The holynes of the Scripture in them selves was never denied by me. Yet their holines doth not justifie any parte of the pope's masse boke or your servise boke where thei are so highly abused to idolatrie.

Page 33. Let the world judge what cause you have to glory in your sufferings: and whether ye be not liker[E] Rabsaka,[2] (who boasted also that God sent him against Jerusalem) than any of the holy martyrs of Christ, [because of Barrow's statement that the Apostles' Creed is a "forged patcherie".]

[E] Christian patience, Mr. Gy[fford], I alwaies thought the whole Worde of God to be the foundation of the faith of Christe's church and servants. And that it ought not to be culled [picked, plucked] upon, limited in, or restreigned unto a few articles only. I called it a forged patchery. For that it is given out in theiz Apostles' names. As though etch one of them

[1] Barrow's harsh statement occurs first in "Four Causes of Separation"—"And even that best part of it they use is but Dagon's stump devoted [destroied, debased, defiled?], but a pece of swyne's flesh, an abhominable sacrifyse unto the Lord."

[2] Rabshakeh. See Isaiah 36:1–10, II Kings 18:17–37; 19:1–37. The Rabshakeh was a high ranking Assyrian officer, sent by King Sennacherib with an army to Jerusalem to demand the surrender of the city.

had set doune his peculier article or symbole,[1] which is not so found in their writings (than which we may receive none other worde, epistle, revelation as from them[)]. I also so called it in reguarde of this most unsavory and unsond article so contrary to the Apostles' doctrines, to the evangelists' writings, to our Saviour's express words, to the truth and ends of his death and passion, and to our whole faith and hope. As no corrupt translation or corruption of that place of the psalme.[2] No popish glosse or devised exposition can hide, as it is there set in your creed, and hath a long time been expounded and received.[3]

Page 33. Others doo hold that our Saviour in soule after his passion descended into hell, though to no such purpose: this is not blasphemie[F] nor heresie.

[F] It is a blasphemous heresy contrary to our Saviour's expres wordes. The consummation of his death and passion, the preaching of the apostles. And to our whole faith and hope. For suer if Christ in soule discended into hel after his passion, then was it [he?] not in paradise, in the hand of his Father. Then were not his soffrings or our redemption finished. Then is he stil in hel for thense is no redemption. And so all our faith and hope vaine.[4]

Page 34. Now Master Barrow, seeing the words be in the Scripture (*thou shalt not leave my soule in hell*[G]) and the matter resteth onely upon the exposition, what immodest and intemporate heat, or rather furiouse outrage is this, to crie out of a blasphemous article, and to terme the articles of our faith, our forged patcherie?

[G] You know a better translation as it seameth. And therfore seing the Hebrue wordes wil beare a better,

[1] See Arthur Cushman McGiffert, *The Apostles' Creed: Its Origin, Its Purpose, and Its Historical Interpretation* (New York, 1902). This creed goes back to an earlier form known as the Roman Symbol. A "symbol" was a sign, a badge, a watchword, and a test of membership.

[2] Psalm 16:10. This is Psalm 15 in the Septuagint version and in the Vulgate. It is Psalm 17 in the Coverdale version of the psalms.

[3] The third of the Thirty-Nine Articles which represent the creed of the Church of England. See Edgar C. S. Gibson, *The Thirty-Nine Articles of the Church of England*, 2nd ed. (London, 1898), pp. 159–180.

[4] The doctrine of Christ's descent into Hell or Sheol is based on the following Scriptural supports: Luke 23:43; Acts 2:24–31; Ephesians 4:9; I Peter 3:18–20 and 4:6.

and al pure translators use a better, you may as wel as Montanus and the Lovanists[1] leave this ould corrupt translation so contrary to the argument of the psalme to the verity of Christe's soffrings an[d] to all sound doctrine.

Page 35. [After a long quotation from Barrow, *A Plaine Refutation*, p. 180, on the singing of psalms, Giffard continues:] Your owne words, Master Barrow, which I have set downe, doo shew themselves so ungodly[H] and prophane unto every christian minde, yea, unto every one which hath but a sparke of humane civility and modesty left in him, that I neede not to say much.

[H] You rather highly abuse and injure me thus to pervert my writings contrary to my wordz and meaning. I have not spoken against the heavenly exercise of singing psalmes but against the riming and paraphrasing the psalmes as in your synagogs. Nor yet so much there against these as against the apochrypha devised erroneous rime songes and ballades songe [sung] commonly in your church in stead of the psalmes and holy songs of the canonical Scriptures. These would rather have been defended than I blamed by you for reproving the same. As to the confuse and prophane rowtes [crowds, rabble] of your communicants I write none otherwise than the Holy Ghost doth of them, Revelation 18:2, allegoricalli according to the type, Leviticus 11. And as the holy prophets doo through out their writings. Neither doth any reproch herby reach unto other churches (of whom I thincke more reverently) except it be by your evil tonge.

Page 35. Moreover, the people in other churches, you make to be but prophane multitudes, as in the assemblies of England, as we shall afterward see where you charge master Calvine

[1] Montanus was a second-century enthusiast who is associated with Ardabau and Pepuza and Phrygia. He emphasized prophecy, the special and continued inspiration of the Holy Ghost, strict asceticism, the early end of the world, and new revelations through himself and his two prophetesses, Prisca and Maximilla. Tertullian was a leading convert.

The reference to the Lovanists is to the Catholic center at Louvain, in Brabant, in the Spanish Netherlands. The Flemish form is Leuven. The University, established in 1423, was famous for its clergy, professors, and teaching.

at Geneva,[I] that with ignorance and rashnes, and disorderly proceedings, hee at the first dash made no scruple to receave all the whole state, even all the prophane ignorant people, into the bosome of the church, which you terme a confuse route, etc.

[I] Mr. Calvine might erre in the first gathering and erecting the church. This practise might be blamed as a pernicious example, yet neither therby Mr. Calvin or the church of Geneva be condemned as you would suggest. Seing first the church may be so pourged by their sincere preaching of the Worde and by the diligent watch and careful oversight of the ministers that have charge. If this be not doone, I can not excuse as until I know the contrary I wil not accuse them.

[A further note on this page is crossed out.][1]

Page 35. All the knowledge which you have is wholly from the writings, expositions, and translations of those whom[K] you terme owles, vultures, dogs, foxes, etc.

[K] You very maliciously slaunder us. We never so spake or thought of them. We thanckfully receive and use their christian laboures, yet are not therin so circumscribed as to receive what soever thei deliver, or not to proceed beyound that thei deliver. As God revealeth further or otherwise.

Page 36. If you have any true grammer sense of the psalmes . . . or of the rest of the Scriptures, which you have not from such owles and foxes, as Master Tremellious, Beza,[2] and other translators, we would be glad to know it. But remember what is said of some, that they are swelling waves of the sea,[L] foming out their owne shame.[3]

[1] Gifford sarcastically says: "Your sufferings are for Christ, so are theirs which lye bound in Bedlem." Barrow's reply, crossed out, is difficult reading, but is as follows: "This phrase so often used against us or [our?] Christian suffrinths who lie and die in yor miserable prisons where we are cast by this horned armed Clergy for withdrawing from this false worship, Antichristian Ministry, and government of these confuse assemblies. And for seaking the tru ministry and Government of Christ, with" [which?].

[2] The Greek and Latin translations of Theodore Beza (de Bèze) and Immanuel Tremellius were widely used. Beza's Latin New Testament appeared in 1560; his Greek New Testament in 1565. In 1580 appeared the first complete Latin Bible printed in England, translated by Immanuel Tremellius and Francis Junius. A second edition appeared in 1581, a third in 1585, which latter version contained both Tremellius' version and Beza's version of the New Testament.

[3] Jude 1:13.

[L] Whether you rather in all your writings have as those fierce waves of the sea fomed out your oun shame in all these slaunders, accusations, charges, blasphemies against our persons and soffrings for reproving your Romish merchandise and worship, etc., let the reader judge.

Page 36. I doo not know, Master Barrow, what your former conversation[M] hath been: but by your speeches a man would judge that you had spent your time, rather in the societies of carding and dicing,[1] than in the schoole of Christ, here therefore I conclude that with ignorance, falsehood and prophane impiety, ye accuse our worship to be blasphemous and idolatrous.

[M] My former lewd education and conversation had in your church is a bad argumente [to] justifie your church. And as I thincke will beare no such conclusions as you here infer. But this let the reader judge. As also what a worthie defence you have here made of your publicke worship and ministration in those points wherof I blamed it.

Page 37. In your preamble, Master Barrow, you doo but babble, and that upon your owne surmises, contrarie to my plaine words, and whether against your conscience looke you; for I doo not allow evill[N] ministers, nor their admitting of open notorious sinners unto the table of the Lord.

[N] Be the minister never so unworthie or ungodly the parish can not avoide him being presented or permitted by the bishop and your repelling notorious offendors is by your popish suspention; yet even those thus repelled you receive to communicate in your publik prayers and worship.

Page 37. Moreover, wee doo not at any hand allow your arguments, which are drawne from the principles[O] of Donatisme, as,

[1] One may well wonder if Gifford is telling the truth in disclaiming knowledge of Barrow's former life. Gifford's previous slur about Barrow's association with the bowling alley makes one suspicious. Barrow's sudden conversion from a dissolute life was well known in court circles. "He made a leap from a vain and libertine youth to a preciseness in the highest degree; the strangeness of which alteration made him very much spoken of." Francis Bacon, "Certain Observations Made upon a Libel Published This Present Year, 1592," in James Spedding, *The Letters and the Life of Francis Bacon*, I (London, 1861), 166; the manuscript sources are Harley MSS. 547 and 6854; see also Alexander Young's *Chronicles of the Pilgrim Fathers*, pp. 424–435.

namely, that wee must separate our selves where wee see any swarve from thier duety, and offend.

[O] These vituperies are drawen from the sincke of your oun corrupt heart, which can put no end or meashure to your slaunderous accusations. We have often shewed you that we hould no such principles. Neither this position wherof you stil accuse us.

Page 37. [Your argument about the second transgression said there was] no[P] power to cast forth any by excommunication.

[P] I doubted not but the heads of your church have that power of the beast which the pope left and used. But I denied and you can not prove that your church hath that power which Christ hath given to excommunicate.

Page 38. He that is excommunicated whether it be by some one assemblie[Q] which hath that power, or by the whole bodie of a church in a kingdom, is hee not cast forth?

[Q] The excommunication of one man. A popish archbishop or bishop his commissary or chancelor is no such.

Page 38. Why doo not you then, (if you will au[n]swere), proove[R] by the Worde of God, that every particular flock in a kingdome or region, is of necessitie for the being of a church to have this power whole and severall by it selfe.

[R] Though this were not harde to doo, yet is it not our question or here necessarie.

Page 38. I take it you shall never be able to proove that it ought to be, much lesse shall you be able to proove them to bee no[S] true churches, which have not in every severall congregation established the power of excommunication.

[S] A true church may at some time be without a ministerie, without the use (I say not now the power) of excommunication. We never denied this, which you to evade and to torne [turn] away the question, brought. But this we denied and you can never prove that the true constituted church may receive a false anti christian ministry or that such ministry may execute excommunication in the church of Christ.

Page 38. For if you had proved that the Church of England hath no[T] power to excommunicate. . . .

[T] Mr. Gyfford, it standes you upon to prove the

excommunication of your lord bishop and the true excommunication of Christ, elz all these evasions wil not helpe you.

Page 39. [In saying the Church of England is no true church because it includes the profane multitudes and ungodly] you doo here conclude[V] a new question.

[V] I here conclude the true question, which you before turned from the gathering and communion of your church, to the excommunication of your church.

There can be said no true constituted church where the people were never gathered unto orderly communion.

Page 40. [The queen compelleth all her subjects to renounce idolatry:] She receiveth not in nor compelleth Turkes, Jewes, or heathen, but onely such as are Christians by profession. And therefore you may see that if you will have your major proposition agree with the Scriptures, it must needes be taken more[W] largely than your minor.

[W] In al this you but cavil. My major is not by just construction to be understood more largely than my minor, both being understood of all the prophane of this land, where all the queen's native subjects are received, baptised in your church.

In the rest I commend her majestie's godly lawes and indevours for the repressing idollatrie. But this maketh the sinne of our prelats and priests the greater that so seduce and abuse her gracious inclination in setting up these reliques of idolatrie and poperie, these limmes and courtes and jurisdiction of Antichrist in her lande over her subjects. This is not like the reformation of the godly kings of Juda.

Page 41. [After reading Barrow's "extreame wordes" about baptizing the children of prophane men] a man would thinke . . . that the whole church were on fire, especially if I should repeate but the one halfe of your speeches, but that we know, Master Barrow, it is but your fashion: If it please God he may give you some spark of modestie.[X]

[X] Your modestie and christian meakness shineth forth in al your writings. I leave to the reader's judgment and censure those my writings. Wherein I justly charged you of falsifying the second commandment[1] and strowing [disseminating] most odious doctrine.

Page 41. You are out of the way, Master Barrow, and the faster you runne, the further: for you should remember that I spake of the seede of such prophane men as remayne[Y] in the church and professe Christ, and are sealed with the seale of the covenant.

[Y] You stil forget your selfe. These members of the church thus professing Christ, thus sealed with the seale of the covenant cannot be said prophane without high injurie and blasphemie. Therfore this excuse wil not helpe you.

Page 42. Will you make no difference[Z] betweene those which were or are without the church uncircumcised, or unbaptized, not professing the God of Abraham, or the faith of Christ, and those which were or be in the church, circumcized or baptized, professing the God of Abraham and the faith of Christ?

[Z] I can put difference betwixt the heathen never called and the apostate from the faith. And yet exclude both the one and the other and their seed from the church and sacraments as in their own right. And therfore for the receiving these apostate and their seed in your church as members you hi[g]hly abuse the second commandement.

Page 42. But . . . what hath the church to do with their children, which are not under her government and power to bring up? The church is to[A] take care that al those children may be instructed in the faith, and guided in the way of godlines, which she admitteth unto baptisme. For the places of Scripture, where I sayd that the covenant[B] with Abraham was made thus, I will be thy God, and the God of thy seede, and that to a thousand generations, Exodus 20. [see verse 6 and also Genesis 17:7, 8.][2]

[A] I never doubted but the servants and others within the charge of the faithful, the faithful so requiring, might be received to baptisme. But what is this to prove the general receiving of all in your church?

[1] Deuteronomy 5:8–9.

[2] Exodus 20:6 speaks of thousands, but not of a thousand generations. But Deuteronomy 7:9 substantiates Gifford here.

[B] The covenant and election of God remaineth firme to the endz of the world, neither can the sinns of the parents divert or frustrate his mercies to the children. But we reason not of God's secret election whom he may or will call, but of the outward covenant wherin he hath called, and who may be judged within that outward covenant of us. And here I would know of you whether you esteam the state and nation of the Jues generally at the times of Acts 3 and Romans 9 the true church within the outward covenant. And that baptisme the seale therof was to be given to al Jues generally and their seed or to the faithful only.

Page 42. Or how could Saint Paule say, that theirs was the adoption and the covenant? If none were outwardly to stand under the covenant but[C] the elect, how should this have been spoken?

[C] It was never thought much less spoken by me that none but the elect stand outwardly under the covenant. These things you but forge[1] (according to your custome) to torne away the tru question which is whether these profane, ignorant, ungodly multitudes may of us be esteamed members of the church and have the sacraments administred to them and their seed in this estate as with you. This I have proved to you, Mr. Gifford, to be most high and wilful sacrilege, and I have fullie aunswered all such proves [proofs] and places as you brought to justifie your church herein.

Page 43. Thus it is your pleasure (Master Barrow) even in your deepe ignorance, and that in the grounds of religion[D], to impugne the stablenes of God's covenant made unto his people.

[D] I am we[a]ry with inculking [inculcating, repeating] the question which you so flee. It is not of the stability of God's covenant according to his election. But whether these prophane multitudes may of us be esteamed as members of the church and within the outward covenant in this estate. Therfore all this railing might be spared.

Page 43. Hereupon it followeth, that as God is become their God,

[1] Either a word of two letters or an erasure follows, or possibly "to."

so they are become his people, and this is required on our part. But now to inferre upon this, that the stablenes[E] of God's covenant dependeth upon this condition, if we keepe his commandements . . . . is most wicked.

[E] You have been often blamed for these cavils and unconscionable surmises in my former [writing],[1] yet without all shame you stil continue and renue them![2] Because I hould that only such as have made profession of the faith and continue in the same faith and obedience are of us to be esteamed within the outward covenant. Therfore doo I heareupon make the stablenes of God's covenant to depend upon our righteousnes. Let the reader judge what faire inferences you make. And how worthely you refute your oun counceits.

Page 44. Alas, Master Barrow, would[F] any man looke for such matter at their hands that had but even read over the Byble? [Barrow had quoted Deuteronomy 32:19, Micah 2:7–9, Amos 8:2, and Ezekiel 16].

[F] You shew your self ether a most unconscionable or ignorant adversarie. I brought not those Scriptures to prove that in the defection thei were not the Lord's people. But to aunswere a most fond reason brought by you from Ezechiel 16:21, where the children of the idolators were called the Lord's sonnz, etc. Therfore all in that estate within the covenant. By these places I expounded that phrase, and further aunswered your reasons.

Page 44. To say that they forfeited the covenant[G] by transgressing his commandements, and recovered it agayne by repentance, and so to be now out, now in, is (that I may say no worse) most foolishly spoken.

[G] Whilest you wil needs reason of God's eternal covenant and I of the outward covenant we shal never agree. Methinckes you should not denie that obstinasie joyned unto sin or error deserveth excommunication. And excommunication seperateth from the outward covenant until publike repentanse be

[1] *A Plaine Refutation.*

[2] The exclamation mark seems out of place, but it is clear. I wonder whether it is a slip of the pen.

made, etc. Although the counsel of God stand suer: yet our judgments may varie as grace or sinne is found in us to prevaile.

Page 44. You[H] will say, that God's covenant was to the elect among them, but the rest were not under the covenant, nor the visible church.

[H] You make me saie what you list. And so but conflict with your oun phantasies. I never doubted but many reprobate should enter the church here. But even those under the visard [mask, countenance] of the common faith and obedience which when thei openly decline from, etc., thei then cease to be members of the visible church so far as we may judge.

Page 44. And for this cause although the great swarme of the Israelites were wicked reprobates, and (as the prophet sayth) but a remnant saved, yet for their outward profession the whole nation was ever[I] sayd to stand under the covenant.

[I] If those wicked infidels that rejected Christ were then of us to be esteamed the visible church, then make you a visible church without Christ the foundation and head corner stone. Then make you members of the church which are not Christians by profession and what not. Be ashamed therfore and cease thus to pervert the Scriptures.

Page 45. And therefore when the bodie of that people should stand no longer under the covenant, to be the visible church, but (as our Saviour sayth) the kingdome[K] of God should be taken from them. Mathew 21: [verse 43].

[K] If you graunt the kingdome of God to be taken from the Jues after thei had murthered the Sonn and Heire, how then wil you reconcile that saying of Peter, Acts 3:25, "yee are the children of the prophets and of the covenant"? How then wil you avoide [the inference] that open rebellion disanulleth the outward covenant, yea, or your own most fond conclusion to make the stablenes of God's covenant to depend of men's righteousnes.

Page 45. The tenne tribes[L] which fell from the house of David, and worshipped idols, were yet in some sort even the whole bodie of them under the covenant, and were so farre the visible church:

[L] A strange position.

Page 45. For when Benhadab[M] [the king of Syria] made warre agaynst Achab.[1]

[M] Stoute reasons to prove it.

Page 45. Now, for the places which[N] you alleage that they became not his people, you doo but pervert them.

[N] Or you rather without conscience abuse my writings. I brought them to shew the follie of your reason drawen from Ezekiel 16:21, where because God calleth the children of the idollators offred to Moloch his sonnes, etc., therfore you would conclude all those idolators in that estate the visible church. Like to your former reasons from I Kings 20 and II Kings 1, which how ridiculous thei are, let the simplest reader judge. And how wel you expound and apply Scriptures.

Page 46. You would have me shewe some place in the Scriptures where God maketh his covenant without this condition, that they shall bee his people and obey him.

That is not the question[O], Master Barrow, but this, whether, when men breake covenant and promise with God by disobeying him, whose covenant yet they chalenge, his covenant be broken and abrogated towards them?

[O] Though great question might be made of the orderly gathering of those parishes at any time into true constitution, yet I hould that open idolatrie, obstinasie, rebellion, doth disanul the outward covenant so far as we may judge. Neither is our question of the stability of God's election and covenant. But whether we may judge such as never came to the faith or such as are fallen from the faith within the outward covenant. Now albeit God in the greatest defection and sinne of men remembreth his mercy and covenant both in the worst times to save some, and in his good time to renue his ordinances and to repaire his church; yet this maketh nothing that the general state and people in publike apostasie and idolatrie is stil of us to be estemed as the true church within the outward covenant. This you have

[1] I Kings 16:29–22:40. Ahab was king of Israel from 874/873 to 853. See Edwin R. Thiele, *The Mysterious Numbers of the Hebrew Kings*, pp. 61, 62, 189.

been often aunswered if truth or reason might take place with you. Neither is it a nue thing in the Scriptures to shew by such sinne the breake [broken] covenant on their parte with God. As psalm 78:10, speaking of the kingdom of Israel in their schisme, thei have not kept the covenant of their God, thei denied to walke in his lawe. And verse 37. Neither was their heart prepared with him, neither remained thei in his covenant, with sondrie places in the Deutronomie, and in the prophets.

Page 47. Cease therefore, Master Barrow, to hang the stablenes of God's covenant[P] upon the obedience of man.

[P] Neither can the infidelity of the Jues at this day make the truth of God of none effect but that he wil performe his promes [promise] also to them. That al Israel might be saved as it is written.[1] Therfore now also by Mr. Gifford's reason thei are of us to be estemed the visible church.

Page 48. I pray you, Mr. Barrow, is not the outward washing the whole baptisme, and the whole[Q] seale of God's covenant?

[Q] No, Mr. Gifford, such outward baptism or circumcision is not a seale of God's covenant unto them in that estate but a fearful prophanation of God's name and ordinance.

Page 48. But you say, "it is no true seale unto them in their apostasie, or it doth not seale God's covenant unto them in that estate, but[R] when the abuse therof is purged away by true repentance." What absurde speeches be these? Can a man devise more[S] grosse folly?

[R] "But when," etc., is a forged addition of your own.[2] We never held your or the popish baptism a true sacrament by repentance. Though we dout not but the sinne committed therin is pardoned to the penitent.

[S] Yea, rather you shew your self absurd, etc., that can not put difference betwix the sacraments rightly delivered in the tru church unto those hypochrites and those adulterate sacraments so corruptly

[1] Romans 11:26.

[2] Barrow seems falsely to accuse Gifford here. See Barrow's words in *A Plaine Refutation*, p. [64]. See Carlson, *The Writings of Henry Barrow, 1590–1591*, p. 125.

adminstred in the false church to open idolators, prophane, etc.

Page 48. [If a man void of faith receive baptism from those who mix it with corruptions,] and after commeth unto true faith, he himselfe is purged by his fayth, and hath the use of that seale which hee had before, but without fruite, we cannot say as you doo, but with most wicked and foule absurditie, that the sacrament it selfe was a false sacrament, and now through fayth is purged and become[T] a true sacrament. That which is the Lord's doth stand in it selfe pure and undefiled[V], even when corruptions be added.

[T] You make no conscience to falsifie our wordz. You are never able to shew that we hould that popish adulterate baptism made a true sacrament by faith and repentance.

[V] This is strange doctrine to be published in these daies. In the pap[ists' or papistical] blasphemous sacrament of the altare there are some partes of a true sacrament. Shal these justifie the rest to make the whole or any part of that execrable action good? What chaffie [worthless matter] and rustie doctrine is this, Mr. Gyfford?

Page 49. And when you say that concerning the outward washing it is true baptisme ministred in popery, which is as much as I have shewed, as to say it is a true sacrament concerning the whole (because the outward washing is the whole, and therefore all that John[W] the Baptist taketh to himselfe is this, "I baptize ye with water").

[W] [1.] John Baptist was a lawful minister. [2.] He delivered to faithful receivers. 3. According to the institution of the Holy Ghost. These things must neads outwardly concur unto a true sacrament. None of these are found with you or in the papistry. Therfore your baptism can be no true sacrament, your parting can not patch out your ministry or sacraments. Yet if you were not to[o] far caried in malice and self wil you mought [might] by the Scriptures cited be taught to put difference betwixt a true sacrament and a false; betwixt a false and no sacrament. And so unlose this knot.

Page 50. The Romish Antichrist usurped an unjust power and tyrannie, and brought in many most wicked abominations, cannot the churches[X] cast him foorth, with his inventions, but they commit[Y] schisme?

[X] You can make no such distinction and seperation betwixt the true ordinances of Christ and the antichristian corruption in the Romish synagogz.

[Y] If the church of Rome be a true constituted church, having the true ministrie and seales of the covenant, as you confes, then can you upon no pretext seperat from it but with open . . .[1]

Page 51. Can any thing be more frivolous? Are all severall kingdomes tied unto Rome, or shall we be tied to joyne where there be some remnants of a church, with idolatrie? And concerning the rest, your self do in effect now[Z] confesse, that some part of Christ's ministry remaineth in the popery, when you say that their baptisme concerning the outward washing, is true baptisme. And moreover what should be, we dispute not, but this proveth that the true seale[A] of God's covenant is given to open idolaters. For the seale is the same in it selfe, but the idolater hath not the fruite of it, untill he come to true faith. And so your next absurdities fall off themselves, seeing the having of the true seale (that is the outward washing in baptisme) dooth not make the papists true Christians, nor prove that God's[B] covenant of peace and love, dooth belong to the Romish harlot.

[Z] I never confessed but alwaies utterly denied any true ministrie of Christ to be in the popery. Nether have I learned but of such teachers as you to make one and the same ministry true in parte and false in an other parte.

[A] [1.] The popish baptism can not be a true seale for that thei have not a true ministrie to deliver it. 2. A faithful people by outward profession to receive it. 3. The pure element injoyned. 4. Nor yet the maner of administration instituted.

[B] The true seale can not be set but to the true covenant. Neither can it be set to by any but the true ministry of Christ. Or in any other place than in the true

[1] Last line at foot of page is cropped.

constituted church of Christ. In allowing therfore baptism in popery a true sacrament, you make the popish sacrificing priests true ministers of Christ; the whore of Rome the true constituted church, the spouse of Christ; those open idolators, baptised true Christians by outward confession.

Page 51. Why, Master Barrow, you wil not deny but that to[C] the elect in the church of Rome Christ is the head.

[C] We speake not of God's secret elect in the church of Rome but of the outward estate of the church of Rome.

Page 51. And so touching the holy sacrament of baptisme in the church of Rome, and so much of the truth as remaineth, Christ is the author of them,[D] and so standeth the head of his own, he is not the head of the apostasie, or to the wicked inventions.

[D] Christ no doubt doth never forsake or denie his own ordinanse. But now our question is whether the publike constitution of the church of Rome in the people, ministrie, ministration, worship, government, etc., be according to the ordinanse of Christ or of Antichrist, you barely affirme. We denie with reason, shewing cause in every perticuler and even in this baptism whie it is not true and according to the ordinans of Christ.

Page 51. And if the papists have quite[E] overth[r]own the one sacrament.

[E] I never heard before that to one and the same covenant might be joyned one true authentike blessed seale and an other forced blasphemous execrable seale, in one and the same church, by one and the same ministry, etc. This divinity I confes passeth my understanding.

Page 52. Hereupon it falleth out in question[F], whether the church of Rome were the visible church of Christ in time of idolatry.

[F] This visible church must neadz be understood of a church constitute for that thei have a communian [*sic*], ministrie, sacraments, government. These whether christian or anti christian is the question.

Page 52. Who be those learned divines, that when they say the church is in the papacy, but the papacy is not the church, doo meane no more but that there be God's elect, as in other places of the world? If you have any modesty, bring forth some one[G] learned devine which is of that judgement.

[G] Bring you rather forth one learned man that by so[u]nd reason is able to approve the constitution of the church of Rome, in the people, ministrie, ministration of the Word and sacraments, worship, faith, government, as you must doo if you wil have it judged of us a true constituted church in time of publike idolatrie.

Page 52. By the church we may not understand only God's elect, but also so[H] much of God's ordinances as remaine, not only in the points of doctrine . . . but also in the holy baptisme.

[H] But how far this antichristian tyrannie and apostasie hath invaded and corrupted to the expelling and adulterating all the ordinances of God, the bringing in and erecting their oun devises in steed therof in the publike ministry, ministration, government, etc., let the wise examine and judge.

Page 53. [Saith Master Calvine:] Such therefore is the certainty and constancy of God's goodnes, that there remained the covenant of the Lord, neither could his faith given, be made voyde by their unfaithfulnes,[I] neither could circumcision be so prophaned by their impure hands, but that it was still the true signe and sacrament of his covenant. Whereupon the Lord called the children which were borne unto them, his sonnes, Ezechiel 16:[20], which nothing at all perteined unto him, but by a speciall blessing. So when he hath left his[K] covenant in France, Italie, Germany, Spayne, England; since these provinces have beene oppressed with the tyrannie of Antichrist, yet that his covenant might remaine inviolable, he first there preserved baptisme,[L] the testimony of his covenant, which being consecrate with his owne mouth, retaineth her owne force, notwithstanding the ungodlines of man: then furthermore he hath by his providence brought to passe, that there should other remnants also remaine, least the church[M] should utterly perish.[1]

[1] The entire quotation is from John Calvin, *Institutes of the Christian Religion*, translated by Henry Beveridge (London, 1949), Book IV, Chapter II, Section

[I] Circumscision in it selfe and so baptism are the true seales of God's covenant. But yt [that] in this estate thei either belong or seale God's favour can not be proved. And then the prophaning them shal rather increase their sin than any way justify or better their outward estate.

[K] How can the Lord's covenant be said left in these contries when thei have so openly forsaken and fallen from the faith?

[L] Can baptism (admitted as good as you suppose it in the outward administration) either bring or seale God's covenant, to such open idolators in that apostate estate?

[M] The church was rather reserved according to God's secret election by the worck of his grace than outwardly appearing in the state of those times.

Page 54. [Calvin] That his [Antichrist's] seate is placed in the temple of God, thereby is meant that his kingdome shall be such, as may abolish neither[N] the name of Christ nor of the church.[1]

[N] But should falsely chaleng to them the name of Christ and of the church.

Page 54. [Calvin] Furthermore in which all things are so confused and out of order, that there appeareth the face[O] of Babylon, rather than of the holie citie of God.[2]

[O] So the church of Rome is called by the Holy Ghost and condemned as that great whore, etc. Now then how she may be judged and saluted of us in this estate as the spouse of Christ without manifest contradiction of the Holy Ghost?

Page 54. [Calvin] Briefelie, I say they be churches, in as much as the Lord dooth there merveilouslie preserve the remnants of his people, howsoever miserably dispersed and scatred: and in as much as there remaine some[P] badges or seales of the church, and these especially, whose efficacy neither the craft of the divell,[Q] nor the wickednes of men, can destroy: but on the other side, because those notes or markes are blotted out, which wee ought chiefely to

11, page 313. Gifford follows closely, but not exactly, the translation of Thomas Norton. I checked the English editions of 1561, 1562, 1578, 1582, and 1587.
[1] *Ibid.*, p. 314. [2] *Ibid.*, p. 314.

respect in this controversie, I say that everie one of their assemblies, and the whole bodie wanteth the lawfull[R] forme of a church.[1]

[P] Their baptism for the reasons above shewed is denied.

[Q] But if baptism and that so hiely prophaned and adulterate be of this vertue to make a true church to seale God's covenant to that idolatrous estate where all other thingz are confessed so out of order, surely it hath a rare vertue and doth more than seale, yea, even confer grace and that to open idolators. This is strange doctrine and agreeth not to Mr. Calvine's sincerity in other things, or to his oun writings elswhere.

[R] How then can it be judged of us a true constituted church? Thus to conclude he maketh it no church to our judgments.

Page 55. Thus farre be Master Calvine's words: tell me now, Master Barrow, is Master Calvine to be accounted among the learned divines? Dooth he say the church is[S] in the papacy, that is no more but that the elect are among them, as in other places of the world?

[S] Mr. Gifford, I did not denie but Mr. Calvin and sondrie others were of this judgment. Therfore you might have made your booke lesse and spared this laboure. I only insisted of your oun wordes that thought it not inough with these learned to hould the church in the papasie. But you to be singuler wil needz hould the papasie to be in the church. How true either of these opinions are let the reader examine and judge.

Page 56. A worthie collection is it not? Because God in righteous judgement for the punishment of those that received not the love of the trueth, giveth power unto Satan and Antichrist to seduce the multitude in the visible church, Christ is not heire of all things, nor raigneth as k[ing][T] upon Mount Sion.

[T] Christ and Antichrist can not both reign in one church at one time. Neither the church at one time beare the yoke of both. But we see Antichrist to have reigned, etc. Therfore this consequens must needz

[1] *Ibid.*, p. 314.

follow. You knew our controversy was not of the triumphant church. Therin therfore you vainly cavil. Sathan also and Antichrist shal reign in the world, but not in the true visible church of Christ. Therfore you bring this as vainly.

Page 56. The next [blasphemy] is: "If Antichrist sit in the church, then Christ is either cast out of his house [or] made subject unto Antichrist, or els devideth with him."[1] Christ is not[V] cast out of his house nor made subject, (these be most frivolous and fantasticall imaginations), but in his most high and soveraigne power he useth Antichrist and Satan as the instruments of his wrath.

[V] If Christ be in that church where Antichrist reigneth, then he must either devide the empire with him or be subject to Antichrist. But neither of these, in Christe's visible constitute churches. Therfore if it be the tru visible church where Antichrist reigneth, the third must needs follow that Christ is cast out. Your evation of the omnipotent power of Christ to use Sathan Antichrist to afflict and destroy his church to seduse the reprobate wil not helpe you to prove that Antechrist shal reigne in the true church of God. For then you might also conclude Antiochus,[2] the Syrian, Assirian, Babylonian, and Persian kingz within the church because God hath used them to destroy his church and afflict his people.

Page 57. He [Antichrist] exerciseth a savage tyrannie,[W] and oppresseth the elect whome yet he cannot bring into his subjection, to make them hang their faith upon him, or his lawes. For God did miraculously preserve a remnant in the poperie, which were not utterly poysoned.

[W] This distinction in this place is vaine. We reason not whether Sathan and his instruments may outwardly oppresse and persecute the whole church; or whether thei may seduce and withdraw some members of the

[1] *A Plaine Refutation*, p. [65]. In Carlson, *op. cit.*, p. 127.

[2] Antiochus IV, Epiphanes (175–163 B.C.). See I Maccabees, Chapter 1. He claimed divine honours as given to Alexander the Great; he pushed the process of hellenization; and he desecrated the Temple of Jerusalem, as Pompey did in 63 B.C. See E. Badian, "Antiochus Epiphanes and the Rebirth of Judea", *History Today*, IX, no. 6 (June, 1959), pp. 415–423. See also *Cambridge Ancient History*, VIII (1930), ch. XVI, 495–518.

true church. But whether the true may beare his yoke, *viz.*, receive his ministry, leitourgie, ordinances, government. And yet of us be held the true established church of Christ.

Page 57. This is fully answered in the former: for his tyrannie and usurpation dooth not make him head[X], but unto those whose head Christ is not, more than by hypocriticall profession of his name.

[X] The whole church receiveth his false ministrie, lawes, ordinances for their ministration, government, procedings.

Page 57. This is also most frivolous: for as Antichrist did almost destroy all, but yet not all, in other things[Y], so in thc ministrie:

[Y] The ministry is wholly antichristian and forged eaven from the pope's person to the lowest parish priest or somner [summoner].[1] Now let the reader judge whether the true constituted church of Christ may receive such a false and antichristian ministry.

Page 58. [Though some of the elect have strayed,] yet their salvation being onely through faith, it cannot be sayd that they were[Z] built upon any other foundation than that which the prophets and Apostles have layd.

[Z] In this stil you but cavil to evade. We reason not whether the Lord's elect in the church of Rome be built upon Antichrist. But whether the publike state and outward constitution of the church of Rome be built upon Antichrist and his lawes. Which seing it can not be denied, the question is whether in this estate it may be estemed the true constituted church of Christ. If you stil aunswere affirmatively, then must this inconvenience which you labour to avoide necessarily follow.

Page 58. The covenant of God[A] is founded upon free grace.

[A] I must stil repete that we reason not of the stability of the covenant on God's parte. But who of us may be judged within that covenant. And how longe we may so judge of them.

Page 58. The Lord would not (even because of his covenant) suffer

[1] A summoner was a petty officer who cited persons to appear in court, *e.g.*, a bishop's summoner or a sheriff's summoner.

the devill and Antichrist utterly to deface his temple: but preserved the holy seede, preserved some of his ordinances, yea, so farre, that in some sorte the covenant was not disanulled to the very reprobate,[B] but that outwardly they stoode under it in their apostasie.

[B] This is strange divinity that we may judge the same men at the same time both under open apostasie and outwardly under the covenant of God. No mervaile if by the same reason you make the Jues at this present also the visible church. Seing the promes [promise] of God can not be made of none effect by the infidelity of men.

Page 59. The prophets complayned that the great multitude both of Juda[C] and the ten tribes were rebels, and that the Lord had but a remnant among them.

[C] Mr. Gyfford, whom we judge members of the church, them we judge members of Christ purged, justified, saved, etc. This you can neither deny nor aunswer. Your cavil of the ten tribes and the state of the Jues in Christe's time is nothing to this purpose, and [serves] but to torne [turn] away the present question after your custome.

Page 59. Whereas I sayd that the apostasie[D] is in the church but not the church: you think it strange repugnancie. Yet indeed there is none, as may appeare by that which I have set down before, and should appeare unto you, if your minde were not so deepely infected with the principles of Donatisme.

[D] You blaspheme not me so much as the pretious faith of Christ to call it a principle of Donatism that no congregation or person ought to be esteamed a tru church or member of Christ when thei are fallen from the true faith of Christ.

Page 59. To your other question I answere, that it is no[E] schisme to depart from the church of Rome, although in some respects they were the visible church.[1]

[E] Whilest you hould the church of Rome a true visible church you can never excuse your selves of schisme and to make a greavous rent in the body of Christ. The church of Christ is not to be left for corruptions,

[1] *A Plaine Refutation*, p. [66]. Carlson, *op. cit.*, p. 128.

etc. If you say you seperat from the corruptions but not from the church, why may not we pretend the same and finde like favour? But whilest you condemn not so mutch the corruptions as the church of Rome it selfe, retaining stil the same Antich[rist or anti-christian] ministry, courtes, cannons, procedings, ministration, worship in the most parte with the pope exercised and left in these parishes. Al which we condemn and forsake as antichristian. Let the christian reader judge whether you or we savour more of Donastistry.

Page 60. The ten tribes remaynedstill in some force the visible church, and under the covenant. . . . but yet they were not such a[F] true church as men might joyne withall in their worship.

[F] I never read of such a true church to which no faithful Christian might joyne in their publike worship. These are strange positions, Mr. Gyfford.

Page 60. Then you come to expound how this may bee taken that Antichrist shal sit in the temple of God. And first as you take it[G] his sitting in the temple of God, may be understood as in regarde that he tooke his originall before he was revealed.

[G] But the Apostle John, I Epistle, *caput* 2:19, saith: Thei went out from us, etc. And Apocalypse[1] 9:1, it is said Antichrist should be a fallen star, an apostata from the true church. Therfore this may be understood in respect of his original.

Page 60. Matthew 24:29. Revelation 6:14.[H] See what two places Master Barrow hath found to prove Antichrist should utterly destroy the visible church.

[H] In the first place Matthew 24, Mr. Gifford, seing you wil needz have it understood literally and of Christe's comming, I would first know of you whether you thincke it possible for so many starres of sutch incomparable greatnes more than the earth or than the soon [sun] it selfe should fall upon the earth which in respect of them is but as a pricke or circle of the centre. Then if these higher or greater stars should thus fall how the soon [sun], mone [moon], aire should abide. Thirdly, how men in these fraile

[1] Revelation 9:1.

bodies should live after all these thingz. Call your wits and university learning abought you and aunswer these thingz. But against your folly and error herein I oppose against you both the adverb of time our savior useth eutheōs, immediatly, etc. And the Apostle Peter's judgment, Epistle II, *caput* 3, as also Genesis 8:22, where it is said that both the heavens and the earth shal remaine in their order until the end of the world, etc. At which instant thei shal all together passe away, melt, and be bornt up. And in that instant our savior come in judgment. II Thessalonians 1:7, 8; and I Thessalonians 4:16, I Corinthians 15:52. The place also Revelation 6:14, wher he speaketh of an earthquake, the darkening of the soon [sun], the torning the mone [moon] to blood, the ronning of earthly men into denns and rockes, shew that it can not be understood literally or of that last comming of Christ. It must needz therfore have an allegorical and spiritual interpretation. Wherfore if any man can justly blame mine or shew a better I wil gladly yeald unto the best.

Page 61. You will not have this place expounded literally,[I] and then what shall we make of it, or howe shall we finde Antichrist?

[I] Mr. Giffard, whilest you wil understand these words literally you wil make either a very blaspheamous sens, or elz more for the pope than I doo. For you know these wordes "Elohim"[1] and "theos" are not properly given to mortal men, but allegorically. Nor yet to all men but only to the civile and soffereign magistrate or judge. So that in the proper sens you can not understand this word "theos" of Antichrist without blasphemy. Nor yet in your allegorical sens but you must greatly befrend the pope and your supreme lord archbishop, who both of them though thei exercise civile authority yet wil not be estemed temporal lords or magistrats. And so by your exposition the pope can not be Antichrist. Again this

[1] Elohim is written in Hebrew consonants and points. Both Barrow and Greenwood use Hebrew words, but their knowledge of Hebrew does not seem equal to that of Greek.

exaltation and apostasie is rather of things ecclesiastical than temporal, rather a spiritual than civile defection, as you construe.

Page 61. The thing which deceiveth you, Master Barrow, is in the word, shewing,[K] for every thing that a shew is made of, is not so in truth.

[K] You know that "apodeiknunta"[1] is to demonstrat or prove by certain arguments, "oti esti theos".[2] So that now, Mr. Gyffard, if you make him God but in shew you wil not understand these words literally as erwhile.

Page 61. And as Josias and other godly kings of Juda by terrour of punishment drave idolaters which outwardly stood under the covenant, being cyrcumcised, from false worship unto the lawes of God:[3] so Queene[L] Elizabeth hath done with her subjects being baptized, and thereby bound to renounce false worship, and to imbrace the holy doctrine of the covenant.

[L] How wel you prelats and priestes have rered the decaied tabernacle of David or pourged it of idolatrie and popish enormities, let the present constitution, administration, and government of your church compared to the rules of God's Word shew to your faces. That you herein call not the name of our sovereign Queen into question.

Page 62. I see you can make your mach [match, counterpart] wisely, Master Barrow, I must make evident[M] demonstration by the Scriptures: of what? Of that which was not mentioned by the Scriptures.

[M] You were there willed to approve by the Scriptures the publike constitution, administration, worship, government, ordinances of your Church of England or elz to shew some time when ever thei were publikly erect in the perticuler congregations of this land. This I tould you if you could not doo you could nether prove the state past nor present to be a true constituted church. So that these two cavils rather shew your captiousnes than your sufficiensie to performe that you undertoke.

[1] Showing, demonstrating. See II Thessalonians 2:4.

[2] That he is God. [3] II Chronicles 34:1–7, 29–33.

Page 62. If the planters of the fayth and discipline of Christ in England did erre it [in] some things (which yet you know not), how can you tell but that they did it in simplicitie?[1]

Page 63. I have shewed that popery did not utterly destroy the visible church. And there be at this day multitudes that so walke in the holy fayth, that no man is able to accuse them. And therfore if either all, or the most part of schismatikes were not obstinate cavillers,[N] their mouthes might be stopped for ever.

[N] It was firmly proved to you that though it were admitted that the Church of England toke not her being of a church from the church of Rome, yet she might take her not being a church from the whore of Rome whilest she received or reteineth her antichristian ministry, ministration, government, courts, cannons, etc. And so to seperate from this antichristian constitution and estate is no schisme to the stopping your blasphemous mouth.

Page 63. Let the reader here consider (Master Barrow) what a worthie champion you[O] are become for the papists, for heretickes and schismaticks, agaynst all the churches which professe the gospell, and agaynst all their teachers.

[O] Or rather, Mr. Gyfford, let the reader judge what a worthy champion you are become for this popish hierarchie, worship, etc., against al the godly.

Page 64. What is or what hath the church of Geneva been,[P] and together with the assemblies of England, all churches in Europe, but heapes of prophane multitudes, no better than heathen or dogs, if your words be true? True Christ they have none, for they fit not his government,[Q] nor his government them (as you say).

[P] These are the graceles collections of your malicious minde.

[Q] Their [there] might be faltes in their government, and yet not to be antichristian as yours is.

Page 64. [As these churches have been able to defend themselves] agaynst the wisest and learnedst reviling Rabsakaes [Rabshakehs], the hereticks and schismaticks; so must you thinke that they shall be able to withstand two or three which are so ignorant[R] in some grounds of religion, as

[1] There is no letter reference, but in the margin is the word "futilitie."

that their bookes are a bundle, or rather a dunghill of absurdities.

[R] Out of the aboundance of your heart your mouth speaketh. Our ignorance excuseth not the donghil of your corruptions wherof you are a minister and defender. For the bundle of errors and absurdities in our writings, when you shal with more truth and judgment shew and convince them, thei shal be acknowledged.

Page 64. Well, then, to conclude this poynt, he that will finde a true church with which he may joyne himselfe, he must not seeke it in the publike assemblies either in England, Scotland, Geneva, or any region of Europe, (for by your judgement they be[S] all prophane heapes) but he must seeke the fellowship, and joyne with the Donatists of England.

[S] Or elz by your slaunder.

Page 64. Now to the second part of the assumption, where you say, that the Church of England hath power to cast foorth none by excommunication.[T]

[T] You confessed the excommunication of your bishops not to be in the power of Christ. I then concluded that it was the power of Sathan and Antichrist. And so no true church.

Page 65. Doo you hold that a man which doth repent him for his adulterie, theft, heresie, or such like, and is cast downe in sorrowe, is yet to be delivered up to Satan? If not, why doo you upbrayd,[V] that there is none cast foorth among us, but for contumacie?

[V] I said not that any with you were excommunicated for obstinacie joyned to sinne or error but only for contempt of your popish courtes. Not paying those ravenors their fees, mulcts [fines], etc.

Page 69. [*sic*, 66] With what face can you say then (Master Barrow) that the bishops and[W] the pope depend upon one line, and build their preheminence upon that promise made unto Peter?

[W] The pope you confesse so buildeth and chaleng[e]th. The bishops derived their powr from the pope, and execute excommunication in your sole name as the pope doth, by a Latine writte, etc. Now let any judge whether thei may be said to depend upon one line. Neither is the excommunication of the bishop al one like in any thing to that of the eldership.

Page 69. [*sic*, 66] This consistorie (say they) is to have and to exercise that power and jurisdiction which[X] the bishops do hold.

[X] You slander the consistory. Thei never alowed of, mutch les chalenged, that antichristian power and jurisdiction which the bishops doo hould.

Page 69. [*sic*, 66] Now (Master Barrow) as you say, the government thus by the bishops is popish, so you grievously[Y] condemne the consistorie: affirming that it is irregular, that it hath no ground or warrant in God's word, but utterly subverteth all order, and openeth a wide gap unto all licentiousnes, etc.

[Y] I condemn not the consistorie, but blame it, setting down my reasons in this poinct.

Page 69. [*sic*, 66] Then come the fourth sort which expound these words ("tell the church")[1] wrong. And those are they which say "tel the church," is tell the congregation of people without the elders. Here you shew some skill also to confute: which is but to fight with your owne shadow, for this fourth sort (I thinke)[Z] have never been heard of, but among your selves.

[Z] It seameth you never read the booke of the *Confirmation of the Ecclesiastical Discipline* used in the Reformed churches in France.[2] As also Dan . . .[3] etc.

Page 67. For if it be true which you say, that the greatest minister hath[A] no more power to bind or loose the sinnes of the least member, than the said member hath to bind or loose his. Or if Christ speake to all, even to the wemen, John 20, "whose sinnes ye forgive, they are forgiven," etc. If the Word have no more efficacie to worke faith delivered[B] by the ministrie, or the sacrament to seale the promises have

[1] This famous phrase (*Dic ecclesiae*) is from Matthew 18:17. It was used frequently as a proof-text to denounce episcopacy, because Christ did not say, "tell it to the bishop," or "tell it to the chancellor or vicar-general" but to the congregation assembled—the church.

[2] Antoine La Roche de Chandieu, *La confirmation de la discipline ecclésiastique, observée ès églises reformées du royaume de France. Avec la response aux obiections proposées alencontre* [Geneva?, 1566].

[3] The end of the word is not clear, but Lambert Daneau (or Danaeus) is intended. See his book, *The Judgement of That Reverend and Godly Lerned Man, M. Lambert Danaeus, Touching Certaine Points Now in Controversie* [Edinburgh?, 1590?], signature A3 *verso*–B4 *verso*.

no more power delivered by a minister, than when the same word is uttered, and those sacraments delivered by any man or by any woman, or if every young man, yea, every maide (which is of the assembly) have equall power with any to excommunicate, we would see wherein the power of any of your officers consisteth: where all or every one have equall[C] power, there all are officers; where all are officers, we may say that in deed none are publick officers. This is Master Barrow's heavenly patterne, by which he hath convinced all our churches, and found them so obstinate for rejecting it, that they be quite separate from Christ. Master Barrow will say he spake not of the sacraments,[D] for he saith a minister onely is to deliver them.

[A] This is true understood of perticuler offences betwixt the pastor and the other members.

[B] Al have not the gift or calling to administer the Word and sacraments. But you must prove that only the ministers have power to reprove and censure sinne. Else you reason vainly.

[C] Equal power and interest in the judgment pronounced though not like power, ability, or calling to pronounce excommunication.

[D] You shew smal learning thus to confound sacraments and censures. If you reason that because the one wholy belongeth to ministers, therfore the other. The consequent is denied.

Page 67. The power of discipline exercised by the presbytery, as it is in the churches of France, Scotland, Geneva, the Low Countries, etc., you most grievously condemne: [saying]—"These men in stead of this grosse antichristian governement, etc., would bring in a new adulterate forged governement in shew, or rather in despite of Christ's blessed governement,[E] which they in their pride, rashnes, ignorance, and sensualitie of their fleshly hearts, most miserably, innovate, corrupt and pervert, etc."[1]

[E] This was not written of those foreign churches as you accuse but of the Reformist sect of your ministry. Their privie classes,[2] synodes and procedings.

[1] *A Brief Discoverie of the False Church*, pp. 189–190. In Barrow's work, there is no comma after "miserably."

[2] The secret classis movement flourished in the 1580s. See Edna Bibby's Manchester University thesis, "The Puritan Classical Movement of Elizabeth's

Page 68. Also (you say) that "many were the reasons, and more the inconveniences that might bee alleaged against this presumptuous[F] irregular consistorie, which hath no ground in the Word of God, but utterly subverteth, destroyeth and corrupteth the whole order and communion of the churches."[1]

[F] This may be sayd of this error in their practise without sutch condemning of your church, ministry, government, as you exclame of.

Page 68. In other places where the governement is by presbyteries, not onely the people (by your sentence) are prophane multitudes, but[G] their ministers proud, rash, ignorant, and in the sensuality of their fleshly hearts, have corrupted Christe's governement, and in despite thereof have set up a divelish forgery, and open the gap unto all prophanenes, etc.[2]

[G] Stil written of your Reformist sect.

Page 68. I must needs tell you againe, that there is not any which hath any sparke of christian[H] modesty, but will say God hath not sent ye, your sufferings are not to be gloried in, you are but Rabasaka [Rabshakeh], that thus reproach the church of Christ. What schismaticks have gone beyond ye?

[H] If in al this you but slaunder and raile, how great then is your sinne?

Page 69. Now followeth the suspension from the sacraments. You must understand, that al your frivolous[I] cavils about this, and all your reproaches reach not alone unto the Church of England, but unto all the reformed churches which practise[I] a suspention. Master Beza in his booke against Erastus,[3] page 10, sheweth the use and practise of it, not onely in their church, but in the auncient churches.

Reign" (1929). See also Roland G. Usher, *The Presbyterian Movement in the Reign of Queen Elizabeth as Illustrated by the Minute Book of the Dedham Classis, 1582–1589.* See also the lengthy, valuable, and careful thesis of Patrick Collinson, "The Puritan Classical Movement in the Reign of Elizabeth I;" University of London thesis, 1957. Issued as *The Elizabethan Puritan Movement* in 1967—one of the best books on Puritanism.

[1] Gifford is quoting Barrow verbatim. See *A Plaine Refutation*, p. [79]. In Carlson, *op. cit.*, pp. 148–149.

[2] *A Briefe Discoverie of the False Church*, pp. 165, 189–190.

[3] Théodore de Bèze, *Tractatus de vera excommunicatione et Christiano Presbyterio, jampridem pacis conciliande causa, T. Erasti centum manuscriptis Thesibus oppositus, et nunc primum . . . editus* (Geneva, 1590), p. 10.

[I] [Two references]. You have not here aunswered one of those frivolous cavils. Those legal seclusions. Nor yet Mr. Beza his authority wil beare up your popish suspention so utterly without ground and contrary to the rules of Christe's Testament.

Page 69. Then next you say that in the times of wicked kings, when idolatry was set up in Juda, the godly did not[K] communicate with the wicked, which is most true, but the wicked did communicate with the godly in God's true worship, in the dayes of godly kings.

[K] Your custome is to cavil, misaledge, leave out, add, etc., rather than to aunswere any thing directly or soundly. Publike repentanse was shewed you to be made of those publike sinnes committed in the wildernes, that it was a greate falte to admit the people that ought to be seperate to the temple, etc. Yet this not to be compared to the false ministrie, ministration, worship, etc., of your church. From which the godly alwaies refreined in those times. These you have not aunswered.

Page 70. And if they [Scribes and Pharisees] had not of some long time before, brought in their[L] owne traditions, how could they have called them the traditions of their Fathers? Mathew 15. Mark 7.

[L] Though sectz may arise and bring in traditions into the true church, yet can not a publike false ministry, ministration, etc., be set up and received in the true church.

Page 70. And what can be more plaine than that our saviour willeth[M] the people to heare them [the Scribes and Pharisees]?

[M] You wil not be made to see how falsly you expound and pervert this place [1.] contrary to our saviour['s] oun doctrine and wordes. 2. Contrary to the scope of that chaptre. 3. Contrary to the apostles' practise. 4. And contrary to the rules given the church. Our savior Matthew 5, 12, 15, 23 chapters openly convinceth them of corrupting and falsly expounding almost the whole lawe, willing his disciples to avoide them and their doctrine as leaven, Matthew 16, as wolves, John 10, not to heare them. In this 23 [of

Matthew] he sheweth them notable sectories, seducers, making their disciples the children of hel. Shutters up of the kingdome of heaven. Blinde guides, etc. Thei also blasphemed him, excommunicate such as beleaved on him. Now how like it is that our savior Christ would commit either his Father's law or his disciples to these sectories, let the godly judg. The apostles, Acts 2:40, seperated the faithful from them. The church is every where commanded to avoide false teachers, false doctrine, humane traditions, wil worship.

Page 71. Do you not know that our saviour by mentioning their sitting in Moses' chayre, doth bind the auditors to receive their doctrine so farre[N] as it was the true doctrine of Moses and the prophets?

[N] There is no heretike but teacheth some truth. Are we for this truth sake to soffer or heare notorius false teachers in the true church? Our saviour never taught sutch doctrine. What notorius false teachers the Pharisies were wel nigh of the whole lawe appeareth, Matthew 5 and 12 and 15 and 19 and 23. How wel also thei understood or taught the prophets the ghospel after John shew. And how likely it is our saviour would send his oun disciples or the poore ignorant people to these guides, let the learned reader or interpretor consider especially in this 23 of Matthew when he soffred within very few dayes after. And had in the 21 chapter cast out the chief priests. In the 22 the Saducies [Matthew 22:23–33].

Page 71. But men were to take heede of their[O] levine [leaven], that is, of their false doctrine and humane traditions. Our saviour doth not at all approove their open wickednes,[P] when hee willeth them to follow that true doctrine which they should deliver out of Moses, and not to follow their workes.

[O] How easely the levine [leaven] may be esc[h]ued [bee saved?] when the bread is chewed [st or?] swalloed let experience teach especially by the ignorant people and yong simple disciple[s].

[P] Nor yet doth he approve the Scribes and Pharisies for

teachers of his Father's lawe. But rather there preserveth the lawe in due veneration, casteth out and accurseth those teachers and their false expositions.

Page 71. And now if it were an[R] abuse that some of these Scribes and Pharisies which did teach, were not Levites, but of some other tribe, as Paul was of Benjamin:

[R] It wil be hard for you to prove this an abuse.

Page 71. Yet there were greater abuses about the high priest, and the rest, and begun long before that time: and yet the whole church and our saviour himself so long as he did live[S] as a private man, frequented the temple and publike worship and heard them expound the Scriptures. Therefore, Master Barrow, albeit you exclaime in this sorte, these blasphemies doth this wicked man publish, his Ordinarie and all the cleargie in England suffer them to passe in print; yet neither you[T] nor all the Donatists and Annabaptists under heaven, shall ever be able with all your shifts to wring this place from us, which indeede overturneth all the chiefe grounds and principles of your sect. Be ashamed therefore to oppose your selves so wickedly against the cleare doctrine of Christ, and cease[V] to imagine absurdities, which are but from your blind mistaking.

[S] What he did as a private man maketh nothing to the exposition of this 23 chapter. Yet wil it be heard [hard] for you to prove that ever our savior continued to heare any notorious false teachers.

[T] Neither wil al your shiftes make your exposition of this place sound, or prove it any more lawful to heare you in your false and antichristian ministrie than the Donatists, Anabaptistes, etc. It pleaseth you to reproch me with sectes and heresies I detest as also your corrupt expounding of the Scriptures.

[V] And now Mr. Gyfford, seing you make sutch boaste of this place: if your understanding were graunted that our saviour there commanded to heare the Pharasies what wil you gaine therby? It followeth not hereupon that a false ministrie. Those Pharasies.[1]

[1] Foot of page cropped.

Page 72. [Christ's instruction to the leprous man was] "goe, shew thy self unto the priest."[1]

Page 72. You do very fondly imagine, that if the priests, the Scribes and Pharisies and Saduces, and the multitude which clave unto them, were the visible church, then were[W] there two churches, unles we will denie that our saviour and his disciples were the church.

[W] If these at that time when thei had conspired and fully resolved to put Christ to death were the visible church, then must their [there] be two true churches. A true church without Christ, etc.[2]

Page 72. Our saviour doth reprehend them and layeth open their wickednes, to the end that men might beware[X] and not be seduced and kept from truth by them.

[X] And yet there also [doth Christ] commande the people and his oun disciples to heare those false teachers? Again, this commandement of our saviour must needs be extended[3] after his death, it being so few dayes before the same. And then after thei had put Christ to death were thei stil to be estemed the true church (which you often in this and other your writings against us deny) or else Christ also commande his disciples to worship God in the false church.

Page 72. And because Master Calvine hath written strongly and plentifully in these matters against the Annabaptists, and such as most wickedly did condemne the churches in his time, you take upon you to confute him,[Y] as if he were the author of these things, and you tearme us his wretched disciples.

[Y] I there indevored not to confute Mr. Calvin so mutch as to shew whie we neither may be pressed with his writings [and to show] which were the Anabaptists that seperated from tru churches for faltes therein arising. And not against sutch as departe from the fals church, their idolatrie, etc. I shewed likewise how I could not condiscend to his

[1] The marginal comment, without reference letter in the text, is "Nothing to the purpose." See Matthew 8:4 and Luke 17:14.

[2] Some words crossed out. The words are: "at y^t time Math. 23."

[3] The word "intended" is written, but the "in" seems crossed out and above these two letters is written "ex" or possibly "en."

judgment that the open prophane wicked and impenitent might be admitted to the Lord's table without blame, sinne, or polution in the other communicants which are but private men.

Page 72. And you lighting into their tents, set very freshly upon the worke, even as a chiefe captayne, to repayre[Z] and fortifie the ruines of that auncient Catharisme[1] and Donatisme, and yet can bring nothing which they brought not.

[Z] This wil be found as untrue as your often slaundring us with their scisme and heresies.

Page 73. Indeed, Master Barrow, these were speciall places which the auncient Fathers stood upon against the Donatists, and Master Calvine against the Annabaptists, and which we[A] in as great right urge against you and your sect.

[A] When you shal have soundly proved your parish assemblies true constituted churches of Christ, and your selves to have the true ministry of Christ, then had you as just cause to write against us as Agustine and Calvine against the Donatists and Anabaptists. But this would have been doon before you had thus blasphemed us, or taken up their wepons against us, which we are perswaded nothing concern us. Yet if the case stood as you immagine, I thinck under correction, you might have used both better grounds and fitter places than those of theirs against us.

Page 73. And so the good seed and the bad are together in the world,[B] but not in the church.

[B] It was never by us denied but that there shal be wicked in the church both secret and open until the end of the world. But our maine question with you is whether your parish assemblies be sutch tru constituted churches. My question with Mr. Calvin[2] was whether the godly might communicate with sutch rowtes [routs, hordes] of prophane wicked impenitent. Hereunto this parable of the field being brought, I denied and doo denie the field to be understood of the church constituted.

Page 73. In deed your exposition,[C] Master Barrow, is the very same

[1] The Catharists were purists, reformers, and frequently schismatics. The term has been applied to the Novatians, Paulicians, Donatists, Waldenses.

[2] See *A Brief Discoverie of the False Church*, pp. 13–45.

which the Donatists made, and obstinately stoode upon. The field is the world, our saviour hath said it, the truth hath saide it, accursed be he that shal gainesay it: but to gather from hence, that the good seed and the bad shal not[D] be together in the church but in the world, is directly to overthrow the whole parable.

[C] My exposition is the same which our saviour teacheth. Of him I learned it and not of the Donatistes.

[D] How doo you slaunder and cavil! I never so gathered, only I denied Mr. Calvin's collection from this place that the open impenitent or prophane might be suffered and communicated wit[h] in the constituted church, seing our savior himself saith that this field is the world.

Page 74. What is it which is here called the kingdome of heaven, is the world[E] so called? Who dare say so?

[E] I did not say the kingdom of heaven was the world: but that the field was the world.

Page 74. It could not then be saide, the kingdome[F] of heaven is like, but the state of the world is like.

[F] There are many readings of the kingdome of heaven and of the church. If you expound this parable of the church constituted, your exposition wil be found contrary to the rules of the Worde for [1.] the gathering. 2. governing. 3. administration. 4. order. 5. and communion of the church. Therfore I held it more safe to understand the kingdom in this parable of the church more generally as it is in this world consisting not only of the members called, but also of the members to be called. And so I set it doun in the *Discoverie*.[1] But if any shal shew me a better sens I will gladly receive the same.

Page 74. Moreover in the exposition of the parable our saviour saith, "as the tares are gathered and burned, so shall it be in the end of this world, the sonne of man shall send his angels, which shall gather out of his kingdome[G] all offences, and those which worke iniquitie," etc.[2] If they shall be gathered out of his kingdome, which is his church (peculiarly so called, though he be Lord of heaven and earth), then are they untill the end of the world[H] in his church.

[1] *A Brief Discoverie of the False Church*, pp. 18–23. [2] Matthew 13:40, 41.

G This kingdome must be understood more largely than of his constituted church.

H Yet is not his church willingly to soffer them or to communicate with them.

Page 75. The power[I] which God hath given unto the civill magistrates to put murtherers and other wicked malefactors to death, is not to be overthrowne: but if Christ will men to let the wicked ones in the world alone, and will have them grow to the harvest, least in plucking them up they destroy the wheate, hee taketh away that power from the magistrates. Therefore this parable must not bee taken of the good and the bad together in the world. And mark how he sayth not, let them alone, because it belongeth not unto ye, but let them[K] alone least ye plucke up the wheate. What then? Shall we neither take it of the church nor of the world, because of an absurditie which seemeth to followe on either side? Of the world[K] indeed it cannot bee taken, . . . because he sayth, not the world is like, but the kingdome of heaven is like, but of the church it is sayd, that as the good seede and the bad are sowen and grow together untill harvest in the man's field, so the good and bad[L] men are mixed in the church so long as it remayneth in the world. How then for these words, let them alone, let them growe unto the harvest? It is plaine[M] (if we will avoyd absurdities on both sides) that our saviour doth not here meddle either with the civill or ecclesiasticall power, but as it is the manner in parables to utter some sayings which are onely to shew some poynt of doctrine,[N] and not to be taken stricktly according to the letter.

I Your reason wanteth both sens and consequence. Wil you conclude that because God commandeth all men to forgive offences upon repentance and to be merciful, therfore the magistrate may not put a murtherer or traitor to death that should make sutch repentanse. You would judg this reason in me Anabaptistical and what not. Consider better therfore of what kinde of plucking up our savior speaketh and reason more proportionably.

K This very reason together with our saviour's commandment, verse 30.[1] "Soffer them both to grow

[1] Matthew 13:30.

together," etc., shewt [showeth] it not to be understood of the church constituted. For these tares are sayd to growe in the field. The field is said to be the world. Again, our saviour hath commanded his houshould servants to roote up and cast out sutch knowen and noysome tares, both for their recovery and the preservation of the church. Matthew 18. John 15. I Corinthians 5.

[L] What of this; therfore, are thei to be soffred in the church? Or communicated with?

[M] It is plaine by these wordes, "gathering, ro[o]ting up, harvest," etc., that our saviour speaketh of a spiritual final judgment in this parable. Which judgment he hath not committed to any mortal men to be executed by them in this life. But hath therunto appointed an other time and other instruments. As the angels; at the end of the world.

[N] You may torne awaye or pervert what Scriptures you liste by sutch glosses as this.

Page 76. Shal we think that damned soules [*e.g.*, the rich man that besought Abraham to send Lazarus to his father's house][1] have such a care that others may repent and be saved? Nay, as I sayd, it is onely[O] to bring in a doctrine.

[O] Our saviour hath most exactly and perfectly expounded this parable in every perticuler. From whose exposition we may not be torned [turned] by sutch vaine allegations and fals collections as you infer.

Page 76. This it is, that when the christian princes have done what they can in reforming the church, and put the wicked malefactors to death; and when the censures ecclesiasticall bee most diligently and wisely[P] executed, yet wil there bee heapes of ungodly ones in the church, and that seeing it cannot be avoyded, men are not to make schismes, and so to rend up the wheate, but meekly to expect the harvest when the full separation shall be made.

[P] How unsound and corrupt this interpretation and collection of yours is, let the godly consider. For my parte I stil deny that where the magistrates and ministers shal diligently watch and performe their duties there wilbe sutch heapes of the open ungodly

[1] Luke 16:27.

suffred to remaine as members in the constituted church. Neither doo I thinck that in this parable is any thing spoken or mente of schismes or disorderly seperation from the church, as you so peremptorily affirme. Which yet if it were graunted could not be inforced against us for our departure from you that hath neither sutch true constituted church, ministry, watch, censures, amongest you.

Page 76. The next place to proove that the open wicked shall alwayes be mixed with the good in the church is the parable of the draw net out of the same chapter.[1] You say this is graunted to be understood of the planted church. Who are they which graunted this? Indeed the Donatists[Q] granted this, and it is some gentlenes that you will graunt so much.

[Q] Whilest you seake to deprave us, you injure the truth. Which is not the worse because the Donatists hold it. We never denied but in the best churches should be open wicked unto the worlde's end. Else were there no use of excommunication. But this we stil affirme that in al true constituted churches sutch ungodly ought to be duly avoyded by orderly excommunication.

Page 76. You say the evil fishes are not open sinners but hypocrites, and so sayd the Donatists. And I mervaile you shewe no reason for it, seeing the divell[R] did suggest this frivolous shewe of reason unto the Donatists.

[R] Your oun conceived fantasies cary you to[o] far. This we sayd and say that the open prophane and ungodly ought not to be received into the church as members. And againe sutch as fal from their faith and obedience ought not to be reteined as members. This you should rather have refuted than reproched us with your oun or the Donatiste's dreames. This parable of the drawnet impugneth not eyther of our positions. Nor yet justifieth the estate and practise of your church herein.

Page 77. Here you make an exposition of your[S] owne, and then take on grievously that Christ's church should be compared to such a floar [floor] as the chaffe and the corne lye together [Matthew 3:12].

[1] Matthew 13:47, 48.

[S] The exposition I have made I partly received from the prophet Esay [Isaiah] 60 and Malachie the third [chapter]. And in the rest as I thincke I have directly drawen from the very scope and words of the Baptist [John]. According to the analogie of faith, the doctrines and rules of the apostles. But here in I refer and submit to the better information of the learned, resting therein until I see it with greater reason impugned.

Page 77. It is certaine that both the civill and ecclesiasticall power ought to bee imployed with all diligence and care that may bee to purge the church; that albeit the floar cannot be cleane rid of the chaffe, yet it may bee rid so farre as men are able. That is not[T] the question: but when these dueties of men have been neglected, and that there be heapes of chaffe in which the graynes of corne doo lye covered, whether it bee not still the visible church?[1]

[T] Our question with you is whether these your parish assemblies be the true constituted churches of Christ or no. This you should rather have proved than intermedled your selfe in an other man's strife that belonged not unto you to shift of[f] your oun taske that you are not able to performe.

Page 77. You thinke you have great hold that hee speaketh of separating the chaffe from the corne: but answere this one question,[V] was it not his floar, that is his visible church out of which he would purge the chaffe?

[V] This is my aunswere unto you, that if it were so it wil not prove your parish assemblies the tru constituted churches of Christ which have not the ordinances of God. And are like them in nothing but in these heapes of wicked, confusion, impiety.

Page 77. I referre[W] the reader to those things which I have noted betweene the ancient churches and the Donatists, where every thing hath been as strongly urged by those Donatists, as you are able, or any of your sect. Seeing then[X] in your

[1] There is no letter note in the text for this underlined passage. But in the left margin there is a printed figure of a hand-pointer. In the right margin, and in a different handwriting, is this note: "Ans. D.B." [Doctor Bancroft?]—"One reason why you condemne us from visible churches, is because of our confucion of people. But this Mr. Gifford sheweth, although it be a falt, yet overthrowes not our church no more than it did the Jewes, for which you answer not."

second accusation your grounds and reasons are flat Donatisme, and that in your blind furie you condemne all churches both of auncient time, and in these dayes, most deepely reviling and rayling at all the most excellent instruments which God hath raised up unto his church, what remayneth, but to warne simple men to take heed they bee not seduced by you? Thus much for the second, now to the third accusation.

[W] And I refer the reader to expres Scriptures and manifould reasons by me brought to prove it heinouse sacrilege in the minister and whole church where the open wicked and impenitent are permitted to the table of the Lord, etc., one of which places or reasons you have not aunswered, or almost mentioned. I refer also the reader to the aunswere of that your unchristian blasphemous pamphlet where he[1]

Page 78. [X] Seing the premises in this and your other writings are but railings and false accusations, and no way carrie this conclusion against us, as weried with the reading them, I shal leave them to your fearful accompt. And now [that] you have ended this second parte, put the reader in minde how in al this you have not proved the gathering or present communion of your parish assemblies by one rule of the Scriptures or Worde of God.

Page 78. Ye are so miserably ignorant, so full of foule errors, being altogether unlearned (this onely excepted, that yee have scraped some things out of other men's writings, which yet ye pervert) that all wise men, both of learned and unlearned, doo playnely see, it is[Y] but mad frensie, by which yee are led.

[Y] Al this neither proveth your ministrie nor spirit to be of God.

Page 79. To one part of this I made answere,[2] that whereas yee doo imagine that all the learned[Z] are afrayd ye would be too hard for them, if they should deale with yee, and therefore they doo not nor dare not meddle, it is nothing so. But as

[1] Foot of page cropped. The "blasphemous pamphlet" is probably Gifford's *A Plaine Declaration*. To this work Greenwood replied in 1591 with his *A Breife Refutation of Mr. George Giffard His Supposed Consimilitude betwene the Donatists and Us*.

[2] Gifford, *A Short Treatise*, p. 71.

one among the beasts (ye know of whome it is sayd) had gotten[A] a lyon's skinne upon him, and went about and frayed all the simpler beasts.

[Z] We trust not in our selves but in God and his truth which no learning is able to withstand.

[A] I before admonished you that these heathen fables neither become the minister of Christ. Prove your ministry. Convince or edifie us, howsoever you may please your self therein.

Page 79. Ye would not have those dreadfull things which ye denounce[B] lesse feared, because they are pronounced by a frayle man; but would have us all know that the lyon roareth.

[B] Which we pronounce out of the Worde of God. Sending the reader there to inquire the truth of our churches. And therfore you deride not me so mutch herein as the Worde and dreadful judgments of God which you can not escape by derision but by repentance.

Page 79. Therfore ye are much deceived in thinking they all feare and tremble at it. They see playnely that it is but mad frensie, and so they disdayne[C] to deale with it. And for mine owne parte, if[D] I did not see what havock the Donatists made, how many Annabaptists seduced, and how weake much of our people are, I should count it great folly to give you anie answere.

[C] Disdayne becommeth not the servants of Christ mutch lesse the learned.

[D] You hearein accuse the learned of great negligence and oversight, or else bewray in your selfe greate presumption to take that worcke upon you which thei refuse and thincke not meete to be doon.

Page 80. I have heard,[E] Master Barrow, by such as have dealt with yee, that ye make no conscience of lying, and nowe it falleth out so here; for one of those which came to prison,[1] comming to the sight of your booke,[2] hath set downe[F] in the margent that ye make a most shameles lie.

[1] John [Stephen] Egerton, who conferred with Barrow and Greenwood in the Fleet prison on March 20, 1589/1590.

[2] *A Collection of Certain Letters and Conferences Lately Passed betwixt Certaine Preachers and Two Prisoners in the Fleet.* See especially pp. 16–30 for the conference with Egerton, and pp. 31–47 for the letters of Barrow, Greenwood, and Egerton.

[E] Mr. Gifford, it seameth you have smal feare of God or reverence of men that dare thus defame me in so high poincts upon so litle proofe.

[F] But not onely my selfe but some other are ready to affirme it upon our oath of the Lord that Mr. Egerton sayde so.

Page 80. But for the letter you speake of which the other two whome ye name, sent unto ye: I have talked with them both,[1] to knowe why they denied conference, and what they had written. They say they denied conference with ye, onely because yee denied[G] them to be Christians, to pray with them, and that ye denied all the preachers in the land to bee Christians and all those which joyne with them.

[G] What opinion we held of thes parishes and them, there yet live twenty credible witnesses that were present at our conference which can make reporte. We there denied these parishes to be true constituted churches and them to be true ministers of Christ. And hereupon according to God's commandment refused to joyne unto their prayers. This notwithstanding thei promised to meete againe to discusse those matters further. Further speach after that promise we had not with them which [speech or controversy] might cause them to breake it. The blame therfore rather resteth upon them for breaking promise and failing to approve their church and ministry, than upon us which were ready to shew reasons of our dislike. Neither wil al your railing against me cleare them of breach of promise, justify your church and ministrie, or make you be estemed an honest man.

Page 81. These may very well be some of those "swelling words of vanitie," which Saint Peter speaketh of,[2] for who (if he know not before the vaine[H] insolencie of Master Barrow and his fellow) reading this wonder, would not judge them to bee men very deepely read?

[H] You stil by rayling or skoffing shift of[f] the point you should prove, *vizt.*, the ministry of your church in

[1] The "other two" would seem to be Thomas Sperin and Mr. Cooper.
[2] II Peter 2:18.

office, entrance, administration, maintenance. This you wil by no meanes be drawen unto.

Page 82. The papists denying that the churches which have rejected popery have any ministry, and requiring proofe thereof, many[I] learned writers,[I] both of other churches, and of our owne nation, have undertaken this matter, and have so directly[I] proved our ministry by the rules of God's Word, as that the papists have no cause to glorie. Now there be two things here which we may wonder at: the one[K], how it should be possible, that such swelling insolency could be found in the hearts of men grosely ignorant, as that having read almost nothing, and understanding lesse by sundry degrees, yet openly vaunt, as if they had read all, and could finde no such matter. The[L] other how men of so contrarie disposition, should use the very same weapon against the church, for this is one weapon of the papists, and now in your hands, "Ye have no ministrie of Christ."[1]

[I] I never see or heard of any foreign writers that approved the ministry of the Church of England in their offices, entrance, administration, maintenance. Al Reformed churches have a quite other and divers ministry, ministration, government. Both yours and theirs can not be of Christ or true.

[K] It is unpossible for us to satisfie you concerning your first wonder whilest sutch prejudice and malice against us abideth in your hearts.

[L] To the other we aunswere that you utterly if not wittingly mistake the matter. The papists deny your ministry not for that your office, entrance, administration, maintenance is false and antichristian, but because you are scismed from and are not ordeined by them. Our reasons against your ministry in these four points remain to be seen from the 104 unto the 148 page of the *Refutation*,[2] very few or scarse any of which I suppose you shal find used by the papists against you.

Page 82. He denieth the ministry of all churches in expresse words: affirming that "there is no[M] ministry in all Europe, nor in all these knowne parts of the world."

[1] Barrow's third accusation or principal transgession. See Gifford, *A Short Treatise*, pp. 70–82. [2] *A Plaine Refutation*, pp. 104–148.

[M] This is a slaunder and is aunswered in your second criminatory article.

Page 83. "The ministry of our church is not" (you say) "the ministry of the gospell, or the ministry of Christ, but the ministry of Antichrist, comming in the life and power of the beast." Your reason is that we[N] are the children of the bishops, and the bishops are the creatures of the pope."[1]

[N] That[2] wil not so mutch as repete our reasons aright mutch lesse aunswere them. How many reasons you balke and leave unaunswered or unmentioned from the 104 page of the *Refutation* to page 148,[3] let the reader serch and judge. Here you only mention a few wordes of the profe of a reason in my first Aunswer, *anno* 1587, unto you,[4] purposely skipping over these mayn reasons in the next wordes immediatly before, page 13; *vizt.*: In Christe's Testament we finde neyther. 1. the names you carry. 2. the offices you beare. 3. the maner of your entrance. 4. of your administration. 5. neither of your supporte and maintenance. [6] your discent and pedegree, etc. Reasons also were there brought of your education, studies, training, presentation, institution, ordination, subjection, etc.[5] Al which in your first booke and this you wil needz passe over, without mention or aunswere, say what I can.

Page 83. But the bishops of the Church of England, have not their ordination,[O] consecration, or power from the pope, but from our church which hath renounced Antichrist.

[O] It was saide unto you that though your bishops fetch not their ordination from the pope's person, yet their office, ordination, consecration, attiring, power, jurisdiction, etc., to be popish and antichristian. These you should have proved by the Word of God, and not in this futility either beg or flee the question.

[1] "A Brief Summe of the Causes of Our Seperation," p. 14; see also Gifford's reply in *A Short Treatise*, p. 74.

[2] First line cropped. [3] *A Plaine Refutation*, pp. 104–148.

[4] "A Brief Summe of the Causes of Our Seperation," p. 14; the date 1587, I believe, is after Barrow's imprisonment, but I am not positive on this point. The probable time is December, 1587, or January–February, 1587/1588.

[5] *Ibid.*, p. 13.

Page 83. It helpeth not our bishops (*'ye*[P] *say'*) any thing, that they have broken their faith and schismed from the pope, and renounced his yoake, even his usurped power and tyrannie, seing they usurpe and retaine (if not the same) yet as antichristian and enormous a power as the pope,* exercising their authoritie and commaundements contrary unto, and above all lawes, both of God and of their prince, page 113.[1] [The asterisk seems to refer to lines written in at the end of the paragraph, as follows: "Adde-whose royal courtes and writtes are not of power to bayle any one committed by the least of their hierarchie. Assuming unto them selves both the swordes, exercising together and at onse both civile and ecclesiastical offices"].

[P] By how many and weity reasons I disproved the ministry of these bishops from the 104 page to 115, let the reader serch and judge.[2] Al these you aunswere or mention not. Further you injure and falsefy my writings in that you alledg by dismembring [and] omitting. After these wordes, "As the pope," you purposely omit, "retaining the same courts, officers, cannons, constitutions, priviledges over al churches, ministers, causes, doctrines, censures. Themselves not subject to the censure of any church." This that you omit proveth their power enormous, antichristian, execrable. This if you had inserted, an end had been put to al your cavils following before thei began.

Page 83. But Master Barrow, remember the old proverb, "a lier needeth to have a good memorie,"[3] for in page 181 and 182 you have quite forgotten what ye had set downe here, for there yee doo affirme, that the bishops which died for the gospell were godly blessed martyres, of whose happie and blessed estate ye doo not doubt. Your[Q] reason is, for that they were not convinced, but did exercise that power ignorantly.[4]

[1] *A Plaine Refutation*, p. 113. [2] *Ibid.*, pp. 104–115.

[3] Quintilian wrote: "there is no doubt about the truth of the proverb that a liar should have a good memory," *The Institutio Oratoria of Quintilian*, translated by H. E. Butler (London: William Heinemann, 1953), volume II, book IV, part II, section 91, page 101. Montaigne's essay, "Of Liars," has the same sentiment. See *The Essays of Montaigne*, translated by E. J. Trechmann (London: Oxford University Press, 1927), I, 29.

[4] Gifford prints Barrow's words in a different fount, as though he were quoting,

[Q] You are either a most ignorant or else the most extreme falsifier that ever I heard of. I did and doo confes those martyres godly men and to have died in blessed estate. Not for the reason by you set doun because thei exercised those antichristian roomes in ignorance. But because the faith they see unto the death.

Page 85. [*sic*, 84] Could[R] they be godly men, exercising as antichristian and enormous a power as the pope?

[R] I have tould you that in utterly condemning an antichristian ministry yet we utterly condemn not every one that doth or hath exercised the same. Good men may of ignorance commit this or other sinnes. Yet cannot the goodnes of any man or angel make that lawful which God condemneth or forbiddeth. These godly men, though thei exercised an unlawful place or power, yet did it not so unlawfully, tyrannously, blasphemously, as these their wicked successors.

Page 85. [*sic*, 84] Here now we must lay open what power the pope dooth exercise, and what power the bishops in our church doo exercise, to see if it be[S] the same, or the like. Also whether the bishops doo exercise any power, but that which Christ hath given to his church, to be exercised by men, that is, either by bishops, or presbyteries. Touching the pope,[T] he hath usurped[V] power[V] over the whole Word of God, affirming that the holy Scriptures have no authority (as they say unto us), no certainty for the sense, no life, but as hee doth give unto them. And for this cause hee doth take upon him to expound them as he will, contrary to the grammer sense. Hee doth take upon him[V] to dispense with all, and to abrogate expresse lawes of God. And further he taketh upon him to make lawes of his owne.[V]

[S] Looke backe to that which in a corrupted conscience thou hast of set purpose to impugne the truth omitted in reciting my writings. And then see if thou canst defend their power.

[T] How soever these things stand in deed and truth, yet wil the pope and papists deny, and hapely with as great if not the same reasons, that your bishops use.

but actually he is paraphrasing. Gifford, *A Short Reply*, p. 3; Barrow, *A Plaine Refutation*, pp. 181 f.

[V] Your bishops also take power over the whole Scriptures to rente, dismember, stinte, apportion them, to exclude out of the church what parte thei please, to bring in the stead apochrypha, homelies, catachismes, injunctions, leitorugies, etc. Thei also abrogate and dispens with God's lawes, forbidding and geving licens to marie [marry], to eate flesh, to preach, limiting what and what not.

Page 85. [*sic*, 84] The power which the byshops of our church do exercise, is first, in examining,[W] approoving and ordaining ministers and authorising them to preach the gospell. Secondly, it is in this, that they are to see the orders[X] of the church, for the publick[X] administration duly observed, and so they have power[X] to excommunicate, suspend and deprive, etc., such as shall transgresse either against doctrine, order, or in manners. Touching lawes, they have not power to make[Y1] any one, not even in things meete [or] indifferent, neither have they power to abrogate, or to take away any one that is made, and by the publick authority of our church established: they can give no[Y2] commaundements of their owne.

[W] Wo to them that speake good of evil. Esaiah 5: [verse 20]. Of their examination, ordination, licences I have largely written, *Refutation*, from the 126 to the 133 page.[1] The forgery, your bishops' procedings, you can not hide or cure with these beggerie ragges you bring.

[X] The forgerie, popery, idolatry of your publike worship and ministration by their patched leitourgie I have shewed, *Refutation*, in the first parte. Their excommunication, suspension, deprivation, orders, in the second, third, forth.[2] These would now rather have bene approved than barely affirmed.

[Y1] [This note is written at the foot of the page; perhaps Barrow was unmindful of the fact that there was another note [Y2] on p. 84 [85], the same page.] These things in deed both by the lawes of God and of our lande thei ought. But there are no lawes or charters wil hould these giants. Therfore Mr.

[1] *A Plaine Refutation*, pp. 126–133.
[2] *Ibid.*, appropriate sections, pp. 25–50, 51–101, 101–158, 158–186.

Gyffard, what thei may doo is one thing but what [cropped] [they actually do is another thing?].

Y2 Whense then al these Mandates Mittimus,[1] etc.

Page 84. [*sic*, 85] That Christ hath given power to ordaine ministers, and to execute the censures ecclesiasticall, you doo not call into question: the controversie[Z] is but, by whome this power should bee executed, whether by bishops[Z] or by presbyteries.[Z]

Z The question betwixt you and the Reformist sect is whether excommunication be to be executed by one bishop or by a presbytry. We deny and have disproved the one and the other. *Refutation*,[2] from page 70 to page 81.

Page 84. [*sic*, 85] About this then must be our speciall question,[A] whether Christ hath given such a power unto the church, as to make lawes or cannons in externall matters, which wee call things indifferent?

A We reproved your bishops' power, courtes, canons, officers, pleadings, jursidiction, procedings, etc. If their deeds were good you nead not flee the light that thei might be made manifest to be wrought according to God. But now because these their doings can not be deffended and by loking into would become more odious to cover these graves, and to shift of[f] the matter you here again change the question and enter into a large discourse whether the church may make lawes in external matters indifferent as you cal them.

Page 84. [*sic*, 85] Yet it shall bee evident, that by seeking an Annabaptisticall[B] freedome, ye do abridge the power of the christian magistrate, and of the church.

B And you by pleading for this antichristian hierarchie seduce the magistrate and subvert the church.

Page 84. [*sic*, 85] For looke what God hath by his lawe[C] commaunded to bee done, it is good, it is holie; no king, nor the whole church, can make any part of it evill, or commaund it not to be done. Looke what God hath forbidden to be done,[D] that same is evill and unholy: no king, nor yet the whole church, can make it good and holy, or command

[1] A *mittimus* was a warrant committing a person to the custody of the jail-keeper.
[2] *A Plaine Refutation*, pp. 70–81.

it to bee done. I say further, that[E] the law of God is so absolutely perfect, that there is no righteousnes[E] for men, but it is therein conteyned; neyther is there any unrighteousnes,[E] but is therein forbidden.

[C] What say you then to the ecclesiastical government, and ordinances of Christ which your lords the bishops so impugn?

[D] What say you to the publike devised worship, administration, government, ordinances of your church injoyned?

[1.E] [1] This mayne groundworck whereupon standeth al your building, though true in it selfe, yet in this place is over scante and guilefully composed to torne [turn] away no smal parte of the truth and dignity of God's Worde. Take therefore this ground with you and then reare up your muddy wall and spare not. In the Worde of God are all necessary and perfect rules for the direction of man's life both concerning the worship of God and al other actions and duties required of al persons in al callings. And this both for the thing to be doone, and for the maner of doing the same.

Page 86. Now if we respect the very nature of these things, no prince or church can change it, as to make them to become necessarily good,[F] or necessarily evill in themselves to the conscience.

[2.F] And not onely so but must also leave the things in that liberty God hath set them. Onely in these things his office is to see this liberty rightly used to God's glory and a publike benefite. Which may be doon without restreining by his lawe that which God by his Worde hath left in liberty. Ponder this ground wel.

Page 86. [About the power of the prince to make laws or the church to make canons about externals], therein lieth our disagreement, and therein ye pleade for your[G] Annabaptisticall freedome, and confusion, I meane that *ataxia*,[2] or overthrowe of all order.

[G] Or you rather that pleade for your antichristian tyrannie, that most pestilent anarchie and overthrow

[1] As text. So the 2 before F and the 3 before K.
[2] The Greek word for disorder, irregularity.

of al order both in church and common wealth.

Page 86. And you [Barrow] say Master Calvine "having very truely set downe, that it is heinous presumption in any mortall man to restrayne or make lawes of such things as the Lord hath left in libertie:"[H]

[H] Let not the reader insist in [rely upon] your recital of our writings but peruse the *Discovery* from page the 86 to the 97. As also the *Refutation*, page 244 unto 251.[1]

Page 87. Alas, poore soules, I can not but[I] lament with pitie to see your blindenes, for I knowe this is of meere ignorance, that ye cannot understand Master Calvine in a doctrine which yet is cleare by the Scriptures. Ye say he invented this politique distinction of the civill court and the court of conscience, least he should keepe princes back from the gospell. Then by your owne words it doth follow, that if it be prooved that princes have power in such matters to make[K] lawes, ye do fouly abridge their sacred power by denying it.

[I] The onely charitable worde (though leavened [with] mutch Ishmaelitish derision) that you have afforded us in your three bookes[2] you have written against us. Whie might you not as wel impute the other poinctes wherein we differ from you to our ignorance as this, and discusse them in like maner.

3.[K] Before you begin to catechise us, let me desire you to take this third ground with you in the way of good speed. Princes may make no lawes which have not warrant in the Worde of God. What lawe soever hath warrant there is not to be said man's lawe but God's lawe, what man soever revive or command it.

Page 87. Ye cannot see how there should be such a distinction[L] of an externall action to respect men, and not to binde the conscience before God. Mark well and see.

[L] The conscience of man is accomptable for every action, yea, for every word and thought before God, be thei never so indifferent, never so secret. And is liable to the judgment of God for the same where in

[1] *A Brief Discoverie of the False Church*, pp. 86–97; see page 93 for Barrow's statement. *A Plaine Refutation*, pp. 244–251. See Calvin, *Institutes*, Book III, Ch. XIX.

[2] *A Short Treatise*, *A Plaine Declaration*, and *A Short Reply*.

thei transgress his Worde. Yet have we in our writings put difference betwixt heavenly and worldly things, ecclesiastical and civile actions, things by law restreined and things by God left in liberty.

Page 88. For betweene God and the conscience, they[M] [the indifferent fashions of garments] remayne as they did.

[M] In that place and use thei remaine forbidden by a positive lawe, "dei ton episkopon sōphrona, kosmion einai."[1] And therfore now thei remaine not as thei did to the conscience.

Page 88. Will ye say because it is evill for a man to doo thus before men, therefore it is evill to his conscience before God, even for the very dooing, not respecting[N] men?

[N] (Not respecting men) is an addition of your oun not found in any assertion of ours. Mr. Gifford, you must consider that God made many things unlawful in respect of men which in reguard of the creature was not so. As theft, etc. Again in respect of the time and place, which absolutely was not so.

Page 88. Nowe when the sight and view of men doth restraine me from dooing them openly, the freedome[O] of my conscience in them is not taken away before God, or my conscience is not bound by them before God: but I am restrayned in the externall use of them before men, because they be not expedient.

[O] In that time and place that God's lawe restreineth or forbiddeth the use of things, then and there your conscience is bound to forbeare, not onely for the presence of men, but also because the wil of God is sutch. Which ought to be a lanthorne to our paths.

Page 88. Then we see by this there are things which are lawful unto our conscience before God, and in which our conscience retayneth[P] still her freedome before God, even when we are restrayned the outward use before men.

[P] Yet hath God given lawes for the use of this liberty. To which lawes the conscience is bound, though it be not subject to the creature. As also in the 7 and 10 commandment. The conscience is not subject to the creatures but to the lawes of God.

[1] It is necessary for a bishop to be prudent, modest. See I Timothy 3:2 and Titus 1:8.

Page 88. When he [Paul, I Corinthians 10:29] sayth, not thine [own conscience], doth he not shew his conscience remayneth[Q] free before God; even when he is restrayned before men?

> [Q] Free concerning the knowledge of God's wil and of that creature, but not free to use it with offence, or where God for any cause (seame it never so outwarde) hat[h] restreined it. Again free, that is, hath no nue lawe concerning the absolute inhibition of the creature layde upon him, as those weake ones thought.

Page 88. And when he sayth, "All things are lawfull, but I will not be brought under the power of any thing:" I Corinthians 6, verse 12; doth he not shew it is some[R] bondage, if a man have not freedome to refrayne the use of a thing lawfull?

> [R] True. And what you here affirme bondage in laying necessity to doo the like also you must neads hould bondage in laying necessity to forbeare what God hath left in freedome. And thus by your oun place and exposition is it unlawful for man to make positive lawes of that [which] God hath left in liberty.

Page 89. Will not the prince make answere, "thou foolish man, I doo not binde thy conscience in the thing before God, but I enjoyne it as a thing[S] expedient and profitable to my common wealth"?

> [S] And so far as it is expedient or profitable to others doth God him selfe injoyne it. By whose lawe etch [each] one is to love his neighbour as him self. To doo good to al men, to further a common utility. The prince then herein but commands the law of God. Teacheth a tru use of liberty. And caleth his subjects unto their duty.

Page 90. There be thousands of such like matters, Master Barrow: and therefore consider how foully ye doo abridge[T] the power of princes, to the overthrowe of common wealths, in denying them authoritie to make permanent lawes, in things indifferent. But ye make one objection more which is of some shewe: and that is that princes' lawes are to be obeyed for conscience: out of which a man may reason thus: seeing none can make lawes to binde the conscience but God: and no lawe but in things good or evill can binde the conscience, and not in things indifferent, for that were to binde where God hath left free: therefore princes have no power to make lawes in things indifferent.[V]

[T] (Beginning cropped) . . . in perticuler the general lawes of God for the right use of our christian power and liberty: calling his subject[s] to their duties herein. And neither maketh nue lawes (as you suggest) in any thing divers from God's lawes, nor abridgeth any jote of that fredome God hath given. So that whilest his perticuler lawes are conteined within God's general lawes, though in some respect in reguarde of his office and authority thei may be sayd the princes' lawes in the perticulers, yet being conteined within the equity and extent of God's lawes, thei are stil to be estemed as God's lawes. From which lawes the prince may not swerve at any hand. As every where in my writings is to be seen. Therfore with great injury you slaunder when you say I abridge the power of princes, whilest I limit it within the lawe of God. [Here follows an obliterated passage—seventeen lines deleted].[1]

[V] This reason is of your oun forging and not of my framing, wherein you but [bait?], sophisticate and cavile abought words. Not being able, at least willing, to see difference betwixt the law of God, and the outward creature or action. Howe the one even to the least jode [jot] therof bindeth the conscience to exact obedience, whether it be in things absolutely commanded or forbidden, or in the use of things indifferent. For the least breach of which lawes the conscience shal accompt before the Lorde, although the creature or outward action it selfe be transitory and no way concern or avayle the conscience. Yet

[1] The marginal note of seventeen lines is heavily crossed out, but most of it can be deciphered. It reads: "You make no conscience to slaunder me . . . I have in al [my writings?] used these [their?] governors, fathers of the common wealth, to hould and defend [?] now and ever as persons and causes in the common wealth, to dispose them to publike utility. I have also shewed every subject bound to obey them. But this withal I shewed that al princes' lawes must be grounded upon the Word of God, which."

eaven these things wil God have holily used, or doon by his servants, according to his commandment. These things, Mr. Gifford, if you had considered, you might have spared this paynes at catechising us. And rather have proved the ministry and government of your church by the rules of the Worde. Except you would perswade that these also are matters indifferent to be framed or changed at the princes' pleasure, whose power yet even in things indifferent you see limited in the rules of God his Worde.

Page 91. Now to come to the lawes ecclesiasticall, which Mr. Greenwood sayth is to goe a note further.[1] The church (as in one [our?] countrey the prince,[W] the nobilitie, and commons assembled in Parliament) doo agree upon some lawes in things indifferent for comelines and order, and edification[X] in God's worship: as in some other places the presbyteries, with the consent of the christian magistrates.

[W] Your lords the bishops and their clergy wil not alowe of this description of your church in your parenthesis; seing thei are not of the nobility and wil not be of the commons.

[X] You wil in deed goo [go, goe] a note further if you permit the presbytrie to make lawes for edification in God's worship.

Page 91. The princes' lawes (as I have shewed) doo[Z] not bind the conscience.

[Z] And I have shewed how the princes' lawes herein binde the conscience to the obedience therof, as wel as other of God's lawes concerning outward and worldly things.

Page 91. Even so hee that violateth a lawfull rule or ceremonie of the church in matters indifferent, which are not layd upon him to bind his conscience before God, but for order and comelines before men, though his conscience touching the things themselves is not bound before God, yet in shewing any contempt[A] agaynst the publike authoritie of the church, and in giving an offence, by

[1] Greenwood, *A Fewe Observations of Mr. Giffard's Last Cavills about Stinted Read Prayers, and Devised Leitourgies*, p. 247.

bringing in uncomelines or disorder, he sinneth, and if he persist obstinatly is to be excommunicate. Tel me, Mr. Greenwood, is it not a thing betweene God and a man's conscience free to weare[B] a gowne of greene cloath, were it not in regard of comelines among men?

[A] But the church receiveth none other rules or ceremonies for their publike administration, worship, order than sutch as are given in God's Worde: which rules whoso breaketh and contemneth, contemneth not man's but God's ordinance and receiveth censure for the same. Neither may any be excommunicated for the breach of any humane tradition whatsoever.

[B] Mr. Greenwood doth not so hould. It [a man's conscience] knoweth such light and angelike attire forbidden the minister by positive lawe.

Page 91. But you say[C] all these things must be left to the discretion of the minister.

[C] You say it, but he [Greenwood] never said it.

Page 91. And now whereas I have shewed by the example of the holy apostles, Acts 15 . . . . that the church hath power[D] to decree in things indifferent, orders for edification:

[D] We say of the church as of the magistrate. Thei are to see the lawes given of God duly executed by all, and not to make nue lawes to them selves. Obedience is better than sacrifice.

Page 92. [There is no underlining or letter [E] in a long paragraph discussing Acts 15 and the power of the church in regard to things indifferent, but the note reads:]

[E] But you are never able to prove by Acts 15 or by any other Scripture that the church hath power to make lawes of any matter other than thei have received. Whereunto Mr. Grenwood rightly aunswered that no men now have either sutch commission, or measure of gifts as the apostles, those arch builders, had thereunto. He further shewed you that Christ was perfect in his Testament, faithful in his house to which nothing may be added. He shewed you that there would be no end of sutch humane devises. Nor any thing in the whole worship of God kept free from them as is to be seen in your and the popish churches this day.[1] With many other reasons and proves al which you either in greate ignorance or evil conscience pass over and aunswere not. Further to your place, Acts 15:[20, 29], the apostles there made no nue or temporary lawes but confirmant [confirmatory] lawes of God touching the true use of things indifferent to be used without offence as in that perticuler. But now to the heape of sutch popish ceremonies in the worship, administration, sacraments, etc., of your church, I hope thei wil neither be approved nor found things indifferent by that place.

Page 92. What sound stuffe ye have brought to warrant[F] your most ungodly presumption, in condemning the Church of England, as also al churches in Europe,[G] let the reader judge. Also that the churches doo in some things differ about the manner of calling and ordaining ministers, how you or any other by this can prove all to be void, would be seene.

[F] Is this all the defense you are able to make for your ministry, or aunsweare to al the reasons brought against it from your highest bishop to your lowest parish clerck in their office, entrance, administration.[2]

[G] It is your common slander that we condemn the ministry of other churches. This you rather doo in that you have a quite other ministry, ["in"—seems to be deleted] office, entranse, administration, other ordinances, government, etc., than thei have. Both which can not be of God. These are no things indifferent or wherein churches may safely differ.

Page 93. Then next the ministry of the Church of England is the ministry of reconciliation[H]; bringing no doctrine, but the doctrine of the holy Scriptures.

[H] You were shewed to reason preposterously of the end of their administration before you had proved either their office, entrance, or administration by the rules of God's Worde. All which I denied and disproved unto you by manyfould testimonies and proves [proofs], one of which you have not aunswered. Neither did I ever say or thinck that you

[1] *Ibid.*, pp. 244–251. [2] There may be another line, but the page is cropped.

taught but as private men. I can put difference betwixt private men and publike false antichristian ministers. Nor yet doo I hould Mr. Luther and Mr. Calvin antechristian [*sic*] ministers so that their example wil not helpe you.

Page 93. Here besides your wicked barking against the ministry of all churches, which God hath ratified: your ignorance is to be noted in this, that you doo not know, that if a man enter not rightly into a publick[I] office, yet the office it selfe is not destroyed: . . . It is more than foolish, that ye say, we have a leiturgy[K] or prescript forme of praier, therfore we bring other doctrine besides the Scriptures.

Thirdly, the ministry of the Church of England dooth bring men[L] to faith, there being joyned with it the effectual power and blessing of the Holy Ghost, etc. In answering this, Master Barrow, yee fall into your former stincking puddle, into which yee draw many a rash ignorant man. I meane ye utterly deny with the ungodly Swinckfeldians,[M] all the whole efficacy, power and blessing, which God hath annexed unto the ministry of the gospell. . . . Why, Master Barrow, do you not know that as God made a promise to his church to the end of the world, and hath given gifts and a ministry, to continue even to the world's end, to build it.

[I] But by how many reasons I have disproved the very offices of your ministry let the reader search and then judg with what equity you may thus refute or invey [rail, declaim].

[K] I thus reasoned you have and receive a popish leitourgie contrary to the rules of God's Word, by the prescript wherof your publike worship and ministration is made. Therfore you bring other doctrines besides the Scriptures.

[L] First you here forsake your third reason of the building up the church by your ministry. Then you repare [repayre?] not this reason in any of the points wherein it was refuted. I shewed how these effects were not to be ascribed so much to the office or person of the minister as to the doctrine taught. Which doctrine taught by other faithful private men, yea, read by the unfaithful, may have like effects in

God's elect. I shewed the papists might by this reason also approve their ministry and preaching also. Seing the like effects follow in the elect amongest them.

[M] As to this Swinckfeldian heresie,[1] it wil prove but your slander. We deny no parte of the power, efficasy, blessing of christian ministry. But we deny yours to be that tru ministry. If you understand this promise locallie in all places where were true churches, then with the papists you grosly mistake it. If you take this promise [to be] made to the christian ministry, we assent. But then it maketh nothing for the Romishe or your ministrie where Antichrist ruleth.

Page 93. How little help this bringeth to the papists, or all those sound points or doctrine that remained and do remaine[N] among them, to prove that the churches which have forsaken them are but schismatiks, . . . I thinke children might be made to see and understand.

[N] Suerly if thei have the seale of the covenant, the true ministrie confirmed with these effects, thei that forsake them upon any pretext must needz be schismatiks.

Page 94. I said the same[O] ["If I be not an apostle unto others, yet am I unto you"] is to be made the defence of the ministry of the churches at this day.

[O] Paule in al his epistles sheweth his office, proveth his calling and administration, and al these in this sentens by you alledged, if you could see it. Whether the false apostles had any true office of ministry, etc., is not to purpose. That the popish ministrie hath such effects in God's elect amongest them you can not denie except you also denie that God hath any elect amongest them. And then wil the reason as wel hould for them as for you.

Page 94. For if the papists can or may[P] as well say, though wee bee no ministers of Christ unto other, yet unto you that feele the comfort and power of our doctrine and joy in it, we are ministers of Christ.

[1] Caspar Schwenkfeld (1490–1561), a German theologian who served the Duke of Liegnitz, in Silesia, was an early Protestant mystic, whose chief doctrine was the deification of the humanity of Christ. Similar to the Quakers in some of their views, the followers suffered persecution, fled to Holland, England, and North America.

[P] The papists no doubt to their converts may say thus. Yet doth this approve neither them nor you to be true ministers, until you bring better profe for your office, entrance, etc.

Page 94. When ye pronounce that there is no such faith nor repentance, nor joy in the Holy Ghost, nor peace of conscience wrought in the hearts of any by the ministry of our church: how far above the clouds doth your swelling[Q] blind pride, lift up her hands?

[Q] Or your tonge rather is set on fire with hel. I never denied but God might worck such effects by a false ministry, onely I denied that God had made such promise of blessing unto a false ministry.

Page 94. I alleadged that the martyrs which suffered in the dayes of Queene Marie, were moved and brought to fayth and repentance, at the preaching[R] of Master [Hugh] Latimer, [Rowland] Taylor, [John] Ho[o]per, [John] Bradford, and others.

[R] This reason dependeth upon the same grounde and hath the same aunswere that the former [had].[1]

Page 95. When it is confessed that they were holy martyrs, and died for the true faith, will it not follow, if the pope[S] could proove that the church of Rome had held still that holy fayth, that it should bee the true church? We hold the same fayth with the holy martyrs. "The motions," ye say[T] "at our preachings are but the illusions of Sathan," and this is the cause that you account the reason to be Annabaptisticall.

[S] The church of Rome verbally stil maketh profession of a true faithe. But such verbal profession maketh not them or you a true constituted church.

[T] Suer you were not led by the Spirit of God when you published these malicious slanders of us, the untruth wherof to your evil consciens may appeare, whilest you doo graunt that you or the preaching freers [friars] may beget faith unto salvation in the elect, may stir up and nourish these heavenly motions in the godly, yet doth not this approve your or their ministery to be of God. And is indeed but a ground of Anabaptistry to justify open transgression or to doo

[1] *A Short Treatise*, p. 82; *A Plaine Refutation*, pp. 157–158.

things without calling or warrant, by inwarde motions. Cease therfore to broch this stuffe or to seduse with such delusions.

Page 95. Lastly, I did advise men to be somewhat moved with the judgement of other churches. "This" (you say) "is an old popish reason."[1]

[V] [No underlining or note letter in text.] Without the imputation of any church this your reason may be reproved as popish. How the papists have with the same assailed our forefathers none can be ignorant. To your testimony I have shewed all the Reformed churches to have a quite other ministry than this popish hi[e]rarchie and Romish clergie your church stil reteineth. Therfore thei must either acknowledg your ministry or their oun to be false. Except thei can shew that Christ hath instituted two so divers and contrary ministries to his church. Cease therfore thus to slaunder them or to patronise your corruptions by them. [In the text, alongside this reply, Barrow has squeezed in three lines between the paragraphs: "or you rather have aunswered no one reason that we have brought against your constitution, ministry, ministration, government of your church."]

Page 95. The foule reproachfull speeches, which yee use to deface all the ministers[W] of Christ's gospell, both of other churches, and of the Church of England, are so many.

[W] My reverent estimation of other churches and learned I often published. Neither can you shew any thing in our writings to the contrary. Neither to my knowledg have I charged you with any one untruth in al my writings. God is witnes to my conscience.

Page 95. The preaching of the gospel it selfe,[X] in our church, ye do most prophanely blaspheme.

[X] I justly have used those places of the prophets against your mercenary, vagrant, most corrupt and abused preaching.

Page 96. Also wheras in many places of this land, but chiefly when the Spaniards came to invade, there were fasts, and the Word of God preached in some places by two, in some by three ministers: this ye call a[Y] stage play.[2]

[1] *A Plaine Refutation*, p. 156. [2] *A Brief Discoverie of the False Church*, p. 97.

[Y] In regard of the maner and abuse of these your hypochritish fastes, I justly might so call them.

Page 96. The truth is you[Z] do agree with them [the Donatists] in the sum and substance of all the fowlest things, which ye cannot denie.

[Z] With what conscience or truth you can write this when your whole vituperious boke hath been so fully refuted and retorted even in that blame upon your selves, as you are not able to repayre it or cleare your selves in any one point, let the reader judge. And in what other points of Donastry you can justly charge, let your oun evil conscience confes or els God that is greater shal eare long judg betwixt us.

[There is much underlining in Gifford's summary, which extends from the middle of page 96 to the end of page 98, but there are no marginal notes. The reason is that these last two and one-half pages contain a list of twenty-eight points or errors which Gifford has summarized against Barrow. These "errors" were refuted in 1592 by Barrow in "A Few Observations," printed only in the 1605 edition of *A Plaine Refutation*, pp. 251–260. They are reproduced in the present volume. See Chapter VI.

VIII

EXCERPT ON CARTWRIGHT FROM BARROW'S PRISON CONFERENCE WITH DR. RAVIS [*CA*. APRIL, 1592]

The date of this excerpt depends on the date of the conference. We know that Reverend Thomas Sperin was successful in arranging a conference between Barrow and Thomas Cartwright.[1] The probable date would be after Sperin's two conferences with Barrow on March 14 and 20, 1589/1590,[2] and before Cartwright's imprisonment in October, 1590. Since Cartwright came to London about May 20, 1590, and was still there on June 23, and was in Warwick on August 5, we have a *terminus a quo* and a *terminus ad quem* (assuming that Cartwright had not made a special trip in March or April to London).[3] Therefore, Cartwright's conference with Barrow was about June, 1590.

At a time when both Barrow and Cartwright were in the Fleet,[4] Dr. Thomas Ravis[5] was directed by Archbishop Whitgift to arrange a second conference between Barrow and

[1] George Paule, *Life of the Most Reverend and Religious Prelate, John Whitgift, Lord Archbishop of Canterbury*, p. 50.

[2] Henry Barrow and John Greenwood, *A Collection of Certain Letters and Conferences*, pp. 1, 26.

[3] Harley MSS. 7042, f. 58; Lansdowne MSS. 64, no. 15, ff. 49, 50; and no. 18, ff. 59, 60. These letters are printed in A. F. Scott Pearson, *Thomas Cartwright*, pp. 445–450.

[4] Cartwright, in a letter of March 5, 1590/1591, says he has been in prison eighteen weeks (Lansdowne MSS. 64, no. 48, ff. 118, 119). Thus, his imprisonment began about October 30, 1590, and continued until March–May, 1592. Since Sir George Paule (p. 50) gives 1592 as the time of Barrow's conference with Dr. Ravis, and since 1592 began on March 25 for Sir George, it would seem that the conference occurred after March 25, 1592, and before May 21, 1592, when Cartwright had been liberated (Lansdowne MSS. 72, no. 51, ff. 142, 143). I conclude therefore that April, 1592, is the approximate date for Barrow's conference with Dr. Ravis and for the excerpt here printed.

[5] Dr. Ravis (1560?–1609) was one of Whitgift's chaplains, vicar of Allhallows Barking (1591–1598), prebendary of Westminster (1593–1607), dean of Christ Church (1596–1605), bishop of Gloucester (1604–1607), and bishop of London (1607–1609).

Cartwright, but the latter "would by no meanes be drawne to further conference with him againe." Therefore, about April, 1592, Dr. Thomas Ravis signified Cartwright's refusal to Barrow, who sighed deeply and expressed his disappointment that Cartwright had forsaken him.

Sir George Paule, comptroller of Archbishop Whitgift's household, and registrar of the Court of High Commission, probably received this story directly from Dr. Ravis, who was bishop of London from 1607 to 1609. Peter Heylin perhaps derived his account from Paule.

EXCERPT ON CARTWRIGHT FROM BARROW'S PRISON CONFERENCE WITH DR. RAVIS [*CA.* APRIL, 1592]

"And will he not? Hath he onely brought me into this brake,[1] and will he now leave me? For from him received I my grounds, and, out of his premises, did I inferre, and make the conclusion of the positions, which I now holde, and for which I suffer bands."

From George Paule, *The Life of the Most Reverend and Religious Prelate, John Whitgift, Lord Archbishop of Canterbury* (London, 1612), p. 50.

"Shal I be thus forsaken by him? Was it not he that brought me first into these briars, and will he now leave me in the same? Was it not from him alone that I took my grounds? Or, did I not out of such premises as he pleased to give me, infer those propositions, and deduce those conclusions for which I am now kept in bonds?"

From Peter Heylin, *Aerius Redivivus: or, the History of the Presbyterians* (Oxford, 1670), p. 323.

[1] Difficulty, dilemma, snare, cage, predicament.

IX

A FRAGMENT DIRECTED TO THE PARLIAMENT

This fragment is in Ellesmere MS. 2097, f. 38. It carries no name or date, but the authorship of Barrow is evident from the language. The series "mynistery, mynistracion, worship, ordinances and government" occurs twice. Barrow speaks of the "cathedrall and parishionall" communion. These expressions are paralleled by similar phraseology in Barrow's letter to the Countess of Warwick, written April 4/5, 1593, and in other works of his.

The date of this fragment is February or March, 1592/1593. Parliament met on Monday, February 19, and continued until Tuesday, April 10, 1593. Barrow may have begun his treatise earlier, and he may have coupled this appeal with his petition "To the Right Honorable the Lords and Others of Her Majestie's Most Honorable Privie Counsell" of January, 1592/1593.

From Penry's *Notebook*, p. 40, we learn that Barrow's prison cell was rifled on March 11. This was the same day that Barrow was examined by Sir John Popham, lord chief justice of the Queen's Bench, and Sir Edmund Anderson, lord chief justice of the Court of Common Pleas. I conjecture that during his examination the prison officials searched his cell and found this fragment, which came into the possession of Thomas Egerton, then Attorney-General.

A FRAGMENT DIRECTED TO THE PARLIAMENT

In a booke meant to have ben printed and directed to the Parliament, is amongest others thus conteyned.

Vid[*elicet*], the publicke cathedrall and parishionall communion, mynistery, mynistracion, worship, ordinances, and government of the Churche of England now by Aucthoritye established in the land, not to be suche as God hathe prescribed in his Worde, but to be antechristian, and suche as oughte not to be receyved or suffered in any Christian State, muche lesse to be inforced or urged upon any godly conscience.

How many and divers bookes have ben published in this land, callinge to the trew ministery and ordynances of Christ's testament, reprovinge also the present ministery, abuses, corrupcions of this churche? Have there not ben Admonicions,[1] Complaynts,[2] Supplications,[3] Humble Mocions[4] to Her Majesty and this honorable courte to caste oute of the churche this Romyshe hierarchie of arche bishops, lord bishops, with theire cleargie colleagues, courts, officers, cannons, jurisdiccions, yea, and this present worshipp and leitourgie by this service book? And also to receyve and establishe Christe's ministery and ordynances in place of theym? What preachinge, fastinge, praiers, have there ben in all places of this land for theise things? Wherein what else is ymplyed but that the present ministery, worshipp, ministracion and governement, ordynances of this churche are false and antechristian? Ells how should they be caste forthe?

[1] John Field and Thomas Wilcox issued the *Admonition to Parliament* in 1572.

[2] The petition of March, 1592/1593, to the High Court of Parliament is called "The Humble, Most Earnest and Lamentable Complaint and Supplication."

[3] Perhaps the petition of March, 1592/1593, is meant, but Penry's *A Viewe of Some Part of Such Publike Wants and Disorders as Are in the Service of God, within Her Majestie's Countrie of Wales, togither with an Humble Petition, unto This High Court of Parliament for Their Speedy Redresse* was published in February 1588/1589, with the running title: "A Supplication unto the High Court of Parliament." It was commonly referred to, not as *A Viewe* but as Penry's *Supplication.*

[4] Humble Mocions may be generic, but Robert Waldegrave printed a work in 1590, *An Humble Motion with Submission unto the Right Honorable Lords of Hir Majestie's Privie Counsell.* Both Waldegrave and Penry were in Edinburgh when the work was published, a fortnight before Whitsuntide, and therefore Penry—erroneously—was regarded as the author. In 1590 Easter fell on April 19 and Whitsun on June 7. See Ellesmere MS. 2148, f. 88 *verso* in the Huntington Library.

X

BARROW'S SIXTH EXAMINATION, MARCH 11, 1592/1593

This examination was conducted by the two lord chief justices, Sir John Popham of the Queen's Bench and Sir Edmund Anderson of the Court of Common Pleas. One ostensible purpose of the examination was to establish by testimony the authorship of three books by Barrow and Greenwood, although the authorship was apparent to any who read the books. But another purpose was to secure damaging evidence against printers, publishers, and collaborating agents. Barrow readily admitted his part in compiling the two volumes which he and Greenwood had issued, and he testified that he had seen Greenwood when he was writing his answer to George Gifford. He was discreetly silent or honestly ignorant about printers and publishers, and divulged as little information as possible. The one exception is that he revealed the name of Ellyn Bowman as the agent who brought him a copy in prison, but inasmuch as she had died the testimony was not damaging.

The original document for this examination is in the Huntington Library, Ellesmere Manuscript 2091. John Payne Collier printed it, in *The Egerton Papers*, pp. 170–171. His transcription is not always accurate, but anyone who seeks to decipher Sir John Popham's difficult hand will readily understand why errors occur.

BARROW'S SIXTH EXAMINATION, MARCH 11, 1592/1593

THE EXAMINATION OF HENRY BARROWE, TAKEN THE XIth DAY OFF MARCHE, 1592 [1593]

A.—He sayeth that the booke showed unto hym, intytuled *A*

Collectyon[1] *off Certein Letters and Conferenc[e]s Lately Passed between Certeyn Prechers and Two Prysoners in the Flete,*[2] was collected by hym and John Grenwood, and delyvered and sent forth by them, but to whom they were delyvered[3] he doth not remember, hys memory ys so decayed, neyther doth he know who printed them;[4] but at the tyme they were collected together the sayed Mr. Grenwood and he were both prysoners together in one chamber.

B.—He sayeth he hath sene of these bookes at two severall tymes, sythes they were printed, in other men's or wemen's hands, but he rather thyncketh at a woman's hand that ys departed, one Ellyn Bowman,[5] and thyncketh those books were not left with hym above an hower [hourr?] or two.

C.—He sayeth he never h[e]ard how many had been printed off them, nor hath enquyred of any such matter.[6]

D.—He sayeth the cause why they were thus sett down and collected was to testefy alwayes to the world what was the treuth off their cause [case?][7] and conferens with those prechers.

E.—He confessyth that he hath sene the book entituled *An Aunswer to Georg Gyfford['s] Pretended Defens of Redde Prayers and Devised Liturgies,*[8] etc., sythes yt was printed, as he thyncketh, when the others were brought, and hath redd some part therof; and sayeth he sawe Mr. Grenwood when he was in wrytyng off that booke,

[1] J. P. Collier, who edited the *Egerton Papers,* erroneously has "Declaratyon" (p. 170).

[2] *A Collection of Certain Letters and Conferences Lately Passed betwixt Certaine Preachers and Two Prisoners in the Fleet.* It was printed at Dort, about June, 1590.

[3] Robert Stokes was the one who defrayed the costs, and Robert Bowle (or Boull) was the agent.

[4] The printer was one "Hanse" or "Hause" and the place was Dort (Dordrecht) in South Holland. He is listed in R. B. McKerrow, *A Dictionary of Printers and Booksellers in England, Scotland and Ireland, and of Foreign Printers of English Books 1557–1640,* p. 123, but with the comment that "it does not seem possible to identify him." I conjecture that his first name was Hans and that his surname, if known, was deliberately concealed by the Barrowists. He may be Hans Stell.

[5] Probably the wife of Christopher Bowman; they were married in the Fleet prison in 1588, without a clergyman, in defiance of the regulations of the Church of England. From 1589 to 1592 Christopher Bowman was in prison himself for having presented with eleven others a strong "Lamentable Petition" to the Queen on March 13, 1588/1589. Ellyn Bowman died about 1591–1592, and Christopher Bowman remarried, about November 1592. He was married in the home of John Penry, in the presence of witnesses, in defiance again of the canons of the Church of England.

[6] There were 500 copies printed.

[7] A difficult manuscript reading; the word is not "speche" as Collier has transcribed it. (*Egerton Papers,* p. 170).

[8] *An Answere to George Gifford's Pretended Defence of Read Praiers and Devised Litourgies.* Printed at Dort about July–August, 1590.

who made thys examinant acquaynted with sundry partes therof, as occasyon fell out in the wrytyng therof, but who putt the same to printyng, or printed it, he knoweth not.[1]

F.—He confessyth also, he hath sene the booke intituled *A Collectyon of Certeyne Slanderous Articles Given out by the Busshopps agaynst Such Faythfull Chrystyans as They Now Unjustly Deteyne in Their Prisons, together with the Aunswer of the Sayed Prisoners Therunto,*[2] and for such part therof as concernyth hym selff he collected yt; and for that which concernyth Mr. Grenwood, he thyncketh Mr. Grenwood collected [yt], for that he saw hym wryting about yt; but knoweth not who printed that booke, or sett yt to print,[3] but sayeth he sawe yt after yt was printed, as he dyd the others.

Henry Barrow

Examined by us,

John Popham
Edmund Anderson

[1] Hanse printed 500 copies at Dort, with Robert Bowle (or Boull) as the agent and Robert Stokes as the one financing the project.

[2] *A Collection of Certaine Sclaunderous Articles Gyven out by the Bisshops against Such Faithfull Christians as They Now Unjustly Deteyne in Their Prisons togeather with the Answeare of the Saide Prisoners Therunto. Also the Some* [*Sum*] *of Certaine Conferences Had in the Fleete according to the Bisshop's Bloudie Mandate with Two Prisoners There.* Issued at Dort about April, 1590.

[3] Also printed by Hanse at Dort, by the agency of Robert Bowle (Boull) and the financial support of Robert Stokes. There were 500 copies printed.

XI

BARROW'S SEVENTH EXAMINATION, MARCH 20, 1592/1593

Nine days after the two lord chief justices had examined Barrow, they re-examined him, with the assistance of Thomas Egerton, attorney-general, William Lewin, a judge of the Prerogative Court of Canterbury, and Edward Stanhope, high commissioner and chancellor of the diocese of London. They questioned Barrow about his most important book, *A Brief Discoverie of the False Church*, and obtained his acknowledgment of authorship. They learned how the book had been written and smuggled out of prison sheet by sheet, who had prepared the copy and who had defrayed the expense. They also questioned him about his second most important book, *A Plaine Refutation of M. G[eorge] Giffard's Reprochful Booke, Intituled,* A SHORT TREATISE AGAINST THE DONATISTS OF ENGLAND, and obtained his admission that he had written most of the book, as well as two drafts of letters exhibited to him. The examiners also sought information about the role of Daniel Studley and James Forrester in preparing the copy for the printer.

The original manuscript is Ellesmere MS. 2099. John Payne Collier first transcribed and printed this examination in *The Egerton Papers*, pp. 177–178. In his transcription, he has "Dyscription" for Dyscovery, "Dudley" for Studley, "Padry" for Studley, "Stephen" for Scipio, and "Stanley" for Stanhope. There are some other minor mistakes and omissions, but the handwriting is so abominable that any careful transcriber is likely to make errors. Judge Popham was trying to take down oral testimony as fast as Barrow spoke, and the judge had used abbreviations, straight lines for letters, and some almost indecipherable flourishes.

BARROW'S SEVENTH EXAMINATION, MARCH 20, 1592/1593

THE EXAMINATION OF HENRY BARROW, TAKEN THE XXTH DAY OF MARCH, 1592 [1592/1593]

A. He confessyth that the booke intituled *A Breiff Dyscovery*[1] *of the False Church*[2] was wryten and sett forth by thys examinant in the Flete.

B. He sayeth he sent out that booke shete by the shete, and that Studley,[3] when it was wryten out, hadd the copy, and sent it out by Studley [sondry].[4]

C. He sayeth that James Fowrester[5] and thys examinant had speche touchyng the wrytyng out of the same booke.

D. He sayeth to hys remembrans he moved not the same Forester to copy out that booke, but sayeth Forester told this examinant he had ben moved to do yt. He thyncketh yt was at Stokes his charges that Forester dyd copy yt out.[6]

E. He sayeth he doth not remember what speche passed betwene thys examinant and Grenwood concernyng any means to have those bookes prynted.

F. He denyeth to hys remembrans that the same Fowrester dyd

[1] John Payne Collier, in *The Egerton Papers*, p. 177, erroneously has "Dyscription."

[2] *A Brief Discoverie of the False Church.*

[3] John Payne Collier erroneously has "Dudley" in *The Egerton Papers*, p. 177.

[4] Collier erroneously reads "Padry," and Powicke, *Henry Barrow, Separatist*, pp. 38, 86, has repeated this error. The word may be "sondry" but not Padry.

[5] James Forrester (or Forester, or Fowrestier) was a physician and a holder of the M.A. degree. He is listed in *A Collection of Certain Sclaunderous Articles Gyven out by the Bisshops*, A iv *verso*. In the deposition of Roger Waterer, April 3, 1593, there is a reference to James Forrester, who did expound the Scriptures at an assembly in a Garden House near Bedlam [Bethlehem Hospital]. The curate in 1589 at Rayleigh, Essex, was James Forester, and he may have been a visiting speaker for the London Separatists. There is one book listed in the *Short-Title Catalogue* by James Forrester, entitled *The Marrow and Juice of Two Hundred and Sixtie Scriptures* (London, 1611). On the title page Forrester is described as "Minister of God's Word at Enderby Neere Bullingbrooke in Lincolnshire, Chapleine to the Queene's Most Excellent Majestie." The tone of the book is strongly anti-Separatist, and in the preface to the reader there is a reference to Barrow's *A Brief Discoverie of the False Church.* Also, in the dedication to King James, there are two pages deriding the Separatists and one reference to mockers who term the *Book of Common Prayer* "a peece of swine's flesh." Since this is Barrow's phrase, one wonders if Forrester had reacted strongly against his former inclinations to Separatism and had become a militant member of the Church of England, in typical proselyte zeal.

[6] The examination of Forrester is given in *The Egerton Papers*, pp. 178–179. The original is Ellesmere MS. 2095 in the Henry E. Huntington Library.

ever lett thys examinant to know that he dyd myslyke any the sharpe stil [style] used in that booke.

G. For the other booke showed hym, intituled, *A Playne Refutacyon of Mr. G. Gifford's Reprochfull Booke, Intituled,* A SHORT TREYTYSE AGAYNST THE DONATYSTS OF ENGLAND,[1] for the former two parts thereof, endyng on the 206 page,[2] was wryten and sett forth by thys examinant and for the resydue therof to the end was wryten and sett forth by Mr. John Grenwood as he taketh yt;[3] but how that came to be putt in prynt he knoweth not.

H. For the two draughts of the letters showed unto hym, the one begynyng, "Brother R, your letters of the xiith," and the other begynyng, "Such and so honorable hath ben," etc., he confessyth they were of hys owne hand wrytyng, and they were draughtes of letters for Scipio[4] Byllet to wryte.[5]

I. He sayeth he he[a]rd the sayed Fowrester dyd copy out the sayed fyrst booke for money, and thys examinant dyd desyer hym to corect yt.

Henry Barrow

Examined by us,[6]

John Popham — Edmund Anderson
Thomas Egerton[7] — Edward Stanhope[8]
W[illiam] Lewyn

[1] *A Plaine Refutation of Mr. George Giffard His Reprochful Booke, Intituled,* A SHORT TREATISE AGAINST THE DONATISTS OF ENGLAND, etc.

[2] In the 1591 edition, after the address to Lord Burghley and the reader, there follow two parts: "A Brief Summe of the Causes of Our Seperation," pp. 1–20; *A Plaine Refutation*, pp. 21–206.

[3] Greenwood wrote *A Briefe Refutation*, pp. 207–234, and *A Fewe Observations of Mr. Giffard's Last Cavills*, pp. 235–255.

[4] Erroneously given as "Stephen" by Collier, *The Egerton Papers*, p. 178.

[5] I have searched in vain through numerous manuscript volumes for these letters, one of which may have been to Roger Rippon (Brother R), but I have been unable to find any clues either in print or manuscript. The most likely place would be in the Ellesmere Manuscripts at the Huntington Library, but they do not seem to be there. I believe that a portion of the Bridgewater House library was retained by the family when the collection was sold to the Huntington Library. I have found no trace of these letters in the Sir John Puckering Manuscripts (Harley MSS. 6848, 6849), nor in the archbishop's library at Lambeth, nor in Dr. Williams's Library, nor in the Congregational Library, Memorial Hall, nor in the Additional MSS. at Oxford and the British Museum.

[6] Sir John Popham was lord chief justice of the Court of Queen's (King's) Bench from 1592 to 1607. William Lewin was judge of the Prerogative Court of Canterbury, dean of the Peculiars, commissary of the Court of Faculties and a master in chancery. His defence of spiritual courts against the two bills prepared by James Morrice is given in D'Ewes, *Journals of All the Parliaments during the Reign of Queen Elizabeth*, pp. 475, 500. Sir Edmund Anderson was chief justice of the Court of Common Pleas from 1582 until his death in 1605.

[7] Thomas Egerton served as solicitor-general from 1581 to 1592; he was appointed attorney-general on June 2, 1592, and was elevated to the bench as Master of the Rolls on April 10, 1594. His signature in the manuscript is followed by an "S" which possibly might be a "G". Conceivably, it might be a terminal flourish, or it might indicate "Serjeant."

[8] Edward Stanhope (not Stanley, as given by J. P. Collier, *Egerton Papers*, pp. 173, 175, 176, 177, 178, 179) was admitted to Doctors' Commons in 1576, sworn as a master in chancery in 1577, appointed vicar-general of the province of Canterbury about 1583, was selected as a member of the Court of High Commission in 1587, was serving as chancellor to the bishop of London in February, 1589/1590, and was named canon and chancellor of St. Paul's Cathedral in 1591. He is mistakenly identified as "Stanley" six different times by J. P. Collier, but the signature is so carelessly written in a series of up and down straight lines that it becomes almost indecipherable. There is an Edward Stanley, younger son of Edward Stanley, third earl of Derby, but he is not a judge or commissioner.

XII

BARROW'S LETTER TO [ATTORNEY-GENERAL THOMAS EGERTON, MARCH 26, 1593]

This letter is in Harley MSS. 6849, f. 211 *recto*. It carries no date or addressee, but the reference to the likelihood that "streames of christian bloode" may be shed indicates a date between March 24 and March 30. From Egerton's letter of March 28 we obtain a reference to his conference with Barrow [on March 26] and to "what disputacion he requyreth," and to "a copy of Barrow's request in that behalfe"—that is, a copy of Barrow's letter of March 27. Thus we can narrow the date of Barrow's first letter to March 24–26. It is unlikely that Barrow wrote a letter on March 24, the day of his reprieve, and it is unlikely that he wrote the letter on Sunday, March 25. Therefore, Monday, March 26, seems the most likely date. Perhaps Barrow gave the letter to Attorney-General Egerton Monday afternoon during their conference in Newgate prison.

The endorsement on the manuscript reads: "of conferens after his condempnation." Barrow's sentence by the court occurred on Friday, March 23, 1592/1593. His request for a "christian and peaceable conference" very likely was made the following Monday, March 26, 1593.

There is a copy of this letter in Harley MSS. 7042, ff. 195 *verso* and 196 *recto*. It is given by Burrage, without date, in *Early English Dissenters*, II, 97–98.

BARROW'S LETTER TO [ATTORNEY-GENERAL THOMAS EGERTON, MARCH 26, 1593]

My humble desier is to any that feare God and even to my greatest adversaries in theis ecclesiasticall controversies (or I hope) but brotherly differences, if we may come to christian and peaccable conference with some learned and moderate persons, where the reasons of each syde may be with deliberacion set downe and expo[u]nded by the Worde of God and so his trueth therin appearinge may be imbraced and we brought to unitei in the treuth. And theis woundes (which now ar made and lykely to shedd eeven streames of christian bloode) may be healed, those faythfull of oure mynde which yet remayne and such as God no doubt will rayse up in this cause of Christe's may be reunited, yea, rather all of us united to Christe oure Head with joye. And what so ever it shall please God and her excellent Majestei to dispose of oure lyves, yet we therby beinge brought to the sight of such faultes as we ar chardged to have committed (but yet see not) may then humbly acknowledge the same and suffer such punishment as ar [*sic*] inflicted to the good example to the good example [*sic*] of others, to the honor of Her Majestei and this state. And this as in sight of Christe I vowe by his grace, and dare assure in the behalf of my christian bretheren. Lyke mynded that you or any of you takinge this christian and brotherly paynes shall recover and lead us by every word of God to agree with you and be obedient unto his whole will.

Henry Barrow

XIII

BARROW'S LETTER TO [ATTORNEY-GENERAL THOMAS EGERTON, MARCH 27, 1593]

This letter is in Harley MSS. 6849, f. 214 *recto*. It may be dated a day after Egerton's letter of March 26 and after Barrow's first letter of March 26. Egerton had the second letter on March 27, and sent a copy to Lord Burghley that same afternoon or evening. In the first sentence Barrow says his "moste humble and submiss[ive] desire unto your Worship was and is, that . . . your Worship would vouchaffe to be a meanes to hir moost excellent Majestie, that a christian and peceable disputacion by the Scriptures might be vouchaffed unto some few of us." The use of the words "was and is" places this letter after that of March 26. Egerton mentions a "disputacion" in his letter of March 28, but may intend a conference, and Barrow uses the words "disputacion" and "conference" as though they were synonymous. The request for a conference in Barrow's letter of March 26 was granted, and the meeting was held March 29 or 30. The request for a public disputation in Barrow's letter of March 27 was refused, perhaps by Archbishop Whitgift himself, if we may consider him the author of "Reasons against Publike Disputacion with [Henry] Barow."

This letter is printed, with minor variations, in F. J. Powicke, *Henry Barrow, Separatist*, pp. 72 f., and without date in Champlin Burrage, *Early English Dissenters*, II, 98 f. There is a copy in Harley MSS. 7042, f. 196 *recto*.

BARROW'S LETTER TO [ATTORNEY-GENERAL THOMAS EGERTON, MARCH 27, 1593]

My moste humble and submiss[ive] desire unto your Worship

was and is, that for so much as there remaine sondrie ecclesiasticall differences of no smale weight betwixt me, with sondrie others Hir Highnes' faithfull subjectes now imprisoned for the same, on the one side, and this present ministerie now by aucthoritie established in this land, on the other, undecided, or as yett indiscussed, your Worship would vouchaffe [*sic*] to be a meanes to hir moost excellent Majestie, that a christian and peceable disputacion by the Scriptures might be vouchaffed unto some fewe of us, with whom or how manie, of our adversaries herein shall in wisedom be thought meete, for the readie and happie deciding or composing the same. Protesting to your Worship in the sight of God, at whose finall judgement I looke howrelie to stand, that I hould not anie thing in thes differences of anie singularitie or pride of spirit, but as I am hetherto certainlie perswaded, by the undoubted groundes of God's Worde, the profession and practise of other reformed churches, and learned of other countreis, wherof if wee, Hir Majestie's said few imprisoned subjectes, shall faile to make evident and assured proofe, and that those learned shall shew anie other thing by the Word of God in the said christian conference desired, that then, I for my parte, vow unto your Worship through God's grace, as also [I] am perswaded, my said imprisoned brethren permitted this conference will do the like, that I will utterlie forsake anie errors I shall be so proved to holde, and in all humble and glad consent to submitt to our now discenting adversaries in all those matters wherin now wee differ, if theie shall approve them unto us by the Word of God. By which charitable acte your Worship maie put end to theise present controversies, reduce as [us?] wherin wee erre and a peace [appease] manie a christian soule.

Your Worship's humble suppliant,
Henry Barrowe

XIV

EXCERPT FROM BARROW'S CONFERENCE WITH SEVERAL CLERGYMEN, MARCH 29/30, 1593.

On March 23, 1592/1593, Barrow was sentenced to death by the court. Early on the morning of March 24 he was made ready for his execution, but the Queen issued a temporary stay.[1] Some time within the next week four clergymen of the Church of England visited him in Newgate prison, to which he had been transferred from the Fleet, to consult with him about his views and the state of his soul. The conference occurred between March 24, the date set for his execution and March 31, the date of his second reprieve. But we can narrow the time limits further. On March 26 Thomas Egerton, the attorney-general, spent the entire afternoon in conferring with the condemned prisoner, and discussed Barrow's request for a disputation.[2] He sent Barrow's request to Lord Burghley on March 27. I conjecture that about March 29/30, the clergymen conferred with Barrow and the other prisoners.[3]

[1] See "Letter to an Honorable Lady and Countesse of His Kin[d]red," in this volume, chapter XV.

[2] See the letter of March 26, 1593, by Thomas Egerton to Sir John Puckering, in the Appendix.

[3] Arthur T. Russell, in his *Memoirs of the Life and Works of the Right Honorable and Right Reverend Father in God Lancelot Andrewes, D.D., Lord Bishop of Winchester* (London, 1863), p. 45, gives the date of this conference as March 21. Evidently Russell follows Jeremy Collier, whom he cites (*Ecclesiastical History*, II, 638). But Barrow says the conference took place after his first reprieve on March 24, 1592/1593 (Barrow's "Letter to an Honorable Lady and Countesse of His Kin[d]red," April 4–5, 1593). If we assume that the conference was held as a consequence of Egerton's discussion with Barrow on Monday afternoon, March 26, 1593, then we may narrow the date to March 27–30. Now, Andrewes preached before the Queen at St. James's either on Wednesday, March 28, or Friday, March 30 ("Library of Anglo-Catholic Theology," Vol. II, *Ninety-Six Sermons* (Oxford, 1841), where the date is erroneously given as Wednesday, March 30, 1593. Wednesday fell on March 28, and March 30 fell on Friday). The correct date probably is Friday, March 30. Therefore, Andrewes would have been more free for a conference on March 29, which is the likely date. Wednesday, March 28, is a slight possibility, but if Egerton notified Lord

Conference with Several Clergymen

There were at least four clergymen who visited Barrow. He himself records that "certaine doctors and deanes [came] to exhort and confer with us." We know definitely that Dr. Lancelot Andrewes,[1] Dr. Philip Bisse,[2] Dr. Henry Parry,[3] and Dr. Thomas White[4] consulted with Barrow, and there may

Burghley on March 27 of Barrow's request for a conference or disputation, this would allow only one day for assembling the clergymen. It is likely that "Reasons against Publike Disputacion with [Henry] Barow" was written on Wednesday, March 28. The conference could have been held on Friday, March 30, even though Dr. Andrewes had a sermon to preach, and even though it was only one day before the date set for the execution of Barrow and Greenwood.

[1] Lancelot Andrewes (1555–1626), later to become Bishop of Chichester, Ely, and Winchester, was appointed in 1589 to St. Giles', Cripplegate, then to a prebend residentiary's place in St. Paul's, and to the mastership of Pembroke Hall, Cambridge University, on the death of William Fulke in 1589. He also was chaplain to Archbishop Whitgift and chaplain in ordinary to the Queen.

Lancelot Andrewes is one of the glories of the Anglican Church. Renowned for his ability as a preacher and for the beauty of his devotional life, he was also an apologist, a controversialist, an episcopal administrator as bishop of Winchester, an educational leader as master of Pembroke Hall, and a scholar. He carried on a written polemic with papal antagonists such as Cardinal Bellarmine and Cardinal Perron. He ranked with Richard Hooker as one of the great religious forces of the Elizabethan and Jacobean periods, though he lacked the style and fluency of his great contemporary. His devotions are more worthwhile than his sermons, and his *Manual of Private Devotions* remains his best loved work, with its example of self-commitment, consecration, dedication, discipline, and worship.

One of the best older biographies is that of Arthur T. Russell, *Memoirs of the Life and Works of the Right Honorable and Right Reverend Father in God Lancelot Andrewes, D.D., Lord Bishop of Winchester* (London, 1863). An interesting biography is that of Florence Higham, *Lancelot Andrewes* (London, 1952). See also Robert L. Ottley, *Lancelot Andrewes* (London, 1894), and Alexander Whyte, *Lancelot Andrewes and His Private Devotions* (Edinburgh, 1896). Mark Pattison gives a good picture of Andrewes in *Isaac Casaubon, 1559–1614* (Oxford, 1892), chapter VII, pp. 347–353.

Andrewes' views on the Anabaptists and Barrowists is given in volume IV of the "Library of Anglo-Catholic Theology," *Ninety-Six Sermons* (Oxford, 1841), pp. 11, 12. Two recent works are Maurice F. Reidy, *Bishop Lancelot Andrewes, Jacobean Court Preacher. A Study in Early Seventeenth-Century Religious Thought* (Chicago: Loyola University Press, 1955), and Paul A. Welsby, *Lancelot Andrewes, 1555–1626* (London: S.P.C.K., 1958).

[2] Philip Bisse (1541–1613), archdeacon of Taunton and sub-dean of Wells. Fellow of Magdalen College, Oxford. B.D., 1569; D.D., 1580.

[3] Henry Parry (1561–1616), became a fellow of Corpus Christi College, Oxford, in 1586, and held a benefice in Monkton, Kent, from 1591 to 1594. Later he became a chaplain to the Queen, was in attendance at her death, became bishop of Gloucester (1607) and Worcester (1610). Lancelot Andrewes' letter to Parry, on November 7, 1600, regarding the death of Richard Hooker on November 2, and regarding Hooker's manuscripts, is printed in the "Library of Anglo-Catholic Theology," *Two Answers to Cardinal Perron and Other Miscellaneous Works* (Oxford, 1854), pp. xl–xli.

[4] Thomas White (1550?–1624), founder of Sion College, was collated to a prebend in St. Paul's in 1588, became canon of Christ Church, Oxford, in 1591,

have been others with Barrow or the other condemned prisoners. If these men expected to see a man of fear or of chastened spirit, they were badly fooled. Barrow bluntly told them his time was limited and not available for controversy. He charged them with taking no interest in him during the more than five years that he had been in prison; he reminded them that he had repeatedly sought a christian conference with them but without avail.[1]

The account below is derived from George Paule, biographer of Archbishop Whitgift, and comptroller of His Grace's household. It is naturally prejudiced by his prelatical views, his anti-Presbyterian and anti-Separatist attitudes.[2]

EXCERPT FROM BARROW'S CONFERENCE WITH SEVERAL CLERGYMEN, MARCH 29/30, 1593

"You are not the men whom I most dislike in these (present)[3] differences. For although you be out of the way,[4] yet you thinke you are in the right (and walk according to that light which God hath given you). But I cannot but complaine of Maister Cartwright and others of his knowledge (opinion), from whom we have received the truth of these things, and (by whose books we) have been taught, that your callings are antichristian; who yet utterly, against their consciences, forsake us in our sufferings, (against their consciences), and will not come out of Babilon, for feare of their lives (and rather chuse to save their lives, than go out of Babylon)."

and canon of Windsor in 1593. He should not be confused with his namesake, who forsook Separatism, and wrote an anti-Separatist book, *A Discovery of Brownisme* (1605).

[1] Barrow, "Letter to an Honorable Lady and Countesse of His Kin[d]red," in the present volume.

[2] George Paule, *Life of . . . John Whitgift* (1612), pp. 50–51.

[3] This statement is taken from George Paule, *Life of . . . John Whitgift*, pp. 50–51. The variations indicated by parentheses indicate the differences as seen in Peter Heylin, *Aerius Redivivus: or the History of the Presbyterians*, second edition (London, 1672), p. 324.

[4] This phrase means the true way, the way of God, the way of Christ, the narrow way of real salvation. In the book of Acts the word takes on the meaning of the christian movement, the new followers of Christ, those embarking on a new mode of life. See Acts 9:2, 19:23, 22:4, 24:14, 24:22.

[It being farther replied by Doctor White, that those callings, which Barrow reproached as antichristian; were the very same, which Archbishop Cranmer, and Ridley, and many other holy bishops, etc. (that suffered martyrdome in Queene Marie's time) did embrace; Barrow replied in this vaineglorious manner;]

"True it is that Cranmer, and others were martyrs in Queen Marie's dayes, but these holy bands of mine" (and therewithall [Barrow] shooke the fetters, which he did weare)[1] "are much more glorious, than any of theirs, because they had the marke of Antichrist in their hands."[2]

[1] In this paragraph the nine words within the parentheses are thus given by Paule. Heylin, who depends on Paule, has ("and therewith shook his fetters").

[2] Paule, who cannot resist the opportunity of pointing out the danger of innovation, as begun by Cartwright and continued by Barrow, comments as follows: "men, therefore, not partially affected, may hereby observe, and conceive what danger Innovation bringeth to the people, and what hazard to a State; when, by little and little, it encreaseth like the swelling, or flowing of the Sea; which if it surpasse the bounds, wherewith it was confined, or gaine never so small a breach, it spreadeth it selfe over a whole Country, and groweth to that violence, and streame, that it cannot, by any contrarie force be kept backe; but without pittie or mercie, putteth all things to wracke, where it rageth. Which, as it seemeth, Maister Cartwright himselfe did now finde; when after his first conference, hee perceived how impossible it was for him to make up the breach, which he had unfortunately begun; for that Barrow, like a tempestuous surge, would have forced him (by finding his owne over-sight and errors) backe againe from his former positions, or drawne him inevitably to his conclusions" (*Life of . . . John Whitgift*, pp. 51–52).

Sir George Paule also comments: "Thus he, in Newgate at that time, in the presence of many, with great insolencie, did triumph" (*Life of . . . John Whitgift*, p. 51).

XV

LETTER TO AN HONORABLE LADY AND COUNTESSE OF HIS KIN[D]RED YET LIVING

This letter is printed in [Henry Ainsworth and Francis Johnson], *An Apologie or Defence of Such Christians as Are Commonly (But Unjustly) Called Brownists* ([Amsterdam?], 1604), pp. 89–95. This is no. 239 in the *Short-Title Catalogue*. There is another edition of this book, no. 238 in the *Short-Title Catalogue*, which is listed first, and which is supposed to have been printed in Amsterdam in the same year. I believe this is the second edition, very likely printed in England, and the date actually may be 1604 or it may be later, with the old date retained. So far as the letter of Barrow is concerned, the variations are minor, the differences being the expansion of words, use of "and" for the ampersand, upper and lower case variations, and slight changes in punctuation. Both editions are in the British Museum and in the Folger Shakespeare Library. In the British Museum Catalogue, the book is not listed under the name of Ainsworth or Johnson, but is listed under "Brownists."

This letter is also reprinted by Burrage, *Early English Dissenters*, II, 100–108; Powicke prints a portion of it in *Henry Barrow, Separatist*, pp. 76–79.

Inasmuch as this letter was Barrow's final appeal, written only a day or two before his execution, we should like to know to whom the appeal was sent. Burrage does not grapple with the problem. Powicke has a footnote in which he asks: "Was she his cousin Agnes, wife of the Lord Keeper's eldest son, Sir Nicholas Bacon?" And Dr. Peel suggested that Lady Anne, second wife of the Lord Keeper of the Great Seal, mother-in-law of Sir Nicholas Bacon (the younger), and mother-in-law of Agnes, was the lady to whom Barrow addressed his last petition. I believe this conjecture by Dr. Peel is incorrect, but Lady Anne was a famous daughter, wife, and mother in her own right. There is an interesting chapter, well worth reading, on "Sir Nicholas and the Lady Anne Bacon, the Puritan Patrons," in William Urwick, *Nonconformity in Herts.*, pp. 75–96.

The letter itself is addressed "To the right honorable, etc." But in printing it, the editors or authors of *An Apologie or Defence of Such True Christians* described it as a "letter to an honorable Lady and Countesse of his kin[d]red yet living" (p. 88). This means that the lady addressed was the wife of an earl, was at least distantly related to Barrow, and was still living in 1603 when these words were written in answer to the Oxford University leaders (see the *Short-Title Catalogue*, no. 19010). Since neither Lady Anne nor Lady Agnes had married an earl, neither one was a countess.

The honorable lady who best meets the conditions is the Countess of Warwick. She was Anne Russell, oldest daughter of Francis Russell, second earl of Bedford. On November 11, 1565, she married Ambrose Dudley, earl of Warwick, and brother to Robert, the earl of Leicester. The earl of Warwick had been married twice previously, but this was Anne's first and only marriage. She was a lady of the bedchamber to Queen Elizabeth almost from the beginning of her reign, and she was with the Queen at her death in 1603. As an intimate friend, close companion, and trusted confidante of the Queen, the Countess of Warwick was the kind of person to whom Barrow would appeal.

The purpose of Barrow's letter to the Countess of Warwick was to declare his loyalty to the Queen and realm, and to protest his innocency of the charges for which he had been sentenced to death. He requested the Countess to inform Her Majesty of his loyalty and sincerity, and urged the Countess to speak to the Queen on behalf of himself and his four fellow-prisoners. Barrow hoped that the Queen would pardon him, or at least remove him from his miserable imprisonment in Newgate "to some more honest and meet place."

Anne Dudley, Countess of Warwick, was evidently an able, courageous, well-educated, sensible, and influential woman. Her father, Francis, the second earl of Bedford, was a generous and powerful Puritan landlord. Her husband, the "Good Lord Warwick," was a friend of the Puritans, and was one of the administrators for the revenues used for the preachers of the gospel in Warwickshire. The Countess had interested herself in the plight of John Udall, and appealed on his behalf to Archbishop Whitgift and Bishop Cooper (Brook, *The Lives of the Puritans*, II, 1, 7, 9). Both she and her father were friends of Thomas Cartwright. When the enthusiast and fanatic, Edmund Copinger, wrote letters in 1590 to the Countess, Lord Burghley, and the Queen, Cartwright warned the Countess about the nature of the man. As one who was close to the Queen, who had served her faithfully for some thirty years, who was a sincere believer in religion, and who had defended Puritans against the persecuting prelates, the Countess of Warwick was one of the reliable persons to whom Barrow could appeal in his dire need. It is possible that Barrow knew the Countess personally during those years when he was a frequenter of the court circles (*ca.* 1576–1585).

Thus, it is apparent that Barrow's letter was addressed to one who was indeed "an Honorable Lady and Countesse." It will also be apparent that the letter was addressed to one "of his kin[d]red" if the reader will observe the family relationships in the tables on p. 241.

From these tables it is manifest that:

1. Henry Barrow is a cousin of Agnes (Butts) Bacon.
2. Agnes (Butts) Bacon by marriage is a relative of Elizabeth (Cooke) Russell. Actually, Elizabeth is the sister-in-law of Sir Nicholas Bacon the Lord Keeper, who is the father-in-law of Agnes.
3. Elizabeth (Cooke) Russell is the sister-in-law of Anne (Russell) Dudley, the Countess of Warwick.
4. Lord Burghley, as the husband of Mildred Cooke, was the brother-in-law of Ann, who was the mother-in-law of Nicholas Bacon the younger, who was the husband of Agnes, Barrow's cousin.
5. Barrow's cousin Agnes is a sister-in-law of Francis Bacon.
6. Barrow is a cousin of Agnes, who is by marriage a relative

Letter to an Honorable Lady

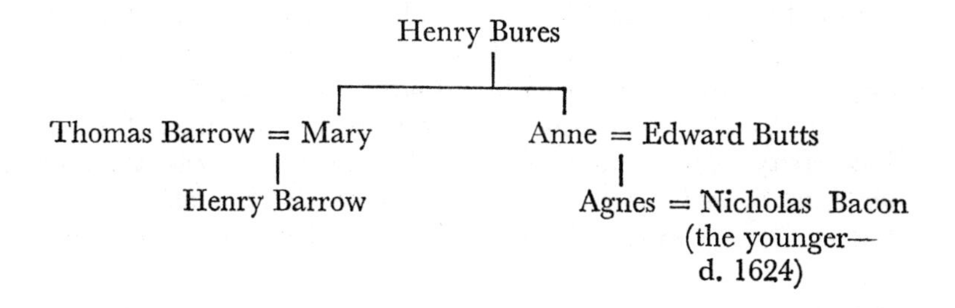

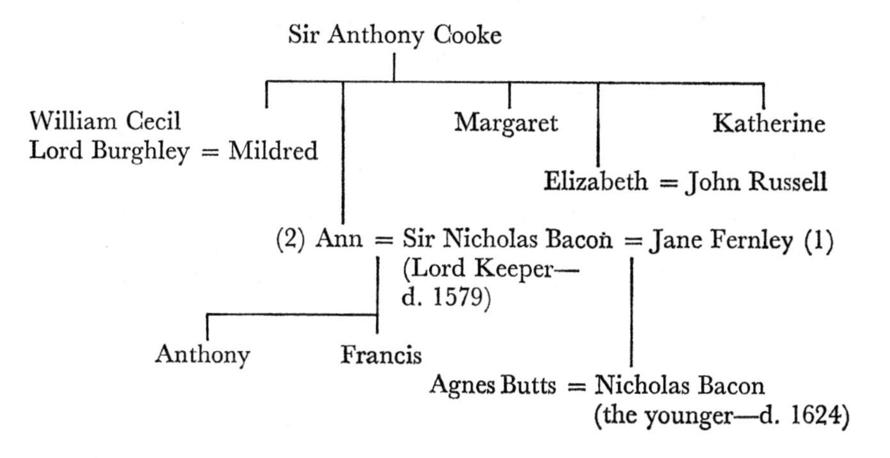

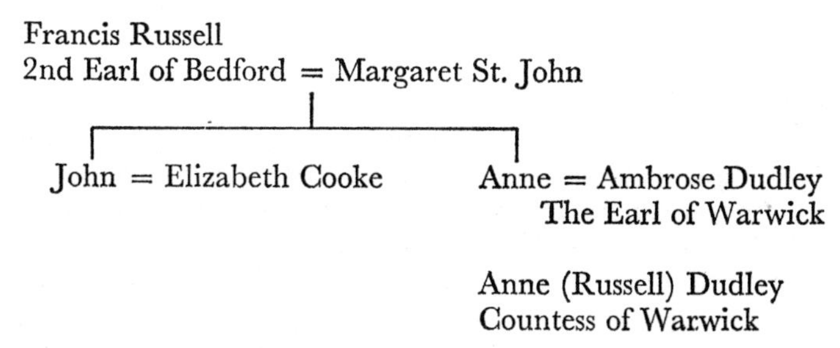

or kindred of Elizabeth Cooke, who is a sister-in-law of Anne, the Countess of Warwick.

One final point may be noted. The phrase "of his kin[d]red yet living" appears in *An Apologie or Defence of Such Christians as Are Commonly (But Unjustly) Called Brownists*, p. 88. This pamphlet was written as a reply to a treatise from Oxford University, *The Answere of the Vicechancelour, the Doctors, Both the Proctors, and Other the Heads of Houses in the Universitie of Oxford.* This work was issued in 1603, and it is likely that the reply was written in the late autumn of 1603, although it was not published until 1604. The Countess of Warwick died February 9, 1603/1604, and the phrase "yet living" may refer to her final illness or it may be simply a reference to her longevity. She died less than a year after the death of Queen Elizabeth, and she outlived Barrow by more than a decade. We do not know if she interceded for Barrow with Queen Elizabeth. Even though she lived in London with her sister, Margaret, who was the wife of George Clifford, Earl of Cumberland, it is possible that the letter came too late or that she had left London because of the serious ravages of the plague. It is probable that the Countess of Warwick made available for the Separatists a copy of Barrow's final writing.

LETTER TO AN HONORABLE LADY AND COUNTESSE OF HIS KIN[D]RED YET LIVING. APRIL 4–5, 1593

Mr. Barrowe's letter written a little before his death

[89] To the right honorable, etc.

Though it be no new or strange doctrine unto you, right honorable and excellent Ladie, who have ben so educated and exercised in the faith and fear of God, that the crosse should be joyned to the gospel, tribulation and persecution to the faith and profession of Christ;[1] yet

[1] Lady Anne Russell had known sorrow, suffering, and tribulation in her own family circle. One brother, Edward, died in 1573; another, John, died in 1584; a third, Francis, was killed July 27, 1585, while fighting along the Scottish borderlands. On the following day, July 28, her father died. On February 20, 1589/1590, her husband died. He had suffered for twenty-seven years from the

may this seem strange unto you, and almost incredible, that in a land professing Christ, such crueltie should be offred unto the servants of Christ for the truth and gospel's sake, and that by the chief ministers of the church, as they pretend. This no doubt doth make sundrie, otherwise wel affected, to think hardly of us and of our cause; and specially, fynding us by their instigation, indicted, arraigned, condemned,[1] and readie to be executed by the secular powers, for moving sedition and disobedience, for diffaming the renowmed [*sic*] person and government of our most gracious soveraigne Queen Elisabeth and this state. But, right honorable, if our adversaries' proceedings, and our suffrings with the true causes therof, might be duly expended [accurately determined or considered] by the Scriptures; I doubt not but their malice and our innocencie should easily appear to al men: howsoever now they think to cover the one and the other, by adding slander unto violence.

Your Ladyship readeth, that the holie prophets who spake in the name of God, yea, our blessed Saviour himself and his apostles, have suffred like usage under the same pretence of sedition, innovation, rebellion against Caesar and the state, at the hands and by the means of the chief ministers of that church, the priests, scribes, and Pharisees; men of no lesse account for holiness, learning and authoritie, than these our adversaries. The faithfull of all ages since, that have witnessed against the malignant synagogue of Antichrist, and stood for the gospel of Christ; have suffred like

effect of a poisoned bullet, and lost both his leg and life in an amputation. See J. H. Wiffen, *Historical Memoirs of the House of Russell; from the Time of the Norman Conquest* (London, 1933), 2 volumes.

Lady Anne lived with her sister Margaret, wife of George Clifford, Earl of Cumberland, who was an absentee and faithless husband. Both sisters were sincerely religious, devout, talented, and serious persons. Spenser dedicated his "Fower Hymnes" to these two sisters—the Countess of Warwick and the Countess of Cumberland. For a portrait of Lady Anne, see Violet A. Wilson, *Society Women of Shakespeare's Time*, p. 140. See also Violet A. Wilson, *Queen Elizabeth's Maids of Honour and Ladies of the Privy Chamber.* There are numerous references to the Countess of Warwick in the calendars of state papers. See further Dorothy Mary Stenton, *The English Woman in History* (London, 1957), pp. 135–136.

[1] March 21–23, 1592/1593. See "The Arraignment of Certaine Puritanes or Brownists" in the Appendix, chapter XXI.

usage, at the hands of the same prelacie and clergie that now is in the land, though possessed of other persons. The quarrel still remayneth betwixt the two opposite kingdomes of Christ and Antichrist; and so long shal endure, as any part of the apostasie and usurped tyrannie of the man of sin shal remayne. The apostasie and tryannie of Antichrist, as it sprung not at once or in a day, but by degrees wrought from his mysterie to his manifestation and exaltation in his throne; so was he not at once wholly discovered or abolished; but as Christ from time to time by the beams of his appearing, discovered the iniquitie, so by the power of his Word, which can not be made of none effect, doth he abolish the same, and shal not cease this warre, until Antichrist with his army, power, and ministerie [mysterie],[1] be wholly cast out of the church. Assurance and manifest revelation herof, we have both in general and particular, in that historical prophesie given of Christ unto his church by John the divine in the book of the Revelation, from the 10 to the 20 chapter:[2] proof and accomplishment hereof, we have hitherto found in the abolishing of al the errors, idolatries, trumperies and forgeries discovered and witnessed against, by the [90] faithfull servants of Christ in former ages. Neither is there cause why we should doubt of the like sequel and event in the present and future times; seing the enormities remayning, are no lesse hateful to God, and contrarie to the kingdome of Christ: and God that condemneth them is a strong Lord to execute his will, which no opposition or tyrannie of his adversaries, shalbe able to hinder or resist.[3]

II Thes. 2:8

Rev. 16

Rev. 19

Rev. 18:8

Whiles then we be in the mercies of God, holding the most holy and glorious cause of Christ against them, that he might reigne in his church by such officers and lawes as he hath prescribed in his Testament; we fear not our adversaries in any thing, knowing that their malice and opposition herein, is made to them a token of perdition, and to us of salvation, and that of God. For this cause we are bold, both to stand for the holy ministerie,

Philip. 1:28, 29. II Thes. 1

[1] The second edition (*S.T.C.*, no. 238), incorrectly has "mysterie." But II Thessalonians 2:7 speaks of "the mystery of lawlessness."

[2] See especially Revelation 17:7–18 and 19:11–21.

[3] Revelation 18:8.

government, and ordinances of Christ prescribed in his Word; and also to withstand and witnesse against this antichristian hierarchie of the prelacie and clergie of this land, in their ministerie, ministration, government, courts, officers, canons, etc., which I by writing,[1] have shewed to have no ground or warrant in God's Word: not to be given, or to belong unto the church of Christ, but to be invented by man; the very same that the pope stil useth, and erewhile used and left in this land. The like, others of us more learned, have offred and do stil offer upon the dispence of our lives, to prove by the expresse Word of God, in any christian and peaceable conference, against any whosoever, that wil there stand for the defence of the same.

The prelats, seing the axe thus layd to the roots of the tree of their pomp, not able to approve their ministerie, ministration, government, which they usurp and exercise in the church, by the Scriptures; sought to turne away this question, and to get rid of their adversaries, by other subtil and hostile practises; as at the first by shutting up the chief of us in their close prisons; by diffaming us in their pulpits, printed books and sparsed libels in the land; by seeking to invegle us with certaine subtil questions to bring our lives into danger;[2] by suborned conferences with certaine their select instruments;[3] not to speak of the manifold molestations, and cruel usage at their commaundment shewed us in the prisons. To their reprochful and slaunderous books, being set of God, though most unworthie, and suffering for the defence of the faith, and being thus provoked by them, I held it my dutie, according to the small measure of grace received, to make answer. Which I also did more than three yeres since.[4] Likewise to deliver our

[1] Especially *A Brief Discoverie of the False Church*, and *A Plaine Refutation.*

[2] A reference to the questions asked at the March 24, 1588/1589, examination. See "Barrow's Fifth Examination," both versions, in Carlson, *The Writings of Henry Barrow, 1587–1590*, pp. 190–202, 203–207.

[3] For a list of preachers selected and for the prisoners interviewed, see *A Collection of Certaine Sclaunderous Articles Gyven Out by the Bisshops*, signature A 4 *verso*, B 1 *recto*, reprinted in Carlson, *The Writings of John Greenwood, 1587–1590*, pp. 115–120, 317–322.

[4] *A Brief Discoverie of the False Church*, written in 1589–1590. *A Plaine Refutation* was mainly written in 1590, completed in 1590/1591, and published in 1591.

selves from the false report and witnes that might be made against us in those Conferences, we thought good to publish them to the land.[1] For these books written more than three yeres since, after well neer six yeres' imprisonment susteined at their hands,[2] have these [91] prelates by their vehement suggestions and accusations, caused us to be now indicted, arrayned, condemned, for writing and publishing sedicious books, upon the same statute made the 23 yere of her Majestie's reigne.[3] Their accusations were drawen into these heads:

First, that I should write and publish the Queene's Majesty to be unbaptized.

Secondly, the state to be wholly corrupted from the crowne of the head to the sole of the foot, in the lawes, judgments, judges, customes, etc., so that none that feared God, could live in peace therein.

Thirdly, that all the people in the land are infidels.

To these indictments I answered, generally, that eyther they were mistaken, or els misconstrued: that neyther in my meaning, matter, or words, any such crime could justly be found. My meaning, being just and without evil towards any man, much more towards my soveraigne and the state, whom I from the hart honored. The matters, being meerly ecclesiastical, controverted betwixt this clergie and us. My words, being eyther in answer of their slanders, or in assertion of such things as I hold. That if I had offended in any of my words, it was rather casual through hast, than of any evil intent.

More particularly, to the first, concerning the Queene's baptisme; I answered, that it was utterly mistaken, both contrary to my meaning and to my expresse words in

[1] *A Collection of Certaine Sclaunderous Articles Gyven Out by the Bisshops*, and also *A Collection of Certain Letters and Conferences*, both published in 1590.

[2] Actually, five and a half years, from October 8 (Greenwood) or November 19, 1587 (Barrow), to April, 1593.

[3] The specific book on which the indictment depended was *A Brief Discoverie of the False Church.* The statute was that of 23 Elizabeth, chapter II, section 4, which enacted that "if any person . . . devise and write, print or set forth any manner of book . . . or writing, containing any false seditious and slanderous matter to the defamation of the Queen's Majesty," such a person was guilty of felony and punishable by death and forfeiture (G. W. Prothero, *Select Statutes and Other Constitutional Documents Illustrative of the Reigns of Elizabeth and James I* (Oxford, 1894), pp. 77–80).

that place of my book,[1] as manifestly there appeareth to any indifferent reader; that I there purposely defended her Maiestie's baptisme received, against such as hold the baptisme given in poperie to be no baptisme at all; where I proved, that it needed not be repeated; yet there I also shewed such baptisme given in poperie, not to seal God's covenant to the church in that estate; and therefore that the abuse ought by all that had there received it, to be repented.[2]

To the second indictment, I shewed the words by me used to be drawen from Isaiah 1 and Revelation 13. That I had no evil mynd towards the state, lawes, or judges; but onely shewed, that wher the ministerie, the salt, the light, is corrupted, the body and all the parts must needs be unsound; which I immediatly in the same place of that book,[3] shewed by the general breach of the lawes of both tables, by all estates, degrees, persons, etc., setting down the particulars.

To the third indictment I answered, that I gladly embraced and beleeved the common faith received and professed in this land, as most holy [92] and sound; that I had reverend estimation of sundrie, and good hope of many hundred thousands in the land; though I utterly disliked the present constitution of this church, in the present communion, ministery, ministration, worship, government and ordinances ecclesiastical of these cathedral and parishional assemblies.

Some other few things, such as they thought might most make against me, were culled out of my writings, and urged: as, that I should hold her Majesty to be antichristian, and her government antichristian. To which I answered, that it was with great and manifest injurie so collected; seing in sundry places of that book, and every where in all my writings and sayings, I have protested my exceeding good opinion and reverend estimation of her Majestie's royal person and government, above al other princes in the world, for her most rare and singular vertues and indowments. I have every where in my writings acknowledged, all dutie and

[1] *A Brief Discoverie*, pp. 112–113. [2] *A Brief Discoverie*, pp. 100–121.
[3] *A Brief Discoverie*, pp. 9–12. See Isaiah 1:6.

obedience to her Majestie's government, as to the sacred ordinance of God, the supreme power he hath set over all causes and persons, whether ecclesiastical or civil, within her dominions. Alwayes desiring [my accusations] to be intended [interpreted] of this false ecclesiastical government, forrayn power, canons, and courts brought in and usurped by the prelates and their accomplices.

But these answers, or whatsoever els I could say or allege, prevayled nothing; all thinges being so hardly construed and urged against me; no doubt through the prelates' former instigations, and malicious accusations. So that I, with my fower other brethren,[1] were the 23 of the third moneth [March, 1592/1593] condemned, and adjudged to suffer death as fellons, upon these indictments aforesaid. Upon the 24, early in the morning, was preparation made for our execution: we [were] brought out of the Limbo,[2] our yrons smitten of[f], and we ready to be bound to the cart; when her Majestie's most gracious pardon came for our repri[e]ve.

After that, the bishops sent unto us certaine doctors and deanes,[3] to exhort and confer with us. We shewed, how they had neglected the time; we had ben well nigh six yeres in their prisons, never refused but alwayes humbly desired of them christian conference, for the peaceable discussing and deciding our differences, but could never obteyne it at their hands; neyther did these men all this time come unto us, or offer any such matter.[4] That our time now was short in this world, neyther were we to bestow it unto controversies, so much as unto more profitable and comfortable considerations. Yet if they desired to have conference with us they were to

[1] John Greenwood, who was executed; Daniel Studley, who was imprisoned until 1597 and then exiled in April to the Magdalen Islands (Ramea, west of Newfoundland) and in September to Holland; Scipio Bellot and Robert Bowle (or Boull), who were imprisoned in Newgate where they died (Henry Ainsworth and Francis Johnson, *An Apologie or Defence*, p. 95).

[2] In Newgate prison, the dungeon. See Harley MSS. 6848, f. 150.

[3] Dr. Lancelot Andrewes, Dr. Henry Parry, Dr. Philip Bisse, and Dr. Thomas White. See "Excerpt from Barrow's Conference with Several Clergymen, March 29/30, 1593," in this volume.

[4] Dr. Lancelot Andrewes had conferred with Barrow in the Fleet on March 18, 1589/1590, and on April 13, 1590. See *A Collection of Certaine Sclaunderous Articles Gyven Out by the Bisshops*, signature D ii *recto*–E ii [F ii] *verso*.

get our lives respited therunto. Then, if they would joyne unto us, two other of our brethren in their prisons, whom we named unto them,[1] we then gladly would condiscend to any christian and orderly conference by the Scriptures, with such or so many of them as should be thought meet.

Upon the last day of the third moneth [Saturday, March 31], my brother Grenewood and I [93] were very early and secretly conveyed to the place of execution.[2] Where being tyed by the necks to the tree, we were permitted to speak a few words. We there, in the sight of that judge that knoweth and sercheth the hart, before whom we were thence immediatly to appear, protested our loyaltie and innocencie towards Her Majestie, our nobles, governors, magistrates, and this whol state. That in our writings we had no malicious or evil intent, so much as in thought, towards any of these, or toward any person in the world. That wherin we had through zele, or unadvisedly, let fall any word or sentence that moved offence, or caried any shew of irreverence, we were hartily sorie, and humbly besought pardon of them so offended for the same. Furder, we exhorted the people to obedience and hartie love of their prince and magistrates, to lay down their lives in their defence against all enemies; yea, at their hands meekly and paciently to receive death, or any punishment they shall inflict, whether justly or unjustly. We exhorted them also unto orderly quiet and peaceable walking, within the limits of their own calling, to the holy fear and true worship of God. For the books written by us, we exhorted all men, no further to receive any thing therin conteyned, than they should find sound proof of the same in the holy Scriptures. Thus craving pardon of al men whome we had any way offended, and freely forgiving the whole world, we used prayer for Her Majesty, the magistrates, people, and even for our adversaries. And having both of us almost finished our last words; behold one was

[1] Probably John Penry and Francis Johnson, but Thomas Settle and William Smithe are also possibilities. All were in prison. All were clergymen, excepting Penry, who was a *de facto* clergyman, theologically trained, but not ordained.

[2] Tyburn, near the present Marble Arch and Hyde Park.

even at that instant come with a repri[e]ve for our lives from Her Majesty. Which was not onely thankfully received of us, but with exceeding rejoysing and applause of all the people, both at the place of execution, and in the wayes, streets, and houses, as we returned.

Thus pleased it God to dispose the uttermost violence of our adversaries, to the manifestation of our innocencie, concerning the crimes whereof we were accused and condemned; and not onely so, but also to the further shewing forth of Her Majestie's princely clemencie, rare vertue, and christian care over her faithful subjects, to the yet further manifesting of her renowmed fame and love amongst all her people. And sure we have no doubt, but the same our gracious God, that hath wrought this marvelous work in Her Majestie's princely hart, to cause her of her owne accord and singular wisdome, even before she knew our innocencie, twice to stay the execution of that rigorous sentence; wil now much more after so assured and wonderful demonstration of our innocencie, move her gracious Majesty freely and fully to pardon the execution thereof, as she that never desired, and alwayes lothly shed the blood of her greatest enemies; much lesse wil she now of her loyal christian and innocent subjects; especially if Her Majesty might be truly informed, both of the things that are passed, and of our lamentable estate and great miserie wherin we now continue in a miserable place and case, in the [94] lothsome gayle of Newgate, under this heavie judgement, every day exspecting execution.

Hereunto if God shall move your noble hart, right vertuous Ladie, not for any worldly cause (which for my present reproch and basenes, I dare not mention to your Honour), so much as for the love and cause of Christ, which we th[r]ough the grace of God professe; to informe Her Majesty of our intire faith unto God, unsteyned loyaltie to Her Highnes, innocencie and good conscience towards all men; in pardoning our offence and judgement, or els in removing our poor worne bodies out of this miserable gayle (the horror wherof is not to be spoken unto your Honour), to some more honest and meet place, if she vouchsafe us longer to live. Your

Ladyship doubtlesse shall herein doe a right christian and gracious act, acceptable to God, behoovefull to your soveraigne prince, comfortable to us the poor condemned prisoners of Christ; yea, to his whol afflicted church, and most of all to your own prayse and comfort in this life, and in the life to come. Hereunto further to exhort your Honor, by the examples of the godly of like condition, in such times of publick distresses and danger, I hope I need not so much, as to stirre up that good gift and grace of God which is in you, not to neglect or put from you this notable occasion sent unto you from God, to shew forth the naturalnes of your faith unto him, of your fidelity to your prince, of your love to the members of Christ in distresse, whom as you succour or neglect herein, so assure your self wil Christ in his glorie esteme it as done or denyed to be done by you to his own sacred person.

Let not therfore, right dear and elect Ladie, any worldly or politick impediments or unlikelyhoods, no fleshly feares, diffidence or delayes, stop or hinder you from speaking to Her Majesty on our behalf, before she go out of this citie;[1] least we by your default herein perish in her absence, having no assured stay or respite of our lives; and our malignant adversaries readie to watch any occasion for the shedding of our blood, as we by those two neer and miraculous escapes have found. Onely, good Madame, do your diligent indevour herein, and commit the successe as we also with you shall, unto God in our prayers; which howsoever it fall out, magnified be the blessed name of God in these our mortall bodies, whether by life or by death. His mighty hand, that hath hitherto upholden us, assist us to the finishing up this last part of our warfare, to the vanquishing of our last

[1] Parliament was in session, but rumours of its impending dissolution may have reached Barrow. Less than a week later, on April 10, Parliament was dissolved by the Queen and Sir John Puckering, the Lord Keeper of the Great Seal. Barrow also may have learned of the Queen's intentions to spend the spring and summer at Windsor because of the dangers from the plague in London. Evidently the Queen decided to remain at St. James, and she deferred her trip to Windsor until the late summer. See G. B. Harrison, *An Elizabethan Journal, Being a Record of Those Things Most Talked of during the Years 1591–1594*, pp. 160, 165, 168, 174–178, 191, 222, 228, 244, 260, 265. See also John Nichols, *The Progresses and Public Processions of Queen Elizabeth*, III, 227–228.

enemie, death, with all his terrors, and to the atteyning of that crowne of glorie which is purchased for us in the bloud of Christ, layd up and surely kept for us in the hand of God; and not onely for us, but for all that keep the faith and commaundements of Jesus. Of which number, noble Ladie, I heare and hope you are; and shal not cease (God willing) whiles I heer live, to [95] further the same unto you by my prayers and utmost indevours. His grace and blessing, the prayers of the saincts, and myne unworthy service be with you.

This 4. or 5. of the 4. moneth. 1593.

Your Honor's humbly at commaundement during life,
condemned of men but received of God:

Henry Barrowe

PART III

APPENDICES

BARROWIST DOCUMENTS

1590–1593

XVI

[A REPLYE BY] A PAPISTE TO BARROWE'S AUNS[WER] OF SOME OF HIS QUESTION[S]

This document is in Additional MSS. 29,546, ff. 119 *recto*–121 *verso*. It carries no author's name and no suggestion of a date. The manuscript itself is in a poor condition, and there are six places where it is torn.

We may conjecture that differences arose between a Catholic and some Separatists. The latter brought their questions, or perhaps a Catholic statement, to Barrow for a reply. When Barrow had completed his answers, a papist wrote the present reply. Evidently he did not know Barrow, since he speaks of him as the answerer. He also suggests that three or four of the Separatists should visit him personally for a conference.

[A REPLYE BY] A PAPISTE TO BARROWE'S AUNS[WER] OF SOME OF HIS QUESTION[S]

The state of the question considered, and understoode, wolde no dowbt have restrayned you in your supposed answere from many impertinent speeches, from manie contrarieties, and absurde paradoxes wherwith your whole paper is in every other line plentifully replenished. But to speake the truthe, yt is moste manifest that the answerer (what soever he was) knewe not [the] state of the question wherunto he pretended an answere.

To anie demaunde that I made there is in the worlde no answere returned but suche as wold pittie anie reasonable consideracion that ignorance sholde so rashlie adventure to play Thersites' parte[1] in censuringe the over[r]each of his meane capacity.

But bycause you shall see that the ignorance of the man is manifest, and the answere nothinge to that it superficially pretendeth,

[1] Thersites, the loud-mouthed Greek, scurrilously reviled Achilles and Odysseus.

I will first sett downe the state of owr question, and after that examine the answere in his over [ever?] ridiculous evasions, suppositions, and affirmations. To examine all were infinite; onely I will geve you a taste of some which shall easely descrie the vanitie of that [which] remayneth.

Concerninge the question whether Scripture discerne or measure the churche, or whether the churche measure, rule, discerne, or interprete Scripture,[1] it is proposed in this sorte and uppon this occasion. Whether when controversies in case of religion doe happen, and heretickes for countenance of theire phantasies, pretende the countenance and color of Scripture, applyinge accordinge to theire opinions the exposition of anie place in Scripture, as we see by experience all hereticks uppon theire owne pryvate spirites have violently wrested the Scriptures in favor of theire errors, in this case to whome doth it appertaine by judiciale powre to determine, not of the truthe of the Scripture but of the true exposition? We say it appertaynethe to the churche assured of the possession of the Holie Ghoste for ever to explicate the sence of that wherof it was the first author. You affirme that the Scripture muste determine Scripture, which can not be, for one and the same thinge restinge in controvercy can have no judiciall authoritie to decyde the controversie. Heruppon I demaunded you [?], attributinge judiciall authoritie unto Scriptures not onely in cases of controversie but censuringe the churche, howe the churche was ruled, directed, etc., before the Scriptures of the Newe Testament were written? To this you answere firste by the Scriptures of the Old Testament. This is very fryvolous, for the Old Testament contayneth but figures of the newe churche to be instituted. And where prove you that the figure is a ruler, a guide, a discerner of the thinge figured? Is this a good argument: Joseph is a figure of owr Saviour, therefore a guide, a discerner, etc., of our Savioure? Besides the Old Testament comprehendinge the prophecies of the future churche are [is] not to limite the maner and qualitie of the same.[2] For if this be true that the churche was by our Saviour fownded not bycause the Scriptures of the Olde Testament dyd foreprophecy of the same, but that because the churche

[1] Evidently Barrow had taken the Protestant position of the supremacy of the Word of God. Thus, he repudiated the doctrine of tradition and rejected the Catholic position that the church was the sole and right interpreter of the Scripture.

[2] The sentence is ambiguous, but I interpret it to be: Furthermore, the Old Testament, in comprehending the prophecies of the future New Testament church, is not intended to limit the manner and quality of that church.

was to have a foundation by owr Savioure the Scriptures dyd forshewe it, uppon this consideration it followeth manifest to common sence that they could not be judges, discerners, etc., uppon the churche to which they were subordinate.

The rest that followeth the answere of this demaunde consisteth that the churche was ruled by the Holie Ghoste remayninge in the churche which is the Cathol. maximi [maxime?].[1] Mannie superfluous speaches are here inserted nothinge appertaininge to owre controversie, as that the apostolicke doctrine ought not to be dowbted, that it was confirmed with signes and wonders.[2] What is this appertayninge to my demaunde?

In my demaunde whether the Holie Ghost were geven at Pentecost, consider with your selves uppon the weight of your sowles howe contrarie you are to Scriptures. Our Savioure promiseth he will sende a Comforter.[3] And againe, excepte I departe hence, that Comforter will not come, with the like.[4] Is not this manifest? Dothe not this prove that they had not yet receyved the Holie Ghoste, who dyd not come except owr Savioure dyd departe? You talke of conference of place with place. What conference is this uppon occasion of one flatlie to denie the other, bycause in some places of Scripture is attributed the receavinge of the Holie Ghoste to the disciples [;] allreadye therefore withowt farder consideration you dyd [119 *verso*] rashely adventure to denie that [which] was manifest. If this answere had not bene very simple, he might have considered eyther that in the Scripture the Holie Ghoste is saide to be receyved when anie operation of the same is performed,[5] in which sence the Apostles had many times receyved the graces of the Holie Ghoste, and so the Holie Ghoste. Or that the Holie Ghoste was to be receyved not onely as before, but with full possession and assurance to continue in the churche for ever, or otherwise he might have knowne that the Holy Ghost is sent two waies, invisibly and visiblie, invisibly before visibly, after his moste glorious ascension. In the one he was sent as to pryvate members, in the other as to extende generally and to principale buylders.

To that demaunde, to what ende the Holie Ghoste was geven, you [affirme, answere?], to comforte, instructe, guide, and direct in all truthe.[6] Where I demaunde whether the Holie Ghost were geven

[1] The Catholic maxime or maxim. That is, Barrow has confirmed the Catholic position.
[2] The reference is to Acts 2:43, 4:30, 5:12, 6:8, 7:36, 8:13, 14:3, 15:12.
[3] John 14:16, 26; 15:26. [4] John 16:7.
[5] Acts 2:38. [6] John 16:13.

to the churche or to the Scriptures, you grante that in that sence as you have sayd, it is geven to the churche and not to Scriptures. Howe agreeth this both with youre position that Scriptures must measure and discerne the churche, or with your wordes followinge after? By which Scriptures God onely nowe speaketh and we trie, discerne, and knowe, etc.

You sayd that in this sence the Holie Ghost could not be geven to Scriptures. What inconstancy and contraryetie is this? Of force you must deny the one or the other.

In your third and fourth answere you talke of disjoyninge God from his worde, of a dangerous devision, unsownde comparison, etc. What could be spoken more fondly? Prove by anie one place or probabilitie that may but pretende a devesion [division]. We demaunde whose office it is to define of the truthe beinge by heresies called in question or controversie? Is the seekinge of proper offices to eyther and application accordinglie any reason to suppose a devision? Because it is sayd that creation is the proper work of God the Father, [do I?] therefore make a division in the b. [blessed] Trinitie? Bycause we say the churche by the Holy Ghoste is to define amongst contrary expositions which is the true sence of Scripture, is this to disjoyne God from his Worde or to make a division, etc., and [an] unsownde comparison? Is there any attributinge of contrary qualities? Is there any comparison in improper offices that I make betwixt the churche and Scriptures? *Quid obmutescis personate?*[1] I yelde truth to eyther. I make no dowt of the certainety of eyther. What reason have you then to suppose seperations, divisions, etc.? The question standeth truely [reely?] which hath judiciale authoritie to decide controversies—churche or Scripture, as in a peece of golde when dyvers do doubt what kinde of mettall it is, whether true or not, etc. Heruppon it is referred to tryall. Is this any unsownde comparison, any division, etc.? Your reasoninge is all one with this. The judge do[th] define or declare the truth of the evidenses. Therefore the judge and the evidenses be contrary. Is this a divesion and [an] unsownde comparison? *Quam velim me cum personato quopiam vel mediocriter erudito se cum personato esset agend*[*um*?] *contulisse*, etc.[2]

[1] The manuscript reading is difficult and uncertain. Perhaps the meaning is: "Why are you speechless—why do you not speak out?" Another possibility is: "Why are you mute, parson?"

[2] How I wish I could have conferred with some individual or moderately educated person himself when action had to be taken. (The manuscipt is torn, and "personato" could be read as personate or personata.) If "se" is "si", and if

To conclude, if [we should] proceede furder, it were to answere a number of absurdities nothinge pertinent to owr question whether the churche or Scripture hath judiciale authoritie in controversies. For that [which] remayneth the answerer fighteth against his own suppositions, as if the churche erre, etc. Then that we must not buyld uppon mortall men, wherin the answerer descryeth open vanitie, not consideringe that members of the churche are one thinge and mortale men an other thinge.

I am here inforced to leave of[f] from wrytinge any more of the answere. If thre or fower of yow will come to me at any time, or findeing [?] oportunytie, and I will come to you. I will peruse your answere *nominale*[1] [?] that [120 *recto*] you shall playnely confesse that the reall answerer, wantinge utterly consideration, hath penned the thinge moste vaynely. If I make not this cleere in conference with you or farther when I have dispatched my earnest affaires that are presently happened, you shall justly account me both a vile and vayne compagnion. In the meane [?time] praye [?] consider of your selves and your sowles. Followe St. Bernard's counsell. Be rather *discipuli veritatis* than *magistri erroris*.[2]

So I leave you.

"personatus" carries the older meaning of "parson", we may translate: How I wish I had conferred with any parson even moderately erudite [himself or if] one had to deal with a parson.

1 Perhaps *nominatim*, particularly.

2 Students of the truth than teachers of error.

XVII
IN THE INDICTEMENT OF BARROWE

This document is in Harley MSS. 6848, f. 8 *recto*. It is a part of the material on which is based the indictment made against Barrow on March 21, 1592/1593, at the Sessions Hall in Old Bailey. The manuscript is interesting for its emphases (shown in italics), probably made for Judge Anderson or Attorney-General Egerton or Serjeant Owen. Most of the extracts—seven of them—come from the conference between Barrow and Thomas Sperin on March 14, 1589/1590, at the Fleet prison. Two of the extracts are taken from Barrow and Greenwood's letters of April 10 and 14, 1590, to Stephen Egerton. Both Sperin and Egerton were conformist Puritans or disaffected Anglicans who had been commissioned by the Bishop of London to interview the prisoners and bring them to conformity. One extract is taken from Barrow's conference on March 18, 1589/1590, with Lancelot Andrewes and William Hutchinson.

IN THE INDICTEMENT OF BARROWE

Page 2	Speryn	"Aunsweared that he ever thought reverentlie of the busshops both for their learninge, as also because her Majestie hath aucthourized them."[1]
	Barrowe	"I shewed their unlawfull, *antichristian beastlyke powre* and aucthouritye. As also their barbarous havocke they excercysed in the church, confounding and subvertinge all good [God's] ordinances, and settinge up theire owne devices in steed [instead] thereof. And therefore *they that reverence theise men, call Christe execrable and worshipp the beaste*."[2]

[1] "A Collection of Certain Letters and Conferences," in Carlson, *The Writings of John Greenwood, 1587–1590*, p. 180. [2] *Ibid.*, p. 180.

Page 4	Barrowe	"Your whole mynistrie and mynistracion is false and antichristian, further you have nether the freedome to practize Christe's Testament, nor the powre or will to redresse anie thinge that is amysse amongest you, but ether runne *to the antichristian powre* and courtes of [the] busshops or ells contynue obstinate, and careless in your synnes."[1]
Page 10	Speryn	"I attribute much to the civell magistrate, I do it because of the civell magistrate, that aucthourizethe the busshoppes."[2]
	Barrow	"But maie the civill magistrate either comaund anie thinge contrary to the comaundment of God, or if he do, is he to be obeyed therin or can he excuse you before the tribunall of Christ, for the breach of God's lawes?"[3]
	Speryn	"Whie, then you affirme that the Queene and the Parliament do *wickedlie, in givinge this powre* and aucthouritie unto the busshops, will you write that?"[4]
	Barrow	"*Yea that I will by the grace of God* [whilest I have breath], and seale it with my bloude also (if so God will), *it beinge directlie contrarye to the Testament of Christe* as your self confesseth, and yet continewe to doe contrarye to your owne conscience."[5]
Page 32 [31]		"You [Stephen Egerton] excercise a mynisteriall *function under Antechrist* in a false office unto a confuse assemblie of all sortes of people."[6]
Page 37		"As to your disordered parishe assemblies wherein you [Stephen Egerton] will needes be stil powered [poured] out in the error of Balaam for wage, wee have longe since proved *them wholie antechristian by sundrie reasons* drawne from the discripcion of the true established church of Christe."[7]
Page 1		"Infidelles are such as ether are never come

[1] *Ibid.*, p. 183. [2] *Ibid.*, p. 190. [3] *Ibid.*, p. 190.
[4] *Ibid.*, pp. 190–191. [5] *Ibid.*, p. 191. [6] *Ibid.*, p. 214.
[7] *Ibid.*, pp. 221–222. The reference to the "true established church of Christe" is to "The True Church and the False Church," printed in Carlson, *op. cit.*, pp. 97–102.

[E1 *recto*] or are fallen from the faith. *Of which sorte I affirme all the people as they thus stand in your parishes to be.*"[1]

Endorsement: Barrowe's fals hereticall and sedicius conclusions in his boke.

[1] "A Collection of Certaine Sclaunderous Articles," Carlson, *op. cit.*, p. 149. The marginal reference to Page 1 should be E1 *recto*, which is p. 149 in the 1962 edition.

XVIII

HENRIE BARROWE TOWCHINGE THE CIVILL MAGISTRATE

This document is in Harley MSS. 6848, f. 10 *recto*. It contains five extracts from Barrow's *A Plaine Refutation* and one from his *A Brief Discoverie of the False Church*. On the question of the role of the magistrate in the reformation of religion there was wide disagreement. Queen Elizabeth, ever concerned about her prerogative in causes ecclesiastical, found it necessary to control Parliament with a strict hand. She lectured her Speakers, berated her committees, and imprisoned those M.P.s who proved too bold, independent, or refractory. The Presbyterian Puritans hoped that Parliament would bring in the new church government, discipline, and liturgy by legal means. Therefore, they petitioned, supplicated, complained, pleaded, lobbied, and preached. Perhaps the high point in their efforts was the presentation of the Bill and Book by Anthony Cope on February 27, 1586/1587. This parliamentary bill and Genevan Prayer Book embodied the hopes of all the zealous advocates of the true reformed church. In fact, it recommended a thoroughgoing ecclesiastical revolution. But the Queen was adamant. The bill was suppressed, the leaders were arrested, and the revolutionary fuse sputtered and died.

The Separatists had scorned the efforts of the Presbyterians to sue unto magistrate and court. Did the Apostles wait upon Nero? Did the martyrs attend upon the wishes of a Domitian, a Decius, or a Diocletian? Then, why should God's true servants await the whims of rulers, godly or ungodly? Let there be reformation without tarrying for any. This was the position of Robert Browne, and this was the policy of the Separatists. Instead of waiting Erasmus-like for reform from within, they separated Luther-like from the adversary. And in this bold drastic policy Barrow was more militant than Browne. Thus, it is not surprising to find frequent interrogations about the magistrate's role in ecclesiastical causes. Since any curtailment of the Queen's prerogative was a dangerous tactic, we find by an easy logic that to question the Queen's episcopal hierarchy was to invite the charge of treason, of felony, of sedition. Elizabeth's generals, judges, and bishops were all extensions of her central prerogative. To question any of them was to incur the wrath of the monarch, and *ira principis mors est*, as the Separatists discovered.

HENRIE BARROWE TOWCHINGE THE CIVILL MAGISTRATE

"That the magistrate's sworde yet wanteth an eye to guyde yt," in his booke agaynste Mr. Giffarde, Folio 139, called *A Playne Refutacion.*[1]

That princes are not to be stayed for, in the busines of reformacion, nor theire restrainte is a sufficient lett. Yea, the crosse of Christe were utterlie abolished, yf the churche and faythfull were not to proceade in theire dueties, untill princes geve leave. Folios 196 *et* 197.[2]

"That the prince maye aswell make a newe religion as newe lawes for religion." Folio 205.[3]

That to accuse them for erectinge this governement is to "accuse Christe of treason, because he saithe he ys a kinge, and his servauntes of sedicion, bicause they sett upp his kingedome withowte the lycense and agaynste the will of prynces, thoughe yt coste them theire lives for the same. Folio 202.[4]

That the prynce for anie transgression of God's lawes is "liable and subjecte to the censures and judgementes of Christe in his

[1] Carlson, *The Writings of Henry Barrow, 1590–1591*, p. 253; the first edition, *A Plaine Refutation*, p. [139]. The quotation should be: "so that if the magistrate's sworde (which yet wanteth an eye to guide it) did not represse some sinnes, there should be no human peace, as there now is no christian order in their church."

[2] *Ibid.*, 349 and [196–197]; "if princes in this business had bene to be stayed for, or their restrainte [197] had bene a sufficient let."

[3] *Ibid.*, 363 and [205].

[4] "Is not this to accuse Christ of treason, because he said he was a King? And his servants of sedition, because he saith he is a Kinge? And his servants of sedition, because they set up his kingdome without the licence, and against the will, of princes, though it cost them their lives for the same?" *Ibid.*, 357 and [202].

churche, which are withowte (all) partialitie or respecte of persones, which censures and judgementes yf the prince contemne, he contemneth them *agaynste his owne sowle*, and ys thereuppon by the same power of Christe *to be disfranchesed* owte of the churche and *to be delivered over unto Sathan*, aswell as anye other offender." In his book intituled *A Dyscoverie of the False Churche*. Folio 14.[1]

"The whole *lande overflowethe with all impietie, vyolence, cruelltie and iniquitie* as in the dayes of Noye [Noah]." *Refutacion of Gyfforde*. Folio 111.[2]

[1] Carlson, *The Writings of Henry Barrow, 1587–1590*, p. 289 and [14].
[2] Carlson, *The Writings of Henry Barrow, 1590–1591*, p. 202 and [111].

XIX

IN THE INDICTEMENT OF GRENEWOOD

This document is in Harley MSS. 6848, f. 112 *recto*. It contains nine extracts, of which two are taken from "A Collection of Certain Letters and Conferences," six from "The True Church and the False Church," and one from "A Collection of Certaine Sclaunderous Articles."

What is interesting about these nine extracts is that they are probably not Greenwood's words. I believe he would subscribe to the ideas, and he would admit collaboration in publishing books with Barrow. But I doubt that he would admit to the phraseology. The first and second extracts come from two letters which Barrow and Greenwood wrote jointly to Stephen Egerton on April 10 and 17, 1590. The following six extracts are from a treatise which is more Barrowist than Greenwoodian. And the last item seems clearly to be by Barrow. Perhaps the judges or attorneys recognized this problem of dual authorship. If so, we may conjecture that greater reliance was placed on those extracts which came from *An Answere to George Gifford's Pretended Defence of Read Praiers and Devised Litourgies*—a work which was clearly and admittedly by Greenwood alone. Greenwood, of course, was culpable even if he wrote none of the extracts inasmuch as he had admitted collaboration with Barrow on the two "Collections." Also, Greenwood was vulnerable because he was an officer of the church—the teacher or assistant pastor.

IN THE INDICTEMENT OF GRENEWOOD

"You [Stephen Egerton] excercise a mynisteriall function *under Antechrist in a false* office unto a confuse assembly of all sortes of people."[1]

[1] "A Collection of Certain Letters and Conferences," in Carlson, *The Writings of John Greenwood, 1587–1590*, p. 214.

"As to your disordred parishe assemblies wherein you will nedes be still powred [poured] out in the error of Balaam for wage we have longe sithence proved them *wholie antechristian by sundrie reasons* drawne from the discripcion of the true established church of Christe."[1]

"Theis parishes consistinge of a companie of profane and ignorant people gathered by the sound of a bell *in the name of Antechriste*, worshippinge God after a false and idolatrous manner, denyinge all obedience unto Christe in his three offices, as their onelie kinge, priest, and prophett, lyvinge in disorder amongest them selfes, standinge in confusion, beinge disordred *and overruled by such lawes and officers as the pope lefte*, and not as Christ left, standinge in bondage to the Romishe courtes and cannons, *havinge no powre to execute the Lorde's judgmentes*, or to redresse the least synne or transgression amongest them selves, but are driven to the commissaries' courtes, and so cast out Sathan by the powre of Sathan."[2]

"They receyve not nor obey not Christ as their kinge, preist, and prophett, not as their kinge, rejectinge his governement, and receyvinge and standinge *under the antechristian yoke of the* [thier] popishe government."[3]

"Not as their priest, sacriligiouslie prophaninge his name with their idolatrie, prosequtinge [prostituting] his bloude, and makinge him a priest and *sacrifice to infidells and the most wicked* offendors."[4]

"Not as theire prophet, givinge no obedience to his Word, usinge it as a mantell to cover their synne, rather than as a rule whereby to directe their lyves, *not seekinge a true mynistrye, but mayntayninge a false, of which sorte the whole ministry of the lande is*, which are permitted to teach in the [*their*] publique places to whom they give eare."[5]

"Theise assemblies are not ruled by the Ould and New Testament, but by the cannons, injunctions and decrees, *of theise antechristian* and popishe courtes. Therefore, etc."[6]

"Theis people stand not in and for theire christian libertie, but all of theyme remaine in *bondage to theis Aegiptian and Babilonishe yoakes*, yeldinge obedience unto theis courtes and theire cannons. Therefore, etc."[7]

The causes of controversie thou maist hereby perceive to be no

[1] *Ibid.*, pp. 221–222. The reference to "the true established church of Christe" is to "The True Church and the False Church," Carlson, *op. cit.*, pp. 97–102.
[2] *Ibid.*, pp. 98–99. [3] *Ibid.*, p. 99. [4] *Ibid.* [5] *Ibid.*
[6] *Ibid.*, p. 100. [7] *Ibid.*

light or small matters, concerninge thinges indifferent, or some few trifflinge ceremonies (as they have longe laboured to make the word [world] beleyve), although even those least litle trifles beinge brought into and thrust by waie of law uppon the chruch [church], havinge no warraunt in the Testament of Christ, ought not to be suffred for the space of one [an] howre, but most high and weightie are theis matters, concernynge the whole bueldinge of the chruch [church], which is *affirmed to be altogether out of order from the verie foundacion to the toppe and not accordinge to the paterne of Christe's Testament* ether in *the people, ministrie, ministracion,* [folio 12 *verso*] *worshipp, government, order,* all thinges out of frame, such as cane [can] *nether stande before the face of Christe, nether maie anny of Gode's children joyne unto with promise of salvacion.*[1]

Endorsement: Grenwoode's fals and sedicious conclusions and sclanders.

[1] "A Collection of Certaine Sclaunderous Articles," in Carlson, *op. cit.*, p. 108.

XX

AN ABSTRACT OUT OF GREENEWOOD'S *AUNSWERE TO GIFFORD*

This document is Harley MSS. 6848, f. 152 *recto*. It has no date, but the subject matter provides the clue for an approximate time. Greenwood was examined on March 11, 1592/1593. He confessed that he was part author of three separate books which were showed unto him. One book was *A Collection of Certaine Sclaunderous Articles Gyven Out by the Bishops*, of which he wrote a portion. A second book was *A Collection of Certain Letters and Conferences*, of which he wrote a part. The third book was *An Answere to George Gifford's Pretended Defence of Read Praiers and Devised Litourgies*. This work was written entirely by Greenwood and carried his name on the title-page, at the close of the preface, and on the final page. Therefore, this work was selected as undoubtedly by Greenwood, and from it were extracted some of the more extreme statements which could be used to prove the charge of seditious and slanderous words, in violation of 23 Elizabeth, chapter II, section 4.

It is a natural deduction, therefore, that these extracts were collected about March 12–15, and given to the two Lord Chief Justices, John Popham of the Queen's Bench, and Edmund Anderson, of the Court of Common Pleas.

On March 20 Greenwood was examined again about two more books. He admitted writing two treatises which were appended to Barrow's *A Plaine Refutation*, but he denied any role in the writing of Barrow's *A Brief Discoverie of the False Church*.

On the basis of these extracts, Greenwood was indicted for writing seditious and slanderous words. The trial was held March 21–23 at Newgate Sessions, and sentence of death was given on March 23, to take effect the following day. On March 24 Greenwood was reprieved for a week, then taken to Tyburn on March 31, when the halter was actually placed around his neck. Once more he was reprieved, but on giving no evidence of submission or fear he was finally executed on April 6.

AN ABSTRACT OUT OF GREENEWOOD'S *AUNSWERE TO GIFFORD*

1. Our *Book of Common Prayer* is Antichrist's masse book Englished,[1] a "counterfeyt shewe of worshippe and of pretended praiers," the "common marchandise" of the antichristian priesthood.[2] Page 1a [Aii *recto* and *verso*].
2. Our church is "a church of worldlings," the *Book of Common Prayer* a Samaritan worshippe, and an Aegiptian calfe,[3] a mockinge of God, a popish mattins.[4] Page 2 [Aii *verso*].
3. Our manner of worshippe is a lothsome drudgerie.[5] "Abbadon is the father of all your prophets of England."[6] Page 17 [and 18].
4. Our assemblies of England as they stand are assemblies of atheists.[7] Page 21. The land is generally brought to atheisme.[8] Page 22.
5. This new worshippe "maketh men fall into dissolutenesse and bloudy tyrannie against God his saintes."[9] Page 22.
6. The ministrie and worshippe of our church (sayth he) "came out of the Divell's forge, and not out of Christ's Testament."[10] Page 26.
7. Our liturgie is "a devise of Antichrist, a dead letter, a quenching of the spirit," idolatrie, etc.[11] Page 34.
8. Our church is a false church, our ministrie false, our goverment false.[12] 41 page.
9. The church is subject to no lawes but such as Christ hath already made.[13] Page *eadem*.

Endorsement: Grenwood's errors and seditious sclaunders out of his boke of *Answer to Gifford*.

[1] Greenwood, *An Answere*, signature A ii *recto*. Also in Carlson, *The Writings of John Greenwood, 1587–1590*, p. 33. [2] Greenwood, signature A ii *verso*; Carlson, 33.
[3] Greenwood, signature A ii *verso*; Carlson, 33.
[4] Greenwood, signature A ii *verso*; Carlson, 34. [5] Greenwood, 17; Carlson, 58.
[6] Greenwood, 18; Carlson, 59. Greenwood really said: "Abbadon is the father of such prophets." [7] Greenwood, 21; Carlson, 64.
[8] Greenwood, 22; Carlson, 64. [9] Greenwood, 22; Carlson, 65.
[10] Greenwood, 26; Carlson, 70. [11] Greenwood, 34; Carlson, 81.
[12] Greenwood, 41; Carlson, 91. [13] Greenwood, 41; Carlson, 91.

XXI

THE ARRAIG[N]MENT OF CERTAINE PURITANES OR BROWNISTS THE SECOND OF APRILL, 1593 [MARCH 23, 1592/1593]

This document is in Stonyhurst College Library, Blackburn, Lancashire, Collectanea B, ff. 87–89—also numbered 343–345. I am indebted to Father Leo Hicks, who first drew my attention to this item and permitted me to make a copy. I am also grateful to Anthony G. Petti, who supplied me with a photostat, and who first printed this document in his helpful edition, *The Letters and Despatches of Richard Verstegan (c. 1550–1640)*, "Publications of the Catholic Record Society," Vol. LII (London, 1959), pp. 144–149. I have used the photostat of the original document, but I have also collated my transcription with that of Mr. Petti as a check on my reading of the manuscript.

We are fortunate in having three reports of the trial of Barrow. One is the summary of Barrow himself, who reported the indictments, the answers, and the conduct of the court, in his "Letter to an Honorable Lady and Countesse of His Kin[d]red," written April 4/5, 1593. We also have a letter from the Attorney-General, Thomas Egerton, to Sir John Puckering, written on the same day after the trial was concluded on March 23. In addition, we have the story of the trial from one who was present at the trial, who took full notes, who reports the arguments of the Queen's Serjeant, Thomas Owen, the replies of Barrow, and the names of nine members of the special commission. This report was sent to Richard Verstegan in Antwerp, who forwarded it to Father Robert Persons in Spain. Thus, we have three eye-witness accounts of the trial. Also we have two documents for the indictment of Barrow, and two for Greenwood's indictment.

The significance of the trial of the five Separatists is indicated by the leading judges who were appointed special commissioners. The two chief justices of the Queen's Bench and the Court of Common Pleas, besides two justices of the Queen's Bench, were in attendance. The Baron and the Chancellor of the Exchequer both sat on the commission. Also, the chancellor for the diocese of London, the Latin Secretary of State, and the Lord Mayor were present. Of the nine judges, two were members of the Privy Council—Sir John Wolley and Sir John Fortescue. Furthermore, Attorney-General Egerton and the Queen's Serjeant, Thomas Owen, conducted the prosecution of the case before the jury and the court.

Two prisoners, examined before the trial, were not arraigned. These were James Fowrestier and Robert Stokes, both deeply implicated in publishing and financing the Separatists' books. Fowrestier had renounced his Separatist connections, and Stokes had abandoned his Separatist views. The latter had also been excommunicated by the newly organized Separatist church in October or November, 1592.

Of the five Separatists sentenced to death, Barrow and Greenwood were executed on April 6, 1593; Scipio Bellot and Robert Boull died in prison about 1594–1595, and one, the scandalous elder, Daniel Studley, was imprisoned from 1593–1597, then exiled, first in April to the Magdalen Islands in the Gulf of St. Lawrence, and then in September to Amsterdam.

THE ARRAIG[N]MENT OF CERTAINE PURITANES OR BROWNISTS THE SECOND OF APRILL, 1593 [MARCH 23, 1592/1593]

The first that was arraigned was Henry Barrow. His indictment was grounded uppon the statute of 23 Elizabeth: that he advisedly and with a malitious intent, had devised, written, caused to be printed, and set forthe one booke called,[1] *The Discovery of the False*

[1] This is the statute of 23 Elizabeth, chapter II, section 4. The language is remarkably close: "That yf any person or persons . . . shall advisedlye and with a maliciouse intente againste our sayd Soveraigne Ladye, devyse and wrighte,

Church [*A Brief Discoverie of the False Church*], wherein first he enveyheth mightely against Her Majestie and the p[rese]nte state, both spirituall and temporall, alleaging that bothe she and the body of the comon welth, now standing as they do, are not christened nor within the rules of Christianity, unles she recall herself and the rest submitt themselves, unto the order of the church,[1] and that it will not be sufficient for Her Majestie to say that she hathe not bene instructed in the same, so long as she runneth on that course she doth, and yet will continew in the same.[2] And further that there is never a man, in whom there is any sparck of the grace of God, or that seeketh to keepe a good conscyence, can live in this comon weale, or use any kynde of trade or lyf whatsoever, for all are corrupted and full of sores, from the highest to the lowest of what estate or degree soever they bee.[3]

An other parte of the indictment was, in that they disallowed the aucthoritie of bishops, and in saying that their lawes were antichristian, and not ruled or directed by the finger of God, and that they, that did reverence the bishops, did reverence the beast spoken of in the Revelation.[4]

He denied the Q[ueen] able to make any lawe concerning the church, alleaging that he that maketh lawes, taketh and arrogateth to himself the office of God, for that is peculier only to God. That all people of this land saving such as were within their church were infidells; an infidell he took to be such as either never was of their churche, or once being thereof did shrinck and fall from the same.[5]

Greenewood was the next, and was indicted for subscribing and publishing of a booke, to which Barrow and he did agree, intituled

print or set forth, any manner of booke, ryme, ballade, letter or writing, conteyning any false, sedicious and slaunderous matter to the defamacion of the Queene's Majestie."

[1] Barrow believed that the Queen was baptized, but not rightly so, because the Roman Catholic clergyman, John Stokesley, Bishop of London, had baptized her on September 10, 1533. He did not believe in rebaptism to make valid a dubious baptizing. Nor did he believe that baptism was essential for salvation. The marrow of salvation was not the rite of baptism but that which baptism signified—God's salvific act which the rite sealed or signified. God seals his covenant or promise in baptism, but the promise is independent of the sealing.

[2] Carlson, *The Writings of Henry Barrow, 1587–1590*, pp. 418–453.

[3] *Ibid.*, pp. 282, 491, 544.

[4] *Ibid.*, pp. 337–339, 504–505, 553, 668. See also Carlson, *The Writings of John Greenwood, 1587–1590*, pp. 180, 212, 223, 228–229, 234, 246.

[5] *Ibid.*, pp. 148–149, 161. Carlson, *The Writings of Henry Barrow, 1587–1590*, pp. 198, 201, 206, 288–289, 291, 401–407, 414, 563, 602, 622, 640–647, 651, 656. Carlson, *The Writings of John Greenwood, 1587–1590*, p. 149.

a conference betwixt him and certaine ministers,[1] wherein first he dissaloweth the *Book of Common Prayer*, allowed both by the lawes of the land as also by the lawes of the churche, since *pri*[*mo*] *Elizabethae*,[2] that he had proved the congregation of England profane and Babell lyke, that it was ruled and governed by the pope's lawes, not by the lawes of Christ, by the power of Satan, not by the powre of Christ, profaning his name through their superstition and idolatry.[3] That there was not the seeking of a true ministrie as their [there] ought to be, but a maintaining of a false, that their assemblies were not ruled, governed, or directed by the Old or New Testament, but by the superstitious canons of popes and councells.[4] That such things as are in the churche, are not to be suffred for an order, to which none of the children of God may come in paine of damnation, that all the lawes of the churche are false and antichristian, that the ministers have no powre to teach, preach, or intermedle in the church of God, in that they are not rightly called. That bothe he and Barrow uppon conference with one Mr. Penry [Sperin] affirmed that the Q[ueen] had donne wickedly in giving powre to the bishops and they said they would seale the same with their blooudes.[5]

Studley an elder of their churche, was indicted, arraigned for publishing of the first.[6]

Billet for the same.[7]

Boules a disciple, for publishing the last.[8]

The Evidence of Serjant [*Thomas*] *Owen against Barrow.*

The lawe of 23° [*anno*] whereof he standeth indicted hathe two partes, the first for advisedly devising of libells, the second for wilfull publishing the same, for the proof of the first he inferred thease

[1] *A Collection of Certain Letters and Conferences Lately Passed Betwixt Certaine Preachers and Two Prisoners in the Fleet.* Actually, the book entitled *A Collection of Certaine Sclaunderous Articles* may be meant; although the word "conferences" does not appear, the book deals with the first conferences, and *A Collection of Certain Letter* continues with further conferences.

[2] Carlson, *The Writings of John Greenwood, 1587–1590*, pp. 123, 163–164, 166–169.

[3] *Ibid.*, pp. 98–101. [4] *Ibid.*, pp. 99–100.

[5] This statement was made by Barrow, not Greenwood, at this conference with Sperin on March 14, 1589/1590. *Ibid.*, pp. 190–191. Penry is mistakenly included, but he was in Scotland in 1590.

[6] That is, for publishing *A Brief Discoverie*. He was convicted.

[7] Scipio Bellot, brother of Arthur. Upon conviction, he alone was penitent and asked for a conference.

[8] Robert Boull, for publishing *A Collection of Certain Letters and Conferences*.

woords, whenas he alleaged Her Majestie not to be baptised, he condemneth the churche, universities, archbishops, bishops, vicars, parsons, cathedralls, churches, and all sortes of persons whatsoever, but themselves; that all that come to the churche are infidells. That the churche and comon weale and all was corrupted, all things oute of order, the publyke lawes and customes of all are corrupted, and that no prince can make new lawes.[1] That he did it malitiously in that it is false.[2] The fact is to be enquired or confessed, that was for the jury. The lawe to be delivered by the judges,[3] that the end and drift of their shooting was to bring in confusion notwithstanding their hypocresy. That the Q[ueen] her government was of God they confesse, but they take away the effect, that is, the making of lawes, and by consequence the government, and therefore don uppon malice insomuch as they alleage that she hathe no aucthoritie, and therefore this their diabolical perswasions tendeth to plaine insurrection and rebellion, and yet forsoothe cloked under the face of religion, as that of Kets[4] [Ket's Rebellion] in Edward VI his tyme, which was for nothing but for the removing of evill councellours from the king, so the rebelles in the north, and so the intended rebellion of thease cormorants, and devourers of men's soules, a fitt company to appoint her Majestie's counsell, beeing never an honest man among them.

That bothe they and the papists were pioners for the king of Spaine, the one begining at the one end, and the other at the other end, and so at the last they would mete at the harte of the midle.

Barrow coming to answere these matters, to some of them, in that they conserned the churche, he required triall by the churche, some he confessed, saying it was an easy matter for a man to fault in speeches. To other some he distinguished as the deniing of Christianity in the Q[ueen] and the rest of her subjects, he said he did not, but confessed althoughe they were christened in the tyme of popery, yet they were not signed before they were called by the spirite which possesseth them into the churche.

[1] Carlson, *The Writings of Henry Barrow, 1587–1590*, pp. 282, 491, 544.

[2] The law stated that if any person "shall advisedlye and with a maliciouse intente, againste our Soveraigne Ladye, devyse and wrighte." Therefore the Queen's Serjeant is seeking to prove intention and malice against the Queen.

[3] I think the sentence ends here and a new one begins.

[4] For Robert Ket, see Frederick W. Russell, *Kett's Rebellion in Norfolk* (London, 1859) and S. T. Bindoff, *Ket's Rebellion, 1549* (London, 1949). See also Joseph Clayton, *Robert Kett and the Norfolk Rising* (London, 1912). Ket was executed at Norwich on December 7, 1549, for resisting the economic encroachments of the manorial lords.

He avouched that our ministers and preachers [*i.e.*, Church of England clergy] were not of the churche, in that they are prescribed their tyme, their forme of prayer, their place to preach in, to wit a tub, in the which they bellow and belch oute, and that the Woord of God was troden under foote by thease beastlyke preachers, with many most damnable vilanous and oprobrious woords.[1]

In saying and writing that the Q[ueen] hathe no aucthoritie to make lawes, proveth malice, for take away her aucthoritie and take away her crowne, and so my Lord [Judge Edmund] Anderson said it was don purposely, *ergo* malitious.[2]

Barrow said that the bishops etc. are so farr from seeing good lawes executed that they seke the abrogating of them. He alleaged that the churche of God cannot have two heads, one in heaven and another in earthe, for by that meanes it would become a monster, much lesse archbishops, bishops and such lyke. And that thease limmes of the devill, meaning the aforesaid p[er]sons, will not acknowlege nor receave any ordinary powre but they will have it allowed them that princes may make lawes not he[a]rd of in the churche before.[3] Yet at the last he came in and was more calme (but that seemed to be but a cloke of hipocresy), for he acknowledged her Majestie's supremacy, and that in this booke written by him he intended not any hurte to Her Majestie. He protested he soughte [f. 89] the salvation of all men, and that he did not go aboute or intend any kynd of sedition and that he detested all Spanish invasion. That he would prove all the lawes made either consonant to the Woord of God or dissonant from the same. That the churche of Grenewood was the true churche, that the Q[ueen] cannot restraine a man from eating of flesh one day.[4] That a man which stealeth privily and for nede is not to be hanged, but he that taketh from a man p[er]force or breaketh his house, his woords were that *fur* might not be hanged, but *latro* might.[5] That all bishops and other spirituall ministers entring into the ministry uncald became antichristians and by

[1] Carlson, *The Writings of Henry Barrow, 1587–1590*, pp. 265, 504–505, 541, 544.
[2] *Ibid.*, pp. 401–407.
[3] *Ibid.*, pp. 442, 515, 601–602.
[4] *Ibid.*, pp. 397–406. By Act of 5 Elizabeth, chapter V, Wednesday was designated as Fish Day, in addition to Friday and Saturday. By Act of 27 Elizabeth, chapter XI, Wednesday was dropped. Barrow regarded abstinence from meat as a popish practice. The law intended to encourage the eating of fish, not as a religious measure but as a furtherance of navigation.
[5] An occasional and unwilling thief (*fur*) should not be hanged, but habitual robbers and inveterate brigands should be treated strictly in accordance with law.

wining [winning] the civill aucthority unto them, they become the beast spoken of in the revealation [Revelation].[1]

Grenewood said that the parishes of Protestants are gathered together in the name of Antichrist by a bell, that they be in bondage to the Egiptians and in Babilonical bondage, which Mr. Attorney [Thomas Egerton] did inferr must bee ment by the Queene. That the disciples did not stand in their christian liberty,[2] (a matter said Mr. Attorney to perswade them unto commotion). Beeing asked by what aucthority Stoke [Robert Stokes] was excommunicated, beeing one of their churche, he answered by the aucthoritie that Christ gave his churche; beeing asked what office he [Greenwood] did beare in the churche, he answered he was a teacher, [Francis] Johnson a pastor, [Daniel] Studley an elder, and that they were elected to thease offices by the congregation; beeing asked where, he answered, in a place free from all trooble, *vidz.*, in the middest of some wood.[3]

Billet was arraigned for publishing the first of the bookes, three of the which he sent to Sir Walter Rawly, and other three to his brother in the country, this man the wiseth of all in this action confessed his fault, and asked mercy.[4]

Boules was arraigned for publishing the second booke, that he paid the mony for the printing, that he had three of them at his returne into England, this man beeing but a yongman, and a fishmonger his prentise, denied to take his othe uppon a booke, but said it was sufficient to sweare by the name of God.[5]

Studley the elder of the churche and yet a linen draper was

[1] Archbishop Whitgift, who was also a Privy Councilor, was regarded by Barrow as the beast, spoken of in Revelation 13:15. In his fourth examination on March 18, 1588/1589, Barrow described the Archbishop to his face as a monster, a miserable compound, that second beast of the Book of Revelation.

[2] Carlson, *The Writings of John Greenwood, 1587–1590*, pp. 98, 100.

[3] Actually, at the house of Mr. Fox in St. Nicholas Lane, in September, 1592.

[4] Scipio Bellot was involved in the publication and distribution of *A Brief Discoverie of the False Church*. Bellot came from Lanteglos-by-Fowey, in Cornwall, and his brother was Arthur, who went to Dort to supervise the printing of the Separatists' books. It is interesting to note that Sir Walter Raleigh received three copies. Raleigh, though from Devon, served as lord lieutenant of Cornwall, warden of the mines and stannaries, and vice-admiral of both Cornwall and Devon. He was urged to aid John Udall in prison. On April 4, 1593, he cautioned against extreme penalties in the "Act to Retain the Queen's Subjects in Obedience," which enforced conformity for sectaries, Brownists, and Separatists, or banishment and exile for non-compliance. See J. E. Neale, *Elizabeth and Her Parliaments, 1584–1601*, pp. 280–297.

[5] Robert Boull was indicted for publishing *A Collection of Certain Letters and Conferences*. All three points are in his examination of March 19, which clearly was used for his indictment. His conviction was evidently a foregone conclusion.

arraigned for publishing the first booke, his office in the churche (as my Lord Anderson said for himself would not tell it in that place, and yet [Studley] had shewed the same to my Lord Anderson) was to see and survey men's houses, their families, their children, and now and then for fassion sake their wyves, with some other things which my Lord Anderson would not utter.[1]

Uppon thease indictments they were arraigned, found guilty and had their judgments as fellons.[2]

Before thease men by spetiall comission.

My Lord Mayor[3]	Sir John Fortescue[8]
Sir John Wolley[4]	Sir John Popham Lord Chief Justice[9]
Lord Anderson[5]	Justice Gaudie[10]
Barron Clerck[6]	Justice Fenner[11]
Doctor Stanhope[7]	with others/

Verstegan's Dispatches
Letter to Father Persons.

Collectanea B, ff. 87–89—also
numbered 343–345
Stonyhurst College Library

See Anthony G. Petti, *The Letters and Despatches of Richard Verstegan* (*c*. 1550–1640). "Publications of the Catholic Record Society," Vol. LII (London, 1959), pp. 144–149.

[1] Daniel Studley received the copy of *A Brief Discoverie of the False Church* from Barrow's hands [not "study"], in the Fleet. He delivered the copy sheet by sheet to James Fowrestier, who prepared the fair copy. Judge Anderson's suspicions about elder Studley's supervisory activities seem prescient. In the Ancient Church at Amsterdam, Studley was a trouble-maker, an elder who overstepped the bounds of decency and propriety. He is severely attacked by Thomas White, Christopher Lawne, and Edward Arber, in their books.

[2] Found guilty by the jury, sentenced to death as guilty of felony, Barrow and Greenwood were sentenced to die the next day, March 24, reprieved until March 31, again reprieved, and hanged on April 6. Boull and Scipio Bellot died in prison before 1596. Studley was banished in 1597, first to the Magdalen Islands in the Gulf of St. Lawrence and then to Amsterdam.

[3] Sir William Roe [Rowe] was lord mayor of London from September 1592 to September 1593.

[4] Sir John Wolley, Latin Secretary of State.

[5] Sir Edmund Anderson, Chief Justice of the Common Pleas.

[6] Sir Robert Clarke, Baron of the Exchequer.

[7] There is a Sir John Stanhope, vice-chamberlain and Baron Stanhope of Harrington, who sat on cases in the Star Chamber. But evidently Dr. Edward Stanhope is intended. He was chancellor in the diocese of London.

[8] Sir John Fortescue, Chancellor of the Exchequer.

[9] Sir John Popham, Chief Justice of the Queen's Bench.

[10] Francis Gawdy, Justice of the Queen's Bench.

[11] Edward Fenner, Justice of the Queen's Bench.

XXII

THOMAS EGERTON TO SIR JOHN PUCKERING, MARCH 23, 1592/1593

This letter of Attorney-General Thomas Egerton to Sir John Puckering, Lord Keeper of the Great Seal of England, is in Harley MSS. 6849, f. 191. It is of special value because it was written by an eye-witness on the same day that the Barrowists were found guilty in court. It reveals the defiance of four of the five defendants, and indicates their denial of any malicious intent against the Queen.

There is a copy of this letter also in Harley MSS. 7042, f. 34. These valuable papers come from the Sir John Puckering manuscripts and were used by John Strype. Edward Arber is wrong in stating that they have disappeared.

THOMAS EGERTON TO SIR JOHN PUCKERING, KEEPER OF THE GREAT SEAL OF ENGLAND, MARCH 23, 1592/1593

My moost humble duetye due to your Lordship. This daye, by vertue of Her Majesty's commyssion of Oyer and Terminer, in London, the court hath p[ro]ceded agaynst Barowe and Grenewood, for devysing,[1] and agaynst Scipio Bellotte, Robert Bowlle, and Danyel Studley, for publyshinge and dispersinge,[2] sedycyous

[1] The Act of 23 Elizabeth, chapter II, section 4, enacted: "That if any person . . . shall advisedly and with a malicious intent against our said Sovereign Lady, devise and write, print or set forth any manner of book . . . or writing, containing any false seditious and slanderous matter to the defamation of the Queen's Majesty that now is, or to the encouraging . . . of any insurrection or rebellion within this realm . . . that then every such offence shall be deemed felony, and the offenders therein . . . shall suffer such pains of death and forfeiture as in case of felony is used, . . ." (Prothero, *Select Statutes*, p. 79).

The authorship of Barrow and Greenwood was readily admitted and needed no proof, but the charge of malicious intent against the Queen was, in my judgment, without foundation.

[2] The Act of 23 Elizabeth, chapter II, section 4, also made it felonious for any person to cause a book containing slanderous and seditious matter to be printed,

bookes, etc. They are all atteynted, by verdicte and judgem[en]t, and direction gyven for execucion to be done to morowe, as in cases of lyke qualyty.

None shewed any token of recognicion of their offences and prayer of mercye, for the same, saving Bellotte alone, who desyreth conference and to be informed of his errors, and, with teares, affyrmeth hymselfe to be sorye that he hath bene mysledd.

The others p[re]tend loyaltye and obedience to Her Majesty, and indevour to drawe all, that [what] they have moost malicyouslye wrytten and publyshed agaynst Her Majesty's gov[er]nem[en]t, [was directed] to the byshopps and mynysters of the churche onlye, and are [were?] not meant agaynst Her Hyghenes, which being moost evydent agaynst them, and so found by the jurye, yet not one of them made any countenance of submission, but rather p[er]systed in that they be convicted of. Thys I have thought good to make knowne to your Lordship, to thende [the end] that yf Her Majesty's pleasure should be to have execucion deferred, it might be knowne this night, and order gyven accordinglye, otherwyse the direction gyven by the judge[1] in open court, will pr[e]vaile. And so I commytte your Lordship to the Almightye. 23 M[ar]tii, 1592 [1592/1593].

Your Lordship's moost humble at commanndment,

Thomas Egerton

published, or set forth. Scipio Bellot is the brother of Arthur Bellot, who was the examiner, or proof-reader, for *A Collection of Certain Letters and Conferences*, for *A Brief Discoverie of the False Church*, and for *A Plaine Refutation* (Collier, *Egerton Papers*, pp. 172, 175). He was also the man who delivered two copies of *A Brief Discoverie of the False Church* to Daniel Studley, and he was the one who made four copies of letters drafted by Barrow. Barrow refers to Scipio Byllet, which is erroneously transcribed by John Payne Collier as Stephen Byllet (*Egerton Papers*, 176, 178). There is a record in the Amsterdam archives of Arthur Billet, who died in February, 1601/1602, and of his widow, Sarah. Robert Bowle (or Boull) arranged for the printing in Dort of *A Collection of Certain Letters and Conferences* and aided in their delivery to England (*Egerton Papers*, 172–174). We have almost no data on Scipio Bellot and his role as distributor of Barrowist books. He died in prison, *c.* 1594–1595.

Daniel Studley received the original copy of *A Brief Discoverie of the False Church*, sheet by sheet, from Barrow in the Fleet, and copied some or all of it for the printer. He also helped to distribute the printed copies (*Egerton Papers*, 175–176). After suffering four years' imprisonment, he was exiled to Amsterdam, where he was a ruling elder—and a troublesome one who occasioned slander—in the Ancient Church with Francis Johnson.

[1] Sir Edmund Anderson, Lord Chief Justice of the Common Pleas, or Sir John Popham, Lord Chief Justice of the Queen's Bench.

XXIII

THOMAS EGERTON TO SIR JOHN PUCKERING, MARCH 26, 1593

This letter is in Harley MSS. 6849, f. 193. It refers to a conference with Barrow, and possibly with the other Barrowists, which proved to be unsuccessful in changing Barrow's attitudes. There is a copy of the same letter in Harley MSS. 7042, f. 34 *recto* and *verso*.

THOMAS EGERTON TO SIR JOHN PUCKERING, LORD KEEPER OF THE GREAT SEAL. MARCH 26, 1593

I have spent this whoale [Monday] aft[er]noon at a fruytles ydle conference,[1] and am but now ret[ur]ned both wearye and weake. Yf my healthe will serve me I will wayte upon your Lordship to morowe mornynge and make report of this daye's exercyse.[2] I have sent to your Lordship herwith, *viz.*, an abstracte of the bille in the Lower House agaynst recusantes,[3] reformed as the committees have brought it agayne into the House. Howe it is in any thinges changed in substance, from the bille as it was fyrst exhybyted, doeth appere in the marginall notes, which to morowe I will more fullye declare to your Lordship, yf it shall please your Lordship to gyve me leave. And so rest in all thinges at your Lordship's commandem[en]t, this 26th of Marche, 1593.

Your Lordship's most humble at commande,

Thomas Egerton

[1] A conference with Barrow, and possibly with John Greenwood, Daniel Studley and Robert Bowle (Boull) as well. Since Bellot acknowledged his errors and placed himself at the mercy of the court, it is unlikely that he was visited by Egerton.

[2] Because of ill health, Egerton may have missed this meeting. He spent March 27 in Parliament and March 28 at home. For this reason, he writes a letter on March 28 to Puckering.

[3] See 35 Elizabeth, chapter II. "An Acte against Popish Recusants." The introductory listing is "An Acte for the Restreyninge of Popish Recusants to Some Certen Places of Aboade." *The Statutes of the Realm*, IV, Part II, pp. 840, 843–846.

XXIV

THOMAS EGERTON TO SIR JOHN PUCKERING, MARCH 28, 1593

This letter is in Harley MSS. 6849, f. 195. It enables us to date Barrow's letter requesting a "christian and peaceable conference with some learned and moderate persons" as March 26 or 27, 1593. It reveals Egerton's concern to keep Sir John Puckering and Lord Burghley informed, and seems to indicate that of the nine known commissioners sitting in trial of Barrow, Sir Edmund Anderson, Lord Chief Justice of the Common Pleas, is the most important judge. There is a copy of this letter in Harley MSS. 7042, f. 34 *verso*.

THOMAS EGERTON TO SIR JOHN PUCKERING, LORD KEEPER OF THE GREAT SEAL MARCH 28, 1593

My moost humble duetye due to your Lordship.[1] Immediatlye after my returne from the p[ar]lement house yesterdaye,[2] I dyd wryte to my Lord Treasorr[er][3] the man[er] and successe [fruyte?] of the conference[4] with Barrowe, and on what termes he stoode, and what disputacion he requyreth, and withall I dyd send to his Lordship [Burghley] a copy of Barrow's request in that behalfe,[5] which together with your letters were deliv[er]ed to his Lordship yesterdaye in the afternoone. So as, so farre as by letters I can informe his Lordship [Burghley], ys alredye done. I am sory this weakenes of healthe falleth unto me at this tyme. But Godd's will must be done. Yf your Lordship thinke good, that my L[ord] Anderson[6] shoulde attende my L[ord] Treasore to informe his

[1] Sir John Puckering, Lord Keeper of the Great Seal.
[2] March 27. [3] Lord Burghley. [4] On March 26.
[5] Barrow's request for a conference is in his letter of March 26 or 27. See chapters XII, XIII.
[6] Sir Edmund Anderson, Chief Justice of the Common Pleas.

Lordship [Burghley] further, I beseche you lette my L[ord] Anderson know your Lordship's pleasure therin, for I would forbeare goinge into the ayre this one day, yf I might, because I am so advised. So restinge [?] [rest upon?] at your Lordship's commandm[en]t in all things. I moost humblye take leave. 28 Martii, 1593.

Your Lordship's moost humble at commande,

Thomas Egerton

XXV

REASONS AGAINST PUBLIKE DISPUTATION WITH [HENRY] BAROW. IT IS NOT EQUALL, SAFE NOR FITTE TO GRAUNT A DISPUTATION TO SECTARIES

This document is in Harley MSS. 6848, f. 212. It is printed in Burrage, *Early English Dissenters*, II, 99–100, and is substantially correct. In points 9 and 12 there is no need of [?], and in point 9 Burrage omits seven words, probably because the manuscript reading is difficult.

On March 23 Barrow was sentenced to death, and reprieved the next day. On Monday, March 26, Attorney-General Thomas Egerton conferred with Barrow. In writing to Sir John Puckering, Egerton described his experience: "I have spent this whoale afternoon at a fruytles ydle conference, and am but now returned both wearye and weake." Evidently Barrow was adamant and defiant, even under sentence of death. In his letter of March 26 Barrow asked for a christian and peaceable conference, and in his letter of March 27 he requested a christian and peaceable disputation by the Scriptures. Egerton informed Sir John Puckering and Lord Burghley, who in turn consulted the Archbishop of Canterbury or the Bishop of London. The resultant reasons for denying the request for a disputation were probably written March 28 by the Archbishop himself, in consultation with his advisers. Richard Cosin may have aided in the composition.

REASONS AGAINST PUBLIKE DISPUTATION WITH [HENRY] BAROW. IT IS NOT EQUALL, SAFE NOR FITTE TO GRAUNT A DISPUTATION TO SECTARIES

1. It hath ever been denied by the state to papistes, a secte that had possession of the church for some hundred yeares before.

2. To call the ministerie, and confession, of the Church of England into question were to call all other churches likewise into question against whom also the[i]r exceptions extend.[1]
3. The Church of England hath submitted her selfe to disputation thrise: 1. in King Edward's tyme, [2.] in Queene Marie, [3.] in Queene Elizabethe's.[2]
4. The erroneous opinions of these men have been already condemned by just treatises of the most famous learned men that have lyved since restitution of relligion.[3]
5. It is no reason that relligion, and the controversies thereof, the same beinge alreadie established by parlament, should be examyned now by an inferiour authoritie by way of disputation.
6. It is no reason (that all the Reformed Churches in Europe acknowledginge our Church of England for a sister) the same should be now brought into question at the will and request of a fewe sectaries.
7. Their principall errours have been already discussed by disputations and writinges in the dayes of Saint Augustine, and that by himselfe, etc.[4]
8. To call the ministerie of England into question is to strengthen the papistes, and to dishable all the exercises of the mysteries of relligion ever synce the establishment thereof.
9. It hath ever been the manner of heretiques to require the same by great importunities, and continuall exclamations, as Novatus,[5] Arrius,[6] Eunomius,[7] Paulus Samosatenus,[8] Campion,[9] and such like.

[1] That is, the reformed Calvinistic churches and the Roman Catholic church.

[2] In the reign of Edward VI, a disputation was held December 14–19, 1548. In the reign of Mary the disputation occurred October 23–30, 1553. In the first year of Elizabeth's accession, a disputation of sorts was conducted on March 31 and April 3, 1559. All three involved points of theology between Roman Catholics and Protestants. See R. W. Dixon, *History of the Church of England,* II (1895), pp. 475–478 and 544–548; IV (1891), pp. 75–92; V (1902), pp. 74–89. See also Francis Aidan Gasquet and Edmund Bishop, *Edward VI and the Book of Common Prayer* (1890 and 1891), chapter XI and Appendix V. Revised edition (1928), chapter IX.

[3] Men such as John Calvin, Theodore Beza, Heinrich Bullinger, William Perkins, Johannes Oecolampadius, John Jewel.

[4] See especially the anti-Donatist and the anti-Pelagian writings of Augustine.

[5] Novatus or Novatian was an anti-pope, a schismatic, and a strict disciplinarian. He opposed Pope Cornelius, after his election in 251, and was unduly strict in advocating purity and rigorous treatment of the *lapsi* after the Decian persecution in 250–251.

[6] Arius was the advocate of the *homoiousian* position at the Council of Nicaea in 325. In his long controversy with Athanasius, he lost the battle but his rationalistic doctrines went marching on.

10. It hath already been discussed by bookes written, out of which the truth may better appear, than by a tumultuarie disputation.[1]
11. They that require disputation of the civill magistrate will not stande to the judgement of the civill magistrate.
12. If the Church should satisfie everie sect that riseth, there were no ende of disputations.

[7] Eunomius of Cappadocia, Bishop of Cyzicus (360–364), was condemned by a council of bishops at Constantinople and banished by Constantius. The emperor Julian the Apostate (361–363) did not regard the Arian views of Eunomius as objectionable, and recalled him.

[8] Paul of Samosata was bishop of Antioch from *ca.* 260 to 269, when he was deposed for his non-Trinitarian and rationalistic views.

[9] Edmund Campion (1540–1581), Catholic recusant and martyr, disputed with William Charke, William Day, William Fulke, Roger Goad, Alexander Nowell, and Dr. John Walker in the Tower on August 31, September 18, 23, 27, 1581. See Richard Simpson, *Edmund Campion, Jesuit Protomartyr of England.* New edition (London, 1907).

[1] Some of the relevant treatises against the Separatists and dissenters are: Richard Alison, *A Plaine Confutation* (1590); Richard Cosin, *Conspiracy for Pretended Reformation* (1591); George Gifford, *A Short Treatise* (1590), *A Plaine Declaration* (1590), and *A Short Reply* (1591); Hadrianus Saravia, *Of the Diverse Degrees of the Ministers of the Gospell* (1591; Latin edition 1590); Robert Some, *A Godly Treatise* (May, 1588; September, 1588; May, 1589); Matthew Sutcliffe, *A Remonstrance* (1590), *A Treatise of Ecclesiasticall Discipline* (1590), and *An Answere to a Certaine Libel Supplicatorie* (1592); Richard Bancroft's *A Survay of the Pretended Holy Discipline* and his *Daungerous Positions and Proceedings* appeared in 1593. Also, Thomas Bilson's *The Perpetual Governement of Christe's Church* and Richard Hooker's *Of the Lawes of Ecclesiasticall Politie* were published in 1593.

XXVI

FOUR LETTERS TO FATHER ROBERT PERSONS MARCH–MAY, 1593

The following four letters were written by Richard Verstegan to Father Robert Persons in Spain. They are quotations or paraphrases from letters sent to Verstegan in Antwerp by one or more London informants. They seem to be based, at least partly, on eye-witness accounts, and they supply new information.

I am indebted to Father Leo Hicks, who first called my attention to these letters and who provided me with photostats. I also am obliged to Anthony G. Petti, who has printed the Verstegan letters *in extenso*. I have given only those extracts relevant to the Separatists, but Mr. Petti has given us all the Verstegan dispatches in his work, *The Letters and Despatches of Richard Verstegan (c. 1550–1640)*, "Publications of the Catholic Record Society," Vol. LII (London, 1959).

VERSTEGAN TO FATHER ROBERT PERSONS, APRIL 1 [MARCH 22, 1592/1593]

The Puritans sent one John Norton[1] into Scotland ther to print

[1] One is tempted to conclude that John Norton is a transcriptional mistake for John Penry. Penry went to Scotland in October–November, 1589, to escape the pursuivants who were seeking the Marprelate press. Penry and Robert Waldegrave printed at least four books in 1590–1591. Penry returned to London about October, 1592, and was imprisoned March 22, 1592/1593. When the writer speaks of the imprisonment of Norton and the capture of Martin Marprelate, he may be thinking of and reporting the same person—Penry.

The difficulty is that there was a John Norton who went to Scotland *ca.* 1587 and set up a bookselling shop in Edinburgh. He was a nephew of William Norton, who may have sent John to Scotland. From David Calderwood, *The History of the Kirk of Scotland*, V (Edinburgh, 1844), page 77, we learn that John Norton's letter to Dr. Richard Bancroft was intercepted. In this letter Norton had expressed his gratitude for Dr. Bancroft's bountifulness. Norton was suspected to be a spy for Dr. Bancroft. Consequently, Norton was examined on February 12, 1589/1590, by Robert Bruce. Norton confessed that, on the

their books, who is returned and imprisoned in London. There were eighty Puritanes lately taken at a sermon in Finisbury Feild and with them Mr. Martin Marprelate is thought to be taken.[1]

There was a Brownist hanged for his seditious tongue and his body was begged by some of his consortes, who did put it in a coffin and covered it over with black clothe and brought it before the doore where the Judge was logd that had condemned him, and on the foure corners of the coffin were fixed rayling libells against the Judge, affirming that this was the sixteenth martir that they had martyred for the profession of the true Gospel of Christ.[2]

Stonyhurst College
Verstegan Dispatches
Collectanea B, f. 86
Antwerp, 1 April, 1593
To Father Persons

London Informant to Verstegan,
ca. March 20, 1593
March 10

VERSTEGAN TO FATHER ROBERT PERSONS, APRIL 28 [APRIL 18], 1593

The second of this moneth [March 23] fyve Brownists or Puritanes were arraigned and condemned to die as fellons.[3] The next day

instigation of Dr. Bancroft, his uncle, William Norton, had sent him to Scotland and had provided him with questions. It is possible that he went to Scotland with the dual purpose of establishing a stationer's shop and of serving as an agent in Dr. Bancroft's espionage network.

John Norton seems to have been in London in 1592 and to have returned to Scotland where he remained until 1596. In 1601 he and his cousin, Bonham Norton, were accused of inducing Andro Hart to send printers to Dordrecht (Dort) in order to print in the Netherlands Bibles and other privileged books. In 1610–1612/1613 John Norton published the beautiful and sumptuous edition, in eight folio volumes, of the works of St. Chrysostom: *S. Ioannis Chrysostomi Opera Graecé, Octo Voluminibus* (Eton). See Henry R. Plomer, *Abstracts from the Wills of English Printers and Stationers from 1492 to 1630* (London, 1903), p. 47; see also H. G. Aldis *et al.*, *A Dictionary of Printers and Booksellers in England and Ireland, and of Foreign Printers of English Books, 1557–1640* (London, 1910), p. 202.

[1] The reference is to the capture of about seventy-two Separatists in the woods at Islington—near Finsbury—on March 4, 1592/1593. In the letter of April 21/May 1, the number is seventy. Penry was captured but escaped the same evening. In the popular mind he was erroneously identified as Martin Marprelate.

[2] This is a reference to Roger Rippon, who died at Newgate on February 16, 1592/1593. He was not hanged, but died of the infection—perhaps the plague or typhoid. The coffin incident occurred on February 17.

[3] On Friday, March 23, at Sessions Hall, in the Old Bailey, Newgate, five Separatists were sentenced; Henry Barrow and John Greenwood, for printing seditious books, and Scipio Bellot, Robert Boull, and Daniel Studley, for publishing and distributing the books.

[April 3, or March 24] was one Penry a Welshman and a principall puritane minister taken, and is undoubtedly the same man that wrote under the name of Martin Marprelate.[1] The fourth of this present [March 25] he was examined before the Counsell[2] and by reason of his apprehension the execution of the others was stayed.[3]

Stonyhurst College
Verstegan Dispatches
Collectanea B, f. 95

London Informant to Verstegan, April 6/March 27, 1593

VERSTEGAN TO FATHER ROBERT PERSONS, APRIL 28 [APRIL 18] 1593

By another letter dated in London[4] the 10 of this moneth of Aprill [March 31] I do understand that two of the Brownists or purest Puritaines (which the 2 of this month [March 23] were condemned to die), were caried unto the place of execution, and the halters beeing put aboute their necks and tyed fast unto the gallowes, they were presently untyed and caried back againe alyve.[5] It seemeth

1 Penry was captured on Thursday, March 22, at Stepney, but he was not Martin Marprelate, as many believed. He was a *de facto* minister, but he was never ordained into any clerical office. He believed that a candidate should be called by a church or congregation. Since he never was able to preach in England for fear of arrest, he was not called, though he wished to be an evangelist in the land of his birth—Wales.

2 He was examined on March 24 before Justice Richard Young and on March 26 by Dr. Richard Vaughan and others, who had been sent to confer with him. Since Sir John Puckering, Lord Keeper of the Great Seal, was a Privy Councillor, and since he had sent Dr. Vaughan to confer with Penry, the report may have spread that he was examined by the Privy Council.

3 The statement may be true, but there is no evidence to indicate a causal connection between the arrest of Penry on March 22 and the reprieve granted early in the morning of March 24. It was probably Judge Anderson who pronounced sentence on March 23, and set the next day for execution. Very likely he knew of the arrest of Penry before sentencing the Separatists. It was the Queen who ordered a reprieve, perhaps during the evening of March 23, to be delivered the following morning.

4 Richard Verstegan in Antwerp received a letter written March 31/April 10—the same day set for the execution. He then summarized this timely letter in his report to Father Persons, who was in Spain.

5 In his letter of April 4/5 to Anne (Russell) Dudley, the Countess of Warwick, Barrow spoke of "being tyed by the necks to the tree." As they completed their final words to the onlookers, a reprieve arrived. "Which was not onely thankfully received of us, but with exceeding rejoysing and applause of all the people, both at the place of execution, and in the wayes, streets, and houses, as we returned."

that the officers durst not execute them by reason of the great multytude of Puritans there present, as also flocking together in the city of London, who began openly to murmur and to give oute threatening speeches, insomuch that a present commotion was feared, and what may yet follow is doubtfull, considering the heate of those purified spirites.

Stonyhurst College
Verstegan Dispatches,
Collectanea B, f. 96.

London Informant to Verstegan,
April 10 / March 31, 1593

VERSTEGAN TO FATHER ROBERT PERSONS, [*CA.* MAY 15 [MAY 5], 1593]

Amonge other accidents there fell oute of late a very strange matter, of two men long since famous for their private opinions, Barrow and Greenwood having thease four or five yeares beene imprisoned in the Fleete.[1] Now uppon the apprehension of 70 of their followers in a woode neere London[2] it came to light that thease men had been publishers of seditious pamphlets,[3] as that they might depose the Queene yf she would not conforme her self to their doctrine[4] and divers other lyke points, for which they were arraigned, condemned, and hanged at Tyborne. They taught it among divers other their doctrines as a thing unlawfull to say the Lord's Prayer, and at their deathes could by no meanes be enduced to say it, no,

[1] Barrow was imprisoned from November 19, 1587, to April 6, 1593—a period of five years, four months, and eighteen days. Greenwood was arrested October 8, 1587, and was executed April 6, 1593. Since he was bailed for about five months in 1592, he was in prison for five years and one month.

[2] The arrest of March 4, 1592/1593, at Islington woods.

[3] The authorship was no secret. Most of the Separatist works carry the names of the writers.

[4] This is a misinterpretation. The Separatists believed in excommunication for those who grievously sinned, who had been warned, and who obstinately resisted any penitence—*provided that they were members of the Separatist church.* As a theoretical or academic question, the examiners asked if the Queen could be excommunicated. The Separatists unflinchingly believed that all *members*—even including the Queen—were subject to God's discipline. Though they never dreamed of excommunicating the Queen, they were compelled to give an academic and theoretical and consistent answer. But they did not advocate deposition. They separated the civil and ecclesiastical powers, and advocated civil obedience even toward an ungodly ruler. In fact, their protestations of loyalty toward the Queen are pathetically sincere.

not with promise of lyf.[1] They were once [March 31] caried to the place of execution afore, where after long prayer which they were permitted to use, and leave to retyre themselves under an hedge, (being redy to be executed), they were caried back againe, but within three or foure dayes[2] after they came againe early to the place, using lyke long protestations of prayer, and thirsting after drinck, which presently was in a redynesse for them, they died obstinately. Their followers, canonizing them for more than martirs, do enveighe privately against the bishops, as the principall procurers thereof. The Q[ueen] lyeth as yet at St. James. The sicknesse beginneth to dispers it self much in the city, their [there] die aboute some 35 of the plague a weeke. It is thought it wilbe the cause of the Queen's sooner remove than she purposed. [By August the death rate was estimated to be 1540 a week around London. *Ibid.*, f. 127].[3]

Stonyhurst College
Verstegan's Dispatches
Collectanea B, ff. 107, 108

London Informant to Verstegan,
ca. May 1/April 21, 1593

[1] The Separatists were constantly maligned because of their attitude towards the Lord's Prayer. They regarded it as the absolute, perfect, and true pattern of prayer. They disliked stinted, rote prayers, and believed in prayer by the Spirit. They taught that the Lord's Prayer was not his personal prayer, because he would not need to pray for the forgiveness of sins or trespasses. The Lord's Prayer to the Separatists was the prayer taught by the Lord to his disciples. This was to be followed as a perfect model, but not to be recited mechanically. Rather, it was to be used for edification.

[2] Actually, six days. The second reprieve was granted on March 31, and the execution occurred April 6, 1593.

[3] John Stow estimated the mortality for 1593 from all causes, for London and the liberties, as 17,844, of which the plague accounted for 10,662—about 888 each month. Another estimate from a later broadside gives a total of 25,886, of which the plague accounted for 15,003—about 1250 a month. The peak month may have been in July or August. See Charles Creighton, *A History of Epidemics in Britain from A.D. 664 to the Extinction of Plague* (Cambridge, 1891), pp. 351–361.

XXVII

EXAMINATIONS IN MARCH, 1592/1593

There are fourteen examinations of the Separatists during March. If we count the two examinations of Barrow and Greenwood on March 11, and their second examinations on March 20 (printed in the main text), there are eighteen examinations in all, and sixteen examinants.

The first nine examinations deal with common material, excepting the one of John Edwardes, which pertains to Penry. The prisoners were asked about the coffin, the affixed libels, and their participation in carrying the coffin to Justice Young's house. The determination of the officials to learn more about this insulting episode perhaps accounts for their early examinations—all on March 6, 7, 8, 9 except Bowman's examination on March 1. The Separatists were questioned about the covenant they had made, how long they had attended the conventicles, where the meetings were held. Daniel Bucke gives the fullest information about officers, members, finance, and celebration of the sacraments. All refused to take the hated *ex officio* oath, which required a man to answer truly whatever questions were put to him, and which usually required the person to incriminate himself and his friends.

Most of the examinants were asked about John Penry. Did they know him? When did they see him last? Did he expound the Word at the March 4 meeting? Where was he? The examination of John Edwardes deals mostly with Penry's journey from Edinburgh to London, halting-places, persons visited, and dates. The examiners are Richard Young, John Ellis, and Henry Towneshend.

The tenth, eleventh, twelfth, and thirteenth examinations are conducted by Sir John Popham, Chief Justice of the Queen's Bench, Sir Edmund Anderson, Chief Justice of the Common Pleas, Thomas Egerton, Attorney-General, and Edward Stanhope, Chancellor to the Bishop of London. They are seeking to establish by confession the role of the men in publishing, dispersing, or financing Separatist books, thus bringing them within compass of the statute of 23 Elizabeth, chapter II, and acquiring data for their forthcoming arraignment.

The last examination is directed by Richard Young. It is Penry's second exam, since he had been interrogated by Young on March 24, but no record is extant of the first interrogation.

Richard Hawton, probably not a Separatist but a curiosity-seeker, is the only prisoner who promises to return to the Church of England.

Of the fourteen examinants, we have a second examination for seven of them: John Nicholas, William Clarke, and George Johnson on April 2; John Barnes and Abraham Pulbery on April 3; Christopher Bowman on April 4; and John Penry on April 5. Also we have two summaries of Bowman's examination of April 4 and of Penry's examination of April 5. There are other examinations and conferences for Penry, but these will be printed in subsequent volumes on his writings.

Of the fourteen examinations, six are given completely by Burrage, two incompletely, and six others are not printed, nor are the four examinations of Barrow and Greenwood published. Perhaps access to the Ellesmere papers was not possible in 1912. Furthermore, John Payne Collier had published some items in *The Egerton Papers*, pp. 166–179.

ALPHABETICAL LIST OF PRISONERS EXAMINED (52)

	Date of Examination	*Age in 1593*	*Date of Imprisonment*	*Main Occupation*
Abraham, Robert	April 3	26	March 4, 1592/3	leather dresser
	April 3			
Barnes, John	March 8	26	March 4, 1592/3	tailor
	April 3			
Barrow, Henry	March 11	42	November 19, 1587	lawyer
	March 20			
Bellot, Arthur	April 5	25	March 22, 1592/3	scholar
Boull, Robert	March 19	*ca.* 23		fishmonger
Bowman, Christopher	March 1	32	*ca.* Feb. 28, 1592/3	goldsmith
	April 4			
Boyse, Edward	April 5	33	October 8, 1587 December 6, 1592	haberdasher

	Date of Examination	*Age in 1593*	*Date of Imprisonment*	*Main Occupation*
Bristowe, David	April 5	30	March 4, 1592/3	tailor
Brodwater, Henry	April 3	29	*ca.* Feb. 19–20, 1592/3	scrivener
Bucke, Daniel	March 9		March 4, 1592/3	scrivener
Clark, John	April 3	50	*ca.* December, 1589	farmer
Clark, William	March 8	40	March 4, 1592/3	caps
	April 2			
Collier, George	April 5	38	October 8, 1587	haberdasher
Curland, William	April 5	30	March 4, 1592/3	shipwright
Dalamore, John	April 3	25	March 4, 1592/3	weaver
Darvall, William	April 6	25	March 4, 1592/3	carpenter
Denford, William	April 6	50	March 4, 1592/3	schoolmaster
Diggins, Christopher	April 3	24	*ca.* Feb. 17–19, 1592/3	weaver
Edwardes, John	March 6		March 4, 1592/3	
Eyles, William	April 4	22	March 4, 1592/3	tailor
Farrot, Thomas	April 3	22	March 4, 1592/3	servant
Fowrestier, James	March 19		December, 1589	physician
Gilbert, Edward	April 4	21	March 4, 1592/3	trunkmaker
Grave, Edward	April 3	25	March 22, 1592/3	fishmonger
Greenwood, John	March 11	*ca.* 33	October 8, 1587	clergyman
	March 20		December 6, 1592	
Hawton, Richard	March 8			shoemaker
Hewett, Thomas	April 4	30	March 4, 1592/3	pursemaker
Hulkes, John	April 4	21	March 4, 1592/3	shipwright
Johnson, Francis	April 5	31	October, 1592	clergyman
			December 6, 1592	
Johnson, George	March 7	29	March 4, 1592/3	schoolteacher
	April 2			
Knyviton, George	April 4	24	March 22, 1592/3	apothecary
Marshall, William	April 4	32	March 4, 1592/3	shipwright
Mason, William	April 4	24	March 4, 1592/3	shipwright
Mihilfeld, Thomas	April 5	33	March 4, 1592/3	joiner
Mitchell, Thomas	April 24	30	March 4, 1592/3	turner
Nicholas, John	March 8	36	March 13, 1588/9	glover
	April 2		March 4, 1592/3	
Parkes, John	April 5	50	March 4, 1592/3	clothworker
Pedder, Leonard	April 5	30	March 4, 1592/3	shoemaker
Penry, John	March 26	30	March 22, 1592/3	writer
	April 5			
Pulbery, Abraham	March 7	25	April, 1592	pursemaker
	April 3	24	March 4, 1592/3	
Settle, Thomas	April 6	38	December 17–24, 1592	clergyman
Smells, George	April 10	40	April 8, 1593	tailor
Smithe, William	April 5	30	*ca.* Feb. 17, 1592/3	clergyman
Smyth, Quintin	April 6	30	March 4, 1592/3	feltmaker
Sparewe, John	April 24	60	March 13, 1588/89	
Stokes, Robert	March 19			
Studley, Daniel	March 20	*ca.* 41	*ca.* December 17, 1592	draper
Symkins, Christopher	April 5	22	March 4, 1592/3	coppersmith
Unwin, Katherin	April 6	35	October 8, 1587	widow
			March 10, 1592/3	
Waterer, Roger	April 3	22	December 1589	haberdasher
Weaver, William	April 6	40	March 4, 1592/3	shoemaker
Wythers, Henry	April 4	27	March 4, 1592/3	shipwright

XXVIII

ROGER RIPPON'S COFFIN LABEL

Roger Rippon, of Southwark, was a prisoner in Newgate, where he died on Friday, February 16, 1592/1593. His body was carried in a coffin on February 17 from Newgate to Cheapside and to the home of Justice Richard Young. A special inscription on the coffin described the Archbishop of Canterbury as that "great ennemye of God" and that "great ennemy of the saints." It characterized Young as one who had "abused his power for the upholding of the Romishe Antichriste, prelacy, and preisthood." Since Rippon was the sixteenth or seventeenth prisoner to die in the malodorous Newgate, 1587–1592, the Separatists called the High Commissioners murderers —including Whitgift and Young. The authorities were deeply incensed and made diligent search for those implicated in any way with the coffin, label, and macabre trek through London.

ROGER RIPPON'S COFFIN LABEL

This is the corps[e] of Roger Ripponn, a servaunt of Christ, and Her Majestie's faithfull subject, who is the last of 16 or 17 which that great enne[m]ye of God, the Archbishop of Canterbury, with the Highe Commissioners, have murdere[d] in Newgate within theise 5 yeares for the testimony of Jesus Christ.

His soule is now with the Lord and his bloud cryeth for spedy vengeance against that great ennemy of the sainctes and against Mr. Richard Younge, who in this and many the like poynts hath abused his power for the upholding of the Romishe Antichriste, prelacy and preisthood.

Endorsement: February 1592 [1592/1593]. Roger Ripponn that dyed in Newgate. Lansdowne MSS. 73, item 27, f. 76.

XXIX

[CHRISTOPHER BOWMAN] CORAM RICHARDE YOUNG PRIMO DIE MARTII 1592 [1592/1593]

Christopher Bowman, goldsmith, age 32 yeares or there aboutes, saith that hee was not at Newgate at the time that Roger Rippin dyed,[1] but hee saieth that the whole congregacion was consentinge to the makinge of the coffine, and this examinant was made acquainted with a further purpose, which hee saieth hee disliked of.

Beinge demaunded who is the congregacion and what bee their names, hee saieth hee will not declare it nor may not disclose his brethren's secretts, nor the place of their meetinge, for hee remembreth it not, nor the time.

Hee saieth hee was never consentinge to the libell or writinge fixed upon the coffine, neither doeth hee allowe of it if any suche writinge were made. The coffine coste four shillings eight pence, which was gathered of the whole congregacion and paid by this examinant.[2]

Hee saieth that hee doeth not thinke that their secrete meetinges and conventicles are contrary to God's lawe or the lawes of the realme. Hee saieth hee cannot take an othe to aunswere to any slight causes as hee thinketh these to bee.

Hee saieth that hee doeth not remember that hee sawe Mr. Penryn within these four dayes, and will not aunswere directly thereunto, althoughe hee bee required, as hee is a Christian, but hath sene him within these fewe dayes.[3] How many dayes hee knoweth not.

[1] Roger Rippon died February 16, 1592/1593.

[2] Bowman was one of those who presented "A Lamentable Petition Delivered to the Queene's Majestye the 13 of March, 1588" [1588/1589]. On the order of the Privy Council, he was imprisoned on March 17 in the Wood Street Counter, "lyinge in the hole," and despite his petition for release, March, 1589/1590, he remained in prison more than three years. At the organization meeting in September, 1592, he was elected deacon, and was responsible for distribution of funds. He was arrested shortly after the coffin episode, about February 17–28, 1592/1593.

[3] The *Calendar of State Papers, Domestic Series, Elizabeth, 1591–1594*, has "five days," p. 324. But then Bowman is saying that he has not seen Penry within four days—February 25–28—but he saw him February 24. Since this seemed unlikely, I checked the manuscript reading at the Public Record Office, S.P. 12, Vol. 244,

Hee saieth hee was lately out of towne but the place where, hee will not declare, sayenge that unles hee were knowen to bee a man of a bad life, hee is not to sett downe the places where hee hath bene.

Hee saieth hee is not persuaded to goe to his parish churche or to Paule's Crosse to heare a sermon, for that hee seeth every man, how wicked soever hee bee, admitted to receive the communion, and hee will not joyne in prayer with that mynister which geveth holy thinges to dogges.[1]

Hee denieth to subscribe this his examinacion.[2]

Rychard Young

Endorsement: The Examinacion of Christofer Bowman.

[THE EXAMINACION OF JOHN EDWARDES ABOUT MARCH 6, 1592/1593]

John Edwardes came out of Scotlande with Penryn and laye by the way every nighte where hee laye,[3] and saieth that Penryn was not banished out of Scotland, but there was banishment decreed againste him,[4] and the mynisters did staye the proclayminge th[e]reof.

item 62. The correct reading is "fewe", and Bowman is exonerated from giving specific information on Penry, who was much sought after by the Court of High Commission, the Privy Council, Archbishop Whitgift, and Chaplain Bancroft.

1 Separation of the godly, the saints, the elect, from the profane multitudes, the ungodly, the sinners, was a basic Barrowist, and Separatist principle, especially for participation in the Lord's Supper.

2 This examination is in the Public Record Office, S.P. 12, Vol. 244, item 62. Most of the original examinations are in the Ellesmere MSS. at the Huntington Library. Most of the copies are in Harley MSS. 6848, and Thomas Baker's transcripts are in Harley MSS. 7041–7042, in the British Museum.

3 This examination is in Harley MSS. 6848, f. 85 *recto*. Burrage prints it in *Early English Dissenters*, II, 57–58, and gives April 5 as the probable date. But I feel certain the examination should be dated about March 6. Edwardes' references to "Sonday nighte" and "Satterday nighte" refer to March 4 and the immediately preceding day, and his reference to Penry suggests that the date is before March 22, when Penry was captured.

There is a letter of 1591, sent by Penry in Scotland to Edwardes in London at the sign of the Sunne in Watling Street. Since the letter refers to Penry's return to Scotland on August 18 and the birth of his daughter Safety on August 26, we may tentatively date the letter in September or October. Four lines are quoted in Ellesmere MS. 2148, f. 89 *recto*. Possibly the letter was intercepted, but more likely it was found after Edwardes' arrest on March 4, 1592/1593.

4 Lord Burghley urged Ambassador Robert Bowes in Edinburgh to put pressure on James VI to banish Penry. As early as April and May, 1590, Bowes and

Hee saieth that Penryn was of this assemblie and was taken by the waye and broughte to the conestable's house and from thence hee escaped away on Sonday nighte and named himselfe John Harries,[1] and there were two or three countreymen comynge towardes them, which were taken by the way, and said they were goinge to Waltham[2] and therefore the Justice discharged them.

Hee saieth that one Jones[3] was taken and wente home to dynner with Caxton[4] Graye and was afterwardes broughte by him to the Justice. Hee saieth that on Satterday nighte [March 3] hee this examinant walked with Penryn alonge Cheapside thoroughe Newgate and they wente to Nicholas Lee's house and there this examinant lefte Penryn and his wife about viii of the clocke. He

Lord Burghley exchanged letters regarding Penry's banishment. When Bowes in July urged James VI to banish Penry, the king said that "great labour had been made to him in favour of Penry." Nevertheless, by the end of July James VI had given order for Penry's banishment, and on August 6 the order was issued that "Johnne Pennerie Inglishman, be oppin proclamatioun at the mercat croceis of the heid burrowis of this realme and utheris placeis neidfull, to depairt and pas furth of this realme, boundis, and dominionis thairof within ten dayis nixt eftir he be chargeit therto." Evidently the order remained unenforced, or Penry was not "chargeit therto," for in November Bowes informed the king that "it was marvelled in England that Penry should be suffered to remain in Scotland" notwithstanding the king's order. The king and chancellor affirmed their belief that Penry had left, but they promised to make search. By December Bowes reported to Burghley that Mrs. Penry was in Edinburgh, but that Penry had departed. It is probable that King James wished to please Queen Elizabeth, Burghley, and Bowes, and at the same time hoped to satisfy the Scottish clergy by not prosecuting Penry, who probably remained secretly in the vicinity of Edinburgh.

Penry continued in hiding, aided by the connivance of Scottish friends and clergy. About July 1, 1591, he left for England and was secretly in London about July 20–28 during the episode involving William Hacket, Henry Arthington, and Edmund Coppinger. Upon the failure of this misguided venture, Penry returned to Scotland—despite the prohibition in his banishment order—and arrived August 18; on August 26 his wife gave birth to a third daughter, who was appropriately named Safety. Penry remained in Scotland another year, and left about September, 1592, for London. See *The Register of the Privy Council of Scotland*, IV, *1585–1592*, Edited by David Masson (Edinburgh, 1881), pp. 517–519; see also *Calendar of the State Papers Relating to Scotland*, Volume II, Edited by M. J. Thorpe (London, 1858), pp. 574, 580, 581; see further *Calendar of State Papers Relating to Scotland and Mary, Queen of Scots, 1547–1603*, Volume X, *1589–1593*, Edited by W. K. Boyd and H. W. Meikle (Edinburgh, 1936), pp. 280–281, 292, 294, 361, 363–364, 368, 380, 383, 420–421, 435. See also Ellesmere MS. 2148, f. 89 *recto*, for Penry's trip in July–August, 1591.

[1] Penry sometimes was called Ap Henry, son of Henry, or Harry, and thus John Harrison, or Harries.

[2] Waltham Holy Cross, including Waltham Abbey, is in Essex, but Waltham Cross, site of an Eleanor Cross, is in Hertford and west of Waltham Abbey.

[3] Most likely Jenkins Jones, Penry's kinsman and servant.

[4] Burrage, *Early English Dissenters*, II, 57, has Captein[?] Graye, but Caxton is the better manuscript reading.

knoweth not who should have exercised that day,[1] nor did not heare of any purpose that they had to goe into the countreye.

His comynge out of Scotland with Penryn was in November laste,[2] and they came firste to one Mr. Yreton's house besides Darby vi miles,[3] and dyned there and came to Northampton to the house of Henry Godley, who is father in lawe to the said Penryn, where the said Penryn lodged, and this examinant lay at the signe of the Bull, and the next day they came from thence to St. Albans and lodged at the signe of the Christofer and the nexte day came to Stratford at Bowe to the signe of the Crosse Keyes where Penryn's wife was and had a chamber,[4] and this examinant lefte them there and came to London and sawe him no more untill a little before Christmas that they mett at a garden house at the Duke's place neere Allgate [Aldgate], where Penryn did preache and (as hee doeth remember) Grenewood did preache there allso[5] and this examinant wente downe into the countrey and came not up untill Satterday was sevenighte[6] and since hath laien at his brother Richford [Rochford?] his house, and upon Wensdaye or Thursday morninge[7] Penryn came to this examinant's chamber before hee was up and was booted.

Hee saieth that hee did heare that Penryn was lodged at Mrs. Settle's house.[8]

Rychard Young

[1] Because of the imprisonment on December 6, 1592, of the pastor, Francis Johnson, and also of John Greenwood the teacher or doctor, the preachers or expounders varied. George Johnson was the preacher on March 4. The Separatists met in the woods or country not for any rebellious or seditious purposes, but simply to escape detection.

[2] Penry, in his April 5 examination, says he came out of Scotland about September, 1592. I think the arrival in London may have been early October. Pierce, in his *John Penry*, p. 306, suggests the middle of September, but he has stretched the evidence in George Kniveton's examination of April 4.

[3] Probably John Ireton, a prominent Puritan of Leicestershire, in or near Derby. See Patrick Collinson, *The Elizabethan Puritan Movement*, pp. 235, 455, 503.

[4] Penry's wife, with two babies—Comfort and Safety—had most likely left Scotland by ship, and landed at one of the towns along the Thames.

[5] If Greenwood preached, the date would be December 3, 1592—a Sunday. On the evening of December 5–6, Greenwood and Francis Johnson were arrested at the home of Edward Boyse in Fleet Street.

[6] Saturday, February 24, 1592/1593. Therefore, a week after the coffin incident.

[7] Wednesday, February 28, or Thursday, March 1, before the arrest on March 4.

[8] Her husband Thomas Settle had been imprisoned about December 17 or 24, 1592. Penry and his wife probably rented rooms in her house in Stepney.

THE EXAMINACION OF GEORGE JOHNSON, SCHOLEMASTER, TAKEN THE DAY AND YEAR AFORESAID [MARCH 7, 1592/1593?]

He saieth that hee was not privy, partie or consentinge to the framinge and settinge forthe of the libell upon the coffine.

And being further examined upon other matters,[1] he said absolutely that hee would annswere nothinge but onely concerninge himselfe.[2]

THE EXAMINACION OF ABRAHAM PULBERY OF LONDON FREE OF THE COWPERS, OF THE AGE OF XXV OR THEREABOUTS, TAKEN VII DIE MARTII 1592 [1592/1593] AS FOLOWETH

Item hee saith that hee was in Cheapeside when the dead corps[e] of Roger Rippon was caried thorowe the same, and saieth further that hee heard there publikely redde the paper which was sett upon the coffine, but hee would not call the same a libell. And the same libell being shewed unto him, hee thinketh that it was in effecte the same hee heard redde in Chepeside.

And beinge examined of what opynion hee was touchinge the same libell, hee saieth that the mainteyninge of the bishops of

[1] George Johnson (1564–1605), born in Richmond, Yorkshire. His father John was mayor of Richmond. Younger brother of Francis. Graduated B.A. and M.A. (1588) from Christ's College, Cambridge. Served as schoolmaster and as teacher or preacher in the assemblies. Imprisoned March 4, 1592/1593. Went to Newfoundland and Cape Breton with his brother Francis, Daniel Studley, and John Clarke in 1597. Returned to London about September 8 and went to Amsterdam about September 20. Sharply criticized his brother's wife in the clothes controversy, caused division in the Ancient Church and was excommunicated. Published in 1603 *A Discourse of Some Troubles*. See *D.N.B.*; *Athenae Cantabrigienses*, II, 435; Arber, *Story of the Pilgrim Fathers*, 107; Powicke, *Henry Barrowe Separatist*, 225, 229, 238–240; Dexter, *Congregationalism*, 74, 121, 263, 272, 277, 283–296, 325, 683; David B. Quinn, "England and the St. Lawrence, 1577 to 1602," in *Merchants and Scholars*, ed. John Parker; David B. Quinn, "The First Pilgrims," *William and Mary Quarterly*, July, 1966, pp. 367–383. John Peile, *Biographical Register of Christ's College*, I, 160.

[2] We have his examination for March 7 before Richard Young and John Ellis; also for April 2 before five judges. He was examined at least on two other occasions. The present examination is in Harley MSS. 6848, f. 43 *verso*, the copy in Harley MSS. 7042, f. 62 *recto*. It is not in the Ellesmere MSS., nor in Burrage, *Early English Dissenters*.

England, as, namely, the Archbishop of Cannterbury and the reste of the bishops whom he termeth to be antichristian bishops as they are, that they are the mainteyners of antichristian authoritie, sayeing further that the said bishops have their authorities as they are bishoppes from Antichriste and not from her Majestie, because there is noe suche authoritie in the Word of God for any princes to make such bishoppes to overrule the churches of God.[1]

And saieth further that when hee heard that paper redde in Chepeside hee heard allso then reported that they mente to carry the said coffine to Mr. Justice Young's house.

And hee saieth further that hee was upon Sonday laste in the morninge at a wood neere Yslington with others that were there, the nomber he knoweth not, and then and there had a sworde about himselfe, and denieth to aunswere how often hee had bene there before, and saieth allso that Mr. Johnson was their expounder that daye.[2]

Item hee saieth that hee hath made a promise to the Lord in the presence of his congregacion when hee entred thereunto that hee would walke with them as they would walke with the Lord.[3]

Rychard Young
John Ellis

THE EXAMINACON OF JOHN BARNS, TAYLER, TAKEN BEFORE US HENRY TOUNSEND, RICHARD YONGE, AND JOHN ELLIS, ESQUIRES, THE VIIITH OF MARCHE 1592 [1592/1593]

Item beinge tendred his oath to aunswher truly to such questions as on the behalfe of the Quene's Majestie might be demaunded of him, denyes to take any oath.

Item he saith he did knowe Roger Ryppon and was at Newgate in

[1] Abraham Pulbery, age 24 or 25, arrested March 4, examined March 7 and April 3. He had been previously arrested in Surrey about April, 1592, suspected as a Brownist, imprisoned at Arundel, Sussex, and indicted before the Judges of Assize. His examination is interesting for three reasons: his implication in the coffin episode, his statement of the simple covenant he made (last paragraph), and his admission of wearing a sword. The judges were interested in any suggestion of sedition and rebellion, but Pulbery is the only one mentioned among the examinants as being armed. Pulbery is unusually frank and outspoken on his attitude towards antichristian bishops.

[2] George Johnson was the preacher or teacher on March 4. His brother Francis was in prison, probably the Clink.

[3] This examination is in Harley MSS. 6848, f. 43 *recto*. It is printed in Burrage, *Early English Dissenters*, II, 31–32. The copy is in Harley MSS. 7042, f. 62 *recto*.

the morninge before he was caried thens but was not prevye of the carrynge of the coffyn to Mr. Yong's, nor of the lybells fixed thereon, nor whoe wrote them.

And beinge demaunded whether he knowes Pendred [Penry] or not, saith he knowes him, and did see him on Sonday last, but will not say where nor what tyme that daye nor will aunswher whether he did here [hear] him read any lecture either that daye or at any tyme els.[1]

Item he saith that at his first entringe into that societie he made noe other vowe, but that he wold followe them soe farr forth as the Word of God did warraunt him.

Beinge demaunded whether he wold repaier to his parishe churche accordinge as he is bound by the lawes of this land, saith he will not, excepte the Word of God weare preached there as it ought, for against that service he stands.

Item he saith that the Bishopp of Canterbery is noe magistrate but a beast[2] and that the said bishopp is noe [Privy] Counceller, and that the Quene's Majestie cannot geve hir aucthoritie or power to any such.[3]

Rychard Young
John Ellis

THE EXAMINACON OF WILLIAM CLERKE [CLARKE], A WORKER OF CAPPS, OF THE PARISHE OF ST. BUTTOLPHE'S, TAKEN BEFORE US HENRY TOWNSEND, RICHARD YONGE, AND JOHN ELLIS, ESQUIRES, THE VIIITH OF MARCHE, 1592 [1592/1593]

Item he beinge tendred his oath to aunswhere truly to such

[1] Penry was arrested on March 4, 1592/1593, but evidently identified himself under the Anglicized form as John Harrison (ap Henry). Somehow he managed to escape. That same evening the Privy Council, which had sought him since 1589, issued a warrant for his arrest. Not until March 22 was he apprehended, through the means of the vicar of Stepney, Anthony Anderson.

[2] The reference to Archbishop Whitgift as a beast is probably to Revelation, chapters 13, 16, 17. The Separatists were strongly opposed to the combining of ecclesiastical and civil functions and offices. Whitgift became a member of the Privy Council in February, 1585/1586, and in the next seven years his civil powers and influence increased, especially after the deaths of Leicester (September 4, 1588) and Walsingham (April 6, 1590).

[3] This original examination is in Harley MSS. 6848, f. 67 *recto*. Of the six paragraphs, Burrage prints two, in *Early English Dissenters*, II, 34. The copy is in Harley MSS. 7042, ff. 59 *verso* and 60 *recto*.

questions as should be demaunded of him on the behalfe of the Quene's Majestie, refuseth to take any oath.

Item he saith he did knowe Roger Ryppon but was not with him duringe his imprisonment nor was at Newgate when the coffyn was carried from thens, nor was previe of yt nor of the lybell fixed theron nor who wrote it.

Item he saith he hath bene of the foresaid congregacon these fower or fyve yeres,[1] and made promise to stand with the said congregacion soe longe as they did stand for the truthe and glory of God, beinge then of that congregacon at that tyme present aboute twentie or thereabouts.

Item beinge demaunded when he did see Pendred [Penry], denies to aunswhere that question.[2]

And beinge demaunded whether he wold geve his consent to repaier to his parishe churche (as he is bound by the lawes of the land), saith he maye not soe suddenly yeld thereunto but (soe that he maye be at libertye)[3] he saith he will put in good securytie to be of good behaviour towards the Quene's Majestie and the state.[4]

THE EXAMINACON OF RICHARD HAWTON, SHOOMAKER, TAKEN BEFORE US HENRY TOWNSEND, RICHARD YONGE, AND JOHN ELLIS, ESQUIRES, THE VIIITH OF MARCHE 1592 [1592/1593]

Item he denyes to take any oath to aunswhere to any question but will aunswher truly soe nere as he can.

[1] William Clerke, or Clark, age 40, joined the Separatists about 1587–1588. He was committed to prison about April, 1589, by the constable without a warrant, for protesting the arrest of Thomas Legate. He is in prison in May, 1589, and also appears on the February, 1589/1590, list of prisoners, but is not on the April, 1590, list.

[2] He was apprehended on March 4, examined on March 8 and on April 2, 1593. He probably saw Penry on March 4.

[3] There are brief references to Clark in Carlson, *The Writings of John Greenwood, 1587–1590*, pp. 117, 314, 320, 323, 328, 330, in Johnson, *A Discourse of Some Troubles*; in Thomas White, *A Discovery of Brownism*, p. 25; in John Fowler *et al.*, *A Shield of Defence*, p. 30. See also Harley MSS. 6848, ff. 20, 21 for Thomas Legate, as well as Carlson, *op. cit.*, pp. 280, 288, 298, 304, 314, 317, 320, 323–325, 328, 331. Clark was excommunicated by Francis Johnson, but remained a member of Henry Ainsworth's church in Amsterdam.

[4] This examination is in Harley MSS. 6848, f. 62 *recto*, and in Burrage, *Early English Dissenters*, II, 33. The copy is in Harley MSS. 7042, f. 60 *verso*.

Item he saith he hath bene of the foresaid congregacion a fortenight or three weeks.[1]

Item he saith he had noe notice of their meetinge at the wood but meetinge with a shoomaker (whome he knowes not) went with them.

Item he saith he knowes not Roger Rippon, nor was at Newgate, nor in Cheepesid, when the coffin was carried from Newgate, but he heard that a coffin was carried throughe the streets and that libells were fixed on yt but was not previe of them nor knowes whoe wrote them.

Item he saith he is nowe contented to repaier to his parishe churche as he ought and will hereafter refraine the company of that congregacion and will observe the Quene's Majesty's lawes.[2]

THE EXAMINACON OF JOHN NICHOLAS OF SMITHFEILD, GLOVER, TAKEN BEFORE US HENRY TOUNSEND, RICHARD YONGE, AND JOHN ELLIS, ESQUIERS THE VIIITH OF MARCHE 1592 [1592/1593]

Item beinge tendred his oath to aunswhere truly to such matters as should be demaunded of him concerninge the Quene's Majestie refuseth to take any oathe.

Item beinge demaunded whether he were at Newgate or in Cheepesid when the coffin was carried to Mr. Yong's, saith he was not, nor was prevye of the makinge of the saide coffin, onely Rippon's wyfe did tell him on Frydaye night (as he thinks) that hir husband was deade.[3]

Item he saith he did not knowe of the makinge of the lybells that were fixed on the coffin, nor did knowe whoe they were that made them.

[1] Richard Hawton was a newcomer, and had evidently joined with the Separatists in February. He refused the oath *ex officio*, but promised to return to the Church of England. Since there is no further record of him, we may conclude he was set free. His name does not appear on the list of eight men who were bailed, in April.

[2] This examination is in Harley MSS. 6848, f. 61 *verso*. The copy is in Harley MSS. 7042, f. 60 *recto* and *verso*. It is printed by Burrage, *Early English Dissenters*, II, 34, but it is not given in the index. Burrage, *op. cit.*, I, 146, says Richard Hawton died before April 3, 1593, but this should be William Howton, or Hawton, or Hutton. Richard conformed.

[3] Roger Rippon died on Friday, February 16, 1592/1593.

Being demaunded whether he knowes Pendred [Penry] or not, saith he hath heard of him but knowes him not.

Item he saith he knowes Abraham Pulbery.

Item he saith he knowes one Jones[1] but hath not bene longe acquainted with him nor doeth he knowe where he dwells.

Item this examinate saith that he with his company were at the wood where they were nowe taken on Sonday was a fortnight.[2]

Item he saith that the Lord's Prayer is noe praier for that (as he saith) Christ did not saie it as a praier.[3]

THE EXAMINACION OF DANIELL BUCKE SCRIVENER OF THE BOUR[O]UGHE OF SOUTHWARKE, TAKEN THE NYNETH DAYE OF MARCHE, BEFORE HENRY TOWNSEND, RICHARD YONGE, AND JOHN ELLYS, ESQUIERS. AND BEINGE REQUIRED TO BE DEPOSED UPPON A BOOKE, REFUSETH TO TAKE ANY OTHER OATH THEN [THAN] TO PROTEST BEFORE GOD THAT ALL HIS SAYINGS WERE TRUE

Beinge examined whether he was with the coffyn at Newgate, denyes that he was there and that he did not see the lybell fixed on the said coffin, but saith that afterwards a straunger shewed unto him the coppie of the same at his owne shop in Southwarke, and denyes that he knewe the name of the straunger, nor any thinge els of him, but that he was a Wiltsheere man and came to see how he did.[4]

[1] This Jones is probably Jenkin Jones, a kinsman of Penry. The authorities were seeking Penry, and wished to question Jones. There are extracts from Jenkin Jones' examination of November 6, 1590, in Ellesmere MS. 2148, ff. 88 *verso* and 89 *recto*, pertaining to his role in distributing Penry's books in 1590.

[2] This statement is ambiguous. From the examination of Nicholas on April 2 we learn that he had been in prison a month. Thus, he was arrested on March 4. When Nicholas refers to "his company," he is probably referring to a separate group which contemplated establishing a second Barrowist church. The guiding spirits were John Nicholas, Thomas Mitchell, John Barnes, and William Collins. See Bancroft, *A Survay of the Pretended Holy Discipline*, p. 249 [429]. This group probably met on February 18 at the Islington woods where Nicholas was captured two weeks later.

[3] This examination is in Harley MSS. 6848, f. 61 *recto*. Printed in full in Burrage, *Early English Dissenters*, II, 32–33. The copy is in Harley MSS. 7042, f. 60 *recto*.

[4] William Smithe, of Bradford, Wiltshire, may be the person mentioned. He had been ordained into the Church of England by William Overton, Bishop of

And saith further that he was uppon Sondaye last in the afternoone in the Cunstable his house in Islington where he did see emongst others of their fraternitie Penrhyn [Penry].

And saith further that George Johnson was reader there in the Cunstable's house as aforesaid. And saith alsoe that there were there above fortye of them together and divers others that were not of their societie. And saith further that he was not in his parishe church thes xii monethes, bycause it is against his conscience unlesse there were reformacion in the churche accordinge as they be warraunted by the Word of God.

And as concerninge the bushopps, he thinks that they have noe spirituall aucthoritie over the rest of the clergie.

Beinge asked what vowe or promise he had made when he came first to their socyetye, he aunswhereth and saith that he made this protestacion, that he wold walke with the rest of that congregacion soe longe as they did walke in the waye of the Lord and as farr as might be warraunted by the Word of God.

Beinge demaunded whether there shold be any motion made by some of their fraternitie that they should goe some where in to the cuntrye wherby they might be in more saftie, denyes that he herd any such matters, but saith that he herd that one [216 *verso*] Millers [or Myllers] a preacher at St. Andreas Underashafte[1] sayd that if they did maynteyne the truth they should not keepe them selves in corners but should shew them selves forth publiquely to defend the same, and he thought that unfitt lest it should be a meane to stirr a rebellion.

And further beinge demaunded whoe was their pastor and by whome he was created, saith that Mr. Francis Johnson was chosen pastor, and Mr. Grenewood doctor, and Bowman and Lee deacons, and Studley and George Knifton potticary [apothecary] were chosen elders, in the house of one Fox[2] in St. Nicholas Lane, London, aboute halfe a yere sithence, all in one day by their congregacion, or at Mr. Bylson's house in Crechurche [Christchurch],[3] he remembreth not whether [which one], and that the sacrament of baptisme was (as he called it) delivered there to the number of vii persons by Johnson, but they had neither godfathers nor godmothers, and he tooke water and washed the faces of them that were

Lichfield and Coventry. Nevertheless, he joined with the Separatists, and was arrested about February 17 for being involved in the Rippon coffin episode.

[1] Miller was the clergyman at St. Andrew's Undershaft.

[2] Possibly Abraham Foxe. See Burrage, *Early English Dissenters*, II, 18.

[3] Christchurch, in Newgate Street.

baptised. The children that were there baptised were the children of Mr. Studley, Mr. Lee,[1] with others, beinge of severall yeres of age, sayinge onely in the administracion of this sacrament, "I doe baptise thee in the name of the Father, of the Sonne, and of the Holy G[h]ost," withoute usinge any other cerimony therin as is now usually observed accordinge to the *Booke of Common Praier*.

Beinge then there p[res]aunte the said Daniel Studley, William Sheppard, William Marshall, John Beche [Bethe?], Roberte Bray, Thomas Lee, Arthur Byllet, Edmund Thompson, Roberte Jackson, William Mason, George Marten, Thomas Michell, Robert Abraham, Henry Wythers, Thomas Digson [Ligson?], Peter Farland [Fairlambe], William Wever, Dauy [Davy] Bristoe, John Nicholas, John Barnes, George Smell, Christofer Roper, Cristofer Sympkins, Christofer Diggins, Roger Rippon, Christofer Bowman, Thomas Settell, John Grenewood aforesaid, Edward Grave, William Collins, Abraham Pulbery, Nicholas Leye [Lee] aforesaid, George Manners, George Knyfton aforesaid, Mrs. Settell, Katherine Onnyon, Mrs. Boyes, Margery Daubin [Danbin?], Ellyn Rowe, Avis Allen, Ann Homes [Honies?], Jone Pulbery, Nicholas Lee his wyfe, Fraunc is Johnes, An Bodkyn, Elizabeth Moore, Barbera Sampford, and others whose names he doeth not remember.[2]

[217 *recto*] Beinge further demaunded the manner of the Lord's Supper administred emongst them, he saith that fyve whight loves [white loaves] or more were sett uppon the table and that the pastor did breake the bread and then delivered yt unto some of them, and the deacons delivered to the rest, some of the said congregacion sittinge and some standinge aboute the table and that the pastor delivered the cupp unto one and he to an other, and soe from one to another till they had all dronken, usinge the words at the deliverye therof accordinge as it is sett downe in the eleventh of the Corinthes the xxiiiith verse.[3]

Beinge demaunded whether they use to make any collection or gatheringe amongst them, said that there is a gatheringe mony of emongst them, the which mony is delivered to the deacons to be

[1] Daniel Studley, the elder of the church, and Nicholas Lee, deacon.

[2] Daniel Bucke was the only one to give the full list of members at the organization meeting in September, 1592. There are thirty-four men and thirteen women listed. If we add the names of Francis Johnson and Daniel Bucke, we have forty-nine, and Bilson was probably also present. Making allowance for those that Bucke could not remember, and for wives unmentioned—*e.g.*, Mrs. Rippon and Mrs. Greenwood—we have approximately sixty charter members.

[3] I Corinthians 11:24. "This is my body, which is for you: this do in remembrance of me."

distributed accordinge to their discretion to the use of the poore.

And he herd saie [said?] that they did use to marry in theire congregacion.

And further refuseth to com to the churche and obeye the forme of service which is used in the *Booke of Common Prayer*, sett oute by the Quene's Majesty's Injunctions, bycause there is not a reformacion accordinge to the Word of God.[1]

Rychard Young

THE EXAMINATION OF ROBERT BOWLE,[2] TAKEN THE XIXTH OF MARCHE, 1592/1593

A.—He sayeth that the boke intituled *A Colleccyon off Certen Letters and Conferences Lately Passed betwene Certen Preachers and Two Prysoners in the Flete,*[3] this examinant caused to be prynted at Dort, in the Low Cuntryes, by the meanes of Robert Stookes.

B.—The copy of that booke thys examinant receaved her[e] in London, but wher ther, or off whom, he remembreth not.

C.—He sayeth Arthur Byllett[4] was the corector for the prent of that boke, and they were prynted by one Hanse.[5] Ther were above two or three hundred off them.

D.—He confessyth he brought these bookes from the presse, which were putt into the sayd Stookes hys clockbag.[6]

[1] This examination is in Harley MSS. 6849, ff. 216 *recto*–217 *recto*, and in Burrage, II, 34–37. The copy is in Harley MSS. 7042, f. 205 *recto* and *verso*.

It is not surprising to learn that Daniel Bucke became an "apostate" and returned to the Church of England. He is compared to Doctor Andrew Perne, the old turncoat, by Francis Johnson, in *An Answer to Maister H. Jacob His Defence of the Churches*, p. v.

[2] Bowle, Bull, or Boull. This examination is not in Burrage, but it is in John Payne Collier, *The Egerton Papers*, pp. 172–173. The original is Ellesmere MS. 2093, in the Huntington Library.

[3] *A Collection of Certain Letters and Conferences Lately Passed betwixt Certaine Preachers and Two Prisoners in the Fleet*, written by Barrow and Greenwood, was printed at Dort. Boull was the agent who supervised the printing, and he helped in the transportation and distribution of the books—about 500 copies.

[4] Arthur Bellot was the examiner or proof-reader. Collier reads the manuscript as "cownter," but "corector" is the better reading.

[5] Hanse may be Hans Stell, who printed books in the Netherlands. See J. Dover Wilson, "Richard Schilders and the English Puritans." *Trans. of the Bibliographical Society*, XI (1909–1911), pp. 72–75.

[6] Stokes carried most of the books from the Netherlands to London, but Boull probably brought over 100–200 copies himself.

E.—Thys examinant layd out the money for the pryntyng therof, which thys examinant had by the means of the sayd Stookes.

F.—He sayeth that he hath hadd thre of those bookes sythens he returned into England, but sayeth he brought them over with hym into England, but whether he brought over any more with hym he remembreth not.

G.—He sayeth he hath one of those bookes leaft, but wher yt ys, or wher he leaft yt, he remembreth not, neyther can he dyrect how yt may be come by, and yet he offereth to gett yt.

H.—He denyeth that he can tell to whom he hath delyvered eyther of the other two bokes, but he sayeth he hath delyvered them to somebody, but doth not remember to whom.

I.—He denyeth to take any othe upon[1] any booke in any case; but wyll swere by the name of God, but not upon any creature.

K.—He confessyth he was one of them that was taken in Seynt James wood upon yesterday was fortnyght.[2]

By me, Robert Boull

Examined by us,

John Popham	Edmund Anderson
Thomas Egerton	Edward Stanhope

THE EXAMINATION OF JAMES FORESTER,[3] PHYSYCYANE AND MASTER OFF ARTE, TAKEN THE XIXTH DAY OF MARCHE, 1592/1593

A.—He confesseth that hym selfe, by the procurement off Henry

[1] Collier has: "He denyeth he toke any other person," but he has misread four out of five words here.

[2] He was captured on March 4, and probably was examined by commissioners. The present examination concentrates on one book, although Boull may have assisted with some of the other five Barrowist books printed at Dort in 1589–1591. Two days later, on March 21, he was indicted, for publishing seditious books, in violation of 23 Elizabeth, chapter II, section 4, and on March 23 was convicted and sentenced to death. Although he was not executed, he remained in Newgate prison where he died before 1596.

[3] Fowrestier, as he signs his name, or Forester, is one of the few educated laymen among the early Separatists. Robert Harrison and Robert Browne, Francis Johnson and John Greenwood, Thomas Settle and William Smithe, were educated clergymen, but Barrow as a lawyer and Fowrestier as a physician and Master of Arts are part of the laity. Penry remained a layman but was a *de facto* clergyman. George Johnson was a schoolteacher with a Master of Arts degree. All were Cambridge men with the possible exception of William Smithe, who may have been an Oxford man.

Barow, wrote out some parte off the booke intituled *A Breiff Discorse* [Discoverie] *of the False Church*, and as one shete was wryten the same was taken away, with the copy therof, and new brought.[1]

B.—Ther were sundry thynges that thys examinant fo[u]nd falte with in respect off the sharpe maner off wrytyng therof, which thys examinant caused to be reformed; but whether he wrote the whole thereof he remembreth not[2] for he sayeth he never sawe the booke beyng prynted. The same were caryed, always as he wrote the copyes, unto one Danyell Studley, or receaved by hym, who had the orygynall copy therof, which thys examinant saw in hys hand at Bridwell,[3] they beyng fellow prysoners ther together; and he saw also the same Studley to wryte out a copy therof for hym selfe: and he sayeth he began to inclyne that way,[4] but hath sythens sene, he thancketh God, their great error.[5]

James Fowrestier

Examined by us,

John Popham	Edmund Anderson
Thomas Egerton	Edward Stanhope

THE EXAMINATION OF ROBERT STOOKES, TAKEN THE XIXTH OF MARCHE, 1592/1593

A. He sayeth he hath bene seduced, and therby became one alowyng off Henry Barowe's opynyons, and hath bene perswaded

[1] Daniel Studley received the original manuscript from Barrow in the Fleet, and Fowrestier prepared the fair copy for the printer. Collier has "Description," but the reading is "Discorse." It should be "Discoverie."

[2] Studley asserts that Fowrestier wrote out the entire copy.

[3] Fowrestier was arrested about December, 1589, and was imprisoned at Newgate. In April, 1590, he is listed as a prisoner in the Bridewell, and there he collaborated with Studley. Evidently they were not "close" prisoners, and were free to exercise in the prison yard, hold meetings, and write out their copy.

[4] On at least one occasion Fowrestier served as the preacher or expounder. He may have saved his life by confessing the error of his ways. In my work, *The Writings of John Greenwood, 1587–1590*, p. 318, note 1, I said that Fowrestier was indicted and convicted, March 21–23, 1592/1593. Inasmuch as Robert Stokes seemingly was not indicted, it may be that Fowrestier also escaped indictment and conviction because of his confession. The documents are incomplete. We have the examination of Fowrestier, who may not have been indicted. We do not have the examination of Scipio Bellot, or Billett, who was indicted and convicted.

[5] The original examination is in Ellesmere MS. 2095. It is printed by John Payne Collier, *The Egerton Papers*, pp. 178–179.

from yt by the space of a yeare and a halff, and was perswaded partyly by Snape, and cheffly by Mr. Aves, my Lord of Canterbury's chaplyn.[1]

B. He sayeth whyles he held that opynyon he was at the pryson with the sayd Henry Barow and John Grenwood, and they moved thys examynat fyrst to procure the boke intituled *A Colleccyon off Certen Slanderous Articles*, etc.,[2] and one other booke intituled *An Answer to Georg Gyfford's Pretended Defens of Red Prayers*,[3] to be prynted, about thys tyme three yeares, which thys examinant dyd cause to be done accordyngly, at thys examinant's owne charg; and ther were printed about fyve hundred of eche off those bokes at Dort, which thys examinant conveyed over into England after they were prynted; some of which bookes the same Henry Barow and John Grenwood had the dysposycyon off to the number of about two or thre hundred.

C. For the boke intituled *A Collectyon of Certeyne Letters and Conferences Lately Passed*, etc.[4]

D. He confessyth that the sayd Barrow and Greneway [Greenwood] dealt with thys examinant to get that prynted also, and that was about mydsommer last was two yeares, at which tyme thys examynant promysed to gett yt done, and the copy therof beyng sent to one Robert Bulle, now in the Counter of the Pultry, to whom thys examinant gave order that what so ever the sayd Barow and Grenwood shold direct hym to do, the same Bull shold do yt at thys examinant's charg. And so the same Barow and Grenwood gave dyrectyon to the same Bull for the doyng therof.

E. And thys examinant comyng into the Low Contryes, to Dort, wher the same also were printed, had about CC [200] of those bookes put into thys examinant's clokebag by Robert Bull; and so

[1] Robert Stokes actively supported the Separatists from 1589 to 1591. He helped to finance the printing of six Separatist books at Dort and aided in the transportation and dispersing of the books. About September, 1591, he weakened in his Separatist beliefs, and in October or November, 1592, he was excommunicated by the newly organized congregation. He was not indicted on March 21, 1592/1593, since he had abandoned the Separatists and they had denounced him. Collier, in *Egerton Papers*, p. 173, has "Sunper" and "Atres," but the manuscript reading is [Edmund] Snape and [Robert] Aves [Avys].

[2] *A Collection of Certaine Sclaunderous Articles Gyven out by the Bisshops* was the second Separatist book to be printed, and was published about June, 1590.

[3] Greenwood's *An Answere to George Gifford's Pretended Defence of Read Praiers and Devised Litourgies* was the fourth Separatist book to be printed, and was published about August, 1590.

[4] *A Collection of Certain Letters and Conferences Lately Passed betwixt Certaine Preachers and Two Prisoners in the Fleet* was the third Separatist book to be printed, and was published about July, 1590.

thys examinant brought them into England, and delyvered sundry of those bookes to one [Mr.?] Nychas Lye [Nicholas Lee or Ley] to be sold.[1] And of those also there were prynted about fyve hundred.

F. He sayth also that the booke intituled *A Breiff Discovery of the False Church*, and the booke intituled *A Playne Refutacyon of Mr. G. Gifford's Book*, etc.,[2] thys examinant procured, at hys charg, to be prynted at Dort about Christmas last was two yeares; which was lykewyse done by the perswasyon of the same Mr. Barow and Grenwood, all which were taken at Flushyng and Burned [Brill].[3] And ther were of those thre thowsand prynted, as thys examinant understood, and Arthure Byllett was the examyner for that impressyon.

G. He sayeth that those severall impressyons stud [stood] thys examinant in about xl^li [40 pounds].

H. He sayeth, also, he caused a little thyng of one shete of paper to be prynted by their procurement before all thys, called *The Descripcion off the Vysyble Church.*[4]

By me, Robert Stokes[5]

Examined by us,

John Popham	Edmund Anderson
Thomas Egerton	Edward Stanhope

THE EXAMINATION OF DANYELL STUDLEY, TAKEN THE XXTH DAY OF MARCH, 1592/1593

A.—He confessyth that he had the orygynall of the booke intituled, *A Breiff Dyscovery off the False Church*, which he receaved shete

[1] Collier, *Egerton Papers*, p. 174, erroneously reads: "to one Mychens, there to be sted."

[2] *A Brief Discoverie of the False Church* was the fifth Separatist book to be printed, and was published about December, 1590, or January–February, 1590/1591. *A Plaine Refutation of Mr. George Giffarde's Reprochful Booke* was the sixth Separatist volume to be printed, and was published about March, 1590/1591, or April, 1591. There were printed 2000 copies of the former and 1000 of the latter.

[3] Not all the books were seized at Flushing [and Brill]. See Carlson, *The Writings of Henry Barrow, 1587–1590*, pp. 261–262. See also Carlson, *The Writings of Henry Barrow, 1590–1591*, pp. 370–377. The better manuscript reading is "Burned," not "Brill," but the word is indistinct. The final "ed" is fairly clear, but the initial letter is a capital "B."

[4] *A True Description out of the Worde of God, of the Visible Church* was the first Separatist book to be printed, and appeared about the end of 1589.

[5] The original examination is in Ellesmere MS. 2094. The examination was printed by John Payne Collier in *The Egerton Papers*, pp. 173–175.

by shete at Mr. Henry Barowe's hands in the Flette, when as he and one Andrew Smyth[1] hadd lycens from the Archbusshopp of Canterbury to have accesse unto hym.

B.—He sayeth that James Forester brought word to thys examinant from the sayd Henry Barowe that he was to have that copy to copy out to be putt in prynt, which thys examinant dyd delyver unto the same James Forester, who wrote out of the same copy an other copy of the whole therof, which copy was that by which yt was prynted.

C.—He confessyth that he had the orygynall under the sayed Barow's hand of the same Forester backe agayne, and began to wryte out a copy therof; but he sayeth he knoweth not what ys become of that copy under the same Barow's hand.

D.—He confessyth he had two off those bookes, after they were printed, off Arthur Byllet,[2] and were delyvered [to] thys examinant at Brydwell.

E.—He sayeth he delyvered the one of those bookes to John Gwalter[3] about two years past in Brydewell, but who hadd the other of this examinant he can not tell at thys present, unles yt were the same John Gwalter.

[F.]—He confessyth that within thys halff year he hath bene chosen by the congregacyon to be one of the elders.[4]

Daniel Studley[5]

Examined by us,

John Popham	Edmund Anderson
William Lewyn	Edward Stanhope

[1] Andrew Smith was a Separatist, imprisoned in the Clink in 1590. He is on the lists for February and April. It is likely that he was arrested in a conventicle about December, 1589. Collier has "Dyssection" and "Letters," but the correct manuscript readings are "Dyscovery" and "lycens." Also, Collier has "study," but the correct reading is "hands." Barrow never did have a study in the Fleet.

[2] Arthur Bellot was the agent in the Netherlands for the supervision and transportation of the books to England. Stokes testified that Bellot was the examiner, or proof-reader.

[3] John Gwalter first appeared as a prisoner in April, 1590, at the Gatehouse. In 1591 he was in the Bridewell prison. Some time before 1596 he died in Newgate. See [Francis Johnson or Henry Ainsworth?], *A True Confession of the Faith*, preface, p. v, margin. Dexter, *Congregationalism*, 207, has John Swaltee, but this is a misreading for Gwalter.

[4] Studley was elected an elder in September, 1592. He was apprehended in December, 1592. On March 23, 1592/1593, he was found guilty of publishing and dispersing Barrowist books. He was in the Newgate in 1595. In 1597 he was liberated, on condition that he go to Newfoundland and the Magdalen Islands. The expedition failed, he returned to England, went to Amsterdam in

THE EXAMINACION OF JOHN PENRYN[1] TAKEN XXVI° MARTII 1593

Beinge enfourmed that Mr. Doctor Vaughan and others were sent by my Lord Keeper one of the principall of Her Majesty's moste honourable Prevy Counsell to have conference charitably

the fall of 1597, and was very active as elder in the Ancient Church and staunch supporter of Francis Johnson. His mortal enemy was George Johnson, who went with him to Newfoundland. In his *Discourse of Some Troubles*, George Johnson blames much of his trouble with Francis on the machinations of Studley. There is no doubt that Studley was a trouble-maker, an aggressive, shrewd, and unscrupulous character. He caused division in the church at Norwich, at London, and at Amsterdam. Serious moral charges were made against him. See his defence in Richard Clyfton, *An Advertisement Concerning a Book Lately Published by C. Lawne and Others, against the English Exiled Church at Amsterdam*, p. 122. See also E. Arber, *Story of the Pilgrim Fathers*, pp. 116, 119, 122–125, and F. J. Powicke, *Henry Barrowe Separatist*, pp. 229, 243, 255, 257, 303. See especially G. Johnson, *A Discourse of Some Troubles*, pp. 44, 205, 206 *et passim*, and Christopher Lawne *et al.*, *The Prophane Schisme of the Brownists or Separatists*, pp. 2–4, 11, 16, 17, 22–41.

[5] The original examination is in Ellesmere MS. 2096. It is printed in John Payne Collier, *The Egerton Papers*, pp. 175–176.

[1] John Penry was captured on March 22, 1592/1593, at Stepney, in the house of Mr. Lewes or Lowes. With him were George Knyviton, Edward Grave, and Arthur Bellot, who were also captured. The man who enabled the authorities to arrest Penry was Anthony Anderson, vicar of Stepney. If Anderson regarded Penry as Martin Marprelate, he may have revenged himself, because he had been ridiculed and charged with immorality by Martin in *The Just Censure and Reproofe* (*Martin Senior*), signature C ii. Penry was taken to the Poultry Counter, where he was subject to Mr. Robert Gittens, keeper of the prison, and to the London sheriffs, John Garret and Robert Taylor.

In the following two months Penry was examined at least ten times. On March 24 he was examined by the notorious Richard Young, probably at his house. On March 26 he received a visit from Dr. Richard Vaughan, his brother, and Richard Young, who offered to confer with him, but Penry demanded a public conference. On March 28 he was summoned by Justice Young to confer with Dr. Nicholas Balgay of the Temple. On April 2 he conferred with Dr. Thomas Crooke, preacher at Gray's Inn, with Richard Greenham of Dry Drayton and London, and Robert Temple, prebendary of St. Paul's and chaplain to John Aylmer, Bishop of London. On April 5 he appeared before Dean Gabriel Goodman and Judges Mathew Dale, John Barne, and Richard Young. One of the longest examinations—about twenty typed pages—was the examination of April 10, before Henry Fanshawe, Remembrancer of the Exchequer, and Richard Young, and reported by Penry himself. On May 15 Penry appeared before six high legal officials—William Aubrey, Edward Coke, Richard Cosin, Thomas Egerton, Edward Stanhope, and Richard Young. On May 21 he was arraigned at the Court of Queen's Bench, then unexpectedly examined on May 24 by Richard Young, and once more arraigned at the Queen's Bench, indicted, convicted, and sentenced on May 25. Of these ten examinations and appearances, Pierce in his *John Penry* discusses or mentions eight, but he omits the examinations of May 15 and May 24. Burrage printed incompletely both the March 26 examination and the April 5 interrogation in *Early English Dissenters*, II, 37, 42, 54–55.

with him, hee saieth that hee reverenceth the Lord Keeper[1] and the reste of Her Majesty's Counsaile, but it is not my Lord Keeper or any one counsailer that can relieve or helpe him and therefore hee requireth that hee may have a publike conference to bee allowed or appointed by Her Majesty and the Lords of the Counsell, if it so please their Honours, or otherwise hee will not conferre for this present.

Hee saieth that there was a peticion delivered[2] and also there is a booke to bee delivered into the Parliament,[3] conteyninge his faith and opinions, and hee expecteth to knowe their censure therof and allowance or disallowance of the same.

Hee saieth that there are some in presence that cannott stande if hee stande, for that they are in a false ecclesiasticall office in the Church of Englande.

Beeinge demaunded if hee bee a mynister, hee saieth hee will not aunswere,[4] and beinge likewise demaunded if hee bee acquainted with Barrowe his booke,[5] hee saieth hee cometh not to bee examined and saieth hee will aunswere to what hee listeth.[6]

Rychard Young

[1] The Lord Keeper of the Great Seal was Sir John Puckering, who was a Privy Councillor.

[2] The petition referred to is "The Humble, Most Earnest and Lamentable Complaint and Supplication, of the Persecuted and Proscribed Church and Servantes of Christ, Falsely Called Brownists: Unto the High Court of Parliament," dated about March 7–10, 1592/1593, in Harley MSS. 6848, f. 150. It is printed in the Appendix.

[3] The "book" to be delivered is Penry's "Declaration of Faith and Allegiance."

[4] Penry was not a formally ordained clergyman. See his examination of April 10 before Fanshawe and Young, in Pierce, *John Penry*, pp. 420–429.

[5] Probably Barrow's *A Brief Discoverie of the False Church.*

[6] Of these four paragraphs, Burrage inexplicably omits more than half of the first one and eliminates the last two paragraphs entirely. See *Early English Dissenters,* II, 37.

This examination is in Harley MSS. 6849, f. 204 *recto,* and in Ellesmere MS. 2113. The latter is the original, the former the copy.

XXX

EXAMINATIONS IN APRIL, 1593

During April forty-three Separatists were examined. The examinations total forty-four, inasmuch as Robert Abraham was examined twice on April 3. Of the forty-three persons, twenty-six had been apprehended in the meeting of March 4. Of the remaining seventeen, one [Collier] had been in prison since 1587; one [Sparrow] since March 1588/1589; two [J. Clark, Waterer] since about January, 1589/1590; three [Boyse, F. Johnson, Settle] since December, 1592; four [Bowman, Brodwater, Diggins, W. Smithe] since February, 1592/1593; five [Bellot, Grave, Knyviton, Penry, Unwen] since March 10–22, 1592/1593; and one [Smells] since April 8, 1593.

Of the fourty-four examinations, Burrage prints twenty-one, of which three are given completely and eighteen incompletely. One should feel grateful to Mr. Burrage for making available much good material on nonconformists, but also one should be cautiously critical of the examinations given by Mr. Burrage. Most of his examinations are based on copies, not originals. Therefore, if the copy carries a transcriptional error, it appears in Burrage's work. Furthermore, most of Burrage's examinations are incompletely given, and he often omits important words, phrases, sentences, and paragraphs. Also, he has omitted annotations—most likely for lack of space.

In April the examiners were less interested in the coffin incident, and did not press the subject, though four Separatists—Brodwater, Bowman, Diggins, and William Smithe—had been suspected of complicity. There were no searching questions about Penry, even though Bellot, Grave, and Knyviton had been arrested with Penry on March 22, but frequently the prisoners were asked if they had any of the books of Barrow, Greenwood, or Penry. There are standard questions, such as: How long have you been in prison? Who committed you? Have you been previously examined or indicted? How long have you been a Separatist? Have you persuaded any to attend conventicles? Was there any suggestion of sedition or rebellion?

The examiners were much interested in the details pertaining to the practices of the Separatists. They asked questions about officers, meeting-places, collections, finance, baptism, communion, marriage, the Lord's Prayer, excommunication, and discipline. They sought information about Separatist attitudes and reasons for leaving the Church of England. Though most of the prisoners refused to incriminate others, yet some divulged the names of preachers who had influenced their thoughts and decisions. There is no mention of Cartwright, Travers, Field, or Fenner, but Cooper, Egerton, Gardener, King, Philips, Snape, Sparke, and Wigginton are designated as "forward" preachers. These clergymen were ordained into the Church of England, but they were Puritans who wished to change the English church from within. They were Presbyterian in polity, Calvinistic in theology, and Englishmen at heart. Thus, they were willing to labour for gradual innovation, but they were unwilling to separate from the national church. They disliked the prospect of division, disruption, and schism, and therefore were willing to make concessions. The thought of exile in 1593 was anathema to them, but their followers carried out the implications of their anti-episcopal ideas, and their sons and grandsons in 1630–1640 even accepted the reality of emigration.

During March most of the Separatists who were examined were questioned about the coffin incident on February 17, or they were examined for their implication in publishing or distributing Separatist books. Among the former group were Bowman, Brodwater, Diggins, and W. Smithe, all arrested in February. But J. Barnes, Bucke, W. Clark, and Pulbery, who were arrested on March 4, were also questioned about the coffin episode. Their examiners were mainly Ellis, Townshend, and especially Young, who were commissioners or lesser legal officials. Among the latter group of Separatists were Boull, Fowrestier, Stokes, and Studley. Since the accusation against them of publishing, distributing, or financing books involved felony, the judges are usually the two chief justices—Popham and Anderson, the attorney-general—Egerton, and the chancellor of the diocese—Stanhope, who was also a Master in Chancery.

In April the roster of judges changes. The reason for this change is that on March 26 the government appointed a special commission to examine Barrowists and Separatists, Catholic recusants, counterfeiters, and vagrants. The commissioners are listed in "De Commissione Speciali Concernente Jesuitas," dated March 26, 1593, and printed in Thomas Rymer, *Foedera, Conventiones, Literae*, 2nd ed., XVI (London, 1727), pp. 201–204. They are also listed in Harley MSS. 6849, f. 239 *recto*, together with the special commissioners appointed in 1594. Of the thirty-six commissioners, eighteen are designated as a group from which one at least must sit on every hearing. Nine special commissioners participated in the examinations of the Separatists. Usually the court consists of four or five judges. The following list includes those special commissioners who examined the Separatists, and the number within the parentheses indicates the number of examinations in which each one participated: John Barne or Barnes (33), Julius Caesar (3), Mathew Dale (30), Dean Gabriell Goodman (33), Robert Forthe (1), Giles Fletcher (3), Owen Hopton (1), Henry Towneshend (8), and Richard Young (33). Thus, Barne, Dale, Goodman, and Young carry the main burden for examining in April, and Young is the most regular participant for both March and April. He also seems to be the one commissioner whom the Separatists despised.

In the *Acts of the Privy Council of England*, New Series, XXIV (1592–1593), p. 145, there is a letter of March 30, 1593, from the Privy Council to the special commissioners, with instructions to take the examinations of recusants, Barrowists, and sectaries. Thus, after the special commission of March 26, the Privy Council acted within four days, and three days later, on April 2, the special commissioners began their examinations of the Separatists.

Of forty-three persons in the April list, thirty-four refused to take an oath before testifying, eight took the oath, and one took the oath after he had testified. Of those who sign their examinations, about one-half sign their own names, and one-half make a mark.

2 Aprilis 1593 [Ellesmere MS. 2101]

THE EXAMINACON OF WILLIAM CLARK OF ST. BUTTOLPHES WITHOUT BUSHOPS GATE, AGED XL YERES OR THERABOUTS, TAKEN BEFORE MR. DEANE OF WESTMINSTER, MR. DOCTOR CESAR, MR. DALE, MR. BARNES AND MR. YOUNG. HE REFUSETH TO ANSWER UPPON HIS OTHE BUT SAIETH:

First, that he hath bene in prison in the Fleet this monthe.

Item, that he was comitted by the Byshop of London and others the high comissioners, beinge taken in the wood beyond Islington, wher he sayeth they prayed and exercised the word of God, and ther George Johnson used the exhortacon and prayer.

Item, he sayeth he was once examined before Mr. Yonge, Mr. Townsend, and Mr. Ellis.[1]

Item, he knoweth not that he is endited for any cause.

Item, he sayeth he hath refrayned to come to churche but half a yere, but hath held his oppynions thes five yeres, beinge drawen therto first by Grenewood then in pryson, and since by one Crane whoe died in Newgate.[2]

Item, being asked wher they used to mete in ther assemblyes, he refuseth to answer.

Item, he refuseth to be conformable or come to churche to heare divine service as it is ther used.

[1] The examination of March 8.

[2] The statement indicates that he was a Separatist in spirit from 1588 to 1593, but in fact he attended the Church of England services from 1588 to 1592—probably to September, when the Separatist church was organized. John Greenwood was imprisoned October 8, 1587, in the Clink and remained there until his execution April 6, 1593, except for a few months in 1592 when he was bailed. Nicholas Crane died in Newgate prison in 1588.

Item, he sayth he hath not nor had any of Barrowe, Grenewood, or Penrye's books, nor knoweth any other that hath.

Item, he sayeth he hath not perswaded any others not to goe to churche.

Item, he sayeth that if the[i]r nomber were increased, yet they ment it not but to the service of God.[1]

sign dci Will Clark
[signum dicti William Clark]

2 Aprilis 1593 [Ellesmere MS. 2102]

THE EXAMINACON OF GEORGE JOHNSON, LATE SCOLEMASTER IN ST. NICHOLAS LANE, LONDON, BORNE IN RICHEMOND SHIRE IN THE COUNTY OF YORK, OF THE AGE OF XXIX YERES OR THER ABOUTS, WHOE REFUSETH TO TAKE AN OTHE BUT SAYETH:

First, he hath bene prisoner in the Fleete a monthe, comitted by the high comissioners for eccl[es]iasticall causes, *viz.*, by the Byshop of London and others for beinge taken in an assemblye [of] people in a wood beyond Islington.

Item, that he was once before the Byshop of London examined, secondly before Mr. Yonge and Mr. Ellis, and thirdly before the Lord Chief Justice of England and my Lord Anderson.[2]

Item, that he is not yet endited for any fact to his knowlege.

Item, beinge asked howe longe he hath absented him self from his parishe church, refuseth to answer.

Item, being demaunded by whome he was drawen into his oppinions, sayth he was drawen therto by the word of God and by the hearinge of Mr. Egerton, preacher, at his sermons.[3]

Item, being asked in what places they met together in the[i]r

[1] This examination is in Burrage, *Early English Dissenters*, II, 45, but of ten paragraphs, Burrage printed only three. The copy or transcript is in Harley MSS. 6848, f. 55 *recto*.

[2] Probably examined about March 6 by John Aylmer, Bishop of London. Examined on March 7 by Richard Young and John Ellis. Probably examined in March by Sir John Popham, Lord Chief Justice of the Queen's Bench and Sir Edmund Anderson, Lord Chief Justice of the Common Pleas.

[3] Stephen Egerton, popular preacher, but not the regular incumbent, at St. Anne in the Blackfriars. As a staunch Puritan, he was not in good standing with Bishop Aylmer.

assemblies, he refuseth to confesse the same nor howe often they have soe assembled.

Item, being asked whether he wilbe contented to conforme him self and be bound to come to devine service nowe used in the parishe churches, he refuseth soe to doe.

Item, being asked whether he have or had any of Barrowe, Greenwood, or Penrye's books, refuseth to answer except he maye have accusers.

Item, being asked whether he hath drawen or procured any others to thes assemblies, refuseth likewise to answer without accusers.

Item, being asked what they intended if they had drawen them selves to a greate number, sayth but only to walke in the ordinance of God accordinge to his worde.[1]

Julius Caesar
Gabriell Goodman
Mathew Dale
John Barne
Richard Young

2 Aprilis 1593 taken before the said comissioners [Ellesmere MS. 2101]

THE EXAMINACON OF JOHN NICHOLAS OF THE PARISHE OF ST. PULCHRES [SEPULCHERS], LONDON, GLOVER, AGED XXXVI YERES OR THERABOUTS, WHO REFUSETH TO ANSWER UPPON HIS OTHE BUT SAYETH:

First, he hath bene in prison a monthe.

Item, that he was comitted by the Lord Byshop of London and others high comissioners for eccle[si]astical causes, beinge taken in the wood beyonde Islington amonge diverse others ther assembled.

Item, that he hath bene examined twice, *viz.*, once before my Lord Bysshop of London and once before Mr. Yonge.[2]

[1] Of these ten paragraphs, Burrage printed only two in *Early English Dissenters*, II, 46, 47, from Harley MSS. 6848, f. 63 *recto*.

[2] Probably examined by Bishop Aylmer about March 5 or 6. Examined on March 8 by Richard Young, Henry Townshend, and John Ellis.

Item, he standeth not endited for any offence to his knowledge.

Item, that he hath refrained from parishe churche assemblies thes foure yeres wherof he hath bene thre yeres and more in prison in the Gate Howse at Westminster, comitted by the Lords of her Majestie's Privy Councell, being one of them that exhibited the suplicacon to her Majesty at the last parliament before this.[1]

Item, being asked by whome he was drawen into his opp[in]ions, and when, sayeth by the worde of God, and that he hath heard George Johnson preache once or twice wherof once was in the wood and hath heard Francis Johnson preache once in St. Nicholas [Lane].

Item, he sayth that they used to meett in the[i]r assemblye in St. Nicholas Lane and in the wood beyond Islington wher he was taken.

Item, he refuseth to be reformed and to come to the churche assemblyes.

Item, he sayeth he hath none of Barrowe, Grenewood, or Penrye's books.

Item, that he hath not perswaded any not to goe to churche, nor drawen any to his oppinions, but sayth he would if he could.

Item, he sayth that one of his sonnes named Nathanyell, beinge fyve yere[s] of age, was baptised by Francis Johnson in Nicholas Lane in the scole howse ther about Xpmas [Christmas] last,[2] and that he was never baptised before that tyme.

Item, he sayth that if they had increased the[i]r nomber, they ment it not but to serve God.[3]

John Nicholas

[1] On March 13, 1588/1589, Nicholas, Christopher Bowman, and John Sparewe, or Sparrow, presented "A Lamentable Petition" to the Queen. All three were committed to prison by the order of the Privy Council. For the petition, see Carlson, *The Writings of John Greenwood, 1587–1590*, pp. 277–282. Nicholas was in the Gatehouse prison at Westminster from March 17, 1588/1589, until about the summer of 1592, when he was bailed or allowed a limited liberty in the custody of a responsible citizen. Arrested again on March 4, 1592/1593.

[2] His son was probably baptized before December 6, 1592, when Francis Johnson was arrested.

[3] The copy of this examination is in Harley MSS. 6848, f. 63 *verso*, from which Burrage omits six paragraphs; see *Early English Dissenters*, II, 46.

XXXI

[3 Aprilis 1593] [Ellesmere MS. 2106]

THE EXAMINACON OF ROBERT ABRAHAM,[1] SERVANT TO THOMAS ROOKES, DWELLING IN ST. OLAVES IN SOUTHWORK, LETHER DRESSER, OF THE AGE OF XXVI YERES, TAKEN THE DAYE AND YERE AFORESAID BEFORE THE SAID COMISSIONERS AND MR. DOCTOR FLETCHER[2] [FORTHE?], WHO REFUSETH TO ANSWER UPPON HIS OTHE BUT SAYETH:

First, that he hath bene in prison in Newgate this month, beinge taken in the wood in the assembly ther, and comitted by Mr. Doctor Stanhop[3] and Mr. Yong.

Item, he was but once examined, which was by the said Mr. Stanhop and Mr. Yonge.[4]

Item, he knoweth not that he is indicted for any cause.

Item, he sayth he hath not bene at any churche this twelve monthes, and hath bene of his oppinions a yere and half.[5]

Item, beinge asked by whome he was drawed [*sic*] into his oppinions, he sayth none but by the worde of God.

Item, beinge asked howe often they have used to meete in the[i]r assemblies, sayeth twice a week comonly except they were otherwise occupied, and sayth they met somtymes at Smythfeld in a howse by the hospitall, alwayes erly in the morninge, and in the winter about iiii[or] [*quattuor*] or five a clock in the morninge, and some tyme by Algate besides Christ churche, and they met by suche direccon as they took always at ther last metings and sometymes about Mooregate. They toke their direccon for meting as they mett ther. And [he] sayth they received the communyon but once, which was in a

[1] Abraham, Aburne, and Aweburne.

[2] There is a Dr. Giles Fletcher and also a Robert Forthe. Fletcher's name is not appended with the signatures of the commissioners, but probably both Fletcher and Forthe are present. Both were appointed special commissioners.

[3] Edward Stanhope, Chancellor to John Aylmer, Bishop of London.

[4] There is no record of this examination. It may have occurred about March 7.

[5] Therefore, he probably began his Separatist association in October, 1591. He is not on any previous prisoner list, but he was present at the organization of the church in September, 1592. Abraham died in Newgate prison before 1596.

howse about Smythfeld, but he remembreth not the howse and it was at the hands of Francis Johnson, the[i]r pastor.[1]

Item, he confesseth that they mett thre or foure tymes at St. Nicholas Lane, and once at Rippon's howse in Sowthwork and in the felds by Detforde sometymes, and often tymes in the felds and wood by Islington.[2]

Item, beinge asked if he wilbe contented to reforme him self and come to his parishe church to devine service, sayth he will if he maye see it reformed and evell persons removed out of the churche assemblies.

Item, he sayth he hath sene some of Barrowe and Grenewood's bookes, but hath none of them and remembreth not whome he hath sene to have the same bookes.

Item, he sayeth he never perswaded any to his oppinions or metings.

Item, beinge asked what they ment to doe if that they were growen to a greater nomber, sayeth but only to serve God.

Item, he sayeth they used to geve the[i]r pastor every man accordinge to his ability.[3]

signum dci [dicti] Roberti Abraham
Gabriell Goodman
Robert Forthe
H. Towneshend
John Barne
Rychard Young

3 Aprilis 1593 [Ellesmere MS. 2104]

THE REEXAMINACON[4] OF ROBERTE ABURNE [ABRAHAM, AWEBURNE] TAKEN THE 3D OF APRILL 1593 BEFORE DOCTOR GOODMAN, DEANE OF WESTMINSTER, MR. TOWNSEND, MR. DALE, MR. BARNE, AND MR. YONGE.

He saith he is by trade a lether dresser and servant to one Mr.

[1] The communion service was held at the home of John Barnes in Smithfield, near St. Bartholomew's.

[2] He mentions eight meeting places, but gives no names of house owners except Roger Rippon, who had died February 16, 1592/1593.

[3] Burrage prints this examination from the copy in Harley 6848, f. 57 *verso*. Of twelve paragraphs, Burrage prints only five. Also, the title and first paragraph are incomplete. See *Early English Dissenters*, II, 47–48.

[4] It is not clear why Abraham was re-examined the same day. His judges are the

Rooks of Southwark. He saith he hath not bene at his parishe churche this yere and half.

He saith the first that ever brought him in to this congregacon was one William Howton, decessed,[1] whoe perswaded him to refraine his parishe churche, and brought him acquainted with the rest of the brethren of that congregacon being at Bridwell, and thether he went to see their orders, beinge then at that tyme Studley with others prisoners there, where he herd at that tyme one Stanhopp[2] preache emongst them in the prison openly, and then this examinant beinge emongst them was receyved and admitted into their societie and congregacon without either examinacon or farther enquirie of his conversacon.

He saith that sithence he hath mett with the said congregacon diverse tymes aswell privately in howses, as in open feilds and woods, some times to the number of 100, some times lx [60] at the least. Once they mett aboute a halfe a yere sithence at Roger Rippon's in Southwarke, twoo other times at Algate quarter of a yere sithence at a house within Algate, on the lefte hand, he knowes not at whose house and that Mr. Johnson was their pastor when they were in Southwarke and after at one other house at Smithfeld almost halfe a yere sithence but knowes not whose house it was, and there they re[ceive]d the communion, Johnson ministeringe unto them, and met once in St. Nich[ol]us Lane, the said Johnson beinge pastor and Grenewood their teacher.

They mett divers times in the feild nere Detford, and aboute the woodsids nere Islington and there have herd younge Johnson[3] preche sithence his brother the elder Johnson was in trouble.

He saith that at their meetinge in St. Nichus [Nicholas] Lane when Mr. Yonge did take them there, they did then make choice of their doctor, techer, deakons and elders and that Johnson the elder was then chosen pastor, Grenewood teacher, Studley and Knifton elders, Lee and Bowman deakons.[4]

same except that Mathew Dale is present in place of Robert Forthe and Giles Fletcher is not present.

[1] William Hawton, or Howton, or Hutton, is a prisoner in the Counter Wood Street in 1590. He died in Newgate about 1592.

[2] This Stanhope or Stanhopp probably was one of the prisoners. His name does not reappear, and we do not have his first name. He should not be confused with Dr. Edward Stanhope, Chancellor to the Bishop of London and persecutor of the Separatists.

[3] George Johnson. The elder brother Francis was arrested on the night of December 5–6, 1592.

[4] There seems to have been an arrest of some Separatists on December 17 or 24, 1592, when Daniel Studley and Thomas Settel were seized. Abraham seems to

He saith that their doctor and pastor weere mainteyned by contribution from emongst them every one as his habillite was by weekly collection, and that he for his parte hath yelded his contribucon this yere and this halfe, and that the collection beinge gathered was delivered to the deakons to be distributed emongst those of that congregacon which the said deakons did thinke good, or most to stand in need.

He saith that they did use to excommunicate emongst them, and that one Roberte Stokes, and one George Collier,[1] and one or twoe more whose names he remembreth not, were excom[mu]nicated for that they discented from them in opinion but in what poynte he remembreth not, and that the said Johnson the elder did denownce [pronounce] the excomunicacon against them, and concerninge the[i]r manner of procedinge to excommunicacon he saith, that they, the said Stokes and the rest, beinge privatly admonished of their pretended errors and not conforminge them selves, and by witnes produced to their congregacon, then the said Johnson with the consent of the whole congregacon did denownce [pronounce] the excommunicacon, and that sithence they were excommunicated, which was a halfe yere and some what more sithence they were not admitted into their churche. And beinge demanded whether he could be contented to forsake the said congregacon and repaier to his parishe churche or not, he saith he knowes not nor can see any cause why he should soe refraine the said congregacon.[2]

the mark of Robert Aburne
Gabriell Goodman
H. Towneshend
Mathew Dale
J. Barne
Richard Young

confuse dates by suggesting an arrest in September, 1592, when the church was organized. Conceivably, it may have been in October, when Francis Johnson was seized by the sheriff of London, in St. Nicholas Lane.

[1] Robert Stokes was excommunicated in the autumn of 1592. George Collier was imprisoned October 8, 1587, and had remained in prison more than five years. On his examination, April 5, 1593, he refused to conform in order to obtain his liberty. Therefore, he is an unlikely candidate for excommunication. There may have been two Colliers, or Abraham may have confused the name. Collins is a possibility.

[2] Burrage prints this re-examination completely from the copy in Harley MSS. 6848, f. 41 *recto* and *verso*. See *Early English Dissenters*, II, 49–51.

3 Aprilis 1593 [Ellesmere MS. 2107]

THE EXAMINACON OF JOHN BARNES OF DUCK LANE, TAYLOR, OF THE AGE OF XXVI YERES OR THERABOUTS, TAKEN BEFORE MR. DEANE OF WESTMINSTER, MR. DOCTOR FORTH, MR. TOWNSHEND, MR. BARNES [BARNE], AND MR. YONGE. WHOE REFUSETH TO TAKE AN OTHE TO ANSWER TREWLY BUT SAYETH:

First, that he hath bene in prison in Newgate a monthe, comitted by the Lord Byshop of London and others, beinge taken in the wood in the assembly ther by Islington.

Item, he sayeth he knoweth not that he is indicted for any cause.

Item, he sayeth that he hath refrayned from comynge to churche thes four yeres last past.[1]

Item, he sayeth he was not perswaded to his oppinions by any but by the word of God and by hearing of others whose names he remembreth not.

Item, beinge asked howe often and wher they used to mete in the[i]r assemblys, sayeth they used wekely to meete, but wher he refuseth to tell.

Item, he refuseth to reforme him self and to come to churche to heare divine service except he sayeth it be reformed accordinge to the worde of God, and sayeth he findeth noe a[u]cthoryty in the worde of God for mayntenance of the name of Lord Byshop.[2]

Item, he denyeth that he hath any of Barrowe, Grenewood, or Penrie's books or ever read any of them, nor knoweth any that hath any of those bookes.

Item, he sayeth he never perswaded or drewe any to ther assemblies.[3]

signum dci [dicti] Johis [Johannis] Barnes
Gabriell Goodman Henry Towneshend
Robert Forthe John Barne Rychard Young

[1] John Barnes joined with the Separatists in 1588 or 1589. In February and April, 1590, he is listed as a prisoner for attending conventicles. He was probably bailed in 1592, and was present at the organization of the church in September, 1592.

[2] Separatists accepted bishops but not lord bishops. They were aware of the use of the word "episkopos" in the New Testament, but this "overseer" was equated with the elder, or presbyter.

[3] But the church met at Barnes' house in Smithfield near St. Bartholomew's.

[3 Aprillis 1593] [Ellesmere MS. 2107]

THE EXAMINACON OF HENRY BRODEWATER OF ST. NICHOLAS LANE, SCRIVENOR, OF THE AGE OF XXIX YERES OR THER ABOUTS, TAKEN BY THE SAID COMISSIONERS THE DAYE AND YERE ABOVE SAID.

First, that he hath bene in prison thes six weekes,[1] comitted by the Byshop of London and other high comissioners for beinge suspected to be privy to a libell lately dispersed concerninge the coffyn brought to Mr. Yonge's doore.

Item, he hath bene twice examined, *viz.*, once before the Byshop of London and others and likewise before Mr. Recorder,[2] Mr. Townshend, and others, and is not indicted for any offence to his knowlege.[3]

Item, he will not be bound to come to anye parishe churche, but sayeth he will consider of that matter.[4]

Item, beinge examined whether he hath or had any of Barrowe, Grenewood, or Penrie's bookes, sayeth he hath nor had any nor hath not sene any of them to his knowlege [sayeth he hath not nor had any nor hath sene any of them to his knowlege].[5]

Per me Henry Brodwater

Also, communion—the Lord's Supper—was administered by Francis Johnson there. Barnes reveals very little in his examination, but he probably was well-informed. He died in Newgate prison—before 1596.

This examination is not in Burrage, *Early English Dissenters*.

[1] He was arrested about February 17–20. The coffin was carried to Justice Young's house on Saturday, February 17, and some of the participants may have been apprehended the same day. February 20 to April 3 would be exactly six weeks.

[2] Edward Drew was the Recorder of London, 1592–1594. William Fleetwood held the office from 1571 to 1591. Edward Coke was elected on October 14, 1591, sworn and accepted into the office on January 14, 1591/1592. Drew succeeded him on June 17, 1592, and resigned the office on March 27, 1594, when he became a Justice of Assize for Kent and Essex.

[3] The examinations before Bishop Aylmer and Recorder Drew probably occurred in the period February 17–March 7.

[4] Brodewater, or Brodwater, was imprisoned in the Clink, in Southwark. When he says "he will consider of that matter," he seems to be wavering. From an undated list—perhaps about April 1593—we know he was bailed upon his conformity. See Harley MSS. 6848, f. 210 *recto*, and chapter XXXVIII, *infra*.

[5] Burrage printed only three lines of this examination from a summary in Harley MSS. 6848, f. 32 *recto*. See *Early English Dissenters*, II, 38. Only one-half of the summary is given.

[3 Aprilis 1593] [Ellesmere MS. 2103]

THE EXAMINACON OF JOHN CLARK OF WALSOTKON IN NORFOLK, HUSBONDMAN, OF THE AGE OF L [50] YERES OR THER ABOUTS, TAKEN THE DAYE AND YERE AFORESAID BEFORE THE SAID COMISSIONERS, WHOE REFUSETH TO BE SWORNE BUT SAYETH:

First, that he hath bene in prison thes thre yeres in Newgate,[1] comitted by the sherifs of London which then were,[2] being taken in an assembly of Brownists.[3]

Item, he sayth he was indicted for a recusant about a yere and a half since.

Item, he hath bene of his oppinions thes thre yeres and refuseth to come to church for that he sayth the ministers are not ordayned by the worde of God.

Item, he saith he was perswaded to his oppinions by the preachinge of one Colshill, preacher.

Item, he refuseth to come to churche to heare divine service or sermons.[4]

Item, he denieth the havinge of any of Barrowe, Grenewood, or Penrie's books, neither hath he perswaded any to his oppinions.[5]

signum dci [dicti]
Johis [Johannis] Clark

[1] Clark, or Clerke, was from the parish of Walsoken in Norfolk, near Wisbech. Probably arrested in January, he first appears as a Separatist prisoner in February, 1589/1590, and in April, 1590, he is in the Bridewell. Then he was transferred to Newgate prison.

[2] The sheriffs of London in 1589–1590 were Richard Gurney and Steven Some, and Sir John Hart was mayor. See William Jaggard, *A View of All the Right Honourable the Lord Mayors of This Honorable Citty of London* (1601).

[3] The phrase "an assembly of Brownists" is correct. In Harley MSS. 6848, f. 32 *recto*, the phrase is "an assembly with Barrowes," evidently a scribal mistake for Barrowists or Brownists. Thus, Burrage concludes erroneously that Henry Barrow must have been temporarily out of prison early in 1590. See *Early English Dissenters*, I, 130.

[4] Evidently Clark was adamant, perhaps belligerent. From the summary of his examination we learn that "yt was thoughte good by the commissioners that hee should bee sente to Bridewell to grinde in the mill." See Harley MSS. 6848, f. 32 *recto*. In 1597 he was banished to Newfoundland.

[5] This examination is not in Burrage, but the summary is given in *Early English Dissenters*, II, 38–39, from Harley MSS. 6848, f. 32 *recto*.

3 Aprilis 1593 [Ellesmere MS. 2106]

THE EXAMINACON OF JOHN DALAMORE OF THE CITTIE OF BATHE, BRODE WEAVER, OF THE AGE OF XXV YERES, WHO LAYE AT THE HOWSE OF ONE GRYFFETH[1] AT THE HARPE WITHIN LUDGATE TWO NIGHTS BEFORE HE WAS TAKEN, TAKEN BEFORE MR. DEANE OF WESTMINSTER, MR. DOCTOR FORD [FORTHE], MR. TOWNSEND, MR. DALE, MR. BARNE, AND MR. YONGE. WHO BEINGE REQUIRED TO ANSWER UPPON HIS OTHE REFUSETH TO BE SWORNE BUT SAYTH:

First, that he hath bene in prison this month, being taken in the wood beyond Islington in the assembly ther and comitted to prison by the Byshop of London and others the high comissioners.[2]

Item, he sayth he was examined before Doctor Stanhop, Mr. Yonge, and others.[3]

Item, he knoweth not that he is indicted for any cause.

Item, he sayeth he used to come to church untill within thes thre monthes and soe long hath refrayned.

Item, beinge asked by whome he was drawen into his oppinions, sayeth by the word of God, and that he hath heard one Smyth[4] and others preache at Kensham and other places in Somersetshire.[5]

Item, beinge asked howe often he hath bene at the[i]r private meetings and conventicles, refuseth to answer.

Item, beinge asked whether he wilbe contented to reforme him self and come to churche to heare divine service, refuseth soe to doe.

Item, he sayeth he doth not knowe whether he did ever see any of Barrowe, Grenewood, or Penrie's books, nor hath any of them.

Item, he sayth he never perswaded any to come to any their conventicles or metings, nor moved any to his oppinions noe further than by the word of God.

[1] Conceivably this is Robert Griffeth, who was arrested October 8, 1587, and bailed in May, 1589, "being very sycke." See Carlson, *The Writings of John Greenwood, 1587–1590*, pp. 280, 308, 313, 317, 327, 330.

[2] Arrested March 4 and imprisoned in the Newgate.

[3] Probably examined by Dr. Edward Stanhope and Richard Young in March.

[4] Possibly William Smith, or Smythe, clergyman from Bradford, Wiltshire. He may be the same Smith who goes to the Netherlands about 1595–1596. See Johnson, *A Discourse of Some Troubles*, 214.

[5] Kensham is Keynsham, near Bristol and Bath and Bradford, in Somersetshire.

Item, he beinge required to saye the Lord's Prayer, he refuseth soe to doe.

Item, beinge asked what was the[i]r intent to doe when they had drawen them selves to a greater nomber, [he] sayeth, to serve God accordinge to his worde.[1]

John Dalemor

3 Aprilis 1593 [Ellesmere MS. 2103]

THE EXAMINACON OF XPOFER [CHRISTOPHER] DIGGINS OF ST. OLIVES IN SOWTHWORK, WEVER, OF THE AGE OF XXIIII YERES OR THER ABOUTS, TAKEN BEFORE MR. DEANE OF WESTMINSTER, MR. TOWNSHEND, MR. DALE, MR. BARNE, AND MR. YONGE. WHOE REFUSETH TO BE SWORNE BUT SAYTH:

First, that he hath bene in prison vi or vii wekes, comitted by Mr. Yonge for the libell and coffyn brought to Mr. Yonge's doore.[2]

Item, he sayeth he knoweth not whether he be indicted for any offence yea or noe.

Item, he sayth he hath not come nor repayred to any parishe church to devine service thes two yeres and soe long hath held his oppinions, but refuseth to tell by whome he was drawen therto.

Item, he sayeth he hath bene at the[i]r assemblyes every saboth daye thes two yeres[3] but refuseth to tell wher they held the[i]r assemblyes.

Item, he sayth that ther were diverse children baptised at the[i]r assemblyes at St. Nicholas Lane, which children were about the age of thre yeres as he supposeth.

Item, he refuseth to come to churche to heare devine service ther used.

[1] Burrage prints two paragraphs out of eleven, from the copy in Harley MSS. 6848, f. 58 *recto*. See *Early English Dissenters*, II, 47.

[2] Diggins, or Dickons, of St. Olave's parish, Southwark, was arrested about February 17, 1592/1593. Thus, he had been in prison for six weeks and three days. The summary of his examination states specifically that Diggins "was one of them that carried the coffine to Mr. Younge's dore." See Harley MSS. 6848, f. 32 *recto*. See also Albert Peel, *The Notebook of John Penry, 1593*, p. 39.

[3] He is not on any list of prisoners in 1590.

Item, he sayeth that he did see one of Barrowe and Grenewood's bookes which one John Wilkinson brought unto him.[1]

Item, he sayth he never perswaded any to his oppinyons.[2]

Item, he sayth if the[i]r nomber should have increased, yet they ment nothinge but the service of God and trewe subjeccon to the Quene's Majesty.[3]

Signum dci [dicti]
xpofir Diggins

[3 Aprilis 1593] [Ellesmere MS. 2103]

THOMAS FARROT SERVANT TO WILLIAM GRENE OF ALDERSGATE STRETE, AGED ABOUT XXII YERES, EXAMINED BEFORE THE SAID COMISSIONERS, BEINGE VERY SICK, SAYETH:

That he was taken in the wood beyond Islington and comitted by the Byshop of London and others, and examined by Mr. Yonge.[4]

Item, he refuseth to reforme him selfe and to come to churche.[5]

Gabriell Goodman
Henry Towneshend
Mathew Dale
John Barne
Richard Young

[1] John Wilkenson, or Wilkinson, was a Separatist and later a Seeker. He had a congregation at Colchester, Essex, was imprisoned there, disputed with John Murton in 1613, and died about 1619. See Walter H. Burgess, *John Smith the Se-Baptist, Thomas Helwys and the First Baptist Church in England. With Fresh Light upon the Pilgrim Fathers' Church* (London, 1911), pp. 299–302. See also the references in Burrage, *Early English Dissenters*, I, 192–194, 370–375 *et passim*.

[2] Diggins joined the Ancient Church in Amsterdam about 1597. See Johnson, *A Discourse of Some Troubles*, pp. 126, 127, 143, 152.

[3] This examination is not in Burrage, but he prints a summary from Harley MSS. 6848, f. 32 *recto*. There are fifty-six words omitted from the summary, in Burrage, *Early English Dissenters*, II, 38.

[4] Farrot, or Farrett, or Farrat, was probably examined about March 6 by Richard Young. About May he was bailed upon his conformity, probably induced by his sickness. See Harley MSS. 6848, f. 210 *recto*.

[5] About 1595–1597 he went to Amsterdam, probably joined the Ancient Church led by Francis Johnson, then joined the small church led by Henoch Clapham in the same city. See Clapham, *The Syn, against the Holy Ghoste*, p. 2. Arber, in his *Story of the Pilgrim Fathers*, p. 99, describes Farrat as one of the "faithful brethren, a poor remnant of the ever visible Catholic and Apostolic Church." There is a

[3 Aprilis 1593] [Ellesmere MS. 2107]

THE EXAMINACON OF EDWARD GRAVE OF ST. BUTTOLPHE'S IN THAMES STRETE, FISHMONGER, OF THE AGE OF XXV OR THER ABOUTS, TAKEN BY THE SAID COMISSIONERS THE DAYE AND YERE AFORESAID, WHO REFUSETH TO BE SWORNE BUT SAYTH:

First, he hath bene in prison but a weke, comitted by Mr. Yonge for being in some of the assemblies, and taken with Penry, Kniveton, and Billet.[1]

Item, he sayth he hath held his oppinions and refrained from any churche this half yere,[2] and was perswaded to his oppinions by Mr. Gardiner,[3] Mr. Phillips,[4] and others the[i]r sermons.

Item, he refuseth to come to churche to heare divine service as it is now used.

Item, he saithe he hath had one of Barrowe and Grenewood's books of conference, but he remembreth not to whome he delivered the same booke.[5]

letter of Henoch Clapham, in Harley MSS. 7581, f. 57, item 4, which gives an interesting criticism of the severity in Francis Johnson's congregation. It is wrongly catalogued under Henry Clay, but the manuscript reading is "Hen. Clap."

This examination has not been published previously.

[1] He was arrested on March 22, 1592/1593, at the house of Mr. Lewes or Lowes, in Stepney, together with John Penry, George Knyviton, and Arthur Bellot.

[2] He was present at the organization of the church in September, 1592.

[3] Richard Gardiner, or Gardener, rector of St. Mary, Matfellon, Whitechapel, staunch Puritan and a leader of the Presbyterian classis movement. See Pearson, *Thomas Cartwright and Elizabethan Puritanism, 1535–1603*, pp. 201, 237, 316. See also Patrick Collinson, *The Elizabethan Puritan Movement*, pp. 320, 411, 412.

[4] Thomas Philips, or Phyllips, was rector at St. Augustine on Watling Street. Edward Philips, or Phillips, was a preacher at St. Saviour's, in Southwark. See Powicke, *Henry Barrowe Separatist*, 81, 155; Collinson, *op. cit.*, 447. Edward Phillips seems to be the better choice. There is material on Edward Philippes for January, 1596/1597, his failure to keep a fast day, his suspension and imprisonment in the Gatehouse, in Lansdowne MSS., item 34, ff. 98–99.

[5] There are four conferences reported in *A Collection of Certaine Sclaunderous Articles Gyven Out by the Bisshops*. There are three more in *A Collection of Certain Letters and Conferences*. Printed in Carlson, *The Writings of John Greenwood, 1587–1590, together with the Joint Writings of Henry Barrow and John Greenwood, 1587–1590*, pp. 103–174, 175–262. He delivered the book to Leonard Pidder, or Pedder.

This examination is not in Burrage, but he prints the summary from Harley MSS. 6848, f. 32 *recto*, wherein he omits twenty words. See *Early English Dissenters*, II, 38.

Item, he sayth he hath not procured or drawen any to his oppinions.

Item, he sayeth he hath bene in the assemblies once in the wood by Islington, once at the wood at Detford, and once at Nicholas Lane, and sayth ther was in Detford wood at that tyme when he was ther lx [60] persons or ther abouts.

Item, he sayth they intended nothing by the[i]r assemblyes but to serve God.

Be me, Edward Grave

3 Aprill 1593 [Ellesmere MS. 2107]

THE EXAMINACON OF ABRAHAM PULBURY OF THE PARISHE OF CHRI[ST]-CHURCH, PURSMAKER BY TRADE BUT FRE OF THE COWPERS, OF THE AGE OF XXIIII^or YERES OR THER ABOUTS, TAKEN BEFORE MR. DEANE OF WESTMINSTER, MR. TOWNSHEND, MR. BARNE, AND MR. YONGE. WHO REFUSETH TO TAKE AN OTHE BUT SAYETH:

First, that he hath bene in prison this month, comitted by the Byshop of London and others, taken in the wood beyond Islington, examined before Mr. Townshend, Mr. Yonge,[1] and others, and sayth he had with him a sworde at the wood.

Item, he sayth he is not indicted to his knowledge.

Item, he sayth he hath not bene at any parishe churche these two yeres.

Item, he saith he hath bene at some of the[i]r assemblies at diverse place[s], *viz.*, once by Smythfeld, erly in the morning, wher they continewed most parte of the daye, and sometymes by Chri[st] church, sometymes by Detford.

Item, he sayth that Francis Johnson was the[i]r pastor, Grenewood the[i]r doctor, Studley and Kniveton the[i]r elders, Nicholas Lee and John [Christopher] Bowman the[i]r decons.[2]

[1] Richard Young and John Ellis signed his first examination of March 7, but Henry Townshend and possibly one or two other commissioners were present.

[2] The officers of the first Separatist church were elected in September, 1592: Francis Johnson, pastor; John Greenwood, teacher or doctor; Daniel Studley and George Knyviton, elders; Nicholas Lee and Christopher Bowman, deacons. The meeting was held in London at the home of a Mr. Fox in St. Nicholas Lane.

Item, he sayth ther hath bene baptised in the[i]r assemblies in Nicholas Lane at one tyme iiii^or [*quattuor*, four] or five children, wherof some were of five yeres old, some of six, and some of vii yeres.

Item, he sayeth he will not come to o[u]r parishes [*sic*] church assemblies, neither will he reforme him self or his oppinions.

Item, being asked whither [whether] he had or hath any of Barrowe, Grenewood, or Penrie's bookes, refuseth to answer, sayenge he will saye neither yea nor noe.

Item, beinge asked whether he hath perswaded any to his oppinions and to those assemblies, sayth he hath not, but would doe what he might to instruct his owne famylye.

Item, he sayeth he was about twelve month[s] since comitted to prison in Sussex, tog[eth]er with one William Collyn,[1] by the Byshop of Chichester[2] and from him sent to Sir Henry Goringe and by him sent to Arrundell, ther to be kept untill the Quarter Sessions, beinge taken in Arrundell as suspected to be a Brownist, and then continewed in prison untill the Assises, wher he was indicted and burned in the eare for a vagabond, and then prest [impressed] for a soldier, which he sayth was done against all lawe and justice.[3]

Abraham Pulbery

3 Aprilis 1593 [Ellesmere MS. 2105]

THE EXAMINACON OF ROGER WATERER, LATE SERVANT TO ROBERT PAVY OF ST. MARTYN, LUDGATE, HABERDASHER, AGED XXII YERES, TAKEN BY MR. DEANE OF WESTMINSTER, MR. TOWNSHEND, MR. DALE, MR. BARNE, AND MR. YONGE, WHOE REFUSETH TO BE SWORNE BUT SAYTH:

First, that he hath bene in prison in Newgate thes thre yeres and a quarter, comitted by Doctor Stanhop and never yet examyned,

1 William Collins was one who planned to begin a second Separatist church in London, with John Nicholas, Thomas Mitchell, and John Barnes. Richard Bancroft refers to one Collins as "not unlearned" and as able to write Latin. See *Survay of the Pretended Holy Discipline*, p. 249 [429] and Harley MSS. 6848, f. 47 *verso*.

2 Thomas Bickley was the Bishop of Chichester, 1586–1596.

3 The copy is in Harley MSS. 6848, ff. 47 *verso* and 48 *recto*. Burrage prints five of the ten paragraphs in *Early English Dissenters*, II, 48–49.

and the cause of his committement was, as he sayth, for not comynge to churche.[1]

Item, he knoweth not that he is indicted for any offence.

Item, he confesseth that before he was comitted to prison he was in an assembly in a garden howse by Bedlem,[2] wher James Forrester[3] expounded before the[i]r churche was setled, and was perswaded to his oppinions by one [Farrot—crossed out] Coppye.[4]

Item, he refuseth as yet to come to church but semeth willinge to be conferred with by some learned men and to be instructed.

Item, he sayeth he hath had one of Barrowe and Grenewood's books, *viz.*, the conferrence,[5] but of whome he had it or what became of it, he sayeth he knoweth not.

Item he sayth [he] never perswaded any to his oppinions.[6]

Roger Waterer

[1] In December, 1589, or January, 1589/1590, he was apprehended, only eighteen years old, and kept in irons in a Newgate dungeon for more than a year. He is on both prison lists for 1590. From January 3, 1589/1590, to April 3, 1593, the time would be exactly three and one-quarter years.

[2] Bedlem or Bethlehem Hospital.

[3] See the examination of Fowrestier for March 19.

[4] Thomas Farrot was examined on April 3, 1593. There is no other reference to the mysterious Coppye, who may be a ghost.

[5] The book, *A Collection of Certain Letters and Conferences*, was published about July, 1590. He must have received it at Newgate prison and read it in the dungeon while still in irons.

[6] Burrage prints this examination from the copy in Harley MSS. 6848, f. 51 *recto*, but he omits 107 words. See *Early English Dissenters*, II, 39, 49.

XXXII

[4 Aprilis 1593] [Ellesmere MS. 2110]

XPOFER [CHRISTOPHER] BOWMAN OF SMYTHFELD, GOLDSMYTH, OF THE AGE OF XXXII YERES, EXAMINED BEFORE THE SAID COMISSIONERS THE DAYE AND YERE AFORESAID, WHOE REFUSETH TO BE SWORNE BUT SAYETH:

First, that he hath bene in prison in the Counter in the Powltry this v wekes, comitted by Mr. Yonge, being suspected to have knowlege whoe made the libell and about the coffyn brought to Mr. Yonge's dore, once examined before Mr. Yonge and others, never indicted to his knowlege.[1]

Item, he sayeth he is a deacon in the congregacion chosen in September last.

Item, he sayeth he hath not bene at churche thes five yeres last past, wherof he was iiii^{or} [four, *quattuor*] yeres in prison, and soe long hath held his oppinions, and was one of them that delivered the supplicacon to the Quene's Majesty the last Parliament before this.[2]

Item, he sayeth he was drawen to his oppinions by the course that the forward preachers tooke, and by a book of a sermon uppon the xiith of the Romans, made by Mr. Chatterton,[3] as he thinketh,

[1] He was examined on March 1. If he had been in prison exactly five weeks, he was arrested on February 28. He paid for the cost of the coffin—4*s.* 8*d.*—in his capacity as deacon, with responsibilities as treasurer.

[2] The supplication, or "A Lamentable Petition," was presented to the Queen on March 13, 1588/1589. On March 17 Bowman was imprisoned in the Counter Wood Street, and a year later he petitioned unsuccessfully to Lord Burghley for his release. These two documents are printed in Carlson, *The Writings of John Greenwood, 1587–1590*, pp. 279–284, and 285–288. He was bailed or given a limited liberty, since he was at the organization meeting of the church in September, 1592. In later years he went to Kampen, Naarden, and Amsterdam.

[3] Laurence Chaderton, venerable master of Emmanuel College, published *A Fruitfull Sermon upon the 3, 4, 5, 6, 7, and 8 Verses of the 12 Chapter of the Epistle of Paul to the Romanes*, in 1584. It was printed by the Puritan printer, Robert Waldegrave in 1584, entered in the *Stationers' Register* August 22, 1586, reissued in 1586 and 1589. Thomas Rogers published a reply to it in 1590. The sermon is not mentioned in the *D.N.B.* article by E. S. Shuckburgh.

Chaderton explained the great ignorance about God in England by the lack of doctors and teachers. Why did sin so much abound in the land? Because the church lacked "elders and governours of every congregation to admonish, correct, suspend and excommunicate such noisome, hurtfull and monstrous,

and by the forward preachers; he sayeth he meaneth one Snape and Kinge,[1] with others, whose course made him enter into further serche of the matter of reformacon.

Item, he sayeth he hath bene at the[i]r metings as often as he could, beinge at liberty and in helth, *viz.*, at Mr. Bilson's howse nere C[h]ri[st]church, at St. Nicholas Lane, in the woods by Detford and Islington, at Penrye's howse, at Lee's howse, and at Rippon's howse, and at Barnes' his howse in Smythfeld by St. Barthelmewes.

Item, he sayeth he had one of Barrowe's bookes of Discovery[2] about two yeres agoe, which book he had of Robert Stokes and, as he remembreth, he redelivered the same to Stokes againe.

Item, being asked howe manye he hath drawen and procured to his oppinions and assemblyes, sayeth he maye use his gyfts to God's glory, and otherwise will not answer.

Item, he sayeth if the[i]r nomber should never soe much have increased, they ment noe reformacon by stronge hand.

Item, he refuseth to reforme him self and to come to his parishe church.

Item, being asked wher he was marryed to his last wief [wife], sayeth in Penrye's howse, wher Mr. Setle used prayer,[3] and that his oppinion is that mariage in a howse without a minister by consent of the parties and frends is sufficient.[4]

Gabriell Goodman Mathew Dale
John Barne Rychard Young

beastes, out of the house of God, without respect of persons." Why were there so many poor, feeble, and weak persons on the verge of death? The answer was: "we want [lack] deacons and merciful men, which should faithfully distribute to the necessitie of the saints, and willingly and cheerefully attend upon the impotent, which are unable to help them selves." Despite good laws for the provision of the poor, "wee [shall] have swarmes of beggars poore and impotent, till we have by authoritie established in every congregation these eternall decrees of Christ, touching the government of his church." (I have used the edition published at Leyden, 1618, published by the Pilgrim Press. See pp. 56–57.

[1] For Edmund Snape and Andrew King and the forward preachers—the Puritan reformers—see Patrick Collinson, *The Elizabethan Puritan Movement*, pp. 143, 144, 323, 326, 409, 412, *et passim*.

[2] *A Brief Discoverie of the False Church*, published about January, 1590/1591, and printed in Carlson, *The Writings of Henry Barrow, 1587–1590*, pp. 259–673.

[3] He was married the second time about November, 1592, after Penry's return from Scotland and before the arrest of Thomas Settel about December 17. The Separatists, who regarded marriage as a civil ceremony, contravened the ecclesiastical law of the Church of England. See Harley MSS. 6848, ff. 33 *verso*, 70 *recto* and *verso*, 84 *recto*.

[4] Burrage prints this examination from the copy in Harley MSS. 6848, f. 70 *recto* and *verso*. He omits part of the title, part of the first paragraph, and three

4 Aprilis 1593 [Ellesmere MS. 2108]

WILLIAM EYLES,[1] SERVANT TO ONE CHERIOT, TAYLOR IN WALBROKE,[2] OF THE AGE OF XXII YERES, EXAMINED BEFORE MR. DEANE OF WESTMINSTER, MR. DALE, MR. BARNES [BARNE], AND MR. YONGE. WHO REFUSETH TO BE SWORNE BUT SAYTH:

First, that he hath bene in prison a monthe,[3] comitted by Mr. Doctor Stanhop and others for goenge to the assembly in the wood by Islington, never examined, nor indicted.

Item, being asked howe longe he hath held his oppinions, refuseth to answer.

Item, being asked howe often he hath bene in the assemblyes, refuseth likewise to answer.

Item, he denyeth that ever he had any of Barrowe, Grenewood, or Penrie's bookes.

Item, he sayeth he never perswaded any to his oppinions.

Item, being asked whether he will goe to church and here [hear] divine service, refuseth to answer directly but prayeth to be pardoned of that.[4]

Item, he refuseth to saye the Lord's Prayer.[5]

Gabriell Goodman Mathew Dale
J. Barne Rychard Young

other paragraphs. He also gives the summary from Harley MSS. 6848, f. 33 *recto and verso*, from which he omits three sentences. One sentence in the summary reads: "Hee saieth hee is one of the confused churche." This is a scribal error in the copy, and should read: "He sayeth he is a deacon in the congregacion chosen." See Burrage, *Early English Dissenters*, II, 40–41, 53–54.

[1] William Eiles or Eyles is sometimes confused with William Giles. The difficulty stems from the manuscript reading where "E" is misread as "G". Burrage lists Eiles and Giles in the index as separate persons, but they are identical.

[2] Walbrook originally was a stream running from Finsbury to the Thames. Then it became a sewer, was covered up, and became a street extending from the Poultry to Cannon Street. See John Stow, *A Survey of the Cities London and Westminster*, ed. John Strype (London, 1720), I, 191–200, and Sugden, *A Topographical Dictionary*, p. 551.

[3] Arrested March 4.

[4] He went to Amsterdam and in January, 1597/1598, was nominated as a deacon, with Robert Jackson, but Francis Johnson and Daniel Studley, who dominated the Ancient Church, preferred Stanshall Mercer and Jacob Johnson. See George Johnson, *A Discourse of Some Troubles*, p. 155.

[5] This examination has not been previously printed. There is a summary of ninety-one words, of which Burrage gives thirty in his *Early English Dissenters*, II, 43. The summary adds one bit of information: "Thomas Emery is his felowe servaunte."

[4 Aprilis 1593] [Ellesmere MS. 2108]

EDWARD GILBERT OF ST. GREGORIE'S PARISH NERE POWLE'S, APPRENTICE TO ISAKE FREESE, TRUNCKMAKE[R], OF THE AGE OF XXI YERES, EXAMINED BEFORE THE SAID COMISSIONERS THE DAYE AND YERE AFORESAID, WHO REFUSETH TO BE SWORN BUT SAYETH:

First, that he hath bene in prison in the Counter in the Poultry a month, comitted by Mr. Doctor Stanhop and others, never examyned nor indicted.[1]

Item, he sayth he hath held his oppinions a quarter of a yere last past, and hath bene often tymes at the assemblyes, *viz.*, twice or thrice at a howse in a garden by Chri[st] church and other places, and hath received the communyon in the assemblyes in the afternoone.

Item, he refuseth to come to church and be reformed.[2]

Item, he denyeth that ever he sawe anye of Barrowe, Grenewood, or Penrye's bookes.

Item, he sayeth he never perswaded any to his oppinions.[3]

signum dci [dicti] Edward Gilbert

[4 Aprilis 1593] [Ellesmere MS. 2109]

THOMAS HEWET OF ST. MARTYNS LE GRAND, PURSEMAKER, AGED XXX YERES, TAKEN BEFORE THE COMISSIONERS AFORESAID THE DAYE AND YERE AFORESAID.

First, he sayeth he hath bene in prison a month, comitted by Mr. Doctor Stanhop, Mr. Yonge, and others, beinge one of them that were taken in the wood by Islington.[4]

[1] Gilbert, or Gilbarte, was apprehended by Dr. Edward Stanhope, Chancellor to the Bishop of London, on March 4, but not examined until April 4.

[2] Although he refused to be reformed, he changed his mind evidently, because he was bailed upon his conformity, probably in April. His employer was Isake Freese, or Isaac Frize, or Isack Frees, who is also described as a tailor.

[3] This examination has not been published, but of the summary in three sentences, Burrage published one sentence. See Harley 6848, f. 34 *verso*, f. 210 *recto*, and *Early English Dissenters*, II, 43.

[4] Hewet, Hewett, or Hewit, was born in Swanton [Swannington?], Leicestershire. In London he was the servant of John Sutton. On March 4 he was apprehended,

Item, he saieth he was never examined before this tyme, and never indicted.

Item, he hath not bene at church this half yere and soe longe he hath held his oppinions and will not shewe by whome he was perswaded to it but only by one Edward Hale, a Hertfordshire man.[1]

Item, he sayeth he hath bene at the[i]r assemblyes every Sondaye this half yere, *viz.*, sometymes in Nicholas Lane, and sometymes at Nicholas Lee's howse by Smythfeld, and sometyme by C[h]ri[st]-church, and once in the woods by Detford, and hathe sene v or sixe children ther baptised of two or thre yeres old.

Item, he sayeth he never had any of Barrowe, Grenewood, or Penrie's books.

Item, he sayeth he never perswaded any to his oppinions, neither if the[i]r nomber should have increased they ment noe ill.

Item, he refuseth to reforme him self and to come to churche.[2]

By me, Thomas Hewit

[4 Aprilis 1593] [Ellesmere MS. 2109]

JOHN HULKES[3] OF DETFORD, SHIPWRIGHT, AGED XXI YERES OR THER ABOUTS, TAKEN THE DAYE AND YERE AFORESAID BEFORE THE SAID COMISSIONERS.

First, he sayeth he hath bene in prison this month and more, comitted by Mr. Stanhop and others for beinge taken in the assembly in the wood, examined before Mr. Yonge and others.[4]

Item, he knoweth not that he is indicted for any offence.

Item, he was never at the assemblyes but twice, *viz.*, once at Algate by C[h]ri[st]church and one other [place] where he was

but was not examined until a month later. He died in the Wood Street Counter before 1596.

[1] This is the only reference to him, and Hewet, perhaps deliberately, omits any reference to a town. See chapter XXXIX for Thomas Hale and John Hale, both from Hertfordshire.

[2] The examination has been previously published, but Burrage prints only two paragraphs out of seven. The copy is in Harley MSS. 6848, f. 76 *recto*, and the summary is in f. 32 *verso*. See Burrage, *Early English Dissenters*, II, 39, 53.

[3] Listed erroneously as Huckes by Burrage.

[4] Probably examined shortly after his arrest on March 4. The examination is not extant.

taken goenge to the wood, and was first brought to the assemblyes by Marshall and Curland.[1]

Item, he sayeth he never had nor sawe any of Barrowe, Grenewood, or Penrie's books.

Item, he sayeth he never drewe nor perswaded any to his oppinions.

Item, he is bound in recognizance of xl^{li} [40 pounds] to come to Rederiff[2] church the next Sondaye in the forenoone to heare divine service ther and to bringe a certificate therof from the minister ther to Mr. Yong.[3]

John Hulkes

[4 Aprilis 1593] [Ellesmere MS. 2109]

GEORGE KNIVETON OF NEWGATE MARKET, POTECARY, OF THE AGE OF XXIIII^{OR} YERES, EXAMYNED BEFORE THE SAID COMISSIONERS THE DAYE AND YERE AFORESAID, WHOE REFUSETH TO BE SWORNE BUT SAYETH:

First, that he hath bene in prison this fortnight, comitted by Mr. Yonge and others, taken in the company of Penrye and others in the howse of one Lewes [Lowes?] in Stepny.[4]

Item, he confesseth that he is one of the elders of the[i]r congregacon.[5]

Item, he hath bene diverse tymes examined, *viz.*, before Mr. Anderson[6] preacher and Mr. Yonge[7] and others.

[1] William Marshall, a shipwright, and William Curland, shipwright. The former was a charter member of the church, the latter upon his conformity was bailed.

[2] Rederiff, Redriff, Redreffe, Rothered, Rotherhithe, on the south bank of the Thames between Deptford and Bermondsey. Hulkes was bailed upon his conformity.

[3] This examination has not been printed previously. The summary is in Harley MSS. 6848, f. 32 *verso*.

[4] Knyviton, Knyfton, Knyveton, Knifton, Kniftton, or Knifeton was arrested on March 22, with Penry, Arthur Bellot, and Edward Grave, in Ratcliffe, a hamlet of Stepney parish.

[5] He was elected an elder in September, 1592.

[6] We do not have these examinations. The reference to Anthony Anderson, vicar of Stepney, is especially relevant since he was the one responsible for the arrest of Penry and Knyviton on March 22. Anderson is harshly treated by Martin Marprelate in *The Just Censure and Reproofe of Martin Junior*, Cii *verso*, where Martin accuses Anderson of having "robbed the poore men's box at Northampton, played the Potter's part in the morrice daunce, and begotte his maide with child in Leicestershire, and these things hee did since he was first Priest."

[7] The examination before Richard Young was probably held about March 22–24.

Item, he knoweth not that he is indicted for any offence.

Item, he hath held his oppinions thes iiii^or [*quattuor*, four] or five yeres,[1] and hath not come to any churche thes two yeres.

Item, he sayeth he hath had conference with Mr. Browne, whoe perswaded him not to receive the comunyon, and since hath had conference with Barrowe and with Grenewood and with Penry,[2] and was made elder about half a yere since, and that he misliketh Cartwright's plat [plan, platform?] of church government.[3]

Item, he sayeth he hath bene at the assemblyes most comonly uppon every Sondaye and sometyme uppon the the weke dayes, sometymes in St. Nicholas Lane, sometyme at Nicholas Lee's, and sometyme at Mr. Bilson's by C[h]ri[st]church, sometyme at the woods by Islington and Detford, and at John Barnes' his howse by St. Barthelmewes.

Item, he sayeth he hath read some parte of Barrowe and Grenewood's books in writinge but hath none of them.[4]

Item, he sayth he never perswaded any to his oppinions.

Item, he sayeth if the[i]r nomber should have muche increased, yet he denyeth that they ment not to have done any thinge but the service of God.

Item, beinge demaunded whether he will come to church or noe to divine service nowe used, sayeth that untill he be resolved by learned men he will not.[5]

George Knyviton

[1] He was probably first arrested at a conventicle in December, 1589, or January, 1589/1590. In February and April, 1590, he is listed as a prisoner in the Counter Poultry.

[2] He probably conferred with Robert Browne in 1589 or 1590, with Barrow and Greenwood 1590–1592, with Penry in October, 1592. Pierce, in his *John Penry*, 359–360, deduces that Knyviton conferred with Penry *before* he accepted the position as elder, but the evidence seems conclusive that Penry arrived *after* the organization meeting. He is not listed as a charter member. He stated in his examination of April 5 that he came out of Scotland about September last, in his examination of May 15, 1593, "that he came to London from Scotlande in September or October last," and his traveling companion, John Edwardes, dated his coming out of Scotland as in November last. See Harley MSS. 6848, f. 86, Ellesmere MS. 2113 and 2146, f. 81.

[3] That is, Thomas Cartwright's Presbyterian system of local consistories, classes or presbyteries, synods, and national assemblies. See A. F. Scott Pearson, *Thomas Cartwright and Elizabethan Puritanism, 1535–1603*, and Patrick Collinson, *The Elizabethan Puritan Movement*, and Albert Peel and Leland H. Carlson, *Cartwrightiana*.

[4] This may imply that he read Barrow and Greenwood's books in manuscript in 1590 when he was in the Counter Poultry prison.

[5] The summary of his examination in Harley MSS. 6848, f. 33 *recto*, states that Knyviton is to be sent to the Dean of Westminster, Gabriel Goodman, to confer. The Dean was unable to convert the young Separatist elder, who chose banish-

4 Aprilis 1593 [Ellesmere MS. 2109]

THE EXAMINACON OF WILLIAM MARSHALL OF WAPPINGE, SHIPWRIGHT, OF THE AGE OF XXXII YERES OR THER ABOUTS, TAKEN BY MR. DEANE OF WESTMINSTER, MR. DALE, MR. BARNE, AND MR. YONGE. WHOE REFUSETH TO BE SWORNE BUT SAYETH:

First, he sayth he hath bene in prison this monthe, comited by Doctor Stanhop and others, beinge taken in the wood nere Islington, examined before the said Doctor Stanhop.[1]

Item, he knoweth not that he is indicted for any cause.

Item, he hath bene of his oppinions this half yere, and sayeth he hath bene at a sermon at Paule's Crosse within thes sixe wekes, and was drawen and perswaded to his oppinions by Roger Rippon of Sowthwork.[2]

Item, he sayeth he hath bene at the[i]r assemblyes fower or fyve tymes in the said wood.

Item, he sayeth he never had any of Barrowe, Grenewood, or Penrye's bookes, but sayeth that he hath heard one John Barrett a seaman read some of those bookes.[3]

Item, he sayeth he never perswaded others to his oppinions.[4]

Item, he sayeth that if the[i]r nomber should have increased, yet he knoweth not that they ment any evill intent but to continewe the[i]r assemblies in the service of God.

Item, he sayeth he will not come to churche because ther be many corrupcons therin.[5]

Signum dci [dicti] William Marshall.

ment, and went to Kampen, Naarden, and Amsterdam. See Francis Johnson, *An Inquirie and Answer of Thomas White*, p. 46, and George Johnson, *A Discourse of Some Troubles*.

From Harley MSS. 6848, f. 76 *verso*, Burrage prints four out of eleven paragraphs, but he prints the summary in full. See *Early English Dissenters*, II, 39, 51–52.

[1] Marshall was present at the organization meeting in September, 1592. He was arrested on March 4, 1592/1593.

[2] He may have attended one of the meetings about October, 1592, at Rippon's house in Southwark. Rippon died February 16, 1592/1593. Also in February he seems to have attended a service at St. Paul's Cross.

[3] There is no other mention of Barrett, who is a literate seaman, whereas Marshall seems to be illiterate, since he does not sign his name but simply makes a mark.

[4] Yet Hulkes testified that Marshall brought him to the assemblies.

[5] This examination has not been printed heretofore. Burrage, *Early English Dissenters*, II, 39, prints one-half of the summary from Harley MSS. 6848, f. 32 *verso*.

4 Aprilis 1593 [Ellesmere MS. 2110]

WILLIAM MASON OF WAPPINGE, SHIPWRIGHT, OF THE AGE OF XXIIII^{OR} YERES OR THER ABOUTS, EXAMINED BEFORE MR. DE[A]NE OF WESTMINSTER, MR. BARNES [BARNE], MR. DALE, AND MR. YONGE, SAYETH:

First, that he hath bene in prison in the Counter in the Poultry, comitted by Mr. Doctor Stanhop and Mr. Yonge and others, being taken in the wood.[1]

Item, that he was never examined nor indicted to his knowledge.

Item, that he was never at church since Christmas last and soe longe he hath held his oppinions,[2] perswaded therto by Edward Chandler a shipwright,[3] and went to the wood with Roger Rippon, and hath bene at the[i]r assemblyes about xii tymes, *viz.*, at Nicholas Lane, at Roger Rippon's [house at Southwark,] at Detford wood, and at the woods by Islington, where he was taken, and at Danyell Buck his howse, a scrivenor by Algate,[4] and hath sene diverse children baptized, and gave to the deacons vi^{d} a weeke when he had money.

Item, he sayeth he hath heard Edward Chandler read some of Barrowe and Grenewood the[i]r books, but hath none of them nor had had any him self.

Item, he is willinge to conferr with any learned men and is conformable,[5] and is bound by recognizance with sewertyes [sureties] to come to churche to divine service.[6]

Signum dci [dicti] William Mason

[1] Arrested March 4, 1592/1593.

[2] Actually, at least since September, 1592, since he is on the list of charter members.

[3] Edward Chandler may be a son of John and Alice Chaundler, who had a family of eight children in 1587. John was arrested at the first Separatist conventicle on October 8, 1587, and died in the Counter Poultry before May, 1589. Alice may be the "widow Ch." who served later in the Amsterdam church as a deaconess. See Dexter, *Congregationalism*, 317, note 103.

[4] In his examination of March 9, Daniel Bucke does not divulge the fact that a conventicle was held in his own home near Aldgate.

[5] He was bailed upon his conformity. His recognizance was probably forty pounds. In the summary of his examination, Harley MSS. 6848, f. 33 *recto*, the clerk ambiguously states that Mason "is bounde with his brother Richard Mason and James Tailor and so discharged." Burrage lists Richard Mason and James Tailor as Separatists, but I believe they are simply sureties for William Mason.

[6] Burrage prints the summary in full, but he gives only two paragraphs out of five from the copy in Harley MSS. 6848, f. 69, *recto*. See *Early English Dissenters*, II, 40, 52.

[4 Aprilis 1593] [Ellesmere MS. 2110]

HENRY WYTHERS OF DETFORD STRAND, SHIPWRIGHT, AGED XXVII YERES OR THER ABOUTS, EXAMYNED THE DAYE AND YER[E] AFORESAID BEFORE THE SAID COMISSIONERS, BEINGE SWORNE, SAYETH:

First, that he hath bene in prison a month, comitted by Doctor Stanhop and Mr. Yonge, beinge taken in the wood, never examined nor indicted to his knowlege.[1]

Item, he sayeth he hath held his oppinions but since Michas [Michaelmas, 29 September] last, and was drawen to his oppinions, perswaded therto by the teaching of Johnson and Grenewood.[2]

Item, he sayeth he was most comonly at the[i]r assemblyes every Sondaye, sometymes at St. Nicholas Lane, at the woods by Islington, at Rippon's howse, and in Smythfeld at Lee's howse, and at the wood by Detford, and sawe diverse children ther baptized.

Item, he hath heard some of Penrie's books read but knoweth not by whome.

Item, he sayth he never procured any to his oppinions.[3]

Item, he denyeth that if the[i]r nomber had growen and increased, he ment noe harme but to serve God.[4]

Signum dci [dicti] Henrie Wythers.

[1] Wythers, or Withers, was apprehended on March 4.

[2] If Wythers is exact in his memory in reference to Michaelmas—September 29, then the organization meeting may have occurred on Sunday, September 17 or 24. September 29 fell on a Friday. No record indicates the day in September when the organization was effected.

[3] Wythers was bailed upon his conformity. He and William Mason, both shipwrights, were the only charter members who conformed.

[4] Burrage prints this examination from the copy in Harley MSS. 6848, f. 69 *verso*. He gives three out of the five paragraphs. He also prints the summary from Harley MSS. 6848, f. 33 *recto*, and omits one sentence of twenty-one words relating to Penry's books. See *Early English Dissenters*, II, 40, 52–53.

XXXIII

[5 Aprilis 1593] [Ellesmere MS. 2114]

ARTHUR BILLET OF LLANTEGLOS BY FOWHEY IN CORNWALL,[1] SCOLLER, OF THE AGE OF XXV YERES OR THER ABOUTS, EXAMYNED BY THE SAID COMISSIONERS THE DAYE AND YERE AFORESAID, WHOE REFUSETH TO BE SWORNE BUT SAYETH:

First, that he hath bene in prison this fortnight, comitted by Mr. Yonge, who was in the wood by Islington, and afterwards taken in the company of Penry and others,[2] examined by Mr. Yong and others, never indicted to his knowlege.

Item, he hath bene drawen to his oppinions thes two yeres, perswaded by certain conferences in the Fleet, betwene Mr. Mullins, Mr. Hutchinson, and Barrowe and Grenewood.[3]

Item, he hath bene at the assemblyes thre or fower tymes, *viz.*, twice at the wood by Islington, in the wood by Detford once, once at Rippon's house, and once by Lee's howse.

Item, he confesseth that he received the communyon once at Barnes his howse by St. Barthelmewes, ministerd by Francis Johnson the[i]r pastor, and sawe diverse children christened, *viz.*, vi or vii, some of thre, some of iiii^{or} [*quattuor*, four] and some of six or vii yeres of age, which baptizing was in St. Nicholas Lane.[4]

Item, he denyeth that he hath or had any of Barrowe's, Grenewood's, or Penrye's books, but hath received some of the written coppies and carried them over into the Lowe Contrye to be printed,

[1] Billet, Byllet, or preferably Bellot, as he signs his petition to Lord Burghley, from Lanteglos-by-Fowey, in Cornwall. He was a gentleman and a scholar, who matriculated at Oxford University from Exeter College on July 30, 1585.

[2] Arrested on March 22 at Ratcliffe, a hamlet of Stepney parish, with Edward Grave, George Knyviton, and John Penry.

[3] Three years. The conferences were held on March 9, 17, 18, 1589/1590, and April 13, 1590. William Hutchinson, archdeacon of St. Albans and rector of St. Botolph's, participated in all four, but John Mullins, archdeacon of London, did not take part. He may have been present, or he may have conferred with other prisoners. See Carlson, *The Writings of John Greenwood, 1587–1590*, pp. 128–162.

[4] He was present at the organization meeting in September, 1592, and he mentions six other meetings himself.

and that he hath sene one of Barrowe's bookes in Nicholas Lee's howse in the hands of a contryman whose name he knoweth not.[1]

Item, he denyeth to have procured any to the assemblyes, nor thinketh that if ther nomber should have increased they would have done nothing but the service of God.[2]

Gabriell Goodman Mathew Dale
John Barne Rychard Young

5 Aprilis 1593 [Ellesmere MS. 2112]

EDWARD BOYS OF ST. BRIDE'S PARISHE, HABERDASHER, OF THE AGE OF XXXIII YERES OR THER ABOUTS, EXAMINED BEFORE MR. DOCTOR CESAR, MR. DOCTOR GOODMAN DEANE OF WESTMINSTER, MR. DALE, MR. BARNE, AND MR. YONG. WHOE REFUSETH TO BE SWORNE BUT SAYETH:

First, that he hath bene in prison these fower monthes in the Clink, comitted by the Lord Archbyshop of Canterbury and others high commissioners by vertue of the[i]r warrant wher in he sayth was conteined that he was taken in an unlawfull assembly.[3]

[1] He probably had all six of the books of Barrow and Greenwood, and perhaps five or six of Penry's works. Daniel Studley testified that in the Bridewell he received from Bellot two copies of Barrow's *A Brief Discoverie of the False Church*.

He was responsible for seeing through the press at Dort 2000 copies of *A Brief Discoverie of the False Church* and 1000 copies of *A Plaine Refutation*. In April, 1591, he revealed the whereabouts of the entire consignment, which was seized by Sir Robert Sidney at Flushing. Bellot was sent as a prisoner to Lord Burghley, who committed him to the custody of Archbishop Whitgift. His petition for release to Lord Burghley is printed in the Appendix.

He joined with the exiles in Amsterdam, and died about 1601. His widow, Sarah, married Hans Hatmercer, or Hatmer, on June 29, 1602. His brother, Scipio, was convicted on March 23, 1592/1593, of dispersing Separatist books, remained in Newgate prison, and died before 1596.

[2] Burrage prints this examination from the copy in Harley MSS. 6848, f. 71 *verso*, but omits half of it. He also gives the summary from Harley MSS. 6848, f. 34 *recto*, and omits only one sentence. See *Early English Dissenters*, II, 42, 59.

[3] Boys, Boyce, Boyse, or Boyes was arrested late at night on December 5–6, 1592. See Lansdowne MSS. 75, item or folio 25. See also Chapter XLI, *infra*. With him at his home were Francis Johnson and John Greenwood, who were also arrested. Boyes implies that the warrant wrongly accused him of being in an unlawful assembly in his own home on Fleet Street. Johnson and Greenwood were immediately imprisoned without a warrant, but Boyes was apprehended the next day, by warrant.

Item, he saieth he was never examined since he was comitted,[1] nor is not indicted to his knowlege.

Item, he sayeth he hath bene drawing to his oppinions thes vii or viii yeres but not throughly setled therin untill thes thre yeres last past, and refuseth to tell howe longe he hath refrained coming to church,[2] and sayeth he holdeth nothing but that which Mr. Egerton, Mr. Cowper, Mr. Wigington and others have taught.[3]

Item, being asked howe often he hath bene at the[i]r assemblyes, desireth that he maye not be drawen to accuse him self, and otherwise refuseth to answer.

Item being asked whether he hath or had any of Barrowe, Grenewood, or Penrie's bookes, sayeth he will not accuse him self and otherwise will not answer.

Item, being asked howe manye he hath procured or perswaded to his oppinions and assemblies, answereth as before that he will not be his owne accuser and otherwise he refuseth to answer.

Item, being asked if he wilbe contented to come to his parishe church to divine service nowe used, refuseth so to doe.[4]

Julius Caesar
Gabriell Goodman
Mathew Dale
John Barne
Rychard Young

1 He was first arrested on October 8, 1587, with Greenwood and twenty others at the home of Henry Martin. He remained a prisoner for nineteen months in the Bridewell, then was transferred to the Clink where he was kept a close prisoner. Since he does not appear on either prison list for 1590, we may conclude he was liberated or bailed at the end of 1589.

2 He does not appear on the list of charter members for September, 1592, but his wife's name is listed. He may have been cautious, or he may be of those other names which Daniel Bucke did not remember.

3 Stephen Egerton, popular Puritan preacher at St. Anne's, Blackfriars; Martin or Robert Cooper, who participated in a prison conference with Barrow and Greenwood on April 3, 1590; Giles Wigginton, a contentious vicar from Sedbergh, Yorkshire, who had been deprived by Archbishop Whitgift.

4 Boyes was a prosperous haberdasher who left a legacy of £300 to his wife. He died in prison in 1593 or 1594. Francis Johnson in the Clink married the widow, Thomasine or Tomison Boyes, about 1594 in the Clink. As the pastor's wife, she figures prominently in the clothes controversy at Amsterdam, and was unmercifully criticized by George Johnson. She appears frequently in Johnson's *A Discourse of Some Troubles*.

This examination has not been printed previously, but Burrage prints one-third of the summary from Harley MSS. 6848, f. 35 *recto*, in *Early English Dissenters*, II, 43–44.

[5 Aprilis 1593] [Ellesmere MS. 2115]

DAVID BRISTOWE OF THE LIBERTY OF ST. MARTYN'S LE GRAND, TAYLOR, OF THE AGE OF XXX YERES OR THER ABOUTS, EXAMINED THE DAYE AND YERE AFORESAID BEFORE MR. DOCTOR GOODMAN, DEANE OF WESTMINSTER, MR. DALE, MR. BARNE, AND MR. YONGE, WHOE REFUSETH TO BE SWORNE BUT SAYETH:

First, that he hath bene in prison this five wekes almost, comitted by the Byshop of London and others, being taken in the wood by Islington, never examined since his imprisonment nor indicted to his knowlege.[1]

Item, he sayeth he hath not bene at his parishe churche this half yere last past,[2] and soe longe hath held his oppinions, but by whome he was perswaded, he will not confesse, but sayeth by the word of God.

Item, he sayeth he hath bene twice at the wood wher he was taken, and diverse tymes at other places, but refuseth to tell wher and when.

Item, beinge asked if ever he received the comunyon in the[i]r assemblies, saieth he will not answer to that.

Item, beinge demaunded whether he had any of Barrowe's, Grenewood's, or Penrie's bookes, sayeth it maye be he had, it maye be he had not, and otherwise will not answer.[3]

Item, being asked howe manye he hath drawen to the assemblyes, refuseth to answer.

Item, he refuseth to goe to his parishe church.[4]

Gabriell Goodman Mathew Dale
John Barne Rychard Young

[1] Bristowe, Bristoe, or Bristow, was arrested on March 4.

[2] He was a charter member, being present at the organization in September, 1592.

[3] This examination is remarkable for its lack of information. Bristow refuses to give any names or places. He refuses to answer about any person influencing him or any whom he may have persuaded. He will not discuss the subject of the administration of the Lord's Supper, nor will he say anything about Separatist books which he probably had read.

[4] He went to Amsterdam, helped to mediate the controversy between Francis and George Johnson, became a wandering star for a while, and about 1608 was elected a deacon of the Amsterdam church. See Johnson, *A Discourse of Some Troubles*, pp. 101–103, and Dexter, *Congregationalism*, p. 317.

This examination has not been published previously. From Harley MSS. 6848, f. 33 *verso*, Burrage prints less than half of the summary, in *Early English Dissenters*, II, 41.

[5 Aprilis 1593] [Ellesmere MS. 2112]

GEORGE COLLIER OF ST. MARTIN'S, LUDGATE, HABERDASHER, OF THE AGE OF XXXVIII YERES, EXAMINED BEFORE THE SAID COMISSIONERS THE DAYE AND YERE AFORESAID, WHOE REFUSETH TO BE SWORNE BUT SAYETH:

First, he sayeth he hath bene thes five yeres in prison in the Clink,[1] comitted by the high comissioners, taken in an assembly in a howse at prayer wher then was Grenewood[2] and Crane[3] and others.

Item, he sayeth he was never examined, nor indicted, to his knowlege.

Item, being demanded howe long he hath held his oppinions, refuseth directly to answer.

Item, he sayeth he was never at any of the assemblies in the woods or other places with Johnson, Grenewood, and the other sectaries of that sort.

Item, he sayeth he sayeth [*sic*] he never had any of Barrowe, Grenewood, or Penrie's bookes.

Item, he sayeth he never perswaded any to the[i]r conventicles or assemblyes.

Item, he refuseth to conforme him self and come to churche.[4]

Gabriell Goodman Mathew Dale
J. Barne Rychard Young

[1] He was arrested on October 8, 1587, at the home of Henry Martin, and was examined or questioned the same day at the Episcopal Palace at London. Of all twenty-two persons, he alone remained continuously in the Clink for five and a half years, without trial, and probably was finally banished about 1593 or 1594. Ann Colyer, a servant girl in Francis Johnson's house in Amsterdam, could be a daughter, since George Collier went to Amsterdam. See Johnson, *A Discourse of Some Troubles*, p. 152.

[2] John Greenwood was also arrested on October 8, 1587, but evidently was out on bail for a few months in 1592. On the late evening of December 5–6, 1592, he was arrested again and remanded to the Fleet, and executed April 6, 1593. Henry Barrow was imprisoned on November 19, 1587, and remained continuously in prison five years, four and a half months, and was executed on April 6, 1593.

[3] Nicholas Crane was ordained a priest by Edmund Grindal, Bishop of London, in April, 1562. Arrested on October 8, 1587, for attending a conventicle where the Scripture was read, he died in 1588 from the infection in Newgate prison, age sixty-six.

[4] This examination has not been published previously. Burrage prints the summary from Harley MSS. 6848, f. 35 *recto*, except for one sentence, in *Early English Dissenters*, II, 44.

[5 Aprilis 1593] [Ellesmere MS. 2111]

WILLIAM CURLAND OF DETFORD, SHIPWRIGHT, OF THE AGE OF XXX^TY YERES OR THER ABOUTS, EXAMYNED BEFORE THE SAID COMISSIONERS THE DAYE AND YERE AFORESAID.

First, that he hath bene in prison this monthe, comitted by Doctor Stanhop and others, being taken in the woods by Islington, examyned the daye after he was taken by Mr. Stanhop and others.[1]

Item, he sayeth he was drawen to his oppinions about vi or vii wekes since,[2] and went to the woods with George Martyn,[3] and hath bene at the assemblies about v or vi tymes, *viz.*, sometymes at Nicholas Lee's howse[4] and sometymes in the wood wher he was taken.

Item, he sayeth he never had any of Barrowe, Grenewood, or Penrie's bookes.

Item, he sayeth he never perswaded any to his oppinions.[5]

Gabriell Goodman
Mathew Dale
John Barne
Rychard Young

[1] Arrested on March 4, and examined by Edward Stanhope, Chancellor to the Bishop of London, on March 5.

[2] Probably six or seven weeks before March 4. He has been in prison almost five weeks.

[3] George Marten, or Martin, was at the organization meeting in September, 1592. He appears again in Amsterdam in December, 1597. See Johnson, *A Discourse of Some Troubles*, pp. 140–141. He may be related to Henry Martin, at whose home the calamitous conventicle of October 8, 1587, was held. See Carlson, *The Writings of John Greenwood, 1587–1590*, pp. 306–309.

[4] Nicholas Lee, who was elected deacon at the organization meeting, lived on Cow Lane in Smithfield. He is the only officer of the congregation who was not imprisoned or examined. *Felix qui bene latuit.*

[5] This examination has not been published previously. The summary is in Harley MSS. 6848, f. 34 *verso*, of which Burrage prints one-fourth of it—fifteen out of sixty words. From the omitted portion we learn that Curland agreed to return to his parish church. He was bailed upon his conformity. See *Early English Dissenters*, II, 24, 43, and Harley MSS. 6848, f. 210 *recto*.

5 Aprilis 1593 [Ellesmere MS. 2115]

FRANCIS JOHNSON, MINISTER, BUT BY THE ASSEMBLIES CHOSEN TO BE A PASTOR OF THE CONGREGACON, BEYNGE OF THE AGE OF XXXI YERES, OR THER ABOUTS, EXAMINED BEFORE MR. DOCTOR CESER, MR. DOCTOR GOODMAN, DEANE OF WESTMINSTER, MR. BARNE, AND MR. YONGE. WHOE REFUSETH TO BE SWORNE BUT SAYTH:

First, that he was first comytted to the Counter in Wood Streete, by the Sherif of London and Mr. Yonge, in October last, beyng taken in an assemblie in St. Nicholas Lane,[1] and lastly comytted by the Lord Archbishop of Canterbury and others, beynge taken in Mr. Boyese's howse in Fleete Streete,[2] and hathe bene twyse examined before the Lord Cheef Justice of England, and my Lord Anderson, *viz.*, once before the Lord Cheefe Justice of England, and once before them bothe.[3]

Item, he sayeth he knoweth not that he is indicted for any offence.

Item, beynge asked howe longe he hath heald his opinions, sayeth he cannot definitely answear, but sayeth he was comytted to prison in Cambridge iiii^{or} [*quattuor*, four] yeres agoe, upon the makinge of a sermon in St. Marie's Churche.[4]

Item, he confesseth he hath baptised diverse children in the[i]r congregacon, and saieth as for mariage he dothe not accompt that an ecclesiasticall matter, nor laide upon the minister of God as a dewtie of his mynistrie, and also saieth they ar not bounde, nor tyed to the words of the Lord's Prayer, and towchinge the comunion of the Lord's Supper, he saieth it may be received at any tyme of

[1] This is the only reference to Johnson's first arrest in October, 1592, by the Sheriff of London. Johnson must have given bond or obtained release, since he officiated in October and November.

[2] His second arrest occurred late at night, December 5–6, at the home of Edward Boyes on Fleet Street. Greenwood and Boyes were also imprisoned, without a warrant. Johnson and Boyes were sent to the Clink, and Greenwood was returned to the Fleet.

[3] The Lord Chief Justice of the Queen's Bench was Sir John Popham, who succeeded Sir Christopher Wray in 1592. The Lord Chief Justice of the Common Pleas was Sir Edmund Anderson. Johnson's importance is indicated by the fact that these two high legal officials are assigned to interrogate him.

[4] See H. C. Porter, *Reformation and Reaction in Tudor Cambridge*, pp. 157–163. Johnson presented his sermon at Great St. Mary's Church, Cambridge, on January 6, 1588/1589.

the day or nyght, when the congregacon is assembled and prepared therunto.[1]

Item, beynge required to shewe in what places they used to meete in their conventicles and assemblies, refusethe to answeare.

Item, beynge asked whether he hath or had any of Barrowe, Greenewood, or Penry's bookes, refuseth also to answear, but desireth he may be accused.[2]

Item, beynge asked, whether he hath not labored and perswaded others to the assemblies and congregacon wherof he is a Pastor, and howe many he hath soe perswaded and drawen, saieth he hath and must doe that which God layeth upon him in dewty, accordinge to his worde, and otherwise refuseth to answeare.

Item, beyng asked whether he will be contented to reforme him selfe, and come to churche, refuseth directly to answear, but sayeth he cannot joyne with this ecclesasticall mynistrie, in this estate of archebushopps, bushopps, parsons, vicars, curats, etc.[3]

Julius Caesar Gabriell Goodman
Mathew Dale John Barne Rychard Young

[5 Aprilis 1593] [Ellesmere MS. 2112]

THOMAS MIHILFELD OF ST. SAVIOR'S, JOYNER, OF THE AGE OF XXXIII YERES OR THER ABOUTS, EXAMINED BEFORE MR. DOCTOR GOODMAN, DEANE OF WESTMINSTER, MR. BARNE, MR. DALE, AND MR. YONG, WHO REFUSETH TO BE SWORN BUT SAYETH:

First, he sayth that he hath bene in prison this monthe, comitted

[1] The views of the Separatists on the sacraments of baptism and the Lord's Supper, on marriage as a civil ceremony, and on spontaneous instead of repetitive stinted prayers were regarded as radical and dangerous.

[2] He probably had read all of them. In April, 1591, he collaborated with Sir Robert Sidney in the seizure, and burning, in June, of 2000 copies of Barrow's *A Briefe Discoverie of the False Church* and 1000 copies of *A Plaine Refutation.* He kept two copies of the latter book for himself and a friend [George Gifford?], was strongly influenced by its arguments, returned to England and became the elected pastor of the Separatists in September, 1592. In 1605, perhaps as an act of atonement and reparation, he reissued *A Plaine Refutation* at his own expense. See Carlson, *The Writings of Henry Barrow, 1590–1591*, pp. 370–377.

[3] Burrage prints the summary from Harley MSS. 6848, ff. 34 *verso* and 35 *recto*, but omits 139 words. He prints the copy in full from Harley MSS. 6848, f. 181 *recto* and *verso*. See *Early English Dissenters*, II, 43, 56–57.

by Mr. Doctor Stanhop and others, being taken goeng to the wood by Islington, examined before Mr. Stanhop and Mr. Yong, never indicted to his knowlege.[1]

Item, he sayeth [he] hath bene of his oppinions this quarter of a yere and noe more, but will not shewe by whome he was drawen therto.[2]

Item, he refuseth to shewe howe often and in what places he hath bene at the assemblies.

Item, he sayeth he never had any of Barrowe, Grenewood, or Penrie's bookes.

Item, he sayth he never perswaded nor drewe any to the assemblies, and that if the[i]r nomber had increased they ment noe ill but the service of God.

Item, he refuseth to be come [*sic*] to his parishe churche.[3]

Signum dci [dicti] Thomas Mihilfeld

[5 Aprilis 1593] [Ellesmere MS. 2114]

JOHN PARKES OF DOELITLE LANE, LONDON, CLOTHWORKER, AGE L [50] YERES OR THER ABOUTS, EXAMINED THE DAYE AND YERE AFORESAID BY THE SAID COMISSIONERS. WHO WILL NOT BE SWORNE BUT SAYETH:

First, that he hath bene a month in prison, comitted by Mr. Doctor Stanhop and others, never examyned since his imprisonment, being taken in the woods by Islington, never indicted to his knowlege.[4]

Item, he hath bene drawne to his oppinions a quarter of a yere, and [was] perswaded partely by the sermons of Mr. Sparkes.[5]

[1] Mihilfeld, Mihilfield, Micklefield, and Mehellfyld, was apprehended on March 4, and examined about March 5–7, though this record is not extant. He lived in St. Mary Overy parish.

[2] In the summary of his examination, he confessed that he was influenced by the popular Puritan preacher, Edward Philips.

[3] He changed his mind, since he was bailed upon his conformity. See Harley MSS. 6848, f. 210 *recto*.

Burrage prints the summary from Harley MSS. 6848, f. 33 *verso*, in *Early English Dissenters*, II, 41, but he omits one-third of it.

[4] Arrested March 4. The summary of his examination states that he served "Mr. Livesey his sonne and hath meate and drinke of him and noe wages and hath no habitacion."

[5] Probably Thomas Sparke, rector of Bletchley in Buckinghamshire and chaplain

Item, he hath bene at at [*sic*] the assemblyes about sixe tymes, and refuseth to tell wher.

Item, he denyeth that ever he had any of Barrowe, Grenewood, or Penrye's bookes.

Item, he sayth he never perswaded any to his oppinyons.

Item, he thinketh if the[i]r nomber had increased, they ment noe harme to the state.

Item, he refuseth to come to churche to heare divine service.[1]

Gabriell Goodman
Mathew Dale
John Barne
Rychard Young

5 Aprilis 1593 [Ellesmere MS. 2113]

THE EXAMINACON OF JOHN PENRYE, CLERKE,[2] OF THE AGE OF XXX YERES OR THER ABOUTS,[3] EXAMINED BEFORE MR. DOCTOR GOODMAN, DEANE OF WESTMINSTER, MR. DALE, MR. BARNE, AND MR. YONGE, WHOE BEING REQUIRED [TO] BE SWORNE TO ANSWER TREWLY [REFUSETH] SOE TO DOE BUT SAYETH:

First, that he was in or [about London][4] the xix^th^ of March, and that he and [Edward] Grave[5] went that night to Hodsdon [where they] laye at the Antelop [and from thence at Ratcliffe].[6]

to Thomas Cooper, Bishop of Lincoln and Winchester. Also, participant at the Hampton Court Conference in 1603/1604 as a nondescript or tired Puritan.

1 Burrage prints the summary from Harley MSS. 6848, f. 34 *recto*, but omits forty-two words. See *Early English Dissenters*, II, 42.

2 Penry was captured on March 22, examined on March 24 by Richard Young, visited on March 26 by Young, Dr. Richard Vaughan and his brother for a private conference and interrogation, conferred with by Dr. Balguy of the Temple [Nicholas Balgay or Balguay, successor to Richard Hooker] on March 28, and conferred with again on April 2 by Dr. Thomas Crooke, Richard Greenham, and Robert Temple. Penry was not a cleric.

3 This examination helps to date Penry's birth in 1563. In the *D.N.B.*, Anthony à Wood's *Athenae Oxonienses*, and Waddington's *John Penry*, his birth is given erroneously as 1559.

4 The items in square brackets have been obtained from the copy in Harley MSS. 6848, f. 86 *recto*. The original manuscript is badly damaged and blotted.

5 See his examination of April 3 in this volume, p. 333.

6 Hodsdon is Hoddesdon in Hertfordshire. Ratcliffe was a hamlet in Stepney parish.

Item, being asked whether [they] went not from thence to one John [Millette's] howse in Hertfordshire, sayeth [he] will not saye whether he went thither [or] not.

Item, he sayeth that blud cannot be clensed out of this land untill the[i]r blud be spilt that procure it.

Item, he sayeth he came out of Scotland about September last in the company of John Edwardes,[1] and came to London and lighted at the Cork at Long Lane end,[2] and that night lodged at Stratford Bowe.[3]

Item, he sayeth he made and caused to be printed, [in] Scotland, a book intituled *A Reformacon* [*noe*] *Enemye to Her Majesty and the State*,[4] and [a boke] which he translated called *Thesis Geneven*[*cium*].[5]

Item, being asked what other bookes [he made] and caused to be printed the[re, he] refuseth to answer.[6]

Item, he sayeth the cause of his [departinge] out of this land was because he [could] not be in quiet here for the eccli[si]asticall [state of the land.[7]

Gabriell Goodman
Mathew Dale
John Barne
Rychard Young

1 See his examination of March 6, in this volume, p. 297.
2 Long Lane extended from West Smithfield to Aldersgate Street.
3 Stratford-at-Bow, a village four or five miles northeast of St. Paul's. They probably arrived early in October, 1592.
4 *A Treatise Wherein Is Manifestlie Proved, That Reformation and Those That Sincerely Fauor the Same, Are Unjustly Charged to Be Enemies, unto Hir Maiestie, and the State.* [Edinburgh], 1590. Printed by Waldegrave.
5 *Theses theologicae in Schola Geneuensi . . . propositae et disputatae.* (Geneuae, 1586). The English edition is entitled: *Propositions and Principles of Divinitie, Propounded and Disputed in the University of Geneva, by Certaine Students of Divinitie There, under M. Theod. Beza, and M. Anthonie Faius, Professors of Divinitie.* Edinburgh, 1591. Also 1595.
6 He wrote and caused to be published *A Briefe Discovery of the Untruthes and Slanders (against the True Governement of the Church of Christ) Contained in a Sermon, Preached the 8.* [*9*] *of Februarie, 1588.* [1588/89] *by D. Bancroft, and Since That Time, Set Forth in Print, with Additions by the Said Authour.* It was published at Edinburgh by Robert Waldegrave in 1590. The evidence for Penry's authorship is in Ellesmere MS. 2148, f. 88 *verso*, and is based upon the examination of H. Kyndall, Robert Waldegrave's assistant, who was examined on October 3, 1591.
7 Burrage prints this examination from the copy in Harley MSS. 6848, f. 86 *recto*, but omits sixty words. He prints the summary from Harley MSS. 6848, f. 34 *recto*, and omits thirty-seven words. See *Early English Dissenters*, II, 42, 54–55.

5 Aprilis 1593 [Ellesmere MS. 2111]

LEONERD PIDDER OF THE BLACKFRIERS, LONDON, SHO[E]MAKER, OF THE AGE OF XXX YERES OR THER ABOUT, EXAMYNED BEFORE MR. DEANE OF WESTMINSTER, MR. DALE, MR. BARNE, AND MR. YONGE. WHOE REFUSETH TO ANSWER UPPON HIS OTHE BUT SAYETH:

First, that he hath bene in prison about a month, comitted by Mr. Doctor Stanhop and others, never examyned nor indicted to his knowlege.[1]

Item, he sayeth he hath held his oppinions but two monthes or ther abouts, and soe long hath forborne comyng to his parishe churche, but by whome he was therto drawen, he sayeth he cannot tell.[2]

Item, he sayeth that he hath not neclected [*sic*] the assemblies eny saboth since he hath bene of his oppinions, but refuseth to tell wher the assemblyes were held.

Item, being asked whether he hath had any of Barrowe, Grenewood, or Penrie's bookes, sayeth he will not accuse him self.[3]

Item, he sayeth he never drewe any to the assemblyes, nor if the[i]r numbers should greatly have encreased, they would not have done any thing against the state.

Item, he refuseth to come to his parishe church.[4]

Leonerd Pedder

[1] Pidder, or Pedder, was arrested on March 4.

[2] He is not listed as a charter member in September, 1592. Since he did not attend his parish church in January and February, 1592/1593, he probably began to attend Separatist conventicles in November or December, 1592. He chose exile to conformity and seems to have gone to Kampen, Naarden, and Amsterdam. In later years he moved toward Anabaptist beliefs. See Christopher Lawne *et al.*, *The Prophane Schisme of the Brownists or Separatists*, pp. 5, 56, and John Payne, *Royall Exchange*, pp. 4, 21, 45.

[3] Edward Grave had stated in his examination on April 2 that he had lent to Pedder one of Barrow's books of conference—probably *A Collection of Certain Letters and Conferences*.

[4] Burrage does not print this examination. From the summary in Harley MSS. 6848, f. 34 *verso*, he prints one sentence and omits eighty-one words. See *Early English Dissenters*, II, 43.

[5 Aprilis 1593] [Ellesmere MS. 2115]

XPOFER [CHRISTOPHER] SIMKINS OF ALDERSGATE STRETE, COPPERSMITH, OF THE AGE OF XXII OR THER ABOUTS, EXAMYNED BEFORE MR. DEANE OF WESTMINSTER, MR. DALE, MR. BARNE, AND MR. YONGE, THE DAYE AND YERE AFORESAID, REFUSETH TO BE SWORNE BUT SAYETH:

First, that he hath bene in prison this month, comitted by Mr. Yonge and others, taken in the wood by Islington, examined before Mr. Doctor Stanhop and others at his comitment and not since, and never indicted to his knowlege.[1]

Item, he sayth he hath not bene at his parishe church this yere and a half last past, and soe long hath held his oppinions,[2] and drawen therto by the preaching of Mr. Sparkes,[3] and Mr. Cowper,[4] and other forward preachers.

Item, he confesseth he hath bene often at the assemblyes, and comonly every saboth daye, but refuseth to tell where.

Item, he refuseth to tell whether he hath had any of Barrowe, Grenewood, or Perrie's [Penrie's] bookes.

Item, he sayeth if the[i]r nomber had increased, they would not have done any other thinge but serve God.

Item, he refuseth to come to his parishe church,[5] and sayeth he is joyned to the[i]r congregacon, from which he will not departe.[6]

Xper [Christopher] Symkins

[1] Simkins, or Simkyn, or Symkins was arrested March 4, and examined about March 5–7.

[2] He began his association with the Separatists in the autumn of 1591, and became a charter member of the congregation in September, 1592.

[3] Thomas Sparke was an early Puritan who gravitated toward conformity. He was rector of Bletchley in Buckinghamshire, chaplain to Bishop Cooper of Lincoln, and a lukewarm representative of the Puritans at the Hampton Court Conference in 1603/1604.

[4] Either Martin or Robert Cooper, who participated in a conference with Barrow and Greenwood in the Fleet on April 3, 1590. He was the incumbent of the parish church near St. Paul's Cathedral—probably St. Gregory's by St. Paul's. See Carlson, *The Writings of John Greenwood, 1587–1590*, pp. 117, 236–262, and 249.

[5] Simkins went as an exile to the Netherlands, entertained Anabaptist views at Kampen or Naarden, and joined the small group led by Henoch Clapham about 1598, in Amsterdam. See Arber, *Story of the Pilgrim Fathers*, p. 99; Francis Johnson, *An Inquirie and Answer of Thomas White*, p. 64; George Johnson, *A Discourse of Some Troubles*, p. 41; Henry M. Dexter, *English Exiles in Amsterdam, 1597–1625* (Cambridge, 1890), p. 21.

[6] Burrage prints all of this examination, omitting only the name of "Grenewood,"

5 Aprilis 1593 [Ellesmere MS. 2114]

WILLIAM SMYTH OF BRADFORD IN WILTSHIRE, MINISTER,[1] OF THE AGE XXX YERES OR THER ABOUTS, MADE A MYNISTER BY THE BYSHOP OF LYCHFELD AND COVENTRY,[2] AND LICENCED TO PREACH BY THE BYSHOP OF SARUM NOWE BEING,[3] TAKEN BY MR. DEANE OF WESTMINSTER, MR. DALE, MR. BARNE, AND MR. YONGE. WHO UPPON HIS OTHE SAYETH:

First, he sayeth he hath bene in prison this viiith weekes or ther abouts,[4] comitted by Mr. Doctor Stanhop and others, for suspicon to be privy to the matters concerninge the coffyn carried to Mr. Yonge's dore.[5]

Item, that he hath bene examyned first before Mr. Yonge and Mr. Townshend, next before my Lord of London [Bishop Aylmer] and others, and lastly before the Lord Chief Justice of England and the Lord Anderson, and never indicted to his knowlege.[6]

Item, he confesseth he hath bene at an assembly at Lee's howse by Smythfeld.

Item, being asked whether he be of that church or congregacon wherof Johnson is pastor, refuseth to answer.

Item, he sayeth he came of purpose to Lee's howse to the assembly ther to here [hear] and see the[i]r orders in those matters.

Item, being demanded whether he hath had any of Barrowe, Grenewood, or Penrie's bookes, refuseth to answer.

from Harley 6849, f. 182 *recto*. He gives the summary from Harley 6848, f. 33 *verso*, and omits fifty-four words. See *Early English Dissenters*, II, 41, 55–56.

[1] John Dalamore testified on April 3 that he had heard one Smythe preach at Keynsham, Somerset; Keynsham is near Bradford.

[2] The Bishop of Lichfield and Coventry from 1589 to 1609 was William Overton.

[3] The Bishop of Salisbury or Sarum was John Coldwell, from 1591 to 1596.

[4] The carrying of the coffin occurred on Saturday, February 17, 1592/1593. Smithe was probably arrested on February 18 or 19. Therefore he had been in prison six weeks and three or four days. See Albert Peel, *The Notebook of John Penry, 1593*, p. 39.

[5] Daniel Bucke admitted that a Wiltshire man showed him the copy of the libel. This was probably Smithe, since there is no other Separatist from Wiltshire.

[6] Smithe, as a clergyman of the Church of England, was examined by the special commissioners, Richard Young and Henry Towneshend, by the Court of High Commission—Bishop Aylmer and others, and also by Sir John Popham, Lord Chief Justice of the Queen's Bench, and by Sir Edmund Anderson, Lord Chief Justice of the Common Pleas.

Item, he sayeth he came up to London to confer with Mr. Johnson, Grenewood, and others.[1]

Item, he refuseth to be bound to be reformed and to come to parishe churche assemblies.[2]

Myne othe was taken after my answers gyven.[3]
By mee, William Smithe

[1] If he attended only one meeting, at the home of the deacon, Nicholas Lee, he probably came to London in February, 1592/1593. Yet it seems surprising that he became involved in the coffin incident, if he had recently arrived in London to confer with the Separatist leaders. Perhaps he had conferred earlier with Francis Johnson and John Greenwood before their arrest on the night of December 5–6, 1592. He is very likely the same Smithe who was with Penry on December 22–23, at the home of Thomas Wilkines in the vicinity of Reading. He also is with Penry about February 17–18 and feared that he would be captured. See Albert Peel, *The Notebook of John Penry, 1593*, pp. 38–39.

[2] In 1593–1595 the Separatist church members went in exile to Kampen and Naarden. Before the arrival of Francis Johnson at Amsterdam in 1597, Smithe served as a pastor or teacher to the exiles.

[3] Burrage prints this examination from the copy in Harley MSS. 6848, f. 71 *recto*, but he omits 107 words. He gives the summary from Harley MSS. 6848, f. 34 *recto*, and omits forty-four words. Burrage does not include this last point about the oath being taken after he had answered the questions.

XXXIV

[6 Aprilis 1593] [Ellesmere MS. 2116]

WILLIAM DARVALL OF SHOREDICHE, CARPENTER, OF THE AGE OF XXV YERES OR THER ABOUTS, EXAMINED THE DAYE AND YERE AFORESAID BEFORE THE SAID COMISSIONERS, WHOE REFUSETH TO BE SWORNE BUT SAYETH:

First, that he hath bene in prison about a month, comitted by Mr. Doctor Stanhop and others, being taken in the woods besides Islington, examined by Mr. Yong and others, and never indicted to his knowlege.[1]

Item, howe longe he hath bene of the congregacon or hath held his oppinions, refuseth to answer.

And to all other questions he sayeth he will not accuse him self and otherwise will not answer.[2]

Gabriell Goodman Mathew Dale
John Barne Rychard Young

6 Aprilis 1593 [Ellesmere MS. 2117]

WILLIAM DENFORD OF FOSTER LANE, SCOLEMASTER, OF THE AGE OF FIFTY YERES OR THER ABOUTS, EXAMINED BEFORE MR. DOCTOR GOODMAN, DEANE OF WESTMINSTER, MR. DALE, MR. BARNE, AND MR. YONGE, REFUSETH TO BE SWORNE BUT SAYETH:

First, that he hath bene in prison in the Gate Howse at Westminster a monthe, comitted by the Byshop of London and others,

[1] Arrested March 4. Probably he was first examined March 5–7, but the examination is not extant.

[2] This examination is one of the briefest—seventy-one words, and the summary, in Harley MSS. 6848, f. 36 *recto*—thirty-two words—adds nothing. Both are omitted by Burrage.

comissioners, being taken in the woods by Islington, examyned once by Mr. Yong and others, never indicted to his knowlege.[1]

Item, that he held most of the oppinions that he holdeth nowe about iiii^or [*quattuor*, four] yeres since,[2] and then departed from the congr[eg]acon and afterwards fell to them againe about fortnight before he was taken, and was never past [more than] twice in the assemblyes, *viz.*, bothe tymes in that wood wher he was taken.

Item, he denyeth that he ever drewe any to his oppinions or to the assemblies.

Item, he refuseth to be reformed and to come to church to heare divine service ther nowe used, neither hath he received the comunyon of the Lord's Supper thes five yeres.[3]

Item, he sayeth we have noe ministers lawfully called.[4]

Item, he sayeth the comunyon maye be received at any tyme either after dynner or after supper.

Item, he confesseth that he had one of Barrowe and Grenewood's bookes of the Discovery,[5] but sayth he borrowed it of one but of whome he nowe remembreth not, and used it not above sennyth, and redelivered him [it] againe to the partye of whome he borrowed him [it].[6]

W. Denford

[1] Arrested March 4 and examined about March 5–7. The Gatehouse in Westminster was near Westminster Abbey. Denford died here before 1596.

[2] He was first apprehended about March, 1588/1589, indicted and convicted as a recusant for neglecting church attendance, and sent to the Newgate as a close prisoner. According to the statute of 23 Elizabeth, chapter I, any schoolmaster who failed to attend church was disabled and subject to imprisonment for one year without bail. In 1589–1590 he is on three lists of prisoners. See Carlson, *The Writings of John Greenwood, 1587–1590,* p. 330. He was probably liberated or bailed in May, 1590.

[3] This indicates he may have become a Separatist in 1588.

[4] That is, the clergy of the Church of England have not been called by a congregation, but have been appointed by a patron, instituted by the bishop, and imposed upon the church without the approbation of the people.

[5] *A Brief Discoverie of the False Church.* Published 1590/1591.

[6] This examination has not been published previously. Burrage prints the summary from Harley MSS. 6848, f. 35 *verso,* but omits one-third of it. See *Early English Dissenters,* II, 44.

[6 Aprilis 1593] [Ellesmere MS. 2117]

THOMAS SETLE, WHOE LATELY DWELT IN COWE LANE, MINISTER, MADE BY BYSHOP FREKE BUT NOWE RENOWNCETH THAT MINISTRY,[1] OF THE AGE OF XXXVIII YERES OR THER ABOUTS, EXAMINED BEFORE THE SAID COMYSSIONERS THE DAYE AND YERE AFORESAID, WHOE REFUSETH TO TAKE AN OTHE BUT SAYETH:

First, that he hath bene in prison this fiftene weekes,[2] comitted by Sir Owen Hopton, knight, for beinge in an assemblye in [a schoolehowse in] St. Nicholas Lane, never examined since his comittment, nor indicted to his knowlege.

Item, he sayeth [he] hath held his oppinions and severed him self from the parish churche congregacons about a yere, but hath not received the comunyon in the parish church assemblyes thes thre yeres, and hath bene againste church discipline thes vii yeres, but whoe hath drawen him hereto, he refuseth to tell.

Item, beinge asked and required uppon his allegiance to shewe whether he hath or had or hath read any of Barrowe, Grenewood, or Penrie's bookes, refuseth to answer but sayeth he will not be his owne accuser.[3]

Item, beinge asked howe many he hath drawen and perswaded to his oppinions, sayeth he is resolute in that which he professeth and his desier is to drawe as manye therto as he maye, and further will not answer.

Item, he confesseth that he was present in the congregacon in a howse nigh Algate within the wall when Robert Stokes was excomunicated,[4] and that he was excomunycate by Francis Johnson,

[1] Settel or Settle, of Queens' College, Cambridge, ordained by Edmund Freake, Bishop of Norwich, was a parish priest at Boxted, Suffolk.

[2] Captured December 17 or 24, 1592. Previously he had been cited before Archbishop Whitgift in 1586, and had been imprisoned in the Gatehouse about December, 1589, or January, 1589/1590. He is on the list of prisoners for February, 1589/1590, but not on the list for April. After December, 1592, he remained in the Gatehouse until 1595 certainly and probably until the spring of 1597. In 1608 or 1609 he is in Norfolk, possibly with the sister church in Norwich. See Henoch Clapham, *A Chronological Discourse*, p. 3.

[3] There is an interesting article in the *Harvard Law Review*, by John H. Wigmore, "Nemo Tenetur Seipsum Prodere." See volume V (1891–1892), pp. 71–88.

[4] This house near Aldgate within the wall was Daniel Bucke's residence. In his examination Bucke testified freely about others but omits that a meeting was

the pastor, the rest of the officers and the congregacon beinge present and consenting, which was done for his apostacy.

Item, he sayth he hath never served in any office in the congregacon, but he hath spoken in prophesye in the congregacon.[1]

Item, he confesseth he hath received the comunyon in the[i]r congregacon which was nere Smythfeld, but sayeth he knoweth not whose howse it was.[2]

Item, he refuseth to come to churche to here [hear] divine service nowe used, and sayeth the cause therof is because he thinketh ther is noe true ministry.[3]

Thomas Settle

6 Aprilis 1593 [Ellesmere MS. 2116]

QUINTIN SMYTH OF SOWTHWORKE, FELTMAKER, OF THE AGE OF XXX YERES OR THER ABOUTS, EXAMINED BEFORE MR. DOCTOR GOODMAN, DEANE OF WESTMINSTER, MR. DALE, MR. BARNE, AND MR. YONG. WHOE REFUSETH TO BE SWORNE BUT SAYETH:

First, that he hath bene in prison a month, comitted by the Byshop of London and others, being taken in the wood by Islington, examyned by Mr. Yong and others, not indicted to his knowlege.[4]

Item, he sayeth he hath held his oppinions about two yeres,[5] but

held in his own home, and he says nothing about the excommunication of Stokes—perhaps because he feared the judges would ask where it occurred!

1 That is, he was the leader in the exercise of prophesying, or interpreting the Scriptures. James Fowrestier, George Johnson, John Penry, John Greenwood, William Smithe, and perhaps William Collins served as expounders of the Word.

2 In the summary of his examination, in Harley MSS. 6848, f. 35 *verso*, he said the communion was received in the house of John Barnes in Smithfield.

3 Burrage prints the summary from Harley MSS. 6848, f. 35 *verso*, but omits thirty-nine words. He prints the examination itself from Harley MSS. 6848, ff. 65 *verso* and 66 *recto*, but of the eight paragraphs he prints only one and even curtails the title. In this case the incompleteness is difficult to understand, because the examination is important and the person significant. Yet Burrage himself referred to various depositions—"cited in full in the volume of documents." See *Early English Dissenters*, I, 142.

4 Arrested March 4, and probably first examined March 5–7.

5 He was first arrested in 1588 or 1588/1589. For distributing Separatist pamphlets in manuscript, he was "taken from his labours, cast into the dungeon with irons, his Bible taken from him by Stanhopp [Dr. Edward Stanhope]." See Carlson,

whoe drewe him therto nor to the woods and assemblyes, he refuseth to tell.

Item, he confesseth he hath bene often in the assemblyes, but wher he will not tell.[1]

Item, he sayeth to his knowlege he never had any of Barrowe, Grenewood, or Penrie's books.

Item, he refuseth to come to church.

Item, he sayeth he did covenant with the congregacon to walke with them in the lawes of God, soe longe as the[i]r doings should be approved by the Word of God, and soe longe would forsake all other assemblyes.[2]

Signum dci [dicti] Quintin Smyth

[6 Aprilis 1593] [Ellesmere MS. 2116]

KATHERIN UNWEN, WIDOWE, LATE OF CHRI[ST]CHURCH,[3] OF THE AGE OF XXXV YERES OR THER ABOUTS, EXAMINED THE DAYE AND YERE AFORESAID BEFORE THE SAID COMISSIONERS.

First, that she hath bene in prison about a monthe in the Gate

The Writings of John Greenwood, 1587–1590, pp. 116, 280, 293, 295, 296, 300, 316, 331. He is on the list of prisoners for May, 1589, February, 1589/1590, and April, 1590. Therefore, he must have held his opinions more than four years.

[1] He is not listed as a charter member in September, 1592, and yet he took the simple covenant, and attended "often in the assemblyes." He may be one of those charter members whom Daniel Bucke did not remember.

[2] Burrage prints this examination from the copy in Harley MSS. 6848, f. 79 *recto*, but he omits three paragraphs and part of the title. From the summary in Harley MSS. 6848, f. 36 *recto* he omits thirty-one words. See *Early English Dissenters*, II, 45, 59–60.

[3] She is listed as Onyon, Onnyon, Owin, Unyon, and Unwen. Owin is probably a scribal error for Ōwin or Onwin. The expression, "late of Christ Church," may indicate that she enjoyed the sermons of Richard Greenham, who resigned his pastorate at Dry Drayton, Cambridgeshire, in 1591, and accepted a position at Christ Church, London.

On October 8, 1587, Mrs. Unwen was first arrested as one of twenty-two persons meeting in a conventicle at the home of Henry Martin. She was liberated, but during the summer of 1588 it was discovered that her twelve-year old son had never been baptized because the mother regarded the regular clergy as false ministers. The case became a *cause célèbre*, and the Chancellor to the Bishop of London, Dr. Edward Stanhope, caused the child to be publicly baptized at St. Andrew's in the Wardrobe, with a special sermon presumably by the incumbent Arthur Williams. Mrs. Unwen ran away because she feared punishment.

Howse at Westminster, comitted by the Lord Chief Justice,[1] for being with Penrie's wief [wife] and others when she delivered the piticon to Lord Keper[2] and not being examyned since she hath bene in prison.

Item, she semeth conformable and to come to church, but wanteth sewertyes[3] [sureties] to be bound for her.[4]

Gabriell Goodman
Mathew Dale
John Barne
Rychard Young

[6 Aprilis 1593] [Ellesmere MS. 2117]

WILLIAM WEAVER OF GRAYE'S INNE LANE, SHO[E]MAKER, OF THE AGE OF XL [40] YERES OR THER ABOUTS, EXAMINED BEFORE THE SAID COMISSIONERS THE DAYE AND YERE AFORESAID, WHO REFUSETH TO BE SWORNE BUT SAYETH:

First, that he hath bene in prison a month, comitted by Doctor Stanhop and other the high comissioners, being taken in the wood nere Islington, examyned once before Mr. Townshend and others, not indicted to his knowlege.[5]

[1] She was arrested about March 10, and sent to the Gatehouse on the order of John Popham, Lord Chief Justice of the Queen's Bench, or by Edmund Anderson, Lord Chief Justice of the Court of Common Pleas.

[2] On March 4 about fifty-six members of the Separatist church were captured and imprisoned, but Penry escaped. He then composed a petition entitled: "The Humble, Most Earnest and Lamentable Complaint and Supplication, of the Persecuted and Proscribed Church and Servantes of Christ, Falsely Called Brownists, unto the High Court of Parliament." Several of the wives of the Separatists presented a copy to the House of Lords, where Sir John Puckering, Lord Keeper of the Great Seal, presided, and to the House of Commons, where Edward Coke served as Speaker. Mrs. Unwen, Mrs. Penry, and probably Mrs. Nicholas Lee were questioned by Justice Young for presenting this bold complaint and supplication. Mrs. Unwen implies that the petition was delivered to Lord Keeper Puckering. Penry suggests a copy was handed to Sir Robert Cecil, who refused it.

[3] Mrs. Unwen may have remained in prison, since she was a widow of limited means, but in 1598 she and her specially baptized son, now aged twenty-two, were in the Ancient Church at Amsterdam.

[4] Burrage prints two lines from the summary in Harley MSS. 6848, f. 36 *recto*. See *Early English Dissenters*, II, 45.

[5] Arrested March 4, and examined about March 5–7.

Item, he hath bene of his oppinions about a yere and a half and some what more, and hath bene often at the assemblies, *viz.*, twice or thrice at the wood wher they were taken and sometymes at St. Nicholas Lane and once at Nicholas Lee's howse in Cowe Lane, and was drawen first to the assemblyes by Robert Bodkin,[1] in Graye's Inne Lane, taylor.

Item, he sayeth he sawe one of Barrowe's books in the said Robert Bodkin's howse.

Item, he sayeth he never drewe any eyther to the assemblyes or to his oppinyons.

Item, he sayeth that if the[i]r nomber had greatly increased, yet he thinketh they ment nothing against the peace or the state.

Item, he sayeth that when he was joyned to the[i]r congregacon,[2] they caused him to use words to this effect, that he should promise to walke with them soe longe as they followed the ordinance of Christ.

Item, he refuseth as yet to come to churche.[3]

Signum dci [dicti] William Weaver

[1] Bodkin, Badkinge, or Batkine was arrested before May, 1589, imprisoned in Newgate, bailed, and arrested again about December, 1589. In February and April, 1590, he was imprisoned in the Fleet. In September, 1592, he probably became a charter member, though he is not listed. Perhaps Daniel Bucke inadvertently omits his name, though he includes An Bodkyn, who may be his wife. Robert and Anne Bodkin joined the exiles in Amsterdam about 1597.

[2] Weaver was a charter member, but in the list for September, 1592, he is called William Weber. Burrage lists Weaver and Weber as two persons, but they are identical.

[3] Burrage prints this examination from the copy in Harley 6848, f. 66, but omits eighty-three words. He prints less than half of the summary from Harley MSS. 6848, f. 35 *verso*. See *Early English Dissenters*, II, 45, 60.

XXXV

10 [20?] Aprilis 1593 [Ellesmere MS. 2121]

GEORGE SMELLS OF FINCHE LANE, TAILOR, OF THE AGE OF XL [40] YERES OR THER ABOUTS, EXAMINED BEFORE SIR OWIN HOPTON, KNIGHT, MR. DOCTOR GOODMAN, DEANE OF WESTMINSTER, MR. DALE, MR. BARNE, AND MR. YONG. WHO REFUSETH TO BE SWORNE BUT SAYTH:

First, he saieth he hath bene in prison ever since Sondaye last, comitted by Mr. Yonge for a sectarie.[1]

Item, he saieth he hath held his oppinions thes iiii^or [*quattuor*, four] yeres,[2] perswaded therto by an old man, one father Graynes [Grayves?], a carpenter as he supposeth, who is deceased.

Item, he sayth he hath bene often at the assemblies, but will not tell howe often nor wher, but comonly he sayth uppon every saboth daye.

Item, beinge demaunded when he was at his parishe churche, refuseth to answer.

Item, he sayth he hath sene one of Barrowe's bookes in the hands of Xpofer [Christopher] Bowman in the prison when they were ther together, and heard Bowman read the same booke.[3]

Item, he sayth he never drewe any to the assemblies or his oppinions, but sayth he would geve good councell to as many as he could.

Item, he refuseth to be bound to come to churche.

Item, he sayeth when he was received into the[i]r congregacon,[4] he sayeth he promised ther before the pastor and the congregacon

[1] Arrested on April 8 or 15. The manuscript reading is doubtful, but April 10 seems preferable. Therefore, the arrest would be April 8.

[2] George Smells was arrested at the conventicle on October 8, 1587, at the home of Henry Martin. Thus, he had been a Separatist for five and a half years. From 1587 to 1590 he is on all four lists of prisoners. See Carlson, *The Writings of John Greenwood, 1587–1590*, pp. 306, 313, 320, 325, 331.

[3] Probably in 1590 or 1591 after Barrow's books were published. Bowman and Smells were both in the Counter Wood Street.

[4] He was present at the organization of the church in September, 1592, and accepted the simple covenant.

to walk with them in the ordinance of God soe longe as they departed not from his word.[1]

Owyn [or Owen] Hopton John Barne
Gabriell Goodman Rychard Young
Mathew Dale

[24 Aprilis 1593] [Ellesmere MS. 2145]

THOMAS MITCHELL OF LONDON, TURNER, OF THE AGE OF XXX YERES OR THER ABOUTS, EXAMINED BEFORE THE SAID COMISSIONERS THE DAYE AND YERE AFORESAID, WHOE REFUSETH TO BE SWORNE BUT SAYTH:

First, that he hath bene in prison in Ludgate thes vii weekes, comitted by the Byshop of London and Mr. Yong and others, and hath bene examined before them and others, but not indicted for any cause to his knowlege, and the cause of his comitting was for beinge taken in the wood beyond Islington.[2]

Item, he sayth he hath not bene at churche thes two or thre yeres and soe longe hath held his oppinions, beinge drawen therto by conferrence with one Forrester, whoe nowe cometh to churche.[3]

Item, he saieth they used to meet in the[i]r assemblies in the wood beside Detford, and in the wood wher he was taken, and was taken once before this tyme [in] an assembly in St. Nicholas,[4] but

[1] Burrage prints this examination from the copy in Harley MSS. 6848, f. 59 *recto*. Of eight paragraphs he gives only two. See *Early English Dissenters*, II, 61.

[2] Mitchell, Michill, Michell, or Michel was arrested March 4, probably examined March 5–7. Whereas most prisoners were sent to Newgate, Bridewell, the Counter Wood Street, the Fleet, and the Counter Poultry, in London, the White Lion and the Clink in Southwark, and the Gatehouse in Westminster, Mitchell is the only one sent to Ludgate prison in London. He is also the only one who was apprehended March 4 and not examined in the period April 2–6 with the others.

[3] He was first apprehended about December, 1589, or January, 1589/1590, at a conventicle meeting in a garden house near Bethelehem Hospital, where James Forrester, or Fowrestier, expounded the Word. See Fowrestier's examination of March 19 for his confession of error. He returned to the Church of England. Mitchell was a charter member in September, 1592.

[4] Abraham, Francis Johnson, and Mitchell refer to a capture in St. Nicholas Lane. This was in October, was short-lived, and involved the pastor, who was bailed. On December 17 or 24 there was a second capture in St. Nicholas Lane of Thomas Settle and Daniel Studley, who were imprisoned, bailed by the sheriff, and then recommitted about December 31, in the Gatehouse. See Lansdowne

remembreth not howe often, but as he thinketh, he hath bene at the assemblies xx tymes.

Item, he refuseth to come to churche or to heare sermons, although it was affirmed by the keper of Ludgate and by him self confessed that he hath bene often called to the sermons in the prison to which he would never come.

Item, he sayth he had one of Grenewood's bookes written against one Gyfford, a preacher in Essex, which he calleth against redd prayer.[1]

Item, he refuseth to come to churche.

Item, he refuseth to use the Lord's Prayer as a prayer.[2]

Signum dci [dicti] Thomas Michill

24 Aprilis 1593 [Ellesmere MS. 2145]

JOHN SPAREWE, CITTIZEN AND FISHE MONGER OF LONDON, OF THE AGE OF LX [60] YERES, EXAMINED BEFORE MR. DOCTOR GOODMAN, DEANE OF WESTMINSTER, MR. DALE, MR. BARNE, AND MR. YONGE. WHOE REFUSETH TO BE DEPOSED [SWORNE] BUT SAYETH:

First, that he hath bene in prison in the White Lyon in Sowthwork and the Clink thes iiii yeres, comitted by the Privy Councell

MSS. 109, no. 12, f. 134, and the petition of January, 1592/1593, printed in this volume.

[1] This book of John Greenwood was his *An Answere to George Gifford's Pretended Defence of Read Praiers and Devised Litourgies*, published in August, 1590, at Dort and reissued in 1603, together with Greenwood's "A Fewe Observations of Mr. Giffard's Last Cavills about Stinted Read Prayers and Devised Leitourgies." It was issued again in 1640 with the title, *More Worke for Priests*.

[2] He was willing to use the Lord's Prayer as a model, as a prayer for personal edification, and as a perfect pattern, but not as a mechanical, stinted, repetitive prayer. The Separatists reacted sharply against written prayers, especially as given in the *Book of Common Prayer*, and urged too strongly and exclusively the use of spontaneous prayers, which were frequently long, ill-conceived, and emotional.

Mitchell was a member of the group which intended to establish a second London Separatist church, with William Collins as the leader, and with John Barnes and John Nicholas as supporters. See Bancroft, *A Survay of the Pretended Holy Discipline*, p. 429 [249]. Mitchell went to Amsterdam, joined with Francis Johnson, then flirted with Baptist views, returned to Norwich, was imprisoned, and evidently went to Amsterdam a second time.

This examination is not given by Burrage.

for deliveringe a peticon to the Quene's Majesty concerninge diverse sectaries, but was never examined since his imprisonment and is not indicted for any cause to his knowlege.[1]

Item, he sayeth he came to churche untill about a week before he was comitted.

Item, he sayeth he hath not nor never had nor sene any of Barrowe, Grenewood, or Penrie's bookes.

Item, he refuseth to come to churche as yet, but desireth conference.[2]

Gabriell Goodman
John Barne
Mathew Dale
Rychard Young

[1] Sparewe, or Sparrow, with John Nicholas and Christopher Bowman, was imprisoned on March 17 for presenting "A Lamentable Petition" of March 13, 1588/1589, to the Queen. He was sent to the White Lion prison in Southwark, and transferred before February, 1589/1590, to the Clink. It is remarkable that he remained in prison more than four years, without trial, inasmuch as Nicholas and Bowman were bailed. It is probable, however, that Stephen Egerton conferred with him in March, 1589/1590. Sparrow, one of the oldest of the prisoners, may not have been a thoroughgoing Separatist, since he stated that up to March, 1588/1589, he attended the Church of England services, and since he desired conference with some learned men of the Church of England.

[2] This examination is not printed by Burrage.

XXXVI

The following document is in Harley MSS. 6848, ff. 32 *recto*–36 *recto*. It is a summary of thirty-two examinations, and was probably prepared for the commissioners who had been appointed to conduct them. The summaries are fairly close to the original examinations, but sometimes they contain new information.

There are eleven examinations for which there are no summaries. For April 2 there are no summaries for W. Clark, G. Johnson, and Nicholas. For April 3 there are no summaries for Abraham, Barnes, Dalamore, Farrot, and Pulbery. Of these eight, Farrot was bailed, but why the others are not included remains unexplained. The examinations of Smells, Mitchell, and Sparewe are not included because they were taken after April 6.

For annotation on these thirty-two Separatists, see their examinations in chapters XXIX–XXXV.

THE EXAMINACION OF SONDRY PERSONS ABIDINGE IN THE PRISONS IN AND ABOUTE LONDON, TAKEN BEFORE DOCTOR GOODMAN DEANE OF WESTMINSTER AND OTHERS, iii°, iiii°, v^to^, et vi^to^ APRILE 1593

Clinke

Henry Broadwater scrivener dwellinge in St. Nicholas Lane aged xxix yeares was committed to prison by the Bishop of London and others aboute vi weekes paste. Hee saieth that hee will not bee bounde to come to any churche. Beinge demaunded whether hee have had any of Barrowe's or Penryn their bookes, hee aunswereth hee never sawe any of them to his knowledge.

Newgate

Edward Grave fishmonger of the parishe of St. Botulph in

Thames streete aged xxv yeares was committed to prison a weeke paste. Item he saieth that hee hath bene of this opinion of the Sectaries this halfe yeare and was persuaded by the sermons of Mr. Gardener and Mr. Phillips, who preached that men were bounde to heare and to bee ruled by their pastor, elders, and deacons. Hee saieth that hee will not goe to churche untill hee bee better persuaded, and confesseth that hee had one of Barrowe's his bookes of conference which hee lent to Pedar the shoemaker, and hee hath bene at their assemblies in the woodes at Detford and Islington, and allso in St. Nicholas Lane.

Christofer Diggins we[a]ver aged xxiiii yeares is servaunte to Nicholas Haveren of the parishe of St. Olave's in Southwarke and was one of them that carried the coffine to Mr. Younge's dore and saieth that hee hath not bene at churche these two yeares. Beinge demaunded whether hee will goe to churche, hee saieth hee will not. Hee saieth that hee was in the assemblies every Lorde's day by the space of two yeares now laste paste. Item hee saieth that hee hath seene one of Barowe's his bookes in the handes of one John Wilkenson. And denieth that hee hath persuaded any man to their opynion.

John Clerke husbandman of the parishe of Wallsoken in the countye of Norfolke was committed three yeares paste by the sheriffes of London, beinge taken in an assembly with Barrowes [Barrowists, Brownists] and not examined untill this time. Hee saieth that hee will not goe to any churche nor to any sermons.

Yt was thoughte good by the commissioners that hee should bee sente to Bridewell to grinde in the mill.

[Folio 32 *verso*] Roger Waterer haberdasher servante to Robert Pavye of the parishe of St. Marten's at Ludgate was committed to Newgate by Doctor Stanhope three yeares and a quarter paste and was never examined. The cause of his imprisonment (as he saith) was for that hee wente not to his parishe churche in three weekes and was fetched out of his master's house. Hee saieth that hee was once at an assembly in a gardeyne house neere Bedlem where James Forester did expounde the Scriptures. Beinge demaunded whether hee will goe to churche hee saieth that hee will so as he may bee persuaded by the Word of God. Hee saieth that hee had the booke of conference, but what is becomme of it hee knoweth not.

William Marshall shipwrighte dwellinge at Wappinge aged xxxii yeares was taken in the wood and was sent to prison by Doctor

Stanhope. Hee saieth he hath bene of these assemblies halfe a yeare and was with them three tymes in the woodes and yet was at churche vi weekes paste. Hee saieth that John Barrett hath had bookes but what were the contentes of them hee knoweth not. Beinge demaunded whether hee will goe to churche, hee saieth hee will not nor will not take any othe.

John Hulkes shipwrighte borne in Chatham aged xxi yeares or thereaboutes was taken in the woodes and committed to prison by Doctor Stanhope and others aboute a moneth paste. Hee saieth that hee hath bene twise in their assemblies, beinge caried thereto by Curlande and Marshall, and is not setled in their company as yet. Beinge demaunded whether hee will goe to churche and sermons, hee saieth hee will and is thereto bounde by recognisance and so discharged.

Thomas Hewett borne in Swanton in the county of Leicester pursemaker of the age of xxx yeares and doth dwell at St. Marten's le Graunde with John Sutton and is his servaunte and was taken with the reste in the wood. Hee denieth to aunswere to any thinge and refuseth to come to the churche.

[33 *recto*] George Knifton apothecarye dwellinge in Newgate markett of the age of [xxiiii] yeares saieth that hee hath mett at the assemblies at Barnes his house, at Billson's house and at Lee's house and at the woodes and at Rippon's house and at Deptford wood, and hee is an elder. Beinge demaunded whether hee will goe to churche, hee aunswereth that hee wilbee content to have conference and before that hee will not goe to the churche, and refusethe to take an othe. Hee is to bee sent to the Deane of Westminster to conferre.

William Mason shipwrighte of the age of xxi yeares was taken in the wood. Hee saieth that hee hath bene of these assemblies since a little before Christmas laste and was persuaded by Roger Rippon and Edward Chaundler, and hath bene at their assemblies xi [xii ?] tymes, *viz.*, in Nicholas Lane, at Daniell Bucke's neer Allgate [Aldgate] and at Nicholas Lee his house, and hee gave vi d. a weeke which the deacons receyved and hee saieth that Chaundler had Barrowe's bookes and did reade them. Beinge demaunded whether hee will goe to churche, hee saieth he will and is bounde with his brother Richard Mason and James Tailor and so discharged.

Henry Withers shipwrighte dwellinge at Deptford Strande of the age of xxvii yeares was committed a moneth paste, beinge taken at the assembly in the woodes. Hee saieth that hee hath bene of the said assemblies this halfe yeare by meanes and persuasion of the shipwrightes and they did assemble themselves every Sabboth daye at dyvers houses. Item he saieth that hee hath seene of Penry his bookes but hee hath none of them nor ever had them. Beinge demaunded whether hee will goe to churche, hee aunswereth that hee is willinge to goe to churche after that hee hath had conference.

Christofer Bowman goldsmithe of the age of xxxii yeares and doeth dwell in Weste Smithfield and was committed by [for] the coffine and libells. Hee saith that hee is one of the confused [confessed, constituted?] churche and is a deacon amongest them, beinge chosen in September laste. Hee saieth hee was imprisoned v [iv] yeares paste for puttinge up a peticion to the Queene's Majestie and continued in prison iiii [iii] yeares for the same. Hee saieth that the forward preachers caused him to fall into these assemblies and that Mr. Chatterton's printed sermon was the cause that made him enter into this action. Hee saieth that hee had the booke of discovery of Barrowe's which hee receyved of Stokes but what is become of it hee doeth not knowe. [33 *verso*] Hee saieth that hee hath beene at their assemblies as often as hee could have time and liberty, *viz.*, at Mr. Billson's house, at Penryn's, Lee's, Rippon's, and Barnes' their houses and in St. Nicholas Lane and in the woodes. Beinge asked whether hee hath drawen any to this churche, hee saieth that hee hath done accordinge to his knowledge. And beinge demaunded whether hee will come to the churche, hee saieth hee will not. Beinge demaunded where hee was maried, hee saieth at Penryn's house, and Settle did pray and Grenewood was presente, and hee denieth to sweare or subscribe.

Thomas Micklefield joyner of the age of xxxiii yeares dwellinge in St. Mary Overie's parishe was taken in the assembly in the woodes and was examined before Mr. Stanhope and others. Hee confesseth that hee hath bene of the company of these sectaries this quarter of a yeare and was persuaded thereto by Mr. Philip's preachings. Beinge required to goe to the churche, hee saieth hee will not, and denyeth that hee hath persuaded any.

David Bristowe tailor of the age of xxx yeares dwellinge in St. Marten's le Graunde was taken in the woodes and committed by the highe commissioners. Beinge required to take an othe, he denieth so to doe or to come to the churche. Hee hath bene in the assemblies vi tymes and beinge demaunded whether hee have receyved the communion with their company, hee saieth hee will not aunswere. Hee hath bene in their company this halfe yeare and saieth hee cannot goe to any churche but to that whereunto he hath joyned himselfe.

Christofer Simkyn coppersmith dwellinge in Aldersgate streete of the age of xxii yeares was taken in the woodes and committed by the Bishop of London and others. Hee denieth to sweare upon any booke and saieth that hee hath not bene at his parishe churche these xviii moneths, beinge thereto persuaded by hearinge Mr. Sparkes, Mr. Cowper and others their sermons. Hee saieth that hee hath bene at these assemblies every Sabaoth but where hee will not tell and denieth to goe to the churche for that hee is joyned with this assembly and hee will not forsake them.

[34 *recto*] William Smithe of Bradford in the com. [county] of Willshire [*sic*] mynister of the age of xxx yeares was made mynister by the Bishop of Coventrye and Litchfield. Hee saieth hee was imprisoned viii weekes since by Mr. Stanhope for the carriage of the coffine and was examined by the Lord Chiefe Justice. Item hee denieth to take his othe and saieth that hee came to heare their opynions. Beinge asked whether hee will goe to the churche hee saieth hee wilbe contented to have conference.

Arthur Billett borne in Flanteclex in the com. [county] of Cornewall aged xxv yeares saieth that hee hath bene a scholler and a souldiour and was taken with Penryn and others at Ratcliffe aboute a fortnighte paste. Hee saieth that hee hath bene in drawen into this society these two yeares and hath bene three or foure tymes at the woodes and in dyvers houses and receyved the communion at Barnes' house. Hee was the man that putt Barrowe's and Grenewood their bookes to the printe at Dorte and hee sawe one of the bookes in a countrey man's handes. Beinge required to take an othe hee refuseth to doe it.

John Parkes clothworker of the age of L [50] yeares was taken in the woodes and committed by the Bishop of London aboute a moneth paste. Hee saieth hee serveth Mr. Livesey his sonne and hath meate and drinke of him and noe wages and hath no habitacion. Hee hath bene of this secte a quarter of a yeare and hath bene at these assemblies vi tymes in sondry places. Beinge demaunded whether hee hath had any of Barrowes his bookes, hee saieth hee had none of them nor seene them. Hee saieth hee will not goe to the churche unles hee may bee persuaded by conference.

John Penryn mynister of the age of xxx yeares or thereaboutes, beinge demaunded where hee was the xixth daye of Marche, hee aunswereth that hee was in London or thereaboutes, and that ther was one Edward Graves who laye with him at Hogsdon and from there at Ratcliffe. The cause of his departure out of the lande to Scotlande was for that hee putt up a petition to the parliament and could not bee heard and therefore hee departed.

[34 *verso*] Leonard Pidder shoemaker of the age of xxx yeares dwellinge at Blacke Friers was taken in the woodes. Hee denieth to take an othe. Hee saieth that hee hath not gone to his parishe churche these two moneths and hath beene of this secte these two moneths and ever since hath bene at their assemblies every Sabaothe daye, but the places where, hee will not name. Beeinge asked whether hee had any of Barrowes and Greenewood their bookes, hee saith hee will not accuse himselfe. Beinge asked whether hee will goe to the churche, hee saieth hee will not.

William Curland shipwrighte of the age of [30] yeares was taken in the woodes neere Islington. Item hee saieth that by the space of a fortnighte before his takinge hee was at their assemblies v or vi tymes in sondry places. Beinge demaunded whether hee will goe to his parishe church, hee saieth hee wilbe persuaded if hee may bee bailed.

William Giles [Eiles] taylor aged xxii yeares servaunte to Mr. Cheryatt of Walbroke was taken as hee was goinge to the assembly in the woodes. Beinge demaunded when he was at the parishe churche or whether hee have bene at their assemblies, hee saieth hee will not aunswere thereto. Beinge demaunded whether hee will goe to the churche hee praieth that hee may bee pardoned for that. Beinge required to saye the Lorde's Prayer, hee likewise praieth that hee may not bee urged to saye it. Thomas Emery is his felowe servaunte.

Edward Gilbarte of the age of xxi yeares servaunte to Isaac Frize tronkemaker was taken in the woodes. Hee saieth that hee hath bene of these assemblies this quarter of a yeare and hath receyved the Lorde's Supper in the afternoone. Hee denieth to goe to his parishe churche.

Frauncis Johnson mynister was so made by the sectaries and chosen their pastor, is of the age of xxxi yeares and is of noe certeine abode. Hee was offered the othe to aunswere to all suche matters as shal bee demaunded of him on Her Majestie's behallfe, but hee refuseth to take it. Hee saieth that it is the power of their churche that they may excommunicate the queene untill shee acknowledge and confesse her selfe, and this is done to save her soule. [35 *recto*] Hee saieth that hee was committed the vth day of December 1592 by the lord of Caunterbury and others, and hee hath bene examined two severall tymes by the Lord Chief Justice at Sergeantes Inne. Item hee saieth that the Lorde's Prayer is a forme of prayer but not to bee used, for the apostles did not use to saye it. Item hee saieth that hee was prisoner in Cambridge for a sermon that hee made to this purpose for that hee would not take an othe foure yeares paste. Beinge demaunded by whom hee was persuaded to these assemblies, hee saieth by the Scriptures and Worde of God. And beinge likewise asked if hee have had any of Barrowes and Grenewood their bookes, hee saieth hee hath aunswered it to the Lordes Chiefe Justices and more hee will not aunswere. Beinge demaunded whom hee hath drawen to these assemblies, hee saieth hee will not aunswere but that hee hath done his duety as hee is bound by the Worde. Beinge asked whether hee will goe to churche there to heare devine service and to receive the sacramentes and whether hee will say the Lord's Prayer, hee saieth that hee will not aunswere and that hee came not hither to pray, neither can hee joyne with these bishops, parsons, and mynisters.

Edward Boys haberdasher aged xxxiii yeares dwellinge in Fleetestreete was committed xvi weekes paste by the Bishop of Caunterbury and others and refuseth to take an othe and saieth that hee was not examined since his committment. Beinge asked how longe hee hath bene drawen from his parish churche, hee saieth that hee hath bene of this societie these three yeares and was moved thereto by Mr. Egerton, Mr. Cowper, and Mr. Wigginton their sermons, and will not aunswere where hee hath bene assembled with them other than the place where he was taken. Hee saieth hee will not aunswere to any question wherein hee may accuse himselfe or others. Beinge demaunded whether hee will goe to his parish church there to heare devine service and receyve the sacramentes, hee aunswereth that hee cannot come to these parishe assemblies.

George Collier haberdasher aged xxxviii yeares of the parishe of St. Marten's at Ludgate was committed by the Bishop of London and others v yeares paste. Beinge required to take an othe hee refuseth to bee sworne. Hee saieth that hee was taken with Grenewood and Crane and others and was never examined in all this time. Beinge required to goe to his parishe church and have his liberty, hee saieth hee will not.

[35 *verso*] William Denford schole master of the age of L [50] yeares, lodged at Mayre's house in Fosterlane, and was taken in the wood and committed by the Bishop of London and others aboute a moneth paste. Hee saieth that hee hath bene twise at the assemblies in the wood and doeth use to saye the Lorde's Prayer, but hee will not goe to churche untill the parishes bee reformed. Hee saieth that the minstery is not duely called. Beinge offered the othe, hee denieth to take it upon a booke, and beinge asked when hee receyved the communion, hee saieth it is v yeares since or thereaboutes.

Thomas Settell mynister of the age of xxxviii yeares hath bene in prison these xv weekes, beinge committed by Sir Owen Hopton, and doeth renounce his mynisterye, and was not examined since his committinge. Hee was taken in an assembly at a schoole house in St. Nicholas Lane. Beinge demaunded how longe he hath absented himselfe from the Church of England, hee aunswereth about a yeare paste and hath not receyved the communion these three yeares and hath bene againste the discipline of the Churche of England these vii yeares, and refuseth to take an othe. Beinge asked whether he hath had any of Barrowe's and Grenewoode's bookes, hee saith hee will not aunswere for that hee will not accuse himselfe. Hee allso saieth that hee was at the excommunicacion of Robert Stokes and the wordes were pronounced by Frauncis Johnson their pastor, and confesseth that hee hath prophecied in their assemblies. Hee saieth that hee did receyve the communion in Barnes his house in Smithfield in the aforenoone, and hath persuaded the people to their assemblies. Hee refuseth to come to the churche for that there is noe true mynister.

William Wever shoemaker of Graye's Inne Lane of the age of xl yeares, serva[un]t to George Smith, beinge required to take an othe, denieth so to doe, was taken in the woodes and examined before Mr. Townesend, Richard Younge and others. Item hee saieth that hee hath frequented these assemblies these xviii monethes and hath bene in the woodes at Deptford and Yslington and in St. Nicholas Lane and at Lee's house, and Robert Bodkyn was the first that persuaded him thereto. And hee hath seene one of Barrowes his bookes in Bodkin's house. Hee saieth that hee hath made a covenaunte to the congregacion to bee of their societie and refuseth to goe to the churche.

[36 *recto*] Quintine Smith feltworker, servaunte to his brother in Southwarke, aged xxx yeares, was taken in the woodes and refuseth to take an othe. Hee saieth that hee hath bene of these assemblies these two yeares and beinge required to goe to the churche hee saieth hee will not till suche time as the churche may bee reformed from the wicked. Hee saieth that hee made a covenaunte with the assembly that as longe as they did walke in the lawes of God hee would forsake all other assemblies and onely folowe them.

William Darvall carpenter of the age of xxv yeares dwellethe in Shorditch and was taken in the wood. Hee saieth hee will not sweare to any thinge nor aunswere to any thinge.

Katherine Onyon spinster, dwellinge at Allgate, is willinge to goe to churche, but shee is not able to putt in suerties.

XXXVII

This summary of examinations is in Ellesmere MS. 2158 at the Huntington Library. The compilation was made by a different person from the one who prepared the previous summary. There are twenty-nine names, and their summaries are similar to the previous ones, but occasionally and surprisingly there is additional material. Missing from this list are the summaries of three persons, Brodwater, Mason, and Wythers, all of whom were bailed.

For annotations on these twenty-nine Separatists, see their examinations in chapters XXIX–XXXV.

A BREFFE NOT[E] OF ALL THE SECTARIES REMENYNG [REMAINING] IN THE PRESONS ABOTTS [ABOUT] LONDON WITH A BREFFE NOT[E] OF THER EXAMINATIONS AS FOLOTHE

1 Thomas Mehellfyld, joyner, aged xxxiii yeares, saieth that hee was drawen into this opynion by hearinge of Mr. Phillips his sermons and hath bene of th[e] assembly not above a quarter of a yeare and refuseth to goe to churche in his parishe.

2 David Bristowe, tailor, aged xxx yeares, hath bene at the assemblies about VI tymes and hath kepte company with them this halfe yeare. Hee will not declare the places where they have mett, and refuseth to goe to any other churche than to that congregacion.

3 Christopher Simkins, coppersmith, of th[e] age of xxii yeares, was drawen to this opynion by the hearinge of Mr. Sparke, Mr. Cowper, and others, and hath bene of this society these XVIII moneths and frequented their assemblies every Sabaoth daye, but where hee will not tell, and refuseth to goe to his parishe churche for that hee is joyned with this assembly and will not forsake them.

4 William Smith of Bradford in the com. [comitatu, county] of Wilt[shire], mynister, aged xxx yeares, hath kepte Penrye in

his house, and refuseth to goe to churche, but is contented to have conference.

5 Arthur Billett gent[leman] aged xxv yeares, was taken with Penry and hath bene of this societie these two yeares and hath bene in dyvers places aswell in houses as in the fieldes at these assemblies, and confesseth that hee did putt Barrowe's and Grenewood their bookes to bee printed at Dorte, and beinge required to take an othe to speake trueth, hee refuseth to sweare.

6 John Sparkes [Parkes], clothworker, aged L [50] yeares, hath no habitacion but hath meate and drink of young Mr. Livesey but no wages. Hee hath bene of this societie these three moneths and hath bene vi tymes at the assemblies in sondry places. Hee refuseth to goe to churche unles hee may bee persuaded by conference.

7 Edward Grave, fishmonger, aged xxv yeares, hath bene of these assemblies this half yeare and was drawen thereunto by the hearing of Mr. Gardener and Mr. Phillips their sermons. Hee refuseth to goe to church untill hee bee better persuaded. Hee had one of Mr. Barrowe's [and Greenwood's] their bookes of conference and sente it abroade.

8 Xrofer [Christopher] Diggins, wever, aged xxiiii yeares, was one of them that caried the coffine, and hath not bene at churche these two yeares, and hath bene duringe that time at their assemblies every Lord's daye. Hee hath seene of Mr. Barrowe's bookes in the handes of one John Wilkenson, and will not goe to churche.

9 John Clerke of the parishe of Wallsokin in the com. [comitatu, county] of Norfolk, husbandman, hath bene in prison three yeares, committed by the sheriffs of London, beinge taken in these assemblies, and refuseth either to goe to churche or to heare sermons.

10 Roger Waterer, haberdasher, aged xxii yeares, hath bene of these assemblies three yeres and a quarter paste, and hath bene in prison three yeares. Hee had the booke of Mr. Barrowe's conferences and what is become of it hee knoweth not, and refuseth to goe to churche unlesse hee may bee persuaded by the Worde of God.

11 William Marshall, shipwrighte, aged xxxii yeares, hath bene of these assemblies vi moneths and hath bene with them in the woodes and other places, and refuseth to take his othe or to goe to the churche.

12 John Hulkes, shipwright, aged xxi yeares, hath bene twise in these assemblies and is not yet settled in their companye. Hee yelded to reforme himself and is discharged upon bonde.

13 Thomas Hewett, pursemaker, of the age of xxx yeares, hath bene of this societie but how long hee will not declare, nor take an othe to aunswere to any thinge, and refuseth to goe to churche.

14 George Knifton, apothecary, aged xxiiii yeares, was an elder in their congregacion and hath frequented their assemblies continually in divers places. Hee refuseth to take an othe or to goe to churche but yeldeth to have conference.

15 Xrofer [Christopher] Bowman, goldsmith, aged xxxii yeares, was a deacon of this confused churche and was brought to these assemblies by readinge of Mr. Chatterton's [Laurence Chaderton's] printed sermons and by the preaching of forward preachers. [He] hath bene in all their assemblies. Hee had Mr. Barrowe his booke of discovery [*A Brief Discoverie of the False Church*] of [Robert] Stokes but knoweth not what is become of it. And beinge demaunded if hee have drawen any others to these assemblies, hee saieth hee hath done accordinge to his knowledge, and was maried in Penry his house, and [Thomas] Settle did praye in [the] presence of [John] Grenewood, and refuseth to take an othe or to goe to churche or to subscribe this his confession.

16 William Giles [Eiles], tailor, aged xxii yeares, will not aunswere howe longe it is since hee was at his parishe churche or whether hee hath bene at these assemblies, and beinge demaunded whether hee will goe to churche hee praieth that hee may bee pardoned, and desireth allso that hee may not bee urged to saye the Lorde's prayer.

17 Edward Gilbert, tronkemaker, aged xxi yeares, hath bene of these assemblies a quarter of a yeare and hath bene at their assemblies and receyved the Lord's Supper in the afternoone. He refuseth to goe to his parishe churche.

18 Frauncis Johnson, mynister, aged xxxi yeares, chosen pastor of this congregacion, saieth that their churche hath power to excommunicate the Queene till shee acknowledge and confesse her selfe, which is done to save her soule, and saieth the Lord's prayer is not to bee used, for the Apostles did not use it, and beinge demaunded whom hee hath drawen to their assemblies, hee saieth hee will not aunswere but hee hath done

his duety as hee is bounde by the Worde, and beinge demaunded whether hee will goe to churche and there to heare devine service and receyve the sacraments and say the Lord's prayer, hee saieth hee came not hither to praye and cannot joyne with these bishops, pastors, and mynisters, and other aunswere hee will not make.

19 Edward Boise, haberdasher, aged xxxiii yeares, refuseth to take an othe and saieth that hee hath bene of this societie these three yeares and since hath not bene at his parishe churche, and will not aunswere where hee hath bene at their assemblies, sayenge that hee will not accuse himselfe or any others, and refuseth to come to the parishe assemblies.

20 George Collier, haberdasher, aged xxxviii yeares, was committed V yeares paste by the Bishop of London, and refuseth to aunswere upon his othe and will not goe to his parishe churche.

21 William Denford, scholemaster, aged L [50] yeares, hath bene twise at their assemblies in the wood, and doeth use to saye the Lorde's prayer, but will not goe to the churche untill the parishes bee reformed and the mynister bee reformed, and denieth to take an othe upon a book and hath not receyved the communion these V yeares.

22 Thomas Settell, mynister, aged xxxviii yeares, doeth renounce the mynisterye, and saieth that hee hath not bene at any parish assemblie these xii moneths, nor receyved the communion these three yeares, for hee hath bene againste the discipline of the Churche of England these seven yeares, and refuseth to take an othe. Hee hath persuaded the people to come to their assemblies, and will not aunswere whether hee had any of Barrowe's or Grenewood their bookes, sayenge hee will not accuse himselfe. Hee was at the excommunicacion of Robert Stokes pronounced by Frauncis Johnson their pastor, and this examinant hath preached amongest them. Hee refuseth to come to the churche for that there is noe true mynister.

23 William Wever, shoemaker, aged xl [40] yeares, hath bene of these assemblies this yeare and an halfe, and hath frequented their assemblies in the woodes and in sondry other places, and was persuaded thereto by Robert Bodkyn, and sawe him have one of Barrowe's his bookes, and will not goe to the churche for hee made a covenaunte to that congregacion to bee of their societie.

24 Quintine Smith, feltmaker, aged xxx yeares, refuseth to take

an othe, and hath bene of these assemblies this two yeares, and refuseth to goe to churche untill such time as the churche bee reformed of the wicked, and hath made a covenant with the assemblye that so longe as they walke in the lawes of God hee will forsake all others and folowe them.

25 William Darvall, carpenter, aged xxv yeares, will not take any othe or aunswere to any thinge.

26 John Penry, mynister, aged xxx yeares, saieth that hee wente into Scotland because hee had exhibited a peticion to the Parliament and coulde not bee hearde, refuseth to take any othe, and refuseth to aunswere for suche places as hee hath frequented, and saieth that bloude cannott bee clensed out of this lande untill their bloud bee spilte that procure it. Hee saieth that in Scotland hee made and caused to bee printed a booke entitled *A Reformacion and No Enemye to Her Majestie and the State*, and another booke which hee translated, called *Thesis Genevensium*, and will not aunswere what other bookes hee hath made or sett forthe.

27 Leonard [Pedder], shoemaker, aged xxx yeares, denieth to take an othe, hath bene of this congregacion these two moneths and since hath not bene at his parishe churche, but hath frequented their assemblies every Sabaoth daye, but in what places hee will not declare nor whether hee had any of Barrowe's or Grenewoode's bookes, and refuseth to goe to the churche.

28 William Curland, shipwrighte, of the age of xxx yeares, hath bene of this societie about x or xi wecks [weeks] and hath bene at these assemblies v or vi times and saieth hee wilbee persuaded to goe to churche if hee may bee bailed.

29 Katherin Onwen, spinster, dwellinge at Allgate, is willinge to goe to churche but is not able to putt in suerties.

XXXVIII

THE NAMES OF SUCHE SECTARIES, AS UPON THE[I]R CONFORMITIE THE COMMISSIONERS HAVE BAYLED

This document is in Harley MSS. 6848, f. 210 *recto*. It lists eight Separatists who were bailed upon promise of conformity. All were arrested on March 4 except Henry Brodwater, who had been apprehended about February 17–20 as a suspected collaborator in the coffin incident. Two of the men were charter members—William Mason and Henry Wythers. All were examined in April. Six evidently took the oath, but Edward Gilbert and Thomas Mihilfield refused to be sworn. Four of the men were shipwrights, from Deptford and Wapping, three were from London, and one from Southwark. They were probably all bailed in April, 1593.

There is one name not given here. This is Richard Hawton, who was examined on March 8, and who agreed to return to his parish church. He was evidently bailed in March. One other border-line case is that of Katherin Unwen, who was examined on April 6. She seemed to be conformable and willing to attend her parish church, but she lacked sureties for her recognizance.

THE NAMES OF SUCHE SECTARIES, AS UPON THE[I]R CONFORMITIE THE COMMISSIONERS HAVE BAYLED

John Hulkes of Detford, shipwright.
William Mason of Wappinge, shipwright.
William Curland of Detford, shipwright.
Edward Gilbert, apprentice to Isack Frees, taylor, of the parishe of St. Gregorie's neere Powle's.

John Greenwood

Henry Brodewater of St. Nicholas Lane, scrivenor.
Thomas Mihilfield of St. Saviour's, joyner.
Thomas Farrot, servant to William Greene of Aldersgate Streete.
Henrye Withers of Detford Strand, shipwright.

XXXIX

THE EXAMINATIONS OF JOHN HALE AND THOMAS HALE

The examination of John Hale is in Harley MSS. 6848, f. 95 *recto*, dated July 28, 1590. His second examination is in f. 95 *verso*, of which there is a copy in Harley MSS. 7042, f. 204 *verso*. It is undated, but probably occurred on July 28 or 31.

The examination of Thomas Hale, July 31, 1590, of Welwyn, Hertfordshire, is in Harley MSS. 6848, f. 95 *recto*, and the copy is in Harley MSS. 7042, f. 204 *verso*.

These examinations are interesting because they indicate sympathy with Barrow and Greenwood in prison. They also reveal an incipient Separatism in Hertfordshire. If John Hale is identical with John Hales, he went to Amsterdam, was excommunicated by Francis Johnson, but remained a member of Henry Ainsworth's church. See John Fowler, Clement Saunders, and Robert Bulwarde, *A Shield of Defence against the Arrowes of Schisme* (Amsterdam, 1612), pp. 27, 29, 30, 36. These examinations are not a part of the examinations held in March and April, 1593, nor do they occur in London. If we count all the examinations, there are three in July, 1590, for two persons; there are eighteen in March, 1592/1593, for sixteen examinants; and there are forty-four examinations in April, 1593, for forty-three persons, of whom seven had been examined also in March. Thus there are sixty-five examinations for fifty-four individuals.

THE EXAMYNACION OF JOHN HALE OF HATFEILD IN THE COUNTIE OF HARTFORDSHIRE, TANNER, TAKEN BEFORE SIR JOHN BROCKET, KNIGHT, ONE OF HER MAJESTIE'S JUSTICES OF PEACE WITHIN THE SAID COUNTY ON THE XXVIIITH DAYE OF JULY IN THE XXXIITH YERE OF THE RAIGNE OF QUEEN ELIZABETH [JULY 28, 1590]

First, being asked howe long it is since he was at his owne churche assemblie, he saieth he cannot nowe remember.

Being asked the cause whie he doth not come to his churche or assemblie, he saith because he cannot see it proved by the Word that it is the true church.

And being asked howe long he hath bene of that mynde, he answereth the tyme certen he cannot tell, but when he did come lately to an assemblie or church, he was accused in his conscience because he did see all men aswell the wicked as others admytted as members of the churche.

Being asked what he thinketh of our mynisters that he so refuseth to come to the churche, he saieth he doth not think them the mynisters of Christ's churche, therfore not to be acknowledged to be that [which] they are not.

And being asked what he holdeth the cyvill majestrate, whether they be christian magestrates and to be obeyed, he saieth he doth acknowledg them to be God's ordynaunces and therfore to be obeyed.

JOHN HALE'S FURTHER EXAMINATION

John Hale of Hatfeild, tanner, saieth that he thinketh the mynisters are not the true mynisters of the church of Christ, nor the church where the[y] serve to be the true and lawefull churches, for that they are no lawfull mynisters of a true church. And that our churches of England are no lawfull churches. And further saieth that he taketh them not to be the lawfull ministers of Christ's churche.

Being demanded whether the Queene be a true lawfull and christian majestrate, he answereth that he thinketh that she is a lawfull governor, but whether she be a true and a christian majestrate he can[n]ot tell because he is not conversant with her and therfore he cannot judge of her.

Being demanded who they were that did instruct him, or who they were that were in his kinsman's company of late at the tyme that he was in conference with Mr. Abbott of Hatfeild, mynister, he answereth that in conscience he ought not accuse his brethren that instructe them in the word of God.

Harry Cock John Brocket
Phillip Butler Harry Coningesby

Endorsement: Copye of John and Thomas Hale's examynacions.

THE EXAMYNACION OF THOMAS HALE OF WELWEYNE AND JOHN HALE OF HATFEILD TAKEN BEFORE SIR HENRY COCKE, SIR JOHN BROCKET, SIR PHILLIP BUTLER, AND SIR HENRY CONINGESBY, KNIGHTS, HARRY BUTLER AND THOMAS SMYTH, ESQUIRES, THE LAST OF JULY IN THE XXXIIth YERE OF QUEEN ELIZABETH [1590]

First, the said Thomas Hale being demanded whether with the rest of the company being before us in number xviii (whereof viii were mynisters) were of the true and faythfull church of God, he saieth that never a one of the mynisters were of the church of God, but were all mynisters of the false churche, having no lawfull church.

[95 *verso*] Being further demanded where the true visible church is, he saieth where faythfull people are, such as Barowe and Grenewood and such other like as are under persecucion at London.

The second Article he affirmeth.

The third Article he saieth that it is lawfull for any pryvate man that hath a gifte to prophecy and to interpret the Scriptures.

To the fourth Article he saieth that tythes are ceased by the comying of Jesus Christ. And that there are other lyvings appointed for them to lyve upon that preach the gospell, that is, to have the reward of them which are fedd by the gospell.

Being demanded what they are which were his teachers and instructors of this doctryne, he saith he may not nor will not confesse. But being further demanded what person he was, and what his name is, that was with him and talked with Mr. Abbott, parson of Hatfeild, he saieth he may not nor will not confesse the same.

XL

ARTHUR BELLOT TO LORD BURGHLEY, *CA*. 1592

This petition of Arthur Bellot is in Lansdowne MSS. 107, item 25, f. 44. It has not been printed previously, and it has not been used by earlier historians. It implies an earlier petition, since Bellot writes: "I do againe (as of right) appeale unto your Honor."

Bellot was twenty-four years old in 1592. He matriculated at Oxford University from Exeter College on July 30, 1585, having come from Lanteglos-by-Fowey in Cornwall. In 1590/1591 he was instrumental in the publishing at Dort of 2000 copies of Barrow's *A Brief Discovery* and 1000 copies of *A Plaine Refutation.* Almost all the books were seized at Flushing in April, 1591, and burned in June. Bellot was captured by Sir Robert Sidney, sent to Lord Burghley, who placed him in the custody of Archbishop Whitgift. We do not know the date of this petition, but we may surmise that the first appeal was made in the autumn of 1591 and the second appeal—the present petition—in the spring of 1592. We do know that he was at liberty in September, 1592, when the church was organized, and that he was a charter member. He was arrested again on March 22, 1592/1593, imprisoned for several years, exiled about 1595–1597, and died in February 1601/1602 at Amsterdam. Scipio is his brother.

ARTHUR BELLOT TO LORD BURGHLEY

Forasmuch (right Honor[a]ble) as the books I caused to be prynted, and which (I doubt not) your Honor hath taken viewe of, were dedicated to your Honor,[1] and committed to your Lordship

[1] *A Plaine Refutation* was dedicated to Lord Burghley but *A Brief Discoverie* has no dedication.

with my poore bodie, and for that your Lordship's wisdom and honorable care of Her Majestie's true subjects in the equitie of their causes, is notably apparant and manefested dayly, I do againe (as of right) appeale unto your Honor (to whom my cause everye way belongeth)[1] to have some just defence and protection, after my long and greivous emprisonment in great miserie and distresse.[2] For being (with much grief of heart), right Honorable, sent from your Lordship to the Archbishop and (as it seemeth) even committed into his hands, I was by him commanded close prysoner unto the Marshalsea, where (because of my povertie, not being able to defray chamber rent, having nothing for the provision or maintenance of life it self), I am cast into the common gaole,[3] and by reason of the same my povertie shall here end my dayes (as I see manie faithfull witnesses of Christ and true subjects to Her Majestie do in other prysons) without hope of release, except your honorable regard and pitie be shewed toward me.

The works themselves I assigne to the authors to be defended in christian tryall.[4] For me, I am both an infant in the faith of Christ, and having according to the corrupt education of gent[lemen] wasted manie of my young yeeres past. If through ignorance in the one, or rashnes in the other, I have offended God or Her Majestie, I would redily humble myself. Only now let it please your honorable Lordship to vouchsafe me some present succor and release, that in Her Majestie's service I might have some meanes to geat my lyving, and not thus to spend my tyme to my utter decay in this miserable emprisonment.

My life (right Honorable) lyeth in your hands, which shall, upon your honorable favor shewed, be at your Lordship's commandement in all things. Yea, howsoever, I shall not cease to pray

[1] The *Injunctions Geven by the Queene's Maiestie. Anno Domini 1559*, Article 51, gave some jurisdiction to the Court of High Commission, especially for pamphlets and ballads. The task of licensing books was essentially a prelatical function. The Star Chamber decree of June 23, 1586, increased the power of the Archbishop of Canterbury and the Bishop of London over printers. The statute of 23 Elizabeth, chapter II, applied to seditious books. Bellot prefers to negotiate with Lord Burghley rather than with Archbishop Whitgift, but he is in error if he is denying the Archbishop's jurisdiction.

[2] This seems to imply an imprisonment of perhaps a year. If so, the petition could be dated April, 1592. Bellot was probably bailed or released about June, 1592.

[3] The Marshalsea was a prison in Southwark, on the east side of Borough High Street, often used for debtors.

[4] *A Brief Discoverie* and *A Plaine Refutation*. For the story of their seizure and the capture of Bellot, see Carlson, *The Writings of Henry Barrow, 1590–1591*, pp. 370–377. See also Francis Johnson's letter of January 8, 1593/1594, to Lord Burghley, in Lansdowne MSS. 75, item 25, ff. 50–51. It is printed in chapter XLVIII.

for your Honor's preservation and prosperitie, to the glorie of God, comfort of his afflicted, and good of the whole land, and in the life to come eternall happines.

Your Lordship's in all humblenes and
respect of dutie
Arthur Bellot

Endorsement: Arthur Bellott imprisoned for printing certain books of religion. In the Marshalsea.

XLI

TO THE RIGHT HONORABLE THE LORDS AND OTHERS OF HER MAJESTIE'S MOST HONORABLE PRIVIE COUNSELL

This supplication is in Lansdowne MSS. 109, no. 12, f. 34. It was written in January, 1592/1593, and delivered, without success, to the Privy Councillors at the Court of Star Chamber in February. From Penry's cryptic and succinct entries in his diary we may glean the information that the petition was delivered to a custodian or clerk of the Star Chamber but not presented to the Privy Councillors or judges.

The occasion of the supplication was the seizure of the Separatist leaders. On the night of December 5–6, 1592, the pursuivants arrested the pastor, Francis Johnson, the teacher, John Greenwood, and a prominent layman, Edward Boyse. On December 17 or 24, Thomas Settle, a clergyman of the Church of England who had become a Separatist, and Daniel Studley, elder of the church, were seized. Thus five leading Separatists, including three officers, were added to the five Separatists already in prison—Henry Barrow, John Clark, George Collier, John Sparrow, and Roger Waterer. We do not know the dates for the arrest of Scipio Bellot, James Fowrestier, and Robert Stokes, but one or two of them also may have been in prison in December—prior to their examination or trial in March, 1592/1593.

When Barrow learned of the arrest of five Separatist leaders in December, 1592, he began thinking of an appeal to the Privy Council. Probably the rearrest of Thomas Settle and Daniel Studley about the first week in January precipitated his decision. One internal clue informs us that "about a moneth since" the pursuivants ransacked the home of Edward Boyse. Since this occurred on the night of December 5–6, 1592, we may date the writing about January 10. From Penry's too brief diary in his *Notebook*, page 39, we learn that it was delivered to the Privy Council in the Court of Star Chamber, February 20, the day after the opening of Elizabeth's eighth Parliament on Monday, February 19.

The author of the petition is clearly Henry Barrow, whose style, spirit, and phraseology are evident. Upon completion of his work, Barrow submitted the draft to Penry, who added the last three paragraphs and perhaps toned down some of Barrow's sharp sentences. The evidence for Barrow's authorship is found in the following statements:

1. "ministrie, ministration, worship, government." This series occurs three times in the petition, and is paralleled by an identical series in Barrow's introduction. See Carlson, *The Writings of John Greenwood, 1587–1590*, p. 108.
2. "put end to these long contynued controversies." This statement is paralleled by Barrow's letter of March 26, 1593, to Attorney-General Thomas Egerton, where he uses the words—"put end to theise present controversies."
3. "the bounds of our owne calling." The parallel, "the lymitts of owre calling" is in Carlson, *op. cit.*, p. 125.
4. "acknowledge her sovereigne and supreme power under God over all persons, causes, and actions civile or ecclesiastical." This is similar to Barrow's reponse: "acknowledg Her Majestie to be the supreame majestrate and governesse of all persons with in the church, and without the church, yea, over all causes ecclesiasticall and civill." See Carlson, *op. cit.*, p. 125.
5. Barrow three times uses the phrase "within the limites of our callings" or a close approximation thereof; once he refers to "the malignant synagogue of Antichrist." Both expressions are paralleled in his "Letter to an Honorable Lady and Countesse of His Kin[d]red Yet Living, April 4–5, 1593."
6. "this christian and peaceable course." In his letter of March 26, 1593, to Attorney-General Thomas Egerton, Barrow speaks of "a christian and peaceable conference."

Again, in his letter of March 28 to Egerton, Barrow pleads for "a christian and peaceable disputacion." In Carlson, *op. cit.*, p. 110, occurs the expression by Barrow of "this peaceable and christian triall."

In the last three paragraphs the tone changes. Barrow speaks as one in prison, but Penry is out of jail. Penry's phrases are apparent: "the Lord of heaven and earth," "justice and equitie," "a wofull charge," "innocent blood to be spilt," "wyves and succorless children." Penry uses such words as "beseech" and "craving" and "sighes and cryes" and "teares." Penry promises, pleads, threatens, and warns, but Barrow is defiant, intransigent, unbending. In the main, Barrow and Penry collaborated, but they may have consulted with Francis Johnson and others for suggestions.

TO THE RIGHT HONORABLE THE LORDS AND OTHERS OF HER MAJESTIE'S MOST HONORABLE PRIVIE COUNSELL

Your Honors' venerable authoritie, gravitie, and wisdome assembled in this high place of counsel for the redresse of abuses, and for the godly and peaceable government of this land under her most excellent Majestie, giveth us her poore oppressed subjects bouldenes, yet in all humilitie, to expose before your Honors our most lamentable usage and distressed estate. Whose intire faith unto God, loyaltie to our sovereigne, obedience to our governors, reverence to our superiors, innocencie in all good conversation toward all men, cannot avayle us for the safetie of our lyves, libertie, or goods, not even by Her Highnes' royall lawes, and the publike charters of this land, from the violence and invasion of our adversaries, Her Majestie's subjects. Whose dealing with us, your Honors shall further understand, when wee have breifly declared the true cause thereof unto you, which is this.

Her Highnes' publishing the holy Scriptures, and exhorting all her subjects to the diligent reading and sincere obedience therof in the[i]r callings, wee therby upon due examination and assured proofe finde the whole publike ministrie, ministration, worship, government, ordinances, and procedings ecclesiasticall of this land, by authoritie established, to be strange, and quite discenting from the rules of Christ's Testament, not to belong unto, or to have anie place, or use, or so much as mention in his church. But rather to belong unto, and to be derived from, the malignant synagogue of Antichrist, beeing the self same that the pope used and left in this land. Wherfore wee dare not by anie meanes defile or submit our selves in anie outward subjection or inward consent therunto; both in regard of the whole first table of God's lawe[1] to the contrarie, and of the wrath denounced, Revelation 14:9, 10, 11. And 18:14.

Againe, wee by the holy Scriptures finde God's absolute commandment that all which heare and beleeve the gospell of our Lord Jesus Christ, should forthwith thereupon forsake their evill wayes, and from thenceforth walke in Christ's holy faith and order together with his faithfull servants, subjecting them selves to that ministrie, those holy lawes and ordinances which the Lord Jesus hath appoincted, and wherby he only is present and reigneth in his church. Wherfore, both for the enjoying that inestimable comfort of his joyful presence and protection, and to shewe our obedience to God's holy commandement, wee have in his reverend feare and love drawen and joined our selves together in that christian faith, order, and communion prescribed in his Word; and subjected our soules and bodies to those holy lawes and ordinances which the Sonne of God hath instituted, and wherby he is present and ruleth his church here beneth. And have chosen to our selves such a ministrie of pastor, teacher, elders, deacons as Christ hath given to his church here on earth to the world's end. Intending through the promised assistance of God's grace (not withstanding anie prohibition of man, or what by man can be don unto us), according to God's holy commandement, to worship him aright, and to frame all our procedings according to the prescript of his Word;[2] and to leade our lyves in holyness and righteousnes before him in all dutifull obedience and humble subjection to their magistrates and governors set over us by the Lord.

Our attempts in both these, as well in forsaking the one as indevoring the other, we undertake and are redie before your

[1] The first table includes the first five commandments or religious prescriptions; the last five of the Ten Commandments are moral commands. See Exodus 20:3–12.

[2] This sentence is similar to the second point in Barrow's "A Breefe Sum of Our Profession." See Carlson, *The Writings of Henry Barrow, 1587–1590*, pp. 84, 119, 214.

Honors [to prove] against all men, as they are publikely avowed in the confession and practise of foreigne churches,[1] so to be warrantable by the Word of God, allowable by Her Majestie's lawes, no way prejudiciall to her sovereigne power, or offensive to the publike peace of this state, injurious to the lawfull authoritie and procedings of anie in the same, or without the limites of our owne place and callings. Likewise, what wee have doon in our publike procedings, the same to have doon in such christian and peaceable maner, as no one of Her Highness' subjects hath cause to complaine of injurie, molestation, or unquietnes doon or intended to them anie maner of way. Thus, right Honorable, standeth our case in all truth and uprightnes. It remayneth that you now heare a breife narration of our usage for the [sake of, shame of?] our adversaries.

Our only speciall adversaries that finde themselves offended hereat are the officers of Antichrist's kingdom, namely, the Romish prelacie and priesthood left in this land with such other their assistants as are made rich by the trafique of that sea [see]. Their dealing with us is and hath been a long time most injurious, outragious, and lawlesse. By the great power and high authoritie they have gotten into their hands, and usurp above all the publike courtes, judges, lawes, and charters of this land, persecuting, imprisoning, there deteyning at their pleasures our poore bodyes without anie tryall, release, or bayle permitted, yet or hitherto without anie cause eyther for error or crime directly objected, much lesse proved against anie one of us. Some of us they have now more than five yeeres thus deteyned in prison, yea, four of these five yeeres in close prison with much miserable usage, as Henry Barrow and John Grenwood it [at] this present in the Fleet. Others they have cast into the Lymbo of Newgate laden with as manie yrons as they could beare; others into the dungeons and lothsome gaole[s] amongst the most facinorous and vile persons.[2] Where it is lamentable to relate how manie of these innocents have perished within these five yeeres; and of those some aged wydowes, aged men, yong maydens, etc.[3] Where so manie as the infection hath spared still

[1] Some of the confessions or creeds of foreign reformed churches to which Barrow alludes were those of Helvetia, Basel, Bohemia, Belgia, Saxony, Augsburg, Württemberg, France, and Scotland.

[2] Quintin Smith was arrested in 1589, put in the dungeon or Lymbo of Newgate, and loaded with irons. Roger Waterer, age eighteen, was kept a full year in the dungeon with irons.

[3] The aged widows were Margaret Maynard and Alice Roe; the aged men were Nicholas Crane and John Debenham. The young maidens were Judith Myller, Anna Tailour, and possibly Margaret Farret.

lye in wofull distresse, like to follow their fellowes, if speedie redresse be not had. Others of us have been greevously beaten with cudgells in the prison, as at Bridewell, and cast into a place called "Little Ease," there for refusing to come to their chappell service; in which prison they and others of us not long after ended their lyves.[1] Upon none of us thus committed by them and dying in their prysons is anie search or inquest suffred to passe, as by lawe in like case is provided, and to all others is doon. Others of us, and those verie aged men, they have a long tyme kept in the White Lyon, where they still remaine without anie tryall, bayle, or pitie.[2]

Their manner of pursuing and apprehending us is with no lesse violence and outrage. Their pursevants with assistants break into our houses at all howers of the night (for such times to these exploits they for the most part chuse to hide their unchristian and cruel dealing with us from the world). There they breake up, ransake, rifle and make havock at their pleasures, under pretence of serching for seditious and unlawfull books. The husbands in the deepe of the night they have plucked out of their bedds from their wyves, and haled them violently to prison. Wherby one of their wyves, an honest and virtuous gentlewoman, being great with childe, and having her husband thus drawen out of her bed from her, who so frighted, as she fell into untimely travayle; the childe miscarid, and she with no smale hazard escaped.[3] Now againe about a moneth since their pursevants late in the night entred in the Queene's name into an honest citizen's house upon Ludgate Hill. Where after they had at their pleasures serched and ransaked all places, chests, etc., of the house, they there apprehended two of our ministers, Francis Johnson with out anie warrant at all, and John Grenwood; both whom, betwixt one and two of the clock after midnight, they with bylles and staves led to the Counter of Woodstreete. Taking assurance of Edward Boyse, the owner of this house, to be true prisoner in his owne house, until the next day that he were sent for. At which

[1] John Purdye was cast into "Little Ease" at Bridewell prison. This was a cell where the prisoner could not stand or walk or sit. His crime was refusing to attend the prison chapel service. He was also compelled to grind in the mill. Worst of all, he was beaten with a "great codgel very extreamly." No wonder he died in Bridewell. See Barrow's "Letter to Mr. Fisher" in Carlson, *The Writings of Henry Barrow, 1587–1590*, pp. 254–256.

[2] John Sparrow, or Sparewe, aged sixty in 1593, was imprisoned in the White Lion in Southwark on March 17, 1588/1589, and had not been tried. His "crime" was that of presenting a petition to the Queen.

[3] Probably a reference to Roger Jackson and his wife. See Carlson, *The Writings of John Greenwood, 1587–1590*, p. 313.

time the archbishop, with certeine doctors his associates, committed them all three to close prison; two unto the Clynke, the third againe to the Fleet, where they remaine in great distresse.[1] Since this they have caused Thomas Settle and Danyell Studley (lately taken in Nicolas Lane upon a Lord's day in our assembly by Mr. Richard Younge and committed to prison, but afterward bayled by the sheriffs of London) to be now againe called for, and committed close prisoners to the Gatehouse.[2] Others of us they have in like maner proscribed, and sent out their pursevants to apprehend.[3] So that there is no safetie to anie of us in anie place, no escaping their violent hands, or getting from them beeing taken, not even by Her Majestie's royall courtes and lawes, except your Honors stretch forth your handes to our succour, now you have heard our case and usage.

It were long to relate unto your Honors all their secret dryftes, and open practises, wherby they seek to draw us into danger and hatred. As by their subtile questions propounded, not having nor knowing anie matter to lay unto our charge. By their subornate conference, now almost three yeeres since, sent into the prisons to wel nie sixty faithfull Christians, whom they there against all law, and without anie cause, deteyned.[4] By indicting upon the statutes made for disloyall, idolatrous, recusant papists (whom yet after 33 yeeres' obstinacie they use not in this maner), though they know that wee sincerely hold all the grounds of religion published by Her Majestie in *Harmonie of Confession*,[5] and never refused anie

[1] On the night of December 5–6, the pursuivants arrested Boyse, Johnson and Greenwood. Boyse was sent to the Clink. Johnson was put in the Counter Wood Street and transferred to the Clink. Greenwood went to the Counter for a day or two and then was recommitted to the Fleet.

[2] Thomas Settle, a clergyman, and Daniel Studley, an elder, were arrested on December 17 or 24, 1592, imprisoned, bailed, and reimprisoned. On April 6 Settle said he had been in prison fifteen weeks. December 24 to April 8 would be exactly the period. But if he enjoyed bail for a week, December 17 is the more likely date for his arrest.

[3] Probably a reference to John Penry, by Penry himself, and possibly to the officers of the congregation still at liberty—George Knyviton, elder, Nicholas Lee and Christopher Bowman, deacons.

[4] This is a reference to fifty-two Separatists who had been imprisoned about January, 1589/1590. On February 25, John Aylmer, Bishop of London, acting by virtue of the archbishop's command and the powers of the Court of High Commission, addressed a letter to forty-three clergymen. They were ordered to go to the prisons and interview the prisoners with the purpose of making them conformable. In this purpose they signally failed. See the two defiant treatises which Barrow and Greenwood published, in Carlson, *The Writings of John Greenwood, 1587–1590*, pp. 103–262.

[5] The *Harmonia Confessionum Fidei, Orthodoxarum et Reformatarum* was published at Geneva in 1581. In 1586 an English translation appeared, "Alowed by Publique Authoritie," *An Harmony of the Confessions of the Faith of the Christian and Reformed*

wholesome doctrine or truth shewed us in God's Word, but only withstand such popish enormities as they bring in and urge contrarie to the Word of God. By defaming and divulging us as Anabaptists, though they be not able to charge us with anie one of their errors to our face.[1] As Donatists and schismatiks, though wee hould christian communion with all that truly hould and walke in the christian faith.[2] And though they will not by anie meanes be drawen to approve their owne ministrie, ministration, worship, government, ordinances, and procedings ecclesiasticall by the Word of God. As seditious conventiclers, though they be not able to detect us of anie action doon against the Word of God, or against the lawes of this land in our meetings. And though themselves by their tyrannie dryve us into these secret places and meetings. As abridgers of, and incrochers upon, the royall power of the Queene, though wee from the heart acknowledge her sovereigne and supreme power under God over all persons, causes, and actions civile or ecclesiasticall within her Highnes' dominions; though wee gladly obey, and never willingly breake anie of her godly lawes; though wee never attempted either secretly or openly of our selves to suppresse or innovate anie thing, how enormouse soever by publike authoritie established, but have alwayes conteyned our selves within the bounds of our owne callings, christianly refrayning such things as God hath forbidden us to doo; and indevoring to doo such things as Christ hath commanded his faithfull servants in his holy worship, patiently soffring whatsoever the arme of injustice shall doo unto us for the same, but alwayse leaving the reformation of the state to those that God hath set to governe the state. Yet are wee also accused as pernicious to the state and publik peace of the land, though wee endevour nothing but the pure worship of God and sincere obedience to the holy gospel of our Lord Jesus Christ, within the limites of our callings. Which though this cannot be made to accord to their kingdome and works of darknes, yett wee hope in anie christian judgment they will not be found contrarie or

Churches (Cambridge: Thomas Thomas, 1586). Later reissues were published in 1643, 1656, and 1842. In the *S.T.C.*, 5155, this item is listed under Christian and Reformed Church. In the British Museum Catalogue, it appears under Europe, Christian and Reformed. Although the book was published by authority, it was unpopular with the archbishop, who sought to suppress it. See John Morris, "Restrictive Practices in the Elizabethan Book Trade: The Stationers' Company *v.* Thomas Thomas, 1583–8," *Transactions of the Cambridge Bibliographical Society*, IV, Part IV, 1967.

[1] Robert Some called the Separatists Anabaptists.

[2] George Gifford denounced the Separatists as Donatists and schismatics.

offensive to anie godly government, or well ordered commonwealth. Likewise they verie untruly suggest that wee by our opinions and procedings utterly cut off and condemne her most excellent Majestie, your Honors, and all others not of our mynde as infidells, reprobates, etc. Wherein they much wrong your Honors and us. God knoweth our reverent judgment, loyall hearts, and intire love to you all, how wee seeke, desire, yea, and have hope of your salvation, as our owne. Wee may reproove and forsake their antichristian wayes and procedings, which God in his Word condempneth, yet not all into such horrible presumption and uncharitable prejudice. Otherwise the holy prophets, apostles, and faithfull men of all times, that have lyved in the feare and spoken in the name of God, shall by their reason fall into the like condemnation.

But, right Honorable, this dealing will not for ever uphold their ruinous kingdom, or (wee hope and pray) long keepe your Honorable Wisdoms from the sight and search of God's truth in these matters. Which if it may please your Honors but to permit to be tryed with them cannot longer be hid. Wee can but in all humble maner beseech, offer, and submit our cause and whole procedings to be tryed by the Scriptures of God with anie that is of contrarie or diverse judgment before your honorable presence. Where wee confidently undertake both to disprove their publike ministrie, ministracion, worship, government, and procedings ecclesiasticall established, as they vaunt, in this land. And also to approve our owne present course and practise by such evidence of Scriptures, as our adversaries shall not be able to withstand or gainesay without denying the most substanciall groundes of religion established by Her Majestie. Protesting if wee fayle herein, not only willingly to susteine such deserved punishment as shalbe inflicted upon us for our disorder and temeritie, but also to become conformable to their line and procedings, if wee overthrow not them, wee will not say, if they overcome us. Wee call not our adversaries herein to an uncerteine or unworthie conflict. For wee directly set downe the cause to be debated. Which is of great weight, as wherein their whole state, and our faithfull obedience to our Lord Jesus Christ, and to our sovereigne Queene in the Lord dependeth. Wee shewe them their adversaries of whom they have some in their hands. Wee lay downe the yssue of the disputation or conference, and the crowne of their reward. Wherby they shall not only approve and confirme their owne estate and doings vehemently now suspected, if not detected to manie, but therby also put end to these long contynued controversies, and confirme the troubled consciences of manie thousands of their owne ministers and others Her Majestie's most virtuous subjects that now stand doubtfully affected, and are dayly inclyning in judgment and practise unto us. This course therfore beeing the only meanes prescribed of God for the discussing and deciding of all doubts and differences that arise emongst his servants, and much better instructing or convincing the conscience than prisons and reproch, they cannot refuse or eschue, especially before your Honors, without great imputation and discredit to themselves and their cause. Our fewnes or unlearnednes (which they so disdeine before proofe) ought to be no let when this maketh the better for them, the more certeine and easie victorie, if they be so learned, and their cause so good, as they pretend.

Neither may your Honors without great charge denye, or anie longer defer, this christian and peaceable course prescribed and commanded of God in these cases. Seeing it tendeth to the appeasing and ending of great contention alreadie begun and like to increase. To the satisfiing manie doubtfull consciences. To thc writing and confirming our discenting myndes in the truth. To the advancement of Christ's kingdome, of God's pure worship. To the reformation of the great enormities and impietie of this land. And to the calling of all men to the obedience of the gospell of Christ in their callings. As these things are esteemed and deare unto your Honors, so wee beseech that our petition herein may be regarded, and this course propounded [may be] assayed for the obteyning the same.[1]

Likewise, right Honorable, in the meantime wee even in the name of God and of our sovereigne Queene beseech for the present safetie of our lyves from our adversaries' outrage and violence the benefit and help of Her Majestie's lawes, and of the publike charter of this land (to the observation and preservation whereof your Honors are sworne), namely, that wee may be received unto bayle until wee be by order of lawe convict of some crime deserving bands or this usage. Wee plight unto you our faith towards God, our allegeance to Her Majestie, and to your Honors, that wee will not commit anie thing willingly unworthie the gospell of Christ, or to the disturbance of the common peace and good order of this land. Also that wee wilbe redily forthcomming at such reasonable warning as your Honors shall command. It standeth not with your honorable estimation or justice to suffer us to be thus oppressed or punished, yea, thus to perish before tryall and judgment, specially imploring

[1] This ends Barrow's portion. The last three paragraphs are by Penry.

and crying out for the same unto you. Wee aske, right Honorable, but justice and equitie (which ought to be administred to the worst) and that for the safetie of our lyves. It were a most dolorous case, and a wofull charge to her Majestie, your Honors, and this whole land (whereat the enemies of God and of Her Majestie at home and abrode would greatly rejoyce, but all the faithfull wheresoever would sorrow and lament), if you shall suffer anie more of our innocent blood to bee spilt in this maner through your defalt, yea, now after this knowledge given and suite made, through your consent, by this malignant generation. Which God put in your hearts to foresee and to prevent.

Howsoever, wee here take the Lord of heaven and earth, and his angells, together with your owne consciences, and all persons in all ages to whom this our supplication may come, to witnes, that wee here have truly advertised your Honors of our cause and usage, and have in all humilitie offred our cause to christian tryall by the Scriptures, submitted our bodies to anie judiciall tryall by the lawes of this land, only craving upon our knees in the meane time the benefit of the lawes unto bayle for the safetie of our lyves. Now if your Honors shall neglect, you cannot from henceforth pleade ignorance, or be held guyltlesse. But all the innocent blood alredy shed by our adversaries together with the sighs and cryes of us your oppressed suppliants, and the teares of our desolate wyves and succorlesse children, shall incessantly day and night crye in the eares of our just Lord, and also rise in judgment against you in the day of all accompts. And wee shall here be inforced to profer our complaint, and appeale from you to our most gracious sovereigne, with whose pleasure or privitie wee are sure it standeth not that her innocent true hearted subjects, Christ's faithfull servants, should be thus used.

Whose gracious reigne God long contynue over us in all prosperitie to the good of his church, and her owne everlasting felicitie. God likewise blesse your Honors, and incline your hearts to commiserate and redresse the lamentable usage of us your distressed suppliants, who from our hearts detest all heresies, schismes, false worship, antichristian devices, and whatsoever is repugnant to God's holy Word, and endevour to obey both our Lord Jesus Christ in the sinceritie of his gloryous gospell revealed in his Word of truth, and our gracious Queene, your Honors, and all lawfull authoritie set over us, in the Lord our God, to whom be all glory, power and dominion for ever. Amen.

XLII

THE HUMBLE, MOST EARNEST, AND LAMENTABLE COMPLAINT AND SUPPLICATION, OF THE PERSECUTED AND PROSCRIBED CHURCH AND SERVANTS OF CHRIST, FALSELY CALLED BROWNISTS: UNTO THE HIGH COURT OF PARLAMENT

This complaint and supplication is in Harley MSS. 6848, f. 150. It was occasioned by the arrest and imprisonment on March 4, 1592/1593, of about fifty-six persons attending a conventicle in the woods at Islington. Penry was captured, but managed to escape the same evening.

In his biography of Barrow, Frederick J. Powicke assigns this petition to Barrow. See *Henry Barrow, Separatist*, p. 64. Powicke relies on a statement in *Mr. Henry Barrowe's Platform* ([Amsterdam?], 1611), D2 *recto*–D4 *recto*, that the draft of this petition, and some copies of it, were in Barrow's handwriting. It is quite possible that Barrow may have written out a copy or two, and it is also possible that he may have revised it. The use of the word "unbayleably" may be from Barrow, as Peel suggests, and the phrase "streames of innocent blood" is paralleled by the phrase "streames of christian bloode" which Barrow uses in his letter of March 26, 1593, addressed to Attorney-General Egerton.

Despite these considerations, we may say with confidence that Penry is the author. Penry himself is fond of the word "blood," and the phrase "streames of inocent bloud" occurs twice in his *Notebook*, p. 47. Barrow may have remembered the phrase and used it three weeks later. Again, we may note the sentence: "There are manie of us by the mercy of God still out of theyr handes." Since Penry was at liberty, and Barrow in jail, it seems highly probable that Penry is autobiographical in this observation. But the clinching argument for Penry's authorship is the presence of two drafts in his notebook, Ellesmere MS. 483, and published by Peel. About two-thirds of the first draft may be closely paralleled in the polished complaint and supplication, which is an expansion of Penry's work. If Powicke had seen the *Notebook*, he would have reconsidered his conclusion.

Penry wrote this petition about March 7. From Penry's diary entries we learn that it was delivered to Speaker Edward Coke of the House of Commons and to Sir John Puckering, Lord Keeper of the Great Seal, in the House of Lords, on March 10. The women who delivered the petition were Katherine Unwen, with Mrs. Penry or Mrs. Lee. It was disliked, especially in the House of Lords, and some of the members seemed to have dealt roughly with the petitioners. Justice Young summoned the women for delivering a copy to Speaker Coke and also to Sir Robert Cecil, who refused it. The next week Penry sent a copy to Lord Burghley, in the vain hope that its reception would be more favourable from the father than from the son.

There is deep indignation and almost frenetic frustration revealed in Penry's petition and letters. There is the spirit of the true Englishman demanding justice and there is the voice of the Welshman pleading for mercy and understanding: "Oh my Lord, yf you knew the misery wherin Hir Majestie's poor subjectes ly now in horrible dungeones and prisones for the testimony of Christ, I know you co[u]ld not but pitty them. Pitty them, my Lord, and deliver them, that the blessing of him that is ready to perish may follow my Lord Burlye and his house, overtake him, and cleave unto him for ever.

By him who unfaynedly desireth the aeternall good of your Lord in Christ Jesus.

John Penry"

Penry was not only willing to bless Lord Burghley, but also ready to perish in the cause. About ten days later he was arrested, and about ten weeks thereafter he died ignominiously at the end of a noose. A tragic injustice was added to the annals of history.

John Greenwood

THE HUMBLE, MOST EARNEST, AND LAMENTABLE COMPLAINT AND SUPPLICATION, OF THE PERSECUTED AND PROSCRIBED CHURCH AND SERVANTS OF CHRIST, FALSELY CALLED BROWNISTS: UNTO THE HIGH COURT OF PARLAMENT

The most high God, possessor of heaven and earth, bringeth at this present before your Lordships and Wisdomes (right Honorable) his owne cause, his owne people, his owne sworne and most trecherous enimies, together with the most shamefull usage of his truth and servantes that ever hath been heard of in the dayes of Sion's professed peace and tranquilitie.

His cause and people He offreth unto your consideration and defence in our profession and persons: his enimies and theyr outrage against his truth and servantes, in the persons and bloody procedinges of the prelates of this land and theyr complices.

Wee professe the same faith and truth of the gospel which Her Majestie, which your Honors, this whole land, and all the reformed churches under heaven this day doo hold and mainteine. Wee goe beyond them (beeing our only falt, even in the judgment of our most tyrannicall and savadge enimies) in the detestation of all popery, that most fearefull antichristian religion; and drawe neerer in some poinctes by our practise unto Christ's holy order and institucion. This is our faith, this is our cause (right Honorable), yea, the Lorde's cause in our sinfull handes.

For the profession and maintenance of which faith, the forenamed enimies of God deteine in theyr handes within the prisons about London (not to speake of other gaoles throughout the land) about threescore and twelve persons,[1] men and woemen, young and old, lying in cold, hunger, dungeons and yrons: of which number they have taken the Lorde's day last, beeing the 4th of this 3 moneth, March 1592 [1592/93], about some 56 persons[2] hearing the Word

[1] Here Penry says seventy-two persons. In Ellesmere MS. 483, which Albert Peel edited, *The Notebook of John Penry, 1593*, p. 48, Penry states that there were "about seventy-six persons, men and weomen, yong and ould, at this day [*ca.* March 7] in the prisons about London."

[2] In Peel, *Notebook*, pp. 46, 48, Penry estimates the number as fifty-six and "about sixty persones," who were committed by John Aylmer, Bishop of London, after the arrest on March 4. We have the names and examinations of thirty male prisoners who were captured. Therefore, we may estimate that the remaining twenty-six were wives and possibly a few servants or visitors. If we subtract fifty-six from seventy-two, we have sixteen persons who were in prison prior to

of God truly taught, praying and praysing God for his favors shewed unto us, unto Her Majestie, your Honors, and this whole land; and desiring our God to be mercifull unto us, unto our gracious Prince, and to our contrey. Beeing employed in these holy actions and no other (as the parties who disturbed them can testifie), they were taken in the very place where the persecuted church and martyres were enforced to use the like exercises in Queene Marye's dayes.[1]

The former nomber are now unbayleably committed by the prelate or Bishop of London etc. unto close (for the most part) severall prisons: as Brydewell, the Lymboe or dungeon in Newgate, the Fleet, the Marshalsea, the Counters, the Gatehouse, the Clynke, the White Lyon:[2] wherein wee willingly acknowledge the lott and inheritance in this life of our forefathers and brethren the holy martires of the former age, and the entayled Aceldema[3] or bloody possession of the Sea of London and that whole linadge. Well, heere our brethren lye (how long Lord, holy and true, thow knowest) in dungeons, in hunger, in cold, in nakednes and all outward distresse:[4] for these bloody men will allowe them neyther meate, drinke, fyre, lodging, nor suffer anie whose heartes the Lord would stirr up for theyr releif to have anie accesse unto them, purposinge belike to emprison them unto death, as they have doon 17 or 18 others in the same noysome gaoles within these 6 yeeres.[5]

March 4. This tallies exactly with the following list of persons who had been imprisoned previously: George Collier, John Greenwood, and Henry Barrow since 1587; John Clark and Roger Waterer since about December, 1589; Edward Boyse, Francis Johnson, Thomas Settle, and Daniel Studley since December, 1592; Christopher Bowman, Henry Brodwater, Christopher Diggins, and William Smithe since February, 1592/1593; Scipio Bellot, James Fowrestier, and Robert Stokes, whose dates of arrest are not given but probably since December, 1592, or 1592/1593. Greenwood was out on bail in 1592 and then remanded to the Fleet on December 6, 1592.

[1] They were captured in the woods at Islington.

[2] Of these prisons, the Bridewell, Newgate, Fleet, Counter Poultry, and Counter Wood Street were in London, as well as Ludgate Prison (unmentioned), where Thomas Mitchell was imprisoned; the Gatehouse was in Westminster; the Marshalsea, the White Lion, and the Clink were in Southwark.

[3] Aceldema, from the Greek *akeldama*, from the Syriac, ōkel damō, the field of blood, the potter's field, which was purchased with the thirty pieces of silver that Judas returned to the chief priests and elders. See Matthew 27:3–10, and Acts 1:16–20.

[4] There is something moving and rhythmical about this simple, realistic, despairing sentence.

[5] Ten died between 1588 and 1590, *viz.*, Georg Brightie, John Chaundler, Nicholas Crane, Richard Jackson, Widow Margaret Maynard, John Purdy, Widow Alice Roe, Thomas Stephens, Jerome Studley, and Henry Thomson.

Fourteen or fifteen died between 1590 and 1596. Of these, eight are not in the

The wife and husband beeing now taken by them, they permit not to be in the same, but have sent them to be closely kept in diverse prisons: what theyr poore familie doth at home in the meane tyme your Lordships may consider and justly pittie. Some of this companie had not anie penie about them when they were sent unto close prison; nor anie thing beeing abrode (which is the case of the most of them, if not of all) to procure themselves and theyr poore families anie maintenance, save only their handy labors and trades. Whereby it is come to passe, that these enimies of God doo not only starve and undooe a number of men in prison, but even a lamentable companie of poore orphanes and servantes abrode. Their unbrydled sclanders; their lawlesse privie serches; their violent breaking open and rifling of our houses; their lamentable and barbarous usage of woemen and young children in these hostile assaultes; theyr uncontrolled theeverye, robbing and taking of whatsoever they thinke meete from us in this case; their unappeased and mercilesse pursuite of us from our houses, trades, wives, children; but specially from the holy societie of the sainctes and Church of God, wee are enforced to omitt, lest wee should bee over tedious unto your Lordships. But theyr dealing this way toward us is so woefull (right Honorable) as wee may truly demaund with greife of heart, whether the forreigne enimie or our naturall contrymen doo possesse and beare rule over us in our deare and native contrey.[1]

Their whole dealing heerein is most barbarous, most inhumane, but especially most unchristian, and such as exceedeth the crueltie of the heathen and popish professed tyrantes and persecutors. The

list of those examined in 1593: Father John Debenham, Margaret Farret, John Gwalter, William Hutton (or Hawton or Howton), Walter Lane, Judith Myller, Roger Rippon, and Anna Tailour. They probably died in 1591 or 1592.

Those who died after April, 1593, were Robert Abraham, John Barnes, Scipio Bellot, Robert Boull, William Denford, Thomas Hewet. Thomas Drewet and Thomas Hewet may be the same person. If so, this would account for the seventeen or eighteen which Penry gives and the figure sixteen or seventeen which was given on the label on Rippon's coffin. The deaths of Anna Tailour, Judith Myller, and Margaret Farret, plus the earlier deaths of Widow Margaret Maynard and Widow Alice Roe, account for five of the twenty-four or twenty-five deaths in the period 1588–1596, plus the executions of Barrow, Greenwood, and Penry.

[1] The home of Edward Boyse was rifled on the night of December 5–6, 1592. About February 18, 1592/1593, the home of Nicholas Lee was ransacked. Mrs. Lee was roughly treated by Justice Young, and Mr. Lee was accused of treason. About February 19 George Johnson was "sorelie assayled by a pursuivant" but he escaped. On March 11, the prison cells of Henry Barrow and Scipio Bellot were rifled. Those involved in the coffin incident were probably harshly treated.

recordes of the heathen persecution under Nero, Trajan, Decius, Galienus, Maximinian,[1] and so forth can scant affoord us anie examples of the like crueltie and havock: for the heathen Romans would murther openly and professedly; these godlesse men have put the blood of warre about them in the day of that peace and truce which this land professeth to hold with Jesus Christ and his servantes. Bishop Boner,[2] Storye,[3] Weston,[4] delt not after this sort: for those whome they committed close, they would also eyther feed, or permit to be fedd by others; and they brought them in short space openly into Smythfeild to end their miserie, and to begin theyr never ending joye. Whereas Bishop Elmar, Doctor Stanope, and Mr. Justice Young,[5] with the rest of that persecuting and blood-thirstie facultie, doo neyther of these. No fellons, no murtherers, no traytors in this land, are thus dealt with.

There are manie of us by the mercy of God still out of theyr handes.[6] The former holy exercises and profession wee purpose not to leave by the assistance of our God. Wee have as good warrant to reject the ordinances of Antichrist, and to labor for the recoverie of Christ's holy institucions, as our fathers and brethren in Queene Marye's dayes had to doo the like. And wee doubt not if our cause were truly knowne unto her Majestie and your Wisdomes, but

[1] Nero (37–54–68), Trajan (52–98–117), Maximimus (173–235–238), Decius (200–249–251), and Gallienus (233–260–268) were all Roman emperors. Trajan in his correspondence with the younger Pliny reveals a cautious policy, and Gallienus permitted Christianity to continue as a *religio licita*. Better examples of persecuting emperors would be Domitian (51–81–96), Septimius Severus (146–193–211), Gallus (*c.* 205–251–253), Diocletian (245–284–305), and his fanatical son-in-law and co-regent Galerius (?–305–311). See Lactantius, *De Mortibus Persecutorum*, available in an English translation by Gilbert Burnet, *A Relation of the Primitive Persecutors* (Amsterdam, 1687). There is also a recent edition by Joseph Moreau, in Latin and French, in two volumes. Paris, 1954. See also Edward Gibbon, *The History of the Decline and Fall of the Roman Empire*, chapter XVI, and Philip Schaff, *History of the Christian Church*, II, *Ante-Nicene Christianity, A.D. 100–325*, chapter II.

[2] Edmund Bonner (1500?–1569), Bishop of London, 1539–1549, 1553–1559, a *bête noire* to Protestants.

[3] John Story (1510?–1571), Chancellor of the London diocese and active collaborator with Bonner in burning heretics. Executed for treason June 1, 1571.

[4] Hugh Weston (1505?–1558), dean of Westminster (1553–1556) and archdeacon of Colchester (1554–1557). Involved in the trial of John Philpot and Thomas Cranmer, and in the disputations with John Bradford, Nicholas Ridley, and Hugh Latimer. Found guilty himself of gross immorality.

[5] John Aylmer, Edward Stanhope, and Richard Young.

[6] This sentence points to Penry as author, since most leaders were in jail. Two officers of the church were at large, Nicholas Lee the deacon and George Knyviton the elder. The latter was captured with Penry on March 22—about two weeks after this supplication. Lee somehow escaped, although his wife was imprisoned for one day on February 17 for her part in the coffin incident.

wee should finde greater favor than they did, whereas our estate now is far more lamentable.

And therfore wee humbly and earnestly crave of her Majestie and your Lordships both for our selves abrode, and for our brethren now in miserable captivitie, but just and equall tryall according to her Majesti's lawes. If wee proove not our adversaries to bee in a most pestilent and godlesse course, both in regard of theyr offices and theyr proceedings in them, and ourselves to bee in the right way, wee desire not to have the benefit of her Majesti's true and faithfull subjects, which of all earthly favors wee accompt to bee one of the greatest. Are wee malefactors? Are wee anie wise undutifull unto our Prince? Maineteine wee anie errors? Let us then bee judicially convicted thereof, and delyvered to the civill authoritie; but let not these bloody men both accuse, condemne and closely murther after this sort, contrarie to lawe, aequitie and conscience, where they alone are the plaintiffes, the accusers, the judges, and the executioners of theyr most fearefull and barbarous tyrannie.

They should not by the lawes of this land goe anie further in cases of religion than theyr owne ecclesiasticall censures, and then referre us unto the civill power. Their fore-fathers, Gardyner,[1] Boner, Story, delt thus equally. And wee crave but this aequitie. Oh let her excellent Majestie our sovereigne and your Honours consider and accord unto this our just petition. For streames of innocent blood are likely to bee spilt in secret by these bloodthirstie men, except Her Majestie and your Honours doo take order with theyr most cruell and inhumane procedinges.

Wee crave for all of us but the libertie eyther to dye openly or to lyve openly in the land of our nativit[i]e. If wee deserve death, it beseemeth the majestie of justice not to see u[s] closely murthered, yea, starved to death with hunger and colde, and stifled in lothsome dongeons. If wee be guyltlesse, wee crave but the benefit of our innocencie, *viz.*, that wee may have peace to serve our God and our Prince in the place of the sepulchres of our fathers.

Thus protesting our innocencie, complayning of violence and wrong, and crying for justice on the behalfe and in the name of that righteous Judge the God of aequitie and justice, wee contynue our prayers unto Him for her Majestie and your Honours, whose heartes wee beseech Him to encline toward this our most aequall and just suite, through CHRIST JESUS our Lord.

[1] Stephen Gardiner (1483?–1555), Bishop of Winchester, faithful to Henry VIII, hostile to Princess Elizabeth, was associated with the statute "De Haeretico Comburendo" and the sentencing and burning of the first Protestant Marian martyr, John Rogers.

XLIII

TO THE MOST HONORABLE AND WORSHIPFULL MAGISTRATES OF OUR MOST MERCIFULL SOVERAIGNE LADY QUEENE ELIZABETH IN THEIR SEVERALL PLACES

This petition is in Harley MSS. 6848, ff. 2–7. It is a general petition, addressed to the magistrates, such as the members of the Privy Council, the judges of the national courts, the Lord Mayor of London, the local judges such as the Recorder of London and Justices of the Peace.

The petition consists of an introduction, together with a humble plea for mercy and understanding. This is followed by four motions or requests: that the Separatists should not be treated as papists, that they should be released from their imprisonment, or that they should be bailed upon security given. If the Separatists cannot be allowed to enjoy the same legal privileges and liberties accorded to the Dutch, French, and Italian churches in London, then let them have the benefit of the highest mercy and compassion.

The motions for mercy are followed by suggestions for achieving unity. In effect, the petitioners asked for a general conference or disputation, or at least a conference in which the Separatist leaders could participate, inasmuch as Edmund Campion and John Hart, both papists, had been granted a conference. They pleaded for an application of the Golden Rule, for ordinary humanitarianism, for persuasion by the Word rather than by the sword. Surely the way to achieve truth was not by dungeons and irons but by understanding and respect for tender consciences.

The date for this petition is April, 1593. The writer refers in graphic terms to the reprieve of Barrow and Greenwood on March 31 and speaks of the Separatists' "late experience" of Her Majesty's clemency. Although the Queen's mercy continued only for six days, the Separatists attributed the execution of Barrow and Greenwood to others—the bishops—who hastened the sad event by their importunity. There is one reference to "this mournefull moneth," which points to April.

The style, phraseology, and ideas all point to Francis Johnson as the author of this petition.

[TO THE MOST HONORABLE AND WORSHIPFULL MAGISTRATES OF OUR MOST MERCIFULL SOVERAIGNE LADY QUEENE ELIZABETH IN THEIR SEVERALL PLACES]

For Godde's sake
For Queene Elizabeth's sake
For Englande's sake and
For your owne sake,
peruse it with favoure;
it tendethe to mercy
and unitie.

THE FIRSTE PARTE OF A TRETISE CONTEYNING MOTIONS TOUCHING MERCIE AND UNITIE.

Sent by a few of those whoe are falslie and maliciouslie called Brownistes. For Christ's sake, for Queene Elizabeth's, for Englande's sake, and for your owne sakes, Peruse it, and neglect it not.

If the confession of offence against Her Majestie, in some falts escaped in those books and the suffering death for it by the two principall doers,[1] may be found sufficient punishment in conscience, for the qualletie of those falts: the Lord graunte that none maye diswade Her Highnes from her wonted mercy, but that some may have will and power to perswade Her Grace to pardon all former offences in theis poincts; and it shalbe a warning to us all to looke better unto that which our

[1] Barrow and Greenwood. The books referred to as faulty were those used in the indictment: (1) *A Brief Discoverie of the False Church*; (2) *A Collection of Certaine Sclaunderous Articles*; (3) *A Collection of Certain Letters and Conferences.*

penns lay downe (*quia litera scripta manet*), and we shall also be the more bounde, to praise our God, and to pray unto Him for her Majestie's most longe and prosperous raigne, and the present and everlasting comfort of her soule and boddie. [folio 2 *verso*]

TO THE MOST HONORABLE AND WORSHIPFULL MAGISTRATES OF OUR MOST MERCIFULL SOVERAIGNE LADY QUEENE ELIZABETH IN THEIR SEVERALL PLACES (SPECIALLY HER HIGHNES' MOSTE HONORABLE PRIVIE COUNSELL, IN THEIR DIGNETIES, HER REVEREND JUDGES IN THEIR SEATES, THE RIGHT HONORABLE THE LORD MAYOR OF LONDON, AND THE WORSHIPFULL JUSTICES THERE IN THEIRE ROOMES), TO ALL AND EVERIE OF THEM, ABOUNDAUNCE OF HEAVENLY WISDOME BE MULTEPLIED. [folio 3 *recto*]

In most humble and lamentable manner beseech your Honnours and Worshipps, a fewe of the poore people, falslie and maliciouslie called Brownistes, in behalfe of our selves at libertie, and more than threskore [three score] poore prisoners now shut up in the severall gaoles and prisons of this most noble cittie.[1] That whereas all the bookes, letters, wrytings, examinacions, speeches, and accions of anie particuler person, or of the whole congregacion, are undoubtedlie knowen to be quite contrarie to infidells, papists, and atheists. And whereas none can prove that we hold anie heresie, or mainteyne filthines amongest us (the thought whereof we thanke our God we abhorre). And lastlie, whereas we doe here protest before His heavenly majestie (whoe knoweth all secretts) that we hartelie desyer the glorie of our God to shine more and more in this nacion by increase of true holines and godliness in all the people thereof even with intire and fervent love to Him, our Queene, and one an other, togeather with the abundant peace, plenty, and prosperretie of our countrie, and all this under the longe and most blessed government of our dread and soveraigne ladie and Queene Elizabeth to Melchisedeche's

[1] My list of prisoners examined totals fifty-two, which is reduced to fifty after the execution of Barrow and Greenwood. I estimate that about twelve wives were also in prison. Scipio Bellot should be added, but we have no examination for him.

age, if such be His good pleasure (whose princelie spirits and boddie we praye that He will refreshe or renew as He doth the eagle's bill). It may therefore please your Honnours and Worshipps for God's sake to increase all charitable thoughts of us, and to be mercifull unto us as our heavenlie Father is mercifull, and as our noble Queene doth plentifully and daylie imitate Him* therein: hereof we have late experience by her Highnes' prolonging our deare Mr. Barrowe's and Mr. Greenewood's life, when the instruments, and man, and sheetes, and flowers, and grave, of death were all prepared, and they both reddie (as they had lived togeather like two turtles) to yeld up their sperits togeather (like two lambs) in all meekenes and obedience;[1] now blessed be our God for such a ruler of his people; let them deepelie repent or perishe forever that once seeke one drop of her bloud, or peece of her land, or blemishe to her renowme.

* Sequens pagina explanat (in fine)

What is our cheife request in this introduction? Having twoe or three motions concerning mercy, and more touching unetie, whereby we verelie hope that this controversie shalbe the sooner taken up, wee most humblie beseech yow to harken unto them with patience and then to favour them so farre as they shalbe found godlie, lawfull, and convenient. Ye reverend magistrates, ye gods (so called in the Scriptures,[2] because yow are in his stede to doe righteous judgment uppon the earth), hath not the Almightie given yow understanding to trye the depth of all attempts within this land? Wee trust He hath, oh search us deeper then, try our wayes, and if none can alleadge anie thinge against us save onelie this one error (if it be so) touching the law of our God.* Deale tenderlie with tender consciences; wee are yet perswaded that we shold shew our selves disobedient and unthankfull to our Maker, except we hold fast this cause: yow know not how rich His mercie hath ben unto us, for we verelie suppose that yow never offended His Divine Majestie so much or so often as most of us have donne (like the prodigall childe, yea, like Mary

* Like Daniel's case Chapter 6:5

[1] This is the reprieve granted on March 31 a few minutes before the intended execution. The halters had been placed around their necks.
[2] See Psalms 82:6 and John 10:34, 35.

Magdelin), but He hath wasshed us and clensed us, and given us unspeakable joye and peace of conscience sence we came to this companie: mervell not then at our zeale, but pittie us and helpe us wherein yow know it to be a misse [amiss, faulty, improper]. Behold a people wholly bent and vowed to serve the God of heaven in that course which they may perceive to be most tending to holiness and righteousnes. If your Honnours and Worshipps can bring anie to shew us that we shall doe more true service to our God, our Queene and countrie, by comyng to the parish assemblies, verelie we will harken unto them without obstinacy (and o that some of yow wold be the witnesses and judges).[1] Alas, it is not our worldlie ease to be thus tossed as we are, it is onely this matter of conscience that causeth all our sufferings, and your troubles with us.

Wherefore for Christe Jesus' sake (whose true servauntes we strive to be), for Queene Elizabeth's sake (whose true subjects we are), for Englande's sake (whose loving countrymen we remaine), and for the honnour of your owne names and helth of your owne soules, let no man cause yow to fixe your eies and your thoughts whollie uppon that our supposed falte (or falt indeede), but rather uppon some holie and mercifull meane whereby this our too much heate may be cooled and tempered (if it be adust [seared]) in all meekenes and love. Howe? As becommeth them, that wold spend their blood against the Pope and Spanishe kinge to deale with those that are most willing to doe the like; as it becometh Englishmen to deale with Englishmen, Protestants with Protestants, fathers with their children, and breifely Christians with Christians; men and fathers, if yow cannot helpe us presentlie, yet suffer us to ease our hartes a little by expressing our wounds, sorrowes, and suits at large (even as a childe mourneth to the nurse) under God, we have no helpe but our Queene and yow. And whoe knoweth whether He will (even this mournefull moneth),[2] by increasing our

[1] That is, let us not be judged by the bishops or the Court of High Commission.
[2] April, 1593. Penry was executed May 29, almost eight weeks after the deaths of Barrow and Greenwood.

afflliccions, cause yow to behold our loyaltie and innocency more than ever yow did, and thereby release us the sooner; the mercy of God, and the mercifull inclinacion of our most gracious Queene, doth feede us with undoubted hope, that so manie of the rest of us as cannot be found traitors or herretickes, shall yet fynde favour and pardon. The God of Daniel, our most mercifull Father, graunte all true wisdome and prosperetie to our most gratious Queene Elizabeth, and to as manie of yow and yours as desyer to increase in true feare and love and service of that mighty God of Izraell. Amen.

MOTIONS TENDING TO MERCY

First that it may please your Honnours and Worships (the promysses christianlie pondered) never to hearken unto them, whoe shall goe aboute to perswade yow that this people deserve the like terror and punishment, as treacherous and idolatrous papistes doe.

Secondlie, that it may please yow to take order for releasing theis pore distressed Protestantes, freelie from those contagious gaoles, yf that may stand with lawe and conscience.

Orels, to baile them uppon sufficient securetie, to answer at a reasonable warning unto whatsoever shall be objected against them.

Lastlie, yf it be not thought convenient that wee her Majestie's naturall and loving subjects shold have the same libertie graunted us in the worship of God, which Her Highnes giveth to strangers, French, Dutche, and Italian (sithe our practise is no other in every cheife poinct, than that of theirs, and Geneva, and all other reformed churches). Yet that we maye have *summam misericordiam*, not *summum ius: sed quorsum hec de gallis*, etc.? *Inuidus alterius? Non equidem inuidemus* (*honoratissimi et nobilissimi viri*) *miramur magis undique totis usque a deo*, etc. *En nos*, etc: (*sed tempus non datur*).[1]

The other motions tending to unitie (which wee trust wilbe acceptable to your Honnours and Worshipps) shalbe now alsoe

[1] Yet that we maye have the highest mercy, not the highest law (or right): but to what purpose these points regarding the Gauls, etc.? Envious of another? Indeed, we are not envious (most honorable and noble men), we marvel the more in all respects, even from God, etc. Among us, etc. (but time is not given).

delivered to yow and more partes,[1] God willing, very shortlie, yf theis firste, and the women that bring them, doe finde such favour in your eies, as not to be turned back or misliked; otherwise wee know not what course to take (so greate is our misery and want of men and meanes to expresse it). Wee are like enough to offend in not writing with such discression as we ought, and they in not delivering with such modestie as they shold; but wee are simple men, and they are silly women.[2] Therefore howsoever either wee now or others of late have failed in manner or matter, wee most humblie beseech your Honnours and Worshipps to be perswaded, that it was not for lack of care and conscience, but onelie for want of judgment and experience, and therefore to pardon us the sooner. If he that hath but his foote out of joynct can scarce doe anie thing currantly, what can they doe whoe have all their cheife members troubled and almoste quite cut of[f]? No marvell yf their acc[i]ons be distempered (some too violent, some too cold). In such a case have we ben theise manie weekes. The knee (as it were) is faine to ronne for the foote and a few little fingers (which co[u]ld never helpe them selves) to labour for the whole bodie; howbeit we truste that in such times and cases, your Lordships and Worshipps will ymmitate all godly men of trades (*si liceat magna paruis*) when children or servaunts are sent unto them, they will give better ware and measure, and dispatch them sooner than yf the parents them selves shold come to buye; necessety compelleth us to make mone [moan] and signes unto yow: ah barre us not of that comfort, for then shall our greate distresse be made unspeakable. *Heu, quanta miseria est, in tormento, nec vocem, nec pennam, nec signum habere: O vos qui dii appellamini, nolite istiusmodi silentiam iniungere: ferme omnes perimus (dolore et paupertate oppressi); iuniores carent gubernatione, et aliqui seniores sepulti sunt: si non remedium statim, saltem lachrymas, suspiria, declarationes, supplicationes, et verba concedite (presertim matri pro filio, sorori pro fratre, uxori pro marito). Aliter, regia (quasi) petendi via obstructa erit, quod adhuc non factum esse vidimus (Deo gratias). Ecce*

[1] This statement implies that the introduction, the "Motions Tending to Mercy" and the "Motions Tending to Unitie" were written first. Included in the "more partes" are the petitions to the Privy Council and the Lord Mayor. See *infra.* On June 12, 1593, when Francis Johnson petitioned Lord Burghley, he wrote: "I have made bolde to send inclosed an humble petition to Her Most Excellent Majestie." See Harley MSS. 6849, f. 143 *recto.*

[2] The petition of January, delivered February 20 to the Privy Council at the Court of Star Chamber, was rejected. The women who presented a petition to both Houses of Parliament on March 10 were roughly treated—especially Mrs. Unwen, who was imprisoned for delivering the petition.

feminas petentes pro charissimis suis in causa lamentabili, cum motionibus honestis, legitimis et piis: Estote misericordes, qui sub Deo et Elizabetha (ipsius Ancilla Regina nostra) judicatis et gubernatis Angliam.[1]

In all humble and pittifull manner wee intreate yow not to make question whoe shold begynne to releive us. But as we have joined yow all in one humble peticion: soe all of yow to joine togeather in one christian compassion and everie one in his place according to his lawfull aucthoritie to helpe us. The cause whie we made our direction thus generall, was, to the ende that one or a few coppies might passe from manie handes to many hartes. Wee beseech yow then, send our papers from one to an other, and lett our lamentable case remaine in your bosome till there be some godlie and mercifull order taken for us.

Whereas we spake of her Majetie's imitacion of God in mercy, lest some might misconster [*sic*] us as liers or flatterers,[2] thus we say. We are persuaded that their reprive as from Her Highnes, was in mercy, and that their execution (sone after) was rather importuned and hastened by others than easily consented unto by her Grace, for hath she not ben alwaies very mercifull to her veriest enemies? Therefore howsoever it fell out, we still retaine a good hope of Her Majestie's favour towards us when God shall find meanes to revele our inocencie unto her, and still we pray that nothing may withdrawe our loiall harts from her. [folio 4 *recto*]

THE SECOND PARTE

MOTIONS TENDING TO UNITIE

1. That yf we maie not heare publique conference for anie in-

[1] Alas, how great is our misery, being in torment, because we do not have any sign, neither a voice nor a pen. O ye who are called gods, do not impose silence of that sort. Almost all of us are perishing, afflicted by grief and poverty. The young people are lacking in governance and some elders have been buried. If there is not relief immediately, at least yield to tears, sighs, declarations, supplications, and words, (especially to a mother for her son, to a sister for her brother, to a wife for her husband). Otherwise, as it were, the royal way of seeking will have been obstructed, which up to the present time we have seen has not come to pass (thanks to God). Behold women seeking for their dearest ones in a mournful cause, with motions (emotions) which are honest, legitimate, and pious. Be ye tender-minded, who serve under God and Elizabeth—His handmaiden, our Queen—for administering and governing England.

[2] That is, to praise the Queen for a temporary reprieve when the leaders were executed seems insincere and inconsistent. The Separatists liked to think that the Queen was their friend and the prelates the enemy.

convenience (in regard whereof it were better we shold suffer mischeif), yet that our teachers may (in our hearing if it be thought meete) have such as was graunted Campion and his fellowes.[1]
2. Orels, that there may be some conference betwene two or three of either side, before a good nomber of your Honnours and Worshipps in some private chamber, the manie questions agreed uppon before hand (with preparacion by fasting and prayer), and when the tyme commes, omytting all tauntes and by matters, onely searching the truth in love. To the touchstone, to the lawe and the Testament.
3. Orels such a conference as was graunted Hart, the papist. Yf it be objected that none of our side are worthie to be thus disputed or wrytten with (publiquelie nor privately), wee thinke that this will prove the contrary, *viz.*, because there are three or four in this cittie and more els where, whoe have been zealous preachers in the parish assemblies, not ignorant in the Lattin, Greeke, and Hebrew tongues (nor otherwayes unlerned) and generally confessed to be of honest conversacion.[2] To be breife, as gentle and lerned Mr. Reynoldes of Oxford[3] and others like him are yet alive, so are there right honorable and godlie disposed personages of Sir Fraunცis Walsingham's minde (and alyance and mynde), whoe have power, wee know, and good will, we hope, to furder such lawfull mocions tending to so good precious [?] purposes.

If these mocions take effect wee are verely perswaded that the controvercy will soone ende (with all or moste of us), for by theis meanes shall wee poore wretches whoe onelie make this sepperacion (as knoweth the Lord) for love we have to kepe His commaundimentes and for feare to disobey Him, perceive more plainely

[1] Edmund Campion was granted four conferences, on August 31, 1581, on September 18, 23, and 27, with two sessions each day. It would be more correct to say they were thrust upon him, with no opportunity for preparation. He was still suffering from severe torture, had no friends to help, and no books to consult. Arrayed against him were some of the most learned men of the times: on August 31, Dean William Day and Dean Alexander Nowell; on September 18 and 23, Provost Roger Goad and Dr. William Fulke; on September 27, Dr. John Walker and William Charke. William Whitaker and John Feild served as notaries. Such a conference would never have been acceptable to the Separatists, who suffered from the illusion that in any free conference their cause would be proved superior and more Scriptural. See [Alexander Nowell and William Day *et al.*], *A True Report of the Disputation or Rather Private Conference Had at the Tower of London with Ed. Campion Iesuite* (London, 1583 or 1583/1584).

[2] Perhaps a reference to Stephen Egerton, Walter Travers, Edward Philips, Thomas Sparke, and Laurence Chaderton.

[3] Dr. John Rainolds, or Reynolds, was president of Corpus Christi College, Oxford. He participated in the conference with John Hart, the papist, in 1582. See his report, *The Summe of the Conference betwene John Rainoldes and John Hart: Touching the Head and the Faith of the Church* (London, 1584).

whether (as men and simple soules) we be deceived by a false light, orells (as his deare children) (for soe we hope) honored and trusted with the first view of and faithfull standing in a cause of holines and righteousnes. Wherefore in most humble and earnest manner, and even as yow feare God and love righteousnes (and as yow strive to resemble Him in liking better of them that are hott, than of those that are luke warme). We intreate your Honnours and Worshipps to labour in obteyning theis or some better mocions for procuring unitie and mercye, that so the blessings, promysed to mercifull men and peacemakers, maye light upon yow and yours, and the curses threatened for the contrarye maye be farre from yow. Ye reverend magistrates and noble guides of this most florrishing common welth, we beseech yow againe and againe in the Lord Jesus, searche your selves narrowlie when you seeke him whome your soule loveth and thinke how yow wold desyer to be dealt with yf yow were in our case, and so deale with us and our teachers; if yow suppose them and us to be in a grevious error, for common humanitie's sake (were there no further cause) let us not perishe either secretly in prisons or openlie by execucion for want of that utermost helpe which lyeth in your power to afford them that are not obstinate.

If anie adversary shall object that we are worthie of close ymprisonments in most contageous ayre, withoute bayle, and unworthie of having or hearing anie greate prepared conference or of anie favour because some of us have ben conferred with alreadie,[1] and yet remaine in greate error as lerned men judge, we make this answer, and praye eache one of tender harte to ponder it deepelie.

God forbid that all they whoe erre greately in some opinions shold have no other meanes to convert them but sodden unequall conferences by startes (with snatching and catching) without good order and indifferent hearing and judges (such have all or the moste of our conferences ben), and then yf they will not by and by yeild, be thought worthie of as bad prisons as theeves and roges: the Holy Ghoste seemeth to be of another mynde, II Timothy 2: 24, 25, 26, even towardes those whoe are in "the snare of the devill taken prisoners by him to doe his will" (can we be worse than such?).

[1] The leaders of the Separatists had been conferred with, or examined, by high legal officials. Francis Johnson had been examined by Judge Popham and once by Judges Anderson and Popham. George Johnson and William Smithe were examined by Popham and Anderson. Boull, Fowrestier, Stokes, and Studley were officially examined by Popham, Anderson, Attorney-General Egerton, and Dr. Stanhope. Penry was questioned by Mathew Dale, John Barne, Henry Fanshawe, Edward Coke, Robert Temple, Richard Vaughan, William Aubrey, Richard Cosin, Thomas Egerton, and Edward Stanhope.

And also Gallatians 6: 1, 2, 3. O that the bisshopes and all the zealous preachers of this land, wold aske their owne harts whether we have ben soundlie and lovinglie delt with according to theise rules. If they be true pastors to us, then though we goe a straye and be intangled in errors (as sillye sheepe with thornes), yet ought they to follow us, seeke us up, and unlose us with all tendernes (not so much for feare of loosing of our fleece as of our soules). The love of a naturall brother is greate, and will not easely cease, but more of a naturall mother but much more of a supernaturall father (such are pastors and therefore they will not easely give over the leaste and leanest of their flocke, though he have a greate disease, a greate error). O why then doe theise or anie of them so revile us in their bookes and common speeches, whie do they wish and perswade the civil magistrate to deale with us by the sword and not by the Word, by prisons and not by perswations, whie doe they use us thus whiles we praye for them and wish them no more harme than we desyer to our owne soules and bodies, naye, whilest we grone and longe to heare some of them, so wee might do it with a saife conscyence? Is there no other remedy but yf wee erre we must be thus dealt with? Alas, our first parents Adam and Eve did fall; the patriarks had their faltes, the holiest prophets were not free from them, the appostles erred and dissented, the auncient fathers of the prymative church retracted divers opinions, greate parliamentes and generall counsells have fouly erred. The lerned of this age, yea, of this land (naye of one profession and church) differ very much in judgment aboute moste of the same poinctes which we doe, and whoe is cleere from synne, error, and ignoraunce?[1] But so longe as men are not in herresy, nor in trechery, nor in filthie conceipts, nor in obstinacy, but erring (yf they doe faile) on the right hand in poincts uncondempned, still hating all falce wayes and loving the pathes of righteousnes, thus long there is apparant mercy in the Moste High, and so is there in those pastors, those magistrates, those people whoe have feeling compassion (when God brings meanes whereby they understand the truth of accions). As for dungeons, irons, close ymprisonment, honger, cold, want of meanes to mainteyne their famulies, theise may cause some to make shipwrack of a good conscience or to lose their life, but they are not fitt wayes to perswade honest men to anie truth or diswade them from errors.

[1] These two sentences about differences in judgment are closely paralleled by the paraphrases in Lansdowne MSS. 109, no. 14, ff. 37–40. See *infra*, p. 429.

Her Majestie hath shewed greate mercy to her undoubted enemies, the trecherous papistes. What then wold her Majestie shew to us yf she knew that which some of yow doe now see. O that Her Grace and yow did understand of all our accions, and did see the severall declaracions of our faith and loyalty (longe sence penned). Wee shold not then be longe in such hazard of utter spoyle to our bodyes and myndes (of evel ayre and dyet) and of the poore remnant of our goods, and of our families' distruccion through lacke of guiding. Doubtles, right Honorable and Worshipfull), unles there be some speedie and mercifull order taken with us, both wee our selves are like to perishe in the gaoles (as divers of our bretheren and sisters have donne) and our families and housholds fall to utter ruen and decaye through want of government and teaching. Alas (reverend fathers), what is youth without governement? And what governement can there be in those howses whose shop windowes are alwaies shut, whose masters are continuall prisoners, whose dames are dayly cold sutors,[1] and whose teachers and overseers are so enclosed as they cannot performe any dutie unto them upon the Lord's day, or wekely from howse to howse? Mercifull magistrates, yf anie of yow fynde the bowells of your christian compassion stirred by theise lamentable yet true reportes, let not your eyes rest untill your hearts have made a promise to cause your tonges to speake, and your bodies to labour for mercy and unetie. And the God of righteousnes graunte that yow maye fynde peace and favour with Him in the dayes of trouble, sicknes, and death (whereto all flesh is subject). Amen

[1] In Lansdowne MSS. 109, the reading is: "Whose dames are contynuall suters.

XLIV

TO THE RIGHT HONORABLE, THE LORDS AND OTHERS OF HER MAJESTIE'S MOST HONORABLE PRIVIE COUNSELL

This petition to the Privy Council is found in Lansdowne MSS. 109, no. 14, ff. 37–40. It includes "A Breife Declaration of Our Faith and Loyaltie to Her Majestie," possibly influenced by Penry's "Confession of Faith" and "Apology," and probably stimulated by a set of fifteen articles which attacked the Separatists. These articles were entitled: "An Abstract of the Opinions Which the Brownists Do Mainteyn." A second part of the petition sought to refute two rumours circulated against the Separatists, *viz.*, that they denied the role of the hierarchy and the magistrates, and that they were heretics and schismatics.

The petitioners denied the rumours and charges. They asked for an impartial trial and requested that the Separatists in prison might be bailed upon adequate security until formal charges were brought against them.

The date of this petition is about April or May. One reference to "this spring tyme" provides a clue. The date probably is subsequent to the execution of Barrow and Greenwood on April 6, to the adjournment of Parliament on April 10, and to the examinations of the Separatists which were concluded on April 24. Perhaps May 10 would be a fairly close conjecture.

The writer of this petition, I believe, was Francis Johnson, imprisoned since December, 1592, in the Clink. Barrow and Greenwood had been executed, and Penry was a close prisoner in the Counter Poultry. Therefore, we may narrow the possible writers to such persons as Thomas Settle, William Smithe, and Johnson. There are similarities in the style of this petition and the writings of Johnson. The parallels found in Johnson's petitions of June 2 and June 12, 1593, and of January 8,

1593/1594, with those of the present petition and the preceding general petition to the magistrates, are sufficiently close in phraseology and ideas to point to Francis Johnson as the author. It is quite possible that other Separatists, in and out of prison, helped to prepare the fair copy, and perhaps to improve and edit the original draft. Nevertheless, certain characteristic phrases and ideas of Johnson are apparent: "be a meane," "humbly beseech," "if such be His will," "pittie our lamentable case," "that you knewe the truth," "the magistrates wee reverence." Several longer striking parallels are indicated in the footnotes.

TO THE RIGHT HONORABLE, THE LORDS AND OTHERS OF HER MAJESTIE'S MOST HONORABLE PRIVIE COUNSELL

Right Honorable, though our extreme calamities by sicknes, wantes, greifes, and troubles in noysome and yrksome prison, would urge us to a large discourse, yet the knowledge of your manifold affaires in the common wealth doo enjoyne us to brevitie. Therfore wee most humbly beseech your Honors at this tyme to reade and consider of a verie short declaration of our loyaltie, twoe breife answeres to certeine rumors, and one petition concerning our present estate. And as your Honors finde our petition reasonable, our answeres christian, and our loyaltie entire to our sovereigne prince, so wee intreate you for God's sake to be a meane to relieve us, especially them who are knowne to be in extreme distresse by sicknes and want.

A BREIFE DECLARATION OF OUR FAITH AND LOYALTIE TO HER MAJESTIE

Christ's lawes

1. Wee fully acknowledge our duties to obey and practise within our callings the lawes of Christ Jesus our heavenly kinge in and about all thinges, worshiping Him according to the rules of Christ's Testament, because the same are perpetuall,

immutable, most holy, just and wise, only thought meete in his owne wisdome for all tymes, places, and persons, and therfore upon payne of damnation to be embraced of all men.[1]

Title

2. Wee fully acknowledge Her Majestie's title to the crowne by right discent [descent] from the undoubted kinges of this realme, her most royall progenitors.[2]

Supremacie

3. Wee fully acknowledge Her Majestie supreme governesse in magistracie over all persons and causes within Her Highnes' dominions, within the church or without.[3]

Prayer for Her Majestie's person

4. Wee fully acknowledge our duties to pray for the preservation of her royall person, and that they are negligent whoe forget this dutie, that they are atheists who contemme it, and that they are traytors who denie it.

Landes and goods

5. Wee fully acknowledge our duties to yeild the halfe or whole of all our landes and goods towardes the maintenance of her princely estate, or other benefit of our contrey, whether by way of benevolence, subsedies, takings or such like, without grudging, being by due order exacted.

Our prince's lawes and statutes

6. Wee fully acknowledge our duties to obey the lawes and statutes of this land so far forth as they are agreeable to Christ's,[4] and patiently to suffer

[1] This is a subtle assertion of the Puritan position on church government and discipline and officers. Johnson may be thinking of Bishop Thomas Cooper's challenge. In his *An Admonition to the People of England, 1589*, Cooper wrote: "Onely this I desire, that they will lay downe out of the worde of God some just proofes, and a direct commaundement, that there should bee in all ages and states of the Church of Christ, one onely forme of outwarde governement. Secondly, that they will note and name some certaine particular churches, either in the Apostles' time, or afterward, wherein the whole governement of the Church was practised, onely by Doctours, Pastours, Elders, and Deacons, and none other, and that in an equalitie, without superioritie in one above an other" (Arber's edition, p. 62).

[2] See the similar language in "A Short and True Answer to the Partycular Slanders Conteyned in These—15—Most False and Malycyous Artycles": "We gladly acknowledge Her Majestie to be our lawfull and soveraigne Prince by right descent from the undoubted right kinges of theis realmes, her royall progenitors." See Burrage, *Early English Dissenters*, II, 78. The author is not Penry but Johnson.

[3] See the letter of Johnson to Lord Burghley, June 2, 1593, p. 439, for a similar statement.

[4] The proviso is important: "so far forth as they are agreeable to Christ's."

for not obeying those which eyther wee rightly take, or (as men may erre) doo mistake, to be contrarie to His, without thought of making newe or altering old ones (how unequall soever they were), which things no subject (say wee) hath anie warrant to doo.

Officers — 7. Wee fully acknowledge our duties to obey all christian civill officers (or the heathen, if wee were under their government) from the prince in the throne, to the meanest officer at his plough or trade, as constable or anie such like.

Bodies — 8. Wee fully acknowledge our duties to be readie at all tymes with our bodies to be employed in peace or in warre, at home or abrode, in anie service to God's glorie, and our Queene and contrey's safetie.

Bodies and lyves to suffer — 9. Wee fully acknowledge our duties to yeild our members and lyves to what maner prison, punishment, or death so ever, whether justly or wrongfully inflicted rather than resist the higher powers.

Our duties generally to all men — 10. Wee fully acknowledge our duties to doo good to all men, as becommeth Christians. Therfore, touching our whole contrey, even the most ignorant, willfull, obstinate and wicked, thus wee say: whatsoever knowledge, good name, health, wealth, joy in this world or in the world to come wee wish for our selves, let us never enjoy anie of these, if wee wish not the same to as manie of them as feare God, love their prince and contrey, and obey Her Majestie and her lawes in such maner as wee have described. Unto the rest wee pray and wish for repentance with amendement of life.

SHORT ANSWERES UNTO TWO RUMORS GYVEN OUT AGAINST US

The rumor goeth that wee differ from all the land in some opinions, gainesaying not only the bishopps and whole clergie, but

Disputations and conferences broke down on the interpretation of Scripture, *e.g.*, Matthew 18:17: "Tell it unto the Church."

magistrates and all the whole land, and therfore no pryson too vile, nor anie punishment too grevious or too long for us.

Right Honorable, the magistrates wee reverence in thought, word, and deede; for the other this consequent is verie hard and unmercifull; blessed be God that hath not made the multitude our judges, or our prince a childe. Indeed wee dissent from all our nation in some doctrines concerning the true worship, offices, officers and government of God in his church. But yet seeing wee have thus layde open our faith and loyaltie to God, our Queene and our contrey, is there no more favour and mercie due unto us, than to languish away in prisons without bayle and tryall (which kynde of persecution is more greivous than death it selfe). The antient fathers have much differed in judgment. The most learned and famous men in England doo differ in judgment.[1] But where no heresie nor schisme is proved, where love and loyaltie remaine, where wickednes is rather hated and reproved, than committed, God forbid that more greivous punishment should be inflicted upon such a people, than upon anie maner malefactors, traytors, idolators, papists, hereticks, adulterers, lyers, swearers and such like.

YEA, BUT THE RUMOR GOETH THAT WEE ARE HERETICKS AND SCHISMATIKES, HOLDING MOST UNGODLY OPINIONS

Right Honorable, this rumor is false. In error it may be that wee are, for wee confesse our selves to be sinfull men, yea, daily to sin.[2] And what man, whether you looke to the first man Adam, or to the patriarchs, prophets, or apostles, or to the most learned and holy of the former, later or present age, what man (say wee) except the man Christ, but hath erred and may erre.[3] Therfore (as men) wee also may fayle in judgment, but hereticks or schismatikes none can prove us. If they could, it were their great fault thus manie yeeres to suffer us to remaine in so manie partes of the realme unconvinced; especially sithe wee contynually desire an equall tryall, for which

[1] This matter of differing in judgment is also found in chapter XLIII, "To the Most Honorable and Worshipfull Magistrates," p. 423.

[2] A denial of the Anabaptist "heresy" of perfectionism. See also Johnson's letter of June 2 to Lord Burghley wherein he denies any "dreaminge of perfection in this lyfe," *infra*, p. 439.

[3] Compare chapter XLIII, p. 423.

cause wee pyne away with astonishment and greife that no more pitifull order is taken with such a people, but one after another to be thrust up in the vilest gaoles (as New-gate, White-Lyon, etc.), emongst the most vagrant roges, the most infectious, facinorous and lewde wretches of all the nation. The Lord our God open the eares and eies of you the civill magistrates to heare and see our miseries, and somway to releive us, that he also may remember you in the day of distresse, sicknes and death, which is the way of all flesh. Amen.[1]

In tender consideration of all the premisses, our lamentable and humble petition unto your Honors is, even for God's cause, as you regard the lyves of Her Majestie's faithfull subjects, that you wilbe a meane to obteine us so much favour as to have equall tryall of the matters in question, which thing was never so long denyed in this realme (for ought wee reade) to the veriest papists and hereticks that ever were, or else that all who are bayleable by lawe, may be bayled from these noysome prisons and gaoles this spring tyme[2] till the later end of the next sommer upon sufficient securitie to answere unto what ever shalbe objected against us. This peticion wee make cheifly for them whose bodies are presently in danger of death by greivous sicknes and want, or els diseased by long emprisonment. Secondly, wee desire it for us all to this end, that wee may labour in our vocations, or at least-wise have an eye to our families, therby to guyde them in better sort than now they can be governed; who by reason of our so long absence from them, may soone fall into some of those heynous crimes, whereof wee and they are now most unjustly slandered. For what is youth without government, and what government can there be in those houses, whose masters are contynuall prysoners, whose dames are contynuall suters, and whose shop-windowes are alwayes shutt (or as good they were)?[3] Right Honorable, wee are perswaded that no cronicles or bookes of monuments or records doo shew a denyall of both these requests to anie sort or sect, who might be drawne or persuaded to yeild such obedience as our Declaration doth manifest. But wee have bene and are willing to subscribe to those pointes, of our owne accord. The greatest supposed hereticks in Queene Marie' dayes, and the vilest malefactors now-adayes, have had and have lawfull examining,

[1] See chapter XLIII, p. 424, where the reading is: "in the dayes of trouble, sicknes, and death (whereto all flesh is subject). Amen."

[2] This suggests April or May, 1593.

[3] Almost the identical language is found in chapter XLIII, p.424. This clearly indicates the authorship of Johnson for the petition.

committing, and triall, and gaole delyverie within a short tyme appointed by statute, the which some of us can prove that wee have not had, nor can have. And shall a people who are found and confessed to be most contrarie in judgment and greatest enemies to the pope's supremacie, the seminaries, and all the broode of that apostaticall throne, with all their trumperies, and to the kinge of Spaigne and all his trecheries, be as hardly, or more cruelly dealt with, than anie popish recusants (and that in Queene Elizabeth['s] dayes); but wee cease to question with our betters. Yet in all humilitie and reverence to your persons and places, we are inforced to stirre up your affections by humble petition thus earnestly, because that through the last commission about Jesuits, seminarie priests, and such as take parte with the pope and Spanish kinge, wee also are sought after, emprisoned and indicted, as if wee were such.[1] Indeed (right Honorable) wee and they both doo refuse to come to the parish assemblies; but with what difference in faith to God, and loyaltie to our prince, our Declaration sheweth.

Now (right Honorable), if wee should set forth at large a manefestation of the particular handling of most of us since Her Majestie's reigne (namely, when wee were committed, by whome, how examined, how manie committed and kept close without warrant, how long after kept in prison by warrants without anie cause shewed, how manie yeeres some have bene thus deteyned without accusation by witnesses or anie publicke tryall, how manie sutes and petitions utterly refused or neglected, how manie proffers of bayle rejected, what usage wee have had by keepers and gaolors, how manie have dyed in prysons, and such like things), wee might bring to open veiwe such procedings of the bishops, and such as they stirre up hereunto, contrarie to all lawe and conscience, as wee hope would make our mercifull Queene and her godly magistrates' hearts to pittie us, when they should but heare or see that which wee have knowne and felt. How long shall our desire of having peace with all men, if it were possible; how long shall our feare of being thought malicious, contentious, and seekers of revenge, cause us to keepe silence, and not make such a greivous complaint as this would be, and not seeke all lawfull meanes to obteine such a

[1] Johnson refers to "the Pope and Spanishe Kinge" in chapter XLIII, p. 417. Johnson is also referring to the "De Commissione Speciali Concernente Jesuitas," which includes as adversaries not only papists and Jesuits, but also vagrants, counterfeiters, sectaries, and Barrowists. The commission, dated March 26, 1593, is printed in Thomas Rymer, *Foedera, Conventiones, Literae,* second edition, XVI (1724), pp. 201–204.

speedie redresse as this would aske? Would to God that you knewe the truth of those things which wee have suffered, then, no doubt, you would pittie our lamentable case. In consideration whereof, and of all our long emprisonments and great miseries, wee humbly entreate for justice, according to Her Majestie's lawes; which thing wee trust will not be denyed us, namely, seeing wee desire nothing touching the libertie of our bodies or myndes, but what the lawes of our God and of our Queene doo allowe, and have provided for us, though wee could not wryte for our selves, nor anie sergeant, counsellor or attorney ever yet durst or would pleade our poore and lamentable cause. For the which mercie and justice shewed, wee all shalbe bounde to pray to God our heavenly Father, that he will multiplie Her Majestie's yeeres (if such be his will)[1] with more blessings and more, and yours with honor added to honor, and establish unitie in true religion and peace of conscience emongst them who professe the name of Jesus Christ. Amen.

Endorsement: The lamentable and humble complaint and petition of certeine faithfull Christians Her Majestie's true subjects in distresse by sickness and want, in Newgate and other prysons in and about London, etc.

[1] "If such be his will"—a favourite proviso in Johnson's writings.

XLV

TO THE RIGHT HONORABLE SYR [WILLIAM] ROE NOWE LORD MAJOR OF LONDON ABUNDANCE OF ALL BLESSINGS BE MULTIPLIED TO GODD'S GLORIE

This document is in Harley MSS. 6848, f. 7. It was written about the end of April, 1593, or early in May and is linked with the general petition sent to the magistrates. The writer is probably Francis Johnson, who also wrote the general petition and the plea to the Privy Council. Although the petition is brief, there are small touches that are characteristic of Johnson's writings: "Beseeche, accounted, noble, vouchsafe, neglect, Her Grace, reverend judges, surely you ought, doubtles you should, godlie meane, prosperities, if it be His will."

Sir William Rowe was mayor of London from September—October, 1592, to 1593. According to Joseph Haydn, *Book of Dignities* (1851), Rowe was mayor in 1592. In the 1890 and 1894 editions the new editor, Horace Ockerby, has added a note stating that the year indicates the time that the incumbent served and that he was elected the year previously. In other words, Rowe was elected in 1591 and served most of his mayoralty in 1592. This is an error. The year indicates the election year and the subsequent year is the main period of service. Burrage evidently was misled by the 1890 edition and accepts 1591–1592 as the period for Mayor Rowe. He solves the problem by conjecturing that the Separatists in their troubles had forgotten that a new mayor had been elected. But the Separatists had lived five months during Rowe's administration before their arrest, and there had been no new election in April–May, 1593. See Burrage, *Early English Dissenters*, II, 124. Rowe's predecessor in office (1591–1592) was Sir William Web and his successors (1593–1594) were Sir Cuthbert Buckle (died in office 1594) and Sir Richard Martin (1594). Sir John

Spencer follows, 1594–1595. In Robert Steele's *Tudor and Stuart Proclamations, 1485–1714* (Oxford, 1910), I, 95, there is a proclamation for April, 1593, with the name of William Rowe.

TO THE RIGHT HONORABLE SYR [WILLIAM] ROE NOWE LORD MAJOR OF LONDON ABUNDANCE OF ALL BLESSINGS BE MULTIPLIED TO GODD'S GLORIE

Right Honorable, seinge God disposeth of everie action (accordinge to His surpassinge wisedome) and sith He and his angells behold all the doings of men, we humblie beseche you to consider with your self that it is not without some providence of His (to your good if you deale mercifullie) that these things touchinge mercy and unitie are first brought to your Lordship's handes.[1] Many of our bretheren are in the prisons belonginge to your libertie; nowe as your citie is accounted the most noble (even as the prince's chamber) and as you are the honorable and chefe officer therein, so we beseche our God that your Lordship may be made a noble honorable and worthy instrument in bringinge these twoe most blessed and acceptable things (in the sight of God and man) to good passe: if we sent you vile things (disho[no]rable to God, our Queene, and contrey), ought you not to make the superior magistrates acquainted with them? Surely you ought: but howe if we acquaint your Lordship with honest motions (tendinge to the glorie of God, the honour of her Majestie and the benefit of our contrey), should you not doe the like? Dowtles you should: if you hide it or neglect it, yet the Almighty may fynd waies to bring it to the sight of her Highnes' right honorable Counsell and her Grace's reverend judges:[2] but if you vouchsafe to be a charitable and godlie meane for effectinge such lawfull and conscionable suites, you shall dischardge the dutie of a most honorable officer of a most famous and populous citie, and we and all ours shalbe the more bound to pray unto our God

[1] The mayor received a copy of the general petition to the magistrates (Harley MSS. 6848, ff. 2–7), including the "Motions Tending to Mercy" and the "Motions Tending to Unitie."

[2] The Almighty had the active cooperation of the Separatists, who addressed their general petition to the Privy Council and the judges. Johnson perhaps had completed his separate petition to the Privy Council and dispatched it in May. In June he sent another petition to Lord Burghley for the Queen herself.

that he will blesse your mayraltie with all manner blessings of trewe peace (both inward and outward) and of healthe, with all other prosperities soe as may tend most to His owne glory and your and our comfort in Hym: and that He will continnewe those blessings to your successors and to all England in such sorte as moche happines may redound to you and us and all her Majestie's dominions for many yeares (if it be His will)[1] under the blessed governement of our most gratious zoveraigne ladie and Queene Elizabeth. Amen.

[1] Johnson frequently uses this qualification in accordance with his belief in Calvinistic predestination and God's absolute sovereignty. It is not distinctly Puritan or Separatist, but a carry-over from Paul and Augustine and Beza—*Deo volente.*

XLVI

[FRANCIS JOHNSON TO LORD BURGHLEY], JUNE 2, 1593

This document carries no name, no addressee, and no endorsement, but it does have a date. It is found in Harley MSS. 6849, f. 145, but is not mentioned in the *Catalogue of the Harleian Manuscripts*, III (1808). Consequently it has not been used and has not been printed.

Fortunately, the subject matter and style make the task easy of assigning the letter to Francis Johnson, who is making suit to Lord Burghley. From a second letter of June 12, we learn that the author was a "brother" of John Penry and a close prisoner. He enclosed a copy of Penry's "Confession of Faith and Allegiance," and also a copy of his "Apologie," but he warns Lord Burghley not to reveal who has sent it to him. Consequently, he does not sign his second letter. But the authorship and addressee are verified by a third letter, dated January 8, 1593 [1593/1594], signed by Francis Johnson, still in close prison at the Clink, and carrying in the endorsement the recipient of the letter—Lord Burghley. From this last letter we learn that the bearer of the missive was John Johnson, father of Francis, who in all likelihood also received the two previous letters at the Clink and delivered them to Lord Burghley.

John Johnson had been a mayor of Richmond in Yorkshire. Lord Burghley seems to have known him and his two sons. When Francis preached his Presbyterian sermon at Cambridge on January 6, 1588/1589, he became enmeshed in campus politics. When he refused to retract his views, he was imprisoned. He then appealed to Lord Burghley as Lord Chancellor, who supported the heads of colleges at Cambridge. Thus, Lord Burghley would have known of Francis Johnson for at least four years.

The letter itself is a plea for liberty, either absolutely or by bail. It reveals a kind of familiarity towards Lord Burghley, a defiance of the prelatical hierarchy, and a justification of the practices of the Separatists.

[FRANCIS JOHNSON TO LORD BURGHLEY], JUNE 2, 1593

Right Honorable, I verily suppose you can not be ignoraunte of our cause and estate, in so great havocke as is made of us at this day, unles you doe beleeve the false and sclaunderous reportes which daylie and every where are spred against us, unto which I am perswaded your Lordship giveth no credite, bycause I am sure you knowe that this is the lott of the truthe and servaunts of God[1] to be persecuted and evill spoken of amonge the chilldren of men. Your Lordship remembreth that the apostle him selfe was accused to be of the secte[2] of the Nazarites, of a sect[3] that was every where spoken against, when indeed the matter was nothinge ells (as he saith)[4] but that they accompted the true worship of the true God to be a secte.

So it falleth owte with my selfe and other poore afflicted Christians at this tyme (Right Honorable), we are accused to be of the sect of the Brownistes, to be schismatickes, heretickes, and what not? We are every where spoken against. And what is the cause? Truly (my Lord) as I shall aunswere in that great day, before God, which searcheth the reynes and knoweth the secretes of all hartes, it is nothinge ells but this, that we endevor to obey the Lord Jesus Christ in his owne ordenaunce of ecclesiasticall ministery, worship, and order, which he hath given unto his churche and prescribed in his laste testament, sealed with his pretious bloude. And bycause to this ende (at his commandement) we departe owte of these false constituted parishionall and cathedrall assemblyes, in their present ministery, worship, and order ecclesiasticall, not daringe to receyve the marke and character of these their ordenaunces and constitucions, nor to subject our bodies and soules thereunto. For which we have not only expresse warraunte and commandment in the

[1] [In chapter XLVIII, which is indisputably by Johnson, we read: "But this hath allwaies bene the lott of the truthe and servants of God."]. Notes in square brackets are my own; the rest are Johnson's marginal annotations.

[2] Acts 24:5, 11 [14]. [3] *Et* [Acts] 28:22. [4] Acts 24:14.

Scriptures[1] of the everlyvinge God (the only rule of all true obedyence) but we have allso the publicke profession of the reformed churches abroade,[2] the testimony of many faithfull and worthie martirs[3] in former ages, the approbacion of many bookes[4] allowed by publicke authoritye in this lande. And finally the consent and direct assertions of many treatyses published by the best and forwardest preachers and professors in these assemblyes.[5] In all which, this present ecclesiasticall ministery, from the highest prelate to the lowest parish preist, or stipendary preacher, is proved to be false and antechristian, to be straunge from the Worde of God, and from the use of all well reformed churches in the worlde, to be such as Christe our Kinge and lawgiver never gave unto nor sett in his church. Finally to be a popish hyerarchi first coyned in the middest of the miserie of iniquity,[6] opposed against and exalted above all the holy thinges and ordenaunces of the Lord Jesus Christe.

The case beinge such, I beseech you well consider (Right Honorable) whether it be not high tyme for every man (at the commandment of God) in the obedience of faithe,[7] to "flee owt of the middest[8] of Babell," and to delyver his soule "from the feirce wrathe of the Lorde." And yet the performaunce hereof (which is our very cause) in the obedience of the holy ordenaunces of Jesus Christe, and in the hatred of all false wayes,[9] and vaine invencions of Antechriste, is nowe with open mouth accompted a secte and a schisme, and every where spoken against. Yea, persecuted even unto death. But thus the Scripture is fullfilled which sayth: "The tyme is come that judgment must begin at the house of God. If it first begin at us,[10] what shall the end be of them which obey not the gospell of God?"

1 Matthew 28:20; I Timothy 6:13, 14; Jeremiah 51:6, 45; Revelation 18:4; II Corinthians 6:17.

2 French, Belgic, Helvetian in *Harmony of Confessions.*

3 Mr. Tindall, Mr. Frithe, Mr. Wickliffe, etc.

4 *Acts and Monuments*, Bertrand de Loques, [*A Treatise of the Church* (1581)], *Harmony of Confessions*, Mr. Rainolde's and Hart's Conference, etc. [John Rainoldes, *The Summe of the Conference betwene John Rainoldes and John Hart: Touching the Head and the Faith of the Church* (London, 1584).]

5 *Admonition to Parliament*, T.C. 1. *Reply* and 2. *Reply*. [Thomas Cartwright, *A Replye to an Answere Made of M. Doctor Whitgifte agaynste the Admonition to the Parliament* (1573); *Second Reply* (1575) and *The Rest of the Second Replie* (1577)]. *Declaration of Ecclesiasticall Discipline* [Cartwright, translator of] Travers, *A Full and Plaine Declaration* (1574) or William Fulke, *A Briefe and Plaine Declaration* (1584). *Demonstration* [John Udall, *A Demonstration of the Trueth of That Discipline* (1588)].

6 II Thessalonians 2:4. [*Cf.* 2:7]. Perhaps Johnson intended "the misterie of iniquity."

7 Romans 16:26. 8 Jeremiah 51:6, 45. Revelation 18:4.

9 Psalms 119:113, 128. 10 [I Peter 4:17].

"If they doe these thinges to [in] a green tree,[1] what shall be done to [in] the drye?" This I thoughte good to make bolde to write to your Lordship touchinge our cause and estate. For in other thinges we holde the same common faith, which is published by Her Majesty, and this state, and hope, in the unity thereof, to be saved.

We doe allso fullye acknowledge Her Majesty to be cheife governor under God over all causes and persons whether ecclesiasticall or civill, within Her Highnes' realmes and dominions.[2] We doe willingly yeeld to Her Majestie's pleasure our bodyes, lands, goods, and lyves, submittinge our selves for conscience sake. We utterly hate and abhorre all popery and antechristianisme. We are so far from dreaminge of perfection[3] in this lyfe, as we feele and acknowledge that we daily need aske of God in Jesus Christe the forgivenes of our manifolde and greivous transgressions into which we fall. Finally, we lothe and deteste all sectes, schismes, heresyes, treasons, rebellions, seditions, and whatsoever is of the lyke nature. For it is written:[4] "Buy the truth, but sell it not, likewise wisedomme, instruction, and understanding." And againe:[5] "My sonne, feare the Lord and the king, and meddle not with them that are seditious."

Yet (Right Honorable) notwithstandinge this our uprightnes and innocency (which we have through the mercy of God), we feare that the prelates and clergie (our greate adversaryes) never bringe our cause before Her Majestie or your Honors, but only under the names of schisme, heresy, treason, fellony, and such lyke. So opposite they are against the blessed truth, and holy ordenaunces of Jesus Christe, and so greedily they thirste after our bloude, which allreadye they have begunne to drink in great measure.

Now, therefore, my most humble and earnest suite unto your Lordship, in the name of the Lord Jesus, is, that as you esteeme and accompte of these thinges, you woulde consider of our lamentable and wofull estate, and put to your helpinge hande for our succor and delyveraunce, in the middest of this fiery triall and most subtile persecution. Oh my Lord, let it not be founde true in Englande, which God hath spoken by the prophet, saying:[6] "I sought for a man among them, that should make up the hedg, and stand in the gappe, before mee, for the lande, that I should not destroy it, but I

[1] [Luke 23:31].
[2] Romans 13:1. I Peter 2:13, 14. [See chapter XLIV for the same idea and similar language—both by Johnson]. [3] Romans 7.
Proverbs 23:23. [5] Proverbs 24:21. [6] Ezekiel 22:30.

found none." For if it be so, assuredlye the tyme will come when it will allso be verified, [that] which there followeth: That God will therefore powre out his indignacion upon such a people, and consume them with the fire of his wrathe, and rendre their owne wayes upon their heades, as sayeth the Lord God.[1] Be carefull therefore (Right Honorable) to shew the truthe and naturallnes of your love, which I am perswaded you beare to the Lord Jesus him selfe, in settinge your selfe to be an helpe and releife of his poore distressed sainctes thus unchristianly intreated and pursued at this tyme.

For my selfe and my brother in particuler (who are knowen and many wayes bounde unto your Lordship) I only desyre this, that we may by your Lordship's meanes, either by your selfe or by the Right Honorable the Earle of Essex,[2] the Lord of Hunsden,[3] the Lord Gray,[4] or whome your Lordship thinketh beste, obteyne this favor and helpe, to be freed owt of prison eyther simply (there beinge now a new statute made) or under bayle for four or five monnethes. We have beene detayned in severall close prisons this longe tyme, so as our friends can not have accesse unto us. The cause I have before sett downe as in the presence of God. My selfe have bene sicke and weake, since the beginninge of August laste,[5] now of late it hath pleased God to beginne to recover my former strength, even in this straight and harde usage. For the contynuaunce and increase of which recovery, I hope my liberty may the sooner be obteyned. If not, the will of God be donne. I am assured there shall not a haire of our heades perish, without God. And therefore seinge by the mercye of God we suffer for welldoeinge, we committe our selves to him as to a faithfull creator. Neither need we feare the malice and opposicion of our adversaries (thought it be to the sheddinge of our bloude) which is to them a token of perdicion but to us of salvacion, and that of God.

Blessed be his name, therefore, who hath not [145 *verso*] in this cause left us withowte comforte (though all men forsake and revile us for it). For it is written: "Though my father and my mother

[1] Ezekiel 22:31.

[2] [Robert Devereux (1567–1601), Second Earl of Essex. He became a member of the Privy Council on February 25, 1592/1593.]

[3] [Henry Carey, (1524?–1596), First Lord Hunsdon, cousin of Queen Elizabeth.]

[4] [Arthur Grey (d. October 14, 1593), Fourteenth Lord Grey of Wilton. His son, Thomas Grey (d. 1614), Fifteenth Lord Grey of Wilton, was pro-Puritan.]

[5] [August, 1592. Johnson probably came to London in July, 1592, from Middelburg. The Separatists organized their church, with Johnson as pastor, in September, 1592.]

shoulde forsake mee, yet the Lord will gather mee up."[1] And agayne he hath sayde: "I will not leave thee, nor forsake thee. So that we may boldly saye: The Lorde is my helper,[2] neyther will I feare what man can doe unto mee." And here indeed "is the pacyence of sainctes, here are they that keep the commandementes of God,[3] and the faythe of Jesus," wherein when we shall by the power and grace of Christe our Saviour have fought a good fight and finished our course (as dyverse of our brethren allready have donne), then shall we with them finde it true which is allso written: "Blessed are the dead that dy in the Lorde, even so sayth the spirit."[4] Amen.

Thus therefore trustinge your Lordship to be of this number, and hopinge that God will give you with Mardochee[5] and Hester to stande in the gappe and open your mouth for the people of God, Her Majestie's loyall subjectes now counted as sheep for the slaughter, and made the chilldren of destruction, I committ your Lordship and all your holy indevors to him who hath sayde, that "whosoever shall gyve to one of his litle ones but a cup of colde water only in the name of a disciple shall not loose his rewarde."[6] The same God of heaven and earth, even the kinge of kinges, blesse and preserve Her Moste Excellent Majestie, your Lordship, and this whole lande, now and for ever. Amen. Mon. [Month] 6. 2. 1593.[7]

[No signature. No endorsement.]

[1] Psalms 27:10. [2] Hebrews 13:5, 6. [3] [Revelation 14:12].
[4] Revelation 14:13. [5] [Mordecai and Esther]. [6] Matthew 10:42.
[7] ["Mon." does not mean Monday. June 2, 1593, was a Saturday. February 6, 1592/1593, was a Tuesday, and February 6, 1593/1594, was a Wednesday.]

XLVII

[FRANCIS JOHNSON TO LORD BURGHLEY], JUNE 12, 1593

This letter of June 12 is a continuation of the letter of June 2. It is unsigned, and it lacks an endorsement. Nevertheless, it is clear from the handwriting, the context, and the ideology that it is written by Francis Johnson to Lord Burghley. The original is in Harley MSS. 6849, f. 143 *recto* and *verso*. Since it has no signature, it is not catalogued in the third volume of the *Catalogue of the Harleian Manuscripts* (1808).

There is a tone of moralizing, of prophetical preaching, and of inner rectitude in the letter. There is no suggestion of yielding to the prelates, of making peace with the hierarchy. Instead, the petitioner asks for the release of the Separatists, either to live within Her Highness' dominions or, if necessary, to suffer banishment and exile, as established in April by the new law of 35 Elizabeth, chapter I: "An Acte to Retayne the Quene's Subje[c]ts in Obedyence." (The introductory listing of of the statutes has an alternative wording: "An Acte to Retayne the Quene's Majestie's Subjects in Their Due Obedyence." See *The Statutes of the Realm, IV*, Part IV, p. 840.)

The letter is interesting for its mention of "An Humble Petition to Her Most Excellent Majestie," which Johnson encloses and urges Lord Burghley to deliver to the Queen so that she may be apprised of the lamentable condition of the imprisoned Separatists. This petition, though unknown, may still be extant in some manuscript collection, perhaps at Hatfield House or Windsor Castle. It is the culmination of the Separatists' appeals, beginning with Barrow's petition of January, Penry's supplication of March, Johnson's general petition to the magistrates, and his specific suits to the Privy Council, the Lord Mayor, Lord Burghley, and finally the Queen herself.

Johnson mentions a second enclosure, which seems both daring and impolitic. This is a copy of Penry's "Confession of Faith and Allegiance" and also his "Apologie." It is surprising to discover that Johnson sent these Separatist charters to Lord Burghley just two weeks after Penry's execution. Johnson probably hoped that Lord Burghley would be convinced of the rightness and righteousness of Penry, but evidently Johnson knew nothing of Burghley's effort through ambassador Robert Bowes to obtain the banishment of Penry from Scotland in 1590. Johnson supports Penry unequivocally, defends his faith and loyalty, and gives him the status of a true martyr for the cause of Jesus Christ. Burghley must have been irritated by the letter, if he read it, and by the request that the identity of the sender of the two enclosures be not revealed because of the danger of vindictive action by the Archbishop and the prelates. We are fortunate in having Penry's items extant, but it would be doubly fortunate if we had knowledge of Burghley's action and reaction. The petition probably never was delivered to the Queen, the Penry items became a part of Burghley's fabulous collection, and Johnson remained in the Clink until 1597.

[FRANCIS JOHNSON TO LORD BURGHLEY], JUNE 12, 1593

Right Honorable and my very good Lorde. The Scripture (which teacheth that "whatsoever[1] thinges were written aforetime were written for our learninge") hath left in recorde that when Jeremiah[2] the prophet was, by the wicked suggestion of the rulers of Judah to Zedekiah the kinge, caste into a dungeon for speakinge the truthe, as the Lord commanded him, then Ebed-melech, one of the kinge's house, went unto the kinge and sayde unto him: "My Lord the King, these men have done evill, in all that they have done, to Jeremiah the prophet, whome they have cast into the dungeon."[3] Wherupon the king commanded Ebed-melech to goe and take Jeremiah owt of the dungeon before he dyed.

[1] Romans 15:4. [These notes are mainly by Johnson; mine are in square brackets.]
[2] Jeremiah 38: [6]. [3] Jeremiah 38:9, 10.

My selfe and my poore distressed brethren, I confesse, are unworthie to be compared with Jeremiah the prophet, yet seeinge God in mercye hath herein made us like unto him in that we are by the prelates and their accomplices cast into the severall prisons (as it were, so many dungeons) in and aboute this citie of London, for bearinge wittnes to the truthe, and in that God hath (as I heare) moved your Lordship's hearte (as the hearte of an other Ebed-melech) to take compassion of our greyvous imprisonments and suffringes. It doth much embolden mee to wryte agayne to your Lordship and most earnestly to beseech the continuaunce and increase of your favor and helpe towards us, the poore afflicted servauntes of Christe Jesus our Lorde and the true loyall subjectes of Elizabeth our gracyous queene.

In this respecte, I have made bolde to send inclosed an humble petition to Her Most Excellent Majestie,[1] with moste earnest suite, in the bowells of Jesus Christe, to your Lordship, that eyther by your selfe, or by some other, whome your Lordship thinketh meete here-unto, you would cause it to be delyvered to the handes of our gracyous soveraigne, and by this meanes make knowen our estate and request unto Her Highnes, as Ebed-melech did Jeremiah's unto the kinge of Judah.

God him selfe is one and the same, his yeares faile not, neither is there any ende of his mercyes; his arme allso is not weakned, that it can not enclyne the hartes of princes to compassion nowe, as then it did, neyther is his hande shortened, that it can not at this day delyver his children owt of pryson, as at that tyme it did Jeremiah owte of the dungeon. Onely there are few (Right Honor-able), yea, to speake the truthe, as in experience we have founde it, there are scante any now a dayes who with Ebed-melech will open their mouthe for the dumbe in the cause of the chilldren of destruction.[2]

Many knowe not our cause and either speake evill of that they knowe not,[3] or at least offer not any way to helpe us,[4] if they doe not allso seeke by all meanes they can to adde to our afflictions. Of them that know it, some thinke us worthie to be caste into dungeons,[5] yea, and to be put to death for it, allthough they be not hable by the

[1] [We do not have this petition, but it may be extant in some of Lord Burghley's papers.]

[2] [The same idea is in chapter XLIV, where Johnson asserts that no "sergeant, counsellor or attorney ever yet durst or would pleade our poore and lamentable cause."] [3] II Peter 2:12. [4] Judges 5:23.

[5] Jeremiah 38:4, 6 *et* 26:8, 11; John 16:2; Acts 22:22.

Scriptures of God either to justefye their owne standinge in their false wayes, or to blame this our walkinge in the wayes of Christe. Others are fearfull[1] of the faces of men, or ells forgetfull of the afflictions of Joseph,[2] not havinge, or at least not shewinge them selves to have, that fellow feelinge[3] which ought to bee in the members of that bodye whereof Christe Jesus is the heade. And thus our misery continueth, yet none at all putt owt their handes to help us, so as we may justly lament and say, as it is written:[4] "They have shutt up our life in the dungeon, and cast a stone upon us." "Yea, for thy sake (O Lord) are wee killed all day long,[5] and are counted as sheepe to the slaughter." But howsoever God for a tyme chastise our sinnes, and try our faith, in stampinge us under feet, and in subvertinge our cause, and overthrowinge our right, before the face of him that is high, yet certeinly there is a tyme when this our warfare shalbe accomplished,[6] and when the Lord will speake comfortablye unto us in Jesus Christe for whose sake we suffer these thinges, though otherwise in our selves we be moste unworthie, by reason of our sinnes.

For doubtles the Lord seeth and judgeth, neyther will he forgett his people for ever. But he will arise and mainteine their cause, he will make enquiry for their bloude. Then shall they perish in his wrath, who woulde not kisse and obey the gospell of his son.[7] Then shall they be blessed that truste in him. And even this comforte allso is gyven in the forsayd historicall prophecy of Jeremiah,[8] who was commanded from the mouth of the Lorde to tell Ebed-melech that God wold bringe his wordes upon that cyty of Jerusalem, for evill and not for good, even in that day, before him. Yet that he would delyver Ebed-melech in that daye, that he shoulde not fall by the sworde, but his life shoulde be unto him for a praye, bycause he had put his truste in the Lorde. And thus allwayes in God (who is one and the same) will justice and mercye kisse eche other when he recompenceth the wayes of his adversaryes upon their owne heades, then will he shew mercye to them that have shewed mercye to his afflicted chilldren, and have put their truste in him.

Remember therefore (Right Honorable), I beseech you, that the Lord hath by expresse commandement[9] layd this duty upon all his servauntes to open their mouth in the cause of his chilldren,

[1] Esa. [Isaiah] 51:12, 13; Revelation 21:8.
[2] Amos 6:6. [3] I Corinthians 12:26.
[4] Lamentations 3:53. [5] Romans 8:36; Psalms 44:22.
[6] Lamentations 3:34, 35, 36; Esa. [Isaiah] 40:1, 2.
[7] Psalms 2:12. [8] Jeremiah 39:15, 16, 17, 18. [9] Proverbs 31:8.

especyally when they are appointed unto destruction, that he hath promised[1] allso and will give a plentifull blessinge and rewarde to the performaunce hereof, that your Lordship have heretofore bene many wayes helpfull to the distressed sainctes of God, that your selfe allso have (through the mercye of God) bene an auntient professor and furtherer of the sinceritye of the gospell (for which we suffer). Finally, that whatsoever in this behalfe[2] is performed or denyed to the least of the servaunts of God, Christe accompeth it performed or denied to him selfe. And as God shall move your hearte with the due consideracion of these thinges, so I humbly beseech your Lordship in the name of Christe to shew your love towards him in beinge helpfull to us, his afflicted and despised chilldren, at this tyme. And here againe on my knees I beseech your Lordship by your selfe, or the Earle of Essex,[3] the Lord Graye,[4] or such others, to be a meanes that this our petition may be delyvered to Her Highnes' handes, that we findinge favor in Her Majestie's eyes thorough the blessing of God, this heavy chayne layde upon our loynes may be removed, and that we be not still forced to goe into fire and water, as hitherto we have bene, and that only for our obedience[5] of the commandements of Christe, but that we may be suffered together with peace,[6] eyther to lyve under Her Majestie's government, in obedience of the gospell, in any place of her dominions (which we moste desyre), or ells to departe[7] whithersoever it shall please God to bringe us, and to gyve us a resting place for the service of his name in peace and tranquillitye. Thus shall the prayers of these poor sainctes, and the blessinges of our God, who proveth and tryeth us, be powred owt for and upon your Lordship thorough Jesus Christe, to whome be prayse for ever. Amen.

[1] Jeremiah 39:18 with *caput* 38:7, 8, 9, 10; Matthew 10:42.
[2] Matthew 25:35, etc.
[3] [Robert Devereux (1567–1601), second Earl of Essex.]
[4] [Arthur Grey (d. 1593), fourteenth Lord Grey of Wilton. His son, Thomas Grey (d. 1614), who became fifteenth Lord Grey of Wilton in 1593, was pro-Puritan.]
[5] Matthew 28:20; I Timothy 6:13, 14; Jeremiah 6:16; Revelation 18:4; II Corinthians 6:17. [6] I Timothy 2:2, 3.
[7] [The law of 35 Elizabeth, chapter I, "An Acte to Retayne the Quene's Majestie's Subjects in Their Due Obedyence," enforced conformity or exile. The law received the Queen's assent on April 10, but it provided for a period of forty days to become effective—from April 10 or 12 to May 20 or 22. Thereafter, anyone convicted and unwilling to conform was to abjure the land after three months. Thus, by August 20–22 the Separatists faced conformity or exile.

In his letter of April 24, 1593, to the Distressed Faithfull Congregation, Penry had tried to prepare the minds of the Separatists for exile, and he urged them to take along his poor desolate widow and his fatherless and friendless orphans. Johnson's suggestion of exile is made after the law had gone into effect.]

This I have made bolde to write unto your Lordship, hopinge that God who hath the heartes and wayes of all men in his hands will increase in your Lordship a compassionate hearte of our lamentable estate, and add strength to your hande, to procure our release.

I am bolde allso to sende to your Lordship a shorte Confession of Faith,[1] and an Apologie,[2] drawen by that faithfull wittnes of Christe, our brother Penry, before his death. By which plainely appereth what his fayth was towards God, and loyallty towardes Her Majestie. So that allthough he were condempned of men, yet I doubt not but he was accepted of God, and nowe is partaker of that crowne of life[3] which is promised by Christe to all them that are faithfull unto deathe. The poor remnaunte of poore Christians (who are falsely called Brownistes) doe all of us generally agree with that our faithfull brother in that Confession of Faith and Allegiance to God and Her Majestie, as we have often declared to the worlde in other lyke confessions which now I have not by mee to sende allso to your Lordship, as otherwise I woulde have done that your Lordship might every way be informed aright in the truthe of our cause. Let it not be tedious to your Lordship, I beseech you, to reade over this Confession of Faith, which allso may be shewed to whome it pleaseth you. Only let mee humbly intreat your Lordship not to make knowen from whome you receyved it. Neither to shew this or my former letter[4] to any till it please God I be freed owte of [143 *verso*] prison eyther alyve or dead in the Lord. One of our brother Penrie's indightments was taken owte of his moste secrete writinges, yea, contrary to his meaninge, as I hearde he protested before God. I scant knowe any scholle[r] to whome your Lordship can shew them that will not make relation of it to the Prelate of Canter[bury] and other our adversaries, who will the more either contynue my restreinte in prison or hasten the ende of my dayes in this lyfe. But I knowe your Lordship will be very carefull thereof, in these daungerous dayes. If it please God so to dispose as nothinge be obtayned in our former generall suite to Her Majestie, yet I humbly

[1] [Penry's "Confession of Faith and Allegiance" begins: "I John Penry do here (as I shall answer before the Lord my God in that great day of judgment)." See Additional MSS. 48064, ff. 15 *verso*–18 *verso*, formerly known as Yelverton MSS. 70, in the British Museum. See also Additional MSS. c. 303, ff. 204–206, in the Bodleian Library.]

[2] [His "Apology" or "Protestation" begins: "Although yt were altogether most reasonable." Johnson's copy may be Lansdowne MSS. 109, no. 13, ff. 35, 36. The original is in Ellesmere MS. 2155, f. 113 *recto* and *verso*.]

[3] Revelation 2:10. [4] [The letter of June 2, 1593.]

beseech your Lordship, be a meanes by your selfe, or the Earle of Essex, to Her Majestie's Counsell, or commissioners,[1] to procure mine owne libertye, if it may be simplye (there beinge nowe a new statute),[2] if not, then under bayle, for four or five monnethes this sommer for benefite of my health.

And thus cravinge pardon for my boldnes, I committ your Lordship and this our suite unto God, who worketh all thinges for the best unto them that love him. To whome be prayse in the churche by Jesus Christe throughowte all generacions forever. Amen. Mon. [Month] 6. 12. 1593.

Your Lordship's moste humble to commande in the Lorde.

A close prisoner for wittnes bearinge to the gospell of Christe against the false hierarchi and abhominacions of Antechrist.

[1] [The Earl of Essex, Robert Devereux, became a Privy Councillor on February 25, 1592/1593. By commissioners Johnson means those persons designated by the Special Commission of March 26, 1593. The commissioners who examined Johnson on April 5, 1593, were John Barne, Julius Caesar, Mathew Dale, Gabriell Goodman, and Richard Young.]

[2] [The statute of 35 Elizabeth, chapter I.]

XLVIII

FRANCIS JOHNSON TO LORD BURGHLEY, JANUARY 8, 1593/1594

This document is in Lansdowne MSS. 75, ff. 50–51. Unlike the two previous letters, this one is signed by Francis Johnson, and it carries an endorsement: "To the Right Honorable, my very good Lorde, the Lord Burghley, Lord High Treasurer of Englande." It is dated from the Clink, where Johnson is "still in close pryson for the gospell of Jesus Christe."

Since this letter is undoubtedly by Johnson, it serves to establish his authorship of the previous two unsigned letters and of several petitions. In the present letter we find certain typical expressions: "who are falsely called Brownists," "I have once agayne made bolde to write," "that faithfull wittnes of Jesus Christ," "thirst after our bloude," "every where spoken against," "this hath allwaies bene the lott of the truthe and servants of God," "prysons and gallowes were no fitt meanes to convince and perswade our consciences," "his poore afflicted children." The parallels are sufficiently close and numerous to confirm Johnson's authorship not only of two letters but also of three or four petitions.

The present letter is a complaint against the harsh dealings of Richard Young, whom the Separatists despised for his arbitrary and vindictive actions. It is also an effort to prove that Johnson is not guilty of violating the recent law, 35 Elizabeth, chapter I. For this proof Johnson encloses a separate treatise "proving" by eleven reasons why he is not in danger of the new statute "Made to Retayne the Queen's Majestie's Subjects in Theyr Due Obedyence."

The letter is blunt and defiant. Johnson refers to his brethren, Barrow, Greenwood, and Penry, "whome they have killed," and he provides a good example of a *post hoc, ergo propter hoc* fallacy when he alleges that "since the shedding of the bloude of those faithfull servants of Christe this year last paste," "the Lord hath allready begunne to pleade against this countrye and people by so contagious and deadly a plague, as in wonderfull manner hath bene brought upon this lande and the inhabitantes thereof." Johnson may not have realized that the rank and file of the people regarded the Separatists as heretics and schismatics. Logic could easily reverse cause and effect. Johnson also denounces the Commissioners as well as Justice Young and other judges, for their unreasonableness, wicked-mindedness, unchristian practices, and bloodthirsty procedures. He even tells Lord Burghley in no uncertain language that it is the duty of his Lordship to stop their wicked purposes—"least otherwyse our bloude and God's curse be upon you and yours bycause you have not holpen the Lord against the mighty."

Johnson's letter is more a complaint than a petition, but he reminds Lord Burghley of his obligation to help, to show his love, and to procure a quiet and godly conference before impartial judges.

John Strype has printed this document in his *Annals*, IV (1824), pp. 187–192. He prints the manuscript in its entirety, but the following mistakes should be noted. On page 187 the date is given as January 18, 1593. It should be January 8, 1593/1594. He has "were to be indicted" for "were indicted." He has "two reasons" for "certayne reasons"—actually, there are eleven reasons to which reference is made. He has one sentence which reads: "With this therefore I thought not needfull to trouble your lordship at that time." It should be: "with which therefore I thought it not needfull to trouble your Lordship agayne at this tyme." He has: "The two that are indicted" for "That two are indighted." Strype reads: "At which time also a preacher, one of us," which should be: "at which tyme also, one of us." On pages 187–188 Strype has: "speeches and demands" for "speeches and commands." On page 188 Strype has garbled a marginal reference by incorporating it in the text. He reads: "that he marvelled, who had been above eleven months prisoner, they should deal with men by imprisonment." It should be: "that he mervayled they would deale with men by imprisonment." Strype has "submit to go to church" for "promyse to goe to churche." He has "if thou wilt" for "if thou wilbe," and "about fourteen months" for "above fowrteen moneths." Strype changes the meaning when he prints: "sued to him but for liberty of the prison. For as he, with the dean." It should be: "sued to him but for liberty of the prysons for us, he with the Dean." The word "unjust" should be "unjustly." On page 189 "Hauns" should be "Haunse"; "three months" should be "three yeares," and "six of them came to that town" should be "six of them were come to that towne." The phrase "some others of his appointment" should be "some other at his appointment." "Gandymer" is an erroneous reading for "Gardiner." On page 140 we read: "But this (alas!) hath been the lot," but the correct clause is: "But this hath allwaies bene the lott." On page 141 "might be converted" should be "might also be converted," and "my brethren" should be "my brother" [George]. Strype has "your good honour" for "your Honor" and "furthering of the truth" for "furthering of His truthe." In addition to these twenty-three errors, there are minor variations which do not need notice since they do not alter the meaning. Good old Strype—he accomplished an enormous task for which we are grateful—but he too is human and fallible.

FRANCIS JOHNSON TO LORD BURGHLEY, JANUARY 8, 1593/1594

[50 *recto*] Although when I last presumed to wryte unto you, Right Honorable, I then thought no more to trouble your Lordship with my letters, yet now of late hearing that if the Sessions had holden at Newgate,[1] the beginninge of the last moneth, as was appointed,

[1] [The Sessions at Newgate at Justice Hall in Old Bailey served for cases of Gaol Delivery, Oyer and Terminer, and special commissions. Since Middlesex was not included in the six circuits served by the Justices of Assize, the Newgate Sessions supplied a real need for the London area. See the helpful introduction in Hugh Bowler, *Recusant Roll No.* 2 (*1593–1594*). "Publications of the Catholic Record Society," no. LVII. London, 1965.]

two of us (who are falsely called Brownists) were indighted,[1] I have once agayne made bolde to write these few lynes unto your Lordship and herewithall to send included certayne reasons[2] by which it is proved that we are not within danger of the statute of 35 Elizabeth, chapter I (whereupon we have thought they would indighte us), much lesse of the statute of 23 Elizabeth, chapter II, as I doubt not but your Lordship evidently perceyved, by the reasons which that faithfull wittnes of Jesus Christe, John Penry, sente unto your Honor, touching that matter, in his lyfe tyme,[3] with which therefore I thought it not needfull to trouble your Lordship agayne at this tyme.

Who they be that are indighted we can not learne. That two are indighted, one of the commissioners[4] openly spake it when he sate [sat] with others at Westminster the fifth of the laste moneth at which tyme also, one[5] of us being called thither, and upon their speeches and commands answering that he mervayled they would deale with men by imprisonment and other rigorous meanes in matter of religion and conscyence rather than by more christian and fitt proceeding, protesting unto them that he should but dissemble with them, and play the hypocrite, if he shoulde, to please them, or to avoyde trouble, promyse to goe to churche, and to joyne with the publicke ministery of these assemblyes, as now it standeth, he being perswaded in conscyence that it was utterly unlawfull. The aforesayd commissioner sayde to him againe: "come then to churche, and obey the Queene's lawes, and be a dissembler, be an hypocrite, or a devill if thou wilbe." Pardon my boldnes in mentioning this, I beseech your Lordship, for their unchristian and heathenish speeches to us and usage of us force me unto it.

Mr. Justice [Richard] Younge also (who among the rest of the

[1] [This sentence seems to be contrary to fact. Yet in the next paragraph Johnson says two men were indicted.]

[2] [This refers to Lansdowne MSS. 75, item 25, ff. 52–53, entitled: "That Fraunces Johnson for His Writings Is Not under the Daunger of the Statute of 35 Elizabeth, Chapter I, Made to Retayne the Queen's Majestie's Subjects in Theyr Due Obedyence, Appereth Thus." Then follow eleven reasons why the statute does not apply to Francis Johnson. See chapter XLIX.]

[3] [Penry's reasons are in Lansdowne MSS. 75, no. 26, ff. 54, 55, entitled: "Penry Not in Danger of the Statute."]

[4] Mr. Wrath. [This is Robert Wroth, who was appointed to a special commission on March 26, 1593. See Harley MSS. 6849, f. 239 *recto*. See also Lansdowne MSS. 85, item 26; 86, item 35; 87, items 60, 83, 84; and 88, items 27, 37, 44.]

[5] Mr. Smyth, a preacher, who hath bene above [almost] eleven moneths prisoner, and yet is in the Marshalsea. [This is William Smithe, who was arrested February 18–19, 1592/1593. See his examination of April 5.]

commissioners that usually sitt with him, seemeth to carry matters as pleaseth him) will neyther alone, nor with the rest (when suite is made unto him) suffer some of us so much as to have the libertye of the prisons, where we are. Insomuch as my brother (called Georg Johnson) hath now bene detayned about eleven moneths, and my selfe above fowrteen moneths, in severall close prysons, he in a noysome [smelly] chamber of the common gaole of the Fleet, and my self in the Clincke.[1] Yea, when our poor olde father (this bearer)[2] sued to him but for liberty of the prysons for us, he with the Dean of Westminster would have sent him to pryson had not Mr. Justice [John] Barnes[3] stayed them. He sent also in Her Majestie's and your Honor's names to take away my papers and bookes (as I wrote to your Lordship heretofore)[4] and still detayneth some of my bookes, although they be allowed by publicke authority, and all my papers, which albeit for the most parte they be against the prelacy and other clergy of this lande, yet are not any way within danger of the statute, as your Lordship may see by the reasons included.[5] Yet it may be they will pretend some thinge (though never so unjustly) owt of them, against mee, as they have dealt with my brethren allready, whome they have killed,[6] and now can doe no more unto them. Otherwyse I can not imagine whereon they will indight mee, unles it be for sending to your Lordship six bookes (touching the Haunse shippes) which came to Middleborough, whilest I was there, about three yeares synce, that is, for doeing the duty of a loyall subjecte.[7] For indeed I remember that when Mr. Barrow and the rest of us were examined the last Lent, I was asked whether I had ever seen of those bookes, whereunto I answered, that being at Middleborough, one Mr. [Thomas] Ferrers, then the Deputy of the Merchant Adventurers there, shewed mee one of them, and bycause

1 [George Johnson was arrested March 4, 1592/1593. Francis Johnson was arrested on the night of December 5–6, 1592. He may be counting part of a month as a full month, but actually the period is thirteen months].

2 [John Johnson is the father, former mayor of Richmond in Yorkshire, and Gabriell Goodman is the Dean.]

3 [John Barne (or Barnes) was one of the special commissioners appointed March 26, 1593, to conduct the examinations of the Separatists.]

4 [This complaint in a previous letter is not found in the letters of June 2 and 12, 1593. Therefore, Johnson must have written to Lord Burghley in the latter half of 1593. The letter is not known, but it may be extant, perhaps unsigned, as is the case with both June letters.]

5 [See chapter XLIX.]

6 Luke 12:4. [Barrow, Greenwood, and Penry had been hanged.]

7 [Johnson is grasping at a straw. There was no intention of indicting him for sending six copies of Barrow's *A Plaine Refutation* to Lord Burghley in April, 1591, when he was minister to the Merchant Adventurers at Middelburg.]

he understood not the Latine tongue, desyred mee to look upon it.[1] Which when I had done, perceyving it to be written against this lande, and he telling mee that six of them were come to that towne, I wished him to buy them all up, and to send them with all speed to your Lordship, which he accordingly did, and caused them to be delyvered to your Honor (as I take it) eyther by Mr. [Richard] Saltonstall, alderman of this citye, and governor of the Company of Merchants [Adventurers] aforesaide, or by some other at his appointment. Your Lordship may thincke it strange that ever we should suspecte them to be so unreasonable and wickedly minded, as to trouble us for those things wherein we have done the duty of good and faythfull subjects. But (my Lord) we have found such unchristian usage at their hands, and perceyved their harts so to thirst after our bloude, as if they were not restrayned, partly for feare of Her Majestie and your Honors, partly for shame of the worlde, and cheifely by the mighty and overruling hand of God. We might justly feare they would bring as much innocent bloude upon this lande at this day, as ever Arrundell,[2] Gardiner,[3] Stokesly,[4] Boner,[5] Story,[6] Dunning,[7] or any such like bloud suckers have done heretofore. Now the Scripture saith that bloude[8] defileth the lande, and that the Lord when He[9] maketh inquisition for bloude, remembreth it. Therefore it behooveth your Lordship for the love which you beare to this land, to Her Majestie, to your selfe, and to your posterity, to be a meanes (according to the authoritye God hath gyven you) in tyme to stay their wicked and bloudthirsty purposes, least otherwyse our bloude and God's curse be upon you

[1] [There is no Latin in *A Brief Discoverie*, but in *A Plaine Refutation*, AA2 *recto*, there is a Latin quotation from Proverbs 18:17. These three lines add a little to the story of the confiscation of 3000 copies of *A Brief Discoverie* and *A Plaine Refutation* at Middelburg by the governor, Sir Robert Sidney. See Carlson, *The Writings of Henry Barrow, 1590–1591*, pp. 370–377.]

[2] [Thomas Arundell (1353–1414), Archbishop of Canterbury and a staunch opponent of the Wycliffites and Lollards. There is a recent book by Margaret Aston, *Thomas Arundel: A Study of Church Life in the Reign of Richard II*. Oxford, 1967.]

[3] [Stephen Gardiner (1483?–1555), Bishop of Winchester.]

[4] [John Stokesley (1475?–1539), Bishop of London and prosecutor of heretics.]

[5] [Edmund Bonner (1500?–1569), Bishop of London and hated persecutor of Protestants in the reign of Mary.]

[6] [John Story (1510?–1571), Dean of Arches and Chancellor to Bishop Bonner; very active in persecution of heretics.]

[7] [Miles Dunning, a vindictive and blustering chancellor to Dr. John Hopton, Bishop of Norwich. He was regarded as one of the "sorest" persecutors, worse than Nicholas Harpsfield, Archdeacon of Canterbury. Dunning died suddenly in Lincolnshire in 1558.]

[8] Numbers 35:33. [9] Psalmes 9:12.

and yours bycause you have not holpen the Lord against the mighty, as it is written.[1]

I know, Right Honorable, that (if you looke at our persons) we are a people despised and reviled of all men, yea, every where spoken against, as schismatickes, sedicyous persons, subverters of the State, and what not? But this hath allwaies[2] bene the lott of the truthe and servants of God (yea, of the prophetts,[3] apostles,[4] and Christe[5] himselfe) thus to be rayled upon and persecuted for the truthe's sake, and that commonly under other color and pretence. Therefore are we not ashamed of the gospell and suffrings of Christe, neyther ought your Lordship to withholde your help from us, in as much as we suffer these things only for refusing to have spirituall communion with the antechristian prelacy and other clergy abyding in this land, and for labouring in all holy and peaceable manner to obey the Lorde Jesus Christe in his owne ordenance of ministery and worship, prescribed in his last Testament, and sealed with his pretious bloude, wherein if we did erre, yet prysons and gallowes were no fitt meanes to convince and perswade our consciences, but rather a quiet and godly conference, or discussing of the matter by deliberate writinge before aequall judges, which we have often sued for but yet could never obteyne it. And now agayne therefore doe in all humble manner sue to your Lordship to procure it for us. Not that we doubte of this cause whereof we are fully perswaded by the Worde of God, and are still ready (by the grace of God) to seale it with our bloude, but to the end that the truthe being found owt and made manifest, the false offices, callings, and workes of the prelacy and other clergie of this land might be quite abolished owt of it, and their lordships and possessions, which (so longe as they are the mainteynance of this false ministery) were fittly of olde, by [Sir John Oldcastle], the Lord Cobham, that blessed martir, [50 *verso*] sayd to be the venime of Judas shed into the churche,[6] might also be converted to Her Majestie's civill uses (to whome of right they belonge) as were not long since the lyke lyvings of the abbatts, monckes, and friers, in these dominions. That thus there might be more free passage to the gospell of Christe, and

[1] Judges 5:23.

[2] II Timothy 3:12. Acts 28:22. *Acts and Monuments* everywhere. [The same idea and the same words: "the lott of the truthe and servaunts of God," are in chapter XLVI.] [3] Jeremiah 38:4. Matthew 5:11, 12.

[4] Acts 17:6, 7 and 24:5, 6. [5] Luke 23:2. John 19:12.

[6] *Acts and Monuments*, edition 4, volume I, page 562. [London, 1583.] [In the editions by George Townsend, and by Josiah Pratt and John Stoughton, the reference is to Volume III, 333, 346–347.]

more peace to his churche, so as no more innocent bloude might be brought upon this land, but God might be worshipped in peace according to his Worde, and Her Majestie obeyed not for wrath only but also for conscyence sake.

And of these things we are bolde to wryte to your Lordship, being perswaded that it is high tyme for your Honors with speed to consyder hereof, specially now that the Lord hath allready begunne to pleade against this countrye and people by so contagious and deadly a plague, as in wonderfull manner hath bene brought upon this lande and the inhabitantes thereof, since the shedding of the bloude of those faithfull servants of Christe this year last paste.[1] And consydering also that Her Majestie (as we heare), in a gracyous and tender compassion of our distressed estate, hath gyven commission to discharge us all.[2] None of which things seeme to be regarded of our adversaryes, at leaste, not so as they oughte.

Unto your Lordship, therefore, I am bolde, in the name also of my brother, once agayne to make this complainte, humbly praying your Honor to shew that love[3] unto Christe at this tyme, in us his poore afflicted children, which he requireth at your hand, accompteth as donne, or denyed to himselfe, and therefore will accordingly recompense in that greate day.

And thus in all humble manner craving pardon for this boldnes, I betake your Lordship to the protection of the Allmightie, praying Him still to lengthen your lyfe in this worlde, to the prayse of his name, and furthering of his truthe, and to gyve you everlasting lyfe, in the worlde to come, to your endles comforte by Jesus Christe. Amen.

From the Clincke, January 8, [1593/1594.]
Your Honor's moste humble suppliante
Frannces Johnson: Pastor of this poore distressed churche, and still in close pryson for the gospell of Jesus Christe.

[1] [The plague was unusually severe and widespread in 1592 and 1593. Johnson seems to establish a causal connection between the execution of three Separatists and the intensifying of the plague, but this is specious reasoning.]

[2] [We have no direct evidence, but it is probable that many of the Separatists were released in 1594, on condition that they should be banished. The leaders remained in prison until 1597. There is some inconclusive evidence of 220 English residents of London who arrived in Middelburg in August, 1593. Most of them seem to be persons fleeing from the plague, but some of them may have been Separatists. The law of 35 Elizabeth, chapter I, began to take effect in August—forty days after April 10 (May 20), and then a period of three months when a Separatist had to decide between conformity or banishment. See *The Fugger News-Letters*. Second Series. Ed. Victor von Klarwill (London, 1926), p. 250.]

[3] Matthew 25:34, 35, etc.

[Endorsement: 52 *verso*]:

To the Right Honorable, my very
good Lorde, the Lord Burghley,
Lord High Treasurer of Englande.

[In another hand]:

8 January [1593/1594].
Franncis Johnson preacher,
prisonner in the Clynck.

XLIX

THAT FRAUNCES JOHNSON FOR HIS WRITING IS NOT UNDER THE DANGER OF THE STATUTE OF 35 ELIZABETH, CHAPTER I, MADE TO RETAYNE THE QUEEN'S MAJESTIE'S SUBJECTS IN THEYR DUE OBEDYENCE, APPERETH THUS.

This document is in Lansdowne MSS. 75, item 25, ff. 52–53. It is a collection of eleven reasons why Francis Johnson considers himself not in danger of the new law of 35 Elizabeth, chapter I, entitled "An Acte to Retayne the Quene's Majestie's Subjects in Theyr Due Obedyence." This statute received the Queen's approval on April 10, 1593. It should not be confused with a previous statute of 23 Elizabeth, chapter I, which carried the similar title: "An Acte to Reteine the Queene's Majestie's Subjectes in Their Due Obedience."

About April, 1593, Penry had sent Lord Burghley a series of arguments indicating why he was not guilty of the statute of 23 Elizabeth, chapter II (Lansdowne MSS. 75, item 26, ff. 54–55). It is evident that Johnson had read this document and was indebted to it, not only for general reasons but also for particular references to earlier martyrs such as Wiclif, Tyndale, and Frith and to three specific legal citations which Penry had given.

John Strype has printed this document in his *Annals*, IV (1824), pp. 192–194. But the reader should be warned that Strype has severely curtailed this document with no indication of omissions. The title is printed correctly except for the omission of the word "Majestie's." The final short paragraph is correct. But the remaining ten paragraphs are all incomplete. After Strype's first paragraph, there are 133 (typewritten) lines, or about five typed pages, double-spaced, omitted. In the following four paragraphs Strype omits about fifty-eight lines, and in the last six paragraphs he omits some ninety-five words.

In paragraph six, Strype reads: "her majesty protesteth." The correct reading is: "her majesty protecteth." In summary, Strype's version is reasonably accurate, with minor mistakes, but he has printed less than a third of the original manuscript.

[52 *recto*]

THAT FRAUNCES JOHNSON FOR HIS WRITING IS NOT UNDER THE DANGER OF THE STATUTE OF 35 ELIZABETH, CHAPTER I, MADE TO RETAYNE THE QUEEN'S MAJESTIE'S SUBJECTS IN THEYR DUE OBEDYENCE, APPERETH THUS.

1. First, by comparing together the words of this statute with the statute of 1° Elizabeth, chapter I, wherein Her Majestie's authority in ecclesiasticall causes is declared, and with the interpretacion and defence thereof, allowed by publicke authority.[1]

First, the words of the statute of 35 Elizabeth, Chapter I, are these: "If any above sixteen yeares, which shall obstinately refuse to repayre to some churche to heare devyne service, established by Her Majestie's lawes, etc., shall by printing, writing, or expresse words or speeches, advisedly and purposely practize, or goe aboute to move or perswade any of Her Majesty's subjectes to deny, withstand, and impugne Her Majestie's power and authority in causes ecclesiasticall, united and annexed to the imperiall crowne of this realme, or to that end and purpose shall advysedly and malyciously move or perswade any other person whatsoever to abstayne from the church, etc., or to come to any unlawfull assemblyes, under colour of religion, contrary to Her Majestie's lawes, etc., being thereof lawfully convicte, shall be committed to pryson,[2] etc." By which it is manyfest that this statute is concerning such writing as whereby one goeth aboute to perswade any "to deny, withstand, or impugne Her Majestie's power and authority in causes ecclesiasticall, united and annexed to the imperiall crowne of this realme."

[1] [See I Elizabeth, chapter I, "An Acte Restoring to the Crowne the Auncyent Jurisdiction over the State Ecclesiasticall and Spirituall," in *Statutes of the Realm*, IV, Part 1, 350–355. Where I have added footnotes, they are put in square brackets to distinguish them from Johnson's annotations.]

[2] [This is taken from the statute, but there are omissions. 1 Elizabeth, chapter I, section 1.]

Next, therefore, we are to consyder the authoritye in ecclesiasticall causes, "annexed to the imperiall crowne of this realme," which appereth evydently by the words of the statute of *anno primo* Elizabeth, chapter I, where having enacted the abolishing of all forreign power, it is added further in these words. "And that also it may [lykewise] please Your Highness that it may be established and enacted by the authority aforesayde, that such jurisdictions, priviledges, superiorityes, and preheminences spirituall and ecclesiasticall, as by any spirituall or ecclesiasticall power or authoritye, hath heretofore bene, or may lawfully be excercysed or used for the visitacion of the ecclesiasticall estate and persons, and for reformacion, order, and correction of the same, and of all manner of errors, heresyes, schismes, abuses, offences, contempts, and enormityes, shall for ever by authoritye of this present parliament, be united and annexed to the imperiall crowne of this realme."[1]

Where it is evydent that there is no other authority annexed to the crowne, in ecclesiasticall causes, than that which hath bene, or may be used lawfully, for the visitacion of the ecclesiasticall estate and persons, and for punnishing all abuses that way. "To the pleasure" (as the statute addeth) "of Allmighty God, the increase of vertue, and the conservacion of the peace and unity of this realme."[2]

By which it appereth that they have not authority to establyshe what ecclesiasticall minystery and lawes they will, and to doe what they please in ecclesiasticall causes. But the warning is, that they have the supreme oversighte under God, over the ecclesiasticall persons and causes, to see that therein all things be ordered according to the lawes of God and of the lande, and to punishe the offenders in this behalfe according to the law of God, and of the lande.

This also further appereth by a particuler example of heresy, which the same statute also mentioneth, to witt, that those who by Her Majestie should be appointed commissioners to excercise this her authoritye should adjudge nothing for heresy but that which heretofore hath bene so adjudged "by the authoritye of the canonicall Scriptures, or by the first fowre generall Councells, [or any of them], or by any other generall Councell, wherein the same was declared heresy by the expresse [and playne] words of the sayd canonicall Scriptures, or such as hereafter shall be [ordredd, judged or] determined to be heresy by the High Courte of Parliament of [52 *verso*] this realme with the assent of the clergye in the

[1] [1 Elizabeth, chapter I, section 8.] [2] [*Ibid.*]

[their] Convocation."[1] Where all these limitacions declare that the authority in ecclesiasticall causes, annexed to the crowne, is only to have the cheife soveraignty therein according to the Worde of God, and not otherwyse.

In the next place we are to see the interpretacion and defence of these lawes, touching Her Majestie's authority in ecclesiasticall causes.

Dr. Billson writing against the Jesuites[2] against whome no doubte he defended it (as he oughte), to the uttermost, first bringeth in the papists' objection in these words: "We confesse princes (say the papists) to be defenders of the faith, and assisters of the churche with their secular might and power. You [Anglicans] avouch them to be supreme moderators and directors of all spirituall things and causes without restraynte." Then Dr. Billson answered, saying, "you finde no such thing in our words or deeds as you reporte of us. We confesse princes to be supreme governors, that is, as we have often tolde you, supreme bearers of the sworde, which was first ordeyned from above to defend and preserve as well godlynes and honesty, as peace and tranquillitye [amongest men]. We gyve princes no power to [devise or] invent new religions, to alter or change sacraments, to decyde or debate doubts of faith, to discusse [disturbe] or infringe the canons of the churche."

And againe he saith:[3] "Against the precepts of Christe, or canons of his church, we gyve princes no power." "Most true, we doe not."

And againe he saith:[4] "As preachers by their office have instruction and direction in all things both temporall and spirituall, to compare them, and pronounce them consonant or dissonant with the lawe of God. So princes have compulsion and correction annexed to their swords, as well for spirituall causes as temporall, or rather of the twayne, to see godlynes and honesty preserved amongst men, then [than] foode and rayment provyded."

And againe he saith,[5] that as for ceremonies, "so for all other ecclesiasticall things and causes, princes be neyther the devysers nor directors of them, but the confirmers and establishers of that which is good, and the displacers and revengers of that which is evill." And all this to be done (as he sheweth before) according to the Scriptures and canons.

Thus we see what the law and interpretacion thereof setteth

[1] [1 Elizabeth, chapter II, section 20.]
[2] Dr. Billson against the Jesuit, page 240, allowed by publicke authority. [Thomas Bilson, *The True Difference betweene Christian Subjection and Unchristian Rebellion* (Oxford, 1585). "Perused and allowed by publike authoritie."]
[3] Page 242. [4] Page 247. [5] Page 252.

downe to be Her Majestie's authoritye in ecclesiasticall causes against which the aforesayd Fraunces Johnson hath not one iote or syllable in any of his writings. But according to the Word of God,[1] and lawe of the lande, [he] acknowledgeth Her Majestie to have power to maintaine all truthe by her sword, to maintayne by her lawes every poynte of God's Worde, his pure religion and true ministery, to suppresse by her lawes all false religions and unlawfull ministeryes, to enforce all persons (whether ecclesiasticall or cyvill) to do their dutyes to God and men.[2] Finally, to have under God the cheife soveraigntie in all causes, and over all persons, to protect the good and punish the evill, according as God hath commanded.[3]

And therefore it necessarily followeth that he is not under the daunger of the statute aforesayde, of 35 Elizabeth, chapter I. Yea, and that in writing against the unlawfullnes of the present ministery of archbishopps, lord byshopps, archdeacons, parsons, vicars, preists, deacons, etc., and for the ministery of pastors, teachers, etc., appointed by Christe in his Word, that herein (I say) he hath done nothing but as he is bound in conscience to God, and Her Majesty, to make knowen the truth owt of the Scriptures according to the talent he hath receyved. 2. Secondly, it will appeare that he is not within daunger of the statute aforesayde, by demaunding this question of the prelates and ministers, to witt, whether Her Majestie with consent of the parliament may suppresse and abolysh this present prelacye and ministery of the lande, and transferre their revenewes [53 *recto*] and possessions to her owne civill uses, as her father of famous memorye, King Henry the Eight, did with abbotts, monckes, etc., and with their lyvings. If it be answered that she may (as indeed shee and all princes[4] may and ought), then it followeth that this present ministery, and their mainteynaunce, is not instituted by Christe, and consequently that it no way impeacheth Her Majestie's authority, in ecclesiasticall causes, to wryte against it. If it be answered that she may not, then (besydes that hereby it appereth them selves doe limite Her Majestie's authoritye in ecclesiasticall causes), it also followeth that eyther them selves must expressely and directly approve their ministery in their severall offices, callings, worcks, and mainteynaunce to be appointed by Christe, in his Worde, or ells they are indeed the denyers, with-

[1] Deuteronomy 17:14, 18, 19, 20. Psalmes 2:10, 11, 12. II Chronicles 29 and 30 and 34. Romans 13:1. I Peter 2:13, 14. Matthew 22:21.
[2] [1 Elizabeth, chapter I, section 8.]
[3] [Romans 13:3, 4.] [4] Revelation 17:16.

standers, and impugners of Her Majestie's authoritye in causes ecclesiasticall, and not such as wryte against the unlawfullnes of their present ministery.

3. Thirdly, his writings are only in defence of such doctrynes of the religion of Christe, as being against the canonicall functions of the pope, were accounted Lollardye and heresye in the holy servants and martirs of Christ in former ages. As for example, John Wicliffe[1] helde that archbishops, bishops, archdeacons, officials, deanes were disciples of Antechriste.

William Swinderby[2] sayde that "what pope, cardinall, byshop, prelate, or preiste, in manner of lyving or teaching, or lawes making, contrary to Christ's lyving and his lawes, or any other ground putt in ruling of the church of Christ but by Christe, and his lawes, is very Antechriste, adversarye to Jesus Christe, and his apostles."

The Lord Cobham[3] (who was hanged and burnte hanging) helde that the byshops, prestes, prelates, and monckes were the body of the great Antechriste, neyther (sayd he) will I in conscyence obey any of you all till I see you with Peter follow Christe in conversacion. Also, he helde that the possessions and lordships of the clergie were the venome of Judas, shed into the churche.

John Claydon[4] (who was burnt in Smithfeilde) helde that "the archbishops and byshops, speaking indifferently, are the seates of the beast Antechriste, when he sitteth in them and raigneth above other people, in the darke caves of errors and heresyes." Also, "that the byshop's lycense for a man to preache the Worde of God is the true character of the beaste, that is, Antechriste."

William Tindall[5] and John Frith[6] helde that archbishops, lord

[1] *Acts and Monuments.* 4 edition. 1 volume, page 450. A. [London, 1583.]

[2] *Ibid.*, page 468. B. [*The Acts and Monuments of John Foxe*, ed. George Townsend, III (1844), pp. 122, 128. The material on Swinderby's trial before John Trefnant, Bishop of Hereford, in 1391, is given on pages 109–128.]

[3] *Ibid.*, page 562 and 563. [In the edition edited by Townsend, see III, 333, 346–347. Sir John Oldcastle, Lord Cobham, was burned in December, 1417. See W. T. Waugh, "Sir John Oldcastle," *English Historical Review*, July, October, 1905. See also two articles by J. G. Waller, "The Lords of Cobham, Their Monuments and the Church," in *Archaeologia Cantiana*, XI (London, 1877), 49–112; and XII (1878), 113–166.]

[4] *Ibid.*, page 639. B. [Townsend edition, III, 532. Claydon was burned in 1415. See the same page in the Josiah Pratt and John Stoughton edition.]

[5] In his treatyses called, *The Obedience of a Christian Man*, and *The Practize of Prelates.* [*The Whole Workes of W. Tyndall, John Frith, and Doct. Barnes* (London, 1573); see "The Obedience," pp. 97–183 and especially 103, 134, 170; see "The Practize," pp. 340–377.]

[6] In his preface before his *Antithesis between Christ and the Pope.* [See *The Whole Workes of W. Tyndall, John Frith, and Doct. Barnes*, pp. 97–98.]

byshops, archdeacons, deanes, officialls, parsons, vicars, and the rest of that sorte are the disciples of Antechriste, yea, very Antechrists themselves. The lyke might be shewed by the testimony of many other the holy servants and wittnesses of Christe in former tymes. But those martirs writing in defence of the sayd doctrynes of Christe did not any way, therein deny, impugne, or withstande the princes' authoritye under whome they lyved. Therefore, etc.

4. Fourthly, seing his writings are only in mainteynaunce of such points of religion as were in the foresayde martirs accounted Lollardy and heresy. Then if by his writings he be in daunger of this statute of 35 Elizabeth, chapter I, it would followe that this statute both revyveth those three statutes[1] of 5 Richard II, chapter 5, and *anno* 2, Henry IV, chapter 15, and *anno* 2, Henry V, chapter 7, and that of 25 Henry VIII, chapter 14, and that also it repealeth that statute of 1 Edward VI, chapter 12, whereby he is delyvered from all penaltyes and forfaytures that he might have incurred for such writings and opinions.[2] But this statute neyther revyveth the one, nor repealeth the other. Therefore, etc.

5. Fifthly, if this statute of 35 Elizabeth be against such writings and bookes as reprove the ecclesiasticall ministery and government of archbyshops, lord bishops, archdeacons, deanes, etc., then the writing and printing of the publicke Confession of the reformed churches of Helvetia, Tiguri, Geneva, Schaphuse, [Schaffhausen], etc., wherein they wryte that as touching archprelates, metropolitanes, archpreistes, [53 *verso*] deanes, subdeacons, and all that rabble, they passe not a rushe.[3] And the publicke Confession of the reformed French and Belgicke churches,[4] which wryte that the churche ought to be governed by that regiment or discipline which Christe hath appointed, to witt, "so that there be in it pastors, ellders,

[1] Repealed in *anno* 1 Elizabeth, chapter I, [section 6].

[2] [5 Richard II, Statute the First, chapter V. "The King's Pardon to Those That Repressed or Punished His Rebels." *Statutes of the Realm*, II, page 20. 2 Henry IV, chapter XV, "Against the Lollards." *Statutes of the Realm*, II, pages 125–128. 2 Henry V, Statute the First, chapter VII. "Suggested Evils from the Religious Sect Called Lollards." *Statutes of the Realm*, II, pp. 181–184. 25 Henry VIII, chapter XIV. "An Acte for Punysshement of Heresye." *Statutes of the Realm*, III, pages 454–455. 1 Edward IV, chapter XII. "An Acte for the Repeale of Certaine Statutes concerninge Treasons, Felonyes, etc." *Statutes of the Realm*, IV, Part 1, pp. 18–22.]

[3] *Harmony of Confessions*, section 11; Helvetia latter, chapter 18. [The Latter Confession of Helvetia, pages 339–340, in *An Harmony of the Confessions of the Faith of the Christian and Reformed Churches* (Cambridge, 1586). *S.T.C.*, no. 5155.]

[4] *Harmony of Confessions*, section 11, French and Belgick Confession. [Pages 359, 363.]

and deacons," yea, and that all men[1] ought to submitt themselves to that ecclesiasticall discipline which Christe hath appointed, allthough the contrary edictes of princes doe forbyd it upon payne of deathe.[2] Then (I say) the printing and writing of these Confessions aforesayde, yea, and of the *Acts and Monuments* and dyvers other bookes wherein infinite such lyke sayings and treatyses be founde should be thought to be within compasse of perswading to deny and impugne Her Majestie's authoritye in ecclesiasticall causes, whereas to the contrary we finde them to be allowed by publicke authoritye and printed by priviledge of Her Majestye.

6. Sixthly, in his writings he hath proved his assertions by the Worde of God which Her Majesty protecteth and defendeth, yea, and alloweth her subjects to wryte in defence of every poynte of christian religion which is taught therein. Therefore he is not within daunger of this statute.

7. Seaventhly, his writings are in defence of the rights and libertyes of the church of Christe, which the greate charter of Englande[3] granteth shall be free and have all her whole rightes and lybertyes inviolable in this lande for evermore. Now this statute of 35 Elizabeth [chapter I] is not any way against the greate charter of Englande, or any thinge therein conteyned. Therefore, etc.

8. If every perswasion not to have spirituall communion with the publicke ministery of these assemblyes be within daunger of this statute, as tending to impugne Her Majestie's authoritye in ecclesiasticall causes, then, if any should perswade another quite to forsake the aforesaide ministery and to joyne himselfe alltogether to the French, Dutch, or Italian churches, allowed by Her Majestie in London, Norwich, Sandwich, etc., he should also incurre the penalty of this statute. But the latter is false, therefore also the former.

9. He never did malicyously perswade any to abstaine from the churche, etc., much lesse to the ende and purpose that they should "deny, withstande, or impugne Her Majestie's [power and] authority in causes ecclesiasticall," unto which he perswadeth all men to submitt themselves in the Lorde, not for wrath only but also for conscyence sake. g° [*ergo*].

10. He never did nor doth obstinately without lawfull cause (but upon conscience grounded upon God's Word and approved by consent of the Confessions both of the reformed churches at this

[1] *Ibidem*, section 10, French and Belgick Confessions. [Pages 319–323.]
[2] [*Ibidem*, page 322.] [3] Magna Charta, *caput* 1.

day and of the faithfull servants and martirs of Christe in former ages) refuse to heare and have spirituall communion with the publicke ministery of these assemblyes, as now it standeth. Therefore, etc.

[11]. Finally, these things standing thus (as is aforesayde), and he having bene close prisoner ever since a longe tyme before this statute of 35 Elizabeth [chapter I] was made, he can not in regard of his writings or any other thinge whatsoever be lawfully convicted to have offended against this statute.[1] And therefore is not under the daunger thereof.

[1] [He was imprisoned on the night of December 5–6, 1592. The law received the Queen's assent on April 10, 1593. The law was not retroactive; in fact, it went into effect only after forty days had elapsed after the end of the Parliament on April 10 or 12, 1593. Johnson is correct in asserting that he cannot be indicted for offending by writing. He is incorrect in saying "or any other thinge whatsoever." The statute enforced conformity or banishment, upon conviction, after three months. Johnson refused conformity, and he was also guilty of holding conventicles and persuading people to attend them.]

L

THE HUMBLE PETITION OF HER HIGHNES' FAITHFULL SUBJECTS FALSLY CALLED BROWNISTES [1597] TO THE RIGHT HONORABLE THE LORDS OF HER MAJESTIE'S MOST HONORABLE PRIVIE COUNCELL

This petition is in the Public Record Office, State Papers Domestic, Elizabeth, Volume 246, Item 56. There is complementary information in the *Acts of the Privy Council of England, New Series*, XXVII, *A.D. 1597* (London, 1903), pp. 5–6, for March 25, 1597.

As a consequence of this petition, probably penned by Francis Johnson, the government permitted four hard-core Separatists to embark on a colonizing project in the Gulf of St. Lawrence, in the vicinity of the island of Ramea or Amherst Island in the Magdalen Islands. The four Separatists had been in prison for varying lengths of time. John Clarke was first apprehended about January, 1589/1590, and had been in Newgate prison for three years when he was examined on April 3, 1593. Since he was especially punished by the high commissioners, to whom "yt was thoughte good . . . that hee should bee sente to Bridewell, to grinde in the mill," it is likely that he had been in prison more than seven years without bail. George Johnson had been in prison since March 4, 1592/1593, and Francis Johnson had been imprisoned since December 6, 1592. Daniel Studley had also been in prison since December 17–24, 1592, and had been sentenced to death on March 23, 1592/1593, for publishing and distributing Separatist books, then reprieved and kept in prison. Francis Johnson was the pastor and Studley the elder of the Separatist Church.

Francis Johnson and Studley sailed on the *Hopewell*, with Charles Leigh as the owner and William Crafton as master. George Johnson and Clarke boarded the *Chancewell*, with

Stephen van Herwick as a merchant-sponsor and Steven Bennet as master. The ships left Gravesend April 8, 1597, arrived at Falmouth in Cornwall on April 28, then continued to Newfoundland, where they arrived on May 18. On June 5 the ships lost touch in a fog, and the *Hopewell* continued westward. It visited St. Paul's Island, Bird Isle and Brion's Isle. On June 18 the *Hopewell* rounded the southwest cape of Amherst Island, which was vaguely thought to be Ramea, and entered the harbour from the south and east. The prospective colonizers were dismayed when they encountered four ships, about 200 Frenchmen and Bretons, and some 300 Indian savages. Obviously, the Englishmen were intruders, and there was no opportunity for exploring. On June 22 the *Hopewell* put to sea, and on June 27 reached St. Ann's Bay on the east side of Cape Breton.

In the meantime the *Chancewell* had sailed south from Newfoundland down the east coast of Cape Breton. On June 23 the ship came eighteen leagues within the Cape—probably St. Ann's—and in broad daylight ran on a rock, evidently by the negligence of the master, Steven Bennet, who had no pilot. The ship was floated off the rock, but the damage to the hull was serious, and the *Chancewell* was run onto a sandy beach. Here it was stripped by Frenchmen who came in their shallops, and the Englishmen were even despoiled of their personal possessions. After four days of privation, eight men from the *Chancewell*, in their shallop, by sheer good fortune sighted the *Hopewell* and were rescued. After two weeks of adventure and exploring, the *Hopewell* sailed for Newfoundland on July 10. In St. Lawrence Bay or Placentia Bay, they seized a Spanish ship, the *Catalina*, but were compelled to give over their prize to some Basques. Despite this set-back, the Englishmen sailed to Cape Saint Mary where they captured another prize on July 25—a Breton ship of 200 ton burden from Belle-Isle. Plans were quickly changed, and the *Hopewell* with Master Crafton set out for the Azores. Charles Leigh, with the four Separatists, boarded the captured vessel and set out for England on August 5. By the end of the month they reached the island of Lundy in the Bristol Channel, and on September 5 the Separatists secretly landed on the south side of the Isle of Wight. They made their way to London, but in a day or two were dismayed to learn that rumours of their arrival had spread to the magistrates. Leaving London, the Separatists sailed from Gravesend to Amsterdam, and joined their fellow Separatists about September 20.

Though the colonizing effort proved abortive, it is of interest because it occurred ten years before the settlement of Jamestown and twenty-three years prior to the settlement at Plymouth in New England. It should be associated with another colonizing effort which the Separatists of the Ancient Church made in 1618. About 180 of the Separatists, under the direction of the elder Francis Blackwell, set out for the New World in September. Blown off their course, decimated by scurvy, desperately short of water, some 130 Separatists died on the voyage, and only about fifty finally arrived in Virginia in March, 1619. The news of this harrowing voyage reached the Separatists at Leyden, and may have been one of the reasons why only about one-sixth of John Robinson's congregation sailed in the *Mayflower* to Plymouth the following year.

The primary source for the voyage to the Magdalen Islands is the narrative of Charles Leigh. See Richard Hakluyt, *The Third and Last Volume of the Voyages, Navigations, Traffiques, and Discoveries of the English Nation* (London, 1600), III, 189–201. See also Hakluyt, *The Principal Navigations*, VIII (Glasgow, 1904), pp. 150–155, 161–162, 166–182. The Separatists are discreetly omitted from the narrative, but their names are given in George Johnson, *A Discourse of Some Troubles and Excommunications in the Banished English Church at Amsterdam*, pp. 109–114. The best work on this early voyage has been done by David B. Quinn. See his four articles: "The English and the St. Lawrence 1577 to 1602," *Merchants and Scholars*, ed. John Parker (Minneapolis, 1965); "The First Pilgrims," *William and Mary Quarterly*, July, 1966; "Charles Leigh" and "George Johnson" in the *Dictionary of Canadian Biography* (Toronto, 1966). See also John D. Rogers, *A Historical Geography of the*

British Colonies. Vol. V—Part IV. *Newfoundland* (Oxford, 1931), and R. Douglas, *Place-Names on Magdalen Islands, Que.* (Ottawa, 1922), which is a reprint from the 17th Report of the Geographic Board, with a very helpful map.

THE HUMBLE PETITION OF HER HIGHNES' FAITHFULL SUBJECTS FALSLY CALLED BROWNISTES [1597] TO THE RIGHT HONORABLE THE LORDS OF HER MAJESTIE'S MOST HONORABLE PRIVIE COUNCELL

Whereas wee Her Majestie's naturall borne subjectes true and loyall nowe lyving many of us in other countries as men exiled [from] Her Highnes' domynions, and the rest which remaine within Her Grace's land greatlie distressed thorough imprisonment and other great troubles sustained onlie for some matters of conscience, in which our most lamentable estate, wee cannot in that measure performe the dutie of subjectes, as wee desier. And also wheareas meanes is now offered for our beeing in a forraigne and farre countrie which lieth to the west from hence in the Province of Canada where by the providence of the Almightie, and Her Majestie's most gratious favour, wee may not onlie worshippe God as wee are in conscience perswaded by his Word, but also doe unto Her Majestie and our country great good service, and in tyme also greatlie annoy that bloodie and persecuting Spaniard about the Baye of Mexico. Our most humble suite is that it may please your Honors to bee a meanes unto her excellent Majestie that with her most gracious favour and protection wee may peaceablie depart thither, and there remayning to bee accounted Her Majestie's faithfull and loving subjectes, to whom wee owe all dutie and obedience in the Lord. Promising heerebie, and takeing God to record who searcheth the hartes of all people, that wheresoever wee be come wee will, by the grace of God, live and die faithfull to Her Highnes and this land of our nativitie.[1]

[1] Although this petition is brief, there are some nine phrases which are paralleled in chapters XLIII–XLVIII, all by Johnson. These expressions are: "falsly called Brownistes, Her Grace, matters of conscience, lamentable estate, in conscience perswaded, to be a meanes, faithfull and loving subjectes, who searcheth the hartes, Almightie." These parallels are not conclusive, but they are indicative of Johnson's authorship. Of the four prisoners who were exiled to the New World, Johnson is the natural choice as the penner of this appeal.

A SELECT BIBLIOGRAPHY

MANUSCRIPTS

BODLEIAN LIBRARY. OXFORD

Additional MSS. c. 303, ff. 204–206
Tanner MSS. 84, ff. 38 *v.*–79

BRITISH MUSEUM. LONDON

Additional MSS.
6394, ff. 106, 107, 114
15891, 17097, f. 15, 17677
24666, ff. 17–19
25465, f. 48
28571, ff. 165 *v.*, 166, 169
29546, ff. 55, 119, 120, 121
38492
48064, ff. 15–18, 50–63, 68, 76–87, 94, 95, 134–143
48096, 48187, 48188

BRITISH MUSEUM. LONDON

Harley MSS.
1552, ff. 43, 47
1912, f. 10
6848, ff. 1–36, 41, 43, 47, 51, 55, 57, 58, 59, 61, 62, 63, 65, 66, 67, 69, 70, 71, 76, 79, 80–6, 89, 95, 96, 112, 150, 152, 181, 210, 212, 220
6849, ff. 143, 145, 181–183, 191, 193, 195, 204, 210, 211, 214, 216, 217, 233 *v.*, 243, 262–264
6993, no. 33, f. 61
7028–7050 (Baker MSS. I–XXIII) (XXIV–XXXVIII at Cambridge University)
7041, ff. 153–159
7042, ff. 9, 10, 13, 14, 34–64, 193–198, 204, 205
7581

BRITISH MUSEUM. LONDON

Lansdowne MSS.
23, f. 12

33, no. 13, f. 26; no. 21, f. 40; no. 24, f. 48; no. 25, f. 50; no. 26, f. 52
46, no. 65, f. 132
57, item 14, f. 50
61, no. 54, f. 151
64, no. 16; no. 48
64, item 19, f. 61
65, item 44, f. 133; item 65, ff. 182 *r.* and *v.*
68, item 48, f. 110
72, item 39; item 51
73, item 27, f. 76
75, ff. 42, 50–53
82, item 63
82, item 69, f. 150
85, items 49, 51, 52, 53
107, item 25, f. 44
109, ff. 1, 23, 34, 37–42
157, item 43
982, ff. 111, 161 *v.*

BRITISH MUSEUM. LONDON
Sloane MSS., 271, f. 20 *v.*, 24 *v.*

CAMBRIDGE UNIVERSITY LIBRARY
George Gifford, *A Short Reply* B b. * 11.29
Barrow's marginalia
Baker MSS., XXIV–XXXVIII
(I–XXIII at B.M., Harley 7028-7050)
St. John's College, M9, no. 392

CONGREGATIONAL LIBRARY, MEMORIAL HALL. LONDON
Giles Wiggenton MSS. I. e. 14

CORPUS CHRISTI COLLEGE. CAMBRIDGE
MS. 547

CORPUS CHRISTI COLLEGE. OXFORD
MS. 318, f. 143

DR. WILLIAMS'S LIBRARY. LONDON
Seconde Part of a Register (B), 441–465
Transcript Volume (C), 533–554

GREATER LONDON RECORD OFFICE
DL/C/359, ff. 210 *v.* and 211 *r.*

HATFIELD HOUSE. HATFIELD, HERTFORDSHIRE

Cecil Papers, Marquis of Salisbury

Vol. 167, ff. 100 *r.* and *v.*, 102

HENRY E. HUNTINGTON LIBRARY. SAN MARINO, CALIFORNIA

Ellesmere MSS. 16b, 483, 1988, 2077, 2091–2117, 2121, 2145–2156, 2158, 11638

JOHN RYLANDS LIBRARY, MANCHESTER

English MS. 874, ff. 40–42

LAMBETH PALACE LIBRARY.

Robert Some, *A Godly Treatise Containing and Deciding Certaine Questions* (1588). This volume contains Barrow's interleaved manuscript replies (30. 6. 12)

MS. Carta Miscell. XII, no. 9, no. 19

Codices Manuscripti Lambethani, no. 273

MSS. 43, f. 18

MSS. 113, no. 11

MSS. 445, f. 438

MSS. 650, no. 232

PIERPONT MORGAN LIBRARY. NEW YORK

Job Throckmorton MS., ff. 13, 17, 18

MS. MA 276 (Phillipps MS. 13891)

PUBLIC RECORD OFFICE. LONDON

State Papers, Domestic, Elizabeth

CXIII, item 8, f. 61

CLVIII, no. 69

CLXX, f. 10

CXC, no. 86

CCIV, item 10

CCXXXIX, item 93

CCXLIV, no. 124; item 62

CCXLVI, items 56, 68, 69, 72, 75

State Papers, Domestic, Addenda, Elizabeth

Vol. XXXI, no. 33

State Papers, Holland

XLI, ff. 349 *r.* and *v.* S.P. 84/41

XLII, f. 82. S.P. 84/42

Star Chamber 5 A 49/34

5 A 56/1

S.P. 12/93/8
S.P. 12/155/5
S.P. 12/223/23
S.P. 14/10A/81
S.P. 15/21/27, 32, 33

ST. JOHN'S COLLEGE. CAMBRIDGE
MS. M9, no. 392

ST. PAUL'S CATHEDRAL LIBRARY. LONDON
Add. MSS. I, IV, VII
MS. Folder No. 11, item 5
Package No. 4—MS. on *ex officio* Oath

STAATSARCHIV. ZURICH, SWITZERLAND
Zurich Letters
Vols. I (E II 335)–LXI (E II 388b)
Vol. XXXVI (E II 369) Anglicanae Litterae, 1538–1641. Best. Mostly available in Parker Society translation
Vols. LXII (E 389)–CXVII (E 436 a) mostly of seventeenth century; last thirteen volumes of the eighteenth century

STONYHURST COLLEGE. BLACKBURN, LANCASHIRE
Verstegan Dispatches
Collectanea B, ff. 87–89

UNIVERSITY OF LEIDEN. THE NETHERLANDS
Papenbroek MSS.
Constantine Huygens MSS.

ARTICLES

BUTTERWORTH, CHARLES C. "The Term 'Lord's Prayer' instead of Pater Noster." *Library Chronicle*, Winter, 1951/1952.

COLLINSON, PATRICK. "John Field and Elizabethan Puritanism." *Elizabethan Government and Society. Essays Presented to Sir John Neale*. Ed. S. T. Bindoff, J. Hurstfield, and C. H. Williams. London, 1961.

CONDON, RICHARD H. "The Fleet Prison." *History Today*, July, 1964.

CONGREGATIONAL HISTORICAL SOCIETY. *Transactions*. See Vol. I, "Lists of Early Separatists"; II, "The Brownists in Amsterdam"; "A Letter of Henry Barrow's to Mr. Fisher";

"Four Causes of Separation"; "A Remarkable Puritan Manuscript"; "A Pastoral Letter from Prison"; III, "Profes of Aparant Church."

DAVIES, J. G. "Deacons, Deaconesses and the Minor Orders." *Journal of Ecclesiastical History*, April, 1963.

DIBDIN, LEWIS T. "Doctor's Commons." *Quarterly Review*, July, 1932.

"The Great Hospital. Norwich." *The Listener*, August 13, 1964.

HARRISON, G. B. "Books and Readers, 1591–4." *Library*, New Series, VIII, No. 3 (December, 1927).

HITCHCOCK, ROSWELL D. "Origin and Growth of Episcopacy." *American Presbyterian and Theological Review*, January, 1867.

HOOPER, WILFRED. "The Court of Faculties." *English Historical Review*, October, 1910.

JAMES, MARGARET. "The Political Importance of the Tithes Controversy in the English Revolution, 1640–60." *History*, June, 1941.

LIGHTFOOT, J. B. "The Christian Ministry." *Saint Paul's Epistle to the Philippians*. London, 1913.

LINSCOTT, ELIZABETH. "The Art of the Tomb." *History Today*, June, 1968. [Thomas Owen, Justice of the Court of Common Pleas. Queen's Serjeant who prosecuted the Separatists in 1593. Died 1598.]

MAITLAND, F. W. "Elizabethan Gleanings. V. Supremacy and Uniformity." *English Historical Review*, July, 1903.

MILLER, PERRY. "The Marrow of Puritan Divinity." Publications of the Colonial Society of Massachusetts. Vol. XXXII. *Transactions 1933–1937*. Boston. 1937.

MØLLER, JENS G. "The Beginnings of Puritan Covenant Theology." *Journal of Ecclesiastical History*, April, 1963.

MORRIS, COLIN. "The Commissary of the Bishop of the Diocese of Lincoln." *Journal of Ecclesiastical History*, April, 1959.

MORRIS, JOHN. "Restrictive Practices in the Elizabethan Book Trade: The Stationers' Company *v.* Thomas Thomas, 1583–8." *Transactions of the Cambridge Bibliographical Society*, IV, Part IV, 1967.

MOULE, C. F. D. "A Reconsideration of the Context of Maranatha." *New Testament Studies*, July, 1960.

MUSS-ARNOLT, WILLIAM. "Puritan Efforts and Struggles, 1550–1603. A Bio-Bibliographical Study." *American Journal of Theology*, July, October, 1919.

NEALE, JOHN E. "The Elizabethan Acts of Supremacy and Uniformity." *English Historical Review*, July, 1950.

NEALE, JOHN E. "Parliament and the Articles of Religion." *English Historical Review*, October, 1952.

NEALE, JOHN E. "Peter Wentworth." *English Historical Review*, January, April, 1924.

OWEN, H. GARETH. "Parochial Curates in Elizabethan London." *Journal of Ecclesiastical History*, April, 1959.

OWEN, THOMAS. Justice of the Common Pleas. *History Today*, June, 1968.

PEEL, ALBERT. "From the Elizabethan Settlement to the Emergence of Separatism." *Essays Congregational and Catholic*. Ed. Albert Peel. London: Congregational Union, [1931].

POWICKE, F. J. "English Congregationalism in Its Greatness and Decline (1592–1770)." *Essays Congregational and Catholic*. Ed. Albert Peel. London: Congregational Union, [1931].

PRICE, F. DOUGLAS. "The Abuses of Excommunication and the Decline of Ecclesiastical Discipline under Queen Elizabeth." *English Historical Review*, January, 1942.

QUINN, DAVID B. "England and the St. Lawrence, 1577 to 1602." *Merchants and Scholars*. Ed. John Parker. Minneapolis: University of Minnesota Press, 1965.

QUINN, DAVID B. "The First Pilgrims." *William and Mary Quarterly*, July, 1966.

ROSS, J. M. "The Elizabethan Elder." *Journal of the Presbyterian Historical Society of England*, X, no. 2 (May, 1953), 59–67, 126–136.

SMITH, ALAN G. R. "Portrait of an Elizabethan. The Career and Character of Sir Michael Hickes." *History Today*, October, 1964.

SMITH, ALAN G. R. "The Secretariats of the Cecils, *circa* 1580–1612." *English Historical Review*, July, 1968.

STENGER, ROBERT P. "The Episcopacy as an Ordo According to the Medieval Canonists." *Mediaeval Studies*, 1967.

TRINTERUD, LEONARD J. "The Origins of Puritanism." *Church History*, March, 1951.

WALTON, BRIAN. "Treatise Concerning the Payment of Tythes and Oblations in London." Samuel Brewster, *Collectanea Ecclesiastica*. London, 1752. The manuscript, no. 273, is at Lambeth Palace Library.

WHITNEY, EDWARD ALLEN. "Erastianism and Divine Right." *Huntington Library Quarterly*, July, 1939.

WILSON, THOMAS. "The State of England *Anno Dom.* 1600." Ed. F. J. Fisher. *Camden Miscellany*, XVI (London, 1936), pp. 1–47.

WRIGHT, LOUIS B. "William Perkins: Elizabethan Apostle of 'Practical Divinity.'" *Huntington Library Quarterly*, January, 1940.

DISSERTATIONS

BABBAGE, STUART BARTON. "The Church of England and Puritanism during the Primacy of Bancroft, 1604–1610." 1941. University of London. (Published, 1962).

BIBBY, EDNA. "The Puritan Classical Movement of Elizabeth's Reign." 1929. University of Manchester.

BREWARD, IAN. "The Life and Theology of William Perkins, 1558–1602." 1963. University of Manchester.

COLLINSON, PATRICK. "The Puritan Classical Movement in the Reign of Elizabeth I." 1957. University of London.

DONALDSON, GORDON. "The Relations between the English and Scottish Presbyterian Movements to 1604." 1938. University of London.

GABRIEL, RICHARD C. "Members of the House of Commons, 1586–7." 1954. University of London.

HUME, MARY BALLANTINE. "The History of the Oath *ex officio* in England." 1923. Radcliffe College, H 922.

MATTHEWS, HAZEL. "Personnel of the Parliament of 1584–1585." 1948. University of London.

MAYOR, STEPHEN H. "The Political Thought of the Elizabethan Separatists." 1951. University of Manchester.

OWEN, H. GARETH. "The London Parish Clergy in the Reign of Elizabeth I." 1957. University of London.

PETTI, ANTHONY G. "A Study of the Life and Writings of Richard Verstegan (c. 1550–1640)." 1957. University of London.

SMITH, ALAN. "Sir Michael Hickes and the Secretariat of the Cecils, 1580–1612." 1962. University of London.

WHITE, B. R. "The Development of the Doctrine of the Church among English Separatists with Special Reference to Robert Browne and John Smyth." 1961. Oxford University.

John Greenwood

BOOKS

ADAMES, JONAS. *The Order of Keeping a Court Leete, and Court Baron . . . with the Charges Appertayning to the Same.* London, 1593.

AINSLIE, JAMES L. *The Doctrines of Ministerial Order in the Reformed Churches of the 16th and 17th Centuries.* Edinburgh, 1940.

AINSWORTH, HENRY. *Counterpoyson.* [Amsterdam?], 1608.

[AINSWORTH, HENRY, and JOHNSON, FRANCIS]. *An Apologie or Defence of Such True Christians as Are Commonly (but Uniustly) Called Brownists: Against Such Imputations as Are Layd upon Them by the Heads and Doctors of the University of Oxford, in Their Answer To the Humble Petition of the Ministers of the Church of England, Desiring Reformation of Certayne Ceremonies and Abuses of the Church.* [Amsterdam], 1604.

[AINSWORTH, HENRY and JOHNSON, FRANCIS?]. *A True Confession of the Faith, and Humble Acknowledgment of the Alegeance, Which Wee Hir Maiesties Subjects, Falsely Called Brownists, Doo Hould towards God, and Yeild to Hir Majestie and All Other That Are Over Us in the Lord.* [Amsterdam?], 1596.

ALISON, RICHARD. *A Plaine Confutation of a Treatise of Brownisme, Published by Some of That Faction, Entitled: A DESCRIPTION OF THE VISIBLE CHURCH. In the Confutation Whereof, Is Shewed, That the Author Hath neither Described a True Government of the Church, nor Yet Proved, That Outward Description Is the Life of the Church.* London, 1590.

ALLEN, JOHN W. *A History of Political Thought in the Sixteenth Century.* 2nd edn. London, 1941.

[ANONYMOUS]. *Master Broughton's Letters, Especially His Last Pamphlet to and against the Lord Archbishop of Canterbury, about Sheol and Hades, for the Descent into Hell, Answered in Their Kind.* London, 1599.

A caustic reply to Broughton's pamphlet, 'An Explication of the Article'.

[ANONYMOUS]. *The Spirit of Libertinism Display'd.* London, 1709. See also *Dangerous Positions.* 1708. Both works are listed under "Christian Church" in the British Museum Catalogue.

ARBER, EDWARD. *An Introductory Sketch to the Martin Marprelate Controversy. 1588–1590.* London, 1879, 1880. Westminster, 1895.

ARBER, EDWARD. *A Transcript of the Registers of the Company of Stationers of London, 1554–1660.* 5 vols. London, 1875–1894.

Bibliography

ASHTON, JOHN. *The Fleet, Its River, Prison and Marriages.* London, 1887.

BABBAGE, STUART BARTON. *Puritanism and Richard Bancroft.* London: S.P.C.K., 1962.

BACON, FRANCIS. "*Certain Observations Made Upon a Libel Published This Present Year, 1592.*" *The Letters and the Life of Francis Bacon, Including All His Occasional Works.* Ed. James Spedding. Vol. I (London: Longmans, Green, and Co., 1890). This is also Vol. VIII in the 14-vol. series. A reply to [*R. Persons?*], *Responsio ad edictum Reginae Angliae.* See also—*A Declaration of the True Causes of the Great Troubles Presupposed to Be Intended against the Realme of England.* This latter work, which Spedding could not find, is listed in the *S.T.C.*, 10,005 and 19,400.

BAKER, HERSCHEL. *The Race of Time; Three Lectures on Renaissance Historiography.* Toronto: University of Toronto Press, 1967.

BANCROFT, RICHARD. *Daungerous Positions and Proceedings.* London, 1593.

BANCROFT, RICHARD. *A Sermon Preached at Paules Crosse the 9 of Februarie, Being the First Sunday in the Parleament, Anno 1588* [*1589*]. London, 1588 [1589].

BANCROFT, RICHARD. *A Survay of the Pretended Holy Discipline.* London, 1593.

BARROW, HENRY. *A Brief Discoverie of the False Church.* [Dort], 1590.

[BARROW, HENRY]. *The Pollution of Universitie Learning, or, Sciences (Falsely So Called).* London, 1642. Extracts from Barrow's two main books.

[BARROW, HENRY *et al.*]. *Mr. Henry Barrowes Platform. Which may serve, as a Preparative to purge away Prelatisme: with some other parts of Poperie. Made ready to be sent from Miles Mickle—bound to Much-beloved England, together with some other memorable things. And, a familiar Dialogue, in and with the which, all the severall matters conteyned in this booke, are set forth and interlaced. After the untimely death of the penman of the foresaid Platforme, and his fellow prisoner; who being constant witnesses in points apperteyning to the true worship of God, and right government of his Church, sealed up their testimony with their bloud: And paciently suffred the stopping of their breath, for their love to the LORD. Anno 1593. Printed for the yeare of better hope.* [London?], 1611.

[BARROW, HENRY]. *A True Description out of the Worde of God, of the Visible Church.* [Dort], 1589. Two copies of the first edition at Lambeth Palace Library.

BARROW, HENRY and GREENWOOD, JOHN. *A Collection of Certain Letters and Conferences Lately Passed betwixt Certaine Preachers and Two Prisoners in the Fleet.* [Dort], 1590.

BARROW, HENRY and GREENWOOD, JOHN. *A Collection of Certaine Sclaunderous Articles Gyven out by the Bisshops against Such Faithfull Christians as They Now Unjustly Deteyne in Their Prisons, Togeather with the Answere of the Saide Prisoners Therunto. Also the Some [Sum] of Certaine Conferences Had in the Fleete, according to the Bishops Bloudie Mandate with Two Prisoners There.* [Dort], 1590.

BARROW, HENRY and GREENWOOD, JOHN. *The Examinations of Henry Barrowe, John Grenewood and John Penrie before the High Commissioners and Lordes of the Counsel. Penned by the Prisoners Themselves before Their Deathes.* [Dort?], *c.* 1593–5. A later edition, dated *c.* 1662, or *c.* 1690, is *c.* 1681, probably edited by Thomas Wall.

BARROW, HENRY and GREENWOOD, JOHN. *A Plaine Refutation of M. Giffords Booke, Intituled, A SHORT TREATISE GAINST THE DONATISTES OF ENGLAND.* [Amsterdam?], 1605, 1606.

BERNARD, RICHARD. *Looke Beyond Luther: or, An Answere to That Question So Often and So Insultingly Proposed by Our Adversaries, Asking Us; Where This Our Religion Was Before Luther's Time?* London, 1623.

BÈZE, THÉODORE DE. *Tractatus pius et moderatus de vera excommunicatione, et christiano presbyterio.* Geneva, 1590. Another edition, London, 1590.

BICKNELL, EDWARD J. *A Theological Introduction to the Thirty-Nine Articles of the Church of England.* 3rd edn. London, 1955.

BILSON, THOMAS. *The Perpetual Governement of Christes Church.* London, 1593.

BILSON, THOMAS. *The Survey of Christs Sufferings for Mans Redemption, and of His Descent to Hades or Hel for Our Deliverance.* London, 1604.

BIRCH, THOMAS. *Memoirs of the Reign of Queen Elizabeth from the Year 1581 till Her Death.* 2 vols. London, 1754.

BOSANQUET, EUSTACE F. *English Printed Almanacks and Prognostications. A Bibliographical History to the Year 1600.* London: Bibliographical Society, 1917.

BOWLER, CYRIL HUGH (ed.). *London Sessions Records, 1605–1685.* "Catholic Record Society," Vol. XXXIV. London, 1934.

BOWLER, CYRIL HUGH (ed.). *Recusant Roll No. 2 (1593–1594).* "Catholic Record Society," Vol. LVII. London, 1965.

BRADSHAW, WILLIAM. *A Shorte Treatise of the Crosse in Baptisme.* Amsterdam, 1604.

BRIDGES, JOHN. *A Defence of the Government Established in the Church of Englande for Ecclesiasticall Matters.* London, 1587.

BROOK, BENJAMIN. *The History of Religious Liberty from the First Propagation of Christianity in Britain, to the Death of George III.* 2 vols. London, [1820].

BROOK, BENJAMIN. *The Lives of the Puritans.* 3 vols. London, 1813.

BROOK, BENJAMIN. *Memoir of the Life and Writings of Thomas Cartwright, B.D., the Distinguished Puritan Reformer; Including the Principal Ecclesiastical Movements in the Reign of Queen Elizabeth.* London, 1845.

BROOKS, ERIC ST. JOHN. *Sir Christopher Hatton, Queen Elizabeth's Favourite.* London: Jonathan Cape, 1946.

BROUGHTON, HUGH. *An Explication of the Article* [*He Descended into Hades*], *of Our Lordes Soules Going from His Body to Paradise.* 2nd edn. [Middelburg?], 1605.

BROWN, JOHN. *The English Puritans.* Cambridge: University Press, 1910.

BROWNE, JOHN. *History of Congregationalism and Memorials of the Churches in Norfolk and Suffolk.* London, 1877.

BURN, JOHN S. *The Fleet Registers.* London, 1833.

BURN, JOHN S. *The High Commission. Notices of the Court and Its Proceedings.* London, 1865.

BURN, JOHN S. *The Star Chamber. Notices of the Court and Its Proceedings; with a Few Additional Notes of the High Commission.* London, 1870.

BURN, RICHARD. *Ecclesiastical Law.* Ed. Simon Fraser; 4 vols. 6th edition, London, 1797. Also, 9th edn., ed. Robert Phillimore, London, 1842.

BURRAGE, CHAMPLIN. *The Early English Dissenters in the Light of Recent Research (1550–1641).* 2 vols. Cambridge: University Press, 1912.

BURRAGE, CHAMPLIN. *The "Retractation" of Robert Browne, Father of Congregationalism, Being "A Reproofe of Certeine Schismatical Persons,* [*i.e.*, Henry Barrowe, John Greenwood, and Their Congregation] *and Their Doctrine Touching the Hearing and Preaching of the Word of God."* Oxford and London, 1907.

CALVIN, JOHN. *The Catechisme, or Maner to Teache Children the Christian Religion.* London, 1580.

CALVIN, JOHN. *Institutes of the Christian Religion.* Trans. Thomas Norton, 1561; by John Allen, 1813; by Henry Beveridge, 1845, 1846; by Ford L. Battles, 1960.

CAMDEN, [CHARLES] CARROLL. *The Elizabethan Woman.* Houston, 1952.

CARDWELL, EDWARD. *Documentary Annals of the Reformed Church of England.* 2 vols. Oxford, 1839.

CARDWELL, EDWARD. *A History of Conferences and Other Proceedings Connected with the Revision of the Book of Common Prayer; from the Year 1558 to the Year 1690.* Oxford: University Press, 1849.

CARDWELL, EDWARD. *Synodalia. A Collection of Articles of Religion, Canons, and Proceedings of Convocation in the Province of Canterbury, from the Year 1547 to the Year 1717.* 2 vols. Oxford, 1842.

CARLILE, CHRISTOPHER. *A Discourse Concerning Two Divine Positions . . . Touching the Descension of Our Saviour Christ into Hell.* London, 1582.

CHADERTON, LAURENCE. *A Fruitfull Sermon, upon the 3. 4. 5. 6. 7. and 8. Verses, of the 12. Chapiter of the Epistle of S. Paul to the Romanes, Very Necessary for These Times to Be Read of All Men, for Their Further Instruction and Edification, in Things concerning Their Faith and Obedience to Salvation.* London, 1584. Also 1586, 1589, 1618.

CHAMBERS, ROBERT. *The Book of Days.* 2 vols. London, 1888.

CHILD, GILBERT W. *Church and State under the Tudors.* London, 1890.

CHRISTIE, JAMES. *Some Account of Parish Clerks.* London, 1893.

CHURCHILL, IRENE JOSEPHINE. *Canterbury Administration.* 2 vols. London: S.P.C.K., 1933.

CHURTON, RALPH. *The Life of Alexander Nowell, Dean of St. Paul's.* Oxford: University Press, 1809.

CLANCY, THOMAS H. *Papist Pamphleteers: The Allen–Persons Party and the Political Thought of the Counter-Reformation in England, 1572–1615.* Chicago: Loyola University Press, 1964.

CLAPHAM, HENOCH. *Errour on the Left Hand, through a Frozen Securitie.* London, 1608.

CLAPHAM, HENOCH. *Errour on the Right Hand, through a Preposterous Zeale.* London, 1608.

CLARKE, M. L. *Classical Education in Britain, 1500–1900.* Cambridge: University Press, 1959.

CLERKE, FRANCISCUS. *Praxis Francisci Clarke.* Ed. Thomas Bladen. Published 1666, but written about 1596. Dublin, 1666.

COLLIER, JEREMY. *An Ecclesiastical History of Great Britain, Chiefly of England, from the First Planting of Christianity to the End of the Reign of King Charles the Second, with a Brief Account of the Affairs of Religion in Ireland.* Ed. Thomas Lathbury. 9 vols. London, 1852.

COLLIER, JOHN PAYNE. *The Egerton Papers.* London: Camden Society, 1840.

COLLINS, ARTHUR. *Letters and Memorials of State.* 2 vols. London, 1746.

COLLINSON, PATRICK. *The Elizabethan Puritan Movement.* London: Jonathan Cape, 1967.

COLLINSON, PATRICK. "*John Field and Elizabethan Puritanism,*" *Elizabethan Government and Society.* Essays Presented to Sir John Neale. Ed. S. T. Bindoff, J. Hurstfield, and C. H. Williams. London, 1961.

CONGREGATIONAL LIBRARY ASSOCIATION. *The Congregational Quarterly.* 20 vols. Ed. J. S. Clark, H. M. Dexter, *et al.* Boston and New York, 1859–1878.

CONGREGATIONAL UNION OF ENGLAND AND WALES. *The Moderators. The Deacon, His Ministry in Our Churches.* London, 1957.

CONSETT, HENRY. *The Practice of the Spiritual or Ecclesiastical Courts.* London, 1685, 1708.

COOPER, CHARLES HENRY. *Annals of Cambridge.* 5 vols. Cambridge, 1842–1852, 1908. Vol. I, to 1547; II, to 1602.

COOPER, CHARLES HENRY and COOPER, THOMPSON. *Athenae Cantabrigienses.* 3 vols. Cambridge, 1858, 1861, 1913.

COOPER, THOMAS. *An Admonition to the People of England.* London, 1589. There are three editions, all bearing the date 1589, with 244, 245, and 252 pages.

COSIN, RICHARD. *An Apologie: of, and for Sundrie Proceedings by Iurisdiction Ecclesiasticall, of Late Times by Some Chalenged, and also Diversly by Them Impugned.* London, 1591. Also issued in 1593. Part III is a defence of the *ex officio* oath.

COSIN, RICHARD. *Conspiracie, for Pretended Reformation:* viz., *Presbyteriall Discipline.* London, 1592.

COSTELLO, WILLIAM T. *The Scholastic Curriculum at Early Seventeenth-Century Cambridge.* Cambridge: Harvard University Press, 1958.

COX, JOHN CHARLES. *The Parish Registers of England.* London: Methuen & Co., 1910.

CREIGHTON, CHARLES. *A History of Epidemics in Britain from A.D. 664 to the Extinction of Plague.* Vol. I. Cambridge, 1891. Pages 351–361 for 1593.

CREMEANS, CHARLES DAVIS. *The Reception of Calvinistic Thought in England.* Urbana: University of Illinois Press, 1949.

CRIPPEN, THOMAS G. *Relics of the Puritan Martyrs, 1593.* London, 1906.

CROSS, FRANK L. (ed.) *The Oxford Dictionary of the Christian Church.* London, 1957.

CUNO, FRIEDRICH WILHELM. *Franciscus Junius der Ältere, Professor der Theologie und Pastor. (1545–1602). Sein Leben und Wirken, seine Schriften und Briefe.* Amsterdam, 1891.

CURTIS, MARK H. *Oxford and Cambridge in Transition, 1558–1642.* Oxford, 1959.

DALE, R. W. *History of English Congregationalism.* Completed and edited by A. W. W. Dale. London: Hodder & Stoughton, 1907.

DANEAU (or DANAEUS), LAMBERT. *The Iudgement of That Reverend and Godly Lerned Man, M. Lambert Danaeus, Touching Certaine Points Now in Controversie, Contained in His Preface before His Commentary upon the First Epistle to Timothie, Written in Latine, and Dedicated by Him to the Prince of Orange.* [Edinburgh, 1590?]

DAVIDS, T. W. *Annals of Evangelical Nonconformity in the County of Essex, from the Time of Wycliffe to the Restoration.* London, 1863.

DAVIES, HORTON. *The English Free Churches.* London, 1952.

DAVIES, HORTON. *The Worship of the English Puritans.* Westminster, 1948.

DAWLEY, POWEL MILLS. *John Whitgift and the English Reformation.* New York: Charles Scribner's Sons, 1954.

D'EWES, SIMONDS. *The Journals of All the Parliaments during the Reign of Queen Elizabeth, Both of the House of Lords and House of Commons.* London, 1682. Also 1693.

DEXTER, HENRY M. *The Congregationalism of the Last Three Hundred Years, as Seen in Its Literature.* New York, 1880.

DIBDIN, LEWIS T. *Church Courts. An Historical Inquiry into the Status of the Ecclesiastical Courts.* 2nd edn. London, 1882.

DIBDIN, LEWIS T. *Establishment in England. Being Essays on Church and State.* London: MacMillan, 1932.

DITCHFIELD, PETER HAMPSON. *The Parish Clerk.* London, 1907.

DIX, GREGORY. *The Shape of the Liturgy*. Second edition. Westminster: Dacre Press, 1945. Chapter XVI on The Reformation and the Anglican Liturgy is relevant to Elizabethan events.

DODD, CHARLES. *Church History of England, 1500–1688*. 5 vols. Ed. M. A. Tierney. London, 1839–1843. 1st edn., 1737–1742. "Dodd" is a pseudonym for Hugh Tootell.

DYSON, HUMFREY. *A Booke Containing All Such Proclamations, as Were Published during the Raigne of the Late Queene Elizabeth*. London, 1618.

EMERSON, EVERETT H. *English Puritanism from John Hooper to John Milton*. Durham: Duke University Press, 1968.

ENGLAND, CHURCH OF. *A Booke of Certaine Canons, Concernying Some Parte of the Discipline of the Church of England. In the Yeare of Our Lord, 1571*. London, [1571].

ENGLAND, CHURCH OF. *The Form and Manner of Making and Consecrating Bishops, Priests, and Deacons: According to the Appointment of the Church of England*. London, 1629. Issued in 1549 and 1552 as part of The Book of Common Prayer, and also published separately.

ENGLAND, CHURCH OF. *The Humble Petition of the Ministers of the Church of England, Desiring Reformation of Certaine Ceremonies and Abuses of the Church*. Oxford, 1603.

ENGLAND, CHURCH OF. *Injunctions Given by the Queene's Majestie. Anno Dom. 1559*. London, 1559.

ENGLAND, CHURCH OF. [Archbishop Matthew Parker]. *Advertisements*. London, [1566]. Also 1571, 1579, 1584. The *S.T.C.*, lists four editions for [1565?] but 1566 is the better date.

FENNER, DUDLEY. *A Defence of the Godlie Ministers, against the Slaunders of D. Bridges*. London, 1587.

FINEGAN, JACK. *Handbook of Biblical Chronology. Principles of Time Reckoning in the Ancient World and Problems of Chronology in the Bible*. Princeton, New Jersey: Princeton University Press, 1964.

FOSTER, JOSEPH. *Alumni Oxonienses: The Members of the University of Oxford, 1500–1714*. 4 vols. Oxford, 1891, 1892.

FOSTER, JOSEPH. *The Register of Admissions to Gray's Inn, 1521–1889, together with the Register of Marriages in Gray's Inn Chapel, 1695–1754*. London, 1889.

FOWLER, JOHN, *et al. A Shield of Defence against the Arrowes of Schisme*. Amsterdam, 1612.

FOXE, JOHN. *The Acts and Monuments of J. Foxe*. Ed. J. Pratt. Introd. by J. Stoughton. 4th edn. 8 vols. London, 1877.

FREND, W. H. C. *The Donatist Church. A Movement of Protest in Roman North Africa.* Oxford, 1952.

FRERE, WALTER HOWARD. *Two Centuries of Stepney History, 1480–1680.* London, 1892.

FRERE, WALTER HOWARD and KENNEDY, W. M. *Visitation Articles and Injunctions of the Period of the Reformation.* 3 vols. London, 1910.

THE FUGGER NEWS-LETTERS. 1st series. *Being a Selection of Unpublished Letters from the Correspondents of the House of Fugger during the Years 1568–1605.* Ed. Victor von Klarwill. Trans. Pauline de Chary. London: John Lane The Bodley Head Ltd., 1928. Vienna edn., 1923.

THE FUGGER NEWS-LETTERS. 2nd series. Ed. Victor von Klarwill. Trans. L. S. R. Byrne. London: John Lane The Bodley Head Ltd., 1926. Letter from Antwerp, August 22, 1593, refers to a Letter of August 19, 1593, and says 220 refugees from England had arrived. Reason—plague—"the great mortality, in London"—p. 250. Letter of September 4/August 25, 1593, for arrival in Middelburg of Barrowists.

FULKE, WILLIAM. *A Briefe and Plaine Declaration Concerning the Desires of All Those Faithful Ministers That Have and Do Seeke for the Discipline and Reformation of the Church of Englande.* London, 1584.

FULLER, THOMAS *et al. Abel Redevivus: or, the Dead Yet Speaking. The Lives and Deaths of the Moderne Divines.* London, 1651.

FUSSNER, F. SMITH. *The Historical Revolution. English Historical Writing and Thought, 1580–1640.* New York and London, 1962.

GIBSON, EDGAR C. S. *The Thirty-Nine Articles of the Church of England.* 2 vols., 1896. 2nd edn. London, 1898.

GIBSON, EDMUND. *A Compleat History of the Convocations, from 1356 to 1689.* Second ed. of *Synodus Anglicana.* London, 1730. Also, edition of Edward Cardwell. Oxford, 1854.

GIBSON, EDMUND. *Synodus Anglicana.* Ed. Edward Cardwell. Oxford, 1854. Also 1702, 1730.

GIFFORD, GEORGE. *A Briefe Discourse of Certaine Points of the Religion, Which Is among the Common Sort of Christians, Which May Bee Termed the Countrie Divinitie.* London, 1581.

GIFFORD, GEORGE. *A Plaine Declaration That Our Brownists Be Full Donatists, by Comparing Them Together from Point to Point out of the Writings of Augustine. Also a Replie to Master Greenwood Touching Read Prayer, Wherein His Grosse Ignorance Is Detected,*

Which Labouring to Purge Himselfe from Former Absurdities, Doth Plunge Himselfe Deeper into the Mire. London, 1590.

GIFFORD, GEORGE. *A Short Reply unto the Last Printed Books of Henry Barrow and John Greenwood, the Chiefe Ringleaders of Our Donatists in England.* London, 1591.

GIFFORD, GEORGE. *A Short Treatise against the Donatists of England, Whome We Call Brownists. Wherein, by the Answeres unto Certayne Writings of Theyrs, Divers of Their Heresies Are Noted, with Sundry Fantasticall Opinions.* London, 1590.

GRACE BOOK (G) (1501–1542). Ed. W. G. Searle. Cambridge, 1908.

GRACE BOOK (D) (1542–1589). Ed. J. Venn. Cambridge, 1910.

GREAT BRITAIN. ECCLESIASTICAL COURTS COMMISSION. *Report of the Commissioners Appointed to Inquire into the Constitution and Working of the Ecclesiastical Courts, with Minutes of Proceedings, Evidence, Returns, Abstracts, Historical and Other Appendices, etc.* 2 vols. London, 1883. This is Command Paper 3760, Parliamentary Papers.

GREAT BRITAIN. RECORD COMMISSION. *Statutes of the Realm.* 9 vols in 12. London, 1810–1828.

GREAT BRITAIN. RECORD COMMISSION. *Valor Ecclesiasticus.* 6 vols. Ed. John Caley and Joseph Hunter. London, 1810–1834.

GREEN, EDMUND TYRRELL. *The Thirty-Nine Articles and the Age of the Reformation.* London, 1896. 2nd edn. 1912.

GREENSLADE, S. L. *The English Reformers and the Fathers of the Church.* Oxford, 1960.

GREG, W. W. *A Companion to Arber: Being a Calendar of Documents in Edward Arber's "Transcript of the Registers of the Company of Stationers of London, 1554–1640" with Text and Calendar of Supplementary Documents.* Oxford: Clarendon Press, 1967.

GREG, W. W. and BOSWELL, E. (eds.) *Records of the Court of the Stationers' Company, 1576 to 1602, from Register B.* London: Bibliographical Society, 1930.

GREENWOOD, JOHN. *An Answere to George Giffords Pretended Defence of Read Praiers and Devised Litourgies with His Ungodlie Cavils and Wicked Sclanders Comprised in the First Parte of His Last Unchristian and Reprochfull Booke Entituled, A SHORT TREATISE AGAINST THE DONATISTS OF ENGLAND.* [Dort], 1590. Reissued in 1603. Printed in 1640 with the title, *More Worke for Priests.*

HALL, HUBERT. *Society in the Elizabethan Age.* London, 1886, 1901.

HANBURY, BENJAMIN. *Historical Memorials Relating to the Independents, or Congregationalists; from Their Rise to the Restoration of the Monarchy, A. D. 1660.* 3 vols. London, 1839–1844.

HANBURY, BENJAMIN. *An Historical Research Concerning the Most Ancient Congregational Church in England, Shewing the Claim of the Church Worshipping in Union Street, Southwark, to That Distinction.* London, 1820.

HANBURY, BENJAMIN. . . . *A Life of Thomas Cartwright.* See Richard Hooker.

HARINGTON, JOHN. *A Briefe View of the State of the Church of England, as It Stood in Q. Elizabeth's and King James His Reigne, to the Yeere 1608.* London, 1653.

An Harmony of the Confessions of the Faith of the Christian and Reformed Churches, Which Purelie Professe the Holy Doctrine of the Gospell in All the Chiefe Kingdomes, Nations, and Provinces of Europe. [Cambridge]: Thomas Thomas, Printer to the University of Cambridge, 1586. *S.T.C.* 5155. First issued in Latin, 1581. In the British Museum Catalogue, this work is listed under "Europe, Christian and Reformed."

HARRISON, G. B. *An Elizabethan Journal; Being a Record of Those Things Most Talked about during the Years 1591–1594.* New York, 1929. Also London, 1928.

HEATON, WILLIAM J. *The Puritan Bible and Other Contemporaneous Protestant Versions.* London: Francis Griffiths, 1913.

HENNESSY, GEORGE. *Novum Repertorium Ecclesiasticum Parochiale Londinense; or, London Diocesan Clergy Succession from the Earliest Time to the Year 1898.* London, 1898.

HESSELS, JOHN HENRY (ed.). *Ecclesiae Londino—Batavae Archivum.* 3 vols. in 4. Cambridge, 1887–1897.

HEYWOOD, JAMES. *Early Cambridge University and College Statutes.* London, 1855.

HEYWOOD, JAMES and WRIGHT, THOMAS. *Cambridge University Transactions during the Puritan Controversies of the 16th and 17th Centuries.* 2 vols. London, 1854.

HIGGINS, JOHN. *An Answere to Master William Perkins Concerning Christ's Descension into Hell.* Oxford, 1602.

HILL, ADAM. *The Defence of the Article: Christ Descended into Hell.* London, 1582.

HILL, CHRISTOPHER. *Economic Problems of the Church from Archbishop Whitgift to the Long Parliament.* Oxford, 1956.

HILL, GEOFFREY. *English Dioceses, A History of Their Limits from the Earliest Times to the Present Day.* London, 1900.

HILL, GEORGE W. and FRERE, WALTER H. (eds). *Memorials of Stepney Parish.* Guildford, 1890–1891.

HOOKER, RICHARD. *The Ecclesiastical Polity and Other Works of Richard Hooker: . . . Accompanied by A Life of Thomas Cartwright, B.D. and Numerous Notes, by Benjamin Hanbury.* 3 vols. London, 1830.

HOWELL, WILBUR S. *Logic and Rhetoric in England, 1500–1700.* Princeton: Princeton University Press, 1956.

HURSTFIELD, JOEL. *The Queen's Wards. Wardship and Marriage under Elizabeth I.* London, 1958.

JACOB, HENRY. *A Defence of the Churches and Ministery of Englande.* Middelburgh, 1599.

JACOB, HENRY. *A Treatise of the Sufferings and Victory of Christ in the Worke of Our Redemption.* [London?], 1598.

JACOB, HENRY. *A Christian and Modest Offer of a Most Indifferent Conference.* [Middelburg?], 1606.

JAGGARD, WILLIAM. *A View of All the Right Honourable the Lord Mayors of This Honorable Citty of London.* London, 1601.

JENKINSON, WILBERFORCE. *London Churches before the Great Fire.* London: S.P.C.K., 1917.

JESSOPP, AUGUSTUS. *The Oeconomy of the Fleete.* Westminster: Camden Society, New Series, No. 25, 1879.

JOHNSON, FRANCIS. *An Answer to Maister H. Jacob His Defence of the Churches and Ministery of England.* [Amsterdam?], 1600.

JOHNSON, FRANCIS. *An Inquiry and Answer of T. White, His Discoverie of Brownisme.* [Amsterdam?], 1606.

JOHNSON, FRANCIS. *A Short Treatise Concerning the Exposition of Those Words of Christ, "Tell the Church."* [Amsterdam?], 1611.

JOHNSON, FRANCIS. *A Treatise of the Ministery of the Church of England. Wherein Is Handled This Question, Whether It Be to Be Separated from, or Ioyned unto. Which Is Discussed in Two Letters, the One Written for It, the Other against It.* [London?], 1595.

JOHNSON, GEORGE. *A Discourse of Some Troubles.* [Amsterdam?], 1603.

JORDAN, W. K. *The Development of Religious Toleration in England.* 4 vols. London: George Allen & Unwin, Ltd., 1932–1940.

KEELING, WILLIAM. *Liturgiae Britannicae, or the Several Editions of the Book of Common Prayer of the Church of England.* 2nd edn. London, 1851.

KENNEDY, W. P. M. *Elizabethan Episcopal Administration. An Essay in Sociology and Politics.* 3 vols. London: A. R. Mowbray & Co., 1924.

KNAPPEN, MARSHALL M. *Tudor Puritanism. A Chapter in the History of Idealism.* Chicago: University of Chicago Press, 1939.

KNOX, S. J. *Walter Travers. Paragon of Elizabethan Puritanism.* London, 1962.

KOCHER, PAUL H. *Science and Religion in Elizabethan England.* San Marino, California: Henry E. Huntington Library, 1953.

LAMBARD, WILLIAM. *The Duties of Constables, Borsholders, Tything-men, and Such Other Lowe and Lay Ministers of the Peace.* London, 1614.

LATHBURY, THOMAS. *A History of the Convocation of the Church of England.* 2[illegible] London, 1853.

LAURENCE, [illegible] *A General Index to the Historical and Biographical Works of John Strype.* 2 vols. in 1. Oxford, 1828.

LAW, JAMES T. *Lectures on the Ecclesiastical Law of England.* London, 1861.

LAWNE, CHRISTOPHER. *Brownisme Turned the In-side Out-ward. Being a Paralell betweene the Profession and Practise of the Brownists Religion.* London, 1613.

LAWNE, CHRISTOPHER, FOWLER, JOHN, SANDERS, CLEMENT, and BULWARD, ROBERT. *The Prophane Schisme of the Brownists or Separatists.* [London?], 1612.

LE NEVE, JOHN. *Fasti Ecclesiae Anglicanae.* London, 1716. Also Oxford, 1854, ed. T. Duffus Hardy, 3 vols.

LECLER, JOSEPH. *Toleration and the Reformation.* Trans. T. L. Westow. 2 vols. New York, 1960.

LEVY, FRED J. *Tudor Historical Thought.* San Marino: Henry E. Huntington Library and Art Gallery, 1967.

LEVY, LEONARD W. *Origins of the Fifth Amendment. The Right against Self-Incrimination.* New York: Oxford University Press, 1968. See especially the excellent discussion, chapters I–VI.

LITTELL, FRANKLIN H. *The Anabaptist View of the Church.* 2nd edn. Boston, 1958. 1st edn., 1952.

LITTELL, FRANKLIN H. *The Free Church.* Boston, 1957.

MCGIFFERT, ARTHUR CUSHMAN. *The Apostles' Creed: Its Origin, Its Purpose, and Its Historical Interpretation.* New York, 1902.

MCGINN, DONALD J. *The Admonition Controversy..* New Brunswick, New Jersey, 1949.

MCKERROW, R. B. *et al. A Dictionary of Printers and Booksellers in England, Scotland and Ireland, and of Foreign Printers of English Books 1557–1640.* London: Bibliographical Society, 1910.

MCNEILL, JOHN T. *The History and Character of Calvinism.* New York: Oxford University Press, 1954.

MAKOWER, FELIX. *The Constitutional History and Constitution of the Church of England.* London, 1895. German edn., 1894.

MARCHANT, RONALD A. *The Puritans and the Church Courts in the Diocese of York, 1560–1642.* London: Longmans, 1960.

MARTEN, ANTHONY. *A Reconciliation of All the Pastors and Cleargy of This Church of England, by Anthony Marten, Sewer of Her Maiesties Most Honorable Chamber.* London, 1590.

MASTERS, ROBERT. *Masters' History of the College of Corpus Christi and the Blessed Virgin Mary in the University of Cambridge. With Additional Matter and a Continuation to* [illegible] *Time by John Lamb, D.D., Master of the College.* London, [illegible]

MEYER, CARL S. *Elizabeth I and the Religious Settlement of 1559.* St. Louis: Concordia Publishing House, 1960.

MORICE, JAMES. *A Briefe Treatise of Oathes Exacted by Ordinaries and Ecclesiastical Iudges, to Answere Generallie to All Such Articles or Interrogatories, as Pleaseth Them to Propound. And of Their Forced and Constrained Oathes* ex officio, *Wherein Is Proued That the Same Are Unlawfull.* [London?, *ca.* 1599].

MORRISON, PAUL G. *Index of Printers, Publishers and Booksellers in A. W. Pollard and G. R. Redgrave, A Short-Title Catalogue of Books Printed in England, Scotland and Ireland and of English Books Printed Abroad, 1475–1640.* Charlottesville, Virginia: Bibliographical Society of the University of Virginia, 1950.

MOSSE, GEORGE L. *The Holy Pretence. A Study in Christianity and Reason of State from William Perkins to John Winthrop.* Oxford: Basil Blackwell, 1957.

MULLINGER, J. B. *The University of Cambridge from the Royal Injunctions of 1535 to the Accession of Charles the First.* Cambridge: University Press, 1884.

NAUNTON, ROBERT. *The Court of Queen Elizabeth: Originally Written by Sir Robert Naunton, under the Title of "Fragmenta Regalia." With Considerable Biographical Additions, by James Caulfield.* London, 1814.

NEAL, DANIEL. *The History of the Puritans.* 5 vols. London, 1822. Other reprints or editions, 1720, 1732–1738, 1747, 1793–1797, 1811, 1837, 1858.

NEALE, J. E. *Elizabeth I and Her Parliaments, 1559–1581.* London: Jonathan Cape, 1953.

NEALE, J. E. *Elizabeth I and Her Parliaments, 1584–1601.* London: Jonathan Cape, 1957.

NEWCOURT, RICHARD. *Repertorium Ecclesiasticum Parochiale Londinense.* 2 vols. London, 1708, 1710.

NICHOLS, JOHN. *The Progresses and Public Processions of Queen Elizabeth.* 3 vols. London, 1788, 1805.

NICOLAS, SIR HARRIS. *Memoirs of the Life and Times of Sir Christopher Hatton, K. G., Vice-Chamberlain and Lord Chancellor to Queen Elizabeth.* London, 1847. Based on Hatton's Letter Book in British Museum, Additional MS. 15891.

NORDEN, JOHN. *Speculum Britanniae.* London, 1593. Has three contemporary maps.

O'CONNELL, MARVIN R. *Thomas Stapleton and the Counter Reformation.* New Haven: Yale University Press, 1964.

O'DONOGHUE, EDWARD GEOFFREY. *Bridewell Hospital, Palace, Prison, Schools from the Earliest Times to the End of the Reign of Elizabeth.* 2 vols. London, 1923, 1929.

OUGHTON, THOMAS. *Ordo Judiciorum.* 2 vols. 1728, 1738. Translated in part by James T. Law, *Forms of Ecclesiastical Law.* London, 1831, 1844.

OXFORD UNIVERSITY. *The Answere of the Vice-chancelour, the Doctors, Both the Proctors, and Other the Heads of Houses in the Universitie of Oxford . . . To the Humble Petition of the Ministers of the Church of England, Desiring Reformation of Certaine Ceremonies and Abuses of the Church.* Oxford, 1603.

PAGET, FRANCIS. *An Introduction to the Fifth Book of Hooker's Treatise of the Laws of Ecclesiastical Polity.* 2nd edn. Oxford, 1907.

PARKER, ROBERT. *A Scholasticall Discourse against Symbolizing with Antichrist in Ceremonies.* [Amsterdam], 1607.

PAULE, SIR GEORGE. *The Life of the Most Reverend and Religious Prelate John Whitgift, Lord Archbishop of Canterbury.* London, 1612. By the comptroller of His Grace's household.

PEARSON, A. F. SCOTT. *Church and State: Political Aspects of Sixteenth Century Puritanism.* Cambridge, 1928.

PEARSON, A. F. SCOTT. *Thomas Cartwright and Elizabethan Puritanism, 1535–1603.* Cambridge, 1925.

PEEL, ALBERT (ed.). *Essays Congregational and Catholic.* London, [1931].

PEEL, ALBERT (ed.). *The Notebook of John Penry, 1593.* London: Royal Historical Society, 1944.

PEEL, ALBERT (ed.). *The Seconde Parte of a Register.* 2 vols. London, 1915.

PEEL, ALBERT (ed.). *Tracts Ascribed to Richard Bancroft.* Cambridge: University Press, 1953.

PEIRCE, JAMES. *A Vindication of the Dissenters.* London, 1717.

PERKINS, WILLIAM. *An Exposition of the Symbole or Creed of the Apostles, According to the Tenour of the Scriptures, and the Consent of Orthodoxe Fathers of the Church.* London, 1595.

PERKINS, WILLIAM. *The Whole Treatise of the Cases of Conscience.* Cambridge, 1606, 1608.

A Petition Directed to Her Most Excellent Majestie, Wherein Is Delivered . . . [*ca.* 1591]. This is listed in the *S.T.C.*, 1521, 1522, 1522a, under Henry Barrow's name, but it is not by Barrow. The date may be 1591/1592 or 1592, the printer is probably Richard Schilders, and the place of publication is probably Middelburg. See J. Dover Wilson, "Richard Schilders and the English Puritans," *Transactions of the Bibliographical Society*, XI (October, 1909, to March, 1911), pp. 97–98.

PETTI, ANTHONY G. (ed.). *The Letters and Despatches of Richard Verstegan* (*c. 1550–1640*). "Catholic Record Society," Vol. LII. London, 1959. He prints eighty-seven letters, with helpful annotations.

PHILLIMORE, SIR ROBERT, PHILLIMORE, SIR WALTER GEORGE FRANK, and JEMMETT, CHARLES FUHR. *The Ecclesiastical Law of the Church of England.* 2 vols. 2nd edn. London, 1895.

PIERCE, WILLIAM. *An Historical Introduction to the Marprelate Tracts.* New York: E. P. Dutton and Co., 1909. London, 1908.

PIERCE, WILLIAM. *The Marprelate Tracts, 1588, 1589.* London, 1911.

PLOMER, HENRY R. *A Dictionary of the Printers and Booksellers Who Were at Work in England, Scotland and Ireland from 1668 to 1725.* Oxford: Bibliographical Society, 1922.

PORTER, HARRY C. *Reformation and Reaction in Tudor Cambridge.* Cambridge, 1958.

POWICKE, F. J. *Henry Barrow, Separatist* (*1550?–1593*), *and the Exiled Church of Amsterdam.* London, 1900.

PROCTER, FRANCIS. *A History of the Book of Common Prayer, with a Ratiaonle of Its Offices.* Cambridge, 1855.

PROCTER, FRANCIS and FRERE, WALTER HOWARD. *A New History of the Book of Common Prayer with a Rationale of Its Offices.* London: Macmillan & Co., 1949.

PROTHERO, G. W. *Select Statutes and Other Constitutional Documents Illustrative of the Reigns of Elizabeth and James I.* Oxford: Clarendon Press, 1894. 4th edn., 1913.

PURVIS, J. S. *An Introduction to Ecclesiastical Records.* London, 1953 [1954].

RATHBAND, WILLIAM (ed.). *A Most Grave, and Modest Confutation of the Errors of the Sect, Commonly Called Brownists, or Separatists.* London, 1644. A printing of a manuscript written about 1592 by T. Cartwright, W. Charke, W. Fludd, and/or Walter Travers. The *S.T.C.* (no. 10,398) and the British Museum Catalogue erroneously list this work as printed in 1592.

REIDY, MAURICE F. *Bishop Lancelot Andrewes, Jacobean Court Preacher. A Study in Early Seventeenth-Century Religious Thought.* Chicago: Loyola University Press, 1955.

RITCHIE, CARSON I. A. *The Ecclesiastical Courts of York.* Arbroath: The Herald Press, 1956.

ROGERS, THOMAS. *The Catholic Doctrine of the Church of England, an Exposition of the Thirty-Nine Articles.* Ed. J. J. S. Perowne for the Parker Society. Cambridge, 1854.

ROGERS, THOMAS. *The English Creede Consenting with the True, Auncient, Catholique and Apostolique Church.* 2 parts. London, 1585, 1587.

ROGERS, THOMAS. *A Sermon upon the 6, 7 and 8 Verses of the 12 Chapter of St. Pauls Epistle unto the Romanes Made to the Confutation of So Much of Another Sermon* [by Chaderton], *Entituled, A FRUITFUL SERMON, etc.* [London], 1590.

RUPP, E. GORDON. *Six Makers of English Religion, 1500–1700.* London, 1957.

RUPP, E. GORDON. *Studies in the Making of the English Protestant Tradition, Mainly in the Reign of Henry VIII.* Cambridge, 1947.

RUSSELL, ARTHUR T. *Memoirs of the Life and Works of the Right Honorable and Right Reverend Father in God Lancelot Andrewes, D.D., Lord Bishop of Winchester.* London, 1863.

RUSSELL, FREDERIC W. *Kett's Rebellion in Norfolk.* London, 1859.

SCHEFFER, JACOB G. DE HOOP. *History of the Free Churchmen Called the Brownists, Pilgrim Fathers and Baptists in the Dutch Republic, 1581–1701.* Ithaca, New York, [1922].

SCHWEIZER, EDUARD. *Church Order in the New Testament.* Naperville, Illinois: Allenson, 1961.

SEGAL, JUDAH B. *The Hebrew Passover, from the Earliest Times to A.D. 70.* London: Oxford University Press, 1963.

SEARLE, W. G. *Grace Book G* [gamma] *Containing the Records of the University for the Years 1501–1542.* Cambridge: University Press, 1908.

SHIRLEY, FREDERICK J. *Richard Hooker and Contemporary Political Ideas.* London: S.P.C.K., 1949.

SKEATS, HERBERT S. *A History of the Free Churches of England, from A.D. 1688–A.D. 1851.* 2nd edn. London, 1869. Chapter I is a background summary. Also [1894].

SOAMES, HENRY. *Elizabethan Religious History.* London, 1839.

SOME, ROBERT. *A Godly Treatise Containing and Deciding Certain Questions, Moved of Late in London and Other Places, Touching the Ministerie, Sacraments, and Church.* London, 1588. Issued in May.

SOME, ROBERT. *A Godly Treatise Containing and Deciding Certaine Questions, Mooved of Late in London and Other Places, Touching the Ministerie, Sacraments, and Church. Whereunto One Proposition More Is Added. After the Ende of This Booke You Shall Finde a Defence of Such Points as M. Penry Hath Dealt against: And a Confutation of Many Grosse Errours Broched in M. Penries Last Treatise.* London, 1588. Issued in September.

SOME, ROBERT. *A Godly Treatise, Wherein Are Examined and Confuted Many Execrable Fancies, Given out and Holden, Partly by Henry Barrow and John Greenewood: Partly, by Other of the Anabaptistical Order.* London, 1589.

SOPHRONISTES. *A Dialogue, Perswading the People to Reverence and Attend the Ordinance of God, in the Ministerie of Their Owne Pastors.* London, 1589.

SOUTHERN, A. C. *Elizabethan Recusant Prose, 1559–1582.* London: Sands & Co., [1950].

STANLEY, ARTHUR PENRHYN. *Historical Memorials of Westminster Abbey.* London: John Murray, 1882.

STILLINGFLEET, EDWARD. *The Mischief of Separation. A Sermon Preached at Guild-Hall Chappel, May 11, 1680. Being the First Sunday in Easter-Term, before the Lord Mayor, etc.* London, 1680.

STILLINGFLEET, EDWARD. *The Unreasonableness of Separation: or, An Impartial Account of the History, Nature, and Pleas of the Present Separation from the Communion of the Church of England.* London, 1681. Second part, continued by T. Long, 1682.

STOW, JOHN. *A Survey of London.* Edited by C. L. Kingsford. 3 vols. Oxford: Clarendon Press, 1908, 1927. John Strype's folio edition of 1720 is still useful, 2 vols.

STRYPE, JOHN. *Historical Collections of the Life and Acts of the Right Reverend Father in God, John Aylmer, Lord Bp. of London in the Reign of Elizabeth.* Oxford: Clarendon Press, 1821.

STRYPE, JOHN. *The Life and Acts of Matthew Parker.* 3 vols. Oxford, 1821.

STRYPE, JOHN. *Annals of the Reformation.* 4 vols. in 7. Oxford: Clarendon Press, 1824.

STRYPE, JOHN. *The History of the Life and Acts of the Most Reverend Father in God, Edmund Grindal.* Oxford, 1821.

STRYPE, JOHN. *The Life and Acts of the Most Reverend Father in God, John Whitgift, D. D.* 3 vols. London, 1822.

STUBBS, WILLIAM. *See* Great Britain, Ecclesiastical Courts Commission. *See also* Tomlinson, John T.

SUGDEN, EDWARD H. *A Topographical Dictionary to the Works of Shakespeare and His Fellow Dramatists.* Manchester, London, New York, 1925.

SUTCLIFFE, MATTHEW. *An Answere to a Certaine Libel Supplicatorie.* London, 1592.

SUTCLIFFE, MATTHEW. *A Treatise of Ecclesiasticall Discipline.* London, 1590; 1591.

THIELE, EDWIN R. *The Mysterious Numbers of the Hebrew Kings.* Chicago: University of Chicago Press, 1951.

THOMPSON, CRAIG R. *Universities in Tudor England.* Washington: Folger Shakespeare Library, 1959.

THOMPSON, JAMES V. P. *Supreme Governor. A Study of Elizabethan Ecclesiastical Policy and Circumstance.* London: S.P.C.K., [1940].

[THROKMORTON, JOB]. *M. Some Laid Open in His Coulers, Wherein the Indifferent Reader May Easily See, How Wretchedly and Loosely He Hath Handeled the Cause against M. Penri. Done by an Oxford Man, to His Friend in Cambridge.* [La Rochelle?], 1589.

TILLEY, MORRIS PALMER. *A Dictionary of the Proverbs in England in the Sixteenth and Seventeenth Centuries.* Ann Arbor, Michigan, 1950.

TITE, WILLIAM and THOMSON, RICHARD. *A Bibliographical and Literary Account of the Volume of Religious Instruction for Children, Usually Denominated Cranmer's Catechism, Printed and Published in A.D. 1548.* London, 1862.

TOMLINSON, JOHN T. *The "Legal History" of Canon Stubbs: Being the Basis of the New Scheme of Ecclesiastical Courts Proposed by the Royal Commissioners of 1881–3.* London, 1884.

TRAVERS, WALTER. *A Defence of the Ecclesiastical Discipline Ordayned of God to be Used in His Church. Against a Replie of Maister Bridges.* [London], 1588.

TRAVERS, WALTER. *A Full and Plaine Declaration of Ecclesiasticall Discipline Owt of the Word of God, and of the Declininge of the Church of England from the Same.* [Zurich: C. Froschauer?, 1574; more likely Heidelberg: Michael Schirat, 1574].

TRIMBLE, WILLIAM RALEIGH. *The Catholic Laity in Elizabethan England, 1558–1603.* Cambridge: Belknap Press of Harvard University Press, 1964.

UDALL, JOHN. *A Demonstration of the Trueth of That Discipline, Which Christe Hath Prescribed in His Worde for the Governement of His Church, in All Times and Places, untill the End of the Worlde.* [East Molesey], 1588. Reprinted in some copies of *A Parte of a Register* [1593]. Arber reprinted it, 1880.

USHER, ROLAND G. *The Presbyterian Movement in the Reign of Queen Elizabeth as Illustrated by the Minute Book of the Dedham Classis, 1582–1589.* "Royal Historical Society," 3rd series, vol. VIII. London, 1905.

USHER, ROLAND G. *The Rise and Fall of the High Commission.* Oxford: Clarendon Press, 1913.

VALOR BENEFICIORUM: *or, a Valuation of All Ecclesiastical Preferments in England and Wales.* London, 1695.

VENN, JOHN. *Biographical History of Gonville and Caius College: 1349–1897.* 3 vols. Cambridge, 1897, 1898, 1901.

VENN, JOHN. *Grace-Book* Δ [Delta] *Containing the Records of the University of Cambridge for the Years 1542–1589.* Cambridge, 1910.

VENN, JOHN and VENN, J. A. *Alumni Cantabrigienses. A Biographical List of All Known Students, Graduates and Holders of Office at the University of Cambridge, from the Earliest Times to 1900.* Part I. *From the Earliest Times to 1751.* 4 vols. Cambridge, 1922–1927. Part II. *From 1752 to 1900.* 6 vols. By J. A. Venn. Cambridge, 1940–1954. Part I has about 76,000 entries. Part II has about 60,000 entries. Most of the articles have about six lines of succinct material.

WADDINGTON, JOHN. *Congregational History, 1567–1700, in Relation to Contemporaneous Events, and the Conflict for Freedom, Purity, and Independence.* London, 1874.

WADDINGTON, JOHN. *Historical Papers (First Series). Congregational Martyrs.* London, 1861.

WALL, THOMAS. *More Work for the Dean.* London, 1681.

WALLACE, RONALD S. *Calvin's Doctrine of the Word and Sacrament.* Edinburgh, 1953.

WALTERS, H. B. *London Churches at the Reformation, with an Account of Their Contents.* London: S.P.C.K., 1939.

WATERS, DAVID WATKIN. *The Art of Navigation in Elizabethan and Early Stuart Times.* New Haven: Yale University Press, 1958.

WELSBY, PAUL A. *Lancelot Andrewes, 1555–1626.* London: S.P.C.K., 1958.

WENDEL, FRANÇOIS. *Calvin. The Origins and Development of His Religious Thought.* Trans. Philip Mairet. New York: Harper & Row, 1963. French edn. 1950.

WESKE, DOROTHY BRUCE. *Convocation of the Clergy.* London: S.P.C.K., 1937.

WHITE, FRANCIS O. *Lives of the Elizabethan Bishops of the Anglican Church.* London, 1898.

WHITGIFT, JOHN. *The Works of John Whitgift.* Edited by John Ayre for the Parker Society. 3 vols. Cambridge, 1851–1853.

WIFFEN, J. H. *Historical Memoirs of the House of Russell; from the Time of the Norman Conquest.* 2 vols. London, 1933.

WILLIAMS, GEORGE H. *The Radical Reformation.* Philadelphia, 1962.

WILLIAMS, GEORGE H. (ed.). *Spiritual and Anabaptist Writers.* Philadelphia and London, 1957.

WILLIAMS, J. ANTHONY. *Bath and Rome: the Living Link. Catholicism in Bath from 1559 to the Present Day.* Bath: St. John's, South Parade, 1963.

WILSON, H. A. *Constitutions and Canons Ecclesiastical, 1604.* Oxford, 1923.

YOUNG, ALEXANDER. *Chronicles of the Pilgrim Fathers of the Colony of Plymouth, from 1602 to 1625.* Boston, 1841. The second "edition" of 1844 is a reprint.[1]

[1] There is a bibliography in Volume II, "Elizabethan Nonconformist Texts;" see Albert Peel and Leland H. Carlson, *The Writings of Robert Harrison and Robert Browne* (1953). Some of the entries there are relevant to the works of Barrow and Greenwood.

A CHRONOLOGICAL SUMMARY

1591

January	*A Brief Discoverie* printed
February 25	Gifford's *A Plaine Declaration* entered in the *Stationers' Register*
February?	*A Plaine Refutation* printed
March	Greenwood's *A Breife Refutation* written
	Greenwood's *A Fewe Observations* written
April 4	Easter
April 20	Arthur Bellot captured at Flushing. About 2000 copies of *A Brief Discoverie* and 1000 copies of *A Plaine Refutation* seized by Sir Robert Sidney
June?	John Mollins, or Mullins, Archdeacon of London, dies
November 20	Sir Christopher Hatton, Lord Chancellor, dies
December	Gifford's *A Short Reply* published

1592

January	Barrow's *A Few Observations* written. Perhaps finished in February
February?	*A Petition Directed* published
March 26	Easter
March	Barrow's "Final Answer to Gifford—Marginalia" written
April	Barrow's conference with Dr. Thomas Ravis
April (?)	Arthur Bellot's petition to Lord Burghley
May 7	Sir Christopher Wray, Lord Chief Justice of the Court of Queen's Bench, dies
June 2	Thomas Egerton becomes Attorney-General
June 2	Sir John Popham becomes Chief Justice of the Court of Queen's Bench. Knighted the same day
July (?)	Some of the Separatists, including Greenwood,

	liberated from prison to the custody of responsible citizens
August (?)	Greenwood's "Notes for a Sermon against Adultery"
September	Separatist church organized, with Johnson as pastor and Greenwood as teacher
October	Penry arrives in London from Scotland about October 1–7
October	Robert Stokes excommunicated by the Separatist church
December 3 (?)	Penry and Greenwood preach in a garden house at Duke's Place, near Aldgate
December 5–6	Francis Johnson, John Greenwood, and Edward Boyse arrested. The date is December 6—after midnight, but the raid may have begun earlier
December 14	Penry and John Edwardes leave London for Reading
December 17 or 24	Thomas Settle and Daniel Studley arrested

1593

January	Barrow's petition to the Privy Council
February 16	Roger Rippon dies in the Newgate prison
February 17	The corpse and coffin of Rippon carried to the door of Justice Richard Young
February 17	Mrs. Nicholas Lee arrested and imprisoned for one day
February 19	Home of Nicholas Lee ransacked
February 19	Elizabeth's eighth Parliament convened
February 20	Barrow's petition delivered to the Privy Council and rejected
February 25	The Separatist church met
March 1	Christopher Bowman examined
March 4	About fifty-four Separatists arrested at Islington woods
March 6	John Edwardes examined
March 7	George Johnson examined
March 7	Abraham Pulbery examined
March 8	John Barnes, William Clarke, Richard Hawton, and John Nicholas examined

March 9	Daniel Buck examined
March 10	Penry's petition presented to Parliament
March 11	Barrow and Greenwood examined
March 11	The cells of Barrow and Scipio Bellot were rifled
March 11?	Barrow's "A Fragment Directed to the Parliament" seized
March 19	Robert Boull, James Fowrestier and Robert Stokes examined
March 20	Daniel Studley examined
March 20	Second Examination of John Greenwood
	Second (seventh) Examination of Henry Barrow
March 22	Penry, Arthur Bellot, Edward Grave, and George Knyviton arrested
March 23	Attorney-General Thomas Egerton's letter to Sir John Puckering
March 23	Barrow and Greenwood convicted of felony for violating the statute of 23 Elizabeth, chapter II
March 24	Barrow and Greenwood reprieved
March 24	Penry examined by Richard Young
March 26	Penry confers with Dr. Richard Vaughan, his brother, and Young
March 26	Barrow's letter to Thomas Egerton, Attorney-General
March 26	A special commission appointed to conduct examinations of Separatists and Recusants
March 26	Egerton's second letter to Puckering
March 27	Barrow's second letter to Thomas Egerton, Attorney-General
March 28	Egerton's third letter to Puckering
March 28	Penry confers with Dr. Nicholas Balgay
March 28	"Reasons against Publike Disputation with Barrow"
March 29 or 30	Barrow's conference in Newgate with several clergymen
March 31	Barrow and Greenwood reprieved a second time
March	Richard Hawton bailed, perhaps on March 8, or shortly thereafter

March (?)	Richard Hooker's work, *Of the Lawes of Ecclesiasticall Politie*, Books I–IV, published
April 2	Penry confers with Dr. Thomas Crooke, Richard Greenham, and Robert Temple
April 2	William Clark (2), George Johnson (2) and John Nicholas (2) examined. (2) = second time
April 3	Robert Abraham examined and re-examined
April 3	John Barnes (2), Henry Brodwater, John Clark, John Dalamore, Christopher Diggins, Thomas Farrot, Edward Grave, Abraham Pulbery (2), and Roger Waterer examined
April 4	Christopher Bowman (2), William Eiles, Edward Gilbert, Thomas Hewet, John Hulkes, George Knyviton, William Marshall, William Mason and Henry Wythers examined
April 4–5	Barrow's letter to Anne (Russell) Dudley, Countess of Warwick
April 5	Arthur Bellot, Edward Boyse, David Bristow, George Collier, William Curland, Francis Johnson, Thomas Mihilfeld, John Parkes, John Penry, Leonard Pedder, Christopher Simkins, and William Smithe examined
April 5	Penry examined by Dean Gabriell Goodman, Matthew Dale, John Barne, and Richard Young
April 6	Barrow and Greenwood hanged
April 6	William Darvall, William Denford, Thomas Settle, Quintin Smyth, Katherine Unwen, and William Weaver examined
April 6	Penry writes his farewell letter to his wife
April 10	Penry examined by Henry Fanshawe and Richard Young
April 10	The statute of 35 Elizabeth, chapter I, providing for banishment of nonconformists, approved by the Queen
April 10	Parliament adjourned
April 10	Penry writes his farewell letter to his four daughters
April 10	George Smells examined

April 15	Easter
April 24	Thomas Mitchell and John Sparewe examined
April 24	Penry writes his farewell letter to the Separatist congregation
April	Henry Brodwater, William Curland, Thomas Farrot, Edward Gilbert, John Hulkes, William Mason, Thomas Mihilfeld, and Henry Wythers bailed upon promise of conformity
May 15	Penry examined by William Aubrey, Edward Coke, Richard Cosin, Thomas Egerton, Edward Stanhope, and Richard Young
May 21	Penry arraigned at the Court of Queen's Bench before Chief Justice John Popham
May 24	Penry examined by Richard Young
May 25	Penry arraigned a second time at the Court of Queen's Bench, indicted, convicted, and sentenced to death
May 28	Penry writes to Chief Justice John Popham. This is his last writing
May 29	Penry hanged at Thomas à Watering in Southwark
May	Petition of Johnson to Sir William Rowe, mayor of London
May	Petition of Francis Johnson to the Privy Council
June 2	Letter of Francis Johnson to Lord Burghley
June 12	Johnson's letter to Lord Burghley
December 1–2	Two Separatists indicted at Newgate Sessions
December 5	William Smithe summoned before the commissioners at Westminster

1594

January 8	Johnson's letter to Lord Burghley. Encloses separate treatise of eleven reasons why he is not in danger of the statute of 35 Elizabeth, Chapter I

1597

March	Petition of four imprisoned Separatists to go to the Province of Canada

April 8	Four Separatists sail from Gravesend for Newfoundland
May 18	Separatists reach Newfoundland
September 20–25	Separatist leaders arrive in Amsterdam

INDEX

Index

Index

Index

Index